COLLECTED WORKS OF JOHN STUART MILL

VOLUME XXII

The Collected Edition of the Works of John Stuart Mill has been planned and is being directed by an editorial committee appointed from the Faculty of Arts and Science of the University of Toronto, and from the University of Toronto Press. The primary aim of the edition is to present fully collated texts of those works which exist in a number of versions, both printed and manuscript, and to provide accurate texts of works previously unpublished or which have become relatively inaccessible.

Newspaper Writings

by JOHN STUART MILL

*

December 1822 – July 1831

Edited by

ANN P. ROBSON

Associate Professor of History,
University of Toronto

and

JOHN M. ROBSON

University Professor and Professor of English,
University of Toronto

Introduction by
ANN P. ROBSON

Textual Introduction by
JOHN M. ROBSON

UNIVERSITY OF TORONTO PRESS
ROUTLEDGE & KEGAN PAUL

© University of Toronto Press 1986
Toronto and Buffalo
Printed in Canada

ISBN 0-8020-2602-8

London: Routledge & Kegan Paul
ISBN 0-7102-0983-5

∞

Printed on acid-free paper

Canadian Cataloguing in Publication Data
Mill, John Stuart, 1806–1873.
[Works]
Collected works of John Stuart Mill
Includes bibliographies and indexes.
Partial contents: v. 22–25. Newspaper writings /
edited by Ann P. Robson and John M. Robson.
ISBN 0-8020-2602-8 (v. 22–25).
1. Philosophy – Collected works.
2. Political science – Collected works.
3. Economics – Collected works.
I. Robson, John M., 1927–
II. Title.
B1602.A2 1963   192   C64-188-2 rev.

This volume has been published
with the assistance of a grant
from the Social Sciences
and Humanities Research Council
of Canada

TO FRANCIS E. MINEKA
HUMANIST, GUIDE, AND FRIEND

Contents

*

*   *

* * * *

December 1847 to July 1858 1089

March 1863 to July 1873 1201

Introduction

ANN P. ROBSON

THIS INTRODUCTION does not attempt to analyze the thought of John Stuart Mill; it attempts to provide the context of his contribution to newspapers. The limited task is quite sufficient. Mill wrote in the papers for more than fifty of his sixty-seven years, twice on a sustained basis, in the 1830s on France and in 1846 on Ireland. From the chaotic early years of the nineteenth century to the more organized life of Victoria's heyday, he contributed practical and theoretical advice, sometimes hopefully, sometimes irately, frequently despairingly, to his stolid countrymen.

Newspapers were not his major medium—periodicals and books were the media he chose for his important writings—but he knew their impact and their value. Their impact was immediate and widespread. The *Morning Chronicle* under John Black in his prime was read over more cups of coffee than *The Times*. Albany Fonblanque's *Examiner* informed radical opinion. There was no other forum but the press influencing the minds of the politically important men and women with an immediacy made all the more potent because in Mill's youth the numbers who proposed and disposed were so small. As the years went by and as numbers grew, individual influence lessened, Mill's not so much as others, but the influence of the press, still unchallenged, increased with its readership.

Influence upon policy was not the most that Mill obtained by his journalism. Of more value to him was the necessity, forced upon him by the political involvement his journalism entailed, of bringing his hypotheses to the bar of actual events. Perhaps opportunity would be the better word because Mill was aware of, and took advantage of, the laboratory provided by "common experience respecting human nature."[1] It is the testing of his theories concerning human behaviour and the progress of human civilization which gives his newspaper writings weight in the development of his thought and interest to its students.

[1]John Stuart Mill, *A System of Logic, Ratiocinative and Inductive, Collected Works* [CW], VII-VIII (Toronto: University of Toronto Press, 1973), VIII, 874.

The London into which John Stuart Mill was born had a population of under one million; by the time he was twenty-five, it had doubled; when he died there were over three million. The changes taking place in England had produced by the beginning of the nineteenth century a turbulence in society rarely experienced before and a radical political press unique in English history. James Mill may have protected his son from the rough and tumble of boys his own age but he brought him up in the centre of the riots, assassinations, treasonous plots, and mass meetings that were the political manifestation of the social upheaval of early industrial England. The world around the young boy—and he lived his boyhood in London in its very vortex, precocious, his father's intellectual shadow, listening to radical arguments and plans—was violent, brutal, anarchic, insecure, filthy, and noisy. His youthful mind was shaped in this environment —he always stressed the influence of circumstances—as was also his vision as a mature Radical.

Mill was born on 20 May, 1806, in a small house in Pentonville. His father was establishing himself amongst the Radicals of London. The times were desperate for radicalism and yet equally desperate for the condition of England; there was little time for reform but never greater need. Insecurity and violence, and the repression and hatred they bred, were everywhere. The rapidly changing basis of wealth brought increased insecurity for rich and poor. It would be fifty years before the technological and administrative knowledge would be developed to make town life secure, and the same was true for the new financial world. Insecurity haunted all levels of society. Consequently, while Mill was growing up, riots were a way of life, in peace or in war.

There were nearly always riots of more or less seriousness at elections; there were food riots; there were riots amongst the prisoners in Dartmoor and Porchester Castle in 1810; there were riots among the theatre-goers, not only the Old Price riots at Drury Lane in 1809, but at Plymouth in 1810 and Peterborough and Liverpool in 1811; that year the East India College students rioted in Hertford and the next year rioters wrecked the newsroom at the Manchester Exchange; there were riots against high food prices, in favour of a minimum wage, against press gangs; handloom weavers, Tyneside keelmen, Suffolk labourers, Bilston colliers, London shipwrights, all rioted in 1814. From 1811 to 1816 the Luddites broke machinery throughout Yorkshire and the Midlands; in Nottinghamshire in 1812 to make their feelings perfectly clear they rioted in celebration of the assassination of Lord Perceval. The Prime Minister was shot, the King was insane, a profligate Prince was regent, and the country was at war. There was reason for violent dissatisfaction and fear, and both continued to increase. The outbreaks fed into the post-war violence.

In 1815 James Mill moved his family to 1 Queen Square Place, to live beside Bentham. A stone's throw from the Houses of Parliament, this was the very heart of political London, so the young Mill was right in the thick of things, not only for the splendid celebrations as the Prince Regent fêted European royalty at the marriage of Princess Charlotte, but also for the activity leading up to the Spa Fields meeting when the Spenceans, led by the two Watsons and joined by some sailors, broke into several gunsmiths' shops, killing one gunsmith, and attempted to seize the Tower and the Bank of England. Unrest is the word most frequently used to describe the outbreaks from 1815 to 1820, but the word does not indicate the tension or explain Government response. In the atmosphere of the times, any outbreak seemed a possible revolutionary spark to both participants and observers. The year 1817 saw the Manchester Blanketeers, the activities of Oliver the Spy, and the Derbyshire insurrection, for which three were executed and many transported. The popularity of the monarchy reached new depths as public sorrow over the death of Princess Charlotte in childbirth turned to anger over the spectacle of the unprepossessing children of George III without a legitimate heir among them. No one was surprised when a missile was hurled at the Prince's carriage along with the boos and jeers. Rumours of an assassination attempt were readily believed. The years 1819 and 1820—the years of John Stuart's thirteenth and fourteenth birthdays—saw Peterloo, the Six Acts, the death of the beloved old mad king, the Cato Street conspiracy, and Queen Caroline's trial. These events may be played down with hindsight, but at the time rumour fed violence and no one was sure when the revolution might ignite. The year 1789, seen through the glare of 1792, was in everyone's mind. How far could repression and prosecution go? Might the suspension of habeas corpus lead a mob to storm the Tower?

No child living in the heart of Westminster in a house that was the centre of a passionately radical group could be unaware of the violence out of doors. So much has been made of the seclusion and concentration of Mill's upbringing and education that it is necessary to give some emphasis to the other side. The image of the child prodigy screened from friends of his own age is dear to a society which holds the untrained mind to be proof of a happy childhood and which delights in the crisis of the trained mind. But Mill's childhood was not unhappy—he is to be believed on this point, his *Autobiography* being painfully honest and happiness being estimable only by the possessor—nor did his crisis necessarily come from the concentration of the education. Indeed a more likely cause is the gap between his father's solutions and the coarse world he grew up in.

James Mill's house was not a place of total seclusion except from children not of his own making; and of those who were, it should be remembered, there were nine. The young boy also had the society of his father's friends.

During this first period of my life [up to the age of fourteen], the habitual frequenters of my father's house were limited to a very few persons, most of them little known to the world, but whom personal worth, and more or less of congeniality with at least his political opinions (not so frequently to be met with then as since) inclined him to cultivate; and his conversations with them I listened to with interest and instruction.

He also mentions being "disputatious" "from having been encouraged in an unusual degree to talk on matters beyond [his] age, and with grown persons."[2] Mill mentions only David Ricardo, Joseph Hume, and Jeremy Bentham (*A*, 55), but there were others.

And if the number who came to the house was small, the much larger world of violent political activity entered with them. The turmoil of England, its causes and its remedies, was the urgent question during John Stuart Mill's formative years and it was the paramount, if not the only topic of conversation amongst his father's friends. They were an extraordinary group of men. They argued the facts and the principles passionately. It was not the talk of abstract philosophers but of men committed to the society, a society on the brink of revolution or dissolution, of which they felt themselves the proper leaders.[3] The young Mill's world was exciting; all about him was radicalism verging on revolution, not necessarily violent but violent if necessary. He dreamt of being a Girondist.[4] The impression Mill gives in the *Autobiography* that life in Queen Square Place was regulated and commonplace is frequently accepted without question because the work is so obviously intellectually honest. But what was commonplace to the young Mill would have been commonplace to few others. (It is doubtful if Mill ever had much idea how uncommonplace he was.) All around him were unconforming, if not eccentric.

The central figure was Jeremy Bentham who, however much his eccentricity stemmed from his rationality, was also a passionate, at times incoherent, denouncer of abuses. History has often made him quaint, concentrating on his foibles and universal constitutions and prisons, giving others the credit for

---

[2]J.S. Mill, *Autobiography* [*A*], in *Autobiography and Literary Essays*, ed. John M. Robson and Jack Stillinger, *CW*, I (Toronto: University of Toronto Press, 1981), 37. Subsequent references to the *Autobiography* are given in the text. References to Mill's newspaper writings are also given in the text by the item number assigned in these volumes.

[3]Young John might well have listened "with interest and instruction" while his father talked over with Francis Place the possible need to form a Committee of Public Safety contingent on the reform meeting they were organizing in September 1816. The meeting was to have Burdett, Cochrane, and Hunt as speakers, proposing the selection of delegates from all districts to come to London, ostensibly bearing petitions for reform, in time for the opening of the official Parliament's session. No one could foresee the result of such a proposal. The meetings continued and led directly to the Spa Fields attempt of the Spenceans. James Mill and Francis Place had by then drawn back. But nonetheless in December 1816 a Convention of Delegates was gathered in London. It was a very thin line between peaceful agitation as it was practised in the London meetings and armed insurrection. Elie Halévy's account of the state of London and Radical agitation is still the best, in his *The Liberal Awakening* (London: Benn, 1949), 9-53. And note the title of Joseph Hamburger's fine study, *James Mill and the Art of Revolution* (New Haven: Yale University Press, 1963).

[4]Mill said of his younger self: "the most transcendant glory I was capable of conceiving, was that of figuring, successful or unsuccessful, as a Girondist in an English Convention" (*A*, 67).

realizing his law reforms in particular and his social reforms in general. History has made Francis Place respectable, but he had at one time been a co-worker of Colonel Despard, hanged for treason in 1803. And it was he who, through his writings on birth control, was, if indirectly, responsible for the young Mill's being arrested for distributing "anti-social" pamphlets. Frequently on Sundays, John Black, a man who as editor of the *Morning Chronicle* was to be long an associate of John Mill's, visited James Mill. They talked politics, but some of the flavour of Black's unconventional personality must have been noticed by the listening and disputatious son. Black's quarrelsome nature had led to twelve challenges to duels before he was thirty. Having failed to win a divorce suit, he was now living with his housekeeper and being blackmailed by his wife. Brougham, Ricardo, Romilly, and Hume, each of marked character and ability, also provided contrast and interest. And of equal interest but possibly more charm, after 1819 there were the neighbours Sarah and John Austin with, two years later, their lovely baby daughter Lucie. Despite the long hours of study, life could not have been dull for the young boy and, even without the rough-and-tumble of his peers (siblings are never peers), he was better fitted than most to go at age fourteen to stay for a week with J.B. Say in Paris, meeting many of the French liberal circle, on his way for an extended visit in the south of France with the eccentric Samuel Benthams, where, however, the turmoil and chaos were domestic.

It may have been somewhat of a relief to leave London in the spring of 1820. Within a week of the death of the Duke of Kent, the old King had died. Arthur Thistlewood, a long-time friend of the Watsons of Spa Fields, advanced his plans and was surprised in Cato Street on the night of 23 February. The opening scenes of the drama of Queen Caroline, an emotional extravaganza orchestrated by Brougham, were drawing large London audiences.[5] But France was in truth not much calmer, although less noisy and, for the moment, seemingly less volatile. The Duke of Berry had been assassinated the week before the Cato Street conspiracy (the Cato Street conspirators now seem farcically inept; but so would Louvel had he missed), and the royalist reaction was benefiting. Under the Ministry of Villèle, Louis XVIII was following his autocratic inclinations fully supported by the old aristocracy. The law of the double vote passed, increasing the influence of the small rich minority which had already seemed impregnable. The talk at the home of J.B. Say would have been of the kind the boy was used to, only in French. Say's household was radical; he was a political economist—in 1822 he became an honorary member of the Political Economy Club in London—a long-time friend of Lafayette's and a befriender of the

---

[5]It is an indication of the precarious state of England and the hatred that existed that the Whigs and Radicals could, for one minute, much less a year, make that indefensible woman their champion. London was illuminated for three nights when the Bill against her was dropped and the House of Commons voted her the enormous annuity of £50,000.

Carbonari. Mill met many of the leaders of the French left, "among whom [he had] pleasure in the recollection of having once seen Saint-Simon, not yet the founder either of a philosophy or a religion, and considered only as a clever *original*" (*A*, 63). He also recorded that he benefited little; this is hardly surprising since he was only fourteen and spoke only English. But although he may have benefited little immediately, the friendship with that family and the acquaintance of the political group to which it belonged were of immense importance to both his thinking and his actions a decade later. And Mill would have benefited more than any other lad his age.

His radical training also stood him in good stead as he started off on his own to the Garonne to join the Samuel Benthams. As a true Radical and a disputatious youngster he knew his rights, and asserted them against a female claimant to an inside seat that was his by seniority in the coach if not in the world.[6] He arrived without mishap and spent an exceedingly happy year in a household that was normal only by Benthamite standards. The success of this year was of immense importance in Mill's intellectual growth; he developed an enduring affection for France and an unwavering belief that she was in the van of European civilization and that all, including England, must follow the path she took. These thoughts were not matured in 1821, but the ground had been prepared and sown. The influence on his political thought was to be crucial. He later said: "the greatest, perhaps, of the many advantages which I owed to this episode in my education, was that of having breathed for a whole year the free and genial atmosphere of Continental life." In England it is taken for granted "that conduct is of course always directed towards low and petty objects" (James Mill's teaching can be heard here); amongst the French elevated sentiments are "the current coin of human intercourse" (*A*, 59-61). That Mill could feel these sentiments unchanged after the French events of 1851 and 1870 shows how powerful were his early impressions. One may also see here feelings which would contribute to the promptings of the "irrepressible self-consciousness" to answer "No!" and trigger his depression in 1826 (*A*, 139). Certainly one can see here the seeds of his later emphasis on the possibility of the improvement of mankind through the cultivation of their higher natures. The method of his thinking was to be altered in another direction also—one which was to be crucial to his youthful journalism. Mill concluded the account of his sojourn in France:

The chief fruit which I carried away from the society I saw, was a strong and permanent interest in Continental Liberalism, of which I ever afterwards kept myself *au courant*, as much as of English politics: a thing not at all usual in those days with Englishmen, and which had a very salutary influence on my development, keeping me free from the error always prevalent in England, and from which even my father with all his superiority to prejudice was not exempt, of judging universal questions by a merely English standard (*A*, 63).

[6]Anna J. Mill, ed., *John Mill's Boyhood Visit to France* (Toronto: University of Toronto Press, 1961), 10.

The England to which the fifteen-year-old Mill returned in June 1821 was a little calmer than the one he had left. Queen Caroline's trial was over and the illuminations extinguished. The royal Dukes' hasty marriages had produced more than one promising successor to the throne. It was hoped that, God and the Duke of Clarence willing, a regency could be avoided; George IV was unlikely to last long enough—certainly everybody hoped that too. England had largely separated herself from the repressive ideas of the great Continental powers and was associating herself with the liberal aspirations asserting themselves in Europe. There were many insurrections, the precise aims of which were not always clear, but it was clear that Europe was far from calm. Greece, Spain, the Spanish colonies, the Two Sicilies, Northern Italy, Portugal, all were providing alternating hope and despair for the Radicals. At home the mood was easier. The pitch of excitement reached by the summer of 1820 could not be maintained, partly because Burdett, Cochrane, and Cobbett had all in their several ways pulled back from the monster demonstrations in London. A brief period of prosperity in both town and country had lowered tempers and reduced the mob.

John Stuart Mill spent two busy years after his return from France, enjoying a wider acquaintance, including many much nearer his own age with whom to match wits. His father's plans for him at that time included as a distinct possibility a career at the bar. Consequently Mill read law to his great benefit with John Austin, a man whose incisive understanding of the subject was best communicated by tutoring, not lecturing. Mill gained more than legal knowledge from the Austin connection. He went to stay with Sarah Austin's family, the Taylors of Norwich. There he met John Austin's brother Charles, a brilliant Cambridge undergraduate, who, Mill says, "attached me among others to his car. Through him I became acquainted with Macaulay, Hyde and Charles Villiers, Strutt (now Lord Belper), Romilly (now Lord Romilly and Master of the Rolls), and various others. . . . It was through him that I first felt myself, not a pupil under teachers, but a man among men." (*A*, 79.) It is small wonder that Mill's writing shows an unusual blend of modesty, certainty, and arrogance when one looks at the contemporaries against whom he measured himself. And they all assumed it their right and their duty to point England the way.

Mill received another benefit from his father's arranging for him to read under Austin. As part of his preparation for law, Mill was given Bentham's principal speculations, as interpreted to the Continent, and indeed to all the world, by Pierre Etienne Louis Dumont, in the *Traités de législation* (1802).

The reading of this book was an epoch in my life; one of the turning points in my mental history. . . . The feeling rushed upon me, that all previous moralists were superseded, and that here indeed was the commencement of a new era in thought. . . . As I proceeded farther, there seemed to be added to this intellectual clearness, the most inspiring prospects of practical improvement in human affairs. . . . Bentham's subject was Legislation . . . and at every page he seemed to open a clearer and broader conception of what human opinions and institutions ought to be, how they might be made what they ought to be, and how far removed from it they now are. When I laid down the last volume of the *Traité* I had become a different being. . . . I now had opinions; a creed, a doctrine, a philosophy; in one among the best senses of the word, a religion; the inculcation and diffusion of which could be made the principal outward purpose of a life. And I had a grand conception laid before me of changes to be effected in the condition of mankind through that doctrine. The *Traité de Legislation* wound up with what was to me a most impressive picture of human life as it would be made by such opinions and such laws as were recommended in the treatise. . . . And the vista of improvement which he did open was sufficiently large and brilliant to light up my life, as well as to give a definite shape to my aspirations. (*A*, 67-71.)

The euphoria of the moment of grace shines through the calculated wording of thirty years later. Not the least of the emotions was relief at now at last understanding what his father had been teaching him. But the paramount effect was the vision; for the young lad of fifteen the feelings he had experienced in his Girondist dreams were now his in reality. For the rest of his life Mill was to be a visionary, at times a very depressed visionary when the future became blurred or the present seemingly regressing, but always beneath the calm, measured analytical philosopher or economist or political scientist, the saint of rationalism would be following the yellow brick road.

The immediate effects of the vision were to inspire Mill to write his first "argumentative essay" (*A*, 73) and to form debating clubs and discussion societies in order to prove and spread the gospel. He was also ready to take his message to the wider public; he was finally confident of what he had been taught and, truly comprehending it for the first time, was not only able "to converse, on general subjects, with the instructed men with whom [he] came in contact" (*A*, 75) but also desirous of instructing the uninstructed. In December of 1822 appeared the first of his newspaper writings.[7]

Journalism was never intended by James Mill to be his son's career. Some time during the winter of 1822-23, he decided that the India House was a more utilitarian career for his son than the bar. Certainly in retrospect John Mill expressed few regrets about the bar and an acute awareness of the drawbacks of journalism, especially when contrasted with the advantages of following in his father's footsteps.

I do not know any one of the occupations by which a subsistence can now be gained, more suitable than such as this to any one who, not being in independent circumstances, desires to devote a part of the twenty-four hours to private intellectual pursuits. Writing for the press, cannot be recommended as a permanent resource to any one qualified to accomplish anything in the higher departments of literature or thought. . . . Those who have to support themselves by their pen must depend on literary drudgery . . . and can employ in the pursuits of their own choice . . . less than the leisure allowed by office occupations, while the effect on the mind is far more enervating and fatiguing. (*A*, 85.)

[7]Some of the early newspaper pieces may well have grown out of papers for the Utilitarian Society.

So John Mill started work, the day after his seventeenth birthday, 21 May, 1823, in the Examiner's Office of the East India Company, and the newspaper was to become for him throughout his life a means of putting his solutions for immediate problems before the public and of educating that public on the broader philosophical and political issues that lay behind the great events of the day.[8]

Journalism also educated Mill; it played an important part in his development by keeping his feet firmly on the ground. He himself was not unaware of the importance of active involvement to prove philosophical speculation. "But the man to lead his age is he who has been familiar with thought directed to the accomplishment of immediate objects, and who has been accustomed to see his theories brought early and promptly to the test of experiment . . . and to make an estimate of means and of obstacles habitually a part of all his theories that have for their object practice, either at the present or at a more distant period."[9] In his newspaper writings, Mill can be watched applying the principles he had acquired to the practical problems of everyday administration and politics: "My practice (learnt from Hobbes and my father) [was] to study abstract principles by means of the best concrete instances I could find . . ." (*A*, 167). The political scientist needed, like every other scientist, to see if the laws or the hypotheses were verified by the facts.[10] Especially in his earlier years the world was Mill's laboratory and the newspapers his daily notebook. There are interesting times in his journalism, in the early 1820s, the early 1830s, the late 1840s, and the early 1850s, when Mill is quite evidently applying a strongly held belief, quite recently worked out, to contemporary events: in the '20s, Bentham's laws; in the '30s, the laws of historical development and social progress; in the '40s, the consequences of systems of land tenure; and in the '50s, the social consequences of sexual inequality. It is his observation of the actual instances around him (and here his work in the India Office greatly added to his journalist's experience) that lies behind his conviction, so often expressed, that all reforms must be chosen for

---

[8]"Writing of a very high order is thrown away when it is buried in periodicals, which are mostly read but once, and that hastily: yet the only access now to the general public, is through periodicals. An article in a newspaper or a magazine, is to the public mind no more than a drop of water on a stone; and like that, it produces its effect by *repetition*.

"The peculiar 'mission' of this age, (if we may be allowed to borrow from the new French school of philosophers a term which they have abused,) is to popularize among the many, the more immediately practical results of the thought and experience of the few." ("Writings of Junius Redivivus [I]," *Monthly Repository*, n.s. VII [Apr. 1833], *CW*, I, 372.)

[9]"Armand Carrel," in *Essays on French History and Historians*, *CW*, XX (Toronto: University of Toronto Press, 1985), 174. In an earlier version his wording had shown even more awareness: "but before his thoughts can be acted upon, they must be recast in the mould of other and more business-like intellects. There is no limit to the chimeras which a man may persuade himself of, whose mind has never had anything to do but to form conceptions, without ever measuring itself and them with realities." (*Ibid.*, 173[k].)

[10]These ideas are developed by Mill in the *Logic*. See also J.M. Robson, *The Improvement of Mankind* (Toronto: University of Toronto Press, 1968), esp. Chap. 6, "Method: Scientist and Artist."

their present practicality, as well as their furthering of the eventual goal. It was not only his early mental training that led him, in spite of his great sympathy, to reject Saint-Simonism in his time.

The radical world of journalism that he now entered was a small world, peopled by figures long familiar to the sixteen-year-old Mill.[11] Radical politics were led by a select, dedicated few, all of whom turned their hands to whatever task needed doing. The persecution of the press had strengthened the bonds of brotherhood, and freedom of the press became a *sine qua non*, if not the *sine qua non*, of the intellectual radical movement. Between 1808 and 1821, there had been 101 prosecutions for seditious libel, many of them unsuccessful thanks to Charles James Fox's amendment of the law in 1792, which gave juries the power to decide if the words in question were libellous. That amendment itself may have spared England revolution. As it was, the trials provided soapboxes, and if sometimes imprisonment followed, Lord Ellenborough found himself thwarted as often as not. But the continuing struggle against repression, the shared prison experiences, the rallying point provided by people like the Carliles, all created an exciting world, not less so for its danger, which the young boy was now to share. His father and his father's allies welcomed the new torch bearer, but journalism was more a rite of passage than a new land.

Small though the world of journalism was, it had a power quite out of proportion to its size. A great deal of influence was wielded by those whose reasoned argument or memorable invective was read over breakfast or coffee. Westminster with its eleven thousand voters could be swayed by a Black or a Barnes, and most constituencies had less than a tenth that number. But even

[11]One brief daisy chain will illustrate the compactness, marginality, and mutual support of the circle. *The Traveller* was owned by Colonel Robert Torrens, an old friend of James Mill's, political economist and founder member of the Political Economy Club; it was edited by Walter Coulson, whose father had worked in the dock yards supervised by Samuel Bentham, who had been instrumental in young Walter's becoming an amanuensis of Jeremy Bentham, who in turn was the connection to Colonel Torrens and the *Traveller* (soon amalgamated with the *Globe*). Because both were close associates of Torrens and James Mill, Coulson would frequently meet John Black, whom he would succeed as editor of the *Chronicle* in the forties. He would also know Albany Fonblanque, who, having written for Black in the *Chronicle* and been a leader writer for the *Examiner*, followed in the footsteps of Leigh Hunt, who also had written for the *Traveller*, and became editor of the *Examiner*. Leigh Hunt, S.T. Coleridge, Charles Lamb, and Thomas Barnes of *The Times* all attended Christ's Hospital, the "Blue Coat" School; it is quite reasonable to believe that if a London journalist were not a Blue Coat, he was a Scot. A young friend of Leigh Hunt's was John Forster, in his early days dramatic critic of the *True Sun*, for which W.J. Fox, editor of the *Monthly Repository* from 1826 to 1836, became leader writer in 1835. Forster then wrote for the *Courier* and the *Examiner* and for Lardner's *Cyclopaedia* before becoming briefly in his later years editor of the *Daily News* (succeeding Dickens) and then, for nine years, editor of the *Examiner*. Forster's successor at the *Daily News* was Eyre Crowe, who had also written for Lardner's *Cyclopaedia* before becoming French correspondent for the *Morning Chronicle*. "They could not have moved in a circle less small had they been inhabitants of a country town" (T.H.S. Escott, *Masters of English Journalism* [London: T. Fisher Unwin, 1911], 142).

more important, if also more intangible, was the amount of pressure that could be exerted on the Government by the political temperature in London. Certainly a succession of ministries thought it worth the risk of increasing their unpopularity by attempting to silence, or keep within bounds, a Leigh Hunt or a Cobbett. It was said that "an epigram in the *Examiner* went off like a great gun, echoing all over the country."[12] In 1835, when the *Chronicle*, which had fallen behind *The Times*, suddenly acquired many readers lost by its rival through a change in policy, Black exclaimed, "Now our readers will follow me anywhere I like to lead them!"[13] A government that ruled in the final analysis by the tolerance of the people could be forced to alter its course by the strong expression of feeling out of doors. Lord Brougham's triumph in the withdrawal of the Bill relating to Queen Caroline was a triumph of the press and the people, certainly not of justice.

John Mill was fully aware of the power of the press. When he pours scorn on the state of the press in England (No. 57) it is just because he was aware of how much good journalists could do and how much evil in his eyes many of them—*The Times* was often in his mind—were doing. Mill's diatribes against the press must be seen in the context of his frustration with England and Englishmen for their "low moral tone" and "absence of high feelings" (*A*, 61). Certainly only a handful of men in England, including himself, employed daily or weekly journalism with the honesty, respect, knowledge, and integrity that would make it an instrument for the advancement of mankind. To Mill's mind one of that handful was John Black, his father's old friend and, to a certain extent, disciple; when considering Mill's own journalism his estimate of Black should be set beside his condemnations of the press.

I have always considered Black as the first journalist who carried criticism & the spirit of reform into the details of English institutions. . . . [He] introduced Bentham's opinions on legal & judicial reform into newspaper discussion. And by doing this he broke the spell. Very early in his editorship he fought a great battle for the freedom of reporting the preliminary investigations in the Police Courts in which Fonblanque . . . occasionally helped him, but he had little other help. . . . Another subject on which his writings were of the greatest service was the freedom of the press in matters of religion. His first years as editor of the Chronicle coincided with the prosecutions of Carlile & his shopmen & Black kept up the fight against those prosecutions with great spirit & power. All these subjects were Black's own. Parl. Reform, Catholic emancipation, free trade, &c, were the liberal topics of the day & on all of these he wrote frequently, as you will see by any file of the Chronicle.[14]

---

[12]Richard Garnett, *Dictionary of National Biography*, *s.v.* Albany Fonblanque.
[13]Robert Harrison, *ibid.*, *s.v.* John Black.
[14]*The Later Letters of John Stuart Mill, 1849-1873* [*LL*], ed. Francis E. Mineka and Dwight N. Lindley, *CW*, XIV-XVII (Toronto: University of Toronto Press, 1972), XV, 979 (12 Dec., 1864). This letter is written to Robert Harrison, who used it in his article on John Black cited above.

The Mills' only worry was that Black might not maintain his influence over the regular purchasers of his paper:[15] "in their weekly talks with their editor, both the Mills insisted as a condescension necessary to the temper of the time" on a lightness of touch. It was feared "that Black and his contributors were habitually writing above the heads of the public."[16]

The readers, it must be kept in mind, were in the dining room or the coffee house at the beginning or end of a busy day. They had the normal physical disadvantages to contend with: dull weather, smoke, poor window glass, flickering candlelight, more-or-less helpful spectacles, and small bad print on fawn paper. To modern eyes it appears (somewhat dimly) strange that so little effort was made to ease the task of the reader. In the first half of the century the leading dailies usually had only four pages of small print in six columns, the first and fourth pages being devoted to advertisements. (Advertisements were integral to a newspaper then as now, bringing in the crucial portion of their revenue; indeed most, like the *Morning Chronicle*, were originally established as advertising media for a trade.) The second page would contain extracts from foreign papers in two columns, with the other four columns containing theatre and current happenings, chiefly domestic politics. A leading article, if there was one, would usually be on page two. Foreign news, society news, sporting news, and the ever-popular detailed description of the seamy side of life from the law courts filled page three. The *Examiner* was a weekly, with more pages but smaller format than the dailies, and appeared every Sunday; it had sixteen pages with only two columns but of equally miserable type-face.

The reader the Mills had in mind, though interested in politics, had other activities to occupy the greater part of his day. He would have intellectual pretensions but not necessarily a profession; most probably he would be to a large extent self-educated after the age of fourteen. He would like to consider himself an independent thinker, keeping abreast of what went on at home and abroad, especially the former and especially politically, standing on his own intellectual feet, and voicing opinions which he could support on intelligible principles. He would consider himself anti-Tory and, although certainly not of the labouring classes himself, was frequently sympathetic to their plight. But he was not a deep thinker and he was a busy man; his attention must be caught and held and his opinion influenced by blunt arguments. For the most part, John Mill keeps the temporary nature of his reader's attention in mind; the largest exception would be the series of articles on the "Spirit of the Age," their length being

---

[15]A circulation of between 3000 and 5000 was adequate for a newspaper in the 1820s; particular brilliance or popular events might raise it to 10,000. The readership was, of course, greater, but one must be uneasy about the estimate of between ten and twenty readers for each purchaser; there must have been an enormous difference on that score between the *Examiner* and the *Northern Star*, to take a somewhat extreme example.

[16]Escott, *Masters of English Journalism*, 159.

unusual even for the *Examiner*—but on Sunday perhaps the reader could be expected to sit somewhat longer over his coffee. (I say "his" coffee, because it is my impression—and I have no hard facts—that newspapers then for the most part addressed themselves consciously or unconsciously to a male audience.)[17]

There are advantages to the student of Mill's thought in the demands that this audience made on him. In a newspaper, the ideas cannot be hedged around with qualifications and elaborations. What a journalist feels, he must say in a limited number of words, in a straightforward manner immediately intelligible to a man of intelligence but lacking learning and sophistication. For the most part, Mill was very successful (although he thought he lacked the light touch [A, 181]) in adapting his writing to this level. In addition, journalism most frequently demands hasty execution and topicality. The hasty execution was not a problem for Mill; from the beginning of his career, he wrote enviably well under pressure. The topicality can occasionally be a barrier for the reader many generations later, because the ambience of an incident is very difficult, if not impossible, to recapture; one cannot live in the past. But this difficulty is more than compensated for by the opportunity to watch Mill's ideas, unequivocally expressed, shape and reshape themselves as they are proved against the facts and the events.

DECEMBER 1822 TO DECEMBER 1824

JOHN STUART MILL began to write for the press in December of 1822. It was not a propitious time, or not seemingly so. The European powers generally were looking for a return to the *status quo ante*; the experience of the French Revolution and the Napoleonic Wars with their economic and political turbulence was much too recent to admit of broad proposals for change. But the time had rays of hope. Although France had invaded Spain to re-establish the autocratic rule of Ferdinand VII, the Spanish constitutionalists were showing considerable strength. The Greeks had risen against Turkey and liberal fervour was wholly on their side. At home, Lord Liverpool was still stolidly sitting in the saddle, but the worst of the post-war economic disruption was over. Prosperity was returning and tension was lessening. The Cabinet now contained considerable liberal talent: Castlereagh's suicide and Liverpool's resistance to the King had brought Canning back to the Foreign Office; Peel, who had endorsed in 1819 a return to cash payments, had replaced Sidmouth at the Home Office; Huskisson was supporting freer trade at the Board of Trade; and Lord John Russell had been successful in disenfranchising the quite rotten borough of

[17]I do not know whether *The Times'* occasional resort to Latin for the details of a particularly lurid crime indicates a solicitude for female readers.

Grampound, thus setting the precedent of eliminating a parliamentary borough. But at the end of 1822 these were little more than straws in the wind; Peterloo and the Six Acts, Cato Street, and Queen Caroline were only yesterday and still fresh in the mind. The unpopularity of George IV, which was if possible increasing with his girth, assured popular dislike of his Ministry. Peel might contemplate reforms in the Home Office but they would have to be accompanied by a watchful eye and a firm hand, especially on the radical press. The stamp duty had been extended after Peterloo and there were continual prosecutions as the war of the unstamped press raged. For most Radicals a cheap press and a free one continued to be the rallying ground in the defence of Englishmen's liberties, for it was still a radicalism largely in the eighteenth-century tradition of John Wilkes. Radicals stood against encroachment by the King and his Ministers upon the constitutional rights of free men; and generally speaking the reforms they proposed were within the system rather than of the system.

Mill was sixteen and a half, a brilliant, gauche, likely lad, the product of one of the best-known educations of any nineteenth-century figure. He was ready to write, having found a message, and his father was nothing loath, perhaps wanting his son to have experience before Bentham's projected radical periodical was started.[18] During the next fifteen months, until the plans for the *Westminster Review* were realized, the young boy wrote thirty-two newspaper pieces, some quite short, but some more than a full column in length. His taking up his post in the East India Office caused only a slight and momentary lessening of his output; the pattern of life that was to prevail until his retirement in 1858 was set in the first months. The pattern of thought was not.

These early attempts are what might be expected, even from a prodigy, of a youth in his seventeenth and eighteenth years. They are clever but not profound or original, giving ample proof of his own assessment:

The first intellectual operation in which I arrived at any proficiency, was dissecting a bad argument, and finding in what part the fallacy lay. . . . It is also a study peculiarly adapted to an early stage in the education of philosophical students, since it does not presuppose the slow process of acquiring, by experience and reflection, valuable thoughts of their own. (*A*, 23.)

Mill's youthful journalism shows as much the thought of the Queen Square Place circle as of the youngest member of it. In these years the young Mill accepted his mentors' view of a mechanistic world whose parts could not be redesigned, but could be realigned by the adjusting of a legal problem here and the promoting of a political economy reform there. The first principle on which their reforms were based was that men, because they put their own interests before the public's,

---

[18]James Mill might well have been anxious for his son's help. He felt he could not desert Bentham but he much doubted John Bowring's ability to edit a political and philosophical review and "augured so ill of the enterprise that he regretted it altogether" (*A*, 93).

abuse a public trust if left unchecked. Mill's articles all assume a dog-eat-dog world wherein every top dog must be prevented from dining off those lower in the hierarchy. The nature of the beast could not be much improved, but the beast's behaviour could be bettered through the judicious provision of punishments and rewards. A second principle was that there are laws of political economy, the correct understanding of which would vastly improve the lot of the greatest number. It was appropriate that Mill, whose name has become inseparable from his *Principles of Political Economy*, should have written publicly first in that field.

> The first writings of mine which got into print were two letters published towards the end of 1822, in the *Traveller* evening newspaper. The *Traveller* (which afterwards grew into the *Globe and Traveller* by the purchase and incorporation of the *Globe*) was then the property of the well known political economist Colonel Torrens. Under the editorship of an able man, Mr. Walter Coulson (who after being an amanuensis of Mr. Bentham, became a reporter, then an editor . . .), it had become one of the most important newspaper organs of liberal politics. Col. Torrens wrote much of the political economy of his paper; and had at this time made an attack upon some opinion of Ricardo and my father, to which at my father's instigation I attempted an answer, and Coulson out of consideration for my father and good will to me, inserted it. There was a reply by Torrens, to which I again rejoined. (*A*, 89.)

Thus his career started off on ground he knew well; he had been educated on and by Ricardo, and was well aware of the controversy over the theory of value which had frequently exercised them all. It is twentieth-century opinion expressed by Lord Robbins that in these first two essays in public controversy, the newcomer received a "thorough trouncing from Torrens, evoked by . . . [the] effort to sustain his father's preposterous view that differences in the period of investment might all be reduced to labour."[19]

The controversy over the causes of price fluctuations—related to that over value—was equally undecided. This controversy had been stimulated rather than settled by the passing of the Corn Law of 1815 and Peel's Currency Act of 1819. Mill's favourable reviews of Thomas Tooke's *Thoughts on High and Low Prices* (Nos. 8 and 12) consist largely of expository, approving synopses of Tooke's influential book. (He was to use Tooke's arguments again in the following year in his *Westminster Review* article, "War Expenditure.")[20] Young Mill next took on the Rev. Thomas Malthus in a review (No. 18) of *The Measure of Value*, which demonstrated the adolescent neophyte's proficiency at dissecting bad logic. Having dismissed one of the established economist's arguments "as a specimen of the obscure and disjointed mode of reasoning which Mr. Malthus has adopted," and referring to "two or three other paragraphs of too little

---

[19]Lord Robbins, Introduction to *Essays on Economics and Society, CW,* IV-V (Toronto: University of Toronto Press, 1967), IV, viii.
[20]"War Expenditure" (1824), *CW,* IV, 3-22.

importance to require a refutation," the youngster concludes with a triumphant reassertion of the orthodox position on the currency question.[21]

Another economic piece, written in June 1823, "The Debate on East and West Indian Sugars" (No. 10), has additional interest as an example of the way Mill's daily articles not infrequently originated. James Mill was Zachary Macaulay's ally in the anti-slavery movement (Macaulay had supported James Mill for the position in the Examiner's Office of the East India Company); in December of 1821 he had been applied to as the natural authority by Macaulay, who was seeking help in the preparation for a debate, scheduled for May 1822, on the West Indian Monopoly.[22] Macaulay then contributed to the pamphlet war,[23] showing a detailed knowledge of India, its manufactures, and its trade. At this distance we cannot know whether John worked to gather information for his father and Macaulay, but certainly James Mill and his radical allies with their constant discussion and planning provided the motivation and put the needed knowledge at John Mill's fingertips for an article on the parliamentary debate in 1823.

Another example is Mill's article on Spanish affairs (No. 13). His easy familiarity with the recent very complicated events came quite naturally. Radical eyes had been watching the revolutionary events in Spain since 1820. Jeremy Bentham had written a pamphlet to impress upon the Cortes the importance of a free press.[24] In April 1823 the French invasion of Spain had outraged radical opinion; Major Cartwright "entreats" (in Alexander Bain's words) James Mill's "intervention," and a meeting was held on 13 June at the London Tavern "for aiding the Spaniards to maintain their independence against France."[25] Consequently, when on 4 August the news came of the capitulation of the constitutionalist general, Ballasteros, heralding the restoration of Ferdinand, the young boy could write a remarkably sure and percipient article without delay.

The young Mill's main interest in 1823, however, was not political economy or foreign affairs but the issues that Bentham's *Traités* had inspired him to fight for. In Mill's account of the thought of the radical writers—he included

---

[21]In a letter to the Grotes the following year, Mill wrote: "Malthus, it seems, has been puffing himself again in the Quarterly—tho' I have not seen the article, it propounds what no other mortal would think of propounding, his *Measure of Value*" (*Mill News Letter*, XX, no. 2 [Summer 1985], 6 [1 Sept., 1824]).

[22]Alexander Bain, *James Mill: A Biography* (London: Longmans, Green, 1882), 196-7.

[23]*East and West India Sugar; or, A Refutation of the Claims of the West India Colonists to a Protecting Duty on East India Sugar* (London: Relfe, and Hatchard and Son, 1823).

[24]Jeremy Bentham, *On the Liberty of the Press and Public Discussion* (1821), in *Works*, ed. John Bowring, 11 vols. (Edinburgh: Tait, 1843), II, 275-97.

[25]Bain, *James Mill*, p. 206. Bain gives 14 June as the date of the meeting, but *The Times* for that date reports on the meeting of the previous evening. James Mill's name does not appear in the list of the important people attending.

himself—associated with the *Westminster Review* founded in 1824 he says, "Their mode of thinking was not characterized by Benthamism in any sense which has relation to Bentham as a chief or guide . . ." (*A*, 107), but his own journalism of 1823 would lead to a qualification of this estimate. Recollecting thirty years later his "considerably more ambitious" articles in the *Morning Chronicle* on freedom of the press, prompted by the prosecution of the Carliles, Mill dismisses his other contributions: "during the whole of this year, 1823, a considerable number of my contributions were printed in the *Chronicle* and *Traveller*: sometimes notices of books, but oftener letters, commenting on some nonsense talked in Parliament, or some defect of the law, or misdoings of the magistracy or the courts of justice" (*A*, 91); however, it is these writings, especially those on "some defect or misdoings" that show the strength of Bentham's influence, be it from his writings or his lips.

A far greater number than Mill implies of his early articles appeared in the *Morning Chronicle* exposing the "defects of the law, and of the administration of justice." "I do not go beyond the mark in saying," Mill comments, "that after Bentham, who supplied the principal materials, the greatest share of the merit of breaking down this wretched superstition belongs to Black, as editor of the *Morning Chronicle*" (*A*, 91).[26] In 1823 seventeen of his twenty-five contributions, at a conservative estimate, are applications of principles enunciated by Bentham, and by James Mill in his articles in Napier's *Supplement to the Encyclopaedia Britannica*.

In his castigation of religious persecution in January of 1823 (No. 3), Mill applied the fundamental lesson learnt from the *Traités*: "What thus impressed me was the chapter in which Bentham passed judgment on the common modes of reasoning in morals and legislation, deduced from phrases like 'law of nature,' 'right reason,' 'the moral sense,' 'natural rectitude,' and the like, and characterized them as dogmatism in disguise . . ." (*A*, 67). The exposure of such fallacious language had become the trademark of a true practising Benthamite.[27] Such a maxim as "Christianity is part and parcel of the law of England," declares

---

[26]Of the changes in both criminal law and the law of juries wrought during the five years after Sir Robert Peel had accepted the Home Office, Mackintosh claimed it was as though he "had lived in two different countries, and conversed with people who spoke two different languages" (George Peel, *Dictionary of National Biography*, *s.v.* Robert Peel).

[27]George Grote earnestly explained in a letter to his nineteen-year-old sister-in-law, Fanny Lewin: "Volney is an excellent book, but take care that his vague expressions (such as *loi naturelle*, *droit invariable et eternel*, etc., etc.,) do not impose themselves upon you as ultimate truths. Never suffer a word or phrase to take the place of a reason, and whenever you meet such an expression, resolve it into the principle of utility." (*The Lewin Letters*, ed. Thomas Herbert Lewin, 2 vols. [London: Constable, 1909], I, 202.) For Mill's repeated reliance on this passage in Bentham, see John M. Robson, "John Stuart Mill and Jeremy Bentham, with Some Observations on James Mill," in *Essays in English Literature Presented to A.S.P. Woodhouse*, ed. M. MacLure and F.W. Watt (Toronto: University of Toronto Press, 1964), 245-68.

Mill to the editor of the *Morning Chronicle*, is "utterly unmeaning and absurd," and no grounds for religious persecution.[28]

As he pursued the argument in the "Letters on Free Discussion" (Nos. 5, 6, and 7) the young disciple laid about him with his master's sword. Bentham's arguments on efficacious causes and truthfulness in witnesses,[29] Quaker honesty,[30] atheists' reliability,[31] and foresworn jurymen when the punishment is too large for the crime,[32] all appear quite recognizably in these letters to the editor. The argument that Christianity is not needed for the basis of a good judicature, since non-Christians keep their word and many Christians ignore their oaths, bolstered by examples of custom-house oaths and university students' oaths, can be found repeatedly in Bentham.[33] Perhaps even in his reusing of examples, Bentham's influence can be seen. When the evidence of a Quaker is refused in July 1823, custom-house oaths and university regulations are called into service again (No. 11). Mill in August applies Bentham's expostulations on the perniciousness of oath-taking as weakening the sin of lying in "The Mischievousness of an Oath" (No. 14). And the following week in yet another letter on oath-taking (No. 16), custom houses and universities bear witness one more time.[34]

The move from oaths to judges (No. 15) gives the young Benthamite many texts to choose from, all vituperative and all based on the axiom so movingly put by George Grote in his letter to Fanny Lewin on her discovery of the true faith, "I

---

[28]Jeremy Bentham had used this example in *"Swear Not at All": Containing an Exposure of the Inutility and Mischievousness, as Well as Anti-Christianity, of the Ceremony of an Oath* (London: Hunter, 1817), in *Works*, V, 187-229. James Mill used the same argument in his article on "Ecclesiastical Establishments" in the *Westminster Review*, V (Apr. 1826), 504-48. This comment is not meant to add to the store of examples of James's using his son's time and brain but rather to illustrate the common body of knowledge on which they all drew.

[29]Pierre Etienne Louis Dumont, *A Treatise on Judicial Evidence, Extracted from the Manuscripts of Jeremy Bentham Esq.* (translated into English) (London: Baldwin, *et al.*, 1825), 81; the argument of efficacious causes also appears in *Introduction to the Principles of Morals and Legislation* (1789), in *Works*, I, 14-15 (Chap. iii). The dates of Bentham's works here cited are not all previous to Mill's articles. The assumption is that the young disciple saw and heard much of Bentham's work before it was ordered for publication; Bentham's habits of composition justify the assumption. For a detailed look at when Mill probably read and where he directly refers to Bentham's works, see J.M. Robson, "Which Bentham Was Mill's Bentham?" *Bentham Newsletter*, no. 7 (May 1983), 15-26. (The phrases and examples in Mill's attacks in 1823 tempt me to question the year—the end of 1824 or beginning of 1825—given in the *Autobiography*, 117, for the year he received the papers from Dumont for the editing of the *Rationale of Judicial Evidence*.)

[30]*A Treatise on Judicial Evidence*, 84-5.

[31]*Rationale of Judicial Evidence, Specially Applied to English Practice. From the Manuscripts of Jeremy Bentham*, ed. J.S. Mill, 5 vols. (London: Hunt and Clarke, 1827), V, 125-6.

[32]*Ibid.*, Bk. II, Chap. vi, sect. 2.

[33]Particular examples appear in *A Treatise on Judicial Evidence*, 81, and in Mill's edition of the *Rationale of Judicial Evidence*, I, 242-6, 375-6.

[34]Mill throughout his life was parsimonious of his time and energy to the extent of occasionally plagiarizing himself. He was a polemicist as well as a philosopher, and if an idea was worth developing once, it was worth developing again and again until it took root in the public mind.

truly rejoice that you have satisfied yourself as to the fact of *amour de soi* being the universal mover, variously modified, of the human race. There is no possibility of correctly appreciating men or motives until this has become a faultless truth."[35] Mill argues, "A Judge must always have much to gain by injustice: and if due securities are not provided, he will do injustice" (No. 15). Bentham said the same thing at greater length in the *Rationale of Judicial Evidence*, especially in Vol. IV, Book VIII, culminating in Chapter XXIX, "Apology for the Above Exposure," which for sheer spluttering indignant abuse cannot be outdone. Mill's solution is Bentham's—publicity.[36] Mill goes so far as to propose "giving to the people, either immediately or through their representatives, the power of removing judges of all descriptions from their offices" (No. 20)—a position he later qualifies.

When Mill objects to the use of the treadmill (No. 26) and reviews a book by Hippisley deploring its use (No. 22), it is Bentham's views of punishment, found also in James Mill's "Prison and Prison Discipline," that he puts forward. The son includes a puff for his father's work, and well he might, since his piece is little more than a rewording of his father's argument that "People of industry, people who love labour, seldom become the criminal inmates of a prison,"[37] and, therefore, to use labour of any kind, even the treadmill, as an instrument of punishment is exceptionable. But he might equally well have acknowledged his erstwhile guardian in whose *Rationale of Punishment* the distinction between reformation and punishment was argued: reformation would be achieved by bringing the slothful to an appreciation of labour.[38]

In September of 1823 (No. 19) Mill took as his text Bentham's expostulation that it is hardly conceivable that a people could be found so stupid as to be persuaded that to serve justice "Nothing more was in any case necessary, than to pronounce one or other of three or four words, such as *null, void, bad, quash, irregularity*";[39] the legal student holds up two cases, one dismissed for the misspelling of a magistrate's name and the other for using "after-forenoon" for "afternoon."

In January of 1824 two more articles (Nos. 29 and 30) echo Bentham. In his review of Francis Place's pamphlet on special juries, which was itself largely based on Bentham,[40] Mill paraphrases Bentham's defence of his personal

---

[35]*Lewin Letters*, 201.

[36]See *A Treatise on Judicial Evidence*, 69, and *Rationale*, I, 279.

[37]James Mill, "Prison and Prison Discipline," in *Essays* (London: printed Innes, [1825]), 8.

[38]Jeremy Bentham, *The Rationale of Punishment* (1830), in *Works*, I, 440.

[39]*Rationale of Judicial Evidence*, IV, 32.

[40]Place's argument is sustained by the example of Middlesex, an example, including the numbers cited, and even Ellenborough's statement at Cobbett's trial, to be found in Bentham's pamphlet, *The Elements of the Art of Packing as Applied to Special Juries, Particularly in Cases of Libel Law* (1821), in *Works*, V, 61-186. Place also quotes Bentham's *Church of Englandism* (1818) and refers to his *Judicial Establishment in France* (1790).

criticism of judges, that he meant no slur on any individual. Bentham wrote: "The fault lies not in the individual, not in any particular taint of improbity seated in the bosom of the individual, but in the system itself";[41] Mill writes: "We cannot sufficiently reprobate the principle itself, of endeavouring to deter men from exposing a bad system, lest their strictures should be construed into imputations upon the character of individuals" (No. 29). Mill pointed out "the absurdity of a system of law which forces the Grand Jury to say one thing when they mean another; and not only to say it, but to swear it. This is innocent perjury, but it is perjury, and though the Jurors do not deserve blame, the law evidently does," and signed himself, "An Enemy to Legal Fictions" (No. 30): in doing so, he must have had Bentham's voice in his ear, the voice that had filled vitriolic pages on "Legal Mendacity" in the _Rationale of Judicial Evidence._[42]

The echoes of James Mill's voice in these articles, though not as resonant as those of Bentham's, are better known, so a few examples will make the point. There is no embarrassment, indeed there is pride, at being the son of his father when Mill writes that this "subject is developed in the most satisfactory manner in Mr. Mill's invaluable Essay on the Liberty of the Press, forming an article in Napier's Supplement to the _Encyclopaedia Britannica_" (No. 5). No thought then of renouncing "sectarian follies" (_A_, 117). The father's essays and the son's articles show a remarkable similarity in word and idea. James Mill: "As the surface of history affords, therefore, no certain principle of decision, we must go beyond the surface, and penetrate to the springs within."[43] John Mill: "Against theories founded upon universal experience, the enemies of improvement hold out—what? Theories founded upon history; that is, upon partial and incomplete experience." (No. 13.) James Mill: "Government is founded upon this, as a law of human nature, that a man, if able, will take from others any thing which they have and he desires. . . ."[44] John Mill: "unless securities are provided, men will neglect the public interest, whenever it interferes with their own" (No. 13). These were the commonplaces of the Philosophic Radicals at the time, be they seventeen-year-old boys or nineteen-year-old girls or fifty-year-old mentors.

Mill's article on parliamentary reform (No. 21) relies heavily on his father's essay on "Government" but with an interesting twist, one of the early examples of the rhetoric that John Mill was frequently to use against wrong thinkers. James Mill dismissed the argument that a king or aristocracy is ever satiated as "an opinion founded upon a partial and incomplete view of the laws of human

[41]_Rationale of Judicial Evidence_, IV, 59.
[42]Bentham's actual words would have been too rich even for John Black: "Fiction of use to justice? Exactly as swindling is to trade," and "The fictions by which . . . the adjective branch is polluted, may be distinguished in the first instance into two great classes: the falsehoods which the judges are in the habit of uttering by themselves, or by the officers under their direction" (_ibid._, IV, 300).
[43]James Mill, "Government," in _Essays_, 9.
[44]_Ibid._, 8.

nature."[45] The son, more subtle than the father, did not use his father's hatred of the aristocracy. He preferred to defeat his opponents by allowing their original premise: that a people would infallibly make so bad a choice "as to render the attainment of good government in this mode utterly hopeless" (No. 21), and to prove that the logical alternative is not an aristocratic government but an absolute monarchy. Mill's consciousness of his potential opponents, undoubtedly heightened by his debating experience, typifies his lifelong rhetorical style. But the clever scoring of points, though undoubtedly a rewarding game, with a serious purpose for the recently unleashed reformer, was still a game, still "dissecting a bad argument, and finding in what part the fallacy lay," rather than examining the principles of good government and "acquiring, by experience and reflection, valuable thoughts" of one's own. In a short while, this game was to prove unsatisfactory, and the young man would be seeking the principles upon which to base the refutation of his opponents' argument.

There may even be an early warning sign of this dissatisfaction in "Old and New Institutions" (No. 24). Mill attacks an innocent Colonel Hughes who, although advocating reform, does so on the grounds of restoring the old, not introducing the new. Mill's views are quite orthodox, but there is rather an abundance of fervour in his Benthamite deluging of "the wisdom of our ancestors" with scorn. "Happily we are much wiser than our ancestors; it were a shame if we were not, seeing that we have all their experience, and much more in addition to it" (No. 24). The words of a cocky young whippersnapper. Does half a century between birth dates make one an ancestor and another an heir? Bentham and his father were essentially improving the springs of the stagecoach rather than designing the steam engine.

Another element in the philosophical radical synthesis, Hartleian metaphysics, lies behind the curious piece that Mill wrote for the newly founded *Lancet*; the uncompromising nature of his assertion is quite startling:

as it is generally admitted that circumstances often overcome the effect of natural predisposition, while no proof has ever been given that natural disposition can overcome external circumstances: we are at liberty to conclude, that in ascribing to any person a natural and original disposition to vice, men are following the very common practice of representing as *natural* that which is only *habitual*, merely because they do not recollect its beginning, and will not take the trouble to inquire into its cause (No. 26).

Although both Bentham and James Mill were Hartleians, John Mill's analysis in this article on the making of a murderer is more than a derivative attempt to argue

---

[45]*Ibid.*, 11. James Mill's views were unlikely to allow the satiation of the aristocracy: "Mr. Mill had the strongest convictions as to the superior advantages of democratic government over the monarchical or the aristocratic; and with these he mingled a scorn and hatred of the ruling classes which amounted to positive fanaticism" (Harriet Grote, *The Personal Life of George Grote* [London: Murray, 1873], 22).

a problem. This question of human nature bothered him all his life (in the *Subjection of Women* he skirted around it),[46] though he was to find a position he could live with: "I saw that though our character is formed by circumstances, our own desires can do much to shape those circumstances . . ." (*A*, 177). Interwoven with his argument was the depressing prospect of reforming a world for people who are of clay, not only their feet but their souls, clay that must be shaped in Benthamite moulds for every generation. No wonder the promptings of the small voice that wanted to believe in the improvement of mankind, not just circumstances, were gathering force.

The teen-age Mill's regular writing for the newspapers ended with the unfurling of the Malthusian banner in combat against the *Black Dwarf* (Nos. 27, 28, 31, and 32). It is still clever debating: Wooler has only to be forced to concede one point—"such matters will always regulate themselves"—and Mill exults in triumph: "This, Sir, is all that I want" (No. 31). But the central issue of the article is powerfully felt and continues to be felt throughout his life; diminution of family size would bring about other and permanent improvement. Many of the principles learnt from Bentham and James Mill are mustered for this debate, and it is fitting that their influence on him should be so clearly illustrated as the first phase of Mill's journalism draws to a close. What makes a government bad is the amount of discomfort it produces. "Until they [the people] are well fed, they cannot be well instructed: and until they are well instructed, they cannot emancipate themselves from the double yoke of priestcraft and of reverence for superiors" (No. 27). Overpopulation, he argues, is in the interest of landowner and manufacturer who will, therefore, oppose any remedy. To the argument that the plan was against the law of nature, Mill rejoined, "To check population is not more unnatural than to make use of an umbrella" (No. 27), an analogy perhaps prompted by Joseph Hanway's being the introducer into London of both brollies and foundling hospitals. And there is a happy echo of Bentham's style in the concluding sentence of his next article, where he protests the application of the word "heartless" to the promoters of limitation, "unless, indeed, the word heartless, be one of the engines of a sentimental cant, invented to discourage all steady pursuit of the general happiness of mankind" (No. 28).

His technique of argument has developed over the last twelve months; he has become cleverer in ticking off one by one the possible objections of probable opponents; he turns their arguments upon them. Neat turns of invective come from his pen ("you have made a much more free use, in this paper, of that easy figure of speech called assertion, than of that more intractable one called proof" [No. 31]—a use at this age he was well qualified to recognize); but some techniques seem to have been instilled with his training. For example, he sets the

---

[46]In an interesting letter to Kate Amberley, Helen Taylor discusses the books she and Mill were reading on the subject of the formation of character in connection with, she implies, the writing of the *Subjection of Women* (29 Mar., 1869; Russell Archives, McMaster University).

onus of an argument upon his opponents ("it is incumbent upon those who declare against toleration to point out some reason which prevents the general rule from being applicable to this particular case" [No. 5])—he uses nearly the same words forty years later when writing *The Subjection of Women*.[47] But the great value of these early writings is their unique witness to the mind created by James Mill's education. It is almost uncomfortably apposite that this period of his apprenticeship should conclude with two letters to the editor, one (No. 33) defending his father's views, and one which reads:

The accompanying paragraphs are destined for insertion in your *Dwarf*. They are extracted from the article "Colonies," in the supplement to the *Encyclopaedia Britannica*; a discourse composed by an eminent friend of the people. They contain, I think, a most conclusive answer to your last article on population; and if you insert them, you will be very well able to dispense with the reply which you would otherwise have received from Sir, your most obedient Servant. (No. 32.)

SEPTEMBER 1825 TO OCTOBER 1828

PARLIAMENTARY EVENTS were the centre of interest in England in the latter half of the decade. The rioting common after the Napoleonic Wars was less so now, though not unknown. There were strikes in 1824 and after the repeal of the Combination Acts that year, engineered by Place and executed by Hume, there were even more strikes in 1825. The middle classes, too, had their griefs. That year saw wild speculation in "bubble" companies, and county banks joined the Bank of England in over-issuing paper money to fuel the dreams. In December the end came; Pole and Company failed and between sixty and seventy banks were sucked under with it. The Bank Act of 1826 authorizing joint-stock banks and providing controls for currency issue was Peel's response. There followed coincidentally a period of prosperity, quickly terminated by a poor harvest. Corn Law agitation revived amongst the manufacturing classes, and the labouring classes again vented their despair by attacks on mills, especially those with power looms. To the economic uncertainty and discontent at all levels was suddenly added political uncertainty and discontent. On 18 February, 1827, Lord Liverpool had a stroke; the hand that had for fifteen years provided a semblance of stability was gone. The Whigs raised their hopes. After six weeks, Canning formed a Government including some Whigs and thus embittered both Tories and the Whigs who were not included. In August he died. For five months the ship of state was guided by Viscount Goderich, "as firm as a bullrush." He was succeeded in January of 1828 by the Duke of Wellington, with the support, until May, of William Huskisson and other Canningites, to whom Canning's widow

[47]*The Subjection of Women* (1869), in *Essays on Equality, Law, and Education*, CW, XXI (Toronto: University of Toronto Press, 1984), 262.

referred publicly as her husband's murderers. It was in this spirit of public animosity that Parliament and the country debated the Corn Law, Repeal of the Test and Corporation Acts, Catholic Emancipation, and electoral reform.

During all the uproar, Mill contributed only a few pieces to the daily press. His newspaper career was in virtual abeyance between 1824 and 1828; during those five years he wrote mostly for the *Westminster Review*, thirteen articles in all, with another four in the *Parliamentary Review*. He also edited the *Rationale of Judicial Evidence*, a formidable task despite his demonstrated familiarity with Bentham's ideas, and contributed to McCulloch's edition of the *Wealth of Nations* an appendix on Adam Smith's views on rent, territory also familiar to him. There is little new in the topics of Mill's articles in the *Westminster* on free trade and the laws of libel,[48] but, significantly, there were three on France, its great revolution, and its historians.[49] And Mill felt that those written in the *Parliamentary History and Review*[50] were also markedly different: "These writings were no longer mere reproductions and applications of the doctrines I had been taught; they were original thinking, as far as that name can be applied to old ideas in new forms and connexions" (*A*, 121-3). Although this impressive output, especially in the light of his other activities, would easily explain the paucity of his newspaper contributions, inclination undoubtedly played a role. He was depressed during 1826; duty occasionally led him to contribute though he was not inspirited—except in his political satire on Wellington's Ministry—but by 1828 the gloom was lifting.

After his hasty closing of the debate with Thomas Wooler over population, he wrote nothing more until the end of 1824, when he wrote one piece (No. 33) correcting Black's misinterpretation in the *Morning Chronicle* of what James Mill had said in the *Westminster Review*. He wrote another piece in September 1825; two others in June and December 1827; and six in 1828. In themselves they are of only minor significance. His defence of McCulloch's views (No. 34) was off the top of a well-stocked head; he had been writing in the *Westminster* on both economics and Ireland, and showed once again that warmed-up leftovers make a palatable enough snack. Ireland was also the topic of "The Brunswick Clubs" (No. 42). He contributed to the *New Times* (No. 35), probably because he could score off *The Times* and help Eugenius Roche, an editor known to his father from the earlier days of persecution of the press, who had just become its editor (again). Both the inhabitants of Queenborough (No. 36) and the

---

[48]"The Corn Laws" (1825), "The Silk Trade" (1826), and "The New Corn Laws" (1827), *CW*, IV, 45-70, 125-39, and 141-59; "Law of Libel and Liberty of the Press" (1825), *CW*, XXI, 1-34.

[49]"Mignet's French Revolution" (1826), "Modern French Historical Works" (1826), and "Scott's Life of Napoleon" (1828), *CW*, XX, 1-14, 15-22, and 53-110.

[50]"Ireland" (1826), in *Essays on England, Ireland, and the Empire*, *CW*, VI (Toronto: University of Toronto Press, 1982), 59-98; "Paper Currency and Commercial Distress" (1826), *CW*, IV, 71-123; "Foreign Dependencies—Trade with India" (1826–27), in the penultimate volume of *CW*; and "Intercourse between the United States and the British Colonies in the West Indies" (1828), *CW*, VI, 121-47.

shopkeepers on the approaches to London Bridge (No. 41) were small people being hurt by sinister interests, but there seems to be no special motivation for the articles. These are desultory pieces. More interesting are the satirical political squibs in 1828 prompted by the resignation of the Canningite faction from Wellington's cabinet (Nos. 37, 38, 39, and 40); perhaps he was cheering up, for they exhibit publicly the clever wit for which John Mill was enjoyed by his intimates but which, one must regret, appeared in his writings usually only as a very neat, sharp turn of phrase.

Gaiety had been certainly missing from the adolescent mind. There have been many analyses of the mental crisis since 1873; the light thrown on it by his early journalism (and vice versa) is all that need be seen here. John Stuart Mill, the teen-age romantic dreaming of the French Revolution (*A*, 65-7), himself playing the lead as the noblest of the Girondists, had spent his days writing letters and leaders. In them he applied the sectarian doctrines of the Utilitarians to a creaking eighteenth-century mechanical model in an attempt to make it run smoothly in the nineteenth. The world of Jeremy Bentham and James Mill was by definition made up of eternally self-seeking, pre-programmed abusers of power, all carefully set to watch over each other so that their selfish desires were controlled and directed towards the greatest happiness of the greatest number, who "will always prefer themselves to their neighbours . . . will indulge their indolence and satiate their rapacity whenever they can do it without fear of detection" (No. 15). Bentham said, "Amend the system, you amend the man." The idealistic teenager wanted more than to prevent a man from abusing his power; he wanted to reform the man and the system would take care of itself. It is no wonder that the small voice of his self-consciousness whispered "No" clearly, distinctly, and brooking no argument. It is no wonder that the brilliance of "the vista of improvement" that Bentham's *Traités* opened, originally sufficient "to light up my life, as well as to give a definite shape to my aspirations" (*A*, 71), began to dim after several years of applying principles to actual cases and evaluating the effects.

From the end of 1828 until the middle of 1830 he wrote very little (both John and James Mill withdrew from the *Westminster Review*) and nothing in the papers, "and great were the advantages which I derived from the intermission. It was of no common importance to me, at this period, to be able to digest and mature my thoughts. . . ." (*A*, 137.) The ideas which he needed to digest had come from a bewildering number of sources, all tending to loosen the moorings of the basically stationary world his father had explained to him. In England, many other influences came upon him: the ideas of people as different as Robert Owen, Samuel Taylor Coleridge, Thomas Carlyle, Thomas Macaulay, John Sterling, William Thompson. Most important were the young men with whom he associated. Change was in the atmosphere for the young—and for some not so young. For there was not one of Mill's thoughtful cotemporaries (as he would say) who did not acknowledge that some change must come. There was vast disagreement about the route to be taken and how far should be travelled, but there was no disagreement that travel one must. There is an enormous sense of the temporary in the first half of the century, especially after about 1820. Mill may have taken up from the French the phrase "age of transition" in his "Spirit of the Age," but it labelled what many in England felt. Everybody was passing through. Be they currency reformers or Corn Law repealers, Cambridge apostles or utilitarians, ten-hours men or socialists, Chartists or trade unionists, muscular Christians or Popish ones, Poor Law bashaws or angels of charity, conservatives or radicals, they were all working for a better tomorrow. One person's tomorrow might look like another person's yesterday, but they would both agree that today could not be the pattern for the future.

The young men who had developed this sense of change into a philosophy were French youths who breathed "the free and genial atmosphere of Continental life" (*A*, 59) so much admired by Mill. He read Auguste Comte's early *Système de politique positive* (1824) and learnt the stages of historical development, the characteristics of an age of transition, and, most importantly, the significance in historical progress of the French Revolution (*A*, 173); he started his lifelong friendship with Gustave d'Eichthal. The Saint-Simonians had a fundamental influence on him. Through their eyes, Mill had seen the promised land, and that vision, indeed obsession (but perhaps all visions are obsessions), he never lost.[51] The writings of the mature man were sustained by the passionate vision vouchsafed to the young man in his late teens. Not the less passionate by its expression being moderate,[52] this vision was dramatically given immediate reality by the French Revolution of 1830. Experience was to make the expected realization of the vision fade into the future, but the vision itself did not fade. The cards of history revealed movement. Mankind would improve; infinite improvement was possible.

JULY 1830 TO JULY 1831

IF LIFE IN LONDON had been less violent for the last decade than in the 1810s, violence was about to threaten once again. In the summer of 1830 the elections in England on the death of George IV were fought on reform and under the excitement of the July Revolution in France. It was thought the Tories had lost, and in November, when Parliament resumed, the issues became absolutely clear.

---

[51]J.A. Roebuck, looking back on these years, gives a sense of the messianic fervour: "I often laugh now at our splendid plans of moral & political regeneration. We frightened all the old people, by our daring doubts and conceptions. . . ." (Bodleian Library, MS Eng., Lett. c. 295, f. 41; quoted in Sarah Wilks, "The Mill-Roebuck Quarrel," *Mill News Letter*, XII, no. 2 [Summer 1978], 9.)

[52]Harriet Taylor was one of those who shared his vision; therein lay the root of Mill's admiration. The shared vision was what drew Mill to two such disparate men as Auguste Comte and William Gladstone.

Earl Grey raised the question of reform; the Duke of Wellington replied that England was perfect. London was so roused that King William's safety was feared for were he to attend the Lord Mayor's dinner accompanied by the Duke. The Duke resigned. Earl Grey formed a government and everybody went home for Christmas and the foxhunting. When Parliament resumed, Lord John Russell introduced the Reform Bill on 1 March, 1831. On 23 March, it passed its second reading by one vote, with the support of the Irish members. In April the Tories defeated the Government. A general election returned a majority for Grey and reform, and in June a second version of the Reform Bill was introduced into the Commons. Throughout the spring and summer of 1831, tension in England mounted. Crowds gathered in the streets; guns were being bought; political unions were formed and their members attended military drills. All watched as the Reform Bill, carried along by the parliamentary process, moved slowly and inexorably towards the House of Lords.

The tension was heightened by events in France.[53] The Polignac Ministry, with Charles X's full encouragement, had attempted to tamper with the elections in July of 1830. When, nevertheless, it became clear that the tiny electorate had defied their King and returned a majority opposed to the present Government, including the 221 recalcitrant Deputies who had signed a protest to the King against Polignac, Charles X issued the fatal ordinances, annulling the elections, constricting the electorate even more, and gagging the press. Paris rose, and for three glorious days, 27, 28, and 29 July, manned the barricades. During an exhilarating, frenetic week, those who had opposed Charles gathered and argued under a Provisional Government. Charles X abdicated, and Lafayette, the republican idol of France, embraced the Duke of Orleans before an immense crowd saying, "Voilà ce que nous avons pu faire de plus républicain."[54] The Duke, son of Philippe Egalité, became Louis Philippe I on 9 August; Lafayette's embrace had established "un trône populaire entouré d'institutions tout à fait républicaines."[55] From that day began the struggle between, as Mill saw it, the party of movement, led in the National Assembly by the old revolutionists and outside it by the young republicans especially the journalists, and the stationary party, led in the Assembly by Guizot and the Doctrinaires—broadly speaking the

---

[53]Details of those events are given in the headnotes to Mill's articles where they will be of more use to readers whose memories are good but short. "One of the major problems in modern French history is the often confusing changes of governments and the appearance of many politicians, men of letters, and military leaders who very briefly play their role upon the stage and disappear. To the English or American mind this appears to be a kaleidoscopic madness which fails to lend itself to themes and steady interpretations. Certainly, there are basic threads within the history of modern France, but almost as certainly there is a certain Gallic tendency to be scattered." (James J. Cooke, *France 1789-1962* [Newton Abbot: David and Charles, 1975], 7.)

[54]Quoted in René de la Croix, duc de Castries, *La Fayette* (Paris: Tallandier, 1981), 443.

[55]Marie Joseph Gilbert du Motier, marquis de Lafayette, *Mémoires, correspondance, et manuscrits du général Lafayette* (Brussels: Hauman, 1839), 525.

221 Deputies who had been the phalanx of the opposition to Charles X—and outside it by Louis Philippe, his Ministry, and the thousands of government place-men throughout the bureaucracy of France. By the summer of 1831, Louis Philippe and the Ministry under Casimir Périer, through relentless persecution of the republican press and brutal repression of insurrections, had established the bourgeois monarchy modelled, to Mill's infinite disgust, on the Whig example in England.

In the spring of 1830 Mill was well on the way to recovery of his equilibrium, although periods of depression would return. The frame of mind in which the French Revolution of July found him (*A*, 163ff.) still showed many of the effects of his depression, but three things elated him: his introduction to Harriet Taylor, whose effect on him, whatever one may think of her, cannot be overestimated; the prorogation of the French Parliament; and the death of George IV, which effectually prorogued the English Parliament. All three events portended for the young man a much brighter future. The *mouvement* of history that he had learnt from his French acquaintances to hold as a faith was clearly about to advance noticeably.

Mill was quite confident that the death of George IV would mean reform in England. He himself took little part directly in advancing the movement of history in England, not even with his pen. But indirectly he did. His articles on France, contributed to the *Examiner* regularly after August 1830, are written with an acute awareness of the happenings and the attitudes around him. Here Mill's new ideas can be seen being put to the test. "The only actual revolution which has ever taken place in my modes of thinking, was already complete. My new tendencies had to be confirmed in some respects, moderated in others: but the only substantial changes of opinion that were yet to come, related to politics. . . ." (*A*, 199.)

Mill's return to journalism (No. 43) was fired by his desire to ensure that the English public were correctly informed about the issues involved in the French elections; misunderstanding of France must not lead to a weakening of resolve at home. Ignorance could mean destruction and bloodshed in England.[56] It is noteworthy that Mill wrote his articles on France for Fonblanque's *Examiner*.[57]

---

[56]Letter to John Sterling, 20-22 Oct., 1831, in *Earlier Letters, 1812-1848* [*EL*], ed. Francis E. Mineka, *CW*, XII-XIII (Toronto: University of Toronto Press, 1963), XII, 78.

[57]"For the next few years I wrote copiously in newspapers. It was about this time that Fonblanque, who had for some time written the political articles in the *Examiner*, became the proprietor and editor of the paper. It is not forgotten with what verve and talent, as well as fine wit, he carried it on, during the whole period of Lord Grey's ministry, and what importance it assumed as the principal representative, in the newspaper press, of radical opinions. The distinguishing character of the paper was given to it entirely by his own articles, which formed at least three fourths of all the original writing contained in it: but of the remaining fourth I contributed during those years a much larger share than any one else. I wrote nearly all the articles on French subjects, including a weekly summary of French politics, often extending to considerable length; together with many leading articles on general politics, commercial and financial legislation, and any miscellaneous subjects in

The *Examiner* was a weekly and therefore occasionally allowed longer articles while demanding a summary of the week's news rather than daily reports. Fonblanque's ardour was more suitable in spirit than Black's heavier touch for the new (born again?) Mill, and his father's shadow over his shoulder was less sensed.

When the French elections turned into confrontation which developed into revolution, "it roused [his] utmost enthusiasm, and gave [him], as it were, a new existence" (*A*, 179). Mill ecstatically travelled to Paris for two weeks, to the very heart of the intellectual excitement he so much admired. He wrote a hagiographic description of the popular uprising to his father in three letters, two of which were printed in the *Examiner*.[58] When Mill returned to London, he was on tenterhooks as France established herself after the Glorious Days. He at first took advantage of the greater space allowed to discuss the Prospects of France, in a series of articles which he wrote from September to November 1830 (Nos. 44, 45, 48, 50, 51, 57, and 61). His philosophy of history, with its belief in progress through alternating transitional and organic stages, was being tested; before his very eyes was passing in fast-forward a transitional stage. Here was a chance not only to explain progress in history but also to further it by providing the broader background needed for a true appreciation of the forces of movement and stagnation that underlay events both in France and in England. Any party that is on the side of movement is on the side of history and must be on the side of the people. It cannot be otherwise. Any party which opposes movement must be against the interests of France, of her people, and therefore of mankind. "The design of these papers was to prepare the English public . . . for the struggle which we knew was approaching between the new oligarchy and the people; to arm them against the misapprehensions . . .; to supply facts . . . without which we are aware that that they could not possibly understand the true character of the events which were coming" (No. 61).

At the beginning of the series, Mill's hopes were high. The French people had behaved in exemplary fashion, showing that they were the unselfish force of the future, willing at present to leave their interests in the hands of their natural leaders, the educated men. As early as 19 September, however, he was aware that there were those who "in every step which it [the Revolution] takes towards the achievement of its destiny . . . are more keenly alive to the dangers which beset it, than to the glory and the happiness towards which it is irresistibly advancing" (No. 44). Two things worried Mill right from the start: one was the

---

which I felt interested, and which were suitable to the paper, including occasional reviews of books." (*A*, 179-81.) For a recent discussion of Mill's contributions on French politics, see Ann P. and John M. Robson, "'Impetuous Eagerness': The Young Mill's Radical Journalism," in *The Victorian Periodical Press*, ed. Joanne Shattock and Michael Wolff (Leicester: University of Leicester Press, 1982), 59-77.

[58]*EL, CW*, XII, 54-67 (13, 20, and 21 Aug., 1830).

apparent jobbing which immediately took place on a grand scale after the change of government. Place hunters poured into the Elysée Palace by the thousands. The power of self-interest was evident, and Mill realized that France was still ruled by an oligarchy, self-interest being the result of oligarchical rule. A second worry was much more serious. Even in an oligarchy, there can be a division between movement and stagnation. But many Frenchmen and nearly all Englishmen mistook the Doctrinaires under Guizot for the party of reform and gave them their support (No. 49); it could even be enough support for the Doctrinaires to dominate in the Chamber of Deputies and in the Government. But Guizot and his constitutionalists were backward looking. The "221" looked to the preservation of the Charter for which they had laudably fought against the encroachments of Charles X. Since the Glorious Days such an attitude was folly, was the result of a misunderstanding of the shift in the balance of power that had taken place when the people realized their strength, was a denial of the movement. Mill heaped abuse on the "fund of stupidity and vulgar prejudice in our principal journalists" (No. 56); especially the *Quarterly Review* and *The Times* constantly misinformed their readers about the true nature of the parties in France (Nos. 44, 49, 54, and 56 in particular).

In the early days, Mill could not believe in spite of his worries that he had misread the effects of revolution and the timing of history. The French would, he believed, "effect their parliamentary reform in two years, perhaps sooner,—not with muskets, but with newspapers and petitions: after which there will be 'tranquility,' if that name can be given to the intense activity of a people which, freed from its shackles, will speedily outstrip all the rest of the world in the career of civilization" (No. 44). His belief in the importance of newspapers was strengthened by his increasing hesitation about the anachronistic Chamber of Deputies; it was in the newspapers edited by young men that one heard the voice of the movement. A new Chamber chosen by an enlarged electorate was an essential first step, to be followed by elected municipal governments and a reformed peerage; these modest planks constituted the republican platform (No. 51).

When Laffitte, whom Mill saw as a liberal and (in spite of his age) more forward-looking than the constitutionalists, left the presidency of the Chamber to join the cabinet at the end of October, Mill was delighted at this sign that Louis Philippe was turning away from the stationary party (No. 55). It may be only a coincidence that Mill started at this time to contribute regular detailed reports on French politics and brought to a close his discursive series on the "Prospects of France." He argued for the domination of the Chamber by the Ministry—not a position English readers would expect a Radical to adopt; he thought Laffitte's Ministry (in which he included Louis Philippe) ought to control the Chamber because its members were more advanced than the majority of the Deputies. It was certainly more than a coincidence that Mill was putting forward these ideas in November when in England the debate on the speech from the throne, the first test of Lord Grey's support, was taking place. In Mill's analysis of the political developments, the popularity that would allow Laffitte to dominate the Government could only come from the popular press. (Mill used "popular" not to mean representing majority opinion among the people, but being on the side of the people, on the side of history.) Most of the popular press was republican—*Le National*, of which Armand Carrel was one of the editors, was his ideal; these young journalists alone dared to question institutions hallowed by time. This was not like the licentious press of England and America where people pursued journalism as a trade, "as they would gin-making," for it was written by the "highly cultivated portion of *la jeune France*" out of the most noble principle (No. 54). Mill is quite carried away by the prospect afforded by the brilliant young men leading "this noble people [who] afford every day some new and splendid example of its progress in humane feelings and enlightened views" (No. 52), even when they were rioting in favour of the death penalty for Polignac and his ministers.

Mill was very disturbed when the rejection at the end of November of Benjamin Constant's Bill to exempt printers from obtaining licences showed that the Chamber was prepared to see the press curbed (No. 62). The rejection led him to question and then qualify the use of the ballot. The Deputies voted on separate clauses openly and every clause passed, but the Bill as a whole failed to pass on the final vote by ballot. The ballot, he concluded, was not suitable for use in a representative assembly where a man's vote should be known to his constituents, but was for the constituents themselves who needed its protection. His position drew him briefly into a debate with the *Standard* (Nos. 63 and 65).

By December the young enthusiast's growing doubts were given a particular issue to cluster around. Because "a revolution carries society farther on its course, and makes greater changes in the popular mind, than half a century of untroubled tranquillity" (No. 48), Louis Philippe and the Ministry must not be content to tinker with the system but must reconstitute it in accordance with the new society. Laffitte's proposed reform of the election law—at least what it was rumoured to include—was far too narrow to satisfy Mill, especially a Mill with one eye on events in England (No. 64).[59] Earl Grey should realize that a far-reaching reform bill was the only way to bring English institutions into harmony with the new society. Mill's growing disillusionment spills over in his reporting of the death of Benjamin Constant: "We are assured that this lamented patriot, almost with his last breath, expressed to the friends who encircled his death-bed, the regret which he felt, while dying, that the revolution of July was *manquée*, and had fallen into the hands of *intrigans*" (No. 68). The champion of

---

[59]Mill kept his gaze on England long enough to write three orthodox articles supporting the stands taken by his old acquaintances Hume and Hyde Villiers, now in Parliament, on the Truck System and on the Poor Law (Nos. 67, 69, and 70).

a free press was dead, and the *intrigans* were persecuting and silencing the young men who stood for the movement.

The King's dismissal of Lafayette at the end of December was followed by Laffitte's replacement in March by the less acceptable—to Mill—Casimir Périer. Mill now set his hopes (as he was to do in English politics after the Reform Bill passed and Parliament changed not) on a radical opposition. Indirectly warning the Whigs at home, he poured vitriol on the head of Guizot, who was attempting to form a middle party between the popular party, led by Lafayette, and the oligarchy, for his "bigotted and coxcombical devotion" (No. 74) to his own ways instead of joining the popular party which had the backing of all under thirty-five and was thus "a power which no one dares despise; and, by earnest and well-directed exertions, is sure of ultimate victory" (No. 72).

There were small improvements, but little to feed Mill's hopes or catch his imagination. The number of judges was to be reduced; the Commissioner who introduced the Bill delighted the heart of the editor of Bentham's *Rationale of Judicial Evidence* by showing a sense "of the immense importance of the principle of undivided responsibility" of judges (No. 76),[60] but the fact that he was the only one in the debate who did so somewhat lessened the delight. There was to be Government retrenchment of salaries. And then there was the municipal bill by which the local bodies were to be elected "by a suffrage tolerably extensive," though "all the good which would otherwise result from the law is neutralised" by their being elected for six years. The amount of moral improvement engendered amongst the people would presumably therefore be minimal. Mill went so far as to argue that it might be better if the municipal officers continued as Crown appointees, because then they could be removed if the popular outcry was strong enough. He was upset but understanding when the people threw the Archbishop's furniture into the Seine. The people, Mill explained, though they loved religion, could not abide political religion—possibly a timely word to the English bishops (No. 87). Again with the reform crisis at home very much in mind—the Bill was to be introduced on 1 March—Mill chastised *The Times* and the *Quarterly Review* for their failure to realize that the Doctrinaires under Guizot were the stationary party: "If the English and the new French government are destined severally to give another lesson to the world on the incapacity of oligarchies, howsoever constituted, to learn wisdom from experience, the trial must be submitted to: but at least those who shall provoke it shall do so knowingly, and must hold themselves prepared to suffer the natural consequences of their own folly" (No. 89).

On 6 March, 1831, Mill wrote on both Lord John Russell's Reform Bill (No. 90) and French electoral reform (No. 91). Mill's reaction to Russell's Bill was

---

[60]See *Rationale of Judicial Evidence*, IV, 444, where Mill himself has a note to this effect; also James Mill, "Jurisprudence" (1821), in *Essays*, 29-30.

surprisingly cool, since it was surely more thorough than he had expected: it should be supported, although limited, because either the new Parliament under it would represent the wishes of the people or the people would force the ballot. (Mill, like his allies and most others at this time, makes no distinction between the middle class to be enfranchised and the lower classes who are not.) When the new French electoral law was introduced, Mill should have been delighted that it was more generous than he had expected, but instead he was depressed as the parties in the Chamber manoeuvred to secure an election date to serve their selfish interests: "The destinies of France are in the hands of men more than nine-tenths of whom are not fit to have any part in the government of a parish" (No. 91).

With such men in power, throughout the spring of 1831 Mill understandably continued in low spirits.[61] The revolution seemed to have stagnated, to have declined into piecemeal reforms extracted from a grudging Ministry, passed by a petty, selfish, factionalized Chamber of Deputies. Even the middle classes were not satisfied "either in respect to men or measures"; consequently there was no feeling of security. Until there was security, "the labouring population will be without work, will be dissatisfied, a prey to agitators, and ready for continual tumults: which tumults, so long as they do not endanger human life or private property, the National Guard [some of whose companies, Mill does not mention, were commanded by young republicans] will give themselves as little trouble as possible to suppress" (No. 89). It was thus the Government's fault that mobs and rioting were once more commonplace. Mill's enthusiasm for the republican youth was not diminished.

Mill never ceased to defend the right of the youth of Paris to speak and write their thoughts, even in extreme cases when the results of their behaviour were dangerous by ordinary standards. At twenty-four, Mill felt he had much in common with the gallant band of young men who had placed themselves in the van of history. As their influence waned and power became established in the hands of the older liberals, Mill became profoundly disturbed. He hardly mentioned the republicans' part in fuelling the December riots during the trial of the ex-Ministers—the reports of which he had at first dismissed as exaggerated rumour (Nos. 72 and 89)—for which they had been arrested, tried, and acquitted. He referred to the "pretended republican conspirators" (No. 100) "who, it has been supposed by good-natured, timid friends of freedom, both in this country and in France, must needs be firebrands and sowers of sedition" (No. 101). Mill translated Cavaignac's speech in his own defence; the appeal to him was obvious: "it is inevitable; . . . all things are moving in that direction; the course of events, the human mind, and outward things. I have perceived, that it

[61]However much Mill's personal life may have determined his writings, it can, for the most part, here receive only occasional mention. This particular spring and summer may have been a little trying on his spirits as Harriet and John Taylor were expecting their third child, Helen, born in July.

is impossible for the movement which now rules the world to end in any thing but a republic." (App. A.)

It is this spirit, this understanding of the forward movement of history to progressively more democratic institutions, the shift in power to greater numbers, that Mill is trying to inculcate in his readers. It is this spirit that is the spirit of the age. In early 1831, to develop these ideas more elaborately, he wrote five long articles under that title.[62] His belief explains his lack of interest—the words are not too strong—in the details of Grey's Reform Bill. The historical process will bring reform to England; with or without revolution is the choice before Englishmen. He wanted to persuade Englishmen to vote on the side of history; the alternative for England was revolution.

The price had been worth paying in France. Mill is so convinced that revolution is always a great leap forward, an advancing of the historical process, that his vision at times must have made his thought a little obscure to his readers. It triumphed over any disappointment, and he assured Englishmen that despite appearances the French Revolution was a good. If at times the young enthusiast felt that history moved in mysterious ways, his prose revealed no hint of irony.

It is not to be denied that, up to this moment, the Revolution of 1830 has brought forth none but bitter fruits;—the ruin of hundreds of opulent families; thousands of industrious workmen thrown out of employment; perpetual apprehension of internal tumults or foreign war; the most grievous disappointments; the most violent political dissensions; and, finally, a Government not more democratic in its constitution—not more popular in its spirit—and, by the necessity of its false position, not less oppressive and anti-national in its acts, than that of Charles X. . . .

To all this, the answer is, that the circumstances of France and the character of the French nation are grievously mistaken, if it is imagined that the people of France made their Revolution under the conception that it was a thing to *gain* by. (No. 98.)

Such sentiments were a far cry from "*amour de soi* being the universal mover."[63]

The universal mover had become the historical process whose agent was the people. Leaders on both sides of the Channel must understand that power was inevitably moving to the people; political democracy would come. The young

[62]"Mere newspaper articles on the occurrences or questions of the moment gave no opportunity for the development of any general mode of thought; but I attempted, in the beginning of 1831, to embody in a series of articles, headed 'The Spirit of the Age,' some of my new opinions, and especially to point out in the character of the present age, the anomalies and evils characteristic of the transition from a system of opinions which had worn out, to another only in process of being formed. These articles were, I fancy, lumbering in style, and not lively or striking enough to be at any time acceptable to newspaper readers; but had they been far more attractive, still, at that particular moment, when great political changes were impending, and engrossing all minds, these discussions were ill timed, and missed fire altogether. The only effect which I know to have been produced by them, was that Carlyle, then living in a secluded part of Scotland, read them in his solitude, and saying to himself (as he afterwards told me) 'here is a new Mystic,' enquired on coming to London that autumn respecting their authorship; an enquiry which was the immediate cause of our becoming personally acquainted." (*A*, 181.)

[63]*Lewin Letters*, 201.

men of France knew this truth and were actually striving to prevent the stationary party from perpetuating unrest in France. In a time of transition, it is the young who question the received ideas and who will eventually develop the new ideas that will bring stability. It is essential, therefore, that they be permitted freedom of speech and action.

The men of the present day rather incline to an opinion than embrace it; few, except the very penetrating, or the very presumptuous, have full confidence in their own convictions. This is not a state of health, but, at the best, of convalescence. It is a necessary stage in the progress of civilization, but it is attended with numerous evils; as one part of a road may be rougher or more dangerous than another, although every step brings the traveller nearer to his desired end. (No. 73.)

It was absolutely essential to keep stepping. If the leaders refused to help the historical process, there would be a long period of disruption, perhaps much bloodshed; the period of transition would be prolonged in all its uncertainty. This was the message Mill delivered in the spring of 1831 as both Louis Philippe and William IV dissolved their parliaments, the former with dignity after the new electoral law had been passed, and the latter in some haste to forestall the Lords after the proposed electoral reform had been thwarted: "in the two greatest nations in the world, general elections will simultaneously take place, and the new legislative bodies will be simultaneously called upon to determine the future constitution of their country" (No. 102). Mill had two elections of great interest to watch.

But he also had to plan a trip to the Lake District for July, an exciting journey involving four days of conversation with Wordsworth, which, along with Harriet Taylor's safe delivery of a daughter, Helen, may have done something to lift his spirits. For the next few years, Mill's annual summer trips coincided naturally with the summer political recess and with, equally naturally, a gap in his political reporting, and they form for editors convenient chapter breaks. Before he went on his trip, he took time to fulfil a few occasional obligations such as an obituary and a review (Nos. 108 and 110), a response to an attack, if oblique, on a principle (Nos. 109 and 111), and puffs for friends or friends of friends (Nos. 104, 106, and 112). These last remind one that Mill was now, as was Harriet, a frequenter of the *Monthly Repository* circle and a close friend of W.J. Fox and Eliza Flower.

AUGUST 1831 TO JULY 1832

BACK FROM HIS HOLIDAY in the Lake District, Mill returned to his France-watching in a somewhat better frame of mind. But he returned to an England that was to come to the brink of revolution in the next nine months. Grey's increased support from that summer's elections meant the reintroduced

Reform Bill easily passed its third reading in the Commons in September; in October the Lords threw it out; the Bristol riots the same month showed how little protection property had against the mob. Throughout the winter, while cholera raged, the country waited to see which way the King would lean: towards the creation of peers, Grey, and reform, or towards the House of Lords, Wellington, and repression. Then in May 1832 came the ten days without a Government, when Wellington tried and failed to form one; this was the turning point. Grey returned to power with William IV's promise to create peers if need be. In June of 1832, the first Reform Bill received Royal Assent. With considerable excitement the country prepared to elect a reformed Parliament.

Mill's curiously detached attitude towards English politics is explained in a long, very personal letter he wrote to John Sterling:

If the ministers flinch or the Peers remain obstinate, I am firmly convinced that in six months a national convention chosen by universal suffrage, will be sitting in London. Should this happen, I have not made up my mind what would be best to do: I incline to think it would be best to lie by and let the tempest blow over, if one could but get a shilling a day to live upon meanwhile: for until the whole of the existing institutions of society are levelled with the ground, there will be nothing for a wise man to do which the most pig-headed fool cannot do much better than he. A Turgot, even, could not do in the present state of England what Turgot himself failed of doing in France—mend the old system. If it goes all at once, let us wait till it is gone: if it goes piece by piece, why, let the blockheads who will compose the first Parliament after the bill passes, do what a blockhead can do, viz. overthrow, & the ground will be cleared, & the passion of destruction sated, & a coalition prepared between the wisest radicals & the wisest anti-radicals, between all the wiser men who agree in their general views & differ only in their estimate of the present condition of this country.—You will perhaps think from this long prosing rambling talk about politics, that they occupy much of my attention: but in fact I am myself often surprised, how little I really care about them. The time is not yet come when a calm & impartial person can intermeddle with advantage in the questions & contests of the day. I never write in the Examiner now except on France, which nobody else that I know of seems to know any thing about; & now & then on some insulated question of political economy. The only thing which I can usefully do at present, & which I am doing more & more every day, is to work out _principles_: which are of use for all times, though to be applied cautiously & circumspectly to any: principles of morals, government, law, education, above all self-education. I am here much more in my element: the only thing that I believe I am really fit for, is the investigation of abstract truth, & the more abstract the better.[64]

Mill's reporting of French affairs could not help but be increasingly coloured by events in England and his attitude to them. During the next twelve months, Mill seems in his articles to be analyzing the political process more than reporting it. He claimed he was only good for the "investigation of abstract truth," but his newspaper articles qualify that claim, because it was from watching the French argue principle and fail to achieve the needed reforms that he began to realize the

[64]_EL, CW,_ XII, 78 (20-22 Oct., 1831).

truths of practical politics. As soon as he returned in August he wrote two pieces on the French elections, which had also resulted in gains for "the popular party." More than ever he thought the Ministerial Party under Casimir Périer was that of resistance and the opposition the party of movement—the Bonapartists and Republicans being insignificant in the Chamber—but he now thought the balance of power would allow reason to prevail and slow change would result. The French should now rest content until "the great step which their institutions have now made, shall have had leisure to produce its fruits" (No. 114). He recommended calm to allow the new French electoral law, although very inadequate, to make its effect felt; Mill did not want a revolution in England, and continuing ferment and further demands in France might stiffen the resistance, especially of the Lords, at home.

The main issue in the French Chamber during the autumn was the abolition of the hereditary peerage, one of the issues that helped Mill to work out principles and their use. In the article he wrote Mill seemed to be thinking out loud, not just about the peerage in England or France, but about leaders in a time of transition in whatever country.[65] "The will of the majority is not to be obeyed as a law, but it is to be attended to as a fact: the opinions and feelings of the nation are entitled to consideration, not for their own sake, but as one of the circumstances of the times . . . which produces effects not to be overlooked; a power, which so largely modifies and interferes with all you do, that unless it is allowed for in your calculations, you can predict nothing" (No. 115). The experience of these years had only confirmed his dislike of those liberal thinkers who were "for making every man his own guide & sovereign master, & letting him think for himself & do exactly as he judges best for himself. . . . It is difficult to conceive a more thorough ignorance of man's nature, & of what is necessary for his happiness or what degree of happiness & virtue he is capable of attaining than this system implies."[66]

He had moved a long way from his earlier radicalism; his observation of the immediate result of the French Revolution made him adjust his theories to fit the actual rather than the abstract consequences of a revolution. He had watched, and reported on, the devolution of an heroic struggle into a depressing battle between stationary liberals and conservatives, with only the people unthinkingly on the side of movement—and their thinking leaders, the young republicans.

The events in France during the months from October 1831 to May 1832 are of less interest than Mill's reaction to them. The temporary excitement he had felt at the uprising in Lyons in December had been quickly evaporated by its

---

[65]The letter to Sterling gives grounds for thinking Mill was pondering his own role.

[66]Again from the long letter to Sterling, *ibid.*, 84. John Austin's influence undoubtedly played a part; see Richard B. Friedman, "An Introduction to Mill's Theory of Authority," in *Mill: A Collection of Critical Essays*, ed. J.B. Schneewind (Garden City, N.Y.: Doubleday, 1968), 379-425.

suppression. Debates on the Civil List and the budget dragged on. The Bill for national education was delayed. Corruption seemed everywhere. All feeling, except disgust, had been dissipated by the rumours of poisoning that had accompanied the devastating outbreak of cholera in Paris in the spring of 1832. Riots had taken place and Paris was placed under martial law; warrants were issued for the arrest of men as different as Armand Carrel and Chateaubriand; Louis Philippe had handed the Government over to the stationary party, that of the Doctrinaires (nominally under Marshal Soult). Mill did not try to hide his contempt:

The French Chambers were prorogued on the 21st of April, after a session of nine months, in which but little that is of any real use has been even talked about; and of that little, nothing but the most paltry and insignificant fraction has been accomplished. The first session of the first Parliament elected under the Citizen King and the *charte-vérité*, has demonstrated nothing but the vices of the institutions of France, and the backwardness of her national mind. (No. 161.)

The fruits which leisure had produced while the French rested content were unpalatable. How could England save herself from a similar fate? By understanding and avoiding the conditions which caused it.

France's failure could be accounted for by the disastrous effect the concentration on the Charter had had, especially on the young men; the majority were mesmerized by its defence throughout the 1820s, so that when

the Revolution of July [came]: the greatest advance which any nation perhaps ever made by a single step—an advance which no one expected, and for which no one's habits and ideas were prepared—a change which gave the French nation a clear field to build on, . . . they had [not] possessed themselves of the materials to build withal; a leap, which cleared in an instant a space of many years journey; and transported France through mid-air, away from the scenes with which she was familiar, into regions unvisited and unknown. (No. 162.)

Tragically for France, power was in the hands of Guizot and the Doctrinaires, who were trying to suppress the only group, the young republicans, who were capable of charting those regions. Particularly, Mill cited the Saint-Simonians, who were "just now, the only association of public writers existing in the world who systematically stir up from the foundation all the great social questions" (No. 158). Mill continued to support those who shared with him the vision of those unknown lands even if he disagreed about how they should be settled.

In his comparison of the French and English intellects (No. 158),[67] Mill was not only lending his support to his fellow travellers but he was also pursuing his work as a political scientist. He needed to learn so that he could help the English Radicals to avoid suffering the same disastrous aftermath when England had

---

[67]The article was planned as the first of a series but *Le Globe* ceased publication on 20 April, 1832, two days after its appearance.

achieved her radical reform as the French had.[68] From this perspective, the differences between the two nations, viewed

in any way in which it can be looked at by an enlarged intellect, and a soul aspiring to indefinite improvement, . . . is a subject of rejoicing; for it furnishes the philosopher with *varied* experiments on the education of the human race; and affords the only mode by which all the parts of our nature are enabled to move forward at once, none of them being choked (as some must be in every attempt to reduce all characters to a single invariable type) by the disproportionate growth of the remainder (No. 158).

He still felt in 1831, or so he told his French friends, that when he wished

to carry discussion into the field of science and philosophy, to state any general principles of politics, or propound doubts tending to put other people upon stating general principles for my instruction, I must go where I find readers capable of understanding and relishing such inquiries, and writers capable of taking part in them. . . . I conceive that, in political philosophy, the initiative belongs to France at this moment; not so much from the number of truths which have yet been practically arrived at, but rather from the far more elevated *terrain* on which the discussion is engaged; a *terrain* from which England is still separated by the whole interval which lies between 1789 and 1832. (No. 158.)[69]

Some English friends, such as Sterling and Carlyle, were capable of understanding and relishing such enquiries, but for the most part

In writing to persuade the English, one must tell them only of the next step they have to take, keeping back all mention of any subsequent step. Whatever we may have to propose, we must contract our reasoning into the most confined limits; we must place the expediency of the particular measure upon the narrowest grounds on which it can rest; and endeavour to let out no more of general truth, than exactly as much as is absolutely indispensable to make out our particular conclusion. (No. 158.)

His lack of active participation in the reform struggle in England can be at least partly attributed to the lack of lofty feelings involved:

The English people have never had their political feelings called out by abstractions. They have fought for particular laws, but never for a *principle* of legislation. The doctrines of the sovereignty of the people, and the rights of man, never had any root in this country. The cry was always for a particular change in the mode of electing members of the House of Commons. . . . (No. 158.)[70]

---

[68]That others saw a parallel between recent events in the two countries is shown clearly in Armand Carrel's toast to "'The People of England,' with expression of the warmest sympathy and congratulation upon our late glorious though pacific Three Days" (No. 169).

[69]His truest companion for walking on elevated terrain—and walking hand-in-hand—was Harriet Taylor: "she possessed in combination, the qualities which in all other persons whom I had known I had been only too happy to find singly. In her, complete emancipation from every kind of superstition . . ., and an earnest protest against many things which are still part of the established constitution of society, resulted not from the hard intellect but from strength of noble and elevated feeling. . . ." (*A*, 195.)

[70]Mill's views on this point only became stronger as his experience grew: "The English are fond of boasting that they do not regard the theory, but only the practice of institutions; but their boast stops short of the truth; they actually prefer that their theory should be at variance with their practice. If any

But once passed, the Reform Act, although limited in its immediate provisions, could effect a bursting of the fetters on the spirit of the English people. By May of 1832 the task of persuading them of the next step had come to seem more attractive—at least more than watching the French politicians. In France there had been "only public discontent and irritation, and a voice perpetually crying out 'Do something,' but not telling what to do, not having any thing to tell" (No. 162). In the Chamber were "scenes of confusion and disturbance" and outside there was no public opinion to pressure the Deputies (No. 164). The riots continued; the Duchess of Berry invaded (No. 171). At the end of the session Mill exclaimed: "The nature and amount of the doings of the French Chambers, during the session which has just expired, raise a serious doubt of the capacity of those assemblies as at present constituted, we will not say to legislate tolerably, but to legislate at all" (No. 172). So when the passage of the English Reform Bill was assured, he writes that it is small wonder that "The interest of foreign politics now fades before that of our own. The theatre of political excitement has changed. The current of the *mouvement* has now shifted to Great Britain: how rapidly to proceed, or in what latitudes to terminate, he must be a bold man who deems that he can foreknow: nor needs he: it is not now the time to *hope* but to DO." (No. 165.)

The immediate "doing" was the election precipitated by the new franchise. Mill's limited contribution was two articles (Nos. 174 and 177) on a question which divided the Radicals: whether candidates should be required to pledge themselves to certain courses of action in return for support. The articles show the influence of Mill's French experience on the development of his ideas, ideas that were later to be incorporated into *Representative Government*. Only a general pledge should "be tendered to a candidate, his acceptance or refusal of which would decide whether he is with us or against us,—whether he is for the Movement or the Resistance,—whether he voted for the Reform Bill as a prop to all our remaining institutions, or as a means of beating down such of them as are bad, and repairing such as are decaying . . ." (No. 177). Mill's ideal electorate would be chosen from among the superior men trained to govern: "Government must be performed by the few, for the benefit of the many: and the security of the many consists in being governed by those who possess the largest share of their confidence, and no longer than while that confidence lasts" (No. 174). To govern well, the legislators must remember that "the test of what is right in

---

one proposed to them to convert their practice into a theory, he would be scouted. It appears to them unnatural and unsafe, either to do the thing which they profess, or to profess the thing which they do. A theory which purports to be the very thing intended to be acted upon, fills them with alarm; it seems to carry with it a boundless extent of unforeseeable consequences. This disagreeable feeling they are only free from, when the principles laid down are obviously matters of convention, which, it is agreed on all parts, are not to be pressed home." ("Vindication of the French Revolution of February 1848" [1849], *CW*, XX, 331-2.)

politics is not the *will* of the people, but the *good* of the people" (No. 177)—a view he had espoused the previous September during the debate over the French peerage.

There is a hint in these articles that he saw himself as a possible candidate. Though it was not until thirty-three years later that he was to fulfil that ambition, when he did, he lived up to the youthful principles:

When all other things are equal, give your votes to him who refuses to degrade himself and you by personal solicitation. To entrust a man with a burthensome duty (unless he means to betray it) is a compliment indeed, but no favour. The man who manifests the highest opinion of the electors, is not he who tries to gain them over individually by civil speeches, but he who assumes that their only object is to choose the fittest man, and abstains from all canvassing, except by laying his pretensions before them collectively, on the hustings, at public meetings, or through the press. (No. 174.)

Although English politics had been neglected by Mill the journalist—of his sixty-five contributions, all to the *Examiner*, between August 1831 and August 1832, all but some fifteen had been on France—he found time for his English friends. The affectionate and loyal side of the young man showed as he again inserted favourable notices of his friends in the *Monthly Repository* circle, Eliza Flower (No. 155), William Pemberton (No. 168), and also two other acquaintances, Charlotte Lewin (another of George Grote's sisters-in-law) (No. 175) and William Hickson (No. 141). He also praised Whately on his promotion (No. 121) and, as was sadly inevitable, Jeremy Bentham on his death (No. 170). His interest in logic dictated lengthy book reviews of Todd (No. 144), Smart (Nos. 151 and 153), and Lewis (No. 159).[71] The other items in this period are disparate, but many of them reveal the shifting sands of Mill's ideas: the Sugar Refinery Bill and the Slave Trade (No. 118) showed that some things changed very little; the one on the Irish character (No. 138), a very nineteenth-century piece, is of interest in light of his later thoughts on national character; the ideas behind "Property in Land" (No. 163) came from his French friends and would underlie the later Irish articles, the *Political Economy*, and his eventual membership in the Land Tenure Reform Association; and some short pieces were perhaps simply the product of Fonblanque's having passed on to Mill items well within his known competence.

Mill had begun the two articles on pledges with a grand flourish suitable for the new era ushered in by the royal signature on the Reform Act: "The steed is at the door, saddled and bridled, and it is time to mount and journey onward" (No. 174). But for the moment, with both the French and English parliaments adjourned, he was content to go on foot for a tour of the New Forest, Hampshire, West Sussex, and the Isle of Wight.

---

[71]Lewis was also reviewed for *Tait's Edinburgh Magazine*, I (May 1832), *CW*, XVIII, 1-13.

SEPTEMBER 1832 TO AUGUST 1833

MILL RETURNED TO LONDON but did not settle down to his journalism
immediately. Presumably he had some India Office correspondence to catch up
with, and he was also planning to go to Cornwall for a couple of weeks with the
Bullers. He took time before he left to write recommendations for some of those
anxious for election under the new dispensation (No. 179). Many of those he
recommended were known to him; all of them, as he made a point of saying,
were young.

On his return in October his writings for the *Examiner* were once more resumed, and once more on France. On English affairs there are only two quite
predictable pieces on the Corn Laws. After what he had said, such an allotment
of his time may seem strange, but in England there was the inevitable delay in
Parliamentary activity: the necessity of registering the enlarged electorate postponed the elections into the fall.[72] Earl Grey's Ministry was unchanged by the
election: the Radicals' old champion, Lord Brougham, was Lord Chancellor,
Russell and Durham were Paymaster-General and Lord Privy Seal, and the
stalwart Viscount Althorp continued as Chancellor of the Exchequer and leader
of the Commons. Parliament did not meet until 29 January, 1833, and when it
did the House appeared little altered overall although, importantly for Mill, it
contained a small but recognizable group of Radicals, among whom stood out
Mill's old friends, George Grote, J.A. Roebuck, and Sir William Molesworth.
For his own part, having appreciated the vital part the young French journalists
played in forwarding the movement, and acknowledging that his position at India
House prevented his entering Parliament himself, he started orchestrating the
radical programme. Such plans as were to mature with the appearance of the
London Review in April 1835 might have crossed his mind as early as 1832; such
a supposition is given substance by his criticism of the English journalists and
praise of the French, especially Armand Carrel, in the article addressed to the
latter, written in December of 1832 (No. 186).

In the glare of the illuminations for the Reform victory, Mill might well have
seen a role for himself as the ginger journalist if his friends were elected[73] and
exuberantly forgotten about the necessary political hiatus. This speculation also

---

[72]And he had turned his attention to England so far as to write three major articles for the *Jurist* and
Tait's Edinburgh Magazine: "The Currency Juggle" (1833), "Corporation and Church Property"
(1833), *CW*, IV, 181-92, 193-222; and "Writings of Junius Redivivus [II]" (1833), *CW*, I, 379-90.

[73]In his *Autobiography* Mill wrote of this time: "In the meanwhile had taken place the election of
the first Reformed Parliament, which included several of the most notable of my Radical friends and
acquaintances; Grote, Roebuck, Buller, Sir William Molesworth, John and Edward Romilly, and
several more; besides Warburton, Strutt, and others, who were in parliament already. Those who
thought themselves, and were called by their friends, the philosophic radicals, had now, it seemed, a
fair opportunity, in a more advantageous position than they had ever before occupied, for shewing

provides perhaps a key to his continued reporting on the French riots, insurrections, and prosecutions of the press.[74] It was important that his English readers know about the ruthless but inevitably futile attempts to bring stability to France. The continuous unedifying prosecutions for libel that attempted to silence the youth of France and the uncivilized behaviour of all parties both in the courtroom and in the streets[75] were instructive as Mill prepared the way for the radical reforms that were vital if England was to reap the benefits of her revolution and avoid France's failure.[76] The Government of the Doctrinaires, he says, "is an instructive experiment upon what is to be expected from those who affect to found their political wisdom principally on history, instead of looking to history merely for *suggestions*, to be brought to the test of a larger and surer experience" (No. 181).[77]

The Guizot party were not, he argued, to be confused with the Whigs, in spite of their own claims. They thought they were modelling themselves on the English Whigs but that was because they thought 1688 and 1830 were comparable and because they thought the Whigs had principles. The first thought was the result of their being

a kind of people for whom history has no lessons, because they bring to its study no real knowledge of the human mind, or of the character of their own age,—[and, therefore they] could hit upon nothing better than erecting into universal maxims the conditions of the compromise which they fancied had been made at our Revolution of 1688, between the monarchical and the popular principle (No. 181).

If Mill's readers had read his "Spirit of the Age," they would have known that the knowledge one got from history was that the character of an age was peculiar

---

what was in them; and I, as well as my father, founded great hopes on them. These hopes were destined to be disappointed." (203.) See also Ann P. and John M. Robson, "Private and Public Goals," in *Innovators and Pioneers: The Role of the Editor in Victorian Britain*, ed. Joel Weiner (Westport, Conn.: Greenwood Press, 1985), 231-57.

[74]He said, revealingly, of the prosecution of the Saint-Simonians, that it was quite unnecessary since they were killing themselves through ridicule—but that they had the right to be left free to do so (No. 180).

[75]One of Mill's harshest criticisms of the French is provoked by their utter disregard of the law—"the first and fundamental condition of good government, and without which any people, however civilized they may imagine themselves, are little other than savages" (No. 173).

[76]Mill also worked privately to improve understanding. He wished to introduce to John Taylor two of his "acquaintances," Jules Bastide and Hippolyte Dussard, "distinguished members of the republican party in France, [who had] been compelled to fly their country for a time in consequence of the affair of the fifth & sixth of June. They were not conspirators," says Mill, "for there was no conspiracy, but when they found the troops and the people at blows, they took the side of the people. Now I am extremely desirous to render their stay here as little disagreeable as possible, and to enable them to profit by it, and to return with a knowledge of England and with those favourable sentiments towards our English *hommes du mouvement* which it is of so much importance that they and their friends should entertain." (*EL, CW*, XII, 115.)

[77]Cf. the statement of the teen-age Mill, "the enemies of improvement hold out—what? Theories founded upon history; that is upon partial and incomplete experience." (No. 13.)

to that age, always changing, evolving into the next stage, and that therefore no such things as universal maxims could be found; especially short-lived were all maxims in an age of transition.

The second thought was the result of confounding the French and the English:⁺ "in England few, except the very greatest thinkers, think systematically, or aim at connecting their scattered opinions into a consistent scheme of general principles. . . . 'Whig principles' simply meant, feeling and acting with the men called Whigs. . . . The Doctrinaires have not the wisdom of the beaver; they will never yield a part to save the remainder. . . . They are the most inflexible and impracticable of politicians." (No. 181.) The inevitable disaster for France under Louis Philippe and his Doctrinaires Mill now sat back to watch, knowing it would come and in coming would prove his analysis of the spirit of the age correct. England should watch and note well the fatal outcome of stationary government.

The ideas he had put forward in the "Spirit of the Age" were being tested against events in France; his hypotheses were being proved correct; his analyses accurately predicted outcomes. Stability could only be restored to a society in transition by completing the revolution. Mill's articles on France were the windows through which Englishmen could see the fate awaiting them if they too arrested the revolution before it was completed. Thus Mill continued until the end of 1832 to report, with an air almost of satisfaction, the signs of deterioration: the corruption in the courts (No. 182), the attempt to shoot Louis Philippe on his way to open the new session (according to Mill all a farce enacted by the Government to gain public support) (Nos. 185 and 188), the manipulation of the election of the President of the Chamber of Deputies (No. 185). He noticed with commendation the re-establishment of the Department of Moral and Political Science in the Institute (No. 183) and also the move towards freer trade (No. 190). But the only times when strong feelings appeared were in a moving obituary of his old friend Say (No. 185) and a biting denunciation of the British press which, he assured Carrel, did not represent British feelings. "The popular party in England think as ill of the present French Government as M. Carrel himself, and are as anxious as he can be that republican institutions, whether with an elective or hereditary chief, should be firmly established in France" (No. 186).[78] Throughout 1833 Mill reported very infrequently on French politics; his reasons are adumbrated in his earlier remark that "we almost doubt whether the scenes that are unfolded took place in a civilized country" (No. 182), and now made plain: "We have discontinued of late our usual notices of French affairs,

---

[78]Mill's sense of "republican" is fifty years earlier than that cited by the *Oxford English Dictionary*, which gives a quotation from the *Quarterly Review* of 1885: "Republic lately came to mean a government resting on a widely extended suffrage."

because all which has been doing in that country is so paltry . . ." (No. 199);[79] "What then has the Session produced? Produced! It has produced money. Its results are the vote of an enormous budget, and an endless series of extraordinary votes of credit." (No. 204.)[80] Throughout these months perhaps only the establishment of national education and municipal institutions gave him concrete grounds for hope for France.

In January of 1833 the first session of the British Parliament since the Reform Act opened. The English political scene seemed promising; Mill had remarked in December:

we see reason to congratulate the friends of improvement upon the definiteness of their objects, and the zeal and unanimity of their exertions. Scarcely a voice has been raised for any causeless or fantastic change, nor has any captiousness been exhibited about mere forms and phrases. This, indeed, would have been inconsistent with the positive, practical, matter-of-fact character of the English mind. (No. 191.)

Mill had had enough for the moment of Frenchmen in debate. His mind, in any case, was distracted,[81] and even on English politics his writing in 1833 lacks the concentration of the past year.[82] There were a number of favourable pieces in the *Examiner* on the *Monthly Repository* (Nos. 198, 200, and 207); the first of these contained a revealing review of the life of Mehetabel Wesley and the tragedy of her indissoluble marriage.[83] The two studious reviews of Eliza Flower's songs (Nos. 197 and 201) and the praise of Beolchi's poetry anthology (No. 206) were also the products of his friendship with W.J. Fox and his circle:

None of these pieces was demanding.[84] During the whole of the session, which lasted until the end of August, only one or two political matters received his attention; his Parliamentary friends were left largely unaided and unguided while the House discussed factory legislation, the Irish Church, education, law reform, and the emancipation of the slaves.

---

[79]When Mill said "we", he spoke for the *Examiner*. It had virtually ignored French affairs since January, thus reinforcing by omission the inference that Mill's views were editorial policy.

[80]He did have favourable comments to make on the Act providing national education which had finally passed the Chamber of Deputies (No. 205).

[81]Mill's relationship with Harriet and John Taylor was in crisis; see F.A. Hayek, *John Stuart Mill and Harriet Taylor* (London: Routledge and Kegan Paul, 1951), 36ff., and M.St.J. Packe, *The Life of John Stuart Mill* (London: Secker and Warburg, 1954), 137ff.

[82]In 1832 Mill had written sixty-one pieces for the newspapers, virtually all on France; in 1833 he wrote only thirty-three and only eight of those were on France. He wrote to Carlyle in April 1833: ". . . I will not if I can help it give way to gloom and morbid despondency. . . . I have allowed myself to be paralysed more than I should, during the last month or two by these gloomy feelings. . . . I have therefore a poor account to render of work done." (*EL, CW*, XII, 149.)

[83]Is it in human nature to read this article in the spring of 1833 and not to think of the entangled affairs of Harriet and John? These affairs were not prospering at this time any better than his health.

[84]Much more demanding were longer articles he contributed to the *Monthly Repository*, but even so his output was far below what had become his norm.

The proposed budget raised his ire in the spring (No. 202) and in the summer he roundly attacked the Government over that old chestnut the Bank Charter Bill (Nos. 208, 209, and 212). His criticisms were not very different from what he might have written ten years earlier, although his skill in vituperation is more assured. And, in spite of his dismay at the French opposition floundering in a sea of principles, he can still be almost equally dismayed at the British lack of them:

no power of grasping any principle; no attempt to ground their proceedings upon any comprehensive, even though false, views; no appearance of understanding the subject, or even of thinking they understand it; nothing contemplated which rises to the dignity of even a half-measure—only quarter and half-quarter measures; a little scratching on the surface of one or two existing evils, but no courage to attempt their excision, because there has been no vigour or skill to probe them to the bottom (No. 209).

In his piece on the commission to make recommendations about municipal institutions (on which sat some of his friends), Mill again stressed that England needed reform but even more needed principles to elevate the tone of public discourse:

A solemn declaration of opinion from an authoritative quarter, going the full length of a great principle, is worth ten paltry practical measures of nibbling amendment. The good which any mere enactment can do, is trifling compared with the effect of whatever helps to mature the public mind . . . and we always find that *gradual* reform proceeds by larger and more rapid steps, when the doctrines of radical reform are most uncompromisingly and intrepidly proclaimed. (No. 211.)

At the end of the parliamentary session, Mill did not go for his usual summer ramble but stayed in town. Not parliamentary affairs but his own affairs determined his movements, and his own affairs had reached a crisis. Harriet and John Taylor had come to an understanding, the precise nature of which cannot be known, but Harriet Taylor was preparing in the spring of 1833 to go to France.[85] The situation was unclear, and John Stuart Mill, an infatuated twenty-six year old, was uncertain of her plans and, therefore, of his. Throughout the spring and summer he hung uncertainly around town.[86]

SEPTEMBER 1833 TO OCTOBER 1834

MILL'S DITHERING IN LONDON continued throughout September; he finally left for Paris on 10 October. After nearly six weeks in Mrs. Taylor's company, he returned alone to London on 18 November. Despite the unsatisfactory state of his

---

[85]The W.J. Fox-Eliza Flower affair also reached a crisis this spring with Mrs. Fox shouting her wrongs from the attic. For a full account, see Richard Garnett, *The Life of W.J. Fox* (London and New York: Lane, 1910), 155ff.
[86]See the letters to Carlyle that summer (*EL, CW*, XII, 161-4, 169-73, 174-7).

heart, Mill's health improved, and he threw himself into his writing, perhaps easing his feelings by producing some acidic articles.

There could be no quarter given. The Radicals must not be associated with the Whigs either in Parliament or in the *Examiner*.[87] The party of movement must not be embraced and disarmed by the stationary party, as had happened in France. But Mill and his father were to be disappointed by the radical group, partly because their row was particularly difficult to hoe without helping the Whig garden to grow. The truth was that, in spite of Mill's acidulous tone, this first reform Ministry was a reforming Ministry; it did not emulate its French counterpart. Many reforms had been introduced dealing with factory children, slaves, the Irish Church, and much else. Frequently, therefore, the Radicals had found themselves voting with the Ministers even if they had not spoken with them. And for Mill such collusion spelled disaster. Grey's Ministry was after all Whig—Melbourne was Grey's successor in July 1834 when, deserted by Stanley and Graham over Ireland, Grey retired. Mill had seen the French Doctrinaires triumph from the confusion in the Chamber of Deputies when the Radicals had failed to coalesce and many had been co-opted by the Ministry. It was his role and that of the Parliamentary Radicals to keep their own principles flying and to prevent the Whigs from stagnating.

Mill's series attacking the Whig Ministry, elicited by the pamphlet he refers to as the *Ministerial Manifesto*,[88] was as much a rallying cry to the Radicals as a criticism of Grey's Ministry (or Althorp's Ministry, as Mill persists in calling it, Grey possibly being too much the popular hero). In this fight against the English counterpart of the Doctrinaires, nothing was to be praised; Mill pours vitriolic criticism indiscriminately on all the Ministry's achievements: "Ten years, or even five years ago, some of these things might have been matter of praise; but now! to hear a Ministry deified for the Irish Church Bill! for the Slave Bill! for the East India Bill! for the Bank Bill! for the Factory Bill!"[89] This Ministry could not

once find in their hearts to commit themselves to a principle, fairly embark themselves with a principle, wed it for better or worse! But no—they are afraid of principles. . . . They are men of shifts and expedients. What they are from the necessity of their own want

[87]Mill comments in the *Autobiography*, "What I could do by writing, I did. During the year 1833 I continued working in the *Examiner* with Fonblanque, who at that time was zealous in keeping up the fight for radicalism against the Whigs" (205).

[88]The series, which started in the *Examiner* in September, went right through October and into November. Perhaps Mill sent copy back from Paris, but it is more likely that he wrote them all at a very rapid rate before he left. In a nice conceit Mill professes to be taken in by the book's having only Le Marchant's name on it, and to wish the Ministers concerned had written it themselves instead of causing it "to be composed and sent forth by an understrapper" (No. 216); it was well known that it had been written by Lord Althorp, *et al*.

[89]In the spring of 1833, Mill had written to Carlyle: "the Reformed Parliament has not disappointed me any more than you; it is (as Miss Martineau, I understand, says of Brougham) so ridiculously like what I expected: but some of our Utilitarian Radicals are downcast enough, having

of knowledge and judgment, they fancy they are from the necessity of the case. It is their notion of statesmanship. (No. 216.)

Here lay the crucial difference between the stationary Whigs and the advanced Radicals who had the capacity of "in the first place choosing right [principles] . . . [and] in the second, of discerning where the dominion of one principle is limited by the conflicting operation of another" (No. 216).

In one cause, however, Mill's praise could not be withheld—well, not altogether; there was too much Bentham in Lord Brougham's law reforms even be he now a Whig Lord Chancellor. "These things, if accomplished, are the greater part of all which is to be desired. Codify the law, common and statute together, and establish Local Courts *with unlimited jurisdiction*, and all that will remain to complete a systematic reform of the law, is to simplify the procedure, and establish good courts of appeal." (No. 218.) Maybe Fonblanque gave a jab; maybe Mill recalled his role of "keeping up the fight for radicalism." The next week, he wrote of Brougham in terms he applied also to Bentham: "He is great as a destroyer; not great as a rebuilder. All that he has overthrown well deserved to fall; nothing that he has established, in the opinion of the most thorough law reformers in the profession, deserves to stand. Not only his reforms are partial and narrow, but they are such as cannot fit into any more comprehensive plan of reform." (No. 219.) But on the whole Mill's article did not bear out such an opening condemnation, although the proposal for more than one judge to hear a case brought a sharp rebuke. The subject had been Mill's for so long that Bentham's voice rang through, perhaps the louder for his French experience:[90]

to set three or four judges on a bench to hear *one* cause, is not only paying three or four persons to do the work of one, but it renders absolutely certain their doing it ill. *One* judge feels the public eye upon him; he is ashamed to be corrupt, or partial, or inattentive; but when there are several, each dares perpetrate under the sanction of the others, wickedness the undivided obloquy of which he would have shrunk from; each trusts that others have been listening though he has not, that others have given their minds to the cause though he has not; and instead of the services of several judges, the public has something considerably less than the best services of one. (No. 219.)

Neither had his French experience given him cause to qualify his father's teaching about the present: the members of Parliament were, "when strong public clamour does not *compel* some regard to the public interest, still as stupidly and as blindly selfish as in the worst times" (No. 219).

---

deemed that the nation had in it more of wisdom and virtue than they now see it has, and that the vicious state of the representation kept this wisdom & virtue out of parliament. At least this good will come out of their disappointment, that they will no longer rely upon the infallibility of Constitution-mongering: they admit that we have as good a House of Commons as *any* mode of election would have given us, in the present state of cultivation of our people." (*EL, CW*, XII, 145.)

[90]See above, l, and also No. 76.

Mill found his row almost as difficult to hoe as did his Parliamentary friends. He again went after Brougham for his Corporation Bill (No. 220), but it was a half-hearted attack and the interest lies more in his advocacy of government by experts, a position that Tocqueville was to reinforce. He could not condemn the Factory Act (drawn up by Chadwick on the recommendations of the commission managed by him) except for the inclusion—not recommended by Chadwick—of certain classes of adults (No. 220). Neither could he condemn the proposed Poor Law reforms based also, he knew, on Chadwick's work. But he could take a column or two to denounce the Labour Rate Bill defeated by the efforts of the Radicals though supported by Althorp. Althorp was a frequent target, unmistakably Whig, unquestionably honest but not fast on his intellectual feet. But it was with some difficulty and a scathing tone[91] that Mill upheld the distinction in a reforming House between the good (the Radical and not in power) and the bad (the Whig and in power).

As always he had time for his radical friends, Harriet Martineau for her *Tale of the Tyne* exposing the evils of impressment (No. 222), Charles Napier for his book on the government proper to colonies, all of which ought to pay for themselves—in this particular case the Ionian Islands (No. 224)—and W.J. Fox for the December 1833 issue of the *Monthly Repository*. The approval of this last was slightly, but significantly, qualified:

In every word . . . we concur; but with the qualification, that not *only* the more vigorous minds in the poorer class, but persons also with the superior opportunities of instruction afforded by a higher station, *may* be, (and of this the writer himself is an example) most efficient instructors of the poorer classes, provided they have sufficient freedom from the littleness of mind which caste-distinctions engender. . . .

One must speak to the working man in Mill's best of all possible worlds as "equals . . . less informed than himself on the particular subject, but with minds quite as capable of understanding it" (No. 225).

At the beginning of 1834, however, Mill had little intention of speaking to the working man. When he and Harriet were in Paris on a dry run as lovers, Mill had visited Armand Carrel, one of the much persecuted editors of the republican journal *Le National*, whom he had long admired and defended in the *Examiner*. Carrel had much to recommend him in Mill's eyes (including a mistress).[92] Carrel's example had inspired Mill; he was the embodiment of the youthful Girondist dream. The meeting with Carrel, the stay in Paris amongst all the elevated youth, the most perfect of beings as his companion, had given a great

[91]Mill's journalist's licence occasionally carried him far, e.g., in his suggestion that the whole diplomatic service be abolished now that statesmen were literate and could write to each other (No. 217).

[92]For a detailed account of Carrel's influence on Mill and his career as editor of the *London and Westminster Review* see Robson and Robson, "Private and Public Goals," 235-7. For Mill's description of his meeting with Carrel in a letter to Carlyle, see *EL*, *CW*, XII, 195-6 (25 Nov., 1833).

impetus to the side of Mill which had brought about the stimulating friendship
with Carlyle.[93] If it had not been for Harriet Taylor and Armand Carrel perhaps
the events in France would have dimmed Mill's vision. The reality of Mill's
return to England alone and Harriet's return to John Taylor would, on the surface
of it, have dimmed most visions. But Harriet loved him, Armand Carrel led
"formidable looking champions,"[94] and, most excitingly, a role similar to
Carrel's was being suggested for him at home: the possibility of organizing and
inspiring the English equivalent of the French left through the establishment of
an English counterpart to *Le National*. Plans were being mooted for a journal to
replace the *Westminster Review*, which in the eyes of the Mills had not under
Bowring been fulfilling its original purpose.

This possibility was the more important because there was danger of the
Examiner, or at least of the *Examiner* as guided by Fonblanque, having to fold.
Even working with the excellent Fonblanque, Mill, now he was in the thick of it,
desperately anxious to play a role, had become increasingly dissatisfied with his
part in the enterprise. When Mill had briefly considered purchasing the *Examiner*
(he had decided that doing so was totally impracticable) he discussed with
Carlyle at some length Fonblanque's problems and the policy of the paper. It is
hard not to apply his description of the paper in general to his own particular
recent articles on the Ministerial Manifesto:

such as do not take a daily paper, require in a weekly one a better abstract of *news*. . . .
Then the more moderate radicals are revolted by the tone of hatred in which the paper is
written. This feeling extends to many who would have no objection to, but would
applaud, the utterance of the bitterest truths, but do not like a *perpetual* carping at little
things, honestly indeed, yet often unfairly & making no personal allowances, sometimes
misstating altogether the *kind* of blame which is deserved, & meting it out in unequal
measures to different people, so as to give an appearance of spleen & personal antipathy to
individuals—especially to some of the Ministers, & among them, most perhaps to some
of those who deserve it rather *less* than the others. . . . At the very time . . . he
[Fonblanque] was offending the moderate radicals by the nature of his attacks on the
ministry. . . .[95]

Carping is the word that certainly springs to mind when reading Mill's attacks on
the Ministry, and equally Althorp could certainly be thought to "deserve it rather
less than the others." These feelings must have made the prospect of a new outlet
for his writing, over which he would have more control, excitingly inviting. The
solution to both the Bowring and Fonblanque situations would be a new radical

[93]Carlyle in an uncharacteristic moment described Harriet Taylor at this time as "a living
romance-heroine, of the clearest insight, of the royallest volition; very interesting, of questionable
destiny, not above twenty-five" (letter to John Carlyle of 22 July, 1834, in *Collected Letters of
Thomas and Jane Welsh Carlyle*, ed. Charles Richard Sanders, *et al.* [Durham, N.C.: Duke
University Press, 1970-], VII, 245-6).
[94]*EL, CW*, XII, 195 (25 Nov., 1833).
[95]*Ibid.*, 201 (22 Dec., 1833).

review: "Roebuck, Strutt, Buller, and other radical members of Parliament have a scheme to start a radical review as their organ, with individual signatures like J.R., in which we should all of us write—the thing looks possible, and everybody seems so eager about it that I really think it will come to pass."[96] And indeed it did, although not quite after the fashion he had expected and not until the spring of 1835.

Meanwhile, Mill's dissatisfaction was by no means great enough in January of 1834 to cause him to cease writing for Fonblanque, although he again concentrated on French affairs that spring, writing little on contemporary English politics after 1833 in the *Examiner*.[97] Many a man watching French politics in 1834 would have thrown up his hands in despair (were that not too Gallic a gesture) and railed against the French and their preference for the thought over the deed. Mill certainly expressed disgust at times. But he was consciously testing his hypotheses and in the process was learning a good deal about representative bodies, their nature, the difficulties of operating within them and through them to achieve reforms. Undoubtedly his visit with Carrel had given him a deeper awareness of the frustrations and hazards of French political life, and the persistent line that Mill took on French affairs during the first eight months of 1834 can be understood only in the light of this experience. His analysis in 1834 of the French Government was soberer and more perceptive than it had been three years earlier: "The Chamber is no place for advocating doctrines in advance of the existing charter; for such the press is the proper organ; in the Chamber an orator, even of the most commanding talents, could not obtain a hearing for such opinions as are held by the ablest opponents of the present French Government" (No. 230). Mill no longer gave vent to feelings of exasperation at the failure of a popular opposition to emerge in the Chamber; he accepted the conservatism of those who actually wielded power. He had said as much in the autumn, more in the English context than the French, but certainly influenced by the "*varied* experiments" in which he had been participating:

There is a third kind of Minister whom we could allow to take to himself, to whom we could cheerfully give, a large share of credit for his administration. This would be a man who, taking the reins of office in a period of transition, a period which is called, according to the opinions of the speaker, an age of reform, of destruction, or of renovation, should deem it his chief duty and his chief wisdom to moderate the shock: to mediate between adverse interests; to make no compromise of *opinions*, except by avoiding any ill-timed declaration of them, but to negotiate the most advantageous compromises possible in actual *measures*: to reform bit-by-bit, when more rapid progress is impracticable, but always with a comprehensive and well-digested plan of thorough reform placed before him as a guide. . . . (No. 216.)[98]

[96]*Ibid.*, 198 (26 Nov., 1833).
[97]In the first half of 1834, twenty-four of his thirty-two contributions were on French affairs.
[98]It was only another short time before he could extend this same understanding to his *bête noire* of 1833, François Guizot: "I confounded the prudence of a wise man who lets some of his maxims go to

But just because a body of elected governors did not and could not represent advanced opinion in an age of transition, it was absolutely essential that the young men outside the Government be allowed to speak out. The reports of French affairs that Mill continued to provide for the *Examiner* throughout the first half of 1834 have these young men as their focus. The Government persecutions of the young journalists drew his wrath, especially those of Armand Carrel's *Le National* (Nos. 232, 237, 238, 241, 247, 249, 266, and 269). Mill was prepared to defend the opposition outside the Chambers even when it went beyond mere words and even when it went beyond Armand Carrel (Nos. 226, 249, 250, and 251). The behaviour of these young men in court or in the streets might seem to some irresponsible and indefensible, but to Mill they had acted in the only way left to them as Louis Philippe and his Ministers tried to muzzle France and thwart the forward march of history. The misrepresentation by "Tory publications" (No. 244) must not delude England into similar disastrous repressions. The extreme activists of the Société des Droits de l'Homme were not to be feared. On the contrary, "The evil we are apprehensive of is stagnation," and therefore those who put forward anti-property doctrines, although Mill could not "give such doctrines any encouragement," performed a needed service: "unless the ruling few can be made and kept 'uneasy,' the many need expect no good" (No. 233). These men were the forces of history itself in an age of transition.

One important force was the Saint-Simonians. Mill's courageous defence, after they had disbanded, of their doctrines, which again he made clear he did not share—or did he?—is very moving. They had dared to develop bold philosophical speculations that led them to "the most hostile scrutiny of the first principles of the social union" (No. 233) and had arrived at a

scheme, impracticable indeed but . . . only in *degree*, not in kind . . . of a perfect human society; the spirit of which will more and more pervade even the *existing* social institutions, as human beings become wiser and better; and which, like any other model of unattainable perfection, everybody is the better for aspiring to, although it be impossible to reach it. We may never get to the north star, but there is much use in turning our faces towards it if we are journeying northward. . . . We have only to imagine the same progression indefinitely continued, and a time would come when St. Simonism would be practicable; and if practicable, desirable. (No. 234.)

He could not deny the vision three times, and he never ceased to defend those

---

sleep while the time is unpropitious for asserting them, with the laxity of principle which resigns them for personal advancement. Thank God I did not wait to know him personally in order to do him justice, for in 1838 & 1839 I saw that he had reasserted all his old principles at the first time at which he could do so with success & without compromising what in his view were more important principles still. I ought to have known better than to have imputed dishonourable inconsistency to a man whom I now see to have been consistent beyond any statesman of our time & altogether a model of the consistency of a statesman as distinguished from that of a fanatic." (*EL, CW,* XIII, 454-5 [23 Dec., 1840].)

who, like him, had the vision of a different and brighter future.[99] In spite of the immediate outcome of the Revolution of 1830, Mill continued to believe in the promised land; he had seen it. And for Mill it was French intellectual speculation that would reveal the path out of the desert. However reactionary the surface of French life might appear, the Revolutions of 1789 and 1830 had broken the bond that had enchained the French spirit and still fettered all others. The movement was, however, temporarily halted in France, and in the summer of 1834 Mill ceased to write regularly both on France and for the *Examiner*. It was fitting that his last article on France reported the acquittal of Armand Carrel on charges of libelling Louis Philippe (No. 269).

Apart from the articles on France, most of what he had contributed since the end of 1833, even possibly his earlier attacks on the Grey Ministry, could come under the heading of helping one's friends, not that such help excludes in the least furthering one's principles. His reviews of Wilson (No. 231) and Sarah Austin (No. 256),[100] of Eliza Flower's new songs (No. 248), and his mention of the German periodical begun by Garnier, a refugee friend of Carrel's (Nos. 267 and 270), are interspersed with defences of the Poor Law proposals of Edwin Chadwick (Nos. 252 and 253) and the colonization scheme of Wakefield and Torrens (Nos. 259, 261, and 263). In his zeal for his friends, Mill broadened his audience by contributing to the *Morning Chronicle* in August an article on the Poor Law (No. 265) and in September one on Australian colonization (No. 271).

The articles on colonization throw very clear light on Mill's view of the best planned society possible in his own time; it is a far cry from the Saint-Simonians' Ménilmontant. He is most concerned, and quotes Wakefield approvingly at length in this cause, that the proper balance between land, labour, and capital be maintained. No country can be civilized and prosperous that does not possess various groups: some who own land; some who employ capital; and some who labour for the first two groups. There was no question here of anti-property doctrines; what was needed for present-day Englishmen at home or overseas was not the north star. But it was nevertheless the north star toward which Mill strove for the rest of his life to turn the faces of his countrymen.

JANUARY 1835 TO JUNE 1846

IT WAS NOT ONLY the state of the revolution in France in the summer of 1834 that led Mill virtually to stop writing for Fonblanque. That summer Sir William

---

[99]See his description of the Saint-Simonians in *Principles of Political Economy*, *CW*, II-III (Toronto: University of Toronto Press, 1965), II, 210-11. The last letter to d'Eichthal was 21 May, 1871 (*LL*, *CW*, XVII, 1820-1). On Harriet's tombstone he had had inscribed, "were there but a few hearts and intellects like hers this earth would already become the hoped-for heaven" (Packe, 408).

[100]In February, Mill had forwarded a "MS on education," presumably Austin's, to Effingham Wilson, who published her work, to say that though he had not had time to read it, he knew it had "the highest character" (unpublished letter in private hands, to E. Wilson, 14 Feb., 1834).

Molesworth, a wealthy, young, devoted Radical, had offered the money for the longed-for periodical if his hero, John Stuart Mill, would edit it. Mill, who had just turned twenty-eight, was still a young man, one who knew his capabilities but had not yet found the proper field for their exertion. Excluded from direct politics, he eagerly took on the task of editing and writing for the *London Review*. His articles in dailies and weeklies became very occasional. In any case, for him England's politics were quite humdrum in the mid-1830s. The fervour surrounding the reform crisis had dissipated. Some good legislation was passed. Ireland was an habitual problem—much the same as always—with Daniel O'Connell providing fireworks in the House but no dangerous blaze in the country. Lord Melbourne had replaced Grey, who gratefully retired back to the north, and was then himself briefly replaced in December by Sir Robert Peel, on the King's initiative.[101] There was a stir over such a royal indiscretion but no one really thought that Silly Billy was plotting to become a despot. An election was held but Peel failed to win a majority despite his Tamworth Manifesto, and in April of 1835 Melbourne was again Prime Minister. The country was enjoying another of its periods of prosperity. Both the Chartists and the Anti-Corn Law Leaguers were no more than gleams in their future leaders' eyes. There was some rioting, of course, but by and large Melbourne was considered to have over-reacted to the Tolpuddle labourers (the Government pardoned the marytrs in 1836 and brought them home again). The Poor Law of 1834 was decidedly unpopular throughout the country, and it was fortunate that for the moment the meetings on the Yorkshire moors where Richard Oastler and James Raynor Stephens led thousands of men and women to demand the Ten Hours Bill had temporarily ceased after the Factory Act of 1833.

By the end of the decade, however, the country was stirring, but Mill did not turn back to newspapers even after he gave up the *Review* in 1840. In 1841 Sir Robert Peel succeeded Melbourne as Prime Minister, having failed to do so in 1839 thanks to the Bedchamber Crisis. Compared with 1819, the times were peaceful. But only in comparison. Mill knew the country could not yet be stable. And quite right he was; in 1842 the Plug Plot gave a taste of the violence the Oastlerites and the Chartists were threatening and the Anti-Corn Law League was predicting. This period of Mill's journalism ends with the outbreak of the Irish famine and the repeal of the Corn Laws. By that time Mill had tried and failed to shape a radical party to complete the revolution—a completion undoubtedly appearing somewhat different to a man in his forties than it had to one in his twenties—and had instead established an unassailable reputation with his *Logic* (1843).

---

[101]Mill himself wrote nothing (though he quoted Senior) on what historians have sometimes seen as a constitutional outrage; possibly compared to Charles X and even Louis Philippe, William IV cast a small shadow. A discussion of what Mill did not write about would be very illuminating. For instance, during these eleven years he hardly touched in his newspaper writings on the three movements—Anti-Corn Law, Ten Hours, and Chartism—which dominate accounts in modern histories.

Understandably Mill did not write regularly for the newspapers during the frantic years of writing and editing the *London Review*.[102] The tale of Mill's hopes and hardships with the *London* and *London and Westminster* has been told elsewhere.[103] He expended an enormous amount of effort and the last of his youthful ambitions as well as hard cash and five years of his life on the *London Review*. He wrote twenty-seven articles and part of eleven others until he withdrew from the editorship in 1840. But in spite of the excitement and work involved in preparing the first number, rather than neglect his friends he found time at the beginning of 1835 for a few newspaper notices. Eliza Flower's *Songs of the Months* were mentioned as usual in the *Examiner* (No. 273); Nassau Senior's pamphlet on National Property was reviewed twice—of course, favourably—in the *Sun* and in the *Morning Chronicle* (Nos. 272 and 275). As was not uncommon, long excerpts made up most of these articles. Senior criticized William IV's independent action, and promoted the reduction of church endowments, municipal reform, and the admission of Dissenters to Oxford and Cambridge. He also advocated, calling forth Mill's great approval, making peers eligible to sit in the House of Commons.

Mill stayed within the circle of his acquaintance when he contributed to the *Globe*; the *Globe* was still the *Globe and Traveller* and was still owned by Colonel Torrens. Walter Coulson had gone, and in 1834 it had come under the editorship of another of Mill's friends, John Wilson (who had just finished working on the factory commission with Edwin Chadwick). Mill wrote eight articles for the *Globe* from February to October 1835—the only paper he wrote for at that time. (Perhaps these articles were a *quid pro quo* for Wilson's contributions to the *London and Westminster Review*.)[104] Being longer leaders than most of those he had written for the *Examiner*, they gave him an opportunity to press his views before a wider and different, in fact, a Whig audience; at least it was widely believed that the *Globe* was used by Melbourne. Occupied as he was, however, he wrote only occasional pieces supporting particular persons or

---

[102]In 1835 he wrote eleven pieces mostly for the *Globe*; in 1836, none; in 1837, six pieces were published, two in the *Globe*, two in the *Examiner*, and one each in the *True Sun* and the *Morning Chronicle*; in 1838, one in the *Examiner*; none in 1839 or 1840; in 1841, two in the *Morning Chronicle*; in 1842, four items, three in the *Morning Chronicle* and one in the *Examiner*; in 1843, two, one each in the *Morning Chronicle* and the *Spectator*; in 1844, four in the *Morning Chronicle*; and in 1845, none. As noted, the *Logic*, on which he had been working intently since 1836, was published in 1843.

[103]See n92. Not all the hopes and hardships were in journalism. Mill's hopes were up and down as he and John and Harriet Taylor tried to sort out their relationship at the same time as W.J. Fox and Mrs. Fox and Eliza Flower and the whole South Place Chapel congregation tried to sort out theirs. It is impossible to conceive of, much less recapture, the scene and conversation when Harriet Taylor visited her father, a member of Fox's congregation, to persuade him to support Flower power. For a discussion of the difficult, if not ornery, team that Mill was trying to drive, see Joseph Hamburger's Introduction to *Essays on England, Ireland, and the Empire*, CW, VI, xl ff.

[104]"Wraxall's Memoirs," *London and Westminster Review*, IV and XXVI (Jan. 1837), 483-501, and "Architectural Competition: The New Royal Exchange," *Westminster Review*, XXXV (Jan. 1841), 52-88.

proposals. However, his article defending the "destructives," a label bestowed on the Radicals by Mill's arch-enemy, *The Times*, contained an illuminating catalogue of what Radicals were made of at the beginning of 1835; Mill was first quoting and then amplifying the list in *The Times*: they were

for the ballot, for the separation of church and state, for the repeal of the union, and, it has the modesty to add, for an "equitable adjustment" with the fundholder . . ., corporation reform . . ., [and] repeal of the corn laws. . . . All who wish the reform bill to be made effectual by the improvement of the registration clauses, by disfranchising the corrupt freemen of such places as Norwich and Liverpool, and by getting rid of such of the smaller constituencies as have already become, beyond hope of redemption, close or rotten boroughs—all who wish that taxes should be taken off the necessaries of the poor instead of the luxuries of the rich—all who wish for local courts, or any other substitute for the irresponsible and incapable jurisdiction of the country magistracy—all who wish to see any measures introduced for the relief of the Dissenters but such as the Dissenters will indignantly reject—all who wish to see *the Universities reformed* . . . all who wish to see the church of England reformed, and all rational persons who do *not* wish to see it destroyed—all who wish to see the church of Ireland reduced to reasonable dimensions, and the national property . . . employed for the benefit of the unhappy oppressed Irish people . . . and, finally, all who will not endure that a dignitary of something calling itself a Protestant and English church shall go forth with armed men and assassinate the children and neighbours of a poor widow because she will not any longer give to him of her scanty substance the wages of a degrading tyranny. (No. 274.)

Although his style was less vituperative than formerly, his ideas were not moderated as he continued to lend his support to radical friends such as Charles Buller. In one article (No. 277), Mill was to help a very close friend indeed, himself. With his now customary practice of having one stone hit a flock of birds, his article promoted the first number of the new *London Review*; the author of one of the articles, J.A. Roebuck; one of his favourite subjects, corporation reform; one of his abiding interests, Ireland; and first and foremost, the Radicals in Parliament, with special mention for the proprietor of the *Review*, Sir William Molesworth, and a hint as to the line he should adopt in the House. All this he did in a long leader, only the first paragraph of which he had to compose; the rest he copied from Roebuck's article in the *London Review*. His skill, acquired in youth, of getting the most for his time and effort was standing him in good stead in these incredibly busy months.

In 1835 he also gave support to two old allies in two articles on the Poor Law (Nos. 278 and 279). The first of these particularly praised Nassau Senior's careful analysis of the differences amongst countries that accounted for the varied success of the systems of relief. Mill stressed that most countries, like England, granted people a legal right to relief, but there was no such thing as a natural right. In October he lent support to the Radicals' proposal for reform of the House of Lords. He drew on the French experience to refute the possibility of the Government's making good appointments and to argue the necessity of those forming the Upper Chamber having the respect of the country. Mill wanted the

House of Commons to choose the members of the House of Lords to ensure complete identity of interest: "But they would be a wiser, a more instructed and discreet body" (No. 281). Mill had been reading Tocqueville—his review in the *London Review* came out in the same month—and was here putting forward one solution to the problem about which he had become increasingly worried by Tocqueville's discussion of democracy (*A*, 199-201). In these letters he waxed eloquent over the virtues of an Upper House which in theory would be chosen by a House of Commons for whose judgment in practice Mill rarely showed much respect. They would choose men "whom they believed the most fitted in point of talents and acquirements," men "in whose intentions and in whose judgment they have full confidence" (No. 281). Such a conclusion seems born of the *a priori* reasoning of the earlier, much younger, Mill. He had not had a social laboratory in which to test this hypothesis.

The last piece of daily journalism Mill wrote that year was also about a friend's work—a laudatory review of two books for teaching young children arithmetic and perception, both published by the Society for the Diffusion of Useful Knowledge and both by Horace Grant, a debating and walking-tour companion who worked beside Mill in the India Office. Mill's praise of Grant's system sounds very like his later description of his own education.

It has, for instance, been long felt that there are two methods of what is called instruction, which are as remote from each other as light from darkness. One of these is the system of *cram*; the other is the system of cultivating mental *power*. One proposes to stuff a child's memory with the results which have been got at by other people; [by] the other . . . the child acquires . . . ideas, and with those ideas the habit of really discovering truths for himself. . . . [H]e should be accustomed not to get by rote without understanding, but to understand, and not merely to understand, but whenever possible to find out for himself. (No. 282.)

Such strong praise from the young man of nearly thirty for a system obviously close to that he had himself experienced adds support to the words of the *Autobiography* and the positive feelings there expressed about the benefits he had received from his father's training (*A*, 33-5).

The son may have been consciously acknowledging a debt of which at that time he must have been acutely aware, for this was the last piece Mill wrote in the newspapers while his father was alive. He did not write for them again until the desolate year, 1836, was passed. James Mill's health had been deteriorating during 1835 and a rapid worsening of his tuberculosis brought his death on 23 June, 1836, one of the few dates Mill specified in the *Autobiography*. The illness and death of his father increased not only the emotional and familial burden on him but also the editorial and literary one imposed by the *London and Westminster Review*.[105] Another shock was sustained the month after his father's

[105]Molesworth had bought the *Westminster* at the beginning of 1836 to merge it with the *London Review*.

death when Armand Carrel, the man who had provided much of the inspiration for assuming his present labours, was killed in a duel.[106] It is hardly surprising that Mill had to take three months' leave of absence to travel.[107] He took his two younger brothers with him as far as Lausanne; they stayed there while he continued to Italy, where Harriet Taylor joined him.

When he had returned, somewhat recovered, he began work on the *Logic*, a book for which he had long been planning. There is something awesome about a man who spends part of each twenty-four hours helping to direct the governing of India, part trying to direct the governing of England, and part analyzing the method of arriving at the principles that direct his directing, while fulfilling family obligations with devotion and sustaining a relationship with a demanding lady. The little that he contributed to the press at this time was written for personal reasons, either his person or a friend's.[108]

Gibbon Wakefield was given a long review (No. 283) in the *Examiner* and a second article (No. 284) in the *True Sun*, now edited by his old friend from the *Monthly Repository*, W.J. Fox, and owned by the long-time radical publisher Daniel Whittle Harvey, Member of Parliament for Southwark and one of Mill's hopes for his radical parliamentary party. Mill had long supported Wakefield's schemes; in addition, he may possibly have had shares in the new colony in South Australia. In return for his article in the *True Sun*, Mill got a long review from Fox for the *London and Westminster*—a brilliant example of multiple cuts with two strokes of the pen. Certainly friendship was the main reason for the placing of his piece on American banks (No. 285); Henry Cole, another old friend, had, under Mill's urging, undertaken a rival to the *Examiner* called the *Guide*. (It survived for only nine issues.)[109] His friends, J.P. Nichol, "who has carried into physical science a sounder philosophy than most mathematicians" (No. 286), William Molesworth, who had given a speech written by Mill at the end of 1834 (No. 287), and Lord Durham, who returned from Canada at the end of 1838 (the *Examiner* had noticed Mill's *London and Westminster Review* article, "Lord Durham and His Assailants," and then printed a long letter, signed

---

[106]On the early days of 1848 in France, Mill wrote to Henry S. Chapman, "In my meditations and feelings on the whole matter, every second thought has been of Carrel—he who perhaps alone in Europe was qualified to direct such a movement . . ." (*EL, CW*, XIII, 731-2 [29 Feb., 1848]).

[107]According to Alexander Bain: "In 1836, his thirtieth year, he was seized with an obstinate derangement of the brain. Among the external symptoms, were involuntary nervous twitchings in the face." (*John Stuart Mill, a Criticism: With Personal Recollections* [London: Longmans, Green, 1882], 42-3.)

[108]He was fortunately relieved of the need to continue his unpaid contributions to the *Monthly Repository*, it having left W.J. Fox's hands in 1836. More strain was added, however, in 1840, when the family was deeply saddened by another death from tuberculosis—of Henry, aged only nineteen. They gathered at Falmouth to be beside him in his last days; Mill was very affected. In addition fears were revived that his own health might be undermined by this family weakness.

[109]The piece is written with such feeling that the assumption would seem justified that the money was already invested that Mill was to lose in 1842 when American debts were repudiated.

"A.," in which Mill continued the discussion [No. 288]), completed the list of people for whom Mill wrote to the papers. Nothing more appeared until the summer of 1841.

Looking back and reassuming the feelings of defeat of the years 1836 to 1840 when he was running the *Review* and trying to forge a radical ginger group in Parliament,[110] Mill forgot how very much he had accomplished both within and without his own head.

I had, at the height of that reaction [against Benthamism], certainly become much more indulgent to the common opinions of society and the world, and more willing to be content with seconding the superficial improvement which had begun to take place in those common opinions, than became one whose convictions, on so many points, differed fundamentally from them. I was much more inclined, than I can now approve, to put in abeyance the more decidedly heretical part of my opinions, which I now look upon as almost the only ones, the assertion of which tends in any way to regenerate society. (*A*, 237-9.)

Mill perhaps did less than justice to himself (as is frequently the case when he is seating himself in the shadow of Harriet). The lesson he had learnt from French politics by 1833 he had applied to English politics: "to make no compromise of *opinions*, except by avoiding any ill-timed declaration of them, but to negotiate the most advantageous compromises possible in actual *measures*" (No. 216).[111] Although in his more direct political commentary he had expressed approval for practical and somewhat limited reforms without presenting the wider philosophical context, and although in forwarding the reforms of his friends (who were fewer than they had been before he began preaching his new radicalism in the *London and Westminster Review* in 1837) he was sometimes less than incisive, he had nonetheless taken many opportunities to express, sometimes obliquely, his vision of the future to which the historical process would bring mankind. To combine an understanding of the art of the possible with a vision is an unusual accomplishment, and it was the basis for Mill's extraordinary attraction and influence over many decades. He had acquired the gift from his father's teaching, reinforced by political participation through journals and periodicals during the crucial revolutionary years.

Betweeen 1841 and 1846 Mill prepared the *Logic* for the press, and then his *Essays on Some Unsettled Questions of Political Economy*, and began the

---

[110]"And now, on a calm retrospect, I can perceive that the men were less in fault than we supposed, and that we had expected too much from them. They were in unfavourable circumstances. Their lot was cast in the ten years of inevitable reaction, when the Reform excitement being over, and the few legislative improvements which the public really cared for having been rapidly effected, power gravitated back in its natural direction, to those who were for keeping things as they were; when the public mind desired rest, and was less disposed than at any other period since the peace, to let itself be moved by attempts to work up the reform feeling into fresh activity in favour of new things." (*A*, 203-5.)

[111]This lesson, reinforced by his English experience, contributed to his generous re-evaluation of Guizot (see above n98).

Principles of Political Economy. Understandably he was still writing very little for the press—what he did write was in the less radical *Morning Chronicle* (both Melbourne and Palmerston were now reputed to be using it). John Black had retired in 1841 but the new editor, Andrew Doyle, was well known to Mill. Quite predictably he wrote on behalf of his friends: his praise of Sterling's poem, *The Election* (No. 290), and his enjoyment of its wit show genuine warmth; the particularity of his defence of Tocqueville and the warmongering of the French against Brougham is skilful if idiosyncratic (No. 296); a strong article (No. 293) drew attention to the *Report on the Sanitary Condition of the Labouring Population of Great Britain* by Edwin Chadwick.[112] More significant and puzzling, for those—and there must have been many—who still did not fully grasp the Radicals' historical point of view, would have been his praise, albeit somewhat backhanded, of Puseyism (Nos. 291 and 292); it would have been even more so had they known it came from the son of James Mill. He praised Newman and the Puseyites for "embracing not only a complete body of theology and philosophy, but a consistent theory of universal history" and he praised the mediaeval Catholic Church. There was more to this particular case than free speech. The fruitfulness of institutions for their own time was an essential part of his philosophy of history, and his friendship with d'Eichthal had recently encouraged more reading in this interest;[113] his review of Michelet[114] and his recently commenced correspondence with Auguste Comte show that the philosophy of history and within it the historical role of religion were occupying more and more of his attention.[115] His heart and mind were not in his journalism.

At the end of 1842, Mill wrote a despondent letter to Robert Barclay Fox:

But these things [public affairs, especially the Corn Laws], important as they are, do not occupy so much of my thoughts as they once did; it is becoming more & more clearly evident to me that the mental regeneration of Europe must precede its social regeneration & also that none of the ways in which that mental regeneration is sought, Bible Societies, Tract Societies, Puseyism, Socialism, Chartism, Benthamism &c. will *do*, though doubtless they have all some elements of truth & good in them. I find quite enough to do in trying to make up my own mind as to the course which must be taken by the present

---

[112]Even more predictably to those who knew that Mill had advised Chadwick on its form: "I have read your report slowly & carefully. I do not find a single erroneous or questionable position in it, while there is the strength & largeness of practical views which are characteristic of all you do. In its present unrevised state it is as you are probably aware, utterly ineffective from the want of unity and of an apparent thread running through it and holding it together. I wish you would learn some of the forms of scientific exposition of which my friend Comte makes such superfluous use, & to *use* without *abusing* which is one of the principal lessons which practice & reflexion have to teach to people like you & me who have to make new trains of thought intelligible." (*EL, CW*, XIII, 516 [Apr. 1842].) Chadwick rearranged it and Mill offered to review it (*ibid.*, 523-4 [8 June, 1842]).

[113]*Ibid.*, 487.

[114]"Michelet's History of France" (1844), *CW*, XX, 217-55.

[115]See especially the letters of 8 November and 18 December, 1841 (*EL, CW*, XIII, 488-90 and 491-3).

great transitional movement of opinion & society. The little which I can dimly see, this country even less than several other European nations is as yet ripe for promulgating.[116]

The lack of enthusiasm can be felt. In a review of Torrens, Mill explained how Continental workmen could compete with the British:

Before a Continental operative can be as steady a workman as an Englishman, his whole nature must be changed: he must acquire both the virtues and the defects of the English labourer; he must become as patient, as conscientious, but also as careworn, as anxious, as joyless, as dull, as exclusively intent upon the main chance, as his British compeer. He will long be of inferior value as a mere machine, because, happily for him, he cares for pleasure as well as gain. (No. 295.)

Mill might not have known what constituted happiness but he knew who had it not, and very depressing it was if prosperity could only be bought through joy-lessness. Nothing seemed advancing; nothing seemed certain, even in banking: "There is a fashion in mercantile, as well as in medical opinions. There is generally a favourite disease and a favourite remedy; and to know what these are we have seldom so much to consider the nature of the case as the date of the year, whether it is 1814 or 1844." (No. 299.)

The most enthusiastic piece Mill wrote in the first half of 1846 and the last in this desultory period of journalism—a review in the *Spectator* of the first volumes of Grote's *History of Greece*—combined his interest in history and in friends.[117] His task was pleasant. His friendship with George and Harriet Grote, going back to his boyhood, had been strained in more recent years and now was under repair.[118] Friendship was strengthened by his genuine admiration of Grote's attempt at a philosophical history. Mill's praise of Grote is based on two virtues of the historian in particular. Grote has an "unbiased opinion," in contrast to Thirlwall, whose "impartiality seems rather that of a person who has no opinion":

We do not say that an author is to write history with a purpose of bringing out illustrations of his own moral and political doctrines, however correct they may be. He cannot too carefully guard himself against any such temptation. . . . But we do say, that the mere facts, even of the most interesting history, are of little value without some attempt to show

---

[116]*Ibid.*, 563-4 (19 Dec., 1842). Later, in January 1846, two pieces in the *Morning Chronicle*, one on the malt tax (No. 301) and one on poor rates (No. 302), could possibly be seen as bearing very indirectly on the corn law issue.

[117]He also wrote at the same time a review of Grote for the *Edinburgh Review* (1846), *CW*, XI, 271-305.

[118]The strain had been increased by both personal and political differences: Harriet Grote was thought to have gossiped about the relationship between Mill and Mrs. Taylor; the Grotes had not approved of Mill's acceptance of Carlyle's "Memoirs of Mirabeau" for the *London and Westminster Review* (IV and XXVI [Jan. 1837], 382-439); and Mill had been critical of George Grote's parliamentary behaviour. After Harriet Taylor Mill's death in 1858, George and Harriet Grote's home was one of the very few Mill visited. They had never by any means ceased altogether to co-operate; in 1844 Grote had obliged Mill by providing financial support for Auguste Comte.

how and why they came to pass; . . . a history of Greece, which does not put in evidence the influences of Grecian institutions and of Grecian opinions and feelings—may be a useful work, but is not *the* history which we look for. . . . (No. 304.)

This unbiased opinion goes hand in glove with Grote's "sympathy with the Greek mind," his ability to recognize historical periods and the concomitant historical differentiation of men's ideas. For instance, Mill praises Grote for not separating legend and history, for recognizing that both are inextricably blended and "formed together the body of belief in the mind of a Greek" (No. 304). The Greeks lived in the infancy of the human race, and their minds are not to be seen simply as Victorian ones in Greek dress.

OCTOBER 1846 TO JUNE 1847

THE POTATO CROP failed in Ireland in the summer of 1845; the people avoided starvation that winter by eating the seed potatoes. The full extent of the disaster became apparent only at the beginning of the following winter and precipitated the repeal of the Corn Laws in June 1846. The next month Lord John Russell's Whigs replaced Peel's bitterly divided Tories. But repeal could not save a potato-less Irish peasantry, and schemes for more direct relief were under consideration by Russell's Government.

Mill's newspaper writing, except for the occasional review, might well have ceased altogether by the mid-1840s. His professional career had prospered; he was now third in rank at the India Office with a handsome salary of £1200, very ample for a bachelor of mild tastes living at home with his mother and sisters. He continued to find the work congenial, leaving him time for his writing. The *Logic* had established his reputation as a serious thinker, and he was working now on the *Principles of Political Economy*. But two pressures acted on him to prevent his abandoning journalism: Ireland and Harriet Taylor.[119]

Mill turned his concentrated attention to influencing the Government's Irish poor-relief policy. Putting aside the *Political Economy* (though he later used in it much of what he now wrote), Mill, between 5 October, 1846, and 7 January, 1847, a period of only ninety-four days, published forty-three articles

in the *Morning Chronicle* (which unexpectedly entered warmly into my purpose) urging the formation of peasant properties on the waste lands of Ireland. This was during the period of the famine, the winter of 1846/47, when the stern necessities of the time seemed to afford a chance of gaining attention for what appeared to me the only mode of

[119]Beginning in 1846 but more frequently in the 1850s, Harriet Taylor and John Stuart Mill wrote articles jointly. These co-operative efforts, of which Nos. 303, 305, 307, 318, 329, and 350 are examples, are best treated out of strict chronological ordering; they are all discussed in the next section.

combining relief to immediate destitution with permanent improvement of the social and economical condition of the Irish people. (*A*, 243.)

Mill shows himself in these articles very much aware that he is arguing a particular case for a particular time in history. The level of civilization which the Irish have reached—a very low one—is constantly before him. His solution is for the Irish as they actually behave in 1846, not as he or anyone else might think they ought to behave; but the more distant goal of the eventual improvement of their character is also constantly before him. Perhaps immediate charity was essential, at least "the whole English people are rushing frantically to expend any number of millions upon the present exigency,"[120] but, as Mill so happily puts it, "Anybody may have a fixed idea, on which he is inaccessible to reason, but it does not follow that he is never to add a second idea to it" (No. 322). This second idea was that any reform, as opposed to a temporary expediency, "must be something operating upon the minds of the people, and not merely upon their stomachs" (No. 316). He rejected the principle of outdoor relief; it had once pauperized the English peasantry and it would be no remedy now in Ireland. He discussed fixity of tenure but saw it as not only unjust to the landlord but also devoid of the beneficial effects of ownership of land. A large emigration of Irish was undesirable: ". . . Ireland must be an altered country at home before we can wish to create an Ireland in every quarter of the globe, and it is not well to select as missionaries of civilization a people who, in so great a degree, yet remain to be civilized" (No. 317).

There remained public works. If these were on roads, the result would be that the Irish labourer would prefer to work for the Government, which paid well, rather than for a landlord or for himself. Neither should these be on a landlord's land at the expense of the Government because such a profit to the landlord was totally unjust (No. 331), nor through loans to the landlord for the same reason—the profit from this tragedy would be all on the one side. "It would be an actual crime to bestow all this wealth upon the landlords, without exacting an equivalent" (No. 324). In addition rents would increase, thus augmenting the injustice to the peasant. Finally Mill argued that the immediate effect of large-scale improvement of agriculture by the landlord was to diminish the number of people employed on the land.[121]

No, what Ireland needed was

something which will stir the minds of the peasantry from one end of Ireland to the other, and cause a rush of all the active spirits to take advantage of the boon for the first time proffered to them. We want something which may be regarded as a great act of national justice—healing the wounds of centuries by *giving*, not *selling*, to the worthiest and most

---

[120]*EL*, *CW*, XIII, 709 (9 Mar., 1847).

[121]This argument was based on information in Torrens's letter to Peel (No. 295), which he had reviewed four years earlier.

aspiring sons of the soil, the unused portion of the inheritance of their conquered ancestors. (No. 321.)

This unused portion was the waste lands of Ireland. Those needing relief should be set to work and provided with tools to reclaim the uncultivated land, much of it bog; drainage projects should be supervised. The advantages of Mill's scheme were manifold, and he pressed them home. The spirit of the Irish would be restored: "Trust to the feeling of proprietorship, that never-failing source of local attachments. When the cottage is theirs—when the land which surrounds it is theirs—there will be a pleasure in enlarging, and improving, and adorning the one and the other." (No. 316.) Mill then outlined the benefits produced by small peasant properties (and at the same time praised his beloved France and his old friend Sismondi). It was at one time predicted that France would be a "pauper-warren," but, quite to the contrary, it has been proved statistically that "the state of her rural population, who are four-fifths of the whole, has improved in every particular; that they are better housed, better clothed, better and more abundantly fed; that their agriculture has improved in quality; that all the productions of the soil have multiplied beyond precedent; that the wealth of the country has advanced, and advances with increasing rapidity, and the population with increasing slowness" (No. 328). It was absolutely vital that the opportunity should not be misused or lost:

We must give over telling the Irish that it is our business to find food for them. We must tell them, now and for ever, that it is *their* business. . . . They have a right, not to support at the public cost, but to aid and furtherance in finding support for themselves. They have a right to a repeal of all laws and a reform of all social systems which improperly impede them in finding it, and they have a right to their fair share of the raw material of the earth. (No. 337.)

At the end of the year Mill thought he had triumphed and that it was now certain that the reclaiming of waste lands and the resettling of the peasantry would form at least part of any Government plan (Nos. 348 and 351). When Mill heard in January that the Treasury was suggesting further loans to landlords, just when he understood the Government to be preparing "a general plan for the reclamation of waste lands, in which the claims of the peasantry to receive some share in the common inheritance of the whole nation are not overlooked," he was appalled (No. 352). The cup of victory was to be dashed from his lips by administrative fiat. On 7 January Mill brought his series to a close; he had done all he could during the parliamentary recess to influence policy.

When Mill ceased to write the leaders on Ireland for the *Morning Chronicle*, he did not give up entirely trying to stay the madness. He wrote four leaders controverting John Wilson Croker, another on the debates in the House of Commons, three condemning the proposed Irish Poor Law, a scathing one on the proposed National Fast, and a melancholy one on emigration from Ireland. On balance, Mill was on the losing side, and the bitterness of the defeat provoked some of his more brilliant displays of verbal acidity. He was not prepared for one minute to admit that peasant proprietors in France or anywhere else in Europe farmed badly. The principal cause of poor agriculture in France, contrary to Croker's view, was "the exclusive taste of the wealthy and middle classes for town life and town pursuits, combined with the general want of enterprise of the French nation with respect to industrial improvements. . . . The thing would be soon done if the love of industrial progress should ever supplant in the French mind the love of national glory, or if the desire of national glorification should take that direction." (No. 357.) France was still beloved, but the years since 1830 had left their mark.

On the proposed National Fast (No. 363), Mill cut loose with controlled satiric venom. He almost found delight in the depths of hypocrisy of a people who, professing to believe that God's wrath had descended upon them for their "manifold sins and provocations," and who, praying with penitent hearts to Him to "withdraw his afflicting hand," could, in order thus to profess and pray, move the Queen's drawing-room from Wednesday to Saturday. Even his friends got the back of his tongue—but only in private. "Roebuck . . . is enlisting his talents in support of the madness. . . . Molesworth, except that he has only made one speech instead of fifty, is just as bad."[122] By the end of March his despair was complete.

The people are all mad, and nothing will bring them to their senses but the terrible consequences they are certain to bring on themselves. . . . Fontenelle said that mankind must pass through all forms of error before arriving at truth. The form of error we are now possessed by is that of making *all* take care of *each*, instead of stimulating and helping each to take care of himself; and now this is going to be put to a terrible trial, which will bring it to a crisis and a termination sooner than could otherwise have been hoped for.[123]

However close Mill was to come to a "qualified Socialism" (*A*, 199), the Irish

---

[122]*EL, CW*, XIII, 709 (9 Mar., 1847).

[123]*Ibid.*, 710-11 (27 Mar., 1847). A few years later he was cheered by the realization that his endeavours had not been an entire failure but had, in fact, furthered his life's work of improving mankind's lot. "Are you [Harriet Taylor] not amused with Peel about Ireland? He sneers down the waste land plan, two years ago, . . . & now he has enfanté a scheme containing that & much more than was then proposed—& the Times supports him & Ireland praises him. I am extremely glad he has done it—I can see that it is working as nothing else has yet worked to break down the superstition about property—& it is the only thing happening in England which promises a step forward—a thing which one may well welcome when things are going so badly for the popular cause in Europe—not that I am discouraged by this—progress of the right kind seems to me quite safe now that Socialism has become *inextinguishable*." (*LL, CW*, XIV, 21 [31 Mar., 1849].)

His assessment in the *Autobiography* is less cheery: "the profound ignorance of English politicians and the English public concerning all social phenomena not generally met with in England (however common elsewhere) made my endeavours an entire failure. Instead of a great operation on the waste lands, and the conversion of cottiers into proprietors, Parliament passed a Poor Law for maintaining them as paupers: and if the nation has not since found itself in inextricable difficulties from the joint operation of the old evils and the quack remedy, it is indebted for its deliverance to that most unexpected and surprising fact, the depopulation of Ireland, commenced by famine, and continued by emigration." (*A*, 243.)

experience when incorporated in the *Political Economy* suggested no more than that property in land was a legitimate area for government intervention. The Saint-Simonian hypothesis might be said to have been tested against the reality of County Clare and the time found far from ripe. Mill's historical sense was reinforced; time determined measures. Whatever the future might hold, whatever form of socialism was to evolve, his view of the Irish peasantry had strengthened his belief that "the object to be principally aimed at in the present stage of human improvement, is not the subversion of the system of individual property, but the improvement of it, and the full participation of every member of the community in its benefits."[124]

Mill's socialism was an integral part of his sense of historical progression, the approaching stage in the human development; that belief had not altered since he had first met Saint-Simonian ideas. But if Bentham has to be watched for his shift in mood from "is" to "ought," a keen eye has to be kept on Mill's tenses. He does not always make clear what is an "actual measure" and what a "plan of thorough reform"; although they are in the same line of progression, the multiplication of peasant proprietors and the nationalization of the land belong to different levels of civilization.

During that spring, Mill wrote for the *Morning Chronicle* only two pieces not on Ireland:[125] a review (No. 360) of the article on "Centralisation" in the *Edinburgh Review* by his old tutor and friend John Austin[126] and a report (No. 366) on the opening of the Prussian Diet. Both are fine examples of Mill's historical relativism, which his less historically-minded friends, and more particularly his enemies, sometimes found puzzling and smacking of inconsistency and radical opportunism.[127] He wrote to Austin, discussing his review: "I have necessarily thought a good deal about it lately for the purposes of a practical treatise on Pol. Economy & I have felt the same difficulty which you feel about the *axiomata media*. I suspect there are none which do not vary with time, place & circumstance."[128] A good example was Austin's discussion of the reform of local government which should have both an immediate end, the provision of "a good administration of local affairs," the means for which might vary between time and place—between, say, France in 1831 and England in 1835, to provide Mill with an example from his own past advocacy—and "its ulterior and

---

[124]*CW*, II, 214.

[125]There were a further two rather curious pieces, one on "Sanitary" versus "Sanatory" (No. 365) in *The Times* and one on enlightened infidelity (No. 367) intended for G.J. Holyoake's *Reasoner* but not published. Some of the phrasing suggests Harriet Taylor's prompting.

[126]*Edinburgh Review*, LXXXV (Jan. 1847), 221-58. The lack of stir caused by Austin's laboriously written article prompted Mill to explain to him: "It seems to me that reviews have had their day, & that nothing is now worth much except the two extremes, newspapers for diffusion & books for accurate thought" (*EL*, *CW*, XIII, 711-12 [13 Apr., 1847]).

[127]Alexander Bain reports that George Grote "would say to me, 'Much as I admire John Mill, my admiration is always mixed with fear'; meaning that he never knew what unexpected turn Mill might take" (*John Stuart Mill*, 83).

[128]*EL*, *CW*, XIII, 712.

paramount object," the "social education of the country at large" (No. 360). In the article on the opening of the Prussian Diet he praised both an enlightened despot and a democratic diet; each benefited the country at the appropriate stage of its development.

This last piece marked the end of an era for Mill; the *Morning Chronicle*, for which he had written from his youth, was to become an organ for the Conservatives under the new ownership of Lord Cardwell and Beresford Hope. Although Mill would still have access to its pages, they were no longer the pages wherein he joined with like-minded men who had "carried criticism & the spirit of reform" into English institutions; the sense of belonging was gone.[129]

Another of Mill's long-time friends and mentors claimed his attention before the summer break. George Grote had published volumes three and four of his *History of Greece* and Mill gave them a long, careful review in the *Spectator* (No. 368), underlining again the historical relativism which informed his understanding and analysis of his own times. He praised once more Grote's understanding of the Greek mind and his ability to communicate that understanding. But above all he lauded Grote's achievement in ascribing the enlightenment in the first place "to her unlimited Democracy" (qualified by a footnote noting the omission of women, aliens, and slaves); "and secondly, to the wise precautions, unknown to the other free states of Greece, by which the sagacity of Solon and of Cleisthenes had guarded the workings of Athenian institutions against the dangers to which they were most liable [from unlimited Democracy],—precautions which insensibly moulded the mind of the Demos itself, and made it capable of its heritage of freedom" (No. 368). Reading the *History*, Mill said, strengthened the arguments that had already led him to complete agreement with the author's conclusions. Grote's *History* no doubt lent added force to some of the passages in *On Liberty* and increased Mill's delight in Hare's proportional representation; but Tocqueville needed little support. For by the summer of 1847 Mill's mind was set in most of its ways. Grote was not altering but confirming Mill's own conclusions by providing more of the necessary "verification and correction" which come "from the general remarks afforded . . . by history respecting times gone by."[130]

DECEMBER 1847 TO JULY 1858

DURING THE NEXT ELEVEN YEARS—years that began with the collapse of the Chartists and ended, after the Indian Mutiny, with the Crown taking over the

[129]*LL, CW*, XV, 978-9. It is an indication of Mill's standing in the world of the press that he was offered joint-proprietorship of the *Chronicle* at this time (Harriet Taylor to John Taylor, 18 Jan., 1848, Mill-Taylor Collection, British Library of Political and Economic Science, London School of Economics, XXVIII, 174).
[130]*CW*, VIII, 874.

East India Company—John Stuart Mill is to the outside eye a rather curious, almost a pathetic, figure. Alexander Bain said bluntly of the forty-one-year-old Mill, "His work, as a great originator, in my opinion, was done."[131] He lived almost in seclusion and was frequently in a low state. Although he had received great respect (as well as money) for his *Logic* and his *Political Economy* and had now an established public reputation, that to which he had devoted his life had not been achieved. The moral elevation of Europe, never mind England, seemed no nearer. Despite his position as a public sage and his vast, almost semi-official, correspondence, he had not been able to inspire the people, or their leaders (or the one leader), with the great principles needed to propel civilization onward. Mill seemed little impressed with the practical reforms that had been achieved. They appear, with hindsight, to have been vast: repeal of the Combination Acts, reform of Parliament, effective factory legislation, the abolition of slavery, an education grant, the new Poor Law (of which indeed he approved at length), rationalized municipal institutions, and repeal of the Corn Laws, none of these—not all of them combined—seemed to bring lasting satisfaction to Mill. The country was better off; prosecutions of the press and of the individual were far less frequent; the labouring classes were of national concern. But to Mill the country was still mean.[132] The practical reforms for which he had once striven in the belief that their effects would be the moral education of mankind had proved ineffectual.

For a considerable time after this [the publication of the *Political Economy*], I published no work of magnitude; though I still occasionally wrote in periodicals. . . . During these years I wrote or commenced various Essays, for eventual publication, on some of the fundamental questions of human and social life. . . . I continued to watch with keen interest the progress of public events. But it was not, on the whole, very encouraging to me. The European reaction after 1848, and the success of an unprincipled usurper in December 1851, put an end, as it seemed, to all present hope for freedom or social improvement in France and the Continent. In England, I had seen and continued to see many of the opinions of my youth obtain general recognition, and many of the reforms in institutions, for which I had through life contended, either effected or in course of being so. But these changes had been attended with much less benefit to human well being than I should formerly have anticipated, because they had produced very little improvement in that which all real amelioration in the lot of mankind depends on, their intellectual and moral state: and it might even be questioned if the various causes of deterioration which had been at work in the meanwhile, had not more than counterbalanced the tendencies to improvement. I had learnt from experience that many false opinions may be exchanged

---

[131]*John Stuart Mill*, 91.

[132]He wrote to John Austin: "I think with you that the English higher classes . . . mean well, 'what little they do mean' as my father said of some person. They have grown good even to goodiness . . . [but show] more & more their *pitoyable* absence of even that very moderate degree of intellect, & that very moderate amount of will & character which are scattered through the other classes. . . . The doctrine of averting revolutions by wise concessions to the people does not need to be preached to the English aristocracy. They have long acted on it to the best of their capacity, & the fruits it produces are soup-kitchen and ten hours bills." (*EL, CW,* XIII, 712-13 [13 Apr., 1847].)

for true ones, without in the least altering the habits of mind of which false opinions are the result. The English public . . . have thrown off certain errors [but] the general discipline of their minds, intellectually and morally, is not altered. I am now convinced, that no great improvements in the lot of mankind are possible, until a great change takes place in the fundamental constitution of their modes of thought. (*A*, 245.)

In this intellectual frame of mind the political events in England during the next eleven years affected him little—at least publicly. The climax, or anti-climax, of the Chartist demonstration rained out on Kennington Common drew no more public comment from him than the political manoeuvrings of the Peelites.[133] He did not comment in the newspapers on the Crimean War with all its mismanagement, even when Roebuck's motion for an inquiry toppled the Government, nor on the Indian Mutiny.

Political events in France in 1848, however, roused him to write three items; Carlyle's views on Ireland prompted two articles; Joseph Hume's motion for Parliamentary reform elicited three articles; and Alexander Bain got a review. Those nine items were all he wrote for the papers in 1848. Although the establishment of a Provisional Government in France in February 1848 had not the effect on Mill of the one eighteen years earlier, he was briefly exhilarated: "I am hardly yet out of breath from reading and thinking about it" was how he put it. "If France succeeds in establishing a republic and reasonable republican government, all the rest of Europe, except England and Russia, will be republicanised in ten years, and England itself probably before we die. There never was a time when so great a drama was being played out in one generation."[134] Perhaps not bliss to be alive but very stirring. However, Mill was prompted initially to no more in the newspapers than a letter to the editor of the *Spectator* (No. 370). In August after the street fighting in June and the suppression of the insurrectionists by General Louis Cavaignac—a name that must have stirred memories for Mill—he denied the Tory press's claim "that the insurrection was something unheard-of for its horrible barbarity" (No. 376). No barbarous actions had taken place and France was advancing rapidly but calmly. Ten days later, France had ceased advancing and Mill was not calm; his tone was one of outrage verging on disbelief as he expostulated against the gagging of the press by the executive commission supported by a democracy which had proved to be conservative. He had seen it all before: "It is the very law of Louis Philippe . . ." (No. 378). Once again, as he had more than a decade earlier, Mill defended the young men who were forced to take up arms against their repressors. But it was a disillusioned voice that asked, "How much longer must we wait for an example, anywhere in Europe, of a ruler or a ruling party who really desire fair

---

[133]In 1842 Mill had written privately to William Lovett offering help although, as he pointed out, he was not a democrat (*EL*, *CW*, XIII, 533-4 [27 July, 1842]).
[134]*Ibid.*, 731-2 (29 Feb., 1848).

play for any opinions contrary to their own?" (No. 378) without which the spark of progress cannot be struck.[135]

Mill's equilibrium was further upset that spring by Carlyle's response to the disturbances in Ireland. The prophet was now prophesying for the wrong tribe, calling for force, preaching false doctrines about Ireland and England and also throwing in a few heresies on France and on the Chartist demonstration. The crowning touch was that his ravings appeared in the *Examiner*—a sad result of Fonblanque's retirement and replacement by John Forster. Just when Mill was feeling that the future direction of Europe hung in the balance—wondering whether in England and in all Europe "faith in improvement, and determination to effect it, will become general, and the watchword of improvement will once more be, as it was of old, the emancipation of the oppressed classes" (No. 376)—Carlyle wrote prophesying anarchy and doom and citing France as proof. Mill trumpeted back, his sarcasm reaching sublime heights as he fought against this political incarnation of intuitionism. Carlyle said it was England's mission to pacify Ireland. Mill first pointed slyly to the example of Cromwell; he who had had the authority and "courage and capacity of the highest order" had not succeeded. "But at present the individual in whom England is personified, and who is to regard himself as the chosen instrument of heaven for making Ireland what it ought to be, and is encouraged to carry fire and sword through Ireland if that assumption should be disputed, is—Lord John Russell!" (No. 372.) And how had England proved herself after four-and-a-half centuries of rule over Ireland fitted to fulfil her mission? "They spent ten millions in effecting what seemed impossible—in making Ireland worse than before. They demoralized and disorganized what little of rational industry the country contained; and the only permanent thing with which they endowed Ireland, was the only curse which her evil destiny seemed previously to have spared her—a bad poor law." (No. 372.) The prophet of rationalism could also thunder from the mountain tops when roused. In his letter to the *Examiner* Mill quoted the Bible three times and Homer once.

A much sunnier note is struck in the three leaders Mill wrote in July 1848 (Nos. 373, 374, and 375) for the *Daily News*, supporting the motion of his father's old friend, Joseph Hume, for Parliamentary reform. The move to the *Daily News* was entirely natural, both the *Morning Chronicle* and the *Examiner* having fallen into less congenial hands. The *Daily News*, whose first leader had been written by W.J. Fox, was the foremost liberal London paper.[136] Its present editor was Eyre Evans Crowe, who had been a resident in France in 1830 and an enthusiastic witness to the street fighting, later Paris correspondent for the

---

[135]Nonetheless Mill wrote a defence of the revolution as forwarding France's history: "Vindication of the French Revolution of February 1848," *CW*, XX, 317-63.

[136]The paper had started in 1846 under the very brief editorship of Charles Dickens, followed for nine months by John Forster, who then took over the *Examiner*.

Morning Chronicle, and writer of a history of France for Lardner's *Cabinet Cyclopaedia*. A congenial editor, obviously, of a paper under the equally congenial ownership of the Dilke family. The *Morning Chronicle* under Black and then Doyle had been serious; the *Daily News* was determined to be popular. It succeeded admirably, and, with a circulation briefly of over ten thousand a day, rivalled the influence of *The Times* and far surpassed that of the *Morning Chronicle*. Mill's style was bright and clever, proving that he was quite master of his pen, able to write to an editor's direction.

Mill's message was the same in 1848 as in 1830: there was nothing to fear from reform; the natural order would not be turned upside down; from historical progress all would benefit. Mill used the example of France, which now had "universal" suffrage (Mill did not stop this time to qualify his use of the term), and yet not twenty members in an assembly of nine hundred were working class.

Then what has France gained, it may be asked, or what would England gain by the admission of the working classes to the franchise? A gain beyond all price, the effects of which may not show themselves in a day, or in a year, but are calculated to spread over and elevate the future. . . .

Grant but a democratic suffrage, and all the conditions of government are changed. . . . The discussions of parliament and of the press would be, what they ought to be, a continued course of political instruction for the working classes. (No. 374.)

Here again speaks the spirit of the age. "The present age . . . is an age of struggle between conflicting principles ["between the instincts and immediate interests of the propertied classes and those of the unpropertied"] which it is the work of this time, and perhaps of many generations more, to bring into a just relation one with another" (No. 374). The peroration also could have been written any time in the last two decades: "The world will rally round a truly great principle, and be as much the better for the contest as for the attainment; but the petty objects by the pursuit of which no principle is asserted, are fruitless even when attained" (No. 375).

Mill's occasional journalism in 1848 ended abruptly in the summer (although in September he managed a promotion of Bain's first of four lectures for a course "On the Application of Physics to Common Life" [No. 379]), when his health, already weak from the labour involved in writing the *Principles*, was further aggravated by a nasty fall. According to Bain,

In treating the hurt, a belladonna plaster was applied. An affection of his eyes soon followed, which he had knowledge enough at once to attribute to the belladonna, and disused the plaster forthwith. For some weeks, however, he was both lame and unable to use his eyes. I never saw him in such a state of despair. Prostration of the nervous system may have aggravated his condition. His elasticity of constitution brought him through once more; but in the following year, 1849, he was still in an invalid condition.[137]

[137]*John Stuart Mill*, 90. Bain introduced Mill to Dr. Thomas Clark who attempted without success to induce Mill to try the water-treatment. Perhaps Harriet remembered the case of Dr. Ellis's patient (see below).

The year 1849 was not a good one for Mill. The first six months were full of disaster, both public and private. Louis Napoleon had beaten Cavaignac by some four million votes to become President of France. England's reforming spirit was buried beneath relief and satisfaction at having withstood unscathed the European upheavals. Mill's health was still very poor: although his leg healed slowly and his eyes gradually improved, his overall depression remained. His friendship with the Austins, which went back to the time when he played with little Lucie in the garden at Queen Square Place, had not survived the disagreements over the Revolution of 1848 in France, and now they were planning to remove with the Guizots to the neighbourhood of Walton-on-Thames, where Harriet Taylor had kept a country home since 1839. Their presence would necessitate her moving, she claimed. To return permanently to Kent Terrace was out of the question; the dedication of the *Political Economy* to her had elicited very sharp words from John Taylor.[138] Her health was poor; her own family upset her beyond enduring; her father was seriously ill (in fact, terminally); her lover was hobbling, partially blind and depressed. She fled to the Continent. Only the prospect of joining her there in April lightened Mill's gloom. That and reading volumes five and six of Grote's *History*. It was hardly surprising, therefore, that no new ideas were developed in the three newspaper articles he wrote in the first six months of 1849. All appeared in March, two in the *Spectator* favourably reviewing Grote (Nos. 380 and 381)—there was far more quotation than review—and one, with Harriet's encouragement, in the *Daily News* on the admission of Jews to Parliament (No. 382).[139]

The year which had begun so badly went steadily downhill. By the summer, Mill's emotional frame of mind was, if anything, worse. Harriet Taylor had refused to accede to her husband's implied request in a letter telling of his increasing ill health that she come home at the end of March.[140] She had replied that she had a duty to Mill and could not consider her own wishes; it was her duty to follow through with the arrangements to meet him at Bagnères in the Pyrenees in April. She arrived home in the middle of May to find her husband in the last stages of cancer. She nursed him hysterically until his death on 18 July, 1849.

[138]Hayek, 120ff. The dedication of the *Political Economy* caused considerable éclat within their small circle; their lives became even more reserved and (coincidentally?) their joint productions for a time ceased.

[139]His comment to Harriet, who had encouraged him to write the last article, illustrates the anonymity they wished to preserve at this time. "As you suggested I wrote an article on Russell's piece of meanness in the Jew Bill & have sent it to Crowe. . . . But I fear the article, even as 'from a correspondent' will be too strong meat for the Daily News, as it declares without mincing the matter, that infidels are perfectly proper persons to be in parliament. I like the article myself. I have carefully avoided any thing disrespectful to Russell personally, or any of the marks known to me, by which my writing can be recognized." (*LL, CW*, XIV, 18 [17 Mar., 1849].)

[140]John Taylor to Harriet Taylor, 30 Mar., 1849, Mill-Taylor Collection, XXVIII, 227.

For the rest of the year, Mill himself published alone[141] just four short pieces, keeping faith with people who had striven for their ideals and been crushed by a philistine world. He added the prestige of his voice to the plea for the Hungarian refugees who had fled to Turkey and were in danger of being handed back to the Czar (Nos. 384 and 385), and with a touch of his old economy got in a slap at France who, "in a moment of insanity, has given herself up for four years to the discretion of the relative (by marriage), and servile tool of the Emperor of Russia, by whose help he hopes to be made Emperor of France" (No. 384), and at the British public who could not be trusted "for support in any energetic and generous course of action in foreign affairs" (No. 385). As always loyal to, and admiring of, any followers of Saint-Simonism, he drew the public's attention to the persecution of Etienne Cabet on trial for fraud in the United States and of Jules Lechevalier prosecuted in France (Nos. 386 and 387). They were men of noble character, dedicated, in the words of Cabet's followers living with him in his utopian community, "to the moral education of mankind" (No. 386). Such dedication was a flame to be cherished in a dark world.

John Taylor's death had done nothing to lighten it, as some might callously have expected. There is no question that it was a dreadful blow to them. It was a sad and very unsettling event; while he was alive, the Mill-Taylor relationship, if far from ideal, had been stable, and custom had made it familiar. Now all was open once more to public speculation, and their small circle of acquaintance and family could not help but be turning on them those prying eyes they both so loathed. They withdrew into even deeper seclusion, and perhaps not surprisingly in 1850 they resumed their joint productions,[142] initiated in 1846 just before the series on Ireland. These articles, mostly on domestic brutality, have been largely overlooked by modern critics. The understandable prejudice against Harriet Taylor, certainly not lessened by Mill's indiscreet praises of her; the instinctive dislike of accepting his reversal of the most obviously reasonable view of their intellectual relationship; the diffuse, if not scattered, composition of parts of the articles; and the offensively Punch and Judy nature of the subject matter—all these factors have led to a somewhat embarrassed ignoring of the roughly twenty articles of their joint production. They are cited very rarely and then mostly only for evidence either of the deleterious influence Harriet Taylor had on John Mill or of his besotted state. These joint productions ought not, however, to be passed over.

---

[141]Just four days before John Taylor's death, they had published an article on corporal punishment (No. 383), their first work designated as a joint production since December 1846—if one discounts the *Principles of Political Economy*.

[142]Mill quite frequently added "very little of which was mine" to the designation "joint production" in his bibliography. Some of these articles would appear to have been drafted by Harriet Taylor and little more than signed by John Stuart Mill.

The passage in the *Autobiography* quoted at the beginning of this section makes clear that in his mid-forties Mill was looking for an explanation of the failure of Europe and England to produce any real improvement in the lot of mankind. Europe had had revolutions; England had had reforms; and yet the expected, eagerly awaited leap forward had not taken place. Why was there so little improvement in the "intellectual and moral state"? How could it be that "the general discipline" of people's minds, "intellectually and morally, [was] not altered"? All the reforms had brought no satisfaction because no "great change" had taken place "in the fundamental constitution of their modes of thought." Mill's convictions would incline him to the conclusion that there must exist an anachronistic social institution—or institutions—that was damming up the historical process, and that he and his fellow Radicals had so far not exposed. Radical analysis had failed to reveal the next step for the improvement of mankind. By intuition Harriet Taylor succeeded.

Mill's disclaimer of having learnt from Harriet Taylor to recognize the claims of women is well known. His acknowledgment of that which he did come to understand through her is almost equally unknown.

Undoubtedly however this conviction was at that time, in my mind, little more than an abstract principle: it was through her teaching that I first perceived and understood its practical bearings; her rare knowledge of human nature, and perception and comprehension of moral and social influences, shewed me (what I should never have found out in more than a very vague way for myself) the mode in which the consequences of the inferior position of women intertwine themselves with all the evils of existing society and with the difficulties of human improvement. Without her I should probably always have held my present opinions on the question, but it would never have become to me as, with the deepest conviction, it now is, the great question of the coming time: the most urgent interest of human progress, involving the removal of a barrier which now stops the way, and renders all the improvements which can be effected while it remains, slight and superficial. (*A*, 252.)

The vast "practical bearings" and "the consequences of the inferior position of women" were illuminated for Mill by the reports of legal proceedings, frequently concerning brutality, to which Harriet Taylor drew his attention. Together they tested the new hypothesis "by common experience respecting human nature in our own age."[143] He became convinced that injustice and tyranny were perpetuated in society by the familial arrangements between the sexes. When these were changed, only then would come about the fundamental reconstitution of modes of thought.[144]

This belief was a natural enough development in Mill's thought. He had been

[143]*CW*, VIII, 874.

[144]It was not perhaps unnatural that during the twenty-one months between John Taylor's death and Harriet Taylor's remarriage to John Mill, the subject of marriage and the laws governing it should have been much on their minds. Only one of their joint productions during those months, "Questionable Charity" (No. 394), was not concerned with domestic relations.

first stirred by the possibilities of reshaping society through law reform; he accepted unreservedly associationist psychology; he lived in a society that believed fervently in the moral superiority of women and their irreplaceable civilizing role in the family. The belief in phases of history and the seeking of causes for the characteristics of each age were essential to his way of thinking; his interest in ethology led him to contemplate a book on the subject; and his faith for the future had always been reliant on the working class. In the most basic of all social relationships, that between man and woman, was to be found the explanation of working-class brutishness and the fundamental cause, and therefore the remedy, of "one of the chief hindrances to human improvement."[145] Equality for women was to become "a badge of advanced liberalism";[146] his having raised the question of women's suffrage, was, he said, "by far the most important, perhaps the only really important public service I performed in the capacity of a Member of Parliament" (*A*, 285).

Their joint productions began to appear, very infrequently, at the beginning of 1846 in a manner quite reminiscent of the youthful Mill's articles in the *Morning Chronicle*. Specific cases were used as springboards to the larger questions lying behind certain legal practices. The acquittal of the brutal Captain Johnstone (No. 303) on a charge of murder led to a discussion of "temporary insanity" as a legal fiction; the conviction by twelve Surrey tradesmen of Dr. Ellis (No. 305) for professional incompetence raised the questions whether medical practitioners ought to be held responsible for the results of treatment sought by the patient and whether a jury picked at random was competent to judge such treatment; and the case of Private Matthewson (No. 307) brought forth once again Mill's theme of the need for disinterested judges. By the end of 1846 the Mill-Taylor interest had become more focused. The three cases of Sarah Brown (No. 318), William Burn (No. 329), and the North family (No. 350) all had to do with family relationships and the iniquitous consequences of the subordinate position of wives and children. Contemplation of these inequalities before the law led to strong conclusions about the married state, the brutality of some husbands, and the helplessness of all wives. Mill had known since he was a boy that the second-class position of women could not be upheld by *a priori* reasoning; through Harriet Taylor he learnt to feel it insupportable, and to understand its consequences. When Mill sent Eugène Sue a copy of his *Political Economy* in 1848 he wrote, "sur le mariage et sur l'entière égalité de droits entre les hommes et les femmes les opinions de l'auteur de 'Martin' et du 'Juif Errant' sont non seulement les miennes mais j'ai la conviction profonde que la liberté, la démocratie, la fraternité, ne sont nulle part si ce n'est dans ces opinions, et que l'avenir du progrès social et moral ne se trouve que là."[147]

[145]*Subjection of Women*, *CW*, XXI, 261.
[146]Letter to Parker Pillsbury, *LL*, *CW*, XVI, 1289 (4 July, 1867).
[147]*EL*, *CW*, XIII, 736 ([May?] 1848).

By 1850 the principle had been more fully developed and was more clearly applied. The persistence in society, especially among the lower classes, of coarseness—a combination of brutality and tyranny—was the result of the formative years being spent in domestic relations where the law recognized the rights of men only, refusing any to wives and children, and where, consequently, mistreatment of those weaker, either because of age or sex, was commonplace, physical chastisement being, if not encouraged, certainly not discouraged by society. In Mill's youth self-interest had been the root cause of evil, circumstances being seen as capable of redirecting it to good. Then political institutions had been blamed for society's lack of progress in civilization. Reform had come but not progress. In these articles, guided by Harriet Taylor's "rare knowledge of human nature, and perception and comprehension of moral and social influences," Mill the scientist traced the flaws in society to the nurturing of its citizens in an atmosphere of brutality, tyranny, and injustice.

The series of letters in 1850[148] starts out with one on the Californian constitution (No. 388); nearly half of the letter is devoted to the granting of married women's property rights. Harriet Taylor herself had suffered greatly in spirit if not in body from the law's most universal injustice to women—the deprivation of all civil rights upon marriage.[149] Women legally disappeared *sous couverture*. The law then had to assume, and it did, that all members of the family were subsumed under the male head. In society generally, but particularly among the lower classes, this fiction was reflected in a common attitude that inflicted degradation and hardship on wives and children:

The baser part of the populace think that when a legal power is given to them over a living creature—when a person, like a thing, is suffered to be spoken of as their own—as *their* wife, or *their* child, or *their* dog—they are allowed to do what they please with it; and in the eye of the law—if such judgments as the preceding are to be taken as its true interpretation—they are justified in supposing that the worst they can do will be accounted but as a case of slight assault. (No. 400; cf. No. 395.)

The law positively encouraged brutality in the family (No. 389). Wife or child beating should be regarded with greater revulsion than common assaults outside the home. Those most affected, tragically, are "the wives and children of the

---

[148]Apart from the co-operative productions, Mill published in the papers on only three occasions during 1850. The first and most significant was a review in the *Spectator* of Volumes VII and VIII of Grote's *History*; it was again favourable. He also wrote two letters to the *Leader* (Nos. 397 and 398) in one of which there was a defence of nonconformity similar to that in *On Liberty*: "No order of society can be in my estimation desirable unless grounded on the maxim, that no man or woman is accountable to others for any conduct by which others are not injured or damaged" (No. 397). There was also one, dated 1 February, 1851 (No. 399), a draft of an unpublished letter to the *Weekly Dispatch*, defending the non-believer, who is undogmatic about religion, from the charge of being "merely a speculative, disquisitive, logical, thinking machine."

[149]On his own marriage to Harriet, Mill wrote a solemn renunciation of any rights over his wife or her property granted him by the law: "Statement on Marriage," *CW*, XXI, 97.

brutal part of the population," and on their torturers the law should be harshest (No. 400).

The law's callous sufferance of wife beating was all the more deplorable because it deprived a woman of any alternative to dependence on her husband. Thanks to the law she could not leave him to escape his brutality because legally all her earnings belonged to him. In these circumstances could there be a greater injustice than that inflicted by a law which fined a husband for a barbarous cruelty but did not protect the wife from future torture? Mill cited the case of a man acquitted on charges of attempted murder on the evidence of his terrified wife, who said he had hanged her only in jest, "for what would have been the consequence to her of having given strong evidence against him, in the event of his acquittal?" (No. 400.)[150] Husbands could beat their wives and, if they chanced to kill them, they would be tried for manslaughter. "Is it because juries are composed of husbands in a low rank of life, that men who kill their wives almost invariably escape—wives who kill their husbands, never? How long will such a state of things be permitted to continue?" (No. 393.) Insidiously destructive was the habitual violence, the daily brutality, that never came to court.

Let any one consider the degrading moral effect, in the midst of these crowded dwellings, of scenes of physical violence, repeated day after day—the debased, spirit-broken, down-trodden condition of the unfortunate woman, the most constant sufferer from domestic brutality in the poorer classes, unaffectedly believing herself to be out of the protection of the law—the children born and bred in this moral atmosphere—with the unchecked indulgence of the most odious passions, the tyranny of physical force in its coarsest manifestations, constantly exhibited as the most familiar facts of their daily life—can it be wondered if they grow up without any of the ideas and feelings which it is the purpose of moral education to infuse, without any sense of justice or affection, any conception of self-restraint. . . . (No. 390.)

Brutal treatment in childhood prepared the victim "for being a bully and a tyrant. He will feel none of that respect for the personality of other human beings which has not been shown towards his own. The object of his respect will be power." (No. 396.)[151] Domestic tyranny and the brutality that accompanied it, encouraged as they were in society by the courts' tolerance, had a profound, an historically crucial, effect on society.

The great majority of the inhabitants of this and of every country—including nearly the whole of one sex, and all the young of both—are, either by law or by circumstances

[150]This piece, entitled "Wife Murder," was the first one written after their marriage.

[151]Another aspect of the case of the illegitimate child, Edward Hyde, who had been brutally beaten by his natural father, Edward Kenealy, roused the Mills as reflecting also on the injustice caused by a wife's legal non-existence. Lord Campbell rejoiced that no stain would be left on Mr. Kenealy's character; on the contrary, Lord Campbell bestowed praise on him for having shown an interest in his son when, by law, an illegitimate child was the responsibility solely of the mother. The injustice was the greater as a legitimate child belonged in law solely to the father because of the wife's legal non-existence.

stronger than the law, subject to some one man's arbitrary will [and] it would show a profound ignorance of the effect of moral agencies on the character not to perceive how deeply depraving must be the influence of such a lesson given from the seat of justice. It cannot be doubted that to this more than to any other single cause is to be attributed the frightful brutality which marks a very large proportion of the poorest class, and no small portion of a class much above the poorest. (No. 390.)

Seen in the light of their belief in its vast social ramifications, Harriet Taylor's plea "that her Majesty would take in hand this vast and vital question of the extinction of personal violence by the best and surest means—the illegalising of corporal punishment, domestic as well as judicial, at any age" (No. 383) was foolish only from its impracticability. Failing the Queen, two acts were needed immediately to reform the law to prevent its continuing inculcation of domestic brutality and tyranny.[152] "There should be a declaratory Act, distinctly setting forth that it is *not* lawful for a man to strike his wife, any more than to strike his brother or his father. . . . It seems almost inconceivable that the smallest blow from a man to a man should be by law a criminal offence, and yet that it should not be—or should not be known to be—unlawful for a man to strike a woman." And there should be "a short Act of Parliament, providing that judicial conviction of gross maltreatment should free the victim from the obligation of living with the oppressor, and from all compulsory subjection to his power—leaving him under the same legal obligation as before of affording the sufferer the means of support, if the circumstances of the case require it" (No. 395). Given the state of the unreformed law, Mill's renunciation of his rights in 1851 seems a little less quixotic.

Harriet Taylor's interest in cases of domestic brutality, whatever its origins, profoundly influenced John Stuart Mill's understanding of the present condition of society and its historical development. It had provided an environmental cause—and hence a remediable one—of the condition of the working classes to refute the anti-democratic assumption of the innate brutishness of the lower orders. In the laboratory of the courts the hypothesis that men and women were not irredeemable brutes by nature but depraved by and, therefore, salvageable by nurture, had been tested and proved (though there remained some question as to the extent of man's redemption). The importance of these ideas for Mill's future thought and actions should not be ignored. The joint productions themselves are not major works, but they should be taken seriously as the exploration of a significant new element that Mill was adding to his basic beliefs about the necessary steps towards the improvement of mankind.

The parallels with the *Subjection of Women* are too obvious to need

---

[152]In 1853, Mill, acting "chiefly as amanuensis to [his] wife," published a pamphlet, *Remarks on Mr. Fitzroy's Bill for the More Effectual Prevention of Assaults on Women and Children* (London: n.p., 1853), *CW*, XXI, 101-8.

elaboration.[153] The very tones were recaptured, although Mill now worked alone: "the wife is the actual bondservant of her husband: no less so, as far as legal obligation goes, than slaves commonly so called"; "the full power of tyranny with which the man is legally invested"; "however brutal a tyrant she may unfortunately be chained to—though she may know that he hates her, though it may be his daily pleasure to torture her, and though she may feel it impossible not to loathe him—he can claim from her and enforce the lowest degradation of a human being. . . . While she is held in this worst description of slavery as to her own person, what is her position in regard to the children in whom she and her master have a joint interest? They are by law *his* children. . . . Not one act can she do towards . . . them, except by delegation from him. Even after he is dead she is not their legal guardian. . . ."[154] "The family is a school of despotism, in which the virtues of despotism, but also its vices, are largely nourished."[155] The book was written to show that "the legal subordination of one sex to the other . . . is wrong in itself, and now one of the chief hindrances to human improvement. . . ."[156] It was from working with Harriet that this truth had been borne in upon him.

Denial of the suffrage was the political side of the legal subordination. Although Mill did not designate as a joint production his letter to the *Leader* (No. 398)[157] of 17 August, 1850, on the stability of society, it certainly dealt with a subject they had talked over together. Harriet Taylor was already working on her article on the enfranchisement of women,[158] and there is no doubt that Mill expressed their mutual views in this early public advocacy of women's suffrage. The letter started as a reply to a gentleman who had written that society without strict divorce laws to guide it would run aground. There was a humorously presented analysis of what society's being on a sandbank could possibly mean: understanding what it meant for a ship to come upon a sandbank, Mill wanted "to have it made equally clear to me what would happen if, in consequence of permitting facility of divorce, 'society' should . . . come upon a sandbank." Mill went on in more serious vein to point out that in two other letters, one in favour of divorce and one in favour of extended suffrage, "the writer shows the most unaffected unconsciousness that anybody has an interest in the matter except the

---

[153]In the final version of the *Autobiography*, Mill wrote: "that perception of the vast practical bearings of women's disabilities which found expression in the book on *The Subjection of Women*, was acquired mainly through her teaching" (*A*, 253n).

[154]*Subjection of Women*, *CW*, XXI, 284-5.

[155]*Ibid.*, 294-5.

[156]*Ibid.*, 261.

[157]The *Leader* had been newly established in 1849, based on a policy of positivist reporting; George Henry Lewes was principal writer, and Marian Evans and Harriet Martineau were regular contributors.

[158]"Enfranchisement of Women" (1851), *CW*, XXI, 393-415.

man," whereas women have more need of facility for divorce, and every argument for men's voting applies equally to women's voting.

But this entire ignoring of women, as if their claim to the same rights as the other half of mankind were not even worth mentioning, stares one in the face from every report of a speech, every column of a newspaper. In your paper of the 27th ultimo, there is a long letter signed Homo, claiming the "right of the suffrage" as justly belonging to every *man*, while there is not one line of his argument which would not be exactly as applicable if "woman" were read instead of "man;" yet the thought never appears to occur to him. In a Conservative this would be intelligible—monopoly, exclusion, privilege, is his general rule; but in one who demands the suffrage on the ground of abstract right, it is an odious dereliction of principle, or an evidence of intellectual incompetence. While the majority of men are excluded, the insult to women of their exclusion as a class is less obvious. But even the present capricious distribution of the franchise has more semblance of justice and rationality than a rule admitting all men to the suffrage and denying it to all women. (No. 398.)

It is little wonder, with the memories of what they had once talked over together, that Mill had noticeably to pause to control his emotions after he began to speak in the House of Commons on 20 May, 1867, moving to substitute "person" for "man" in the Representation of the People Bill.

After their marriage in April 1851 until Harriet's death in November 1858 Mill wrote for the papers hardly at all: eight pieces in as many years; in 1851 he wrote only one piece. The question of street organs would perhaps be deemed an odd choice for the solitary contribution to the newspapers in over a year by the author of the *Logic* and the *Principles of Political Economy*, but that was the subject upon which Mill contributed an article—to the *Morning Chronicle*—in 1851 (No. 401). Miscarriages of justice and the limited understandings of magistrates had been the subject of their joint letters, and perhaps this was a sequel drafted or suggested by his wife. In 1852 he took time for only two letters (Nos. 402 and 403), very short, supporting free trade in the book trade and opposing the control exercised by the Booksellers' Association. The following year, 1853, plagued by ill health, but intensely loyal to the East India Company through which he genuinely believed India was getting as good a government as was humanly available, he published two articles (Nos. 404 and 405) during the debate on the India Bill to defend the Company against the meddling fingers of a harassed Government. In the spring of 1854 he was told his life was in danger from consumption, and from then on he and Harriet tried to put on paper for posterity their best thoughts, and only twice were their thoughts sent to the newspapers for their contemporaries. Time, they felt, was running out. Harriet's health was weak; she nearly died of a lung haemorrhage at Nice in 1853 and now John was threatened. His father and one brother had already died of tuberculosis, and another brother was living abroad but with no hope of curing the disease, only delaying its progress. Mill's health remained unreliable even after the consumption was arrested (seemingly by 1856); splitting headaches continued to make his India Office duties more onerous than normal. There was less time for writing: he was frequently travelling for his health and when he was not, she was. The newlyweds worked hard outlining the ideas they wished to leave to the future—even on their separate trips.[159]

When they were together, they lived very private lives. In November 1854 in the *Morning Post* they published one more joint effort (No. 406). It was a short letter expressing distress and disgust that even after the passing of the new Act to protect battered wives, magistrates would not hand down hard sentences. Mill did not write again for the daily press until, somewhat unexpectedly after three-and-a-half years of silence, on 31 July, 1858, he sent a letter to the *Daily News* on the Laws of Lunacy (No. 407). The surprise results from the sudden break in the silence, not from the topic; recent incidents in which "refractory wives" had been declared insane prompted the letter. Criticism of the Lunacy Laws was not uncommon at this time but it was rarely presented from the women's point of view. This was the last piece in the papers published with his wife's encouragement.

In October they left for a long, warm winter in southern Europe; at Avignon, Harriet Mill collapsed and on 3 November she died.

MARCH 1863 TO MAY 1873

WHEN JOHN STUART MILL returned to public life, he had beside him his stepdaughter, Helen Taylor. She had been born in 1831 and, still in her twenties when her mother died, had already developed great strength of character. (She had abandoned an apprenticeship as an actress to join Mill in his despair.) Mill referred to her somewhat inappropriately as a "prize in the lottery of life" (*A*, 264). For the next six and a half years, the grieving pair lived quiet lives, half the year in Blackheath and half in Avignon. They travelled together and on one occasion, in 1862, took a genuinely daring trip through the Greek interior. She helped him in many ways after her mother's death, one of which was with his correspondence; the echo of Taylor phrasing can still be heard, therefore, in some of his later public letters, though less in those concerning international affairs. After he recovered from the shock of his loss, Mill devoted himself to

[159]In the late fall of 1853 Mill had accompanied his wife and stepdaughter to Nice, returning alone to London in December. Harriet Mill's health made the avoidance of a Blackheath winter necessary (in a letter to her daughter in the winter of 1857, Harriet Mill apologized for her handwriting, explaining that the temperature in the room in front of the fire was 36°F. [Mill-Taylor Collection, LII, 103 (29 Jan., 1857)]), and mother and daughter did not return until the spring of 1854. Mill then, having waited until their return to tell them that he had consumption, left for two months in Brittany, returning home in July. They separated again in December—John Stuart Mill to Greece for six months for his health and Harriet Mill to Torquay for hers, she being too weak for the extended trip.

making ready for publication works he and Harriet had planned.[160] He was only fifty-two, but Harriet's death halted his mental development—at least he felt so—and those developments in his thought which took place are not best seen in his sporadic journalism. The general set of his thinking was established. He was a highly respected philosopher and Radical. Commentary on contemporary events was no longer of value to his own development, nor was daily journalism the medium most effective for the exercise of his influence, especially when he was in Parliament. Mill's concern was less to influence immediate actions than to complete mankind's guides to the future. His final pieces, then, have interest but little cohesion, being disparate and few. Events in England seem not to provide the occasion; Europe, friends, and ideas are the stimulants.[161]

The year 1865 saw the realization of an ambition he had first dreamt of thirty years earlier; he was asked to stand for Parliament. His candidacy gave him an excellent chance to express his views on matters for which the occasion might not otherwise have presented itself. He had been promoting Thomas Hare's system of proportional representation ever since, in the spring of 1859, he had first received and read Hare's book, which had, "for the first time, solved the difficulty of popular representation; and by doing so, [had] raised up the cloud of gloom and uncertainty which hung over the futurity of representative government and therefore of civilization."[162] In contradiction to a writer in the *Spectator*, he affirmed that Hare's system "is equally suitable to the state of things under which we now live, since it would at once assure to that minority in the constituencies which consists of the operative classes, the share in the representation which you demand for them," as it will be to that state when the operatives far outnumber those likely to support the eminent men (No. 411).

He attacked the ballot when reviewing Henry Romilly's pamphlet favouring it (No. 413).[163] His arguments are very similar in one way to the arguments he had put forward on the opposite side under his father's tutelage forty years earlier. In the old days the good of the country was served by diminishing the power of the aristocracy through giving a man a ballot and thus removing influence and bribery at one stroke. But now Mill saw man's actions as not determined solely by his selfish interests but—in keeping, in fact, with Bentham's list of influences that make a judge a good judge too—people were influenced by the desire to stand well with their fellows. This social motive would be weakened "when the

[160]Most notably, *On Liberty* (1859), *Thoughts on Parliamentary Reform* (1859), *Dissertations and Discussions* (1859), and *Utilitarianism* (1861).

[161]For example, in 1863 Mill wrote on Poland for the *Penny Newsman*, edited by Edwin Chadwick: one of the revolutionary journalists, Ogareff, whom he was praising for "shaking the whole fabric of Russian despotism," was a follower of Saint-Simon (No. 408).

[162]*LL*, *CW*, XV, 598-9 (3 Mar., 1859).

[163]Mill was continuing his policy of supporting his friends by aiding in the establishment of new journalistic ventures. A group including Herbert Spencer, Thomas Huxley, John Cairnes, and Mill himself had attempted to rescue the failing *Reader* in 1865.

act is done in secret, and he can neither be admired for disinterested, nor blamed for mean and selfish conduct" (No. 413). He repeated his unequivocal denial whenever asked (No. 425).

But the real, the great reward of his candidacy was his election on 12 July, 1865. His letter thanking the Liberal electors of Westminster is warming to read over a century later. All Mill had feared about democracy had been (at least temporarily) assuaged and all he had claimed about Radicals and workers had been triumphantly vindicated—and by a personal triumph. It must have been a sweet moment when, after a long stationary period, the historical process, with him as its agent, seemed to be visibly advancing. "I should join . . . in hearty and grateful acknowledgments to the Liberal electors generally, and especially to the great number who, by their strenuous and disinterested personal exertions, renewed the lesson so often forgotten, of the power of a high and generous purpose over bodies of citizens accustomed to free political action. . . . That I may not fall so far below your hopes as to make you regret your choice, will be my constant and earnest endeavour." (No. 414.) The knight's armour was slightly loose, the limbs not so lithe, but he rose to do battle against the "personal and pecuniary influences" who had won a majority in the House with the same conviction and sense of righteousness with which he had wielded his pen for the last forty years.

While Mill was a sitting member of Parliament, he does not appear to have written for or to the newspapers. During the election of 1868, he published two letters.[164] In September he wrote a letter to the borough of Greenwich which had emulated Westminster and further rekindled Mill's hope for the future by "electing a public man, without any solicitation on his part" (No. 416). The only other public letter from this time published in England was an attempt to mop up the hot water boiled over by his support of Chadwick for a riding in which there was a sitting Liberal member, albeit an Adullamite (also a leader in the anti-feminist forces). The letter, published in *The Times*, had some fine hits by the Avignon team; the tone of Helen Taylor is evident in the sharp riposte to Bouverie: "For my part I never presumed to give you any advice, nor did I 'invite' you to retire in Mr. Chadwick's favour, because I had no idea that you were in the least likely to do so; I merely, in reply to a communication from yourself, shewed how very public spirited a proceeding I should consider it if you did."[165]

The memories evoked by Mill's active role promoting women's right to vote,

[164]A third (*LL*, *CW*, XVI, 1443-8 [24 Sept., 1868]) was published in the United States, solicited by Charles Eliot Norton, expressing strong disapprobation of the proposal for the American Government to pay its debts in debased currency and to cancel the interest. His sentiments are unchanged over thirty years although he now had nothing to lose.

[165]*LL*, *CW*, XVI, 1461. In *LL* the reading is "'incite' you to retire" but the version in *The Times*, 22 Oct., 1868, 3, gives "'invite' you to retire"; Bouverie's own letter supports the latter reading.

especially his preparation of the *Subjection of Women*, surely must relate to a letter intended for the *Daily News* in January of 1870 (No. 419), which seems to put the calendar back twenty years. The attention of the readers was drawn to the case of William Smith, a policeman, sentenced for (according to the magistrate) an "unprovoked, brutal, and unjustifiable" assault upon a man who had knocked his wife down in the street. Though now Mill could write also to the Attorney-General, the Solicitor-General, and the Recorder of the City of London, he could not secure the unfortunate policeman's reinstatement in the force when he came out of prison.

Now a distinguished philosopher in his sixties, Mill had no need and no desire to put his ideas before the public through the newspapers. He preferred to develop his thoughts in longer form and published, apart from books,[166] lengthy essays in the *Fortnightly Review* edited by his disciple John Morley.[167] In 1870 he commented on the Education Bill (No. 420) and Russia's threatened abrogation of the Treaty of 1856 (Nos. 421 and 422).[168]

Mill did not speak out again in newspapers until the last year of his life.[169] It was a singularly appropriate ending to his long association with the newspapers: he wrote for the *Examiner*, and on a subject that was part of his vision, land tenure. Since his youth many advances in public thinking had been made on the question, promoted in part by the state of Ireland and Mill's writings on it; it had been possible for Gladstone to introduce an Irish Land Act. To advance the public attitude further, Mill now actively promoted a Land Tenure Reform Association, for which he had drawn up and published the programme.[170] The justification for restricting the rights in land already in private hands is vintage Mill:

The land not having been made by the owner, nor by any one to whose rights he has succeeded, and the justification of private ownership in land being the interest it gives to the owner in the good cultivation of the land, the rights of the owner ought not to be stretched farther than this purpose requires. No rights to the land should be recognised which do not act as a motive to the person who has power over it, to make it as productive, or otherwise as useful to mankind, as possible. Anything beyond this exceeds the reason of the case, and is an injustice to the remainder of the community. (No. 427.)

[166]The most significant being *The Examination of Sir William Hamilton's Philosophy* (1865), *Auguste Comte and Positivism* (1865), the *Inaugural Address* (1867), his edition of James Mill's *Analysis* (1869), and *The Subjection of Women* (1869).

[167]"Endowments" (1869) and "Thornton on Labour and Its Claims" (1869), *CW*, V, 613-29 and 680-700; and reviews of Cliffe Leslie (*CW*, X, 669–85), Taine (*CW*, XI, 441-7), Berkeley (*ibid.*, 449-71), Grote (*ibid.*, 473-510), and Maine (in the penultimate volume of *CW*).

[168]Mill also published "Treaty Obligations" (1870), *CW*, XXI, 341-8.

[169]Mill's denial in 1871 (No. 424) that he was to take the chair at a meeting to be addressed by Emily Faithfull probably reflects Helen's views of her—views perhaps determined by the somewhat colourful episodes in Faithfull's past.

[170]*Programme of the Land Tenure Reform Association, with an Explanatory Statement by John Stuart Mill* (London: Longmans, *et al.*, 1871), *CW*, V, 687-95.

All his life he had pitted reason against injustice.

Mill died quite unexpectedly on 7 May, 1873, after a long walk botanizing. He died while still enjoying the full vigour of a mind that analyzed with logical precision each next step forward for mankind's betterment. His advocacy had been extraordinarily influential, because his dreams of the future had been tempered by his knowledge of present possibilities. This commonsensical approach to the millenium was the reward he reaped from all his arduous efforts to instruct his countrymen through the newspapers, because awareness of his readers never allowed him to forget that reforms had to be designed for, and accepted by, his fallible contemporaries. His career as a journalist ensured that he kept his feet firmly on the ground while he urged mankind forward towards his hoped-for heaven.

Textual Introduction

JOHN M. ROBSON

THE ARTICLES IN THESE VOLUMES span more than fifty years, from Mill's first published letter in 1822 when he was sixteen years old, until his last leading article in 1873, the year of his death. The subjects range from abstract economics (with which he began) and practical economics (with which he ended), through French and British politics, reviews of music and theatre, and Irish land reform, to domestic cruelty, with glances at a multitude of events and ideas important to the nineteenth century. They therefore provide a needed perspective on his life and thought, giving a record of his ideas and of the development of his argumentative skills, as well as revealing his attitude to public persuasion through the newspaper press, a medium of increasing importance in his lifetime.

Identification of most of these articles as Mill's would be impossible had he not kept a list of his published writings.[1] This list is markedly reliable, but it presents a few problems in identifying newspaper writings. For example, some of the very early entries lack dates, and a few have wrong dates or lack other elements. Inference and other bits of evidence, however, make it possible to make corrections and to identify with confidence all the items except two.

One of these two has defied identification: "An article on wages and profits, capital and prices, which appeared in the Edinburgh Times of   May 1825." The problem is not the missing date; we have not been able to locate any

---

[1]The surviving scribal copy, in the London School of Economics, edited by Ney MacMinn, *et al.*, as *Bibliography of the Published Writings of J.S. Mill* (Evanston: Northwestern University Press, 1945), will be found in re-edited form in the concluding volume of the *Collected Works*. The entries in this list are given in headnotes to individual items, with the scribal wording corrected (the original and amended versions are listed in Appendix G). In some cases the scribal list is mistaken or lacks information (usually a date is involved): our policy has been (a) if the missing information is obvious, to give it in square brackets; (b) if there is doubt about the exact reading, to leave a blank space between square brackets; and (c) to add "[*sic*]" to mistaken dates (the correct dates being given in the articles' headings). The copyist sometimes, like all of us, tended to drift away; for example, in the entry for No. 239 "9th" is cancelled and "2d" substituted. Another probable example of the wandering mind is seen in the entry for No. 14, where the signature is given as "A Lover of Caution," whereas the copy-text reading is "A Friend to Caution"; because that for No. 15 (properly) gives "A Lover of Justice," it seems likely that the scribe's eye skipped.

issue of a paper of that name, though it appeared for at least a few weeks early in 1825.[2]

The other problem concerns Nos. 53 and 54. The entry in Mill's list gives the title "The Quarterly Review and France," with the date of No. 53 (24 Oct., 1830). In the *Examiner* No. 53 is actually entitled "The Quarterly Review versus France," whereas an article in the next week's issue (our No. 54) is entitled "France and the Quarterly Review." One would be tempted to accept Mill's date, ignore the slight difference in the title, and so to include No. 53 and exclude No. 54, were it not that in Mill's own bound set of the *Examiner* (discussed below) he has made an inked correction in No. 54 (and there are elsewhere no such corrections in articles not by him). No. 54 begins with a reference back to No. 53, using the journalistic "we," but such evidence of continued authorship is weak. On stylistic grounds, both are possibly Mill's, though it might be held that No. 53 shows some signs of Albany Fonblanque's lighter tone (he was then the editor of and principal writer for the *Examiner*). Faced with this conflicting evidence, and recognizing the possibility that the scribe who copied Mill's list made an error of omission (there are many easily identifiable errors throughout), we have included both as probably Mill's.

Most of Mill's entries in his list identify single items, but occasionally, and particularly in the case of four series of his news reports on French political life, he groups articles in a general statement. For example, as the headnote to No. 55 indicates, the first such entry reads: "The summary of French affairs in the *Examiner* from 7th November 1830 to 17th April 1831, inclusive: comprising several long articles." We have gone through the *Examiner* (as did MacMinn) to locate the items in these series, and have, in the absence of confirming or disconfirming evidence, accepted all the articles between the bracketing dates as Mill's. In a few cases, we have had to conclude that there are errors in Mill's entries: first, there is no account of French politics in the *Examiner* for 3 April, 1831 (the news report is concerned with other European matters, including one sentence signalling a French response to Belgian events). Second, the entry quoted in the headnote to No. 113 says that between 4 September, 1831, and 15 July, 1832, Mill wrote on all Sundays but one (1 July, 1832); however, there is no article on France in the number for 13 November, 1831. Finally, the articles for 11 and 18 November, 1832, which would be covered by the entry quoted in the headnote to No. 181, are not included because they are not marked by Mill as his in his set of the *Examiner*.

Confirmation of Mill's list so far as the important early writings in the *Examiner* are concerned is possible because of markings in that set, which is in

---

[2]In a review of MacMinn's edition, Jacob Viner calls attention to the announcement in the *Examiner* that the *Edinburgh Times* would appear on 22 January (*Modern Philology*, XLIII [1945], 150; the notice is in the *Examiner* of 16 Jan., 1825, 48). Specific issues of the *Edinburgh Times* are mentioned in the *Examiner* on 20 Feb., 1825, 122, and on 10 Apr., 1825, 233.

the collection of materials from his library housed in Somerville College, Oxford.[3] On the front flyleaves of all but the 1830 volume Mill listed his own articles, and (for the volumes for 1831-33) enclosed the parts of the text by him in inked square brackets. Also he made some inked corrections in the texts themselves. For the most part these three sets of information confirm the other, independent list, but the Somerville material enabled us to add seven items to that list.

Other evidence enabled us to add twenty more. Signatures contributed ten of these: "J.S. Mill" adds nine late items (Nos. 414-18, 420, 423-4, and 427), all but the last, an article, being letters to the editor; and, in conjunction with internal evidence, a common signature ("S.") led us to another (No. 32). (Also, identification of No. 33, vaguely described in Mill's list, was possible because of a combination of signature and internal evidence.) Identifications of part of one (the *addendum* to No. 34) and all of another (No. 49) were made through comments by the editors of the newspapers in which they appeared, and one more (No. 285) was made through the editor's entry in his own file copy. Mill's correspondence led to identification of No. 101 as his (and also Appendices A and C, not included in this count). One further, a review (No. 379), is said to be Mill's by Alexander Bain, the author reviewed. Finally, Mill's list gives only *published* writings; we have included the five unpublished letters intended for newspapers that remain in manuscript (Nos. 367, 371, 399, 412, and 419, as well as Appendix D).[4]

These successes have not made us blind to the possibility that some newspaper items remain unidentified, particularly in the final years of Mill's life. Indeed, Mill's list contains a disturbing entry: "From this time no memorandum has been made of my letters which have appeared in print: numbers of my public or private letters having found their way into newspapers, of all of which (I believe) the original drafts have remained in my possession."[5] Unfortunately, Mill does not specify exactly what "this time" means; the comment comes in a section evidently added longer after the fact than usual, between the listing for his *Examination of Sir William Hamilton's Philosophy* (published on 13 Apr., 1865) and the entry which, as he says, is misplaced, of his "Austin on Jurisprudence" (Oct. 1863). The two items that bracket these are for 29 April, 1865 (No. 413) and April 1866 ("Grote's Plato"; in *CW*, XI, 375-440). What Mill actually had in his possession when he wrote the entry we of course do not know; still

[3]See Ann P. and John M. Robson, "John Stuart Mill's Annotated *Examiner* Articles," *Victorian Periodicals Newsletter*, X (Sept. 1977), 122-9. We there describe the three volumes for 1830, 1832, and 1833; subsequently we located two more, for 1831 and 1834.

[4]It may be added that in his list but not identified as his in the Somerville College *Examiner* are Nos. 158 and 245.

[5]MacMinn, 96. In fact, three such letters are in the list, Nos. 421 and 422, and a letter printed in the *Nation* (15 Oct., 1868), which is in *LL*, *CW*, XVI, 1443-8.

surviving are many drafts and some clippings from newspapers, most of which, as originally private letters, are in the final volumes of *Later Letters*. We have therefore scanned newspapers most thoroughly for the period from April 1865 to May 1873 (when Mill died); the result is a disappointingly small number, but Mill seems not to have used the periodical press very much in his years in Parliament or subsequently.

In his bibliographic list, Mill carefully designates fifteen of these items, like other of his writings, as "joint productions" with Harriet Taylor, who married him in 1851 after twenty years of close friendship.[6] He actually uses three formulations, saying just a "joint production" in three cases (Nos. 318, 393, and 394), commenting "very little of this [article] was mine" in eight (Nos. 305, 329, 350, 389, 390, 392, 395, and 396), and combining these two descriptions in three (Nos. 303, 307, and 383); No. 400, the last one to which such a comment is attached, has a comment that has defied particular analysis: "This, like all my newspaper articles on similar subjects, and most of my articles on all subjects, was a joint production with my wife." On that basis, however, one may speculate that nine others (Nos. 367, 369, 371, 397, 398, 399, 401, 406, and 407) were at least influenced by her, and that two more (Nos. 363 and 386) might also be included, as well as Appendix D, which, as unpublished, is not in his list. Furthermore, external evidence of the share that her daughter, Helen Taylor, had in his work after her mother's death, and the similar tone of the letters in question to letters known to be hers, make it reasonable to think of Nos. 417 and 424 as "joint productions" with her.[7]

There are in total 427 items in the text proper: these are taken from twenty-seven newspapers, seventeen of them daily and ten weekly. The greater number, 261, appeared in weeklies, most the result of Mill's dedication to the *Examiner*, especially from 1830 through 1834, which resulted in 235 contributions to that paper over his lifetime. In fact, after Mill's first few years of writing for newspapers (much of it consisting of letters to the editor of the *Morning Chronicle*), contributions to weeklies dominate the record through the 1830s, Mill's busiest period as a journalist. Beginning in the 1840s, he contributed more commonly to dailies, with leading articles for the *Morning Chronicle* and a variety of letters to editors making up the bulk. Among the dailies the *Morning Chronicle*, which provides 114 items in all, is as dominant as the *Examiner* is among the weeklies. The only other weekly with a significant number of items is the *Spectator* with 12; among the dailies important to this record are the *Daily News* with 16 items, the *Globe and Traveller* with 11, and *The Times* with 8.[8]

[6]The first of these is dated 10 February, 1846; the last, 28 August, 1851.

[7]See *CW*, I, 286-7, for Mill's imprecise account of her share in his writings.

[8]The other weeklies here represented are the *Black Dwarf* (four items), the *Leader* and the *Sunday Times* (two each), and the *Lancet*, the *Reader*, the *Reasoner*, the *Republican*, and the *Weekly*

The distribution over time is significant: 42 of the items appeared in the 1820s, 246 in the 1830s, 99 in the 1840s, 20 in the 1850s, 11 in the 1860s, and 9 in the 1870s. Equally significant is the distribution of genres: 182 are leading articles, 106 news reports, 72 letters, 47 reviews, and 6 obituaries; 14 may be called miscellaneous. These two distributions are combined in Table 1.

Table 1

	1820s	1830s	1840s	1850s	1860s	1870s	Total
Leaders	5	86	78	10	0	3	182
News Reports	0	106	0	0	0	0	106
Letters	29	6	13	9	9	6	72
Reviews	4	34	7	1	1	0	47
Obituaries	0	6	0	0	0	0	6
Miscellaneous	4	8	1	0	1	0	14
Total	42	246	99	20	11	9	427

Referring to the contents of the volumes simply as "newspaper writings" disguises some problems. The basic definition, "those of Mill's writings that appeared in daily or weekly newspapers," needs refinement. First, we have included letters that, in view of their intended audience, can be called "public," even though they were initially directed to private individuals, and even if they exist only in draft form.[9] Similarly, we have included letters to editors that failed to be published, because, though some of them are obviously drafts, they were intended for newspaper publication. Another problem arises concerning articles or parts of articles that were reprinted in newspapers from other of Mill's writings. If one were to see these volumes as gathering together the total materials that revealed Mill to newspaper readers, it would be regretted that some very telling pieces are excluded as extracted reprints. But actually no one reader would have been able to see Mill the journalist whole, for most of his writings were anonymous, and they were scattered over such a period of time and in so many papers that the likelihood of anyone's reading them all is so small as to be

---

Dispatch, all with one. The other dailies are the *Sun* with two items and, with one each, the *British Traveller*, *Le Globe*, the *Guide*, the *Morning Post*, *Le National*, the *New Times*, the *New York Tribune*, *Our Daily Fare*, the *Penny Newsman*, the *True Sun*, and the *Voix des Femmes*. The total of these is 424: there are three anomalous items, explained in n9. The items are attributed to the papers for which they were intended, so the unpublished items are included in these counts; one piece (No. 255), intended for *Le National*, in fact appeared in the *Monthly Repository*.

[9]The three exceptions mentioned above are two public letters (Nos. 402 and 403) which did not appear in newspapers, written in 1852 concerning the dispute over publishers' restrictive practices, and a draft concerning the Westminster election of 1865 (No. 412), enclosed in a letter to Edwin Chadwick and clearly intended for public use, though it has not been found in a newspaper.

negligible. Furthermore, we cannot pretend that we have found all examples of such reprints: the newspapers of the day commonly made extracts of this kind (often with the intention of puffing), and Mill was a popular author.[10] Finally, we have been reluctant to reprint anything that appears elsewhere in the *Collected Works*, even though it could be argued that some items should have been saved for this volume. We have, therefore, excluded letters that might be judged to be "public" if they are in the correspondence volumes of this edition, Volumes XII to XVII. But in a few cases we have included material also in other volumes of the *Collected Works*: for instance, Mill used some of his leading articles on French agriculture in an appendix to his *Principles of Political Economy*; these were collated for Volumes II and III of the *Collected Works*, where the substantive variants are given. But it is appropriate to give the original versions here, because they are part of a series, not all of which was used in the *Principles*, and because the rewriting altered the form of the argument, though not its substance.[11]

Mill reprinted very few of his newspaper writings, undoubtedly judging them to fall within the area of proscription he defines for his periodical essays in *Dissertations and Discussions*. Those excluded from the volumes, he says, "were either of too little value at any time, or what value they might have was too exclusively temporary, or the thoughts they contained were inextricably mixed up with comments, now totally uninteresting, on passing events, or on some book not generally known; or lastly, any utility they may have possessed has since been superseded by other and more mature writings of the author."[12] While recognizing Mill's wisdom in many matters, we are not disposed to heed him here. At the very least, the bulk of these materials gives them very considerable significance, and we trust that Mill refutes his own vivid indictment of reprinted journalism: "The Spartan in the story, who, for the crime of using two words where one would have sufficed, was sentenced to read from beginning to end the history of Guicciardini, and at the end of a few pages begged to commute his punishment for the galleys, would have prayed to exchange it for death if he had been condemned to read a file of English newspapers five years old."[13] He exempts Albany Fonblanque's writings, and we here dogmatically assert that in his case too any commutation would be a punishment in itself.

That the items are arranged chronologically needs little explanation: such

[10]Those that we have located have been collated with the copy-texts, though there is no evidence that Mill had anything to do with the text of the reprints; we have found nothing of textual interest.

[11]In two other instances we have overridden the criterion: Mill's obituary of Bentham (No. 170) is also in an appendix to Volume X, where it is a useful companion to his other assessments of his great teacher; and his petition for free trade (No. 289) is in an appendix to Volume V, where it serves as an added indication of his economic views.

[12]*Essays on Ethics, Religion and Society*, *Collected Works*, X (Toronto: Univerity of Toronto Press, 1969), 493.

[13]"Fonblanque's England under Seven Administrations," *CW*, VI, 352.

heterogeneous materials resist division into themes or subjects, though two major subjects dominate, French politics in the early 1830s and Irish land in the late 1840s. However, these two themes are so densely grouped in time that they cohere even within a chronological ordering. Furthermore, some other groupings would be quite arbitrary, and there would be a ragtail remnant for a miscellaneous category that would be more irritating than helpful. More determining is the positive benefit of reading the items in the order of their appearance, for their cumulative value lies in their recording Mill's development and emphases; interesting as many of them are in their own right, the total effect in this arrangement is much more than the sum of the individual effects.

This arrangement makes separation into "chapters" somewhat arbitrary. The divisions we have made serve only to suggest relatively important phases in this aspect of Mill's life, reflecting, as the Introduction makes clear, changes and influences of various sorts in his behaviour and thought that reveal thematic and cross-generic affinities.

The titles of the items are taken, when possible, from the copy-text (or from another version of the text that Mill oversaw), even though there is a strong likelihood that a large number of the headings were not chosen by him. The guides to identification mentioned above, Mill's bibliography of his writings and the copy of the *Examiner* in Somerville College, are the authorities for many titles that exactly or closely follow his own wording. Some modifications are easily justified: for example, in his bibliographic list Mill uses two wordings for his news reports on French politics: "summary of French affairs" and (usually after No. 116) "summary of French news"; in the *Examiner* he normally lists each of these same items as "article on France": we have for convenience adopted "French News" with a bracketed serial number for all of them. In the case of the series on Ireland, which he lists in his bibliography as being on "Irish affairs," we have chosen a more descriptive title drawn from the contents of the articles, "Condition of Ireland," again with serial numbers to distinguish them one from another. In both these cases the serial numbers are editorially added; in a few cases ("The Spirit of the Age" for instance) Mill or the newspaper provided numbers for series: to indicate the difference in origin of the numbers, we use roman numerals for those in the copy-text and arabic for those editorially supplied.[14] To distinguish it from the seven-part series "Prospects of France," which begins with No. 44, we have entitled No. 98, which does not belong with the series, "The Prospects of France." A few titles derive from references to the articles by Mill in letters, and finally some are editorially chosen as appropriate to the contents and genre. The reviews, for example, which are normally headed in the copy-text by bibliographical identifications, are here given titles

---

[14]We have altered the copy-text title of No. 404, "The India Bill," by adding "I" to make it consistent with that of No. 405, "The India Bill, II."

combining the author's name and the short title of the work under review. The obituary notices are (in conformity to Mill's occasional usage) headed "Death of" the deceased.

Beneath the title appear the provenance and date of publication of the item, while the headnotes indicate briefly the place of the item in relation to others in these volumes and give the minimal historical information needed as background (a broader view is given in the Introduction, and more detail in the footnotes). Each headnote also gives the evidence that the item is by Mill and justifies (usually implicitly) the choice of title. The context in the newspaper from which it is extracted is sketched (location within a section and headings, for instance) and, when appropriate, mention is made of the choice and treatment of the text.

Two kinds of footnote are appended to the items. Those from the copy-text, that is, Mill's own notes or those by the editors of the newspapers, are signalled by the series *, †, etc., beginning anew in each item. When necessary, the source of such notes is added in square brackets (e.g., "[Editor's note.]"). While there are far more quotations in Mill's newspaper writings than one would expect in such a genre, he does not give references to many of them; in a few cases his references need correction.[15] When he is quoting only or mainly from one source (as in the reviews), page references are given in the text to reduce the number of footnotes.

The footnotes that are editorially supplied are signalled by a separate series of arabic numbers in each item. In accordance with the practice throughout the edition, we attempt to identify in these notes all Mill's allusions to people and references to and quotations from written works and speeches, trying to specify where possible the edition he used or may be presumed to have used; to his notes we add (in square brackets) missing identifications and correct mistaken ones. In the interest of economy, when Mill quotes from newspaper leading articles and letters to the editor, the references (which are almost invariably to only one page) are given in the headnotes. In the footnotes only the primary place of publication is given, and publishers' names are limited to the first two in a longer series; full information is given in Appendix J. Also the full titles of statutes are given only in Appendix J.

In these volumes we have followed the practice, established in the correspondence volumes, of giving additional contextual information of an historical and biographical (as well as bibliographic) kind, in an attempt, necessarily falling short of perfection, to give the reader the perspective of a nineteenth-century newspaper reader. We have restricted our enthusiasm by giving only information (including biographical detail) up to the time of the

---

[15]The corrections are (page and line number, followed by the copy-text reading and then, in square brackets, the corrected reading): 38.35   8 [8-9], 74.4   120 [120n], 413.23   37 [37-8], 711.6   9 [9-10] (the reference is moved to the end of the quotation), 789.10   26-46 [26-47], and 789.12   87 [87-97].

article in cases when Mill continues the story later, but have tried to intimate the conclusion when there is no further allusion. After long contemplation, we decided not to translate foreign words and phrases; it is easier to annoy than to please in such matters, and all the terms Mill uses may be quickly located in dictionaries. We are aware that in falling short of the ideal we shall frustrate some legitimate expectations, but we have aimed a little higher than did James Mill, whose confidence in his readers was as astonishing as was his bland insouciance; in one not untypical note he says: "See the writings of Kant and his followers, *passim*; see also Degerando, and others of his school, in various parts of their works."[16]

Cross-reference within the text and the Introductions is by item number rather than page; to make such reference easier, the running titles include the item numbers and the dates.

As indicated above, there is little problem in choosing copy-text for these items: there is normally only one version. In only nineteen cases are there competing texts:[17] ten appeared in part in other writings of Mill's (three of these in the posthumous fourth volume of *Dissertations and Discussions*; one of them also in a pamphlet and a printed version of a lost manuscript), five appeared in more than one newspaper, two have surviving manuscript versions, and two exist in both English and French versions. These last are given in both versions (in text and appendices); the others, almost all different in kind, are printed with variant notes.

Our practice is to indicate only substantive variants, defined as all changes of text except spelling, hyphenation, punctuation, demonstrable typographical errors, and such printing-house concerns as type size, etc. Paragraphing is considered substantive, as are changes in italicization for emphasis. The variants are indicated in the following ways:

Later addition of a word or words: see 356^d. In the text, the passage appears as "20 per cent; ^{d}"; the variant note reads "^{d}MS   [*footnote:*]" followed by a footnote Mill added to the manuscript used in the preparation of his *Principles of Political Economy* (here signalled by "MS"). As the footnote is not in the copy-text, the implication is that it was added to the later version.

Deletion of a word or words: see 356$^{i\text{-}i}$. Here the passage reads "cause ^{i}amply^i sufficient"; the variant note reads "$^{i\text{-}i}$–MS". The interpretation is that in the manuscript used for the *Principles* Mill altered the passage by deleting "amply".

---

[16]"Jurisprudence," in *Essays*, 4n.

[17]One potentially maddening possibility, variations between editions of newspapers, has not been pursued to its depths. The *Examiner* occasionally had different pagination for Mill's articles in second editions (not so identified in the paper), but we found no variants except the deletion (or addition) of subheadings. No words can express our palpitating sympathy for anyone who attempts collation of twentieth-century newspapers through their several editions.

Substitution of a word or words: see 356[j-j]. In the text, the passage appears as "a [j]much larger[j] increase"; the variant note reads "[j-j]MS   considerable portion of this". Placing the example in context, the interpretation is that the reading between the variant indicators was altered to that of the variant note in the manuscript used in the *Principles*.

In these volumes, exceptionally, there are no places where there are additions (requiring a plus sign) resulting from rewritings of an earlier version for the copy-text version.

The benefit of having normally no choice of copy-text is balanced by the need to intervene editorially. While the spelling and punctuation of the copy-texts are generally followed (without the use of *sic*), there is no point in ignoring the fact that Mill's newspaper writings are flawed in all the ways typical of their genre: characters are dropped or broken, sorts are mixed or lacking, compositors (one may legitimately infer) were inexperienced or careless, and Mill's hand (again one may infer) has been misread. Also, newspapers differed in their treatment of some conventions of the genre and the period, and even within one paper they vary inexplicably and over time; in addition, some non-substantive practices are annoying to readers not habituated to nineteenth-century newspapers. Many of the emendations permit of general description and are made silently, except when a correction was indicated by Mill, or when there is a possible ambiguity, or when one such correction is contained within a more significant one; in these cases they are listed with others in Appendix F. Unnoted common trivial corrections are:

1. Dropped and misplaced characters, and misplaced or absent word spaces (e.g., "discharge sthe" to "discharges the"; "o fchildren" to "of children"; or "allthose" to "all those").

2. Missing or misplaced French accents, including those on proper names. Mill's French was very good, and undoubtedly better than that of most compositors, who, moreover, seem often not to have had the types (or enough of them) to hand. (In this context, it may be mentioned that the habit of setting names in small capitals meant that accents usually could not be indicated.) Also, there is inconsistency in nineteenth-century accentuation, which also differs in unpredictable but disturbing ways from later usage.

3. French proper names. Once more it seems probable that most of the variant spellings were introduced by compositors, and occasionally more than one spelling was acceptable. To avoid annoyance, we always give, for instance, Jean Paul Courier (never Courrier), Casimir Périer (not Casimer or Perrier), Jacques Laffitte (not Lafitte), and (to illustrate what are more clearly compositors' errors) Cormenin (not Cormerin) and Cauchois-Lemaire (not Cauchors-Lemaire).

4. Majuscule / minuscule changes of initial letter. These have been made sparingly and only to make individual passages (not the volumes as a whole) consistent, on the grounds that Mill's hand is not infrequently ambiguous in this

regard for some letters, and that the change in these specific words cannot be seen as emphatic.

Other emendations not signalled in the apparatus result only from the desire for easy reading, without any implication of error in the copy-text. For example, the titles of works are italicized; definite articles are not treated as part of the titles of newspapers, except for *The Times* and for those French newspapers whose titles are visually English homographs (for the same reason the English *Globe* is given its full title, *Globe and Traveller*); monarchs are identified in the form "Louis XVI" rather than "Louis the Sixteenth"; names appearing in small capitals in the copy-text are given in upper and lower case; italics are substituted for small capitals indicating emphasis except when the small capitals are themselves italicized (in which case they are retained in roman); in transcribing manuscripts, "&" has been rendered as "and" and superscripts in abbreviations have been lowered to the line; indications of ellipsis have been normalized to three dots plus, when necessary, terminal punctuation; double quotation marks are used where single appear in the copy-text (except, of course, for quotations within quotations); long quotations are set in reduced type and the quotation marks are removed (in consequence, occasionally Mill's words have to be enclosed in square brackets, but there is no likelihood that these will be mistaken for editorial intrusions, as we have added only volume and page references); terminal punctuation in italic type has been given in roman except when the punctuation functions as part of the italic passage; abbreviations for monetary units are always italicized ("50l." becomes "50*l.*"); and long quoted passages (which are set down, with square brackets around Mill's inserted comments) are introduced by a colon only, rather than a colon and dash. The styling done by different newspapers is also not preserved; so, for instance, the salutations in letters to the editor are always given as "SIR,—"; and the publishing information in the headnotes is regularized.

Appendices. The appended materials are of two kinds, texts (given in chronological order) and lists. Appendices A and C are translations by Mill from the French of Cavaignac's and Enfantin's speeches; Appendix B is the French version of an item by Mill; Appendix D (properly seen as a "joint production" with Harriet Taylor) is the English version of an item also extant in French; while Appendix E is an item attributed to Mill by George Holyoake without any cited evidence of authorship. The other appendices are guides of various kinds to the text: Appendix F gives the textual emendations not covered by the general rules cited above; Appendix G lists the editorial corrections to Mill's bibliography of his published writings; Appendix H is a guide to the signatures Mill used in newspapers; Appendix I lists all the newspapers for which Mill wrote; and Appendix J provides (as in all our volumes) an index of the persons and works cited in the newspaper writings. Finally, there is an analytic Index, prepared by Dr. Jean O'Grady with her habitual diligent equanimity.

ACKNOWLEDGMENTS

FOR PERMISSION to publish manuscript material we thank the National Provincial
Bank (residual legatees of Mary Taylor, Mill's step-granddaughter), the British
Library of Political and Economic Science (London School of Economics), the
Library of University College London, the Library of the University of Illinois at
Urbana-Champaign, the Brotherton Collection of the University of Leeds, and
Yale University Library. We have been as ever blessed by superb co-operation
from not only these libraries but also from many other institutions and their
staffs, including, in Britain: the British Library, the Royal College of Surgeons
of England, the Somerville College Library, the University of London Library;
in Canada: the Robarts Library of the University of Toronto, the St. Michael's
College Library, the Trinity College Library, the Victoria University Library; in
France: the Archives du Ministère de l'Economie; the Archives de l'Ordre des
Avocats à la Cour de Paris; the Archives Départementales de la Gironde, du Jura,
de la Loire-Atlantique, de Meurthe et Moselle, du Puy-de-Dôme, and du Rhône;
the Archives Municipales de Grenoble; the Bibliothèque Nationale; the
Bibliothèque Nationale et Universitaire de Strasbourg; and the Service
d'Archives de Paris; in Germany: the Albert-Ludwigs-Universität (Freiburg), the
Generallandesarchiv Karlsruhe, and the Universitätsbibliothek and the Staats-
und Stadtbibliothek (Augsburg). For the illustrations, we express our gratitude
to the British Library Newspaper Library, the Principal and Fellows of Somerville College, Oxford, the Pierpont Morgan Library, and the Yale University
Library. Never have the research and editorial assistants on this edition deserved
more credit than for these testing volumes: without the dedicated and inventive
labours of Marion Filipiuk, Jean O'Grady, and Rea Wilmshurst publication
would never have occurred. The student assistants have also contributed greatly,
not least by their easy and cheerful accommodation to what must have sometimes
seemed unreasonable requests: Allison Taylor, Jonathan Cutmore, Margaret
Paternek, Mary-Elizabeth Shaw, Marion Halmos, and Jannifer Smith-Rubenzahl;
we thank them now as we have during their labours. Other scholars and friends
who have answered requests promptly and unselfishly include the gifted
members of the Editorial Committee, especially Margaret Parker, copy-editor of
these volumes, and others: Frank Baker, T.D. Barnes, R.D. Collison Black, the
Rev. Leonard Boyle, O.P., Maureen Clarke, G.M. Craig, John Cronin, Eileen
Curran, the Rev. J.L. Dewan, Robert Fenn, William Filipiuk, F.T. Flahiff,
Joseph Hamburger, Helen Hatton, Eleanor Higa, Dwight Lindley, Muriel
Mineka, Albert C. Outler, A.C.W. Robson, J.S.P. Robson, Catherine Sharrock,
and Cecelia Sieverts.

When plans for these volumes were made, Francis E. Mineka was asked to
share the editing with us. With the dedicated help of Cecelia Sieverts, he worked

on the annotation for some time, until his health failed and he was obliged to retire from the project. Their labours lie behind much of these volumes, all their notes having been made available to us, and their generosity of spirit having inspired us. The death of Francis Mineka early in October 1985 was a serious loss to Victorian scholarship generally, and to us a sad deprivation, only partially balanced by the widespread recognition of the high quality of his scholarly legacy. To him we dedicate these volumes.

Our final acknowledgment is of our mutual debt; this, like most of our other writings, is, as someone has said, "a joint production, very little of which is mine."

bers who have been universally returned wherever the principles of a free election have prevailed, the country must stand or fall by it; for, undoubtedly, should this bill fail, there is an end of the constitution,—we, the people of England, and William IV., the King of England, are governed by an oligarchy, whose despotism is founded only on corruption; but on corruption so deeply rooted, that the whole efforts of king and people cannot eradicate or shake it by ordinary process. We are sure that we are supported in this reasoning, and that others will think so, when we state, that the accession of strength to the king's ministers is expected to amount to ten from Scotland, to twelve from Ireland,—and that, upon the whole, the majority in the House of Commons cannot be less than one hundred and sixty!

"Is there, then, under these circumstances, the slightest probability that, with a parliament thus chosen by the people for the express purpose of supporting their bill, ministers should recede even from the least important of its provisions,—should desert their own pledge, and deceive the expectant country? However, it is not as an inference which we deduce, but as a positive fact which we assert, that the bill is to be supported by his majesty's ministers as it is now before the country; and we, with this knowledge, are therefore the more surprised, not that the *Courier* newspaper should make an erroneous unauthorised statement, but that such a man as the Lord Advocate of Scotland should have committed the grievous error of intimating that a change might be made in the amount of the qualification. We sincerely hope he will see this correction of his mistake, and set himself right."—*Times.*

Upon this the *Globe* remarks, what we have from the first observed, that the 10*l.* qualification, in many places, will be quite narrow enough as it stands, and cannot be raised without injurious effect. It proceeds to say—"The only mode by which the qualification could be raised, and a sufficient number of voters procured, would be by altogether abolishing the distinctions of cities and boroughs, and throwing the whole kingdom into electoral districts, with a property or income qualification, on the plan formerly suggested by many advocates of Reform. But this, of course, cannot *now* be done, for the great national charter has been proposed to, and accepted by, the people. No one will disturb so satisfactory a compact."—There is no compact in legislation. Expediency is the rule, and satisfaction with a measure can be no bar to improvement upon it. The people are fixed to no bargain, but to what may be for their good, which is the present character of the Reform Bill.

THE SPIRIT OF THE AGE.

No. V.

[In commencing this series of papers, I intended, and attempted, that the divisions of my discourse should correspond with those of my subject, and that each number should comprehend within its own limits all which was necessary to the expansion and illustration of one single idea. The nature of the publication, which, as being read by more persons capable of understanding the drift of such speculations (and by fewer, in proportion, who are unfit for them) than any other single work, I considered myself fortunate in being enabled to adopt as a vehicle for my ideas, compels n:s to limit the length of each article more than is compatible with my original plan. I can no longer always hope that every paper should be complete within itself; and the present number, had it appeared in its proper place, would have formed the continuation of the last.

In endeavouring to give an intelligible notion of what I have termed the *natural* state of society, in respect of moral influence—namely, that state in which the opinions and feelings of the people are, with their voluntary acquiescence, formed *for* them, by the most cultivated minds which the intelligence and morality of the times call into existence; and in drawing attention to the striking differences between this *natural* state and our present *transitional* condition, in which there are no persons to whom the mass of the uninstructed habitually defer, and in whom they trust for finding the right, and for pointing it out; I have hitherto illustrated the former state only by the example of those commonwealths, in which the most qualified men are studiously picked out because of their qualifications, and invested with that worldly power, which, if it were in any other hands, would divide or eclipse their moral influence: but which, placed in theirs, and acting partly as a *certificate* of authority, and partly as a *cause*, tends naturally to render their power over the minds of their fellow-citizens paramount and irresistible.

But it is not solely in such societies that there is found a united body of moral authority, sufficient to extort acquiescence from the unenquiring, or uninformed majority. It is found, likewise, in all societies where religion possesses a sufficient ascendency, to subdue the minds of the possessors of worldly power, and where the spirit of the prevailing religion is such as excludes the possibility of material conflict of opinion among its teachers.

These conditions exist among two great stationary communities—the Hindoos and the Turks; and are doubtless the chief cause which keeps those communities stationary. The same union of circumstances has been hitherto found only in one *progressive* society—but that, the greatest which had ever existed; Christendom in the middle ages.

For many centuries, undivided moral influence over the nations of Europe, the unquestioned privilege of forming the opinions and feelings of the Christian world, was enjoyed, and most efficiently exercised by the Catholic clergy. Their word inspired in the rest of mankind the most fervent faith. It not only absolutely excluded doubt, but caused the doubter to be regarded with sentiments of profound abhorrence, which moralists had never succeeded in inspiring for the most revolting of crimes. It is certainly possible to feel perfectly sure of an opinion, without believing that whosoever doubts it will be damned, and should be burnt: and this last is by no means one of those peculiarities of a natural state of society which I am at all anxious to see restored. But the deep earnest feeling of firm and unwavering conviction, which it pre-supposes, we may, without being unreasonable, lament that it was impossible, and could not *but* be impossible, in the intellectual anarchy of a general revolution in opinion, to transfer unimpaired to the truth.

The priesthood did not claim a right to dictate to mankind, either in belief or practice, beyond the province of religion and morals; but the political interests of mankind came not the less within their pale, because they seldom assumed the authority to regulate those concerns by specific precepts. They gave the sanction of their irresistible authority to one comprehensive rule, that which enjoined unlimited obedience to the temporal sovereign: an obligation from which they absolved the conscience of the believer, only when the sovereign disputed their authority within their peculiar province: and in that case they were invariably triumphant, like all those to whom it is given to call forth the moral sentiments of mankind in all their energy, against the inducements of mere physical hopes and fears.

The Catholic clergy, at the time when they possessed this undisputed authority in matters of conscience and belief, were, in point of fact, the fittest persons who *could* have possessed it—the then state of society, in respect of moral influence, answers to the description of a *natural* state.

Now, When we consider for how long a period the Catholic clergy were the only members of the European community who could even read; that they were the sole depositaries of all the treasures of thought, and reservoirs of intellectual delight, handed down to us from the ancients; that the sanctity of their persons permitted to them alone, among nations of semi-barbarians, the tranquil pursuit of peaceful occupations and studies; that, howsoever defective the morality which they taught, they had at least a mission for curbing the unruly passions of mankind, and teaching them to set a value upon a distant end, paramount to immediate temptations, and to prize gratifications consisting of mental feelings above bodily sensation; that, situate in the position of the rivals to the temporal sovereign, drafted chiefly from the inferior classes of society, from men who otherwise would have been serfs, and the most lowly among them all having the road open before him even to the papal chair, they had the strongest motives to avail themselves of the means afforded by Christianity, for inculcating the natural equality of mankind, the superiority of love and sacrifice above mere courage and bodily prowess, and menacing the great with the only terrors to which they were accessible, and speaking to their consciences in the name of the only superior whom they acknowledged, in behalf of the low. Reflecting on these things, I cannot persuade myself to doubt that the ascendancy of the Catholic clergy was to be desired, for that day, even by the philosopher; and that it has been a potent cause, if even it was not an indispensable condition, of the present civilization of Europe. Nor is this an apology for the vices of the Catholic religion: those vices were great and flagrant, and there was no natural connection between them and the more civilizing and humanizing features in which all that there was of good in it resided. We may regret that the influence of the priesthood was not superseded by a better influence: but alas in those days did any such influence exist?

I conclude, therefore, that, during a part of the middle ages, not only worldly power, as already shown, but moral influence also, was indisputedly exercised by the most competent persons; and that the conditions of a natural state of society were then fully realized.

But the age of transition arrived. A time came when that which had overmatched and borne down the strongest obstacles to improvement, became itself incompatible with improvement. Mankind outgrew their religion, and that, too, at a period when they had not yet outgrown their government, because the texture of the latter was more yielding, and could be stretched. We all know how lamentably effectual an instrument the influence of the Catholic priesthood then became, for restraining that expansion of the human intellect, which could not any longer consist with their ascendancy, or with the belief of the doctrines which they taught.

The more advanced communities of Europe succeeded, after a terrific struggle, in effecting their total or partial emancipation: in some, the Reformation achieved a victory—in others, a toleration; while, by a fate unhappily too common, the flame which had been kindled where the pile awaited the spark, spread into countries where the materials were not yet sufficiently prepared; and instead of burning down the hateful edifice, it consumed all that existed capable of nourishing itself, and was extinguished. The germs of civilization to come were scorched up and destroyed; the hierarchy reigned stronger than ever, amidst the intellectual solitude which it had made: and the countries which were thus denuded of the means of further advancement, fell back into barbarism irretrievable—except by foreign conquest. Such is the inevitable end, when, unhappily, changes to which the spirit of the age is favourable, can be successfully resisted. Civilization becomes the terror of the ruling powers, and that they may retain their seat, it must be their deliberate endeavour to barbarize mankind. There has been, since that day, one such attempt, and only one, which has had a momentary success: it was that of a man in whom all the evil influences of his age were concentered with an intensity and energy truly terrific, less tempered by any of its good influences than could appear possible in the times in which he lived—I need scarcely say that I refer to Napoleon. May his abortive effort to uncivilize human nature, to uncultivate the mind of man, and turn it into a desolate waste, be the last!

It remains to trace the history of moral influence in the nations of Europe, subsequently to the Reformation.]

Harmless Enjoyment of Dignity.—During the last few days a gentleman, availing himself of a strong resemblance to the late Emperor, both in person and features, has amused himself with parading about the town in high military boots, a gray redingote, and the never failing cocked hat, with his hands behind his back, while the vagabond boys of the town run after him, shouting "Vive l'Empereur," which he acknowledges with smiles of complacency, and a nose daubed with snuff.—*Spectateur of Dijon.*

The Spirit of the Age, V [Part 1]
Examiner, 15 May, 1831, p. 307
Somerville College Library

NEWSPAPER WRITINGS BY JOHN STUART MILL

December 1822 to July 1831

··· December 1822 to December 1824 ···

1. EXCHANGEABLE VALUE [1]

TRAVELLER, 6 DEC., 1822, P. 3

This and the next letter, Mill's first published writings, were occasioned by "Political Economy Club," *Traveller*, 2 Dec., p. 3, by Robert Torrens (1780-1864), co-proprietor of the newspaper and a founding member of the Political Economy Club; the subject of Torrens's article was the meeting of that Club to be held later that day. Mill's reply brought forth a retort from Torrens in "Exchangeable Value," *Traveller*, 7 Dec., p. 3, and the series terminated with a note by Torrens appended to Mill's second letter. The exchange centred on the theory of value advanced in *Elements of Political Economy* (London: Baldwin, *et al.*, 1821) by James Mill (1773-1836), J.S. Mill's father; in his *Autobiography* Mill says his reply to Torrens was at his father's "instigation" (*CW*, Vol. I, p. 89). Headed as title, with the subhead "To the Editor of the Traveller," the items are described in Mill's bibliography as "Two letters in the Traveller of [6th Dec.] and [13th Dec.] 1822 containing a controversy with Col. Torrens on the question whether value depends on quantity of labour. Signed S." (MacMinn, p. 1.)

SIR,—In your notice of the late Meeting of the Political Economy Club, you have inserted a disquisition, which professes to be a refutation of Mr. Mill's theory of value. I take the liberty of submitting to you several remarks which occurred to me on reading your article.

In the first place, if I rightly understand Mr. Mill's chapter on Exchangeable Value,[1] he cannot be said with propriety to have any theory of value—at least, in that sense in which the word theory is applied to Mr. Ricardo's doctrines on this subject. Mr. R. renders the word *value*, as synonymous with *productive cost*[2]—thus introducing a new, and as it appears to me, a needless ambiguity of language. Mr. Mill, on the other hand, never uses the word value in any other than its vulgar acceptation. I am not aware that there is any passage in the *Elements of Political Economy*, in which the words *power of purchasing* may not be substituted for the word *value*, without in any degree affecting the truth of Mr. Mill's positions.

But though the word value is never employed by Mr. Mill, in any other sense

---

[1]*Elements*, Chap. iii, Sect. 2, pp. 69-74.

[2]David Ricardo, *On the Principles of Political Economy and Taxation* (London: Murray, 1817), Chap. i, "On Value," esp. pp. 19-21. Ricardo (1772-1823), the great economist, M.P. for Portarlington, was a close friend of James Mill, and, like him, a member of the Political Economy Club.

than purchasing power, it is nevertheless true that he endeavours to ascertain what are the circumstances which regulate the purchasing power of commodities.[3] He agrees with the distinguished political economist whom we have cited, in considering the regulating circumstance to be cost of production. This cost he considers as resolvable into quantity of labour, and it is to this part of his doctrine that your strictures refer. As your arguments on this subject do not appear to me to be conclusive, I beg leave to offer my objections to their validity.

You say, "Let the rate of profit be 20 per cent.; let a manufacturer in silver and a manufacturer in iron each advance a capital of a thousand pounds, and let the advance of the former consist of ninety days' hoarded labour, in the form of material, and ten days' hoarded labour in the form of subsistence, while the advance of the latter consists of ten days' hoarded labour in the form of material, and ninety in the form of subsistence." [P. 3.]

You observe that the manufacturer in silver, with ten days' labour of subsistence, must employ twelve days of immediate labour, in order to realize a profit of 20 per cent.; and that the manufacturer in iron, with his 90 days' labour of subsistence, will employ 108 days of immediate labour: that therefore the silver goods, when completed, will be the produce of twelve days of immediate labour, and 90 of hoarded labour, in the form of material; while the iron goods will be the produce of 108 days of immediate labour, and 120 of hoarded labour, also in the form of material; forming the two different sums total of 102 and 118 days' labour.

This being the case, you assert that the silver and the iron goods will exchange for one another. To this I cannot assent. You appear to have forgotten, that if profits are taken into the account at all, we must suppose the two manufacturers to make a profit, not merely on that portion of their capital which they expend in maintaining labour, but also on that portion which they expend in furnishing the raw material. By supposition, the capital of each producer consisted of one hundred days' labour. You assert that when the production is completed, the silver manufacturer has only the produce of 102 days' labour, while the iron manufacturer has the produce of 118 days' labour, in remuneration for their capital. The former then has only a profit of 2 per cent. on his whole capital, the latter has a profit of 18 per cent. on the whole. It is evident that, under these circumstances, the two commodities will not exchange for one another: their values will be in the proportion of 102 to 118—that is, of the quantities of labour by which they were produced. This, at least, will be the case, if profits are to be considered as forming one ingredient in cost of production, the position on which your whole argument is founded.

If profits are equal in the two cases, as the principle of competition will render them, it is unnecessary to take them into the calculation of exchangeable value,

[3]*Elements*, Chap. iii, Sect. 7, pp. 95-8.

which is, by the force of the term, not something absolute, but something relative. If the whole produce of the one capital exchanges for the whole produce of the other, those parts of them which remain when profits are deducted, will also exchange for one another. But if we exclude profits, your objection falls to the ground. Mr. Mill's argument must, therefore, be considered as resting on the same foundation as before.

You have also started an objection against another of Mr. Mill's arguments. The value of commodities (says Mr. M.) cannot depend upon capital, since capital is commodities, and if the value of commodities depends on the value of capital, it depends on the value of commodities—that is, on itself.[4] You observe, that this argument cuts both ways. If the value of commodities depends upon labour, as the value of labour can only be estimated in commodities, this (say you) is to assert that the value of labour depends on the value of labour. This would be true if Mr. M. had asserted that the value of commodities depends on the value of labour. But he says, that it depends, not on the *value* but on the *quantity* of labour:[5] there is here no inconsistency. The value of commodities depends upon the quantity of labour employed in producing them. The value of labour, which is not itself produced by labour, cannot be subject to the same laws. Mr. M. in his Chapter on Wages, has expounded the laws which regulate the value of labour.[6]

S.

2. EXCHANGEABLE VALUE [2]
TRAVELLER, 13 DEC., 1822, P. 2

For the context, heading, and bibliographical information, see No. 1.

SIR,—In your Paper of Saturday you inserted an article professing to be a refutation of that which you did me the honour of inserting on Friday. Permit me, however, to say, that if I was before convinced of the truth of Mr. Mill's conclusions, my conviction is strengthened by the weakness of the arguments which are brought against them by the ablest of their opponents.

You accuse me of having misunderstood your arguments. I am at a loss to conceive what interpretation can be put upon them, different from that which I have given. In the argument of your first article I can see only two things: first, an elaborate attempt to prove what no one ever thought of disputing—namely, that labour produces more than is necessary for the maintenance of the labourers:

[4]*Ibid.*, Chap. iii, Sect. 2, pp. 70-1, 74.
[5]*Ibid.*, p. 73.
[6]*Ibid.*, Chap. ii, Sect. 2, pp. 24-53.

and secondly, an inference drawn from this—namely, that labour does not regulate exchangeable value. Your reasoning amounts to this—labour is productive, therefore labour does not regulate value. I hope you will excuse me if I confess that I do not see the connection between these two propositions. One man by one day's labour may possibly produce food which will maintain him for ten days; but it does not follow from this, that one day's labour of food will not exchange for one day's labour of any other commodity.

In your last article, you put a different case. You suppose A to have wine, the produce of 100 days' labour, and B to have food, the produce of equal labour. A keeps his wine in his cellar to improve by age; B employs his capital in maintaining 120 days of labour in the production of a commodity. These commodities, you say, will exchange for one another; and you conceive that here labour does not regulate value. It seems to me, however, that this is not an exception to Mr. Mill's doctrine. You virtually admit that the value of B's commodity is regulated by the quantity of labour expended in its production. But if the wine produced by equal capital, and deposited in the cellar of the merchant, did not command the same price, no wine would ever be kept. The value, therefore, of A's wine is regulated by that of B's commodity. But the value of B's commodity depends on quantity of labour. Is it not, therefore, evident that the value of A's wine also depends on quantity of labour?

S.

3. RELIGIOUS PERSECUTION
MORNING CHRONICLE, 1 JAN., 1823, P. 1

This letter was occasioned by a series of prosecutions for blasphemous libel that received considerable attention in the press (see, e.g., in the last part of 1822, *Examiner*, 27 Oct., pp. 685-6, 3 Nov., pp. 709-10, 17 Nov., pp. 721-4, 726, 734, 24 Nov., pp. 748-9, 764-5, 15 Dec., pp. 788ff.). Headed as title, with the subhead "To the Editor of the Morning Chronicle," the letter was the first of Mill's many contributions to the *Morning Chronicle*. The item is described in Mill's bibliography as "A letter in the Morning Chronicle of 1st January 1823 on Free Discussion, signed, An Enemy to Religious Persecution" (MacMinn, p. 1).

SIR,—I beg leave to submit to you some observations, which may, perhaps, appear too obvious to be deserving of insertion. The importance, however, of the subject, and the state of vagueness in which every thing connected with it has been hitherto suffered to remain, must plead my apology for intruding upon your notice.

The late persecutions for matters of opinion have frequently been defended, on the ground that "Christianity is part and parcel of the law of England."[1] This sentence, put together by a Judge, passed from Judge to Judge with solemn and appalling gravity, will be found, on examination, to be, like the many other high-sounding maxims with which our law abounds, utterly unmeaning and absurd. This is so evident, that nothing but the extreme vagueness of the language in which this doctrine is conveyed could have protected it from detection and exposure.

A law is a precept, to the non-observance of which, pains and penalties are attached by the Government. Against this definition, I apprehend, no objection can be brought. And the law of England, collectively considered, is a collection of the precepts, thus sanctioned by legal authority.

Having thus settled the meaning of one of the words employed, let us pass to the other. Christianity then consists of two parts—a collection of precepts and a collection of opinions. When we speak of the spirit of christianity, of its morality, &c., we allude more particularly to the precepts. When we speak of the doctrines, the dogmas, the truths of christianity, this is with reference to the opinions which it inculcates. This division appears to me to be complete. No one can mention any thing connected with christianity, which is not either matter of precept, or matter of opinion.

Now when it is asserted by Judges that christianity is part and parcel of the law, is this meant of the *precepts* of christianity?—No, certainly: for if so, it would mean that every moral duty is enforced by the law of England; of the impossibility of this, it is scarcely necessary to produce any illustration. Not to notice the frequent admonitions which we find in the Gospel for preserving *purity of heart,*[2] it will not be denied that sobriety and chastity are among the first of moral duties. But what would be the consequence of erecting them into a law? It is enough to say that it would be necessary to place a spy in every house.

But if not the *precepts*, perhaps the *opinions* which christianity inculcates, may be said with propriety to be "part and parcel of the law." And how? The law is a collection of precepts. In what sense can an opinion be part of a collection of precepts?—Surely this maxim, which has been made the foundation of proceedings such as we have lately witnessed, is either palpably false, or wholly without a meaning. Unfortunately the protection, as it is sacrilegiously termed, of the christian doctrines, by the persecution of those who hold contrary opinions, *is* part and parcel of the law. But this, the only intelligible sense in which the maxim can be taken, ought not thus to be made a foundation for itself.—The Judge argues as follows:—I punish infidelity, because christianity

[1]The phrase, frequently used in courts, originated evidently with Matthew Hale (1609-76), in his judgment in the case of K. *v.* Taylor, 1676 (86 *English Reports* 189).

[2]See, e.g., Matthew, 5:8, I Timothy, 1:5, II Timothy, 2:22, and Titus, 1:15.

is part and parcel of the law. This is as much as to say, I punish infidelity, because such punishment is part of the law.—This may be a very good defence for the particular Judge who pronounces the sentence, but is it not absurd to give it as a justification of the persecuting law?

An Enemy to Religious Persecution

4. THE WORD "NATURE"

REPUBLICAN, 3 JAN., 1823, PP. 25-6

This letter, which reflects Mill's contemporaneous study of law with John Austin, is addressed to Richard Carlile (1790-1843), the free-thinker, who was editing the *Republican* from Dorchester Gaol, where he had been imprisoned for publishing the works of Thomas Paine and other writings held to be seditious. Mill seems to have been mistaken in attributing to Carlile the view expressed in his opening paragraph; Carlile appended to the letter a signed note: "My Atheistical friend is, I think, wrong in supposing that I wrote such an assertion as that, there must be a cause to be attributed. I may have said the phenomena of the material world: or that the constant charges [*sic*] which we behold in materials argue the existence of a cause or active power that pervades them. But I have again and again renounced the notion of that power being intelligent or designing." The letter, Mill's only one to the *Republican*, is headed "To Mr. R. Carlile, Dorchester Gaol," and is described in Mill's bibliography as "A letter in the Republican of [3 Jan., 1823,] on the word Nature" (MacMinn, p. 1).

SIR,—Admiring as I do the firmness with which you maintain, and the astonishing candour with which you defend your principles, sympathising in your opinions and feelings both on the subject of politics and on that of religion; I deeply regret, in common with your correspondent Gallus,[1] that you should ever have given currency to doctrines in direct opposition to your other opinions. From among many such doctrines, I select one, which appears to me to be the stumbling block of a great number of Infidels. This is to be gathered from the use which you frequently make of the word *Nature* as denoting some positive, active, if not intelligent being. In a former No. of *The Republican*, in allusion to the application which has been made to you of the word Atheist, you observe that although you do not reject this appellation, you consider it as a very absurd one, as you conceive that every man must acknowledge, under the name either of God, or of nature some cause to which the material world is to be attributed. Your exact words I do not remember, but I am certain that this was the import of what you said.

Now as I do not myself acknowledge any such cause, I would if it were necessary, endeavour to convince you that there is no foundation for any such belief. But I rejoice to see that this labour is spared me by the admirable letter of

[1]*Republican*, 29 Nov., 1822, pp. 835-42.

Gallus. I will therefore confine myself to a brief examination of the import and application of the word Nature.

All human knowledge consists in facts, or phenomena, observed by the senses and recorded by means of language. The study of these phenomena is what is called the study of Nature: the aggregate of the phenomena, or human knowledge as it stands, is called Nature in the abstract. If this be true, you must at once see the absurdity of supposing any thing to be *caused* by Nature. Nature is that for which the cause is to be sought; or rather, it is that for which it is needless to seek any cause, as if it has any, this must remain for ever unknown.

The phenomena which we observe are found to follow one another in a certain order; the same event is invariably observed to be preceded by the same event. When a sufficient number of these sequences has been observed, it becomes possible to express them by a certain number of general propositions, which have been metaphorically termed Laws of Nature, but which have in reality no resemblance to laws. A law is a general command laid down by a superior, most commonly by the governors of a nation. The analogy is very distant between this and a verbal expression for a series of phenomena; which is absurdly called a law of Nature.

When once this phraseology was introduced, the poets and mythologists soon took hold of it, and made it subservient to their purposes. Nature was personified: the phrase law of Nature, which originally meant no more than a law for the regulation of Nature, or of the natural world, became a law laid down by the goddess Nature to be obeyed by her creatures. From the poets, this fictitious personage speedily penetrated into the closets of the philosopher, and hence arose the error of attributing a creative power to nature. To make any use of this word, in the explanation of the material phenomena, is only substituting for rational scepticism, a mystical and poetical kind of Theism. Of course, the arguments which serve to explode the belief in an ante-material and intelligent Being, will also suffice to destroy the unmeaning word *Nature*.

Yours, with the greatest respect,
An Atheist

5. FREE DISCUSSION, LETTER I

MORNING CHRONICLE, 28 JAN., 1823, P. 3

The series made up of this and the next two letters is referred to in Mill's *Autobiography* after his mention of his first publications, Nos. 1 and 2: "I soon after attempted something considerably more ambitious. The prosecutions of Richard Carlile and his wife and sister for publications hostile to Christianity, were then exciting much attention, and nowhere more than among the people I frequented. Freedom of discussion, even in politics, much more in religion, was at that time far from being, even in theory, the conceded point which it at least seems to be now; and the holders of noxious opinions had to be always ready to argue and reargue for the liberty of expressing them. I wrote a series of five letters, under the signature of Wickliffe [*sic*], going over the whole length and breadth of the question of free publication of all opinions on religion, and offered them to the *Morning Chronicle*. Three of them were published in January and February 1823; the other two containing things too outspoken for that journal, never appeared at all." (*CW*, Vol. I, pp. 89-91.) The two final letters seem not to have survived. All headed as title and subheaded "To the Editor of the Morning Chronicle," the letters are described in Mill's bibliography as "Three letters, signed Wickliff, on the same subject [as that of No. 3, i.e., freedom of religious discussion], inserted in the Morning Chronicle of 28th January [, 8th February and 12th February,] 1823" (MacMinn, p. 1).

SIR,—At a time when the question of free discussion on religious subjects is agitated with unusual perseverance, and is therefore peculiarly interesting, I think it highly useful to call the public attention to the nothingness of the arguments which have been brought against unlimited toleration; arguments which, though they have been refuted many times already, are daily repeated, and by a very common artifice represented as never having been answered.

I shall first observe, that as it is generally allowed that free discussion contributes to the propagation of truth, and as this assertion is never controverted on the great majority of subjects, it is incumbent on those who declare against toleration to point out some reason which prevents the general rule from being applicable to this particular case; to shew that free discussion, which on almost every other subject is confessedly advantageous to truth, in this particular case unfortunately contributes to the progress of error. If they cannot produce any satisfactory reason, the general rule ought unquestionably to be observed; and that, even if it were not necessary to employ fine and imprisonment in support of the exception; much more when so great a mass of evil is produced by it.

The puerility of the reasons which have hitherto been brought against religious toleration, is perfectly surprising, and proves most satisfactorily that the cause in support of which they are brought is a bad one. The most common of all is the worn-out fallacy, that there is greater danger of mistake on these subjects than on others.

This assertion, it is to be observed, is wholly destitute of proof. In a subsequent letter I will endeavour to prove, not only that the danger of mistake is not *greater*, but that it is much less in the case of religion than in any other.[1] Admitting, however, for the present, that there is greater danger of mistake, I shall proceed to shew, that if free discussion be excluded, the danger is greatly increased.

For if you determine before-hand that opinions shall be promulgated only on one side of the question, in whom will you rest the power of determining which side shall be chosen? The answer is, in those who are most enlightened and best

[1]See No. 7.

qualified to judge. But there are no determinable and universal marks by which wisdom is to be known. To whom will you give the power of determining what men are the most enlightened?

What is meant, though it is not openly avowed, by the assertion that the wisest men shall chuse opinions for the people, is that the Government shall chuse them. But if the Government is allowed to chuse opinions for the people, the Government is despotic. To say that there is no danger in permitting the Government to chuse religious opinions for the people, is to assert what is notoriously untrue: since there is no conceivable opinion, true or false, which may not, at some time or other, be made a religious doctrine. There is scarcely a single improvement, either in physical or in political science, which has not at one time or another been opposed by religion. The Ptolemaean astronomy was at one time a part of religion.[2] A professor was imprisoned within these last two years at Rome for maintaining the truth of the Newtonian system, which is still condemned by the Papal Court.[3] The doctrine of passive obedience and non-resistance was generally a religious doctrine, and is still that of the prevailing party of the Church of England.[4]

But if you exclude discussion on any one doctrine of religion, you must, by parity of reason, exclude it on all. It is in vain to say that Atheistical opinions shall alone be excluded. What reason is there why this more than any other subject should be prevented from undergoing a thorough examination? There is, if not a reason, at least a cause, why Atheism now undergoes that persecution to which other less obnoxious doctrines were formerly subjected. But this cause is merely that the persuasion of its falsehood is more general than in the case of any other obnoxious opinion. To bring this as a reason for preventing discussion, is to say that the people are better qualified to judge before discussion than after it: which is absurd, since before discussion, if their opinions are true it is only by accident, whereas after it they hold them with a complete conviction, and perfect knowledge of the proofs on which they are grounded.

That the evils incurred by permitting any person or persons to chuse opinions

[2]The geocentric astronomy of Claudius Ptolemaeus, 2nd-century Alexandrian mathematician, had been incorporated into traditional Christian cosmology.

[3]The reference is presumably to Giuseppe Settele (d. 1841), teacher and astronomer at the University of Rome. In 1820 the Holy Office withheld the *imprimatur* from his *Elementi di Ottica e di Astronomia*, 2 vols. (Rome, 1818–19), though he was neither permanently condemned nor imprisoned. For the original ruling, see Giovanni Battista Riccioli, *Almagestum novum*, 2 vols. (Bologna: Haeredis Victorii Benatii, 1651), Vol. II, p. 497.

[4]The High Church party in the Church of England saw itself as the heir of the "non-jurors," those clergy who refused after the Revolution of 1688 to swear allegiance to William and Mary on the grounds that their oath to James II, whose title was of divine right, was still in effect. Their opposition, however, was passive, according to their reading of Scripture, esp. I Samuel, 15:23, Romans, 13:1-2, and I Peter, 2:13-14.

for the people are evils of the greatest magnitude, is evident from the arguments which I have adduced. This subject is developed in the most satisfactory manner in Mr. Mill's invaluable Essay on the Liberty of the Press, forming an article in Napier's Supplement to the *Encyclopaedia Britannica.*[5]

The only other argument of any plausibility which the anti-tolerationists adduce in favour of the present persecutions, is the incalculable mischievousness of the doctrines persecuted, which they conceive to outweigh the evil we have proved to arise from allowing the Government to chuse opinions for the people.

I, therefore, propose to examine whether the mischievous effects of these doctrines are so great as to justify persecution; secondly, whether there are not many other doctrines attended with mischiefs infinitely greater, and which, nevertheless, it would be reckoned, and with justice, highly improper to persecute; thirdly, to prove that there is scarcely any kind of mischievous opinion, be it what it may, which the ignorant are not more likely to adopt, if it be tolerated, than atheism and deism; and lastly, to refute some of the minor fallacies which have been brought in defence of persecution.

These four objects I shall endeavour to attain in as many letters, if they should be thought worthy of insertion in your admirable paper, which, in addition to the other benefits it is continually rendering to mankind, has uniformly stood forward in a most manly and most Christian manner in defence of free discussion.

Wickliff

6. FREE DISCUSSION, LETTER II
MORNING CHRONICLE, 8 FEB., 1823, P. 3

This letter, centring on the utility of oaths, draws heavily on *"Swear not at all": Containing an Exposure of the Inutility and Mischievousness, as Well as Anti-Christianity, of the Ceremony of an Oath* (London: Hunter, 1817), by Jeremy Bentham (1748-1832); in his *Works*, ed. John Bowring, 11 vols. (Edinburgh: Tait, 1843), Vol. V, pp. 187-229. (This work was printed in 1813, and a copy given to the Head of an Oxford College in that year, almost certainly during the tour on which Bentham took Mill and his father; see *CW*, Vol. I, pp. 55-7.) In the tract Bentham refers to all the issues cited by Mill: jurymen's oaths, pp. 204-5, custom-house oaths, p. 195, university oaths, pp. 195-7, 209-12, 213-19, and 224-9 (all dealing with Oxford, Bentham's university, except pp. 213-19, on Cambridge), and Quakers' affirmations, p. 201. For the context, heading, and entry in Mill's bibliography, see No. 5.

[5]"F.F." (James Mill), "Liberty of the Press," in *Supplement to the Fourth, Fifth and Sixth Editions of the Encyclopaedia Britannica*, ed. Macvey Napier, 6 vols. (Edinburgh: Constable, 1824), Vol. V, pp. 258-72. The Supplement was first issued in fascicles, this article appearing in that published in July 1821.

sir,—In my first letter I endeavoured to give a general conception of the plan which I intend to pursue in advocating the cause of free discussion. This plan I will now endeavour to carry into execution.

Persecutors do not usually attempt to justify their intolerance under pretence of avenging the cause of God. The absurdity of this pretension would be too obvious, since it would imply that God is unable to avenge his own cause; and since it is also evident, that Christianity rejects this method of defence. If there was any reason which could justify persecution in the eyes of a man of sense, that reason must be its utility to man; and it is upon this circumstance accordingly, that the greatest stress has been laid. By permitting the propagation of infidel doctrines, you destroy, it is said, the principal security for good judicature, and for the practice of private morality.

How far this assertion is true it shall be our business to inquire; and first as to judicature—among those requisites without which good judicature cannot exist, the principal is true and complete evidence. A great part of the evidence delivered in a Court of Justice consists in the testimony of witnesses. To secure veracity on the part of witnesses is therefore one of the most important ends to which the Legislator can direct his endeavours.

For insuring the veracity of witnesses, among other securities the ceremony of an oath has been resorted to. That the desired effect is attained in a very considerable degree is certain—that this beneficial result is to be attributed to the ceremony of swearing, is by no means a legitimate conclusion. There are several motives which tend to produce veracity on the part of witnesses. Even those who attribute the effect principally to the ceremony of swearing will admit, that the fear of punishment and the fear of shame in this instance co-operate with the religious inducement.—Since, then, it is allowed on all hands, that the veracity of witnesses is the joint result of several causes, it is for them to shew why it is to be attributed to one of these more than to another.

When a number of different causes co-operate in the production of a given effect, it is often a matter of some difficulty to determine which of the causes is principally instrumental in bringing it about. This difficulty, however, is removed, if an opportunity presents itself of examining the effects produced by each of the causes, taken separately. If we find that one of the causes, when unsupported by the others, is not followed by any degree of the effect in question, we shall be intitled to conclude, that in all those cases in which the effect really takes place, it is to the other causes, and not to this one, that it ought to be attributed.

This opportunity fortunately presents itself in the case we are considering. There are several instances in which, although the ceremony of an oath is employed, neither the laws nor the popular voice enforce observance of it. If it should appear that in all these cases truth is uniformly and openly violated, then we ought to conclude, that whenever judicial mendacity is prevented, we owe this benefit to the laws and to popular opinion, not to the ceremony of swearing.

I. It is notorious, that from motives of humanity, but in defiance of the strongest evidence, Juries frequently condemn a criminal to a milder punishment than the laws have appropriated to his offence, by finding him guilty of stealing under the value of 40s. Here the oath of the Jurymen is flagrantly violated. They have sworn to judge according to the evidence; but humanity, which dictates the perjury, also prevents public opinion from censuring the perjured Jurymen. This instance, therefore, makes it apparent, how slender is the security which an oath affords, when unsupported by, or at variance with, public opinion.

II. Another most striking instance of the inefficacy of oaths is, the abuse which is made of them at the Custom House. So notoriously does every merchant, who imports or exports goods, swear falsely to their quality and amount, that Custom House oaths have almost passed into a proverb.[1] This perjury, indeed, has for its object to evade certain laws, which are so admirably contrived for the purpose of fettering commerce, that if they were rigidly enforced, certain commodities could not possibly be exported or imported. From the acknowledged absurdity of the laws, this perjurious evasion of them is not reprobated by public opinion.

III. Every young man, at his admission into the University of Oxford, swears to obey certain statutes, drawn up by Archbishop Laud for the government of the University.[2] Now it is well known that no one of these students ever bestows a single thought upon the observance of these statutes. The cause of this non-observance is, that from the uselessness and absurdity of the statutes, public opinion does not enforce obedience to them. If, however, the ceremony of an oath was of any efficacy in preventing mendacity, this efficacy would shew itself even in a case where the obligation is not sanctioned by public opinion. The violation of the University oath, in every case where its observance interferes in the slightest degree with the convenience of the swearer, is a complete proof that the ceremony of swearing affords no security whatever for veracity in any other case, and that whenever witnesses speak the truth, it is not because they have sworn, but because they fear punishment and shame.

The inefficiency of an oath is practically recognized by English Legislators, and by English Judges, when they admit persons of all religious denominations to give evidence, after taking an oath according to the form prescribed by their own religion. For there are some religions which are acknowledged to have little or no efficacy in preventing mendacity. Yet we do not find that, *ceteris paribus*,

[1]For the Custom House oaths, see, e.g., 1 George IV, c. 8 (1820).
[2]See *Statuta selecta e corpore statuorum universitatis Oxoniensis* (Oxford: Webb, 1638) for the statutes as codified in 1636 by William Laud (1573-1645), Chancellor of the University of Oxford from 1629; later (1633) Archbishop of Canterbury. Bentham refers to several revisions and forms of the statutes in *"Swear not at all"*; see esp. pp. 195n and 224-9.

less reliance is to be placed on the oaths of one set of religionists, than of another.

But the law is not even applicable to all Christians, which amounts to an admission of the inefficacy of oaths to secure good evidence. The respectable sect of Quakers is freed from the necessity of swearing,[3] and yet it is always understood that there is proportionably less false evidence on the part of the members of that body, than on the part of the members of any of the swearing sects.

Having thus made it appear that it is not to the influence of religious motives that good evidence is to be attributed, we might conclude from analogy that the security we have for useful actions is chiefly referrable to other sources. This conclusion is farther supported by the frequency with which duelling and fornication are practised, notwithstanding the positive manner in which they are forbidden by Christianity. They are practised merely because public opinion does not, in these instances, support the dictates of religion. The drinking of wine in Mahometan countries is another equally striking instance.

From the considerations which we have adduced, all of them notorious results of experience, it is evident how ill-founded is the argument of those who defend persecution on the ground which we have combated.

In my next I will endeavour to shew that persecution is not necessary for the support of Christianity.

Wickliff

7. FREE DISCUSSION, LETTER III
MORNING CHRONICLE, 12 FEB., 1823, P. 3

For the context, heading, and entry in Mill's bibliography, see No. 5.

SIR,—I shall now endeavour to prove that persecution is not necessary for the preservation of Christianity.

The Christian Religion may be contemplated in two points of view. We may direct our attention to those peculiar characteristics which distinguish it from all other doctrines, true or false; or we may consider it with reference to those properties which it has in common with all true doctrines, as contradistinguished from false ones.

Not one, but many, arguments might be adduced to prove that Christianity, considered merely as a true doctrine, could not, under the influence of free discussion, fail of prevailing over falsehood. This ground, however, has already been gone over by far abler pens than mine; and a truth which has been

[3]Under Sect. 36 of 22 George II, c. 46 (1749).

maintained (not to speak of other writers) by Divines so eminent as Tillotson, Taylor, Chillingworth, Campbell, Lardner, Lowth, Warburton, Paley, Watson, and more recently by Hall, cannot stand in need of such feeble support as I can afford.[1]

In the present Letter I shall therefore confine myself to the consideration of those qualities peculiar to Christianity, which render persecution even less necessary for its support than for that of any other true doctrine.

And first, let me observe, that the only supposition on which persecution can be defended—by such of its advocates, I mean, as are Christians—is that of the utter incapacity and incorrigible imbecility of the people. That infidels should think persecution essential to the being of Christianity, can be matter of no surprise; but one who believes in the truth of the doctrine he supports, can not for a moment entertain any such opinion, unless he believes what no man, whose judgment is not biassed by interest, can believe, that the people are incapable of distinguishing truth from falsehood.

The fact, that the utility of persecution rests on such a basis, would alone induce every reasonable man to scout the idea of it; but, even though we were to allow the incapacity of the people, to admit the truth of all which their worst calumniators have ever imputed to them; it would not be less true that Christianity can support itself without persecution, nor, consequently, would the arguments in favour of toleration be a whit less conclusive.

If a true proposition, and the false one which is opposed to it, are presented at the same time to the mind of a man who is utterly incapable of distinguishing truth from error, which of the two is he most likely to embrace? This question will be found to admit of an easy answer. If he was before prepossessed in favour of either opinion, that one he will still continue to hold. If both were equally new to him, he will choose that which is most flattering to his prevailing passion.

All the prepossessions of those whom it is wished to protect by persecution from the danger of becoming infidels are uniformly and confessedly favourable to religion. No where is education, even partially, in the hands of infidels. There is no place where religion does not form one of the most essential parts of education. It is not, therefore, upon this ground, that persecution can be justified.

To counteract the effect of early impressions, it will, no doubt, be affirmed that infidelity is peculiarly flattering to the passions, and that those who wish to throw off the shackles of morality will be glad, in the first instance, to emancipate themselves from the salutary restraint which religion imposes.

[1]John Tillotson (1630-94), Archbishop of Canterbury (1691); Jeremy Taylor (1613-67); William Chillingworth (1602-44); George Campbell (1719-96); Nathaniel Lardner (1684-1768); Robert Lowth (1710-87), Bishop of Oxford (1766-77) and of London (1777-87); William Warburton (1698-1779), Bishop of Gloucester (1760-79); William Paley (1743-1805), Archdeacon of Carlisle (1782-1805); Richard Watson (1737-1816), Bishop of Llandaff (1782-1816); and Robert Hall (1764-1831).

It was partly with the intention of obviating this objection that my last letter was penned. There is no use in representing the evils of infidelity as greater than they really are: nor does a disposition to do so evince, on the part of him who shews it, any very great anxiety to vindicate either himself or his religion from the imputation of want of candour. That infidelity excludes us from the blessings of a future life, would surely be a sufficient reason to induce every reasonable man to reject it. I have endeavoured to shew that even if (which God forbid) all sense of religion were to die away among men, there would still remain abundant motives to ensure good conduct in this life. The passions, therefore, are not interested in throwing off religious belief, or all our ethical writers have been employing their labour to very little purpose.

Nor is this all. Infidel doctrines are peculiarly ill fitted for making converts among that portion of mankind who are most in danger of mistaking falsehood for truth. They bear a greater analogy to general abstract propositions in metaphysics than to any thing which can immediately affect the sensitive faculties. Besides, they superinduce what, to all men not convinced of the necessity of it by the habit of scientific disquisitions, is the most painful of all states of mind, a state of doubt. On the other hand, one of the strongest feelings in every uneducated mind is the appetite for wonder, the love of the marvellous. Witness the rapid progress of so many religions, which we now think so unutterably absurd that we wonder how any human being can ever have given credit to them. This passion is gratified in the most eminent degree by the Christian religion; for what is there in Christianity which is not in the highest degree sublime and mysterious?

Against so general and so powerful a feeling, what has scepticism to oppose? It is not peculiarly fitted to take hold of the imagination; on the contrary, it is eminently and almost universally repelled by it. If, then, it had not been evident before, I trust that the considerations I have adduced will suffice to make it so, that of all the doctrines which the invention of man ever devised, none is so little likely to prevail over the contrary doctrine as religious infidelity.

Doctrines which, if left to themselves, have no chance of prevailing, may be saved from oblivion by persecution. The advocates of infidelity are active and fearless: no persecution can daunt, no ignominy can restrain them. By persecution they are raised to an importance which they could never otherwise have attained: by ignominy they are only advertised that it is impossible for them to retreat. To prevent them from diffusing infidelity through the whole kingdom, what has been done by our well-paid divines? I am not aware that they have yet employed any other weapon than vague and declamatory abuse. Books indeed there are; but, alas! what avails a mass of ponderous volumes, written in a style as little suited to the capacity, as the price at which they are sold is to the purses, of those for whose use they are principally required? It is true abuse is far easier, and requires less time and application than argument. But unless my knowledge of the duties of Christian Clergymen is very imperfect, they do not receive one-tenth of the produce of the soil in order that they may attack infidels by coarse and disgusting abuse, but that they may bring them back by gentle persuasion within the pale of the Church.

Wickliff

8. TOOKE'S THOUGHTS ON HIGH AND LOW PRICES [1]

GLOBE AND TRAVELLER, 4 MAR., 1823, P. 1

Thomas Tooke (1774-1858), another founding member of the Political Economy Club, became best known for his *History of Prices*, 6 vols. (1838-57). His *Thoughts and Details on the High and Low Prices of the Last Thirty Years* was published in London by Murray in 1823, with the Parts separately issued and paginated. This, Mill's first published review, appeared in two parts, both headed "*Thoughts and Details on the High and Low Prices of the Last Thirty Years,*" with subheadings for the first, "*Part 1.—On the Alterations in the Currency.* By Thomas Tooke, F.R.S.," and for the second (No. 12), "In Four Parts. Parts II, III, and IV. By Thomas Tooke, F.R.S." The first part was his first contribution to the newly amalgamated *Globe and Traveller*. The two-part unsigned review is described in Mill's bibliography as "A Notice of Part I of Mr. Tooke's work on High and Low Prices, which appeared in the Traveller of 4th March 1823" and "A notice of Part II of Mr. Tooke's work on High and Low Prices, which appeared in the Chronicle of 9th August 1823" (MacMinn, p. 2).

MR. TOOKE'S NEW WORK on the High and Low Prices of the last Thirty Years, promises to be of so great utility in furnishing answers to many of the usual fallacies, on what is called "the Agricultural Question," that we cannot devote our columns to a better purpose than that of giving a short outline of its contents. The questions, it is true, which regarded the operation of the Bank Restriction, and subsequently of Mr. Peel's Bill,[1] were settled long ago by general reasoning to the satisfaction of every thinking man. As, however, several well-intentioned, but mistaken individuals, have brought forward in opposition to conclusions borne out by the most convincing arguments, certain facts which they assert to be inconsistent with them, we think that Mr. Tooke has rendered a great service to the British public, in proving that of these facts, a great proportion are incorrect, and the remainder perfectly reconcileable to the results of general reasoning.

On the fluctuations of prices during the last thirty years, there are, says Mr. Tooke, two prevailing opinions. The one attributes the high prices wholly to the excess of paper, and the present low ones to the resumption of cash payments. The other ascribes the high prices wholly to the war, and the low ones to the transition from war to peace. The advocates of both opinions agree in attributing very little to the varieties of the seasons.

[1]37 George III, cc. 45, 91 (1797), known as the Bank Restriction Acts, and 59 George III, c. 49 (1819), introduced by Robert Peel (1788-1850), and known as Peel's Act.

These opinions Mr. T. considers as erroneous. He enumerates three principal causes of the variations in prices:—

1. Alterations in the currency; 2. War, and the return to peace; 3. Varieties of the seasons. [Pt. I, p. 4.] In the present volume, however, he confines himself to the first of these causes.

It is allowed on all hands that the Bank Restriction, by producing over-issues of paper, raised prices to the extent at least of the difference between the market and Mint prices of gold—that is, to the degree in which more paper was required to buy an ounce of gold than was equal to it in nominal amount. This difference, during the whole period from 1797 to 1814, never exceeded 20 per cent. on the average of three years, and during the first twelve years after the suspension of cash payments, averaged no more than about 4 per cent.

But it is a common opinion that the Bank Restriction was the cause, not only of a rise of prices to this extent, but of a much greater rise. There is no doubt that many commodities rose in price, not twenty per cent. merely, but as much as cent. per cent. To prove that this rise was owing to the Bank Restriction, and consequently the present low prices to the resumption of cash payments, three arguments are employed:—

1. That the value of the precious metals, in the commercial world, was lowered by the exportation of gold from England, in consequence of the Bank Restriction, and raised again by the re-importation produced by a return to a metallic currency. The value, therefore, of the currency varied more than is indicated by its fall relatively to gold, since gold itself had fallen in value.

2. That the compulsory paper system lowered the value of money by introducing expedients to economise the use of it, which was equivalent to an increase of its quantity.

3. That a progressive rise of prices accompanied a progressive increase of paper, which affords a strong presumption that the latter was the cause of the former.[2]

Mr. Tooke proceeds to examine these arguments.

The first he answers by showing that the quantity of gold set at liberty by the Bank Restriction was not sufficient to lower the value of gold above one per cent.; that this was compensated by the great demand for gold, for the use of the Continental armies, &c. That in like manner the drain of gold on the Continent, for re-importation into England, was compensated by the cessation of the extraordinary demand. These conclusions he further confirms by an adduction of facts relative to the value of precious metals in France. [Pt. I, pp. 21-42, and 212-15.]

[2]Pt. I, pp. 18-19; Tooke is expounding, in order to refute, the position of Edward Copleston (1776-1849), Provost of Oriel College and Bishop of Llandaff (one of the "several well-intentioned but mistaken individuals" Mill refers to above), in "State of the Currency," *Quarterly Review*, XXVII (July 1822), 239-67.

As to the second alleged effect, that of heightening the expedients for economising the circulating medium, Mr. T. admits that it took place; but he proves by conclusive arguments that it did not arise from the Bank Restriction; that, moreover, at the time when it occurred, and for some years after, the amount of currency was not increased, but diminished, while, from the increased money transactions of the country, the demand for currency was increased—two circumstances which fully compensated for the virtual increase of the circulating medium. The expedients for economising the currency are still in operation as before. If they had raised prices, they ought to have prevented them from falling. [Pt. I, pp. 43-50.]

The Bank Restriction is supposed to have further contributed to lower the value of money by increasing the issue of country paper, and thus substituting credit for currency. Mr. T. however, proves, that except to the degree indicated by the price of gold, the increase and diminution of country paper, which took place at various periods during the Restriction, were not simultaneous with the increase and diminution of Bank of England paper, and depended upon causes entirely different. [Pt. I, pp. 50-62.]

Mr. T. next considers the alleged connection between the Bank Restriction and a progressive rise of prices. In order to meet this assertion, he passes in review all the variations of prices which have taken place during the last 30 years: he shows that during the first seven years after the Bank Restriction, instead of a progressive rise, there was a decided fall in the price of corn: that the subsequent fluctuations were in no way dependent on the Bank Restriction, except to the degree indicated by the price of gold; but were referable to other causes. These are, the variations of the seasons, and the variations in the amount of private paper and credit, arising from speculation and over-trading; which Mr. Tooke also analyses, and refers to their real sources. [Pt. I, pp. 63-168.]

He then anticipates an objection, viz. that were it not for the Bank Restriction, these variations of private paper and credit would either not have taken place, or not to so great a degree.—Mr. T. however, proves, from the examples of Hamburg, the United States of America, and this country before the Bank Restriction, that great variations in private credit are by no means peculiar to a system of unconvertible paper money. [Pt. I, pp. 169-76.]

Finally, he inquires into the immediate cause of the present low prices, and shows that they are by no means lower than the excess of supply over demand, which is well ascertained to exist, will account for. [Pt. I, pp. 184-98.]

We must now take our leave of Mr. Tooke for the present; we shall take an early opportunity to resume the consideration of this important subject.[3] In the mean time, we earnestly recommend to such of our readers as desire to understand thoroughly the Agricultural and Currency questions, to peruse with attention this well-timed and highly-useful production.

[3]See No. 12.

9. THE DEBATE ON THE PETITION OF MARY ANN CARLILE

MORNING CHRONICLE, 9 MAY, 1823, P. 3

Mill's article is associated by him in the *Autobiography* with his letters on Free Discussion (Nos. 5-7): "a paper which I wrote soon after [them] on the same subject, *à propos* of a debate in the House of Commons, was inserted as a leading article" (*CW*, Vol. I, p. 91). The occasion was the debate, initiated by Joseph Hume (1777-1855), Radical M.P. and lifelong friend of James Mill, in speeches of 26 Mar., presenting the Petition of Mary Ann Carlile for Release from Imprisonment (*PD*, n.s., Vol. 8, cols. 709-16), and of 8 May, presenting the Petition of Richard Carlile Complaining of the Seizure of His Property (*ibid.*, Vol. 9, cols. 114-15). Richard Carlile complained that, as a result of the seizure of his goods, he was unable to pay his fine and was subject to perpetual imprisonment. Mary Ann Carlile (b. 1794), his sister, on the instigation of the Society for the Suppression of Vice, had been sentenced to one year's imprisonment and a fine of £500 for selling, in her brother's shop, a pamphlet, *An Appendix to the Theological Works of Thomas Paine.* Mill's first leading article, unheaded and anonymous as they are in all such journals, is described in his bibliography as "Observations on the debate concerning the petition of Mary Ann Carlile, which appeared as a leading article in the Chronicle of [9th May] 1823" (MacMinn, p. 2).

WE ARE NOT OF THE NUMBER of those who have no praise but for the times that are past. We think, on the contrary, the present time, on the whole, better than any former time. There are, for instance, unquestionably a much greater number of intelligent and enlightened men in this country now than it has ever contained at any former period. But while we willingly admit the general superiority of the age, we are not blind to its defects. There is, in particular, one feature belonging to it which we cannot contemplate with satisfaction. We allude to the mental cowardice which prevents men from giving expression to their conviction, and the insincerity which leads them to express what they do not think. A certain assembly has fully its share of this want of singleness of heart and pusillanimity. No man who knows any thing of the world can listen for any length of time to the language used in the assembly in question, without perceiving that the fear of offending in this quarter, and the desire to please in that, rather than conscientious conviction, too often actuates the speakers. There are certainly some distinguished exceptions, who scorn to sacrifice on the altar of timidity or machiavelism, and of these we think Mr. Hume unquestionably one. The unshrinking firmness with which he grapples with the subjects that come before him, without turning to the right hand or the left, has indeed not been lost, either on the country or on the House. We doubt, for instance, whether another Member of any standing in the House could have been found to present and enforce the Petition from Mary Ann Carlile which he brought forward some weeks ago, though the grounds on which he supported that Petition were such as to make a strong impression on the House, and a still stronger on the country. But taking counsel only from his own conscience, being actuated by a sincere desire to rescue that religion of which we deem him a sincere believer and friend, from the odium which false or less judicious friends were throwing on it, and listening to the counsel of the most eminent advocates of Christianity, the most illustrious ornaments of the Church of England, when its higher places were not deemed the almost exclusive portion of the Nobility, he hesitated not to raise his voice in favour of equal law and free discussion, which were wounded in the case of this individual. The result proved, that it was a mere phantom, at which others had taken fright, and the advocates of persecution and of partiality were found unequal to a contest which only exposed them to ridicule.

Last night he presented a Petition from Richard Carlile, an individual whom an injudicious activity has of late brought so much into notice. Alluding to the prejudices against this man, he stated as the result of his inquiries respecting him, that "he was one of the best moral characters in England," that "his religious opinion might differ from that of some other persons, but that that did not affect his moral character; and he would dare any one to contradict him, when he said that as a husband, as a father, as head of a family, and as a neighbour, Mr. Carlile might challenge calumny itself."[1] This was cheered by the Ministerial Benches, not probably because they who cheered knew whether Carlile was a moral or immoral man, but because they thought Mr. Hume had got on ticklish ground, by allowing the probability of a notorious infidel being moral. But we are not to hold religion in less esteem, when we find that faith does not uniformly produce good works, any more than we are to deem it unnecessary to the support of morality, because we find occasionally moral individuals without a due sense of religion. "An unbeliever [says Bishop Sanderson], awed sometimes by the law of natural conscience, may manifest much simplicity and integrity of heart; and the true child of God, swayed sometimes with the law of sinful concupiscence, may bewray much foul hypocrisie and infidelity."[2] It is only injuring the cause of religion to attribute more either to it, or to the absence of it, than is consistent with the truth; and the most respectable Christian writers, though they justly observe that religion and honesty are most frequently found together, are ready at the same time to allow that they are sometimes found separate. We never for instance heard it questioned that Mr. Owen of New Lanark is a very moral man.[3] On the other hand, we have doubts whether M. de Chateaubriand was a much more honest man when he brought water from the River Jordan for the baptism of the King of Rome, or is so even now, than when "shocked at the abuse of some of the Institutions of Christianity and at the vices

[1]Hume, speech of 8 May, 1823, col. 114.

[2]Robert Sanderson (1587-1663), Bishop of Lincoln, "The Sixth Sermon ad Populum" (1627), in *Fourteen Sermons Heretofore Preached* (London: Seile, 1657), p. 342.

[3]Robert Owen (1771-1858), an acquaintance of James Mill's, socialist and free-thinker, whose experiments in improving the environment and providing incentives for his employees at his mills in New Lanark were increasingly favourably publicized.

of some of its professors, he suffered himself to be misled by sophistry and gave way to declamation."[4]

It is curious to see what very different notions have prevailed on this subject within a comparatively short period. Addison thought Catholicism worse than infidelity, because the former was incompatible with morality, while the latter was not.[5] Bishop Sanderson seemed to think the Atheists, whom he supposed to be more numerous than either Papists or Sectaries, principally dangerous from the possibility of their joining the Catholics.

Neither, [says he,] will the supposed (and I fear truly supposed) greater number of Atheists, than either Papists or Sectaries, be any hinderance to the Papists for finally prevailing. Because it is not for the interest of the Atheist and his religion (pardon the boldness of the catachresis) to engage either for or against any side farther than a jeer, but to let them fight it out, keep himself quiet till they have done, and then clap in with him that getteth the day. He that is of no religion can make a shift to be of any rather than suffer. And the Atheist, though he be in truth and in heart neither Protestant nor Papist, nor any thing else; yet can he be in face and outward comportment either Protestant or Papist, or any thing else (Jew or Turk, if need be) as will best serve his present turn.[6]

If Catholicism were incompatible with morality, we should be rather in an awkward plight in the present day, for notwithstanding the aid which infidelity has received of late by the publicity given to it at the expence of the Constitutional Association,[7] we suspect (so much has Atheism gone down since the worthy Bishop's time), that the Atheists are now less numerous than even the Priests of the Catholics, leaving out of the account the flocks. We say nothing of the number of the other sectaries, as this is a much sorer point than that of the number of Atheists, from which we believe no Church Establishment will ever be in much danger.

The question of last night, however, was not so much free discussion itself, as the injustice which had been committed under a sentence levelled against it. On the subject of the severity which had been displayed, Mr. Lennard forcibly

[4]The source of the quotation has not been identified. François René, vicomte de Chateaubriand (1768-1848), writer and statesman, in 1811 provided baptismal water for the christening of François Charles Joseph Bonaparte (Napoleon II), King of Rome (1811-32). As Minister of Foreign Affairs, Chateaubriand had recently been under attack in the English press for his defence of the French intervention in Spain. See *The Times*, 28 Feb., pp. 2-3, and 16 Apr., p. 4; and *Morning Chronicle*, 1 Mar., p. 3 (where there is reference to the episode of the Jordan water), and 5 May, p. 3.

[5]Joseph Addison (1672-1719), essayist and poet; see *The Spectator*, No. 459 (16 Aug., 1712), pp. 1-2.

[6]Sanderson, *Fourteen Sermons*, Preface, pp. xxxviii-xxxix.

[7]The Constitutional Association for Opposing the Progress of Disloyal and Seditious Principles, founded in January 1821, was supported by many aristocrats, including Henry Pelham Clinton, Duke of Newcastle; Sir John Sewell was its President. Operating virtually as a secret society, it instituted proceedings for libel (against Hone and Carlile, for instance); itself accused of illegality, it dissolved before the end of 1821.

observed "that the supporters of the Six Acts, having failed in their efforts to procure the punishment of perpetual banishment, as was contemplated, had still continued through the agency of the Judges to supply that deficiency by sentences which amounted to perpetual imprisonment."[8] Mr. Denman, indeed, offered an apology for the Judges that "had they been aware of the inability of Mr. Carlile to pay the fine at the time judgment was passed, he was sure they never would have passed it."[9] But this apology does not, at all events, apply to the case of Mary Ann Carlile, with respect to whose means to pay the fine imposed on her there never could be the smallest doubt.

Religion disclaims those who would advance her cause by the mean expedients to which Mr. Hume alluded last night. Let good ends be promoted by fair and upright means. The equal administration of law is due to the Infidel as well as to the Christian. Give not to the Infidel any advantage from your disgracing a good cause by disreputable means. In the words of Bishop Warburton, "Can any but an enthusiast believe that he may use guile to promote the glory of God—the wisdom from above is without partiality and without hypocrisy. Partiality consists in dispensing an unequal measure in our transactions with others: *hypocrisy in attempting to cover that unequal measure by prevarication and false pretences.*"[10] And in the words of a man less learned, perhaps, but not less upright than Bishop Warburton, we mean the worthy John Wesley, "no man living is authorised to break or dispensed with in breaking any law of morality."[11]

The discussions have done, and will do, good, and we trust Mr. Hume will return to the subject. The Courts of Law must profit by them. "Shame, albeit the daughter of sinne, becomes sometimes the mother of conversion; and when all good motions else seem mere strangers, this one is admitted as a profitable, though unwelcome guest."[12]

[8]Thomas Barrett Lennard (1788-1865), M.P. for Ipswich, Speech on the Petition of Richard Carlile (8 May, 1823), *PD*, n.s., Vol. 9, col. 116. The "Six Acts" are 60 George III & 1 George IV, cc. 1, 2, 4, 6, 8, and 9 (1819).

[9]Thomas Denman (1779-1854), M.P. for Nottingham (later Lord Chief Justice), Speech on the Petition of Richard Carlile, *PD*, n.s., Vol. 9, col. 116.

[10]Adapted from William Warburton, *The Doctrine of Grace* (1762), in *Works*, 12 vols. (London: Cadell and Davies, 1811), Vol. VIII, pp. 382, 383.

[11]John Wesley (1703-91), founder of Methodism, *A Letter to the Right Reverend the Lord Bishop of Gloucester* (London: n.p., 1763), p. 38.

[12]This quotation has not been located.

10. THE DEBATE ON EAST AND WEST INDIA SUGARS
GLOBE AND TRAVELLER, 7 JUNE, 1823, P. 3

This article was preceded by an editorial comment: "The following article on this question, from our Correspondent, has long been omitted for want of room. Though our Correspondent treats the interests of the West Indians rather cavalierly, the power of his arguments entitle [*sic*] him to attention." The delay was not very long, for the debate in the House of Commons took place on 22 May (*PD*, n.s., Vol. 9, cols. 444-67), just two days after Mill's seventeenth birthday, on which day he joined his father in the Examiner's Office of the East India Company (which was interested in East India sugar). The leading article, headed "East and West India Sugars," is described in Mill's bibliography as "Strictures on the Debate concerning East and West India sugars, which appeared in the Globe and Traveller of [7th June] 1823" (MacMinn, p. 2).

THE DEBATE IN THE HOUSE OF COMMONS, on Thursday the 22d ult., upon Mr. Whitmore's proposal for equalizing the duties on East and West India Sugar, is remarkable, not only for the able and argumentative speeches of Mr. Ricardo and Mr. Whitmore, but for the unprecedented exposure which their opponents made of the weakness of their cause.[1]

There are two arguments against the monopoly, either of which would be conclusive, but when combined, they are irresistible. One of these applies to this in common with all other monopolies, that they enhance the price to the consumer. The other argument applies peculiarly to the West India monopoly, that it perpetuates Negro Slavery.

To these arguments, no answer was or could be made. A cry, however, could be raised against them; and this has been done. The great objection of the West India Gentlemen to the abrogation of the monopoly is this: "IT WOULD RUIN US." Supposing this to be true, it accounts perfectly for their disapprobation of the measure; but it may not, perhaps, be so all-important a consideration in the eyes of the philosopher as it is in theirs. When a Government has made laws for the *protection* of a particular class—that is, laws to enable them to pillage the rest of the community for their own benefit, it can never happen that no expectations will be founded on those laws, no calculations bottomed upon their stability. This may be a reason for making the abrogation a gradual one; but it can never be a reason for allowing the nuisance to be perpetual, inasmuch as the interest of the

---

[1]William Wolryche Whitmore (1787-1858), M.P. for Bridgenorth, an advocate of free trade, Speech in Introducing a Motion on East and West India Sugars (22 May, 1823), *PD*, n.s., Vol. 9, cols. 444-56; David Ricardo, Speech on East and West India Sugars, *ibid.*, cols. 457-9. Mill's references and quotations are not identical to the reports in *PD*, but they are cited for ease of reference. The West India monopoly was established by 1 & 2 George IV, c. 106 (1821), and continued by 3 George IV, c. 106 (1822).

many is preferable to that of the few. No great reform can ever be effected without producing distress somewhere; and the greater the benefit the greater will be the distress. If the public has been robbed of a great advantage, to retard the ruin of the West India Planters, this advantage cannot be restored to the public without deeply affecting the interest of those Gentlemen. But if this were a reason for allowing the abuse which perpetuates Slavery to exist, there are few abuses for which as good an argument might not be found.

In point of fact, however, it is not by the rejection of Mr. Whitmore's motion, that the ruin can be averted which has so long been impending over our Sugar Colonies. It is not many years since the whole continent of Europe was supplied with Sugar from the West Indies. Our Colonies not only possessed a monopoly of the English market, but furnished a large supply for re-exportation. These were the days of West Indian prosperity. But for some time past, the Continent of Europe has derived by far the greater part of its supply from other sources; and the price of Sugar on the Continent has fallen below the lowest rate at which the West Indies could supply it. Excluded thus from the Continental market, colonial Sugar experienced an unexampled depression of price, which was further enhanced by the influx from Demerara and the other newly-acquired Colonies.

This depression must be permanent, or can be remedied only by the removal of a large capital from the production of Sugar to other employments: for at present our Colonies produce and send annually to market a far greater quantity than the consumption of England requires. Hence it is that Mr. Marryatt had to present a petition from a body of Planters in Trinidad, "who did not derive one shilling of profit from four hundred thousand pounds of capital which they had invested, but, on the contrary, sustained considerable losses from the depression in the price of Colonial produce."[2] At present, therefore, as Mr. Ricardo has justly observed, the admission of East India produce would not enhance the distress, for the price is already as low as it would be if the competition were open.[3] But it would do what is of equal importance; it would prevent Sugar from ever rising again to a monopoly price. To reject a measure from its tendency to lower the price of Sugar, when Sugar is at a losing price, and cannot for many years be expected to rise again, might only tend to delude the West India Planters by false hopes, and aggravate their distress by disappointment.

The minor objections of the West India Gentlemen are to the last degree futile. It is scarcely necessary to give more than a bare statement of them.

As for instance—Mr. Ellis says that by acquiring new colonies we pledged

---

[2]Joseph Marryatt (1758-1824; referred to in *PD* as James Marryatt), M.P. for Sandwich, colonial agent for Grenada and Trinidad, Speech on East and West India Sugars, *PD*, n.s., Vol. 9, cols. 460-1.
[3]*Ibid.*, cols. 458-9.

ourselves to support the colonial system.[4] This is to say, that if we ever were ignorant enough to think Colonies an advantage, and to act upon that persuasion, we thereby pledge ourselves never to correct our errors.

For another specimen of this Gentleman's mode of arguing, he tells us that it is unjust to deprive the Colonies of their peculiar advantages, unless, at the same time, we take off the peculiar restrictions under which they labour.[5] This is not a reason for leaving both evils, but for taking them both away. The monopoly is an evil; the restrictions are another, and a very great evil. There is nothing which we more ardently desire than to get rid of both. But, according to Mr. Ellis, we are to retain the one evil on its own account, and the other because it would be unjust to take it away and leave the former alone.

Another argument of a similar stamp was used by Mr. Marryatt—namely, that the East India Company is a monopoly: "Gentlemen who deprecated monopoly, with the profits of monopoly in their pockets, would be much better employed in declaiming against it in Leadenhall-street than in that House."[6] And why not in both? Should the existence of one evil secure another from attack? Nay, more—if we can obtain the co-operation in destroying one evil, even of those who profit by the other, why should we not gratefully accept of it? Evils would seldom be removed if those who attack them were to refuse all aid but from persons who agree in all their opinions.

It is worthy of remark, that while Mr. Ellis opposes the admission of East India Sugar, because too much would come, Mr. Robertson opposes it because no Sugar would come at all. If we may believe him, the East Indies are not only incapable of exporting Sugar—they are even under the necessity of importing it.[7] Be it so. Mr. Ellis's alarm, then, is ill-founded; and there is no danger of ruining the Colonies by granting a permission of which no use can be made. We desire no more than a fair trial. But Mr. Robertson, in his wisdom, has discovered, that "the consumers of this country would be materially injured."[8] How injured? By purchasing their Sugar too cheap? But they desire no better than to be injured in this way. By being forced to pay too high a price for it? But how can this be, when, at the worst, they can obtain it from the West Indies at the same price as before!

It would appear that the West India Gentlemen differ in every thing else, and agree only in condemning the proposed measure. While Mr. Robertson contends

[4]Charles Rose Ellis (1771-1845), M.P. for Seaford, head of the West Indian interest, Speech on East and West India Sugars, *ibid.*, cols. 453-4.

[5]*Ibid.*, col. 452.

[6]*Ibid.*, cols. 459-60. The offices of the East India Co. were in Leadenhall Street.

[7]Alexander Robertson (d. 1856), M.P. for Grampound, Speech on East and West India Sugars, *ibid.*, col. 456.

[8]*Ibid.*

that do what we will we can never get an ounce of Sugar from the East Indies, Mr. Marryatt thinks that the admission of East India Sugars would "lead to so general a growth of Sugars, as must prove highly injurious, by glutting the markets both here and on the Continent."[9] It is the ruined West India Planters, we suppose, who are thus all on a sudden to extend their cultivation. Or if the glut is to come from the East Indies, this proves that—in the opinion, at least, of Mr. Marryatt—Sugar can be grown cheaper in the East Indies than in the West.—We would recommend to this Gentleman the propriety of imposing restrictions upon the trade of making shoes, with a view to prevent a glut of that article. To whom is this glut, as it is called, injurious? To the consumer? No; to him it is a benefit. To the producer? But it is quite evident that the East India cultivator can never permanently sell his Sugar below the price which will repay the cost of production with the ordinary profit. And the consumer would be greatly injured if he could sell it higher. If, indeed, a merchant has a stock of Sugar on sale, the proposed measure may be injurious to him. But why? Simply because it lowers the price, and benefits the consumer. Mr. Marryatt's reasoning would go to prevent all improvements in agriculture or manufactures. There is none of these which does not cause a "glut"—that is, lower the price to the consumer.

Mr. K. Douglas treats the subject as if it were a question of charity. The Sugar Trade can be "no object" either to the Hindoos or the British residents. Mr. Whitmore has proved conclusively, that, far from being no object, it is among the greatest of objects to the East Indies.[10] Suppose, however, that it really were "no object" to the natives or British residents, unfortunately for the argument of Mr. Douglas, there is a third class of persons—namely, the consumers. What should we think if we were compelled to buy hats or shoes, not where we could get them best or cheapest, but where it is the greatest "object" to the seller?

We are informed by Mr. Ellis and Mr. Marryatt, that the "mercantile marine of the West Indies, contributed to support the naval power of Great Britain."[11] We had thought that the day for this sort of cant was gone by; that even in the House of Commons, at this time of day, the mention of the Navigation Laws[12] would excite a laugh. Surely no one can now be deceived by it. Can any one seriously think it possible, that a country rich and commercial like Great Britain, can labour under so great a deficiency of ships and seamen, that it should be

---

[9]These remarks seem to have been made not by Marryatt, but by William Robert Keith Douglas (1783-1859), M.P. for Dumfries Burghs, 1812-32, in his Speech on East and West India Sugars, *ibid.*, col. 455.

[10]*Ibid.*, cols. 446-8.

[11]See Ellis, *ibid.*, col. 453; Marryatt, *ibid.*, col. 460.

[12]See 3 George IV, c. 44 (1822) and, for the earlier navigation laws, 12 Charles II, c. 18 (1660), and 15 Charles II, c. 7 (1663).

necessary for her to continue a branch of commerce where there is not only no gain, but an actual loss, merely for the purpose of having a nursery for seamen! Who can doubt that even if the West India commerce were to cease altogether, the ships and seamen now employed by it would speedily find employment in bringing from the East Indies what they formerly brought from the West! For the longer voyage, indeed, more ships and seamen would be required; and if they be Lascars, what then?—Are not Lascars as good as any other seamen?

Mr. Ellis, moreover, tells us that the proposed measure would deprive the negroes of employment.[13] Can any thing more effectually deprive them of employment, than the present unexampled, but permanent, depression of price? Waiving, however, this consideration, the calamity with which we are menaced by Mr. Ellis is no calamity, but one of the greatest of blessings. We desire nothing more than that the negroes should be without employment. It is the prelude to their final emancipation. What was impracticable when the labour of negroes produced an abundant profit, will be easy when they are a dead weight about the necks of their employers. This alone would be far more than a counterpoise to the most terrific evil which could befal a few West India Planters. They could scarcely be put in a worse condition than their own slaves.

That Mr. Ellis, or any of his supporters, should talk rather unwisely, can be matter of surprise to no one; but we confess we did not expect to hear such a sentence as the following from the mouth of Mr. Huskisson: "If it was true that the production of slavery was more costly than that of free labour, that would be an additional reason for not depriving him [the slave holder] of the advantage of his protecting duty."[14] That is, the greater the mischief the greater the reward. What! is it not enough that we should be compelled to fee the planter for employing slaves? Must the fee be even *greater* because that kind of labour is not only cruel but unproductive? Is he to be rewarded not only for doing evil, but for going out of his way to do it?

To crown all, Mr. Douglas thinks, that "a great deal of mischief is likely to result from the frequent agitation of this question."[15] What a speech for a legislator! We remember that when a cry was first raised against the abominations of the Slave Trade—when benevolent Philanthropists, both in and out of Parliament, lifted up their voices, for a long time unsuccessfully, in earnest reprobation of that atrocious traffic—then too we were warned of the "mischief which was likely to result from the frequent agitation of this

[13] Ellis, speech of 22 May, col. 453.
[14] Speech on East and West India Sugars, *ibid.*, cols. 464-5, by William Huskisson (1770-1830), M.P. for Liverpool, Treasurer of the Navy and President of the Board of Trade (1823-27), advocate of free trade.
[15] Cf. Douglas, *ibid.*, col. 456.

question."[16] The slave-owners, indeed, felt, very deservedly, the mischief which resulted to *them* from it. But we have learned to be suspicious of those questions from the agitation of which mischief ensues.

To conclude—this debate is a striking exemplification of the evils arising from the present constitution of the House of Commons. On one side are liberal principles—the interest of the consumer, and above all, the interest of the slave, for which so many Members express unbounded zeal, and which all affect to consider of supreme importance—on the other side is the personal interest of a few West India Planters and Merchants—personal interest and *nothing more*. There are few evils at all comparable in magnitude to this, and the removal of which, at the present moment, would produce so little suffering; yet personal interest carries the day by a majority of 161 to 34.

It has been urged as an objection against plans for giving the people a control over their Representatives, that the people would certainly be in error on certain questions of political economy. On some, perhaps, they might, though even this is doubtful; but in a case like the present, where the contest is between liberal principles and the interest of a small number of individuals, the worst enemies of the people cannot affirm that they would be in error. Yet, on such questions, the House of Commons almost uniformly goes wrong; and there can be no doubt that personal interest, if it does not immediately dictate the vote, at least prevents the voter from applying his mind so as to understand the subject, and leaves him, even when well-intentioned, to the artful guidance of an interested Minister.

11. JUDICIAL OATHS
MORNING CHRONICLE, 25 JULY, 1823, P. 3

This letter was occasioned by the assize report in the *Morning Chronicle*, 22 July, p. 4, under the heading "Worcester, July 18th (Last Day.) / Before Mr. Justice Park. / Forgery," of the trial of Thomas Pidgeon, a cattle dealer, for forgery, before James Alan Park (1763-1838). Headed as title and subheaded "To the Editor of the Morning Chronicle," the letter is described in Mill's bibliography as "A letter on Judicial Oaths, signed *No Lawyer*, which appeared in the Chronicle of 23d [*sic*] July 1823" (MacMinn, p. 2).

SIR,—In your paper of Tuesday, 22d July, I see a new instance of the mode in which the ends of justice are frustrated by the useless and demoralising, not to say unchristian, ceremony of an oath.

---

[16]See James Baillie (ca. 1737-93), M.P. for Horsham and agent for Grenada, Speech on the Slave Trade (2 Apr., 1792), in *Parliamentary History of England*, ed. William Cobbett and John Wright, 36 vols. (London: Bagshaw, Longmans, 1806-20), Vol. XXIX, col. 1074.

An individual who was capitally indicted for presenting a forged check to a Quaker clerk in the banking-house of Whitehead and Co. at Shipston-upon-Stour, was acquitted from the insufficiency of evidence; the Judge, however, appearing convinced that if the scruples of the Quakers had permitted them to give evidence upon oath, the prisoner would in all probability have been convicted.

The express prohibition of oaths, which we find in the Gospel, couched in the emphatic words "Swear not at all,"[1] has been disregarded, on the ground of expediency, under the supposition that our Saviour could never have intended to prohibit oaths, in any case where they could be proved to be expedient.

To the general principle of this assumption I cannot object, as it would be impiety to ascribe to our Saviour any injunction, the observance of which is not consistent with that greatest of blessings, a good administration of justice. I have noticed the assumption merely to shew, that if oaths can be justified, it must be on the ground of expediency, and if they cannot be supported on this ground, they ought to be abolished altogether.

Now it has long been recognised by all men of understanding, that an honest man's word is as good as his oath. And the same may be said of a rogue. But it has been supposed that between these extremes there is a middle point; that some who are sunk low enough in guilt to have lost all compunction at simple mendacity, still retain a degree of reverence for the ceremony of an oath.

It is well known that public opinion sets more strongly against the violation of an oath, than against that of a simple affirmation; and what if this circumstance should be adequate to account for the difference in the binding force of the two engagements?

When several motives co-operate in producing a given line of action, and when it is desired to ascertain which of the given causes contributes most to their joint effect, there is, I apprehend, only one course to be pursued. The several motives are to be observed when acting separately, and the effects are to be compared which each of them produces, when divested of the co-operating inducements.

When I apply this analytic process to the two sanctions, that of an oath, and that of public opinion, I find the latter continually producing effects of the most tremendous magnitude—I find men readily marching up to the cannon's mouth in the pursuit of public esteem and applause; but if I consider the ceremony of an oath when disjoined from the co-operating force of public opinion, I find it utterly disregarded, without the hesitation of a moment.

Of this, one of the most remarkable examples is that of Custom-house oaths. It is well known that the individuals who are sent with goods to the Custom-house, swear readily to their nature and amount, without having ever opened the chests

---

[1]Matthew, 5:33-5. Taken by Bentham as the title of his anti-oath tract, *"Swear not at all,"* from which Mill derived this and other references; see No. 6.

in which they are contained. In Scotland, a country where the religious spirit certainly is not deficient, a law once existed, which imposed higher duties upon French than upon Spanish wine. The inconveniences of this law were soon felt; public opinion ceased to enforce its observation, and we are told by Lord Kaimes that it was constantly evaded by all who were interested in doing so, through the simple expedient of swearing the French wine to be Spanish.[2] The statutes of the University of Oxford, which were drawn up by Archbishop Laud, contain a variety of regulations of a frivolous and harassing nature.[3] These statutes, all the students swear to observe; but from their absurdity, they are not supported by public opinion; accordingly they are openly violated, not on some occasions merely, but whenever their observance involves the most trifling sacrifice either of ease or of pleasure. Who, then, will venture to assert that the binding force of oaths can be ascribed to the religious obligation? The religious part of the ceremony is not more binding in a judicial, than in a Custom-house oath. But in the former case the obligation is enforced by public opinion; in the latter it is not: accordingly, in the one case it is openly violated; in the other it is observed.

Since then the ceremony does not contribute in any degree to secure the veracity of witnesses, it may be, and ought to be, abolished. Nor is this profanation of the name of God frivolous only and nugatory, it is productive of many very serious mischiefs. Of these I shall instance only one, but that one is of unspeakable importance; whenever an oath is part of the formalities of a judicial affirmation, people soon learn to consider it as the binding part. When Judges charge the jury, or address the prisoner in cases of perjury, they take no notice of the misery which he has in all probability occasioned, the ruin possibly of many individuals—they do not remind him that he has done all which depended upon him to poison the fountain of security and happiness to the people, by frustrating the ends of judicature, by causing the acquittal of a guilty, or the punishment of an innocent individual. It is not from these circumstances that they draw the aggravation, or even the original criminality of the offence. No; it is because he has forsworn himself before the Deity—it is because he has disregarded the awful name of God, that he is guilty and deserving of punishment; a reason equally applicable to the blasphemous exclamations of dustmen and coalheavers in the streets, and tending to place these trivial indiscretions on a level with the most pernicious, without exception, of all crimes—judicial perjury.

Such being the style in which the obligation of judicial veracity is spoken of by the Judges themselves—the people soon learn to consider the profanation of the religious ceremony as the principal part of the crime. This cannot increase their

[2]Henry Home, Lord Kames (1696-1782), Scottish judge and author, *Sketches of the History of Man*, 2 vols. (Edinburgh: Creech, 1774), Vol. I, pp. 480-1. Kames was Scottish, but the Act (as he himself says) was British: 7 & 8 William III, c. 20 (1696).
[3]For background, see No. 6.

detestation of mendacity, when aggravated by perjury: but it greatly diminishes their abhorrence of the same offence, whenever the ceremony of an oath has been omitted. Examine the cases in which judicial evidence is taken, without the aid of an oath; and if you find mendacity, in those instances, more frequent, you cannot ascribe it to the absence of the religious ceremony, which the Custom-house and University oaths prove to be wholly void of influence; but you must necessarily attribute this lamentable effect to the demoralizing influence of judicial oaths, which, by diverting the minds of men from the real to the nominal guilt, greatly diminish the horror with which false evidence, as such, would otherwise be regarded.

Mr. Justice Park, with his accustomed liberality, took occasion from the trial in question to inveigh against the prejudices of the Quakers. I myself, Sir, am no Quaker; but I think that a man to whom justice is thus denied, because he will not violate what he considers to be his duty, deserves more tender treatment, at the hands at least of Mr. Justice Park, and might fairly retort the accusation of prejudice upon his Lordship, who is willing thus openly to frustrate the ends of justice, for the preservation of a frivolous, nugatory, and demoralizing ceremony.

The absurdity of the exclusion is recognised by the law itself, since Quakers are admitted, in civil cases, to give evidence by simple affirmation.[4] The law does not presume that on a civil action, a Quaker will give false evidence, because he will not profane the name of God; why should it set up a contrary presumption in criminal cases, where the accused party having more at stake, a conscientious man (and the Quakers are generally speaking the most conscientious of all religious sects) would be, if possible, more cautious than ever in giving his evidence? It is absurd to suppose that criminal cases are either of more importance, or more exposed to the danger of perjury, than civil ones. A cause where the whole earthly resources, perhaps, of innumerable families concerned may well compete in importance with a prosecution for stealing a cow or a sheep. And where the interests at stake are equal, the motives to perjury are the same.

In the instance of Quakers, and in all similar instances, it has been well remarked by Mr. Ricardo, in his able speech in favour of free discussion, that the presumption of veracity is not weaker, but stronger, from the very circumstance of their not consenting to violate what they conceive to be a sacred duty of the highest order.[5]

I am, Sir, yours, with the greatest respect,
No Lawyer.

[4]For background, see No. 6.
[5]Ricardo, Speech on Free Discussion (1 July, 1823), *PD*, n.s., Vol. 9, cols. 1386-91, 1399.

12. TOOKE'S THOUGHTS ON HIGH AND LOW PRICES [2]
MORNING CHRONICLE, 9 AUG., 1823, P. 3

For the context, heading, and entry in Mill's bibliography for this second half of a two-part review, see No. 8.

IT WILL BE REMEMBERED that we have already noticed the First Part of this well-timed and highly useful production.[1] The remaining Three Parts are now before the public.

Three opinions prevail concerning the circumstances which occasioned the prosperity of the Agricultural Classes during the interval from 1792 to 1812, and their distress during the greater part of the ten years which followed that period.

By Mr. Western, Mr. Attwood, and their followers, the prosperity of the agriculturists is attributed to the depreciation of the currency, and their distress to the resumption of cash payments.[2] By another class of reasoners, the high prices are attributed to the operation of the war—the low prices to the transition from war to peace. There is still another opinion, that the variations of prices were owing to circumstances of temporary operation, principally to the vicissitudes of the seasons.

In Part I of his work, published a few months since, Mr. Tooke gave a detailed examination of the opinion which attributes the high and low prices to the variations in the amount of the currency. He undertook to prove that these variations could not affect prices to any greater extent than was indicated by the difference in value between paper and gold. In support of this assertion, he first adduced general reasoning, which alone sufficed to prove the absurdity of attributing to depreciation any greater effect: but as there are many, who, not being capable of comprehending general reasoning, are inclined to regard it with distrust, Mr. Tooke fortified his position by a statement of facts, proving conclusively that during the last 30 years enhancement of prices was seldom, if ever, coincident with increase in the issues of Bank paper, but was sometimes coincident with a diminution. To attribute, therefore, any considerable part of the

[1]Mill's form of words is odd, since this review is in the *Morning Chronicle*, while the earlier one (No. 8) was in the *Globe and Traveller*, and neither was reprinted in the other paper.
[2]See, e.g., *Observations on the Speech of the Right Hon. W. Huskisson* (London: Ridgway, *et al.*, 1823), by Charles Callis Western (1767-1844), M.P. for Essex, writing in reply to Huskisson, Speech on Resumption of Cash Payments (11 June, 1822), *PD*, n.s., Vol. 7, cols. 897-925; and *A Letter to the Right Honourable Nicholas Vansittart, on the Creation of Money, and on Its Action upon National Prosperity* (Birmingham: Wrightson, 1817), and *Prosperity Restored; or, Reflections on the Cause of the Public Distresses, and on the Only Means of Relieving Them* (London: Baldwin, *et al.*, 1817), by Thomas Attwood (1783-1856), banker, economic and political reformer.

enhancement to depreciation, is inconsistent not only with principle, but with facts—not only with general, but with specific experience.

In Part II just published, Mr. T. proceeds to the examination of the doctrine which attributes the high prices to the effect of war, and the subsequent fall to the transition from war to peace.

Two questions here arise. First—Whether the taxation attending a state of war is calculated to raise prices? Next—How far prices can be affected by war, through the medium of supply and demand?

First, as to taxation. [Pt. II, pp. 1-6.] Direct taxes, such as an income tax, if equally levied upon all classes, are never supposed to affect prices. Taxes levied upon particular commodities will usually raise the prices of those commodities, but there is never any reason why they should raise general prices, while, under some circumstances, they may lower them. If the commodities taxed be the instruments of production, the effect upon prices will vary according to circumstances. If, for instance, the taxes apply equally, or nearly equally, to all branches of industry, they cannot raise prices; but, if they are laid on the instruments of production of some particular article, and not of others, that article must advance in price.

From this analysis of the influence of taxation upon prices, it appears that the high range of general prices during the war cannot be attributed to taxation. To this argument Mr. T. adds a further confirmation, by the fact, that with the exception of the Income Tax, the amount of taxation (including Land Tax, Tithe and Poor-rate,) down to last summer was as great as during the war. [P. 4.] If therefore taxation had raised prices, taxation must have prevented them from falling.

Independently of taxation war could have raised prices only by creating demand, or by obstructing supply.

Those who affirm that war increased demand, think that the whole of the extra government expenditure creates a new source of demand; that not only the prices of naval and military stores are raised, but that the additional consumption of fleets and armies must raise the price of food; that the demand for soldiers and sailors must raise wages; also the increased demand for manufactures to supply fleets and armies must farther raise wages, and thus increase the consumption by the labouring classes, &c.

This would be true if the extra government expenditure consisted of new funds; but these reasoners forget that what is consumed by government comes out of the pockets of the people, and would by them have been expended in the purchase of labour and commodities. In this way, therefore, war cannot raise prices. It can only raise those commodities which are the objects of sudden demand, such as naval and military stores, and these only until the supply has accommodated itself to the demand.

Accordingly, it appears that for 100 years previous to 1793, exclusively of taxed or imported commodities, and naval or military stores, there was as low a range of prices during war as during peace. This Mr. T. proves by a table of prices. [Pp. 14-20.]—Wheat, indeed, was at a lower price during the expensive war preceding the peace of Aix-la-Chapelle[3] than during any other part of the whole period from 1688 to 1792.

Besides, it is notorious that the consumption of food has been considerably increased during the low prices since the peace. It is not, therefore, extra consumption which raised prices during the war, since in that case it would have prevented them from falling during the peace.

It has also been contended, that prices were greatly affected by the monopoly which, from our ascendancy at sea, the war conferred on our trade. But the very articles which were the subject of that monopoly were more depressed in 1810 and 1812, than they have been either before or since. An ordinary monopoly raises prices by limiting the supply; but the supply of Colonial produce, and the other commodities which were the objects of our exclusive trade, was greatly increased during the war, while it was only the export of them which was restricted. The price therefore fell.

Mr. Tooke next considers to what extent war may have operated in raising prices by limiting the supply. [Pp. 47-61.]

This it may have done, either by a diminution of reproduction or by impeding commerce. Now although the tendency of war is to diminish production, no one asserts that the country has retrograded during the war: production cannot, therefore, have been actually diminished. The only mode in which the war can have affected supply must have been by impeding commerce. And it is certain that by enhancing greatly the cost of importation, it did operate to raise the prices of imported commodities. In ordinary years, however, we never imported agricultural produce. War, therefore, could raise agricultural prices only by preventing relief from abroad, to that scarcity which was produced by other causes at home.

Mr. T. therefore concludes that war could affect prices only in as far as it obstructed importation, and created a demand for naval and military stores. [Pp. 58-60.] It is therefore wholly inadequate to account for the high range of prices during the 20 years following 1793.

Part III is devoted to the examination of that opinion which attributes principally to the vicissitudes of the season the great variations in prices during the last ten years. [Pt. III, pp. 9-48.] This opinion Mr. T. has, we think, proved to be perfectly correct, and adequate to the explanation of all the phenomena of prices.

He furnishes a concise character of every season from 1688 to 1792 inclusive, from which it appears, that during that time good and bad seasons occurred as it

[3]The peace, established 18 Oct., 1748, ended the War of the Austrian Succession.

were in clusters, thus producing ranges of high and low prices, which lasted not a few years merely, but for considerable periods.

From 1686 to 1691, prices gradually declined, producing considerable agricultural distress. But in 1692 began a series of seven very bad seasons, which raised prices to an unusually high level. On the whole, from 1692 to 1713 there were no fewer than twelve years of bad or indifferent produce, and consequent high prices. From 1730 to 1739, on the contrary, there was not one decidedly bad season. Accordingly wheat was low. The winter of 1739-1740 was very severe; and the following harvest was bad, which produced a considerable rise, but from 1741 to 1751, were ten abundant seasons. Again, from 1765 to 1776, bad seasons frequently recurred, both in this country and on the continent. From 1776 to 1782, the seasons appear to have been favourable, because with an increased and increasing population, the produce was sufficient for the consumption.—From 1782 to 1792 inclusive, there was a large proportion of severe winters and backward springs, and with the exception of 1791, not one very abundant season. Now, it appears, that during these 105 years, in all the periods when bad seasons were comparatively frequent, Corn was permanently at a high price, and during the periods when they were rare, it was uniformly low.

The analogy of this long period affords reason to conjecture that the high and low prices from 1792 to 1822, may be attributed to similar causes. This is what Mr. Tooke proceeds to establish by a minute character of the seasons during the last thirty years. [Pp. 49-86.][4]

The harvest of 1793 was barely an average, and that of 1794 was deficient, which, combined with unfavourable prospects for the following year, raised prices very high; but the Government sent agents to buy corn in the Baltic, and the harvest of 1795 turning out better than had been expected, prices declined. They followed the variations of the seasons until 1799, when two very bad harvests raised them to an enormous height. On the whole, from 1793 to 1800 inclusive, there were four very bad, and only two good crops, with four very severe winters, producing increased consumption. This surely accounts for a permanence of high prices during all this period.

Three tolerable harvests, with a small importation, lowered prices, and produced agricultural distress. But the six seasons from 1807 to 1812 were all deficient, at a time when the difficulties of importation were very great. On a general review of the whole period of twenty years from 1793 to 1812, there were eleven more or less deficient, six of average produce, and three only of abundant crops. Surely it does not require the supposition of an extra war demand, or a depreciation of the currency beyond the difference between paper and gold, to account for high prices during these 20 years.

[4]Tooke actually covers 1783-1821.

If prices had risen only in proportion to the deficiency of produce, then the farmer and the landlord, while they would have suffered as consumers, would not have gained as agriculturists by the rise. But when the necessaries of life are concerned, prices always rise more than in proportion to the deficiency. The Agricultural classes, therefore, gained by the high prices, and concluding their gains to be permanent, they applied much new capital to the land, thereby increasing the quantity of produce, and aggravating their distress when low prices returned.

Of the nine seasons, from 1813 to 1821 inclusive, one only, that of 1816, was bad, while three were very abundant, and five of fair average produce. Comparing these with the nine years preceding, the difference of produce is abundantly sufficient to account for a great difference of price. As, when the produce was scanty, the price rose; so, when it was abundant, the price fell in a greater proportion than was indicated by the variation in the amount of produce. The Agriculturists, who before gained, now lost by the state of prices. There can, therefore, be no difficulty in accounting for the prosperity of Agriculture during the first twenty years, and for its depression during the last ten of the period from 1792 to 1822, from the vicissitudes of the seasons.

It may be objected that the lowest prices sometimes coincide with the smallest stock for sale, and the highest prices with the largest stocks. This may occasionally happen, but Mr. T. has shewn that it is perfectly reconcilable with the principles which he has laid down. [Pt. III, pp. 87-112; Pt. IV, pp. 4-10.] Demand and supply, as affecting prices, are either actual or prospective. If the supply on hand has been under-rated, more especially if one or more seasons of increased supply should follow, they who have bought before the fall of price, find that they would have done better to postpone their demand, and fearing a still greater fall, they think it their interest not to buy more than they can help in advance.

Thus [says Mr. T.] although the supply may, in consequence of long protracted discouragement, be falling off, that part of the demand which consists in the anticipation of future want, falls off in a still greater degree, till both reach their minimum; the consumption all the time going on at its wonted rate, or more probably increasing in consequence of cheapness; and in such cases it may be only when the stock is at length discovered to be below the immediate want for actual consumption, while fresh supplies are remote or uncertain, that any decided improvement takes place. (Part IV, pp. 8-9.)

In general, Mr. Tooke remarks, that after a glut has been once fully established, it cannot be carried off without a "period of falling prices and diminishing supplies, till it may so happen, though perhaps rarely, that the lowest prices and the smallest stocks may coincide." (P. 9.)

Mr. Tooke subjoins a table of the prices of various commodities, from 1782 to 1822, with explanations, from which it appears that the difference in the relative proportions of supply and demand is quite sufficient to account for the fluctuations in price. [Appendix No. 1 to Pt. IV, pp. 1-69.] Mr. T. has thus the merit of having solved a number of the phenomena of prices, which Gentlemen both in and out of Parliament have frequently quoted, to prove the fallaciousness of the doctrines of political economy. Mr. T. has shewn, that far from being inconsistent with those doctrines, they afford still farther illustrations and confirmations of them, and could not be explained upon any principles except those which they are brought to impugn. It becomes no one, but least of all the Agriculturists, who have suffered so recently from their ignorance of Political Economy, to affect contempt for that important science. Had these gentlemen, in the days of their prosperity, been aware that a succession of deficient harvests was the only cause of the high prices, they would have foreseen that a revulsion would finally take place; and they would neither have expended upon the land a quantity of capital which is now irrecoverably gone, nor entered into contracts, and made provisions for their younger children, on the supposition that their rents would always continue at the existing elevation.

13. ERRORS OF THE SPANISH GOVERNMENT
MORNING CHRONICLE, 12 AUG., 1823, PP. 2-3

This letter was occasioned by the results of the invasion of Spain by France in April 1823, in support of Ferdinand VII (1784-1833). Having been briefly on the throne in 1808, he ruled again from 1814 until he was captured and held prisoner by the revolutionaries of 1820. Attempts at constitutional government from 1820 to 1823 produced meagre results, all of which, as Mill predicts, were erased when Ferdinand was released by the Cortes in October, and took vengeance on the constitutionalists. Headed as title, subheaded "To the Editor of the Morning Chronicle," the item is described in Mill's bibliography as "A letter on the errors of the Spanish Government in the Chronicle of 12th August 1823, signed M" (MacMinn, p. 2).

SIR,—The conduct by which the Spanish Government have brought their affairs to so dangerous a crisis, will afford a salutary lesson both to themselves, if they should ultimately succeed in weathering the storm, and to all who may hereafter throw off the shackles of despotism, and establish a Constitutional Government. It will prove to them the danger of trusting to historical evidence, that is, to the narrow and precipitate theories of unenlightened historians, in preference to those general principles of human nature, of which any one may convince himself by his personal experience, unless he looks at human actions and motives through the coloured medium of prejudice.

They whose interest compels them to oppose improvement, and they who, in the emphatic language of Sir J. Mackintosh, "entangled by the habits of detail in which they have been reared, possess not that erect and intrepid spirit, those enlarged and original views, which adapt themselves to new combinations of circumstances, and sway in the great convulsions of human affairs:"* these two classes of individuals are constantly holding up *practice* in opposition to *theory*, and descanting on the necessity of following the dictates of experience.—They know not what they say. They think they are combatting theories by experience, while in fact they are combatting good theories by bad ones.

Experience, the most certain and the most extensive which we have, proves to us, that unless securities are provided, men will neglect the public interest, whenever it interferes with their own. The same experience enables us to determine what motives will be sufficient to counteract this propensity. On this experience we build a theory of government. Such a theory is least of all entitled to the epithet so liberally applied to it of Utopianism. A Utopian theory is one which is founded not upon our experience of mankind, but upon something inconsistent with experience—upon the supposition that by some wondrous scheme of education which is to be established, men may be induced to act with a view to the public interest, even when it is inconsistent with their own. The real Utopians are they who recommend to vest all power in the hands of Kings and Aristocracies—to annihilate all securities for their acting conformably to the public good,[1] in order to have the satisfaction of seeing them, through patriotism and pure benevolence, sacrifice their dearest interests to the promotion of human welfare.

Against theories founded upon universal experience, the enemies of improvement hold out—what? Theories founded upon history; that is, upon partial and incomplete experience. Has a measure, in any age or nation, appeared to be followed by good effects? they think no farther justification required for adopting it. Has another measure (however conformable to sound and enlarged experience) had the misfortune to be adopted by a nation, the affairs of which, afterwards, took a bad turn? they make no allowance for altered circumstances, but precipitately and peremptorily reject it.

These observations are intended to illustrate the conduct of the Spanish Government since the revolution of 1820, particularly of the Ministry of Count Toreno, and that of Martinez de la Rosa.[2] Terrified at the result of the French

---

*Vindiciae Gallicae [: Defence of the French Revolution and Its English Admirers against the Accusations of the Right Hon. Edmund Burke (1791), 2nd ed. (London: Robinson, 1791)], p. 30 [by James Mackintosh (1765-1832), Whig writer, whose initial enthusiasm for the French Revolution faded, but who favoured the Spanish constitutionalists].

[1]"Securities" used in this sense is a hallmark of the Philosophic Radicals: see, for example, James Mill, "Government" (1820), in *Essays* (London: Innes, 1825), and Jeremy Bentham, *Constitutional Code* (1827, 1841), in *Works*, Vol. IX, p. 9. Further uses of the term in these volumes (see, e.g., the title of No. 20) are not noted, but are listed in App. G *s.v.* these titles.

[2]José María Queipo de Llano Ruiz de Saravia, conde de Toreno (1786-1843), politician and historian, one of Bentham's correspondents, who had been exiled 1814-20,

Revolution, they trembled at every measure which could be made a handle by their opponents for accusing them of violence; as if they could believe, that either the wishes or the designs of those whom they had deprived of their mischievous power, could for a moment be affected by the extension of mercy to a few malefactors, or the silencing of a few Republican Orators in the Fontana d'Oro at Madrid![3]

Yet these pusillanimous statesmen, as if they did not already stand committed in the eyes of their former masters, by accepting power under a Revolutionary Government, still appear to have cherished the hope of securing their own persons and property, if despotism should ever be restored. They had heard that the Jacobin Clubs occasioned the excesses of the French Revolution—and in a spirit of compromise, unworthy of the Ministers of a regenerated country, they stopped that freedom of public discussion, which, in a country where the circulation of books is so limited, was the only available means of enlisting a body of public opinion in their behalf.[4] Their eyes were opened too late by the conspiracy of the 7th of July;[5] and a few months before the moment when they were to feel the want of that popular opinion which timely vigour would have roused, the Ministry of San Miguel re-established the Patriotic Societies.[6]

It was in the same compromising spirit, and from the same irrational dread of imitating the French, that the ruffian Elio was for three years suffered to disgrace by his existence that country which had streamed with the blood of his fellow-citizens slaughtered by his command.[7] This wretch, as much superior in guilt to an assassin as the murder of hundreds is more atrocious than that of one individual—at length, in September, 1822, received the just reward of his

---

returned in the Revolution of 1820 and joined the Cortes; Francisco de Paula Martínez de la Rosa (1789-1862), statesman and dramatist, also exiled 1814-20, was Prime Minister from February to August 1822, when he followed a course unpopular with both conservatives and liberals.

[3]La Fontana de Oro (also known as La Sociedad de los Amigos del Orden), one of the Patriotic Societies established in March 1820, in imitation of the French Jacobin clubs, was ordered closed on 18 Sept., 1821.

[4]Freedom had been granted by Decreto LV (22 Oct., 1820), Reglamento acerca de la libertad de imprenta (*Colección de los decretos y órdenes generales espedidos por las Cortes*, 10 vols. [Madrid, 1820-23]), Vol. VI, pp. 234-46; on 12 Feb., 1822, the Cortes passed Decretos LXVII, LXVIII, and LXIX, limiting freedom of the press and of petitioning (*ibid.*, Vol. VIII, pp. 262, 263, 265).

[5]The Royal Guard, probably at the instigation of Ferdinand VII, attempted an uprising on 7 July, 1822.

[6]Evaristo de San Miguel (1785-1862), Prime Minister and Foreign Secretary (August 1822-February 1823), brought forward Decreto VII (1 Nov., 1822), Lay que prescribe las formalidades con que las personas pueden reunirse en público para discutir materias politicas (*Colección*, Vol. X, pp. 19-20).

[7]Francisco Javier Elio (1767-1822), Royalist general responsible for many atrocities, was executed on 7 Sept., 1822.

crimes. But who can blame a *delay* of punishment, when the perpetrators of the massacre at Cadiz[8] still glory in their atrocious deeds? Had these been visited by the hand of justice, the Spanish Patriots might not now have seen in arms against them so many adventurers, whom experience has taught, that the greatest atrocities may be committed without dread of punishment.

In fact, the idea of a bloodless Revolution is, when rightly considered, visionary and absurd. All great Reforms must injure many private interests, and cannot, therefore, fail to raise many enemies. Nor can those enemies be safely permitted to mature their machinations in security. We do not mean that the people should be excited to massacre. We are not the apologists of the 2d of September, 1792; but, whenever treason against the Constitution can be clearly brought home to any individual, to spare that individual is not mercy but weakness. It cannot alter the hostility of the despots, while it increases their power by evincing an ill-timed indecision. The Spanish Government must now bitterly regret that dread of the accusation of shedding blood, which prevented them from bringing the Duke del Infantado to condign punishment for his notorious complicity in the treason of the 7th of July.[9] Enough has been done to exasperate, but nothing to weaken; and if San Miguel and his colleagues should eventually fall into the hands of the traitor whom they so injudiciously spared, they will scarce have the folly to expect, that he will forget from whose hands he received his degradation and banishment, and remember only that those hands left him life, after taking all, which, to a mind habituated like his, to mischievous power, could render that life an object of desire.

M.

14. THE MISCHIEVOUSNESS OF AN OATH
MORNING CHRONICLE, 15 AUG., 1823, P. 3

Mill here continues the argument of "Judicial Oaths" (No. 11), to which he refers in the opening sentence, by citing a case reported in the Police News of the *Morning Chronicle*, 14 Aug., 1823, p. 4. The letter, headed "To the Editor of the Morning Chronicle," is described in Mill's bibliography as "A short letter signed A Lover of Caution pointing out a case of the mischievousness of an oath in the Chronicle of 15th August 1823" (MacMinn, p. 2). As is evident in the text, the letter is actually signed "A Friend to Caution."

[8] After a successful revolt at Cadiz, a crowd gathered in the Plaza de San Antonio to celebrate the Constitution of 1812; troops suddenly opened fire on them, and over 400 citizens were killed. Those responsible were Manuel Freire (1765-1834), Captain General of Andalusia, and Cayetano Valdés y Flórez (1767-1835), *ad interim* Governor of Cadiz.

[9] Don Pedro Alcántara de Toledo, duque del Infantado (1773-1841), was reported to have incited peasants in support of absolutism and religion during the abortive rebellion (*The Times*, 16 July, 1822, p. 3).

SIR,—In a Letter signed "No Lawyer," which you inserted in your Paper of the 23d July, among the many ill effects of the ceremony of an oath, considerable stress was laid upon the false estimate which it occasions of the credibility of witnesses. When they speak the truth, it is not because they have sworn (for if that were the reason Custom House and University oaths would be observed), but because they fear the shame and the penalties of perjury.[1] It is, however, too commonly believed, that if a man has *sworn*, no other security is required.

An instance of this appeared in your Paper of August 14. A gentleman who complained of a fraud practised on him at a mock auction in Lime-street, stated that he had neglected to make himself acquainted with the name of the auctioneer, because he presumed, that all auctioneers *being sworn*, were therefore respectable.[2] Yet it must appear to all unprejudiced minds, that if the other circumstances were insufficient to remove the possibility of suspicion, the circumstance of the *oath* added nothing to the security. If there were motives sufficient for fraud, they were sufficient for fraud and perjury both.

A Friend To Caution

15. BLESSINGS OF EQUAL JUSTICE
MORNING CHRONICLE, 20 AUG., 1823, P. 2

This letter was prompted by the reports (*Morning Chronicle*, 15 Aug., 1823, p. 4; "Police; Queen Square," *The Times*, 11 and 15 Aug., 1823, both p. 3; "Police: Queen-Square," *Examiner*, 17 Aug., 1823, p. 543) of the handling by Mr. White, the magistrate, of a complaint on 10 Aug. by Mrs. Lang (alias Miss Drummond), a servant of Lady Caroline Lamb (1785-1828), that had been rebutted by her husband, William Lamb (1779-1848), later Lord Melbourne. The letter, headed as title and subheaded "To the Editor of the Morning Chronicle," is described in Mill's bibliography as "A letter on publicity in judicature, and its infraction by a Queen Square magistrate, in the Chronicle of 20 August 1823" (MacMinn, p. 3).

SIR,—Among the numberless blessings which we are continually told that we owe to our glorious Constitution, a good administration of justice has always been considered as the most valuable. While the judicature of every other nation is corrupt, profligate and oppressive—a ready tool in the hands of power; it has been our boast that ours alone is pure and undefiled; that it gives ear alike to the rich and to the poor, that neither the interests nor the prejudices of rank and station ever divert our Judges from the straight path of equity and impartiality.

A practical illustration of this inestimable blessing occurred some days since at the Queen-square Police-office; and although several papers, and you, Sir,

[1]For background, see No. 6.
[2]For auctioneers' oaths, see 19 George III, c. 56, sect. 7 (1779).

among the rest, have taken up the subject, far too little stress has, in my opinion, been laid upon it.

A servant of a lady of rank presented herself at the office, to complain of ill-treatment received from her Ladyship. Her statement appeared in the papers. A day or two after the husband of the lady appeared, and denied the story told by the servant.[1] So far both parties stood upon the same ground. On one side was the woman's affirmation; on the other, that of her master. The woman's story was probably false: that is not the question. It is not sufficient that it should be *presumed* to be false; there ought to be *evidence*, and *conclusive* evidence of its falsehood, before a Magistrate, who sits to act as a Judge, should take upon himself to reject her application. Observe now the conduct of Mr. White: not only does he without farther inquiry pronounce in favour of the gentleman, *upon his own affirmation* only; he does more—because the newspapers *inserted* the woman's story, being equally ready to insert that of her master, he declares that reporters shall be no longer admitted into Court.

That defect of publicity should occasion defect of evidence against criminals, by preventing many persons from hearing of the trial, who would otherwise have come forward as witnesses, is the least of the mischiefs which will arise out of this precedent. The impunity which it will secure to a corrupt Judge, is the greatest.

Although it is the prevailing cry of the English Aristocracy that the Judges are immaculate, and although a deluded people have too long given them credit for any quantity of virtue which they think fit to claim, the public now at length begin to learn that it is absurd to expect from men the qualities of angels. To make a man a Judge, does not change his nature. Judges, like other men, will always prefer themselves to their neighbours. Judges, like other men, will indulge their indolence and satiate their rapacity whenever they can do it without fear of detection. The judicial office offers not fewer, but more numerous, and far more immediate temptations, than one who is not a Judge can easily be subject to. Allow any man to profit by injustice, and it is not the name of Judge which will shield the people from his oppression. When we see how soon almost any virtue yields to continued temptation, there needs little to persuade us, that if every Magistrate were to follow the example of Mr. White, and administer justice with closed doors, Magistrates would ere long be again what they were in the time of Fielding and of Smollett[2]—leagued with every thief in London.

---

[1]For the complaint by Mrs. Lang, see, e.g., "Police. Queen-Square. Lady Caroline Lamb," *British Press*, 11 Aug., 1823, p. 4, an account that William Lamb cited as libellous in his complaint, which is given in "Police. Queen Square," *Morning Chronicle*, 15 Aug., p. 4.

[2]Henry Fielding (1707-54), novelist and magistrate, whose portrait of Justice Thrasher as a "Trading Justice" in *Amelia*, Bk. I, Chap. ii (*Works*, 12 vols. [London: Richards, 1824], Vol. X, pp. 9-15), is cited by James Mill in his Commonplace Book, Vol. I, f.

To illustrate the tendency of the precedent, I will put a case; and it is one which might easily have occurred.— Suppose that the woman's story had been correct, and that of her master false; it will not be denied that *there are* masters who would not scruple to tell a lie, if they knew that, as in this case, their simple affirmation would put an end to the dispute. But it is only a rich man, it is only a member of the aristocracy, whose word is to be taken as conclusive evidence in his own cause. Thus then, whenever a rich individual and a poor one contradict each other on a matter of fact, the poor man is to be disbelieved, and the rich man suffered to carry off (perhaps) the wages of mendacity. And, to crown all, this iniquity is to be covered with the veil of secrecy. Then, perhaps, other motives than aristocratic sympathies may mix themselves in the decision of causes; again, perhaps, we may see a judicial controversy transformed into a competition between the purses of the parties, which can best satisfy the rapacity of the Judge.

Mr. White may derive a precedent, though not an excuse, for the violation of almost the only security we have for the purity of judicature, from the example which has been set by higher authorities, of prohibiting the publication of trials, until the whole of the evidence shall have been given,* for the benevolent purpose, forsooth, of preventing *ex parte* statements from going forth to the world, and giving a false impression of the state of the case. I am not aware that it is a recognised maxim of jurisprudence, however frequently it may be acted upon in practice, that occasional and partial evil shall preponderate over universal good. There might be some reason indeed, for preventing *ex parte* statements from going forth, if the Judges could invent any method of hearing both parties at once. Until, however, some such method shall have been discovered, I shall continue to think that if Juries, who are taken from among the public, can hear first one party, and then the other, and yet decide justly, there cannot be much danger in presenting the evidence to the public, in precisely the same order as it comes before the Jury.

A Judge must always have much to gain by injustice: and if due securities are not provided, he will do injustice. The only efficient security which our Constitution provides is publicity: it is the disgrace which a Judge incurs by an unjust decision. This disgrace is greater or less, according as the public attention

---

137v (London Library); Tobias George Smollett (1721-71), novelist, who like Fielding wrote of criminal life, comments on the failings of judges in his *History of England* (1757), 5 vols. (London: Cadell and Baldwin, 1790), Vol. III, pp. 330-1.

*The proprietor of *The Observer* Newspaper was reprimanded by the Court, for publishing one part of the trial of Thistlewood and others, before the trial was closed. [William Innell Clement (d. 1852) was reprimanded by Charles Abbott (1762-1832) on 17 Apr., 1820; a fine was levied by the Court of High Commission. (See "Old Bailey," *Examiner*, 23 Apr., 1820, p. 270.) Arthur Thistlewood (1770-1820), the leader of the Cato St. conspiracy to murder Lord Liverpool's cabinet, was executed for high treason and murder.]

is more or less drawn to the case. Now it is well known that after a cause is decided, the interest taken in it to a great degree subsides. The prohibition of *ex parte* statements is, therefore, a contrivance to avert the public attention from abuses of judicial authority: to protect the Judges from that odium which their conduct may deserve.[†] Encouraged by the success of this *indirect* attack upon the only security for good judicature, Mr. White, more boldly, has cut the Gordian knot, and destroyed that security altogether.

This is not, however, an affair to be passed over in silence. The securities against abuse, which, in the present state of our Government, we possess, are not so numerous that we can afford to lose one, and that one the most important of them. He is not a lover of good judicature, or he is a very blind one, who does not cry shame upon Mr. White, for setting a precedent so destructive of all security for justice; that if he himself were deliberately planning the most flagrant abuses of power, he could not have hit upon an expedient better calculated to serve his purpose.

A Lover of Justice

N.B. Since writing the above, I have had the pleasure to learn that Reporters still continue to attend the Office, notwithstanding the injunction of Mr. White.

16. PERSECUTION FOR RELIGIOUS SCRUPLES
MORNING CHRONICLE, 26 AUG., 1823, P. 3

Mill's third discussion of oaths (see esp. No. 6), this letter was occasioned by "Imposition of a Fine for Refusing to Take a Judicial Oath," *Morning Chronicle*, 22 Aug., 1823, p. 4. It reported the fining on 16 Aug. of Connell, a pawnbroker, by Richard Pennefather (1773-1859), K.C., Chief Baron of the Irish Court of Exchequer, in the Cork City Criminal Court on 16 Aug., 1823. Headed as title and subheaded "To the Editor of the Morning Chronicle," the item is described in Mill's bibliography as "A letter on the conduct of an Irish judge in fining a witness for refusing to take an oath, in the Chronicle of 26th August 1823, signed *the Censor* of the Judges" (MacMinn, p. 3).

SIR,—I observed in your Paper of Friday last, a conspicuous instance of the mischiefs of judicial oaths. These mischiefs you have frequently adverted to, but I question whether so glaring an instance of them ever yet presented itself to your notice.

A man was called to give evidence at a Court of Justice in Ireland on a cause of no extraordinary interest. He declined taking an oath on the ground of religious scruples: upon which Mr. Baron Pennyfather fined him 100*l.*

[†]That they may be themselves *bonâ fide*, and may not *think* they deserve odium, does not affect the question. The *consequences* to the public are the only thing which deserves attention.

Either this man was conscientiously averse to taking an oath, or he wished, under that pretext, to evade the necessity of giving testimony.

On the former supposition, every discerning lover of justice must lament that, by the imposition of a ceremony which (as we see in the case of Custom-house and University oaths)[1] adds no security whatever, the testimony of a highly conscientious witness should have been excluded.

This supposition appears the most probable, as persons appeared to certify that the witness was known to have these scruples. But even if he really wished, under this pretence, to frustrate the ends of justice, the consequence is not less deplorable. If he had avowed his determination not to give evidence, he would have incurred the infamy which so pernicious a resolution deserves. By covering the wickedness of his intention under the cloak of religion, he screened himself from well merited disgrace.

If there were nothing more, therefore, than the exclusion of his evidence, this were surely enough: but when to the exclusion we add the fine, it ought to inspire every man with serious reflections. It will stand upon record that in the nineteenth century, a fine of 100*l.* was imposed upon a man because his religious opinions differed from those of Mr. Baron Pennyfather. I blame not the Judge, but the law, for excluding the witness. The glory, however, of the fine, belongs wholly to the Judge, who, instead of labouring to effect the amendment of a law which excludes the conscientious while it lets in the unprincipled witness, took upon himself to imitate the Court of Ecclesiastical Commission, and punish Heresy with a fine of 100*l.*[2]

The lawyers may quibble—they may say that he was fined, not for heresy, but for contempt of Court. Contempt of Court is a mere cant phrase, and, in most instances, a phrase employed for the worst of purposes. On this principle, the Judges under Charles II might be justified, who repeatedly fined the Jury because they would not condemn those whom it suited the "Court" and their employers to oppress.[3] All the quirks with which the English law, more than any other, abounds, will not alter the fact, that a man has been fined one hundred pounds *for his religious scruples*; not for refusing to give evidence—he did not refuse this. He never hesitated to give a *solemn affirmation* of all which he knew; he scrupled only the oath. The Judge had not power to dispense with the ceremony, but he was under no obligation to impose on a pawnbroker, not likely to be in very

---

[1] See No. 6.

[2] The Court of High Commission, created by 1 Elizabeth I, c. 1 (1558), was given this power in ecclesiastical matters; it had been abolished by 16 Charles I, c. 11 (1640).

[3] The practice of judges' fining juries developed under the Star Chamber and spread to other courts; it was stopped in 1670 in the case of Bushell (see *A Complete Collection of State Trials*, ed. Thomas Bayly Howell, 34 vols. [London: Longman, *et al.*, 1809-28], Vol. VI, cols. 999-1026).

opulent circumstances, a fine which may amount to the ruin of all his prospects in life.

When I consider that the class to whom Mr. Baron Pennyfather belongs, are continually holding up the importance of encouraging the spirit of religion among the people, continually lamenting the little influence which religious motives exert over human conduct, I cannot help thinking that they should be the last to impose a ruinous fine upon a man on account of the peculiar strength of his religious principles, and thus hold out encouragement to the disregard of those principles.

In discussing this subject, I have avoided considering the question whether oaths are or are not consistent with Christianity—for even supposing the witness to have been in error, a man is not to be fined 100*l.* for being in error.

The administration of justice in Ireland has so long been a scene of all which is unjust and oppressive, that an occurrence, which, if performed at our doors, would have excited attention, may, perhaps, be passed over, when happening amid so many others still more atrocious than itself. But the law is the same in England as in Ireland. In both countries the lawyers are equally ignorant and equally prejudiced; and what has happened in the County of Cork, may, ere long, perhaps, be imitated in that of Middlesex.

                                                    The Censor of the Judges

17. RESURRECTION-MEN

MORNING CHRONICLE, 1 SEPT. 1823, P. 2

This letter was prompted by "Disturbers of the Dead," *Morning Chronicle*, 25 Aug., 1823, p. 4, which reported the trial and sentence of Cornelius Bryant and William Millard for opening a grave in the burial ground of the London Hospital. Those who, by disinterment or other means, procured corpses for sale to schools of anatomy, were known as "resurrection-men." Dissection of non-criminal corpses was an offence under common and ecclesiastical law; under 32 Henry VIII, c. 42 (1540), Sect. 2, four executed felons could be dissected each year; under 25 George II, c. 37 (1752), all executed murderers were to be "dissected and anatomized." Mill may have known that Jeremy Bentham had made provision in his will that his body be used for medical purposes, as Mill recommends in the letter. The letter, headed as title, subheaded "To the Editor of the Morning Chronicle," is described in Mill's bibliography as "A letter on the punishment of body-stealers, in the Chronicle of 1st September 1823, signed a Friend to Science" (MacMinn, p. 3).

SIR,—In your Paper of Monday last, I observed one among a great number of recent cases, where the description of persons called resurrection-men had been sacrificed to popular prejudice.

If it be admitted, and I do not see how it can be called in question, that a knowledge of medicine and surgery cannot be acquired without an acquaintance with the phenomena which the human organs present, both in health and in disease; if it be allowed, that, in order to become acquainted with these phenomena, it is necessary to have ocular demonstration of them, and that dissection is the only mode in which ocular demonstration can be had; it is obvious that every thing which tends to prevent subjects from being obtained in sufficient quantity for the purposes of anatomy, must tend materially to diminish the facilities of acquiring medical and surgical knowledge, and to throw back those sciences into their pristine barbarism.

If bodies had never been dissected, sentimentalists could not have appealed to our hearts in behalf of the sanctity of the tomb, for whether we have or have not such an organ, would probably to this day have remained a problem.

We should have been equally ignorant that we have a brain, lungs, a stomach, nerves, a venous and arterial system, &c. At all events, the structure and position of those organs must have remained for ever unknown to us. The internal processes of animal life—respiration, digestion, the circulation of the blood, all the various secretions, must have continued among the arcana of nature, and all internal diseases must, from want of the requisite knowledge, have been incurable. A man feels, for instance, an acute pain, and shows symptoms of general ill health, from an obstruction in his liver; how can the surgeon, who has never seen a dissection, discover where the remedy is to be applied? The utmost which he could infer would be that the source of evil is somewhere on the right side; and even of this he could not be assured, for the seat of a disease is frequently at a considerable distance from the place of its external manifestation. He might endeavour to cure a liver complaint by a remedy calculated to act on the urinary glands; or to remove the rheumatism by means of an emetic.

If dissection had never taken place, the art of medicine could scarcely have existed. And if it were now to cease, the evil would not be confined to preventing it from ever improving. If, indeed, the present race of practitioners were immortal, this might be the utmost limit of the evil. But there is another generation rising up, who must receive equal instruction with their predecessors, if it is expected that they shall be equally skilful. If dissection were to cease, the death of the latest survivor among the practitioners now living, would be the date of the extinction of medical skill in the world. Instead of ascertaining by actual examination the structure and positions of the organs, physicians would be reduced to guess at them from the imperfect accounts left to them by their predecessors, and the grossest errors would continually be committed.

That bodies should be dissected, is, therefore, absolutely necessary; and the only question is in what way the interests of science and the feelings of individuals may best be conciliated? For any one to attempt confining dissectors to the dead bodies of criminals, displays a degree of ignorance on the subject, which renders it presumption in a person so ill qualified to give an opinion at all on it. Every Middlesex and Old Bailey Sessions produce perhaps two, perhaps three, executions. Is it expected that these shall supply bodies for all the dissections which are necessary to make the rising generation of medical students acquainted with the structure of the human body?

Subjects must, therefore, be provided, and if so, that way is the best which is least offensive to the relatives of the deceased. It implies, indeed, considerable weakness of mind to transfer the associations of pain, which are connected with wounding a living body, to the cold and insensible organs of the dead; as if to be dissected were more shocking than to be eaten by worms! If an attempt were made to dissect a living human creature, there would then be some cause for raising an outcry. It could scarcely then be louder or more widely propagated than it is. But since the feeling exists, the best mode of obtaining subjects is undoubtedly through the resurrection-men. There is nothing here to hurt the feelings of any one. No one knows that the body of his friend or relative has been taken. He cannot acquire this disagreeable piece of information unless he takes considerable trouble for that purpose. Yet these men, who pursue an occupation so useful to the interests of science, and which can give pain to no one unless by his own fault, are condemned to that place of torments incalculable, the tread mill!

What they would not be were it not for the popular prejudice, that prejudice itself compels them to become. A man who will brave such a mass of odium, a man who will expose himself to be stoned to death by the rabble, cannot have much character to lose. Subjects must be had, and as long as there is a demand for medical-surgical knowledge, they will be had, no matter at what cost. Body-stealing cannot, therefore, be prevented, but the price of subjects may be raised, and while the expence of a medical education is enhanced, temptation is held out to persons in distress to expose themselves to such a degree of odium, as cannot be increased by the most vicious conduct on their part, and which by a natural consequence removes all the inducement to a moral and virtuous life. Hence, if the resurrection-men are for the most part low and vicious characters, it is the absurd prejudice, and that alone, which ought to be blamed.

To conclude, I earnestly recommend, as the only effectual mode of destroying the prejudice, that such as are superior to it adopt the practice of leaving their own bodies to the surgeons. If men known to the world for their exalted qualities would do this the prejudice might in time be removed. Such provisions by will have occasionally been made, but from their rarity they are still considered as eccentricities. When they become more common they may perhaps be recognised as proceeding from no other eccentricity than that which is implied in being exempt from, and in wishing to annihilate one of the most vulgar of all prejudices.

A Friend to Science

18. MALTHUS'S MEASURE OF VALUE

MORNING CHRONICLE, 5 SEPT., 1823, P. 2

Thomas Robert Malthus (1766-1834) was a political economist whose views, especially on population, were often discussed by Mill. This lengthy review is headed "*The Measure of Value Stated and Illustrated, with an Application of It to the Alterations in the Value of the English Currency since 1790*, by the Rev. T.R. Malthus, M.A. F.R.S. [London:] Murray, 1823." It is described in Mill's bibliography as "A review of Mr. Malthus's pamphlet on the 'Measure of Value' which appeared in the Chronicle of 5th September 1823" (MacMinn, p. 3).

WHEN TWO COMMODITIES VARY in their relative value, it is often necessary to obtain information of two things. First, the extent of the variation—this may easily be determined, without calling in the assistance of a third commodity. So far, therefore, there is no need of a measure. But it may also be desirable to know whether the cause of the variation is in the one article or in the other, or if in both, to what degree it is in each. And here it is, that a Measure of Value is chiefly useful.

If a commodity can be found exempt from the influence of all causes of variation, such a commodity may safely be taken as a measure. If any article varies in value with respect to it, we shall know that the cause of variation cannot be in the measure, and must, therefore, be wholly in the other commodity.

The received opinion, however, is, that no such commodity is to be found, every article being subject, not only to temporary, but also to permanent causes of variation.

Mr. Malthus is of a different opinion; we shall proceed to give an outline of his argument.

Commodities, he says, will not be produced, unless their value is sufficient to pay the wages, profits, and rents, necessary to their production. Rent, however, is paid only for a certain class of commodities, and of these, the value is regulated by that part of the produce which is almost exclusively resolvable into wages and profits, and pays very little rent.

The *natural* value, therefore, of commodities, is composed of labour and profits.

If labour were the only requisite to production, and if the interval between the exertion of the labour and its remuneration in the completed commodity were inconsiderable, commodities would, on an average, exchange with each other according to the quantity of labour employed in producing them. [Pp. 3-6.]

But two circumstances, he says, render this rule inaccurate, in all cases different from that which we just supposed.

1. A considerable interval must elapse between the exertion of some sorts of labour, and the completion of the article on which they are employed. If A and B

are two commodities produced by equal labour, but requiring different intervals of time; the values of the two commodities must be different in order to yield the same rate of profits.

2. Capital being accumulated labour, it follows that when fixed capital comes to be employed, the immediate labour expended on a commodity, together with the wear and tear which the fixed capital has undergone in its production, may be considered as the amount of labour expended on the commodity. Suppose this amount to be the same for two articles, yet as the profits must be charged upon the whole capital, whether all consumed in the production or not, it follows, that if the amount of fixed capital is unequal for the two commodities, the values must also be different, as there are unequal amounts of profit to pay. [Pp. 8-12.]

Having for these reasons set aside the doctrine, that the values of commodities depend upon the quantities of labour expended in producing them, Mr. Malthus proceeds to state what he considers as the correct expression. Value, he says, depends upon labour and profits. [P. 14.] Two commodities exchange for one another, although the one is produced by less labour than the other, provided the deficiency of labour is compensated by the greater amount of profits.

If this be true, it follows that whatever is capable of measuring labour and profits, is fitted to be an accurate measure of value. Such a measure Mr. Malthus thinks he has found in the quantity of labour which a commodity will purchase in the market. This, he says, is equal to the quantity of labour expended in its production, together with the ordinary profits. This, therefore, is an accurate measure of value. [Pp. 15-16.]

Such is the outline of Mr. Malthus's argument. The remainder of his work consists of illustrations and applications.

For duly appreciating the merits of this doctrine, it is necessary to have clear conceptions with regard to the nature of profits. Under ordinary circumstances, the labourer and the capitalist being the only persons whose services are requisite for the production of commodities, they alone can have any claim upon the commodities when produced. The joint produce of labour and capital is therefore divided between the labourer and the capitalist, between wages and profits. The whole, indeed, of the produce usually appears to belong to the capitalist; but this is only because he has purchased the labourer's share. Whatever is paid to the labourer, to obtain his co-operation in the work of production, is to be considered as the labourer's share of the produce, paid however in advance. What remains is the share of the capitalist, usually called his profits.

After this preliminary explanation we must readily assent to the first position of Mr. Malthus, that value is *composed* of labour and profits, since, if we may trust his own explanation, he only means that the produce, or what amounts to the same thing, its value, composes wages and profits; in other words, that it is divided between the labourer and the capitalist. Thus understood, the position is self-evident, and has never been disputed by any political economist.

We cannot so readily admit the second position, that value *depends* upon labour and profits. The opinion now generally received among political economists is that value depends upon the quantity of labour expended in production. To this expression Mr. Malthus objects, because it does not include a particular fact, namely, the difference of values, which is occasioned by difference in the quickness of the returns, or in the proportion of fixed capital.

The fact itself is indisputable; nor is it less certain, that the expression does not include it. But it may be annexed as a modification; and such must be its fate, unless some expression shall be devised, which shall include this and all other facts, without being liable to any other objection.

Tried by this test, Mr. Malthus's expression appears to us objectionable. It expresses much more than is intended.

When we say that value depends upon labour, we mean, that according as the quantity of labour expended in producing a commodity is increased or diminished, *ceteris paribus*, its value rises or falls. In like manner, if we say that value depends, wholly or partially, upon profits, it is implied, that when profits rise values shall rise; when profits fall, values shall fall. But if profits rise or fall, the variation must be, not in some particular profits, but in all profits. This is universally acknowledged. Mr. Malthus's expression therefore implies, that a rise or fall of profits raises or lowers all values; which is impossible: for values are relative, and the rise of some values imports the fall of others.

Having thus shewn what Mr. M.'s expression really means, let us consider what he intends it to mean; and let us remember that the sole basis of his doctrine is a case of difference in values, arising from a difference in profits. What is meant to be expressed therefore is, that not absolute profits, but differences of profits, and these not in the rate, but in the total amount of profits, as compared with the immediate expenditure, have some influence on values. This is all which Mr. Malthus's fact can be made to prove; but this is no more than the fact itself, and by no method of reasoning can the fact be made to prove any thing more than itself. It is, therefore, totally inadequate to form the basis of a new theory of value, and can only be admitted as a modification of the old one. But, as a modification, it has been universally received among political economists, and is much more fully stated by Mr. Ricardo, the principal supporter of the old theory, than by Mr. Malthus or any other opponent of that theory.[1]

For these reasons, Mr. M.'s second position appears to us unsupported by sufficient proof. Other considerations, of equal strength, also present themselves in opposition to it. To say that value depends upon profits, seeing that profits are the capitalist's share of the produce, is to say that the value of the whole produce depends upon the proportion in which it is divided between the labourer and the capitalist. This doctrine would appear scarcely to merit a serious refutation.

[1]David Ricardo, *On the Principles of Political Economy and Taxation*, Chap. i, "On Value," *passim*.

The doctrine concerning a measure of value, which Mr. Malthus builds upon premises so unsound, it may appear unnecessary, after what has been said, formally to refute. We cannot, however, refrain from offering a few remarks on this part also of Mr. M.'s doctrine.

The measure of value, as proposed by Mr. Malthus, is the quantity of labour which an article commands in the market; because, says he, this includes the labour expended in production, together with ordinary profits.

Mr. M. has indeed shewn, which is not difficult, that labour possesses this property, but he has not shewn that it is peculiar to labour. It would appear, that not labour merely, but cloth, and all other commodities, are on a par in this respect. If the quantity of labour which a commodity will purchase, includes the labour expended in production, together with profits, the quantity of cloth which it will purchase does the like, for, by the very supposition, it is of the same value.

Mr. M. has anticipated this objection, and has provided the following answer:

If the advances of capitalists consisted specifically in cloth, then these advances would always have the effect required in production; and as profits are calculated upon the advances necessary to production, whatever they may be, the quantity of cloth advanced, with the addition of the ordinary profits, estimated also in quantity of cloth, would represent both the natural and relative value of the commodity. But the specific advances of capitalists do not consist of cloth but of labour. (P. 17.)

In point of fact, however, the advances of capitalists do not consist of labour—they consist of wages; that is, of the food, clothing, and lodging of the labourer, and if capital is called accumulated labour, this only means, that it is the accumulated produce of labour. Any of the necessaries of life must, therefore, if this argument be correct, be equally fitted with labour to be a measure of value.

It is, however, really immaterial whether the advances are in one commodity or in another. Whatever be the nature of the returns—be they in Corn, in Cloth, or in any other commodity, they must always be such as to repay the expences of production, together with the ordinary profits of stock; or, to use Mr. M.'s expression, they must include labour and profits. Labour, therefore, in this respect, possesses no advantage over any other commodity.

If, indeed, Mr. M. could prove that no causes of variation can operate upon labour, his position would be established without farther trouble. But this, we apprehend, is impossible. There are two causes which operate upon the value of labour; first, a variation in the relative amount of population and capital; this tends to alter the real reward of the labourer; and 2dly, a variation in the cost of producing the articles consumed by the labourer; this tends to change its value. So long as labour shall be subject to the influence of these causes, so long will it be liable to variations, and therefore equally unfit with almost any commodity to be an accurate measure of value.

Mr. M. admits that the labourer receives, at different times, very different quantities of produce; but this variable amount of produce, he affirms to be constant in value; an assertion, at least in appearance, contradictory to all our experience. In support of this allegation, he argues as follows. The reward of the labourer has been itself produced by labour, and its value, therefore, is resolvable into labour and profits. But if the quantity of labour employed in producing it be increased, profits must fall; if it be diminished, profits must rise, and so as to leave the sum absolutely constant. The value of wages, therefore, is constant. [Pp. 26-8.]

The remark which obviously suggests itself is that, like some of the former arguments, so also this, if it proves any thing, proves too much. There is no reason here given why labour, rather than any other commodity, should be the measure. If it be true of the produce, which is the labourer's reward, that its value is composed of labour and profits, it must, we apprehend, be equally true of all other commodities. It may with equal justice be argued, that any amount, constant or variable, of corn, of cloth, or of iron, is always of the same value.

For if the quantity of labour employed in producing it be increased, so that a greater share of the completed commodity must go to wages, there obviously remains a smaller share for profits. Does this prove that the value of the commodity is constant? Certainly not: for value does not depend upon the proportion in which the produce is divided between the labourer and the capitalist; it depends upon the demand and supply of the market, regulated and limited by cost of production.

The whole chain of reasoning depends upon this position, that the value of the labourer's reward resolves itself into labour and profits. Wages, we have seen to be, that share of the produce which is allotted to the labourer, purchased, however, beforehand by the capitalist. What, therefore, is true of the labourer's share, when purchased by the capitalist, would also be true of it, if the commodity were actually divided between them. Let us make this supposition. The value of the labourer's share cannot then be said to be made up of labour and profits, since profits do not enter into it, being wholly on the side of the capitalist. Suppose now the labour necessary for producing the commodity to increase, the value of the labourer's share can no longer remain constant, since the increase of labour cannot be balanced by a fall of profits. But if the labourer's share is not constant in value, when he waits to receive it until the production is completed; neither can it be constant, when he receives it beforehand in the shape of wages.

Mr. Malthus, however, subjoins a numerical table, by which he thinks he has proved the value of wages to be constant. This table he prefaces by the following obscure paragraph:

If, instead of referring to commodities generally, we refer to the variable quantity of produce which under different circumstances forms the wages of a given number of labourers, we shall find that the variable quantity of labour required to obtain this produce, will always exactly agree with the proportion of the whole produce which goes to labour; because, however variable may be the amount of this produce, it will be divided into a number of parts equal to the number of labourers which it will command; and as the first set of labourers who produced these wages may be considered as having been paid at the same rate as the second set, whose labour the produce commands, it is obvious that if to obtain the produce which commands ten labourers, 6, 7, 8, or 9 labourers be required, the proportion of the produce which goes to labour, in these different cases, will be 6/10, 7/10, 8/10, or 9/10, leaving 4/10, 3/10, 2/10, or 1/10 for profits. (Pp. 30-1.)

As far as the above paragraph has any meaning, it appears to be this:—If the labour of six men is required to produce the wages of ten, what remains for profits must be equal to the wages of four: if the labour of seven men is required to produce the wages of ten, profits will be equal to the wages of three; and so on. But this, one would imagine, scarcely needs a long paragraph, and a table which fills a whole page to prove it. Let us see, however, the inference which he builds upon it. If the labour required to obtain the produce be increased, then, says he, profits will fall, so as to leave the value of the whole produce constant. Why is it constant? Because, if wages are 6/10ths, profits are 4/10ths: if wages are 7/10ths, profits are 3/10ths; if wages are 8/10ths, profits are 2/10ths; and so on. Now the sum of 6/10ths and 4/10ths, the sum of 7/10ths and 3/10ths, and the sum of 8/10ths and 2/10ths, are all equal. Equal to what? to 10/10ths. The value, therefore, of the produce is constant, because it is always equal to 10/10ths of the produce, that is, to itself!

The same identical proposition, and nothing more, results from Mr. Malthus's redoubtable table, from which we extract part of several of the columns. [P. 38.]

Rate of profits	Quantity of labour required to produce the wages of ten men	Quantity of profits on the advances of labour	Invariable value of the wages of a given number of men
25 per cent.	8	2	10
15.38	8.66	1.34	10
50	6.6	3.4	10
16.66	8.6	1.4	10
27.2	7.85	2.15	10

From these elaborate computations he proves that the wages of ten men are in value always equal to ten. To ten quarters of corn, or ten suits of clothing? No.—To ten of what? This we shall see. The number 8 in the second column represents a certain quantity of labour, the labour, namely, of eight men; the number 2 in the next column represents the labour of two men; the number 10, therefore, which is obtained by adding the 8 and the 2, represents the labour of ten men; and Mr. Malthus informs us that the wages of ten men are invariable in value, because they are always equal in value to the labour of ten men! In other words, the wages of a day's labour are always of the same value, because they are the wages of a day's labour!

It is therefore evident that the whole of Mr. Malthus's argument is a begging of the question. His object is to prove that labour is an accurate measure of value, because the value of wages is invariable. But in order to prove this, he covertly assumes labour as the standard; and then, of course, he can easily prove that the wages of ten men, as compared with labour, are always of the same value, because they can always purchase the labour of ten men. But although wages are invariable in value with respect to labour, they are not invariable with respect to commodities in general.

If Mr. Malthus had stated his premises and his conclusion, in the simple form in which we have now stated them, no one could have been misled by so palpable a *petitio principii*.—But many who can see through a fallacy, in a concise and clear piece of argument, are not able to resist a long succession of obscure paragraphs, and a numerical table of no less than nine columns.

To us, therefore, Mr. M. appears to have entirely failed in proving that labour, as a measure of value, is preferable to any other commodity.

The principle itself being erroneous, we shall give no more than a hasty view of the applications.

"1. On the subject of rents," says he, "such a standard would determine, among other things, that as the increase in the value of corn is only measured by a decrease in the corn wages of labour, such increase of value is a very inconsiderable source of the increase of rents compared with improvements in agriculture." (P. 54.) It is difficult to trace the connexion between the premises and the conclusion of this argument. However, the whole must fall to the ground, as the premises themselves are erroneous. There may be an increase in the value of corn, without any decrease in corn wages. When corn rises permanently in exchangeable value, the wages of labour almost uniformly rise along with it. The rise of wages is indeed less than that of corn, but it bears a very considerable proportion to it. The most important practical errors must therefore be the consequence of estimating the rise in corn by a comparison with labour, a commodity which always rises along with it.

"2. If tithes do not fall mainly on the labourer, the acknowledged diminution in the *corn* rents of the landlord, occasioned by tithes, cannot be balanced by an increase of their value, and consequently tithes must fall mainly on the landlord." (Pp. 54-5.)—Another most important practical mistake. *Corn* rents, indeed, are diminished by tithes. But if the exchangeable value of corn is raised, the landlord is indemnified. And although corn may not rise as compared with labour—and therefore, by Mr. Malthus, may be said not to have risen at all—there can be no doubt that, with reference to commodities in general, it has risen, and the landlord, consequently, is indemnified.

The next paragraph we transcribe, as a specimen of the obscure and disjointed mode of reasoning which Mr. Malthus has adopted.

As one consequence of his doctrine concerning the measure of value, he states,

that the increasing *value* of the funds destined for the maintenance of labour can alone occasion an increase in the demand for it, or the will and power to employ a greater number of labourers; and that it is consistent with theory, as well as general experience, that high corn wages, in proportion to the work done, should frequently occur with a very slack demand for labour; or, in other words, that when the *value* of the whole produce falls from excess of supply compared with the demand, it cannot have the power of setting the same number of labourers to work. (P. 55.)

This is Mr. M.'s favourite doctrine of over-production.[2] A more mischievous doctrine, we think, has scarcely ever been broached in political economy: since, if we are liable to have too large a produce, a Government must be highly praiseworthy, which in its loving kindness steps forward to relieve us of one part of this insupportable burden. On other occasions, Mr. M. has adduced, in proof of this doctrine, arguments which have at least the merit of being intelligible. That, however, which is couched in the above paragraph, would require the exercise of no small sagacity in its interpretation, were not this task happily rendered unnecessary by the utter unmeaningness of the phrase upon which the whole argument, such as it is, appears to turn. "The value of the whole produce falls." What does this mean? The exchangeable value? No: for the *whole produce* can have no exchangeable value, as it is never, at least collectively, exchanged. Any other kind of value? But with no other kind have we any thing to do. By value, we uniformly mean exchangeable value. This is the only legitimate use of the term.

There is another paragraph in proof of the same position.

If the increase of capital be measured by the increase of its materials, such as corn, clothing, &c. then it is obvious that the supply of these materials may, by saving, increase so rapidly, compared with labour and the wants of the effective demanders, that with a greater quantity of materials, the capitalist will neither have the power nor the will to set in motion the same quantity of labour, and that consequently the progress of wealth will be checked, but that if the increase of capital be measured as it ought to be, by the increase of its power to command labour, then accumulation so limited, cannot possibly go on too fast. (P. 57.)

The above assertion, for there is no attempt at argument, may easily be

[2]See, e.g., Malthus, *An Inquiry into the Nature and Progress of Rent* (London: Murray, and Johnson, 1815), pp. 8-17, and *Principles of Political Economy* (London: Murray, 1820), pp. 63-72.

disproved; but this is not the place for it. The difficulty is, to see why Mr. M. should have given this as a consequence of his doctrine concerning the measure of value, between which and this paragraph we can see no sort of connexion. If, however, it be such a consequence, it must fall with the doctrine which supports it.

Soon after, he continues, "If commodities and the materials of capital increase faster than the effectual demand for them [faster than labour, we presume, he means], profits fall prematurely, and capitalists are ruined, without a proportionate benefit to the labouring classes, because an increasing demand for labour cannot go on under such circumstances." (P. 59.) Again, we ask, what has this to do with the measure of value? As, however, it can be refuted in few words, we will not grudge the necessary space.

Why do profits fall prematurely? Because, from the increase of capital faster than labour, wages rise. There is no other cause which can lower profits. And yet, in the same breath, Mr. M. tells us, that there is no proportionate benefit to the labouring classes!

If this case were to happen, the only consequence would be, that accumulation would cease to go on at this enormous rate, and would be continued only at the same rate with the increase of population. If Mr. M. confines to this case his doctrine of over-production, we may make the concession with perfect safety.

Another application.

On the subject of foreign trade, it [the doctrine of the measure] would shew that its universally acknowledged effect in giving a stimulus to production, generally, is mainly owing to its increasing the value of the produce of a country's labour, by the extension of demand, before the value of its labour is increased by the increase of its quantity; and that the effect of every extension of demand, whether foreign or domestic, is always, as far as it goes, to increase the average rate of profits till this increase is counteracted by a further accumulation of capital. (Pp. 56-7.)

Many and important are the errors contained in this short paragraph. But it would be loss of time to point them out, as all the proof which Mr. M. has given falls to the ground with his doctrine of the measure. All which he himself asserts is, that if that doctrine is true, these applications are also true.

In another paragraph, Mr. M. says, that value does not depend upon cost of production, because value is proportioned, not to the advances merely, but to the advances, together with variable profits. That allowance is to be made for all cases of difference in the amount of profits, as compared with immediate expenditure, is allowed on all hands; but the necessity of this modification does not authorize our rejecting the general expression, unless Mr. Malthus can point out a better one, which he has not even attempted to do, but has contented himself with saying that, "we must have recourse to demand and supply." [P. 58.] But this is to stop short at the surface of the science. What regulates supply? Surely it is the cost of production, and if we cannot find an accurate expression in one word, or in two, we are not for that reason to content ourselves with a superficial view of the subject.

There are two or three other paragraphs of too little importance to require a refutation. The last and most elaborate of Mr. M.'s *applications* relates to the variations in the currency. He dissents from those who think that paper was depreciated no more than to the extent of the difference between its value and that of bullion; because, he says, when compared with labour, it had fallen to a greater extent. [P. 67.] Those, therefore, who think that Mr. Malthus has failed in proving that the value of labour is constant, will not be prevented, by any thing which is here stated (though here too there are tables [p. 75]) from attributing to labour, and not to the currency, the whole of the depreciation with respect to labour, over and above the difference between the market and mint prices of gold.

19. TECHNICALITIES OF ENGLISH LAW
MORNING CHRONICLE, 18 SEPT. 1823, P. 2

Arguing one of Bentham's central tenets, the absurdity of some English legal practices, Mill in this letter comments on the quashing of cases on technical grounds. He refers to two accounts in the *Morning Chronicle*, "Police News. Hatton-Garden," 9 Sept., p. 4, and "Police. Hatton-Garden," 16 Sept., p. 4. Headed as title, subheaded "To the Editor of the Morning Chronicle," the letter is described in Mill's bibliography as "A letter on the Technicalities of English Law, wch. appeared in the Chronicle of 18th September 1823. Not signed." (MacMinn, p. 3.)

SIR,—In your Paper of Tuesday, the 9th of September, I observed a new instance of legal quashing. A number of bakers were brought up, on the charge of selling bread otherwise than by weight. It was discovered that the Magistrate's name had not been inserted in the indictment, and in consequence of this omission, the charge fell to the ground. I also found in your Paper of Tuesday the 16th, a similar instance of quashing, because an illiterate informer, instead of writing the word afternoon, had written after-forenoon.[1]

If English law were really "the perfection of human reason,"[2] no one would be acquitted, but because he was innocent—no one condemned, but because he was

[1]It would appear that only one baker, Joseph Rose, was brought up (the account on 9 Sept. was, however, entitled "Bakers Must Not Sell Quartern Loaves"), though he had three informations laid against him; he was released because the magistrate had not signed two of the informations. Rose was also the baker brought up in the second case (reported on 16 Sept.); in both cases William Johnson was the informer.
[2]Edward Coke (1552-1634), *The First Part of the Institutes of the Lawes of England; or, A Commentarie upon Littleton* (London: Society of Stationers, 1628), p. 97 (Lib. II, Cap. vi, Sect. 138).

guilty. To praise a system under which men are acquitted on any ground, except the insufficiency of the evidence of guilt, implies either the grossest insincerity, or the most depraved understanding. All formalities which do not facilitate the attainment of truth, are utterly useless, and as they almost always enhance the trouble and expence, they amount to a tax upon justice, and frequently to the utter denial of it. To this we must add the complicated evils which ensue, if it be discovered that a formality has been omitted. The previous proceedings are invalidated, the chance of impunity to the guilty is increased, and additional trouble and expence are occasioned to the innocent, by the recommencement of proceedings which may already have cost them far more than they can bear.

Will any one assert that the omission of the Magistrate's name in the indictment, renders it a whit more difficult to determine whether the parties are guilty or innocent? And if it does not, on what principle can the quashing of the indictment be justified?

But quashing is the favourite pastime of lawyers; nor is the motive difficult to divine. Every new indictment brings new fees into the pockets of Learned Gentlemen. Who can wonder, that a circumstance of such importance should outweigh in their minds the ruin of a thousand families.

Quashing is not confined to the prosecution of bakers for selling bread in an illegal manner. A law suit which has lasted for years may be rendered useless by the discovery that an insignificant formality has been omitted at the commencement. And so numerous are these formalities, that no inconsiderable proportion of the law proceedings which are instituted in this country terminate in that way. A gentleman may be deprived of his estate by the discovery of a technical flaw in his title; so frequently does this occur, that there are few estates, in Great Britain, the title to which is not liable to dispute, and Mr. Canning, in Parliament, spoke of an inquiry into the title deeds of estates as being one of the grossest iniquities which can be perpetrated.[3]

When it is proposed to substitute for the present confused and heterogeneous mass of statutes and cases, a Code constructed, not on a view of what has been done heretofore, but of what ought to be done hereafter—a cry is usually raised that such a reform would annihilate existing rights. Never was accusation more ill-founded, nor does any thing prove more conclusively than the currency which it has obtained, how readily mankind consent to take the opinions of the "constituted authorities" for gospel, on subjects upon which they may and ought to judge for themselves. The fact is, that the first step of an efficient reform of the law would be to pass an Act confirming and establishing all titles in which no flaw could be detected on a retrospect of a very limited number of years.

But now the omission of an unmeaning formality at a distance of forty or fifty

---

[3]Cf. George Canning (1770-1827), Speech on the Freehold Estates Bill (28 Jan., 1807), *PD*, 1st ser., Vol. 8, cols. 857-8.

years, may cast opulent families into the depth of poverty; and so far is the English law from securing rights, that every owner of land pays, at an average, 5 per cent. on his annual rent into the hands of lawyers, on account of the badness of the law. All this happens under a system which is, notwithstanding, "the perfection of human reason," although its rules were all framed six or seven centuries ago, and although there is not one of them which, in accuracy, precision, or, if rigidly enforced, even in justice, rises one step above the level of the age in which it was composed.

20. SECURITIES FOR GOOD GOVERNMENT
MORNING CHRONICLE, 25 SEPT., 1823, P. 2

This letter, like No. 19, employs a particular instance in support of an idea of Bentham's, in this case the popular removal of judges (see his *Draught of a New Plan for the Organization of the Judicial Establishment in France* [1790], in *Works*, Vol. IV, p. 359). The case was that of Richard Battlebar, a tradesman, and Jane Ashwood, "a perfectly respectable woman" (*Examiner*, 14 Sept., 1823, p. 605), who were sentenced on 12 Sept. to one month's imprisonment at the treadmill, on suspicion of indecent exposure, by Maurice Swabey (1785-1864), magistrate at Union Hall, Southwark. Mill picks up the argument of a letter to the Editor, "Revision of the Magistracy," *Morning Chronicle*, 22 Sept., 1823, p. 4, signed "A True Friend of Morality and Social Order" (not "to Morality," as Mill says). The case had occasioned much earlier comment in the *Morning Chronicle*: see 13 Sept., p. 4, 15 Sept., p. 3, and 16 Sept., p. 3 (a letter and a satirical poem, "Love and Justice"). Headed as title, subheaded "To the Editor of the Morning Chronicle," the item is described in Mill's bibliography as "A letter on the advantages of a judicial establishment consisting of judges removeable by the people, in the Chronicle of 24th [*sic*] September [1823.] Signed a Friend to Responsible Governments." (MacMinn, p. 3.)

SIR,—I perused with great satisfaction the Letter inserted in your Paper of Monday, the 22d, on Police Abuses, signed "A True Friend to Morality and Social Order." One passage, however, in that very able Letter, appears to me objectionable. The writer recommends as a remedy for police abuses, that several of the individuals at present in the Magistracy should be removed.

Now, Sir, I am one of those who look at *measures* rather than *men*,[1] and who reprobate the former when I conceive them to merit reprobation, without feeling any peculiar animosity against the latter. My appetite for change would be

---

[1]The catch-phrase, "not men but measures," seems to have originated in "Stentor Telltruth," *The Herald; or, Patriot-Proclaimer*, 2 vols. (London: Wilkie, 1758), Vol. II, p. 247, but was much used in the later eighteenth century, for instance by Edmund Burke (1729-97), the political philosopher, who refers to it as cant in his *Thoughts on the Cause of the Present Discontents* (1770), in *Works*, 8 vols. (London: Dodsley, Rivington, 1792-1827), Vol. I, p. 499.

satisfied, if the welfare of the community were exclusively consulted, no matter whether by one man or another. I know that although some men will yield to a small temptation, while others cannot be moved but by a great one, yet upon the whole there are few exceptions, or rather none at all, to the principle that all men who have power will infallibly abuse it; a principle the truth of which every one admits with regard to other men, although each considers himself to be an exception. My object, therefore, is, to obtain *securities* for the good conduct of Legislators, Judges, and Ministers; not to substitute one set of men for another set, leaving to those whom you nominate the same facilities for abuse of power which were enjoyed by those whom you remove.

Unless the abuses of the judicial power are such as indicate a radically unsound and depraved intellect, there is no reason for removing the individual, although there is great reason for subjecting him to such responsibility as will effectually prevent the recurrence either of the same or of other abuses. And if there is no particular reason for removing him, there is always this reason *against* it, that the experience which he has acquired in the exercise of his office, gives him (*ceteris paribus*) an advantage over any unpractised candidate.

Now in the recent instances of police abuses, no greater weakness of intellect appears, than that which is evinced by sacrificing the public good to the desire of gratifying the whole, or some particular section of the Aristocracy. When Mr. White dismissed the complaint of Lady Caroline Lamb's waiting-woman, on the word of her Ladyship's husband, and expelled the Reporters from the Police Office because they had reported the woman's story,[2] it is easy to see that the feeling uppermost in the mind of the Worthy Magistrate was a desire of gratifying such Honourables and Right Honourables as may hereafter be pleased to quarrel with their servants. In like manner when Mr. Swabey consigned two low vulgar people to a month's torture at the tread mill for indulging in gratifications which their superiors are suffered to enjoy without restraint, a discerning eye might detect in this specimen of Magisterial delicacy, a disposition to curry favour with a certain Society,[3] and with the numerous and powerful portion of the Aristocracy by which that Society is patronized. And I am persuaded that this puerile ambition is at the bottom of almost every instance of injustice which is perpetrated in this country by what are called Courts of Justice as well as of Law, but which should only be termed Courts of Law.

Far be it from me to object the desire of pleasing great people to these Magistrates as a crime. It is the unavoidable result of their situation. In a country

[2]For details, see No. 15.
[3]The Society for the Suppression of Vice was founded in 1802 as an auxiliary of Samuel Wilberforce's Proclamation Society (which it soon superseded). Originally much concerned with blasphemy and obscene publications, it later, using vigilante methods, pressed for greater control over prostitution. It had support from aristocrats and, it was said, from the government.

where there is an aristocracy interested in injustice, and where the judges are dependent upon the aristocracy, the judges will be unjust. Alter the circumstances, and they will be unjust no longer. Place the judicial office on such a footing that it shall not be necessary for them to conciliate the favour of the aristocracy, and that it shall be necessary for them to obtain that of the people; and then it will be no longer the interest of the aristocracy, but that of the people, which will be consulted. For the attainment of this object, I see no other expedient, than that of giving to the people, either immediately or through their representatives, the power of removing judges of all descriptions from their offices. Let the *power* be given, and the necessity for the *exercise* of it will rarely occur. If it be not given, then even if the popular voice made itself heard so strongly as to effect the removal of one or a few obnoxious magistrates, there would be no permanent good, for there would be no *securities* for good judicature, and as soon as the violent excitement of the public mind subsided, misgovernment would return with undiminished vigour.

A Friend to Responsible Governments

21. PARLIAMENTARY REFORM
MORNING CHRONICLE, 3 OCT., 1823, P. 4

This letter may be read as a Radical corollary of James Mill's "Government." Many of its arguments appeared in J.S. Mill's writings in this period (e.g., the assertion of an unlimited desire for power is also in No. 20). The signature "Quesnai" presumably alludes to François Quesnay (1694-1774), the French economist, who argued that the principle of general interest should govern the economic life of nations, and looked to liberty, security, and justice as the means to prosperity for all classes of society. Headed as title, subheaded "To the Editor of the Morning Chronicle," the item is described in Mill's bibliography as "A letter signed Quesnai, on the consequences of denying the capacity of the people, in the Chronicle of 3d October 1823" (MacMinn, p. 4).

SIR,—The difference between the Reformers and the Anti-Reformers of this country is, that the former are friends to a popular government, and the latter to an aristocracy.

The only ground on which Reform can stand, is the assumption that if the people had the power of choosing their representatives, they would make, if not the best, at least a good choice. This accordingly is the doctrine of the Reformers; and if this be true, it is evident that the question as to reform admits of no farther debate. The Anti-Reformers on the other hand, allege that the people are factious, turbulent, inimical to social order, and to the existence of property. On this ground they maintain that the existing form of Government, over which the people exercise no controul, and which is in the strictest sense of the word Aristocratical, should be preserved.

Let us grant to the Anti-Reformers, the full benefit of the assumption upon which their resistance to the Reformers is grounded. Let us admit that the people, if they had the choice of their Rulers, would infallibly make a bad choice, and so bad a choice, as to render the attainment of good Government in this mode utterly hopeless. That this would silence the claims of the Reformers is unquestionable. Let us examine, however, whether it is not equally unfavourable to the pretensions of their opponents.

It is indisputable, that if any person has the power of pillaging the people for his own benefit, and of forcing them to act in entire subservience to his interests, he will do so. This is implied in the common outcry against despotism. And if this be admitted of one man, it cannot be denied of any set of men less than the majority of the whole population. Against this propensity to pillage the people, and to reduce them to subservience, no check can be opposed, because the people alone have an interest in establishing a check; and the people, by supposition, are not to be trusted. All which can be done, is to vest unrestrained power in such hands, that the motive to abuse it shall be reduced within the narrowest possible limits.

Now it is evident, that as far as pillage is concerned, far less will suffice to satiate the rapacity of one man than of a thousand; and then, as to personal subservience, it is a smaller evil to serve one master than a great number. In so far, therefore, as the personal desires of the Sovereign are concerned, less mischief is likely to arise from the rule of one, than of an irresponsible few.

This appears at first sight inconsistent with history. But if we look back to the annals of despotism, we shall find that the oppressions which they exhibit have been severe exactly in proportion as the Monarch has been insecure. The tyrants in Greece were so sanguinary, only because they were in continual danger of being overthrown. The Pachas in Turkey plunder the people with such grinding extortion, only because they do not hold their office on a week's tenure. In fact, it is evident, that if the Monarch were perfectly secure, perfectly certain of never being molested in the exercise of his power, he would be satisfied with extracting from the people such a portion of the annual produce of land and labour as would abundantly supply all his appetites and passions; and when there is but one man to satiate, this is but a small portion. Despotism would be very moderately oppressive, if the despot were perfectly secure, but not being so, he is under the necessity of purchasing support by the plunder of the people. He must maintain a large military force to compel passive obedience—a large ecclesiastical establishment to inculcate it.

But as this Army and this Priesthood will employ their power, not for him, but against him, unless he can make it their interest to do otherwise, he cannot support his dominion unless he satiates, not himself alone, but them, with the spoil of the people. Despotism, therefore, owes by far the greatest part of its mischievousness to the insecurity of the Monarch. If he could be made perfectly secure—if he were released, not only from all legal, but from all moral responsibility—if men could be persuaded, that to oppose the behest of their Sovereign, or even to speak of him or of his acts with any thing short of the most unbounded and submissive veneration, was a most important violation of morality—then the Monarchs would be to them nearly as a shepherd to his flock. He would oppress them no farther than by extorting from them the means of satiating every possible desire, and in every other respect, it would be decidedly his interest to leave them perfect freedom of action.

It appears then, that if the people are not to be trusted, the least bad of all possible Governments must be, that in which all the powers of Government are concentrated in the hands of one man, and when that man is entirely exempt from all controul, either from the laws or from public opinion, a more unlimited despotism than has ever yet existed in the world.

There would, it is true, be grave inconveniences attending on this form of government. First, pillage even by one man is an evil, but this is not the worst. An absolute King, having little or no motive to acquire distinguished intellect, weak Monarchs would frequently fill the throne; and although they would not oppress the people more than Monarchs of vigorous intellect, they would be less capable of protecting them from the aggressions of one another. But although the folly and weakness of the Monarch would prove highly mischievous, it could not produce such lamentable effects as infallibly arise from an aristocratic government, whose interest it is to extract from the people as much in every way as they can be prevailed on to part with, and who, in proportion as they are wiser and better instructed, will only pursue that interest with more unerring certainty.

Thus, then, it appears that, to a man who reasons consistently, there is no medium between advocating a popular government, and standing up for absolute despotism. If the people are capable of making a good choice, with them the choice ought to rest. If they are not capable, he with whom the general happiness is the regulating principle of his judgments, will stop no where short of the completest conceivable despotism. But, he who, while he professes a horror of absolute power, opposes all propositions tending to vest an effective checking power in the people—such a man leaves no inference to be drawn, save either that his reasoning faculty is in a deplorable state of depravation, or that he is blinded by being himself a member of the governing aristocracy, whose rule is far more inimical to happiness than a secure and unlimited despotism. Hobbes, who is branded by all Englishmen as the advocate of despotism, had this advantage over the anti-reformers of the present day, that he reasoned consistently from the principle of the incapacity of the people,[1] which they equally with him adopt, but from which they reason only so far as suits the particular end which they have in view.

Quesnai

[1]Thomas Hobbes (1588-1679), *Leviathan* (1651), in *English Works*, ed. William Molesworth, 11 vols. (London: Bohn, 1839), Vol. III, pp. 153-70 (Pt. II, Chaps. xvii-xviii).

22. ATROCITIES OF THE TREAD WHEEL

GLOBE AND TRAVELLER, 3 OCT., 1823, P. 3

This article is based on Bentham's ideas as developed in James Mill's "Prisons and Prison Discipline" (1823), written for the *Supplement to the Fourth, Fifth, and Sixth Editions of the Encyclopaedia Britannica*, Vol. VI, pp. 385-95. Both the quotation from and reference to the ideas in *Prison Labour, Etc.: Correspondence and Communications Addressed to His Majesty's Principal Secretary of State for the Home Department, Concerning the Introduction of Tread-Mills into Prisons* (London: Nicol, 1823) by John Coxe Hippisley (1748-1825), M.P. for Sudbury, magistrate, actually derive from a letter to Hippisley of 7 June, 1823 (on pp. 23-66 of the work) from Dr. John Mason Good (1764-1867), physician and medical writer. The tread wheel (or treadmill) had been introduced to prisons only five years earlier, in 1818. Headed "Tread Wheel. [From a Correspondent.]," the unsigned article is described in Mill's bibliography as "An article on the atrocities of the Tread Wheel which appeared in the Globe & Traveller of 4th [*sic*] October 1823" (MacMinn, p. 4).

BY THE PUBLICATION of Sir J.C. Hippisley's work on Prison Discipline, the public attention has been called to the mischievous effects of a punishment which has been hailed as the great modern improvement in penal legislation—the Tread Wheel.

There are strong objections to the employment of labour, in any case, as a punishment. If we consider from what causes men are induced to commit that species of crimes which are most common—petty violations of property—it will be found that in the great majority of cases, it is *aversion to labour* which has been the operating motive. To prevent crime, means ought to be taken to counteract the painful associations which give rise to this aversion. For such a purpose no contrivance can be worse chosen than that of forcing labour, and that of the severest kind, upon the offender as a punishment.

When a poor man is at large, earning his bread by his exertions, unless his labour be excessive, there are many circumstances which tend to make it agreeable to him. It is to labour that he owes all the comforts and enjoyments of existence. By labour alone can he hope to advance himself in life and raise the prospects of his family. All this has not been sufficient to counteract his habits of indolence, for those habits have prevailed, and instead of labouring he has turned thief; and yet in order to cure him of his aversion to labour, he is placed in a situation where, instead of being the source of his enjoyments, it becomes an engine of unrequited misery to him, and of misery of the most intense description.

This objection applies strongly to all kinds of labour, when considered merely as a punishment; but most of all, to the tread-mill, the horrors of which, as described by Sir John Cox Hippisley, appear unequalled in the modern annals of *legalized* torture.

I inspected the men as they descended in rotation from the wheel, at the end of the quarter of an hour's task-work, and made room for fresh relays. Every one of them was perspiring—some in a dripping sweat. On asking them separately, and at a distance from each other, where was the chief stress of labour, they stated, in succession, and without the least variation, that they suffered great pain in the calf of the leg and in the ham; while most of them, though not all, complained of distress also in the instep. On examining the bottom of their shoes, it was manifest that the line of tread had not extended farther than from the extremity of the toes to about one-third of the bottom of the foot; for in several instances the shoes were new, and between this line and the heel altogether unsoiled—a fact, however, that was as obvious from the position of the foot while at work, as from the appearance of the shoe at rest. Several of the workers seemed to aim at supporting their weight by bringing the heel into action, the feet being twisted outwards; and on inquiring why this was not oftener accomplished, the reply was, that though they could gain a little in this way, it was with so painful a stress of the knees that they could only try it occasionally. The palms of their hands, in consequence of holding tight to the rail, were in every instance hardened, in many horny, in some blistered, and discharging water. The keeper, who accompanied us, admitted the truth of all these statements, and added that it was the ordinary result of the labour; and that use did not seem to render it less severe; for those who had been confined long appeared to suffer nearly or altogether as much as those who were new to the work. [Pp. 31-2.]

Sir J.C. Hippisley also states on good medical authority, that this kind of labour has a strong tendency to produce varicose tumours and ruptures, also, that the tortuous attitude and uneasy motion totally deprive the prisoner of the healthful advantage of athletic exercise.

On the female prisoners the effects are of a still more serious and distressing nature, in as much, that in the greater number of counties where tread-wheel labour exists, it has not been deemed safe to extend it to females. Nor are these evils chimerical. Sir J.C. Hippisley mentions the particular prisons in which they have been experienced, and gives various details concerning the Cold-bath Fields House of Correction, for which we refer our readers to the work itself. [Pp. 33-7.]

It is true that the communications received from the Governors of the various prisons in which the tread-wheel is in use, in answer to the official circular of Mr. Peel, have not been in any great degree unfavourable to the tread-mill.[1] The admissions, however, which they have made, and which are stated by Sir J.C. Hippisley, are fully sufficient to justify the inferences which Sir J. has drawn from them. And were it otherwise, Ilchester gaol has taught us not to judge of prison arrangements on the word of the prison authorities[2]—more especially of

---

[1] "Copy of a Letter, Addressed, by Mr. Secretary Peel's Directions, to the Visiting Magistrates of the Several Gaols and Houses of Correction, Where Tread Wheels Have Been Established" (18 Jan., 1823), *PP*, 1823, XV, 308.

[2] See "Report from the Commissioners Appointed to Inquire into the State of Ilchester Gaol" (8 Feb., 1822), *PP*, 1822, XI, 277-311, for an account of the abuses and misrepresentations by William Bridle, the Governor from 1808 to 1821.

arrangements so well calculated as the tread-mill to be instruments of oppression in the hands of those authorities themselves.

Among other circumstances which essentially unfit the tread-mill to be a good engine of punishment is the extreme inequality of the labour; which, it is plain, does not admit of being proportioned with any exactness to the constitution and previous habits of the prisoner, nor can it be proportioned at all, without leaving much to the discretion of the gaoler. "A man who has been accustomed to running up stairs all his life, with good lungs and muscular legs, will scarcely suffer by it, while an asthmatic tailor, weaver, or other sedentary artisan, will be half killed by the exercise."*

As if it had been endeavoured to devise a mode of punishment which should unite the fewest possible advantages, the tread-mill discipline, besides its cruelty, its inequality, and its injurious effects upon health, has not even the advantage of being an efficient kind of labour. There are many ways of turning a mill more advantageously than by human labour. Moreover, it does not, like the hand crank-mill, exercise the muscles which are of use in ordinary labour. It does not give those bodily habits which will render labour less irksome after release, while, as we have shown, it strongly tends to give such habits of mind as will render it more so. Nor is the tread-wheel labour efficient in the way of example. To be so, it should be visible to every eye. But it is unavoidably shut up within the walls of a prison, and can operate directly upon the minds of none but the prisoners.

Let it not be inferred, however, that we are adverse to the employment of labour in prison discipline. Labour, not tread-wheel labour, but mild, and at the same time efficient and productive labour, though highly unfit for purposes of punishment, is the best of all engines of reformation. But these two kinds of discipline must be kept entirely separate. The object of punishment is to inflict *pain*—pain sufficient to counteract the motives to vice. The object of reformatory discipline is to break pernicious habits, and to substitute useful ones. If, as has been observed, the *habit* which brings criminals to gaol is usually an *aversion to labour*, the grand object of reformatory discipline should be to *destroy* that aversion. The mode of destroying it is not by making labour an engine of torture. It is by making it a source of pleasure; by suffering the labourer to partake of the *fruits* of his labour, and that in sufficient quantity to make him think of labour with some degree of *pleasure*. It is evident, then, that if punishment, which is intended merely as an infliction of pain, be mixed up with reformatory discipline, which can be made effectual only by rendering the condition of the prisoner a state of pleasure, either the one of these two objects must be entirely sacrificed to the other, or the ends of both must be incompletely

Medical Jurisprudence, by Dr. [John Ayrton] Paris and Mr. [John Samuel Martin de Grenier] Fonblanque, [3 vols. (London: Phillips, 1823),] Vol. III, p. 131.

and inefficiently attained. In fact, we think that nearly all the failures which have taken place in the organization of prison arrangements, may be attributed to an ignorance of this fundamental rule, that *punishment* and *reformation* are two different objects, and as such, should be kept distinct: a position which appears to have occurred to no writer antecedent to the publication of the article "Prisons" in the Supplement to the *Encyclopaedia Britannica*, to which, for farther illustrations we beg to refer our readers.

23. PRACTICABILITY OF REFORM IN THE LAW
MORNING CHRONICLE, 8 OCT., 1823, P. 4

This letter, reflecting Mill's continuing interest in Benthamite law reform and his tutoring in the preceding year by John Austin (1790-1859), Benthamite disciple and close acquaintance of the Mills, appears to have no occasional cause. Headed as title, subheaded "To the Editor of the Morning Chronicle," it is described in Mill's bibliography as "A letter on the practicability of reform in the law, which appeared in the Chronicle of 8th October 1823. Not signed." (MacMinn, p. 4.)

SIR,—That numerous and powerful body, the practising Lawyers, whose opinions the public adopt far too implicitly on the subject of Legislation, have an evident interest in the permanence of the confused and unintelligible mass which now bears the name of law in this country. In proportion as the law is complicated, the influence of the only class who can interpret it must increase; and it is as little to be expected that Lawyers should advocate the adoption of an intelligible system of law, as it was in the time of the Reformation, that the Priests should consent to suffer the Laity to peruse the sacred volume.

We need not therefore be surprised that lawyers should have a number of fallacies at command, with which they combat all attempts at reform in the law. Of these dicta, one of the most frequent is, that it is impossible to devise general rules which shall include all particular cases.

This notion originates in a confusion between questions of law and questions of fact. The latter are innumerable: there is no one case which in all its circumstances exactly resembles another case. It is therefore impracticable to make rules for the decision of all questions of fact. But the questions of law which arise may easily be reduced under a very small number of heads.

Let us consider on what questions every law-suit must necessarily turn. In civil cases the subject of the dispute is, to which of two persons a particular right belongs. Each of them, in order to prove the justice of his claim, affirms that one of those events has happened which give commencement to the right; in the case of an article of property, for instance, that he has bought it, inherited it, and the like. His adversary either denies this event, or affirms that another event has occurred, which gives termination to the right, that he has sold the property, or forfeited it by some subsequent transaction. The question of fact, therefore, is, whether the alleged events have happened, which of course must be determined by the evidence. The questions of law are, in the first place, what the right is; and next, whether the alleged events, supposing them to have happened, are of the number of those which commence, or which terminate the right?

The problem, therefore, of making a *Civil* Code, consists of two parts. It must be determined what rights it is expedient to create; and it must be determined what events shall give commencement, and what shall give termination to a man's enjoyment of the rights.

Neither of these is surely an impossible task. A *right* is the permission, granted by the law, to make a particular *use* of a person or of a thing. Now it may surely be determined what uses a man shall be suffered to make of his property, what rights he shall be allowed to exercise over his servants, his family, &c.; and reciprocally, what services they shall have the power of exacting from him. The *events* also, on the occurrence of which these rights shall begin or terminate, may surely be defined. These are, the modes of acquiring and of losing property, and the like.

To determine all these questions is to make a civil code, which will apply to every individual case that can be conceived; since there is no case in which, when the state of the facts is ascertained, the dispute can turn on any question, except the extent of a right, the facts which confer the right, or the facts which take it away.

Nor is it more difficult to construct a body of *penal* legislation which shall extend to all cases whatever. All rights having been defined, it only remains to assign an appropriate punishment to every violation of those rights.

It appears, then, that there is not that inherent impossibility in devising general rules to fit particular cases, which is affirmed by lawyers to exist. Moreover, it is evident that in all cases which are not left absolutely to the discretion of the Judge, whenever any rule is consulted, even if one decision is made a rule for another, this is applying a *general* rule to a particular case. The Judge says, A shall enjoy a certain right, in consequence of a certain event; because, Sir Matthew Hale says,[1] that this event is sufficient to confer the right; or because Lord Chief Justice somebody declared in the case B versus C, that B became entitled to enjoy the same right, in consequence of the same event. Is it not evident that in both these cases, the Judge is deciding according to a general rule laid down by his predecessors, that the event in question shall always confer the right in question? So that the dispute between the Lawyers and the Reformers of the Law, is not whether it is possible to devise general rules, for this is done by

[1]Matthew Hale, Lord Chief Baron of the Exchequer (1660) and Lord Chief Justice (1671), a major legal authority.

both parties alike; but whether these general rules shall be fixed or variable; and whether they shall be formed upon the universal experience of mankind,—in other words, upon philosophic principles, or upon an induction of one or two instances only,—in other words upon precedents and cases.

24. OLD AND NEW INSTITUTIONS
MORNING CHRONICLE, 17 OCT., 1823, P. 2

This letter is in response to the speech on 9 Oct. to the Chester Whig Club by Colonel William Lewis Hughes (1767-1852), M.P. for Wallingford (1806-31), reported in the *Morning Chronicle*, 13 Oct., 1823, p. 2, in which Hughes was at pains to put distance between the terms "Whig" and "Radical, and Rebel." In the passage referred to by Mill, Hughes said, "We seek no new institutions—we claim only for the people their inalienable rights," a remark galling to the Philosophic Radicals. Headed as title, subheaded "To the Editor of the Morning Chronicle," the item is described in Mill's bibliography as "A letter on Old and New Institutions signed 'No Worshipper of Antiquity,' which appeared in the Chronicle of 17th October 1823" (MacMinn, p. 4).

SIR,—In Colonel Hughes's late speech at the Chester Whig Meeting, most of the principles of which meet with my warmest approbation, I however find one passage to which I cannot agree. The Colonel disclaims a wish to introduce *new* institutions, and only wishes to restore the Constitution to its pristine purity.

I am well aware that this is the ordinary language of those with whom Reform is only the watchword of a party—of those who wish for the removal only of *trifling* abuses, leaving untouched those *great* ones in which all the others originate. But that such a man as Colonel Hughes should give in to this CANT is what, certainly, I did not expect.

I am one of those, Sir, who are friends, and not enemies to innovation; for I wish to see the human race well governed—which would certainly be the greatest of innovations. All history proves, that in every nation of the earth, the powers of Government have uniformly been monopolized in the hands of a privileged few, who, accordingly, never failed to abuse those powers for the benefit of themselves and of their connections, with only one difference, that of old, when the public were far more ignorant and prejudiced than they now are, misgovernment was proportionally more flagrant.

We are told of the wisdom of our ancestors. Let us look back to what by an abuse of terms is called venerable antiquity, and which in fact was the nonage of the world; let us consider for a moment who and of what use were these ancestors, whom it is incumbent on us in the nineteenth century to reverence and worship. Those sages who firmly believed, that St. Dunstan tweaked the evil spirit by the nose,[1] that Aves and Credos, holy water, and the relics of saints were infallible safeguards in the hour of danger, and that a comet or an eclipse portended the ruin of an Empire—those worthies, whose brutality and licentiousness mastered every good feeling, and yielded only to slavish reverence for ascetic and bigotted Priests. Such "ancestors" as these are indeed worthy of being held up as patterns for us their degenerate "sons." Why are we not also required, in imitation of them, to put thousands to death by the most excruciating torments, for heresy, magic, witchcraft and sorcery?

Let us consider for one moment what would have been the consequence, if reverence for our ancestors had prevented us from adopting improvements in the physical, as it has in the moral sciences. We should never then have been initiated into the wonders of chemistry and of natural philosophy. We should never have seen the air pump, the spinning jenny, or the steam engine. No canals, no bridges, should we have had; and our roads would have remained inferior to the worst lanes of the present day. The press, and all the wonders which it has produced, would never have had existence.

It were indeed strange, if at that period of our history, when all the other arts and sciences were in their infancy—when the earth was believed to be a flat surface in the centre of the universe, and the sea to flow round its outer circumference—when the philosopher's stone and the universal medicine were the only objects of chemistry, and to foretel events by the stars, the sole purpose of astronomy; when wool, the only material of clothing, was carded and spun by hand, and when navigators rarely trusted themselves out of sight of the shore. It were strange, I say, if a people among whom these things were, should, amid all their ignorance, superstition, and barbarism, have taken enlarged views of human nature and of human society—should have foreseen all possible modes of oppression, and have provided efficient securities against all—should, in a word, have established a Constitution which could secure in perpetuity the blessings of good government to mankind.

Happily we are much wiser than our ancestors; it were a shame if we were not, seeing that we have all their experience, and much more in addition to it. We look back with contempt upon all which they did in the field of physical and mechanical knowledge. It is only in moral and political science that we are not ashamed to bow submission to their authority.

This will not appear strange, if it be considered what influence the ruling few

---

[1]Mill probably got the story about St. Dunstan (ca. 924-88), Archbishop of Canterbury, from *The History of England* (1754-62), 8 vols. (London: Cadell, Rivington, *et al.*, 1823), Vol. I, p. 112, by David Hume (1711-76), whose source was Osbern, "Vita Sancti Dunstani," in *Anglia sacra*, ed. Henry Wharton, 2 vols. (London: Chiswell, 1691), Vol. II, p. 97.

must necessarily exercise over the opinions and feelings of the subject many. The few profit by the existing Government; if a better were substituted, they would cease to receive more than their due share of the benefit.

Sir James Mackintosh, in his *Vindiciae Gallicae* ([2nd ed.,] p. 120n), makes the following observations:

Mechanics, because no passion or interest is concerned in the perpetuity of abuse, always yield to scientific improvement. Politics, for the contrary reason, always resist it. It was the remark of Hobbes, that if any interest or passion were concerned in disputing the theorems of geometry, different opinions would be maintained regarding them. It has actually happened (as if to justify the remark of that great man), that under the administration of Turgot, *a financial reform, grounded on a mathematical demonstration, was derided as visionary nonsense.* So much for the sage preference of practice to theory.[2]

One word more on innovation. They who do not fall into the egregious absurdity of throwing indiscriminate censure upon innovation, as if it were a necessary inference—because a thing is new, therefore it is bad; but who, nevertheless, wish to keep some measures with those who raise the cry against improvement; these half-and-half-men frequently repel the charge of loving innovation, by giving us to understand that they do not love it *for its own sake*. A most extraordinary merit, in truth! I will venture to affirm, that I have never yet either seen or heard of any one who loved innovation for its own sake. I have seen men who desired to effect *pernicious* innovations; but it was always from a view of some real or imaginary good, either to society, or to themselves individually.

To conclude, whenever I hear the cry against innovation, I always presume that the cause, in defence of which it is raised, is a bad one. For I am sure, that if it were a good one, its advocates could find some more substantial reason in its defence than merely the *antiquity* of the opinions which favour it, and the *novelty* of contrary opinions. And I cannot but consider, that he who, like Colonel Hughes, has a good cause to defend, calculates very ill if he avails himself of an argument which will serve a bad cause with as much success as a good one, when so many cogent arguments may be drawn from the real merits of the case.

No Worshipper of Antiquity

[2]Mackintosh's references are to Hobbes, *Leviathan*, in *English Works*, Vol. III, p. 91 (Pt. I, Chap. xi); and Anne Robert Jacques Turgot, baron de l'Aulne (1727-81), French statesman and economist, Controller General (1774-76) under Louis XVI. For the derision of Turgot's proposals for taxation based on mathematics, see *Vie de M. Turgot* (London: n.p., 1786), pp. 112-14, by Marie Jean Antoine Nicolas Caritat, marquis de Condorcet (1743-94).

25. REPUTED THIEVES

MORNING CHRONICLE, 30 OCT., 1823, P. 2

This letter glosses "Liberty of the Subject," a letter by "Vindex" (of St. John's Square), dated 20 Oct., that appeared in the *Morning Chronicle* of 23 Oct., p. 4. (In that letter Vindex, the employer of the boy sent to the treadmill, refers to his earlier letter, "Unjustifiable Conduct of a Constable," which was sent to the *Morning Chronicle*, but not published.) Rogers, the magistrate, is linked by Mill with Maurice Swabey (see No. 20), the quashing of whose convictions is reported in "The Late Convictions under the Vagrant Act," *The Times*, 20 Oct., 1823, p. 3. The apprehension of "reputed thieves" by a constable was provided for by 3 George IV, c. 55, Sect. 21 (1822), an addition to the Temporary Vagrancy Act, 3 George IV, c. 40 (1822). Mill's letter, signed "The Censor of the Judges" as is No. 16, is headed as title, subheaded "To the Editor of the Morning Chronicle," and is described in Mill's bibliography as "A letter on the practice of sending reputed thieves to the treadmill, signed the Censor of the Judges, which appeared in the Chronicle of 29th [*sic*] October 1823" (MacMinn, p. 4).

SIR,—The case which was communicated to you by your correspondent Vindex, on Thursday the 23d instant, is worthy of attention, as a specimen of the paternal solicitude of Magistrates for the safety of our property. A boy was seen by a petty constable in the street looking at a game at marbles. For this heinous offence, he was carried before the sitting magistrate, Mr. Rogers; and on the oath of the constable that he was a reputed thief (although his master was so entirely ignorant of his true character, as to speak highly in his praise), he was sent by Mr. Rogers to solace himself at the Tread Mill.

This vigilant Magistrate probably took example from one of the Swabey convictions, recently quashed at the Kingston Sessions. On a public occasion, an individual was seen in a crowd by a police officer. He was not, indeed, attempting to commit any criminal act, by the confession of the officer he was merely standing in the crowd like any one else. But then the officer knew him to be a reputed thief, or, at least, to keep company with reputed thieves: besides, on searching his pockets, he discovered a pair of scissors, inclosed in a sheath, whereupon he carried him before that active guardian of public morals, Mr. Swabey, by whom he was sent to the Tread-mill, under the Vagrant Act.

Some incredulous critics, indeed, have presumed to insinuate that a reputed thief means a person thought or said to be a thief, and that it is somewhat hard to punish a man for being so unfortunate as to fall under suspicion; they have farther ventured to hint that a man may have an enemy, sufficiently unprincipled to affirm, in the hearing of an officer, that he is a thief; or that, in a moment of irritation, any one may apply to him that name; and that, in all these cases, an officer of little discernment might, with a safe conscience, swear him to be a reputed thief. Nay, these sceptical reasoners have carried their audacity so far, as to doubt whether the veracity of a police officer always deserves implicit confidence; seeing that he has a strong interest in perjury, as a means of acquiring (not to speak of bribes), a character for zeal and activity, without the trouble of hunting out real offenders; seeing, moreover, that he may perjure himself with perfect safety, since it is utterly impossible for any one to prove that he is not a reputed thief.

But Mr. Swabey and Mr. Rogers are well aware that scepticism is an infallible sign of a narrow understanding. Superior to vulgar prejudices, they know how to place a proper degree of confidence in the virtue of mankind: and indeed it were strange, if that perfect veracity which so eminently distinguishes watchmen, did not extend to their fellow labourers in the cause of social order, the police officers.

With all due deference, however, to such high authorities, I cannot help thinking that this anxiety to punish *reputed thieves* implies an incapability of detecting *real ones*. If the perpetrators of every offence were duly brought to trial and punished, is it not clear that every one who is convicted as a reputed thief would, if innocent, be punished for no crime at all, and, if guilty, be punished twice for the same offence? One of two things, therefore, is the case—either the punishing of reputed thieves is utterly absurd and wicked; or the state of the law is such, that crimes frequently escape detection and punishment.

The case is, that the laws against theft are so disproportionately severe, that out of ten who are robbed, nine are unwilling to prosecute; that the expences of the law are so enormous, that out of a hundred who are willing to prosecute, ninety-nine have it not in their power; and, lastly, that be the fact as clear as the sun at noon-day, it is much more than an even chance that the thief escapes by a quibble.

To remove these obstacles, the wise framers of the Vagrant Act permit summary convictions, not for actual, but for reputed theft. There is ingenuity in the contrivance; but I venture to submit as a sort of insinuation, whether it would not be better to remove the obstacles to the detection of criminals, by mitigating the Penal Code, by abolishing law taxes,[1] by simplifying the law so that hired advocates shall not be needed, and by abolishing all the absurd fictions, all the quirks and quibbles, by which justice is so often eluded in the English Courts of Law.

They will not do this; it would hurt the interest of Learned Gentlemen. But to see men of unblemished character treading at the mill for being *reputed* by a Police officer to be thieves, neither hurts their interests nor their feelings. When

---

[1]As was done by 5 George IV, c. 41 (1824). In a note to Jeremy Bentham's *Rationale of Judicial Evidence*, 5 vols. (London: Hunt and Clarke, 1827), which he edited in the next few years, Mill comments that Bentham had written a passage "before the late repeal of the stamp duties on law proceedings, . . . one of the most meritorious acts of the present enlightened administration" (Vol. IV, p. 624).

will the public learn to think for themselves, instead of trusting to those who are interested in deceiving them?

The Censor of the Judges

26. EFFECTS OF GAMBLING

LANCET, 9 NOV., 1823, PP. 214-16

This article gives early indication of Mill's participation in the nature vs. nurture debate, in which he enlisted on the side of education and environment, without endorsing the views of the necessitarians or Owenites. The case here referred to is that of John Thurtell (1794-1824), who murdered a fellow-swindler, William Weare, on 24 Oct., 1823, and was hanged on 9 Jan., 1824. Mill's reference to "students of our profession" is surely a guise intended to associate his argument with the concerns of medicine (or it may have been added by the editor); he had no medical training, and his brief legal training is not specially germane. The article, Mill's only contribution to the *Lancet*, the (initially) weekly radical medical journal, is headed "[From a Correspondent] / The Late Murder / *Effects of Gambling*," and is described in Mill's bibliography as "An article on the evil consequences of gaming which appeared in the Lancet of 9th November 1823" (MacMinn, p. 4).

WHEN HUMAN NATURE EXHIBITS, as she occasionally does, an example of all kinds of wickedness concentrated in one man, we feel a melancholy interest in looking back upon the events of his life, and tracing the various circumstances which, by their conspiring influence, formed his mind to guilt, and eradicated all those associations, or prevented them from being formed, which cause an ordinary character to shudder at the thought of shedding the blood of a fellow creature.

Indolent and superficial reasoners would willingly arrest the inquiring mind in the search after those hidden causes by which the human character is formed. If a shocking instance of depravity presents itself to their notice, they do not say, That man was an idler, a drunkard, or a gamester; but That man was naturally of a bad disposition: as if men were robbers and murderers by constitution, and gave proof in the cradle of the atrocities which they were destined to commit.

With what face can a man who believes in innate depravity, hold up the fate of a murderer as an example, and warn all who are witnesses of it, to beware of the vices which conduct men to such an end? As consistently might a believer in fatality enlarge upon the necessity of obeying the dictates of prudence. The person to whom the admonition is addressed, might well reply, that it is unnecessary, since, if his nature is corrupt, it is in vain to struggle against it; but if he has a natural disposition to virtue, all exhortation to follow that disposition is superfluous. This doctrine, therefore, must raise up a blind confidence in the minds of the innocent, and must prevent them from taking the necessary precautions against those baneful habits which lead to vice: while they, who have already entered into the downhill path of wickedness, are prevented from a timely reform, by the thought that all their efforts would be unavailing.

Nor is the doctrine which we are combating less unfounded than mischievous. It is truly astonishing upon how little evidence this opinion has obtained currency in the world—such currency that the phraseology to which it has given rise, is, perhaps, equally universal with the use of language. It remains yet to be proved, that men are born either virtuous or wicked—either predisposed to morality or to vice. The only proof which it has ever been attempted to assign, is the enormous difference which exists between the most virtuous and the most vicious of men. The differences of character are indeed great; but so are the differences of external circumstances. And as it is generally admitted that circumstances often overcome the effect of natural predisposition, while no proof has ever been given that natural predisposition can overcome external circumstances: we are at liberty to conclude, that in ascribing to any person a natural and original disposition to vice, men are following the very common practice of representing as *natural* that which is only *habitual*, merely because they do not recollect its beginning, and will not take the trouble to inquire into its cause.

If, then, wickedness is not the effect of nature, but of external circumstances, that inquiry cannot fail to be interesting, which traces up that complicated and lamentable effect to the several causes which produced it. But most of all will such an inquiry be valuable, if it points out to us as the original root of all the evil, not some circumstances peculiar to the guilty individual, but habits and practices common to him with a great number; and which, although they do not conduct their votaries either to equal depravity or to equal punishment, infallibly bring about a radical corruption of character, and lead them continually to the brink of the most atrocious crimes.

Our readers will have long ago anticipated the subject of our present observations. The principal perpetrator of the late murder, John Thurtell, was a murderer only *after* he had been a gamester, and only, as it appears, *because* he had been a gamester.

The process by which gaming effects so complete a corruption of the character is two-fold. First, It reduces the gamester, not gradually, but suddenly, to that necessitous state where the temptation to crime is the strongest. Secondly, There is no practice capable of being pointed out, which so entirely roots out all good habits, and implants in their stead so many bad ones.

We are satisfied that if the unfortunate men who are executed for theft, or forgery, were interrogated concerning the original and primary cause of the distress which occasioned the crime, it would be found, in a great proportion of instances, that this distress was brought on by gaming. But it is not even by the distress which it creates, and the temptation which it frequently holds out to crime, that this destructive vice produces its worst effects. A mind which experiences the agonizing vicissitudes of the gaming table, soon becomes so habituated to strong excitement, that, like the body of the habitual drunkard, it is insensible to every stimulus of a gentler kind. It is totally and for ever unfitted to resume habits of diligence and industry; and the habits which it has acquired are in themselves, such as, above all others, tend to produce crime. Continually liable to perish by starvation, the gamester does not consider his perils much enhanced when, to be released from that danger, he exposes himself to the terrors of the law. And the habit of relying upon chance makes him trust to the chance of escape, even when the possibility is next to nothing. In no other way can the apparent coolness and indifference of Thurtell be accounted for, where it must be evident that the chance of escaping detection scarcely deserved the name of a possibility.

It is a question well deserving of consideration, how far Government or its officers are justified in any direct interference to prevent these practices. It would be a chimerical expectation, that the vice of gaming could be eradicated by positive enactment. But there can be no doubt, that public gaming-houses contribute greatly to the encouragement of this vice. Unwary persons, perhaps, recently arrived in London, (and we particularly address our observations to students of our profession,) and not yet aware of the dangers to which they are exposed, are frequently entrapped, and carried into one of these houses, where they are made drunk, cheated of their money, and, perhaps, by frequent repetition, reduced to poverty, while they contract, at the same time, inveterate habits of gaming. We think that the exertions used for the suppression of these houses are not by any means so active as they ought to be. Many notorious hot-beds of vice are still permitted to exist; and we are convinced, that upon diligent inquiry, their existence would be found to be connived at by the police officers, who have no interest in diminishing the number of offences, though they have in obtaining possession of the persons of the offenders. We think that Mr. Dyer, Mr. Swabey, and Mr. Rogers, would be better employed in extirpating this nuisance, than by sending respectable men to the tread-mill for having the misfortune to be taken ill in Hyde Park,[1] or for being considered by police officers "reputed thieves."[2]

[1]John Watts (in his 77th year), "a most respectable individual," being "taken with a violent pain in the bowels" while in Hyde Park on 20 Aug., "was constrained . . . to obey the imperative call of nature." Taken up by a police officer, he was committed by Dyer, the magistrate in the Marylebone Street office, to a month's hard labour in Coldbath Fields prison. He was not allowed even to notify his family of his whereabouts for more than twenty-four hours and was released only on 31 Aug., without, however, having endured the treadmill. See "Liberty of the Subject," *Globe and Traveller*, 30 Sept., 1823, p. 2.

[2]See No. 25.

27. QUESTION OF POPULATION [1]
BLACK DWARF, 27 NOV., 1823, PP. 748-56

This letter is the first of four by Mill to Thomas Jonathan Wooler (1786?-1853), editor and publisher of the populist weekly *Black Dwarf*, an opponent of the Malthusian principles and practices that Mill had adopted to the point of being arrested for distribution of birth-control literature (probably in May 1823). Mill takes exception to the second part of Wooler's "Inquiry into the Principles of Population," printed in two instalments: the first (including a letter by Francis Place, who was responsible for the printing of the Neo-Malthusian literature Mill had distributed) in *Black Dwarf*, 12 Nov., 1823, pp. 661-3, and the second *ibid.*, 19 Nov., pp. 693-706. The page references in the text are to this second part. For further stages in the controversy, see Nos. 28, 31, and 32. The letter, headed as title, is described in Mill's bibliography as "A letter on the necessity of checking population, which appeared in the Black Dwarf of November 20th [*sic*] 1823, signed A.M." (MacMinn, p. 4).

SIR,—Although I do not agree in the view which you take of the important subject of population, I cannot sufficiently applaud your liberality in leaving your pages open to the discussion of the question; a degree of toleration, which, I am sorry to say, few persons who take your side of this question, can be prevailed on to allow. I hasten to avail myself of this liberty of discussion, for the purpose of combating the objections which you stated in your last number against the plan of checking population [pp. 695-9]; objections which appear to me founded on a mistaken view of the circumstances upon which the condition of the labouring classes depends.

It is unnecessary for me to prove, that the working people are in a state of miserable poverty, since you admit this, and have long been exerting yourself for the benevolent purpose of improving their condition. We differ only as to the cause of the distress; which I maintain to be, excess of population, as compared with the means of subsistence. You, on the contrary, affirm, that population has no tendency to increase beyond the means of subsistence; and that misgovernment is the only cause of the distressed condition of the working classes.

I should be very sorry to extenuate the miseries of misgovernment. I am, equally with yourself, a friend to a Radical Reform in the Commons House of Parliament;—and if I could believe, as you appear to do, that such a Reform can only be effected by keeping the people in poverty, I should perhaps hesitate to urge the plan of checking population, until after a Reform should have been obtained. But I cannot agree with you, that the working classes will not reform the government unless they are miserable. On the contrary, I think that so long as they are in poverty, Reform may be delayed for an unlimited period; but if they were in the receipt of high wages, they would have leisure to turn their attention to the abuses of government; and those abuses could not fail of being speedily reformed.

I.—You maintain that population has no tendency to increase beyond the means of subsistence. [Pp. 694-6.] I feel convinced that you are entirely mistaken; but this is a question of some complication; and although I shall be ready to discuss it whenever you please, the practical conclusion, as far as regards the poor man may be shown without making it depend on this question; and to this point attention is now requested.

You admit the fact of the distress; but you ascribe it to misgovernment [pp. 697-8, 703, 705]; meaning, I presume, over-taxation. Now over-taxation cannot lower wages. It may, indeed, you will say, raise the prices of the necessaries of life. It will thus injure the working classes as much as if it operated directly to reduce wages. I shall not enter into this question at present. I shall concede the point. But I hope to convince you that it does not affect the question. I admit, for argument's sake, that the present rate of wages is such as would enable the labourer to live in comfort and happiness, but for the pressure of taxation.

My argument remains the same:—the labourer is now in distress. If he had double his present wages, with only the same amount of taxation, he would be in distress no longer. Now each man would have double his present wages, if the numbers of the people had not been too rapidly increased.

Does not every working man know, that his employer would give him higher wages, if he were not sure of obtaining as many men as he wants at the present rates? And is it not clear that he could not obtain men, if men in sufficient quantity and out of employment, were not to be had?

There is now a certain quantity of employment. There are as many men as can be employed, and more; for there is a great number of men out of work. These men, who are out of work, must either starve, or agree to take lower wages than their neighbours. The consequence is, that wages are low, and employment being regarded as a favor, the working man is often compelled to submit to incivility and insolence from his employer.

Suppose that, instead of *excess*, there was a *deficiency* of labourers. At present a capitalist can always obtain workmen, but a workman cannot always find an employer. Suppose this order of things reversed: suppose that there were fewer men than are wanted for the purpose of production. All the labourers would then be fully employed, and as more would be wanted than it would be possible to procure, some capitalists, in order to allure the men from their former employers, would offer high wages; this would compel the former employers to do the same. Wages would therefore be high, and employment would no longer be considered as a favor, but on the contrary, a labourer would be doing a favor to a capitalist, by working for him, and the capitalists would be compelled to treat their workmen well.

I infer that it is always wise in the labourers, to keep down their numbers a little below the means of employment. No men would then be ever out of work; the difficulty of procuring workmen would compel the capitalists to offer high wages, and this they would do in spite of any law to the contrary, however severe that law might be.

If then so much good is to be done by keeping down the numbers of the working people, the only question is, between one mode of keeping them down, and another. It is for the people themselves to decide. For my own part, I consider the plan of checking population, to be that which unites the most advantages with the fewest disadvantages.

All this, you see, does not depend in any degree upon the tendency of population to increase beyond the means of subsistence. It depends upon nothing but what every working man must know: that if there were fewer men, there would not be any men out of work; and that if there were no men out of employment, the men who are in employment could make their own terms with the capitalists.

II.—You say, that it would be better to take off the taxes than to diminish the population.[1] I too am desirous that the taxes should be taken off: but if there were no taxes upon the working classes at all, there would be as many men out of employment as before: although they who are employed would be better off as long as their present wages continued; but, as there would still be more labourers than could obtain employment, the same process of bidding at lower wages against one another would continue, and wages speedily be reduced again to the lowest possible amount; reduced too, observe, by the competition of the working people themselves. Besides, when a mode of benefiting the working classes, viz. by limiting their numbers, is pointed out, it is no answer to point to another mode of benefiting them, viz. by taking off the taxes: for this, unfortunately, you have not yet in your power, (and yet there is no reason why the people should be kept miserable in the interim:) and besides, if you had, why not do both?

I cannot agree in the sentiments which you express in the following sentence; "We do not wish men to be comfortable, if they could be so for a period under a *bad system.*" [P. 705.] I *do* wish men to be comfortable, whether under a bad system or a good one. What is it that constitutes a bad system, if it is not the *discomfort* which it produces. Good government is not the end of all human actions. Though a highly important means, it is still only a means, to an end: and that end is happiness.

I admit that I should desire for the people *something more* than merely good clothing and plenty of food. But it remains to be shewn that their chance of obtaining that *something more*, will be in any degree diminished by their being well fed and clothed. I feel confident that it will be increased. Until they are well fed, they cannot be well instructed: and until they are well instructed, they cannot emancipate themselves from the double yoke of priestcraft and of reverence for superiors.

[1]Wooler, "Inquiry into the Principles of Population, No. 1," *Black Dwarf*, 12 Nov., 1823, p. 662.

Placed as is your observation, just quoted, among many others of similar import, I cannot but view it as a sort of acknowledgment, that the people would be made more comfortable by limiting their numbers. If they, too, can be convinced of this, I have no fear of their hesitating to adopt the means from apprehension of its retarding the epoch of a Radical Reform.

A circumstance which appears to weigh with you, is, that you think the plan of checking population a device of the rich to oppress the poor. [P. 705.] So far is this from being the case, that it is entirely contrary to the interests of the rich that any check to population should come into general adoption.

It is the interest of the master manufacturers, that a great number of hands should readily offer themselves at low wages. Now I have shewn, that if the numbers of the people were limited to a sufficient degree, wages would be high, and workmen could not always be readily obtained.

III.—You say, "Wages have decreased in England, in a ratio with the accumulation of capital; not because there are too many labourers, but because capital, being the ruling principle, can compel them to labour upon its own conditions." [P. 701.] It is true, that when the population is excessive, the capitalist can lose nothing by dismissing him—that another man, of equal bodily powers, will immediately offer himself at the same, or even lower wages,—he is forced to cringe to his master, and submit to any indignity rather than be turned out. If labourers were few in comparison to the demand for them—if labour, and not employment for labour, were the article in request:—if every working man knew that when dismissed he could easily obtain employment, while his master could not so readily obtain another labourer, he would then be as independent as his employer.

Look at North America! Is the labourer there the slave of the capitalist? You will say, this is owing to good government. To prove the contrary, I refer you to the English colonies, to Nova Scotia, for instance; and the English colonies are among the worst governed countries in the universe. Yet in Nova Scotia the labourer is highly paid, and perfectly independent; nor does any rich man dare to oppress or insult him. This is only because there is a deficiency of labourers, below the number which capitalists wish to employ.

In some parts of the south of France, the working people are well paid, and well provided with necessaries and comforts. This I affirm from my own observation.[2] There however, *population is regulated.* Yet there the government is not good. The same is the case is some parts of the Austrian dominions, under one of the most despotic governments upon record. In both these countries the people are kept, through the efforts of bad government, in a state of great mental degradation, and consequently unable to avail themselves of the advantages they

---

[2]Mill is referring to his stay in the South of France with Samuel Bentham's family in 1820-21. The journal and notebook recording that period will be found in *CW*, in the first volume of *Journals and Speeches*.

might otherwise possess, which in time they will possess, and which the people of this country might almost immediately possess.

Not only the *master* manufacturer *but the landowner also, has an interest in over-population*. A large population implies a high state of cultivation, and dear corn. Now a high price of corn is the cause of high rents; an highly cultivated farm will yield an increased rent at the expiration of the lease. Both sections of the rich—the landowners and manufacturers—are thus interested in the excessive population; the former for high rents; the latter for low wages, and high profits.

Nor is this all. Both landlords and manufacturers have an obvious interest in keeping the working classes in a state of abject poverty. These gentlemen know that while the great body of the people are compelled to work fourteen hours a day, they cannot turn their attention to the abuses of the government. They can neither instruct themselves, nor send their children to be instructed. From want of leisure, their thinking powers can never be sufficiently developed, to repel the prejudices which make them the slaves of priests and kings.

So long as excess of population was regarded as an irremediable evil, the doctrine was taken up and patronized by the aristocracy: who wished the people to infer, that misgovernment was but a trivial evil, and that it was idle to oppose it, since the *lower classes* must always be in poverty, under a good, or under a bad government. But now that remedy is pointed out, for excess of population; a remedy, which, if adopted, would produce high wages, and would enable the people to instruct themselves, and to reform their government; I venture to predict that the rich, but above all, the clergy will do all in their power to prevent the adoption of the plan, so well calculated to elevate the scale of being. As soon as they shall perceive that it is coming into use, they will rail against it in the pulpit, will persecute in every possible way, and without mercy all whom they suspect to have made use of it. But all their efforts will be useless; and if the superstitions of the nursery are discarded, we may hope ere long to see the English people well paid, well instructed, and eventually well governed.

IV.—I have only room to say a few words against the objection that this plan is a violation of the laws of nature. [Pp. 700, 705.] Those laws are no more violated by checking population than by any other mode of turning to useful purposes the properties of matter. It is not in the power of man, a being of limited faculties, to violate the laws of nature. But he can avail himself of one law to counteract another. It is a law of nature that the sexual intercourse, if not artificially prevented, occasions the generation of children. But it is also a law of nature, that man shall seek happiness; and that he shall avail himself, for that purpose, of other laws of nature.

You say, in a former article; "With all due deference to those who wish to keep down the population to the means of subsistence, I think this might be very safely left to Providence which has spread so plentiful a table for all his creatures:"[3] and in a later article; "We can trust the Ruler of all things, not only with 'his sky' but all the principles which he has called into action, to regulate themselves."[4]

You do not trust the Almighty with "his sky." You do not indeed prevent the rain from falling at unseasonable times: the true reason of which I take to be that you cannot. But you do all in your power to shelter yourself from its fall: you put up an umbrella, and cover your house with a roof, to prevent the rain, which Providence has sent, from injuring your person or your property. The charge of violating the laws of nature may thus be retorted upon yourself. To check population is not more unnatural than to make use of an umbrella. If either of these operations is a counteraction of the designs of Providence, both are equally so. Again, when you speak of leaving to Providence the care of checking population, you seem not to be aware of the length to which this argument may be carried. A man who leaves every thing to Providence, will not succeed in many of his undertakings. "God helps those who help themselves:" and you might as well leave to Providence the care of producing food, as that of preventing either the waste or useless consumption of it.

A.M.

28. QUESTION OF POPULATION [2]
BLACK DWARF, 10 DEC., 1823, PP. 791-8

This is the second of Mill's responses to the opinions of Thomas Wooler (see No. 27). Wooler had replied to No. 27 in "The Black Dwarf to 'A.M.' against the Preventive System," *Black Dwarf*, 3 Dec., 1823, pp. 772-83, to which the interpolated page numbers refer. Headed "Question of Population / Arguments of the Anti-Populationists," the letter is subheaded "To the Editor of the Black Dwarf," and is described in Mill's bibliography as "A second letter on the same subject which appeared in the Black Dwarf of December 10th 1823, signed A.M." (MacMinn, p. 5).

SIR,—I have perused with attention your reply to my former letter on the plan of regulating the numbers of the people; and I proceed to state the reasons which induce me, notwithstanding all which you have said, to adhere to my former opinion, that any increase of population beyond the actual increase of the means of subsistence and employment, would be highly injurious to the labouring classes, by whatever circumstances the increase of the subsistence may be promoted or retarded.

Before replying, however, to your objections, I think it necessary to correct

---

[3]Wooler, "Practical Endeavours to Apply the System of Mr. Malthus, in Checking Population," *Black Dwarf*, 17 Sept., 1823, p. 405.
[4]Wooler, "Inquiry . . ., No. 1," p. 661.

two mistakes into which you have fallen in your statement of my views. You observe, that it is not the labourer alone who multiplies the candidates for labour; and you quote the instances of Mr. T. Courtenay, and Mr. Canning.[1] You then observe, "It is only those who *are poor*, who are recommended to abstinence. A class almost as numerous, namely, *those who may become so*, are never taken into the calculation." [P. 776.] Now, Sir, I have to remark, that I *do* take into the calculation not only the poor, but all men; and I think it highly unwise in any person, rich or poor, to have more than a certain number of children. But I certainly think it still more unwise in a poor man to have a family whom he cannot maintain, than in a rich man to have a family which he can.

The other instance of misinterpretation to which I allude, is the following:— You say, "you would be satisfied if the people could be made comfortable under a bad system; and while no discomfort is actually felt, you seem to infer that it ought not to be feared, no matter how certain to result from a bad system." [Pp. 777-8.] Now, Sir, on turning to my former letter, I do, indeed, find these words: "I *wish* the people to be comfortable under any system, good or bad;" but I also find the following words: "I admit that I should desire *something more* for the people than merely good clothing and plenty of food. But it rests with you to prove, that their chance of obtaining that *something more* will be in any degree diminished by their being well fed and clothed."[2] I also avowed myself,[3] and again avow myself, a friend to a Radical Reform in the Commons House of Parliament. So much for my views and your misinterpretations. I now proceed to comment upon your arguments.

You say that I have avoided the discussion of the question whether population has ever pressed against the means of subsistence; and yet you say this is the *only* ground upon which my arguments in favour of keeping down the numbers of the people can be maintained. [P. 783.]

It may, perhaps, be necessary to inform you, that when population is said to press against the means of subsistence, the meaning is, that it presses against the means of employment; in short, that there are more men in existence than can be employed and maintained, in comfort, by the productive capital of the country. That such is the fact, is sufficiently proved, by the universal prevalence of low wages.—There is no country on the earth, if we except America and other newly cultivated countries, where (if no check is in use) the labourer is not underpaid. Now, I ask, how could this possibly be the case, if the population did not press on the means of employment? If there had been fewer workmen than the capital of the world is able to employ, the capitalists would have found great difficulty in obtaining men; they would have been eager to obtain them almost at any cost,

---

[1]Thomas Peregrine Courtenay (1782-1841), politician and author, M.P. for Totnes, had thirteen children; George Canning had four.
[2]Mill, "Question of Population [1]," p. 752 (No. 27).
[3]*Ibid.*, p. 749 (No. 27).

and would have bid against one another until wages were raised very high. This, however, is very far from being the case. In every old country, the lowest class of labourers are barely provided with the necessaries of life. This could never be the case, if there were not more than the capital of the country could employ; in consequence of which they bid against one another, and obtain lower wages: nor can they all be employed, even at a low rate, for many are constantly out of work. If now they would adopt means for regulating their numbers, they would have it in their power to make their own terms with their employers; for they could always keep their number below that which can be employed with the present capital. Labour would then always be in request, and wages high.

But you affirm (if I understand you rightly), that even in this case, the employers could keep down wages. [P. 775.] I feel no such apprehensions. The capitalists have been enabled, hitherto, to keep down wages, only by the mutual competition of the labourers. Slaves are at the mercy of their employers, and will be worked as it may suit the convenience of those employers. They can be forced to work. Free labourers cannot.

When there is no excess of population—no competition among the labourers, they are not at the mercy of their employers. Among many proofs of this fact which our history affords, I shall only quote one. After the great plague, in the reign of Edward III, by which the numbers of the people were greatly reduced, complaints were made of a deficiency of workmen, and it was found that they would no longer work without high wages. On this an Act of Parliament was made to prohibit them from taking higher wages than they took before the plague: this Act being found ineffectual, the penalties were raised higher and higher, until, at last, the offence was made capital; and still it was all in vain.[4] A

---

[4] After the Great Plague of 1349 had reduced the English population by almost half, the Statutes of Labourers of 1349 (23 Edward III, Stat. 1, cc. 1, 2, 3, 5, 8) and 1350 (25 Edward III, Stat. 1, cc. 1-5) were enacted to prevent the remaining labouring population from demanding exorbitant wages. Both wages and prices were fixed, and work became compulsory. In 1388 (12 Richard II, cc. 3, 4, 7), these laws were enlarged; punishments were increased in severity, and restrictions on the movement of labourers imposed, to prevent desertion of the land through the seeking of higher wages elsewhere. Begging was limited to the aged and infirm. These efforts were largely unsuccessful, and legislation was enacted throughout the fifteenth century to broaden the applicability of the laws, and increase the punishments for breaking them. By 1530 (22 Henry VIII, c. 12) it became necessary to license beggars, and to punish vagabonds who left their homes and work by whipping and setting in the stocks. Refusal to work for reasonable wages led to punishment as a vagabond. Vagabondage resulting from a third escape from service became punishable by death in 1547 (1 Edward VI, c. 3), and though this Act was repealed in 1549 (3 & 4 Edward VI, c. 16), it was restored in 1572 (14 Elizabeth I, c. 5) and remained in force until 1593 (35 Elizabeth I, c. 7). Thereafter the punishments of 22 Henry VIII, c. 12 (1530) were restored. When Mill refers to the capital offence of taking higher wages, he appears to mean these Acts which punished by death a third refusal to work wherever required for whatever wages were offered.

striking proof of the disposition of the higher classes to keep down wages, but an equally striking proof of their inability to do so. It may serve as an answer to your assertion, that if half the population of Ireland were cut off by a pestilence, the remainder would not be benefited. I think it very clear that they would be benefited; as the English people were benefited by the plague in the time of Edward III.

I have your own authority, to corroborate my assertion,[5] that it is the competition of the labourers which enables their employers to keep down wages. You say

no labour was ever *long profitable* to the labourer in this country. All sorts of labour, at the same period, cannot be so, particularly in manufactures; the demand for which is influenced by fashions; and the labourer must eat or starve as fashion pleases. When a trade is supposed to be profitable, a rush is made on the part of the rising population to partake of its advantages. This destroys them. Another is rising and the crowd turns in that direction. [P. 782.]

Is it not clear, from your own statement, that if the "rising population" were not so numerous—if the "crowd" were smaller, their "rush" to partake of high wages would not, as at present, have the effect of lowering those high wages? Is it possible to admit more explicitly than you do, that the lowness of wages is owing to the competition among the people, from which it is a necessary inference, that if the people were less numerous, the competition would be much smaller, and wages would not be so much reduced?

I do not think it necessary to reply to any of the arguments which you have adduced to show that this "check to population"[6] would not have the effect of checking population. Whatever other objections may be urged against it, this, at least, is a merit which certainly must be allowed to it. I do not see how you can well doubt that if the people could be prevailed upon to use the method of keeping down their numbers, they would infallibly succeed.

You endeavour to shew that I am wrong in asserting that it is the interest of the landowners and manufacturers, that the country should be over-peopled;[7] you do not, however, deny, either that low wages are favourable to the manufacturer, or high rents to the landlord: and it is clear that when there are many mouths to feed, a high state of cultivation is required, which implies dear corn, and high rents.

[5]Mill, "Question of Population [1]," p. 750 (No. 27).
[6]Wooler uses cognates of this term throughout "The Black Dwarf to 'A.M.,'" e.g., in his conclusion on p. 783. Malthus introduced the term in the 1st ed. of his *Essay on the Principle of Population* (London: Johnson, 1798), where he refers in the heading to Chap. iv to the "two principal checks to population" (p. 53), i.e., the "preventive check" (associated with vice) and the "positive check" (associated with misery). Five years later in the much enlarged new ed. of the *Essay*, divided into four Books (*ibid.*, 1803), he introduced "moral restraint" as an additional check (of a preventive but non-vicious kind); see, e.g., p. 11 (Bk. I, Chap. ii), and pp. 483-93 (Bk. IV, Chap. i).
[7]"Question of Population [1]," p. 754 (No. 27).

Your only argument is, that Dennis Browne says, that Ireland could spare two millions of its inhabitants.[8] Now I cannot hold it to be any proof, that some thousands of men will not see and act according to their interest, because one man, and he, not one of the wisest, either does not see it, or seeing it, affects to preach against it. But without pushing this argument farther, I admit that Ireland is *rather too much* over-peopled, even for the aristocracy; for their own persons and property are endangered by the despair of a starving people.

You still think that the people will not effect reform until they are driven to desperation by poverty; and you quote the apathy and indifference of the middle classes. [P. 773.] I might quote the apathy and indifference of the agricultural labourers, who are by far the poorest of the working people. Notwithstanding all that you have said, I really cannot admit that the middling classes of this country are more indifferent than the working classes to the blessings of good government; and I am sure that in every other country of Europe the middle classes ALONE feel any desire for a better government than they possess.

As to the condition of the people in the South of France, and in the Austrian States, you do not deny the truth of my statement, that they regulate their numbers, and that they are well paid and comfortable.[9] But you say they are in a state of great mental degradation. [P. 779.] This is true. But who ever asserted, that superstition and mis-government will not brutalize a people? They are the slaves of the priests; and, moreover, the Government, which knows what it has to fear from their mental improvement, discourages the introduction of schools and other means of instruction among them. Our working classes are, by no means, equally priest-ridden, and have much greater facilities for instructing themselves.—You say, "it remains to be proved, that until men are well fed they cannot be well instructed." [P. 778.] In support of which you quote Shakspeare, rather an extraordinary authority in a question of philosophy. I reply, that if *fat paunches make lean pates*;[10] still it is not the less true, that so long as men stand in need of all the money which they can command, to secure a bare subsistence, they are not likely to spend much, either upon books or upon the instruction of their children. Nor is this all. A man who is compelled to work fourteen hours out of the twenty-four to obtain bread, has no time to instruct himself, and is too much harassed and fatigued to turn his attention to important affairs. How can it be otherwise?

A few words more on the specific plan which has been proposed for the regulation of population. You see in it a tendency to moral evils of the most aggravated description; and you insinuate, that it would lead to infanticide, and

[8]Denis Browne (1763-1828), M.P. for Kilkenny, alluded to by Wooler, p. 779. The source of the remark has not been located.

[9]"Question of Population [1]," pp. 754 and 752 (No. 27).

[10]William Shakespeare, *Love's Labour's Lost*, I, i, 26; in *The Riverside Shakespeare*, ed. G. Blakemore Evans (Boston: Houghton Mifflin, 1974), p. 179.

even to murder. [P. 780.] You might as well say, that to give true evidence before a Court of Justice, might lead to perjury; that to write your name would lead to forgery; or, in fact, that any useful act might terminate in any mischievous one, if some insignificant collateral circumstance is, in both cases, the same. This looks very like a reason made to justify a feeling. Can you discover any but a fantastic resemblance between checking population, and committing murder? Do you think, that what deters people from committing murder, is an aversion to reduce the population of the country? for this is the only deterring motive, which would be removed by checking population. As to infanticide, I leave you to judge, whether a parent, who has a larger family than it is possible to maintain, or a parent who has only a small family, is most likely to be tempted to destroy a child. I thus retort upon yourself your remark, that men should keep as far as possible from the temptation to commit any crime. [P. 780.]

In my last letter, I replied to the objection, that to check population is to violate the laws of nature, by observing that it is equally a violation of the law of nature to hold up an umbrella.[11] This you deny; and you say "I am no party to the operation of the law; and I cannot violate it. The law is, that rain should descend; and I only avoid its descending upon my own head." [P. 782.] The law is, that rain shall descend upon every man's head, and every where. But if you do not like this illustration, I will give you another. It is a law of nature that man should go naked. He is born naked; like other animals, all of whom go naked. To put on clothes is clearly a counteraction of the designs of Providence, if Providence intended that we should not violate the laws of nature. Accordingly, upon this principle, some self-called philosophers have written in defence of the savage state, and have exclaimed against every step in the progress of civilization as being an infraction of the laws of nature.

You also say that there is "a great difference between the different laws of nature: and that you do not suspect me of asserting that you have an equal right to hold up an umbrella, and to procure abortion, or to kill a fellow creature." [P. 782.] This is precisely what I want. You have now brought your doctrines to the same test with myself. I too, affirm, that "there is a great difference between *different laws* of nature." The difference is this, there are two sets of actions both of which you chuse to call violations of the law of nature. By the one set misery is inflicted, by the other set, no evil whatever is occasioned. Thus by killing a fellow-creature, pain is inflicted on the murdered person and his connexions, and other persons are alarmed for their own safety. By checking population, no pain is inflicted, no alarm excited, no security infringed. It cannot, therefore, on any principles, be termed immoral; and if the above arguments be correct—if it tends to elevate the working people from poverty and ignorance to affluence and

[11]"Question of Population [1]," pp. 755-6 (No. 27).

instruction, I am compelled to regard it as highly moral and virtuous; nor can I agree with you in treating as "heartless," [p. 781] the desire of seeing so inestimable a benefit conferred upon mankind; unless, indeed, the word heartless, be one of the engines of a sentimental cant, invented to discourage all steady pursuit of the general happiness of mankind.

A.M.

29. PLACE'S ON THE LAW OF LIBEL

MORNING CHRONICLE, 1 JAN., 1824, P. 2

This review deals with a subject that occupied much of James Mill's attention. The anonymous pamphlet (by Francis Place, as Mill certainly knew) is made up of eight parts published in the *British Luminary and Weekly Intelligencer* in weekly first-page, unsigned instalments from 3 Nov. to 22 Dec., 1822, under the title "Constitutional Association. Practice of the Courts.—Trial by Jury in Libel Cases," plus an article added for the pamphlet publication. Francis Place (1771-1854), "the Radical tailor of Charing Cross," was a loyal associate of Bentham and James Mill, and championed popular causes throughout his life. Mill again reviewed Place's pamphlet (with Richard Mence's *The Law of Libel*) in "Law of Libel and Liberty of the Press," *Westminster Review*, III (Apr. 1825), 285-321 (*CW*, Vol. XXI, pp. 1-34). The unsigned review in the *Morning Chronicle* is headed "*On the Law of Libel, with Strictures on the Self-Styled Constitutional Association*, pp. 73. London, John Hunt, 1823" and is described in Mill's bibliography as "A review of Place's pamphlet on the Law of Libel which appeared in the Chronicle of January 1st 1824" (MacMinn, p. 5).

THIS PAMPHLET consists of a series of Essays, all of which, except the last, appeared some months ago in a periodical publication. We recommend it strongly to the attentive perusal of every one who desires to know the extent of that boasted liberty of the press, which, we are taught to believe, is the birthright of Englishmen. He will learn from this pamphlet, that the rulers of this country possess as great a power of suppressing obnoxious publications by fine and imprisonment as they can desire: that the comparative free discussion which we enjoy exists only by connivance, and would not exist at all, were it not forced upon the Government by an enlightened public opinion.

A short abstract will convey a better idea, than any general remarks, of the view taken of the subject in this very able production.

There is no statute law on the subject of libel. There is nothing but common or unwritten law. Where the law is unwritten, definition is evidently impossible; much more, accurate and precise definition. What is to be gathered from precedents and cases can be known only to lawyers. Jurymen are not lawyers. They cannot therefore judge for themselves whether a publication is or is not libellous, but are compelled to decide the one way or the other, according to the directions of the Judge. Now, the Judge, in giving these directions, not only is not restrained by any definition of libel, but is not even restrained by precedents and cases; since there is scarcely a single point of law, on both sides of which many decisions are not to be found. Whether then the Judge shall direct the Jury to decide according to the precedents on one side, or according to the precedents on the other, depends almost entirely upon his own good will and pleasure. The law of libel, therefore, is actually and in fact made by the Judge.

When a person is tried for publishing a libel, some one swears that he has purchased a book, and the Judge tells the Jury that he considers it to be a libel. But does the Judge tell the Jury what a libel is? No; for there is no definition of it. If, therefore, the Jury find the prisoner guilty, it is not upon the testimony of witnesses, but upon the authority of the Judge. The witness swears that the prisoner sold the book; but to sell a book is not punishable, unless that book is a libel. For the fact of its being so, the Jury have nothing but the word of the Judge. The latitude which Judges allow themselves in declaring publications to be libellous, may be judged of by the example of the late Lord Ellenborough, who said that a libel was *any thing which hurts the feelings of any body.*[1] Under this definition, if it be one, it is easy to see that all publications disagreeable to the Government may be included. The only legal check, then, upon the Judge, is the disposition of the Jury to *set aside* his opinion, and refuse to consign a man to imprisonment and fine, merely upon the faith of the Judge's opinion. But there is a mode of rendering this check equally nugatory with all others, and this mode is constantly resorted to in cases of libel. It is by employing a packed Special Jury. The pamphlet before us contains the most complete exposure in the smallest compass which we have yet seen, of the packing system.[2] It investigates the origin of the practice, demonstrates that it was originally an abuse, that the grounds on which it was professedly introduced, have long since ceased to exist, and that Special Jurymen, far from being, as in *theory* they ought to be, superior in education and respectability to the Common Juries, are for the most part greatly deficient in both. It also explains the mode in which the system is acted upon at present. The Special Jury list is composed in counties, of freeholders; and in Middlesex, of some descriptions of leaseholders also; in London, it consists of all whom it is thought proper to term merchants. From this list, the Jury is selected; in Middlesex and London, by the Master of the Crown Office, who names forty-eight persons, twelve of whom form the Special Jury. It is

[1]See the Charge to the Jury in the Trial of William Cobbett, 1804, by Edward Law (1750-1818), Lord Ellenborough, Lord Chief Justice, in *State Trials*, ed. Howell, Vol. XXIX, col. 49. Mill is taking the quotation from Place, p. 9.

[2]Place, pp. 36-50. The practice of having specially qualified jurors began in the seventeenth century, with the particular procedures Mill mentions being laid down in a declaration by the Court of King's Bench in 1670. The practice was given statutory sanction by 3 George II, c. 25 (1730). Both Place and Mill are indebted to Bentham's *The Elements of the Art of Packing, as Applied to Special Juries, Particularly in Cases of Libel Law* (1821), in *Works*, Vol. V, pp. 61-186.

proved in this pamphlet, from indisputable authority, that the Juries are constantly selected out of a certain very small number of persons known to the selector, who make it a regular trade; and as each receives a guinea for every cause he decides, we leave it to the reader to judge how often he will return a verdict contrary to the will of his employers, knowing well that if he does so, he will be summoned no more.

Since the publication of the bulk of these Essays in *The British Luminary*, the subject of Special Juries has been brought before the House of Commons; and the *facts* stated above were met by *protestations* of the unblemished integrity of Mr. Lushington, the present Master of the Crown Office.[3] This, it is to be observed, is the constant practice of all the defenders of abuses; they always endeavour to turn a *public* into a *personal* question; to confound attacks upon a system, with attacks upon the character of individuals. We will not merely say that the administration of justice ought not only to be pure, but unsuspected, and that suspicion of injustice is an evil, second only in magnitude to injustice itself: we will not content ourselves with saying, that if Mr. Lushington be a man of honour, future Masters of the Crown Office may be otherwise. We will not confine ourselves to these arguments, though these, were there no others, would be conclusive. We cannot sufficiently reprobate the principle itself, of endeavouring to deter men from exposing a bad system, lest their strictures should be construed into imputations upon the character of individuals.

We assert, that, if a public officer is placed in a situation where his employers will expect him to serve them at the expence of the public—where he must content them or forfeit his subsistence, evil cannot fail to ensue. We are told, in reply, that Mr. Lushington is a pure, a virtuous, an honourable man, and the upshot of the whole is, that we are to surrender up our liberty and our property into the hands of this honourable man; that we are to trust him with a power over us, which no man could, consistently with prudence, confide to his own brother. We give Mr. Lushington full credit for as much virtue as falls to the share of any other man.—But we confess, we think it rather too much for Mr. Lushington's friends, in his behalf, to lay claim to more, and to think him insulted if the public does not acquiesce in this modest claim. Really, one would think, to hear this language, that a preference of their private interest to that of the community, were something totally unheard of in public men; and that there were no instances of persons who have acquitted themselves admirably well of the ordinary duties of life, but who, nevertheless, when their subsistence depended upon their becoming instruments of misgovernment, have easily persuaded

[3]In a speech of 28 May, 1823 (*PD*, n.s., Vol. 9, cols. 563-7), on special juries (introducing a petition from John Hunt), Joseph Hume was thought to have impugned the integrity of Edmund Henry Lushington (1766-1839); Lushington was defended by his friends, George Richard Philips (1789-1883), then M.P. for Steyning (*ibid.*, cols. 567-8), and Thomas Creevey (1768-1838), then M.P. for Appleby (*ibid.*, col. 568).

themselves that it was their duty to do so. We do not blame Mr. Lushington for doing what every man in his situation would do: but we cannot help reminding his overwarm supporters, that for men to strain every nerve for the attainment and preservation of power, which never can be desired for any good purpose, is not the conduct of all others best calculated to raise an expectation, that if allowed to retain it they will not make a bad use of it.

If they could prove that Mr. Lushington *cannot* abuse his power, they would not take so much pains to prove that he *will not*. But we are to believe that the situation holds out temptations against which no virtue would be proof, save his who actually holds the situation. Another succeeds him; that other is equally immaculate. By this argument, if such it can be called, no abuse would ever be reformed: for there must always be some one in a situation to profit by it; and if the honour of one man is a sufficient guarantee against abuse, it were an affront to suppose that the honour of another was inferior. What tyranny, what oppression, might not be justified in this way? You dare not accuse the man; and if you accuse the system, you are met with protestations that the man is perfectly immaculate.

Where has Mr. Lushington given proofs of such exalted heroism? It is easy to ascertain whether he prefers the public interest to his own, for if so, his salary still remains untouched in the Exchequer. But there is no need of surmises, when facts are before us. Let us look to the list of those who have served on Special Juries for the last ten years:—Let us ask ourselves how it happens that the same small number of men have been always summoned?[4] What Judge would listen to attestations of character, when he has positive evidence before him? Nay, the very circumstance of Mr. Lushington's still remaining Master of the Crown Office, is in itself a sufficient proof that his conduct has been conformable to the interests of his employers: unless Ministers also lay claim to the same super-human virtue for which we are to give credit to Mr. Lushington?

It is probable that this gentleman sincerely believes the custom of packing juries to be right; at all events, we are sure, that he never would set up for himself the same lofty pretensions which are set up for him by his over officious friends; that he desires to be judged by his actions, not by the allegations of his friends as to his character; and that, if he is wise, he wishes for nothing more strongly than to be relieved from a duty which it is scarcely possible to execute without incurring a degree of odium, which, we have no reason to believe, that he personally deserves.

[4]For information about the revelations of abuses found by the inquiry by the Court of Common Council of London referred to by Place, see "Special Juries," *The Times*, 12 Dec., 1817, p. 3.

30. PLEADINGS
MORNING CHRONICLE, 5 JAN., 1824, P. 3

This letter, using one of Bentham's catch-phrases as signature, is in response to a letter, headed "Pleadings" and signed "Hibernicus," *Morning Chronicle*, 3 Jan., 1824, p. 3, which is a rebuttal of another letter headed "Pleadings," signed "G.J.G. Gray's Inn," *ibid.*, 26 Dec., 1823, p. 4. Headed as title, subheaded "To the Editor of the Morning Chronicle," the item is described in Mill's bibliography as "A short letter on Indictments, signed an Enemy to Legal Fictions, whch. appeared in the Chronicle of January 5th 1824" (MacMinn, p. 5).

SIR,—In answer to the letter which you inserted some days ago on the subject of Pleadings, your Correspondent, Hibernicus, observes, that it is incorrect to affirm the Grand Jury to be perjurers, when they return upon oath that the prisoner is guilty; because, in fact, *all which they mean* is, not that he is guilty, but that a *prima facie* case is made out against him. I, too, have read the letter on Pleadings, and I am sure that the writer agrees with Hibernicus on this subject. All which he intended was, to shew the absurdity of a system of law which forces the Grand Jury to say one thing when they mean another; and not only to say it, but to swear it. This is innocent perjury, but it is perjury, and though the Jurors do not deserve blame, the law evidently does.

An Enemy to Legal Fictions

31. QUESTION OF POPULATION [3]
BLACK DWARF, 7 JAN., 1824, PP. 21-3

For the context of this third response to Thomas Wooler, see No. 27. Wooler had replied to No. 28 with "The Black Dwarf to A.M.," *Black Dwarf*, 31 Dec., 1823, pp. 905-10, to which the interpolated page numbers refer. The letter by another correspondent that Mill refers to in the opening and penultimate paragraphs immediately precedes Mill's own letter; headed "Question of Population," and signed "A Friend to the 'Lower Classes,'" it appears on pp. 15-21 of the issue for 7 Jan. How Mill became aware of its existence is not known. Mill's letter is headed as title, subheaded "To the Editor of the Black Dwarf," and described in his bibliography as "A third letter on the necessity of checking population whch. appeared in the Black Dwarf of January 9th [*sic*] 1824, signed A.M." (MacMinn, p. 5).

SIR,—I shall not extend my remarks on your last letter to any great length, as I know that you have on hand another letter on the same subject, which will probably consider the question as you wish it to be considered, with reference to the relative powers of increase possessed by population and subsistence.

I shall only at present remark, that you have made a much more free use, in this paper, of that easy figure of speech called assertion, than of that more intractable one called proof. With reference indeed to the laws of nature, you have, I am pleased to see, given up the point; for although you still dislike the remedy which I propose, you observe, "if it can be proved necessary to check population at all, your means may be the best, and therefore may be tolerated." [P. 909.] At this also I am well pleased. But you maintain that if three-fourths of the inhabitants of Ireland were to be swept off, and the remainder were sufficient to do all the work required by the rich, the price of labour would not advance. This seems to me rather an extraordinary assertion. First, it supposes a case which can never happen. One-fourth of the Irish population COULD NOT POSSIBLY do all the work required by the rich, as the whole population does now.* In the next place, I can safely appeal to the experience of every working man (as well as to the reason of the case), whether, if three out of every four of his competitors were removed, he would not feel a very sensible addition to his wages. You admit that if the population is greatly reduced by a plague, wages will rise. [Pp. 907-8.] Surely then, if it is reduced by means less shocking to humanity than a plague, the effect will be the same.

You observe that it is neither wise nor politic to consider "whether a family of two or ten children, were more convenient to the individual, since such matters will always regulate themselves." [P. 905.] This, Sir, is all that I want. I am far from wishing to regulate population by law, or by compulsion in any shape. I am aware that it will, and I think that it ought, to regulate itself: but you forget that it cannot regulate itself unless the means are known; a man cannot accommodate the numbers of his family to his means of supporting it, unless he knows how to limit those numbers; for *I have no belief in the efficacy of Mr. Malthus's moral check,*[1] so long as the great mass of the people are so uneducated as they are at present. Therefore I think it highly desirable that the physical check should be known to the people; and I agree with you that each man will then be the best judge of his own convenience.

I consider the question to be practically decided by this admission. If you allow that such things ought to regulate themselves, you cannot consistently object to the diffusion among the people of any information calculated to throw light upon the subject. Nevertheless, if you challenge me to the discussion of the other question, whether population has a tendency to increase faster than subsistence, I am perfectly ready to discuss this question also, when I shall have

---

*It can be proved that the great majority of the agricultural population of Ireland have not one quarter as much employment as could be performed by them. Three-fourths of the number of *this* class, then, could be dispensed with, without any injury to the rich, but to their great benefit. [Wooler's note.]

[1]See No. 28, n6.

perused the arguments of your other correspondent, and such remarks as you may think proper to make upon those arguments.

At present I shall trouble you with very few words more, in answer to another of your observations. I consider it a mere play upon words, to say, as you have done, that labour is capital. [P. 907.] Capital is that portion of the annual produce which is set apart for the maintenance of productive labour. Capital, you say, might be made to increase faster than at present. I admit that for a limited time it might; but capital can only be increased from savings. Would you, then, force accumulation? Would you have sumptuary laws? When you shall have answered this question, whether in the negative or in the affirmative, the basis of the discussion will be narrowed, and I shall know what arguments to put forward, among the many which bear upon the case.

A.M.

32. JAMES MILL ON THE QUESTION OF POPULATION
BLACK DWARF, 25 FEB., 1824, PP. 238-44

For the context of this final letter in Mill's series (Nos. 27, 28, and 31) in response to Thomas Wooler, see No. 27. Wooler's response to No. 31, "Further Inquiry into the Principles of Population," *Black Dwarf*, 4 Feb., 1824, pp. 143-9, is here answered by Mill with his strongest weapon, an extensive extract (pp. 260-1) from James Mill's "Colony" (1818), written for the *Supplement to the Fourth, Fifth, and Sixth Editions of the Encyclopaedia Britannica*, Vol. III, pp. 257-73. Because J.S. Mill says his father's comment is in effect his own reply to Wooler, the extract is here included, with Wooler's editorial notes in reply. Headed "Question on [*sic*] Population Resumed," with a subhead, "To the Editor," the letter is not in Mill's bibliography, but its signature ("A.M.") and contents leave no doubt that it is Mill's.

SIR,—The accompanying paragraphs are destined for insertion in your *Dwarf*. They are extracted from the article "Colonies," in the supplement to the *Encyclopaedia Britannica*; a discourse composed by an eminent friend of the people. They contain, I think, a most conclusive answer to your last article on population; and if you insert them, you will be very well able to dispense with the reply which you would otherwise have received from

Sir, your most obedient servant,
A.M.

It should be very distinctly understood what it is we mean, when we say, in regard to such a country as Great Britain, for example, that the supply of food is too small for the population. Because it may be said immediately, that the quantity of food may be increased in Great Britain; a proposition which no man will think of denying.

On this proposition, let us suppose, that in any given year, this year for example, the food in Great Britain is too small for the people, by 10,000 individuals. It is, no doubt, true, that additional food, sufficient to supply 10,000 individuals, might be raised next year; but where would be the amelioration, if 10,000 individuals were, at the same time, added to the numbers to be fed?* Now, the tendency of population is such as to make, in almost all cases, the real state of the facts correspond with this supposition. Population not only rises to the level of the present supply of food; but, if you go on every year increasing the quantity of food, population goes on increasing at the same time, and so fast, that the food is commonly still too small for the people. This is the grand proposition of Mr. Malthus's book: it is not only quite original, but it is that point of the subject from which all the more important consequences flow,—consequences which, till that point was made known, could not be understood.[†]

When we say that the quantity of food, in any country, is too small for the quantity of the people, and that, though we may increase the quantity of food, the population will, at the same time, increase so fast, that the food will still be too small for the people; we may be encountered with another proposition. It may be said, that we may increase food still faster than it is possible to increase population. And there are situations in which we must allow that the proposition is true.

In countries newly inhabited, or in which there is a small number of people, there is commonly a quantity of land yielding a large produce for a given portion of labour. So long as the land continues to yield in this liberal manner, how fast soever population increases, food may increase with equal rapidity, and plenty remain. When population, however, has increased to a certain extent, all the best land is occupied; if it increases any farther, land of a worse quality must be taken in hand; when land of the next best quality is all exhausted, land of a still inferior quality must be employed, till at last you come to that which is exceedingly barren. In this progression, it is very evident, that it is always gradually becoming more and more difficult to make food increase, with any given degree of rapidity, and that you must come, at last, to a point, where it is altogether impossible.[‡]

It may, however, be said, and has been said in substance, though not very clearly, by some of Mr. Malthus's opponents, that it is improper to speak of food as too small for the population, so long as food can be made to increase at an equal pace with population; and though it is no doubt true, that, in the states of modern Europe, food does not actually increase so fast as the population endeavours to increase, and hence the poverty and wretchedness of that population; yet it would be very possible to make food increase as fast as the tendency of population, and hence to make the people happy without diminishing their numbers by colonization; and that it is owing wholly to unfavourable, to ill-contrived institutions, that such is not the effect universally experienced. As this

---

*Nothing is easier than supposition: but it is here necessary to shew that *not more* than food for 10,000 additional mouths could be raised. As one man can raise food for ten, with scope for his labour, the more rational supposition would be, that for every *one* thousand added to the population, enough food for 10,000 *could* be provided, with sufficient scope for labour. It is calculated that every labouring agriculturist has *fifteen persons* to carry on his shoulders; or in other words, that he labours one day for himself, and fifteen for other people.—Ed. [Wooler.]

[†]It is not now understood, because it is not true that population, on the average of European states, outruns the supply of food. There is a *tendency* to an enormous encrease; but this tendency is held in check by so many other tendencies, that population in some instances actually decreases, though there be food in plenty.—Ed. [Wooler.]

[‡]That is, when you can exhaust the surface of the globe; when the time shall arrive in which there shall at least be a hundred times as many human beings as there exist at present.—Ed. [Wooler.]

observation has in it a remarkable combination of truth and error, it is worthy of a little pains to make the separation.§

There can be no doubt that, by employing next year a greater proportion of the people upon the land than this year, we should raise a greater quantity of food; by employing a still greater proportion the year following, we should produce a still greater quantity of food: and, in this way, it would be possible to go on for some time, increasing food as fast as it would be possible for the population to increase. But observe at what cost this would be. As the land, in this course, yields gradually less and less, to every new portion of labour bestowed upon it, it would be necessary to employ gradually not only a greater and greater number, but a greater and greater proportion of the people in raising food. But the greater the proportion of the people which is employed in raising food, the smaller is the proportion which can be employed in producing any thing else. You can only, therefore, increase the quantity of food to meet the demand of an increasing population, by diminishing the supply of those other things which minister to human desires.¶

There can be no doubt, that, by increasing every year the proportion of the population which you employ in raising food, and diminishing every year the proportion employed in everything else, you may go on increasing food as fast as population increases, till the labour of a man, added upon the land, is just sufficient to add as much to the produce, as will maintain himself and raise a family. Suppose, where the principle of population is free from all restriction, the average number of children reared in a family is five; in that case, so long as the man's labour, added to the labour already employed upon the land, can produce food sufficient for himself and the rearing of five children, food may be made to keep pace with population. But if things were made to go on in such an order, till they arrived at that pass, men would have food, but they would have nothing else. They would have neither clothes, nor houses, nor furniture. There would be nothing for elegance, nothing for ease, nothing for pleasure. There would be no class exempt from the necessity of perpetual labour, by whom knowledge might be cultivated, and discoveries useful to mankind.‖

It is of no use, then, to tell us that we have the physical power of increasing food as fast as population. As soon as we have arrived at that point at which the due distribution of the population is made between those who raise food, and those who are in other ways employed in contributing to the well-being of the members of the community, any increase of the food, faster than is consistent with that distribution, can only be made at the expense of those other things, by the enjoyment of which the life of man is preferable to that of the brutes. At this point the progress of population ought to be restrained. Population may still increase, because the quantity of food may still be capable of being

---

§I have not met with any persons who deny that emigration and colonization are not useful; and, in particular cases, absolutely necessary. It is necessary to the defence of Mr. Malthus's proposition to say that colonization would not remedy the evil; for if it would, why have recourse to a worse remedy.—Ed. [Wooler.]

¶This seems begging the question. The original wants of man, are food, clothes, and fire. I shall not discuss what luxuries may be deemed necessary by a few. I look to the mass.—Ed. [Wooler.]

‖Why not? it is not time, so much as space, that is required for the production of food. With the aid of modern improvements in science, it would not be difficult for one to raise food for a hundred. What, then, should hinder the building of houses, and the cultivation of the arts?—Ed. [Wooler.]

increased, though not beyond a certain slowness of rate, without requiring, to the production of it, a greater than the due proportion of the population.

Suppose, then, when the due proportion of the population is allotted to the raising of food, and the due proportion to other desirable occupations, that the institutions of society were such as to prevent a greater proportion from being withdrawn from these occupations to the raising of food. This it would, surely, be very desirable that they should effect. What now would be the consequence, should population, in that case, go on at its full rate of increase,—in other words, faster than with that distribution of the population, it would be possible for food to be increased? The answer is abundantly plain: all those effects would take place which have already been described as following upon the existence of a redundant population in modern Europe, and in all countries in which the great body of those who have nothing to give for food but labour, are free labourers;—that is to say, wages would fall, poverty would overspread the population, and all those horrid phenomena would exhibit themselves which are the never-failing attendants on a poor population.

It is of no great importance, though the institutions of society may be such as to make the proportion of the population, kept back from the providing of food, rather greater than it might be. All that happens is, that the redundancy of population begins a little earlier. The unrestrained progress of population would soon have added the deficient number to the proportion employed in the raising of food; and, at whatever point the redundancy begins, the effects are always the same.**

What are the best means of checking the progress of population, when it cannot go on unrestrained, without producing one or other of two most undesirable effects; either drawing an undue proportion of the population to the mere raising of food, or producing poverty and wretchedness, it is not now the place to inquire.

It is, indeed, the most important practical problem to which the wisdom of the politician and moralist can be applied. It has, till this time, been miserably evaded by all those who have meddled with the subject, as well as by all those who were called upon, by their situation, to find a remedy for the evils to which it relates. And yet, if the superstitions of the nursery were discarded, and the principle of utility kept steadily in view, a solution might not be very difficult to be found; and the means of drying up one of the most copious sources of human evil, a source which, if all other sources of evil were taken away, would alone suffice to retain the great mass of human beings in misery, might be seen to be neither doubtful nor difficult to be applied.††

33. EFFECTS OF PERIODICAL LITERATURE
MORNING CHRONICLE, 27 DEC., 1824, P. 3

In this letter Mill quotes from the article "Periodical Literature: *Edinburgh Review*," by James Mill, *Westminster Review*, I (Jan. 1824), 206-68, and defends it against a misinterpretation in an unheaded leader in the *Morning Chronicle*, 16 Dec., 1824, p. 2.

**When this point can be reached, then emigration and colonization become necessary; as the bees swarm when the hive is too full.—Ed. [Wooler.]

††My argument is, first *do justice to the labourer*, by reforming the institutions that oppress him, and then deal with the population as imperious circumstances shall dictate.—Ed. [Wooler.]

The personal tone in the references to the editor are not *pro forma*, being addressed to John Black (1783-1855), at this time closely allied to James Mill, who constantly advised him on political matters. The letter is headed "Periodical Literature. / To the Editor of the Morning Chronicle." There are several indications that this letter corresponds to the entry in Mill's bibliography, unidentified by MacMinn, which reads "A short letter on [   ] which appeared in the Morning Chronicle of 1824" (MacMinn, p. 6): the signature "A.B." favoured by Mill, the personal interest, and the use of Benthamite phraseology. The cryptic entry appears in the bibliography between items dated October 1824 and January 1825.

SIR,—In your paper of this day (Thursday, Dec. 16th), you controvert certain opinions relative to the probable tendency and effects of Periodical Literature, which were propounded in the first number of the *Westminster Review*. And you bring forward the inestimable service which you have yourself rendered to mankind by criticizing the conduct of the unpaid magistracy, as an instance of the beneficial effects which sometimes arise from periodical literature.

Now, Sir, you must have interpreted the words of the writer in the *Westminster Review* in a very different sense from that in which I understand them, if you suppose that he meant to affirm that periodical literature can *never* be productive of good. His object, as it seems to me, was to point out the motives (hitherto little attended to) which tend to draw the periodical writer out of the path of utility; motives so strong that he did not merely go too far in characterizing them as a *sort of necessity; an inducement which generally operates as necessity.*

That it is possible for a periodical writer to pursue steadily the greatest good of the greatest number, you, Sir, afford a striking example. But this is no more than the Westminster Reviewer has himself acknowledged, in a passage, which, taking the view which you have done of the article, you ought, I think, in fairness to have quoted.

One word of a personal nature seems to be required. We have described the interests which operate to withdraw periodical writers from the line of utility, and we have represented it as nearly impossible for them to keep true to it. What! Are we, it may be asked, superior to seducements to which all other men succumb? If periodical writing is by its nature so imbued with evil, why is it that we propose to add to the supply of a noxious commodity? Do we promise to keep out the poison which all other men yield to the temptation of putting in? If we made such a pretension, our countrymen would do right in laughing it to scorn; and we hope they would not fail to adopt so proper a course. We have no claim to be trusted any more than any one among our contemporaries; but we have a claim to be tried. Men have diversities of taste; and it is not impossible that a man should exist who really has a taste for the establishment of securities for good government, and would derive more pleasure from the success of this pursuit, than of any other pursuit in which he could engage, wealth or power not excepted. All that we desire is, that it may not be reckoned impossible that we may belong to a class of this description.

There is another motive, as selfish as that which we ascribe to any body, by which we may be actuated. We may be sanguine enough, or silly enough, or clear-sighted enough, to believe, that intellectual and moral qualities have made a great progress among the people of this country; and that the class who will really approve endeavours in favour of good government, and of the happiness and intelligence of men, are a class sufficiently numerous to reward our endeavours. [P. 222.]

Even had there been no such passage as the foregoing, the very circumstance that the work which thus criticises periodical publications, is itself a periodical publication, might have convinced you, that in ascribing to periodical works a tendency to advocate false and mischievous, rather than true and important opinions, it spoke of the general rule, not of the particular exceptions—of the motives which act upon all mankind, not of those which may govern particular individuals.

I have been induced to trouble you with these few words, because I regretted that two such efficient friends of mankind, as the writer in the *Westminster Review* and yourself, should appear to be at variance, when I am persuaded that they really agree.

A.B.

34. ABSENTEEISM

MORNING CHRONICLE, 16 SEPT., 1825, P. 3

The letter, dated 15 Sept. (with an additional paragraph oddly inserted in a leading article, *Morning Chronicle*, 22 Sept., 1825, p. 2), responds to two leading articles in the *Morning Chronicle*, 7 Sept., p. 2, and 14 Sept., p. 2 (and probably also to "Absenteeism," a letter signed "A," that appeared in the *Morning Chronicle*, 12 Sept., p. 4), all critical of John Ramsay McCulloch's evidence in "Fourth Report from the Select Committee Appointed to Inquire into the State of Ireland," *PP*, 1825, VIII, 807-38. McCulloch (1789-1864), the Scottish economist and statistician, was closely allied to the Philosophic Radicals at this time. Headed as title, subheaded "To the Editor of the Morning Chronicle," the letter is described in Mill's bibliography as "A letter on Absenteeism, signed J.S. which appeared in the Chronicle of 16 September 1825" (MacMinn, p. 7); the additional paragraph is not there mentioned.

SIR,—In several of your recent Papers you have combated the opinion expressed by Mr. M'Culloch in his evidence, concerning the effect of the expenditure of Irish absentees on the prosperity of that country from which their incomes are drawn.[1] As I agree almost in every particular with Mr. M'Culloch, and think that the arguments which you have urged against him are fallacious, and that the notions which they inculcate are as pernicious as they are, unhappily, common, I submit to your well-known candour the following statement of my reasons for dissenting from your conclusion.

The income of a landlord, like any other income, may be expended in two ways; in the hiring of labourers, or, in the purchase of commodities. In point of fact, it is expended partly in the former way, and partly in the latter; but in one or other of these ways it must be expended, if it be expended at all, unless, indeed, it were given away.

Now I admit that in so far as the income of the landlord is expended in the hiring of labourers, whether these are employed in building a house, in digging a garden, in making or keeping a park, in shooting Catholics or poachers, in washing dishes, or in blacking shoes; to that extent it does give employment to a certain number of persons who would be thrown out of employment if the landlord were to go abroad, and consequently tends to keep wages somewhat higher, or to enable a somewhat larger population to be maintained at the same

[1]McCulloch, "Evidence," pp. 815, 818.

wages, than would be the case if he were to live in London or Paris, and employ English or French labourers for the above purposes, instead of Irish.

What I do not admit is, that (in so far as his income is expended, not in the hiring of labourers, but in the *purchase of commodities*,) it has the slightest tendency to keep wages higher, or to give employment to as much as one labourer more, than if he were living at the antipodes: nor do I believe that (in so far as this part of his expenditure is concerned) as much as one man would be thrown out of employment, if every resident landlord in the island were to go abroad, or to send abroad for every article which he had a mind to consume.

If the landlord remained in Ireland, he would (we shall suppose) eat Irish bread and beef, wear Irish shirts and breeches, sit on Irish chairs, and drink his wine off an Irish table. Now, then, I will put a case:—Suppose that he goes to London, leaving directions behind him that all the bread and beef which he would have eaten, all the shirts and breeches which he would have worn, all the chairs which he would have sat upon, and all the tables off which he would have drank his wine, should be regularly sent to him in London. You will not deny, I suppose, that he would give just as much employment to Irish labour as if he had consumed all these articles in the true orthodox way, close to the doors of the very people who produced them.

It would puzzle you, I think, to discover any error in this proposition, or to shew any difference which it can make to the Irish producers, provided they supply the commodities, whether they are consumed on the spot, or at a thousand miles distance. I would advise you to ponder well, however, before you admit this; since you will find, if you do admit it, that you have conceded the whole question.

In fact, this case, which I have put as an imaginary one, exactly corresponds in every thing that is material to the purpose, with the actual state of the facts. The Irish do not, indeed, always send the identical bread, beef, chairs, tables, &c. which the landlord would have consumed on the spot, to be consumed by him in the foreign country; but they either send those very articles, or, what comes to the same thing, they send other articles of exactly the same value. Some readers will say (I do not impute to yourself such a degree of ignorance) that they do not send goods, but money; to which my answer is short—if they sent any money, they could not send much, because Ireland has no gold and silver mines, and, therefore, cannot continue to export money to one place, without getting it back again from another. Every body knows that if a quantity of the precious metals is exported, unless its place is supplied by paper, it always comes back again. In point of fact, however, every body who knows any thing about the way in which the matter is actually managed, knows that no money whatever is sent. The landlord's steward sends over to him a Bill of Exchange, drawn upon a mercantile house; and the drawer of the bill sends over a quantity of goods to the drawee, to meet the bill when it becomes due.

It appears, therefore, conclusively, that the only difference between the expenditure of the resident landlord, and that of the absentee, is this: the one buys, let us say, a thousand pounds worth of Irish goods, every year on the spot; the other has a thousand pounds worth of Irish goods every year sent to him. Perhaps you may be able to discover some great difference which this makes to the capitalists and labourers in Ireland. Perhaps you may—but if you can, you can do more than I can.

This error (for unless the above argument be incorrect, you must give me leave so to denominate your opinion) appears to me to be a relic of the now exploded mercantile system; of that system, from which emanated those wise prohibitions of the importation of foreign commodities, which might have remained to this day monuments of ancestorial wisdom upon our statute-book, had not Mr. Huskisson been somewhat wiser than that Hibernian genius, whose lucubrations you honoured yesterday by a place in your columns.[2] The theory on which these sage regulations were founded, was exactly the same with that which this declaimer and yourself maintain in opposition to Mr. M'Culloch. By consuming foreign commodities, you employ foreign labour; by consuming British commodities, you employ British labour. What Englishman, then, it was triumphantly asked, can be so lost to patriotism as to lay out that money upon foreigners, which might have helped to enrich his native country? Admirably argued, truly; one thing, however, which these sagacious reasoners did not advert to, was, that, in buying foreign commodities, you are giving just the same employment to British labour as if you laid out your whole income in commodities of home growth; you are giving employment, namely, to that labourer which was employed in making the British commodities, with which the foreign commodities, that you consume, were bought.

The case of the man who has French goods sent to him in Ireland, and that of the man who goes himself and consumes them at Paris, are precisely similar. If the one be criminal, so must the other be. If the absentee landlord be an enemy to his country, so is every resident landlord who expends a shilling upon any article that is not produced—I was going to say in Ireland—but even on his own estate; and just in proportion to the number of shillings which he so spends, in that same proportion is the mischief which he does. We ought, therefore, if this notion be correct, not only to reimpose upon commerce all the shackles which Ministers have earned such high and such deserved praise for taking off, but we ought to do, what I suppose no Government ever did, prohibit absolutely all foreign, not to say all internal trade. Such is, perhaps, the wise course that we should pursue,

[2]The "Hibernian genius" identified in the *Morning Chronicle*'s leading article on 14 Sept. as an anonymous writer in the *Dublin Evening Post*, is probably William James MacNeven (1763-1841), a medical practitioner and active participant in the United Irish movement, who had been banished to the United States in 1805 but continued to be interested in Irish affairs. The many British laws giving force to the mercantilist policy were replaced in 1825 (see especially 6 George IV, cc. 105 and 107) by Huskisson, who had begun the attack in 1824 by reducing some duties (see 5 George IV, cc. 21 and 47).

if the councils of the nations were taken out of the hands of his Majesty's
Ministers, and placed in those of a set of declaimers, who either are desirous to
mislead, or whose incurable ignorance renders them just as mischievous as if
they were.

I am not so unjust, Sir, as to confound you with such as these; and I regret the
more that you should have given your powerful support to an opinion so utterly
inconsistent with those principles of political economy which you habitually
maintain; an opinion which has had, as I believe, so great a share in blinding the
public to the real causes of the evils by which Ireland is afflicted.

I remain, Sir, your's, with the greatest respect,

J.S.

———

[*Addendum*]³

What feeds the journeyman tailors, who make the landlord's coat, is not the
rent of the landlord, but the capital of the master tailor; and if the landlord's rent
were all thrown into the sea, the capital of the tailor would remain, and would
employ, if not as many tailors, as many labourers of some sort as it did
before.—What employs labourers is *capital*. More *income*, unless saved, and
added to capital, employs nobody; except menial servants. Ireland has just the
same capital when her landlords live in Paris as when they live in Dublin. She,
therefore, employs as many labourers, except menial servants, as above.

35. BLUNDERS OF THE TIMES
NEW TIMES, 6 JUNE, 1827, P. 3

This letter, Mill's only one to the *New Times* (which he calls "a Tory paper" in No. 41),
is also his first to a newspaper editor for almost two years. The *New Times* frequently
criticized *The Times* (which it often called "The Old Times"); see, e.g., 24 May, 1827, p.
2, and 31 May, p. 3. Mill's letter, headed "To the Editor of the New Times," is described
in his bibliography as "A letter on the blunders of the 'Times' newspaper which app. in
the New Times of 6th June 1827, signed A.B." (MacMinn, p. 8).

SIR,—Having frequently admired the happy irony with which you expose the
profound ignorance and ludicrous self-importance of the *Times*, I address to you
a few lines on the new specimen which it has recently afforded of these qualities.

In one of its late articles, it is pleased to place under the ban of its censure,
persons, whom it designates, with characteristic elegance of language, as "those
louts and coxcombs united, the landlords, and political economists."

³In the *Morning Chronicle* of 22 Sept., this paragraph is introduced: "Our
correspondent J.S. has sent us the following addition to his communication:".

The poor farmers, [it adds,] have been dragooned into all these petitions against the new Corn Bill, for the mere purpose of keeping up rents, by those two factions of men, whom we above cited; the one, duller than the earth they tread; and the other, a mere batch of fantastical coxcombs, incapable of attaining literature, or fathoming science; and, therefore, distorting and sophisticating common sense, by every kind of paradox and extravagance.[1]

Leaving, Sir, the defence of the landlords in your hands, which are much more capable of doing it justice than mine, I request your attention to the following sentence, extracted from the very next paragraph to that of which I have already quoted the conclusion:

We are well assured, that there is no resting place for our feet; there is no firm principle upon which our commercial pre-eminence can be based, or even the landed community rest free from shocks, but the *unrestricted and untaxed circulation of all the necessaries of life, both for man and beast, throughout the world; and to this point we hope our steps are tending.*

I now submit two questions, not to the Editor of the *Times*, but to every man, who is capable of being disgusted by insolent and ignorant *charlatanerie.*

1. Here is the *Times*, professing itself a determined partisan of the most extreme of all the extreme opinions, which were ever maintained by ultra-political economists on the Corn Laws, and, in the same breath, declaring, that the political economists are "fantastical coxcombs," "louts and coxcombs united," for professing the same opinion on the same subject. I ask, then, is not that Journal admirably qualified for the office of a public instructor, which ridicules men for their opinions without knowing that their opinions are the same with its own?

My other question is, whether the accusation of being "incapable of fathoming science" does not come with an admirable grace from the Journal, which, only a few months ago, expressed the utmost surprise that the expectation of a war should have depressed the Funds?[2] That the expected creation of an immense quantity of new Stock, by new Loans, should lower the price of the Stock already in existence, was too recondite a truth for this sage, who, nevertheless, thinks himself entitled to *trancher du maître,* and denounce others as ignorant of *science!*

Your Constant Reader,
A.B.

---

[1]Leading article on the Corn Bill, *The Times*, 28 May, 1827, p. 2. "A Bill to Permit, until 1st May, 1828, Certain Corn, Meal, and Flour to Be Entered for Home Consumption," 7 & 8 George IV (19 June, 1827), *PP*, 1827-28, II, 573-6, was passed by both Houses in June, and enacted as 7 & 8 George IV, c. 57 (1827).

[2]See "The Money Market," *The Times*, 13 Mar., 1827, p. 3.

36. THE INHABITANTS OF QUEENBOROUGH

THE TIMES, 28 DEC., 1827, P. 3

This letter and its enclosed £1 were elicited by "Meeting of the Inhabitants of Queen-borough," *The Times*, 26 Dec., 1827, p. 3, in which a subscription was suggested. On 27 Dec., p. 3, *The Times* printed three letters with subscriptions, with an editorial note saying a responsible gentleman would distribute the money. *The Times'* account of the long-lasting distress of the fishing town in the Isle of Sheppy, Kent, emphasized the restrictions on the trade enacted by the ruling "select body," the kind of closed corporation to which the Philosophic Radicals strongly objected. The letter, Mill's first to *The Times*, is headed as title, subheaded "To the Editor of The Times," and described in his bibliography as "A letter on the Queenborough case, inclosing a subscription for the inhabitants of Queenborough, signed Ph., in the Times of 28th December 1827" (MacMinn, p. 8).

SIR,—I shall feel obliged by your consenting to be the depositary of the enclosed subscription, towards an object which a nation, which makes greater pretension to humanity than any other will not, I trust, disgrace itself by neglecting—the relief of the ruined and destitute inhabitants of Queenborough, whose misery is so affectingly depicted in your paper of Wednesday.

But if it be a duty to relieve the miserable, the punishment of those who have rendered them so is a still more imperative one. And the 1*l*. herewith transmitted shall cheerfully be increased to 10*l*., so soon as any practicable course shall be entered upon to effect that righteous purpose.

Can it be endured that proprietary rights, on which thousands depended as their sole means of support, should be seized by a self-elected body of seven persons, under pretence that the common property of the corporation is their property—that they, the trustees, the depositaries, the executive officers, the servants of the burgesses, have a right to say to their masters, "Go and starve"? Is it to be borne, that when those whom a court of law has declared to have a right to employment in the fisheries, are compelled by starvation to sue for it as a favour, they should be told, with an oath, by one of their magistrates, that he would never give them any employment while breath was in his body, or tauntingly exhorted to go and ask employment of him for whom they had voted? Can Englishmen suffer this, and listen without a blush to the congratulations of foreigners on the felicity with which our Constitution has reconciled the apparently conflicting advantages of freedom and law? No, Sir, I cannot persuade myself that the means of enforcing their right will be withheld from these unfortunate people by a nation which maintains more charitable institutions than all the rest of the world taken together. Our countrymen, whatever may be their faults, have rarely forgotten their reverence for the two great blessings of human life—liberty and property. And will they tamely suffer the whole population of a considerable town to be illegally deprived of the one as a punishment for their inflexible constancy in adhering to the other?

Ph.

Received a pound [Editor].

37. NEW MINISTERIAL PUBLICATIONS
MORNING CHRONICLE, 31 MAY, 1828, P. 3

These satirical comments (see also Nos. 38, 39, and 40) were prompted by the actions of the Tory ministry formed in January 1828 by Arthur Wellesley (1769-1852), the 1st Duke of Wellington, a target of Radical criticism. The unsigned article is Mill's first contribution to the *Morning Chronicle* since September 1825. It is headed as title and described in his bibliography as "A squib on the Wellington ministry, headed New Publications—and two following paragraphs in the Morning Chronicle of 31st May 1828" (MacMinn, p. 9). A printer's rule (here reproduced) appears in the *Morning Chronicle* after the 9th paragraph; it is followed by three further paragraphs. Assuming that the entry in the bibliography is accurate, we have excluded the final paragraph from the text, but included it in a footnote.

IT IS CURRENTLY REPORTED, that the Duke of Wellington, having become sensible of the detriment which his new Ministry is likely to sustain in public estimation, from the vulgar prejudice, that none except men of talents and information are qualified to administer the affairs of the State, has resolved to establish an office for the publication and distribution of works of a practical character, suited to the composition of the Ministry, and to the exigencies of the times. Doctor Croker being the only Member of the New Administration who can write,[1] has undertaken the office of correcting the press; and the following works are confidently announced as shortly about to appear:—

The Dunce's Manual, or *Politics made level with the meanest Capacity*: For the use of elderly Gentlemen appointed Cabinet Ministers at a short notice.

Bob Short's Rules for Governing a State, whereby the whole Science of Government may be learned in a quarter of an hour, without hindrance of amusements, or knowledge of a bookseller.[2]

The Inutility of Ideas to Public Men, Stated and Exemplified: being an attempt to prove that none but persons totally ignorant of public affairs are competent to

[1]John Wilson Croker (1780-1857), M.P. and writer of Irish origin, one of the mainstays of the Tory *Quarterly Review*, was a friend and adviser to Wellington, who, on acceding to power, had him sworn as a Privy Councillor.

[2]Bob Short was the pseudonym of the author (or authors) of such works as *Twelve Short Standing Rules, for Ladies [and Gentlemen] with Short Memories, at the Game of Whist* (Salisbury: Fowler, 1801); *Hoyle Abridged: A Treatise on Backgammon; or, Short Rules for Short Memories* (London: Allman, 1820); and *Hoyle Abridged: A Treatise on the Game of Chess; or, Short Rules for Short Memories* (London: Allman, 1824).

administer them. Under the immediate patronage of the Lords of the Treasury, and the three Secretaries of State.

A new edition of *Erasmus's Moriae Encomium*, or *Praise of Folly*:[3] with portraits of the New Ministers, beautifully engraven on brass, by George Cruikshank,[4] and an Appendix, shewing the peculiar applicability of the author's Principles to the Government of the British Empire.

Murray's First Book for Statesmen: Being a Compendious Treatise on the Cavalry Exercise, for the use of Young Members of Parliament, and Candidates for Public Employment. By Lieutentant-General Sir George Murray, K.G.H. and T.S., Col. of the 42d Foot, and Principal Secretary of State for the Colonies.[5]

Shoulder Arms! A Tyrtaean Poem,[6] addressed to the Nobility, Gentry, and Clergy of Great Britain and Ireland. By Field-Marshal his Grace the Duke of Wellington, Drill-Serjeant to the Bench of Bishops, and to both Houses of Parliament.

Moderate Talents best fitted for Affairs of State: an Essay, shewing, from practical Experience, the Dangerousness of confiding political Employments to clever Men. Addressed to the moderately-informed. With Remarks on the unexceptionable Character of the present Administration, in this respect.—Also, by the same Author,

The Vanity of Human Learning; or, The Wonderful Worldly Wisdom of Knowing Nothing:[7] wherein are set forth the manifold Advantages, in a practical Point of View, of Ignorance over Knowledge, and the Sufficiency of Reading, Writing, and the Manual Exercise, for the Education of a Cabinet Minister. With a comparative View of Mr. Canning, and the Duke of Wellington, Mr. Huskisson, and Sir George Murray, Turgot, and Sir Thomas Gooch:[8] shewing

[3]Desiderius Erasmus (1466-1536), the great humanist, friend of Thomas More, whose name is played on in the title of *Moriae encomium* (Paris: Gourmont, 1511), Englished as *In Praise of Folly*.

[4]George Cruikshank (1792-1878), the best-known caricaturist and engraver of the time.

[5]Mill is playfully conflating Lindley Murray (1745-1826), author of such well-known elementary texts as *English Grammar, Adapted to the Different Classes of Learners* (York: Wilson, et al., 1795) and *An English Spelling Book; with Reading Lessons* (London: Longman, et al., 1804), and Sir George Murray (1772-1846), general and statesman, Colonial Secretary in Wellington's cabinet.

[6]Tyrtaeus, a Spartan general and poet (ca. 640 B.C.), was known for his war-songs in the epic tradition; see *Elegies of Tyrtaeus*, trans. William Cleaver (London: Payne, 1761). The *Morning Chronicle* here reads "Tyriaean" rather than "Tyrtaean," but the fragments of the *Tyrian Annals* do not suit the reference, and a printer's error seems probable.

[7]Cf. *The Vanity of Human Wishes* (London: Dodsley, 1749), an imitation of Juvenal's Tenth Satire by Samuel Johnson (1709-84), English poet and critic.

[8]Thomas Sherlock Gooch (1767-1851), M.P. for Suffolk, a supporter of Wellington and spokesman for the landed gentry. The concluding ironical "comparative View" in the

the extreme Ignorance of the latter Statesmen, and calling upon all Persons of moderate Intellect to support them.

———

On the occasion of a recent schism in the Ministry,[9] the Duke of Wellington is reported to have said, "There shall be but one head to my Administration." Dr. Croker, who was accidentally present, was heard to mutter, "Fait, and sure now, that won't be your Grace's own, Duke dear."

Another *on dit* of the day is, that in the course of the late Cabinet disputes, Mr. Huskisson formally accused Messrs. Dawson and Goulburn[10] of a conspiracy to set the Thames on fire—which those Gentlemen indignantly denied, protesting that all their friends could avouch them to be altogether incapable of such a proceeding.[11]

38. ADVERTISEMENTS FREE OF DUTY
MORNING CHRONICLE, 3 JUNE, 1828, P. 4

The second of Mill's short satiric attacks on the Wellington ministers (see Nos. 37, 39, and 40), this item is described in his bibliography as "Another squib on the same subject, headed Advertisements Free of Duty, in the Morning Chronicle of 3d June 1828" (MacMinn, p. 9).

WANTED immediately, a person qualified to teach Arithmetic with rapidity. The advertiser is desirous to proceed as far as Long Division. Expedition is

———

subtitle reflects a common element in titles such as John Gregory's popular *A Comparative View of the State and Faculties of Man, with Those of the Animal World* (London: Dodsley, 1765).

[9]A split in Wellington's cabinet arose over the disfranchisement of the corrupt boroughs of Penryn and East Retford. Huskisson's resignation as Colonial Secretary and leader of the House of Commons was followed by those of Lord Palmerston as Secretary of War, Charles Grant as President of the Board of Trade, and William Lamb (later Lord Melbourne) as Irish Secretary.

[10]George Robert Dawson (1790-1856) was Secretary to the Treasury; Henry Goulburn (1784-1856) was Chancellor of the Exchequer.

[11]The following paragraph (see the headnote to this item) concludes the article: "It has been observed, that a large proportion of the *'Squire Wrongheads*, who were present at the annual bamboozlement called the Pitt Club—where fools entrapped by knaves assemble to honour (as they fancy) the memory of one who supported through life principles which they themselves now oppose with all their power—came from Essex, a county of well known *vituline* celebrity." (The ultra-Tory Pitt Club was named for William Pitt [1708-78], 1st Earl of Chatham.)

indispensable, the Budget being positively fixed for this month.—Apply to H. Goulburn, at the Treasury, Whitehall.

————

Just Published

To the Right About Face; or, Decision. A Farce, in one act, recently performed with unqualified success at the Theatre Royal, Downing-street; the principal characters by the Duke of Wellington and Mr. Huskisson; with the words of the original Laughing Cantata, executed at the conclusion of the performance by Mr. Peel, accompanied by Messrs. Goulburn, Herries,[1] Dawson, and the remainder of the Commander-in-Chief's band.—N.B. It is expected that on the next representation, this piece of music will be repeated by the same performer, on the other side of his mouth.

————

ONE GUINEA REWARD.—Lost or stolen, from a Cabinet of Curiosities near the Treasury, a Skull. It is extremely thick, and the eyes are so fixed in it, as to be unable to see beyond the length of the nose. It is also remarkably soft to the touch, and the organ of *place* is very strongly developed. It is entirely empty, and of no use to any person, except the owner. The reward offered, greatly exceeds the value of the article, as the owner having recently been appointed Chancellor of the Exchequer, cannot conveniently do without it.

————

[Advertisement.]² —In consequence of the repeated complaints against divided Cabinets, Wellington, Cabinet-maker to his Majesty, has the honour to inform the Nobility and Gentry, that after several unsuccessful experiments, he has at length succeeded in constructing one which is *all of a piece*. This excellent article of furniture is entirely cut out of the *old block*, and is composed of pure logwood, without the slightest mixture of any other material, except in the *facing*, which is of brass. One trial will prove the fact.—Exhibited daily at St. Stephen's Chapel, Westminster.³ Doors open at Three in the afternoon, begin at Four. Seats may be procured at Gatton and Old Sarum, or of Messrs. Hertford and Lonsdale, House Agents, next door to the premises.⁴

————

¹John Charles Herries (1778-1855), M.P. for Harwich (1823-41), was, like the others named, a Tory politician; Chancellor of the Exchequer (1827-Jan. 1828) in Goderich's cabinet, he became Master of the Mint in Wellington's. Robert Peel was Home Secretary in Wellington's cabinet.

²Square brackets in original.

³The House of Commons met in St. Stephen's Chapel from 1547 until its destruction in the fire of 1834.

⁴Gatton and Old Sarum were the most celebrated of the corrupt "pocket" boroughs,

39. DR. CROKER'S OPINION
MORNING CHRONICLE, 4 JUNE, 1828, P. 3

This brief satire on the Wellington ministry (see Nos. 37, 38, and 40), headed "Doctor Croker's Opinion on the Cause of the Late Ministerial Dispute," is described in Mill's bibliography as "A third short squib on the same subject in the same paper of 4th June consisting of two paragraphs, beginning, Dr. Croker's opinion on the cause of the late ministerial dispute" (MacMinn, p. 9).

DOCTOR CROKER'S OPINION on the Cause of the Late Ministerial Dispute.—Sorrow a bit could he understand how the payple could so desayve themselves, as to fancy that his Grace, dare cratur, was no arithmetician. Sure it was himself that was mad with Mr. Huskisson, about nothing in life, barring that he couldn't tache him a lesson of *cyphering*, by Jasus!

Report says, that Sir George Murray, the new Colonial Secretary, yesterday presented the Duke of Wellington with a handsome copy of his *English Spelling Book*,[1] accompanied by a note, recommending to the Duke's particular attention that part which treats of *letters*, it appearing, from recent transactions, that his Grace cannot at present understand them.[2]

40. ANOTHER OPINION OF DR. CROKER'S
MORNING CHRONICLE, 5 JUNE, 1828, P. 3

The final satire in this series on the Wellington ministry (see Nos. 37, 38, and 39) is an unheaded paragraph described in Mill's bibliography as "A fourth short squib, on the same subject in the same paper of 5th June, only one paragraph concerning Dr. Croker" (MacMinn, p. 10).

SOME PERSON having expressed his surprise that any Minister should have thought of placing the finances of the State under the charge of Mr. George Dawson and of Mr. Goulburn, it being extremely problematical whether those gentlemen had been sufficiently successful in their arithmetical studies, to admit

---

with almost no voters (or even inhabitants). Francis Charles Seymour-Conway (1777-1842), 3rd Marquis of Hertford, controlled two boroughs; William Lowther (1787-1872), Lord Lonsdale, controlled nine.

---

[1]See No. 37, n5.

[2]The sarcasm here plays on the misunderstanding (intentional or not) by the Duke of a letter from Huskisson offering to resign if such an action would serve the government's interest; he eagerly took the letter as proffering resignation, which he accepted, and maintained his reading even after Huskisson's denial. See *PD*, n.s., Vol. 19, cols. 917-44 (2 June, 1828).

of their being pronounced well-grounded in the multiplication table, Dr. Croker replied, that "He couldn't spake, any how, consarning that same; but it was themselves that were nate lads at a *division*, by St. Patrick."

41. COMPENSATION TO THE SHOPKEEPERS ON THE APPROACHES TO LONDON BRIDGE
BRITISH TRAVELLER, 29 SEPT., 1828, P. 3

This article is Mill's contribution to the public controversy (see, e.g., *The Times*, 10 Sept., p. 3, 11 Sept., p. 3, 17 Sept., pp. 3-4, 23 Sept., p. 3, 2 Oct., p. 3) over a proposal that was enacted as 10 George IV, Private Acts, c. 136 (1829). The expensive and potentially litigious proposal was opposed by the small tradesmen of the area, which included Fish Street Hill; Mill contrasts their position with that of the wealthy of Grosvenor Square in the West End, remote from this governmental interference with the rights of property. The unsigned, unheaded leading article is Mill's only contribution to the *British Traveller*. It is described in his bibliography as "A leading article in the British Traveller of 27th September [*sic*] 1828 on the question of compensation to the shopkeepers on the approaches to London Bridge" (MacMinn, p. 10).

THE APPROACHES TO THE NEW LONDON BRIDGE are every day becoming the subject of increased discussion. Perhaps if in deciding upon this point, nothing were requisite to be taken into the account except public convenience, it would have been disposed of in a more summary manner. But it seems that in this, as in so many other projects of improvement, a consideration has intruded itself, which, under our national institutions, and with our national modes of thinking, is apt to be esteemed far more important than public convenience, and this is, the convenience of particular individuals.

Nobody, in this or in any other country, is so impudent as to say, that his individual interest ought to be attended to first, and the public interest afterwards. But instead of one man, put the case that there are two or three score, much more if there be two or three hundred, and what no one of them would have the face to claim for himself, every man among them will boldly demand for himself and company.

If nobody felt and acted in this manner, except the grocers and cheesemongers of Fish street hill, no doubt it would be very justly considered a flagrant enormity. If, however, these shopkeepers are only following the admired and applauded example of their betters, it might be expected that what is thought very proper and patriotic in those betters, would hardly be stigmatized as unjust and selfish in *them*. We were therefore surprised to find an attempt made, in a recent number of a Tory paper, to hold up these respectable persons to public disapprobation, because they, too, thought it proper to stand up for the interests of their "order."[1]

[1]See the leading article on the New London Bridge, *New Times*, 24 Sept., 1828, p. 2.

But there is a distinction running through the whole frame of English society, which, when it is fully seized, explains no small quantity of what would otherwise appear altogether enigmatical in the workings of that society. Fielding describes Bridewell as "that house where the inferior sort of people may learn one good lesson, viz.—respect and deference to their superiors, since it must show them the wide distinction fortune intends between those persons who are to be corrected for their faults, and those who are not."[2] The *New Times*, in its animadversions upon the Fish street hill shopkeepers, intends, no doubt, to read them a similar lesson; to put them in mind of the wide distinction which our institutions intend between those who are to have their interest preferred to the general interest, and those who are not.

There is no other country in the world, says the *New Times*, in which the best avenues to such a structure as London Bridge would be rejected, for fear of affecting the paltry interests of a few shopkeepers. We hope not; and we hope, likewise, that there is no other country in the world in which the public would be taxed ten or twelve millions in the price of their bread, and exposed to incessant vicissitudes of glut and famine, for fear of affecting the paltry interests of a few landlords.[3] We are sure that there is no other country in which a bill, such as the County Courts' Bill, for extending the benefits of an administration of justice to the largest portion of the people, to whom at present it may be said, with scarcely any exaggeration, to be altogether inaccessible, would be rejected year after year by the legislature on the avowed ground, that it would affect the paltry interests of Lord Ellenborough, and two or three other holders of law sinecures.[4]

It was doubtless a great piece of presumption in the persons whom the *New Times* reprehends, to imagine that what might be proper and commendable in so exalted a personage as Lord Ellenborough, was allowable in persons who were no better than shopkeepers, and who lived in no other street than Fish street hill. If the proposed approaches had encroached upon a Nobleman's park, or had passed so much as within a quarter of a mile of his game preserves, it is probable

[2] Henry Fielding, *The History of Tom Jones a Foundling* (1749), Bk. IV, Chap. xi, in *Works*, Vol. VI, p. 191.

[3] The reference is to the Corn Laws, which included 55 George III, c. 26 (1815), 3 George IV, c. 60 (1822), and 7 & 8 George IV, c. 57 (1827). The most recent, 9 George IV, c. 60 (1828), established a sliding scale starting from a nominal duty of 1*s.* on imported grain when the price at home reached 73*s.*

[4] Between 1823 and 1828 five bills pertaining to County Courts were introduced, but none passed. The most recent was "A Bill for the More Easy Recovery of Small Debts in the County Courts of England and Wales, and for Extending the Jurisdiction Thereof," 9 George IV (13 June, 1828), *PP*, 1828, II, 445-58. While the issue of sinecures was clearly central in these bills' failure, the topic was treated gingerly in the debates; perhaps the most forthcoming admission is subsequent to Mill's comment, in Peel's Speech on Small Debts (8 May, 1829), *PD*, n.s., Vol. 21, cols. 1165-6. Edward Law, Lord Ellenborough (1790-1871), son of the former Lord Chief Justice, was Lord Privy Seal in Wellington's administration; at this time, as Chairman of The Approaches to London Bridge Committee, he opposed the suggested improvements.

that we should have heard another story about paltry interests. But it is a mistake, to suppose that cheesemongers can have vested rights. Cheesemongers are only virtually represented. Lords and Landlords not only are actually represented, but virtually represent the Cheesemongers themselves. They may, therefore, possess vested rights: if they possess any thing which they do not like to give up, it is a vested right: and having received this name, however little they may be entitled to it, or however imperatively the public interest may require the sacrifice of it, to demand it would be to infringe upon the sacred rights of property. All this, to the *New Times*, is gospel: but that journal is far too acute not to seize the distinction between Fish street hill, and Grosvenor square, and to perceive, that with lawgivers as well as other men, there is all the difference in the world between doing a dishonest thing for their own interest, and doing exactly the same thing for the interest of other people.

42. THE BRUNSWICK CLUBS
MORNING CHRONICLE, 30 OCT., 1828, P. 3

This letter is in response to the agitations promoted by the Brunswick Clubs in opposition to Catholic Emancipation (which was enacted, to the outrage of a large section of his party, by the Duke of Wellington in 1829, 10 George IV, c. 7). The Brunswick Clubs, founded in Ireland in 1827 as an offshoot of the Orange Society, and named for the German House of Brunswick, were spreading rapidly in England in the autumn of 1828 under the active patronage of the Duke of Cumberland (1771-1851), fifth son of George III. The agitation reached a head with a large meeting on Penenden Heath, Kent, on 24 Oct., 1828, at which the attendance was variously estimated between 25,000 and 60,000. The analogy with military "musters" is in "Brunswick Agitation in the Country of Kent," *Spectator*, 16 Oct., p. 247. Mill's signature, "Lamoignon," probably refers to Nicolas de Lamoignon (1648-1724), Intendant of Montauban, whose administration was marked by vigorous measures against the Camisards, extreme Protestants who took up arms after the revocation of the Edict of Nantes. The letter is headed "To the Editor of the Morning Chronicle" and is described in Mill's bibliography as "A letter signed Lamoignon in the Morning Chronicle of 30th October 1828 on the Brunswick Clubs" (MacMinn, p. 10). For nearly two years following this letter, Mill published nothing (see No. 43).

SIR,—The "Brunswick muster," as it is aptly denominated by your contemporary, *The Spectator*, has at length taken place. The party not having, as they are well aware, any great strength to boast of on the score of *heads*, are at least determined to let the country see how great a number of *hands* they can put in requisition on an emergency. Their first exploit has given, it appears, great satisfaction to their own minds. They are as elate with their triumph, as if any part of it had been due to the force of their logic, or to the brilliancy of their oratory. They hug themselves on their majority, as if the number of their votes were a proof of any thing whatever but the number of their acres. Had the Freeholders of Kent been free agents, these personages could not have raised a greater din of self-gratulation. They talk as magnificently of public opinion as if every child did not know, that all the opinion in the matter is their own opinion reflected back from their tenantry. The boast of the moment is, that the nation is with them; and the nation is every thing that is excellent and respectable, till it suits their purpose that it should be directly the reverse.

This signal respect for popular opinion, considering from what quarter it comes, is at least new. We were not always accustomed to so much deference, in certain personages, for the will of the people. Expressions of popular feeling were not deemed worthy of so much obedience when the feeling expressed was a reluctance to be starved by a bread-tax for the benefit of rent, and buried in a gaol "on suspicion of being suspected" of an encroachment upon the landlord's monopoly of game.[1] It was not respect which was felt for the voice of the nation, when it complained that the life-blood of the nation was drained from it in exorbitant taxation, to be profligately expended in affording a patrimony to the younger branches of certain families.[2] There was a time when public opinion was only named to be insulted; only interfered with to be bound down and gagged. I congratulate these Lords and Gentlemen on their conversion. It is somewhat tardy; but it still is welcome. Some slight shew of external respect towards a people whose bread so many of their relations eat, is at least decent. Pity that they did not see at a somewhat earlier period the error of their ways. The country might have been spared the recollection of more than one act, which will not redound to the honour of the British Aristocracy in future ages, nor perhaps of the nation, which an Aristocracy of such a stamp could so quietly rule.

What strange destiny! By what marvellous overturning and reversing of the established relations of things have English Borough Lords given in their adhesion to the "sovereignty of the people;" and the men who cheered the declaration of the Duke of Wellington, that county meetings were a farce,[3] appealed from the Duke of Wellington to a county meeting? I am not one of those who profess a sort of instinctive horror of "new lights;"[4] I think little of the

---

[1]The first reference is to the Corn Laws; the second is to the Game Laws, of which 22 & 23 Charles II, c. 25 (1671), 57 George III, c. 90 (1817), and 7 & 8 George IV, c. 27 (1827) were the most important prior to the passing, in July 1828, of 9 George IV, c. 69.

[2]Radical objections to the expenditures of the Civil List had been most prominently expressed by John Wade (1788-1875), author and periodical writer, in *The Black Book; or, Corruption Unmasked!*, 2 vols. (London: Fairburn, 1820, 1823), Vol. I, pp. 110-41, and Vol. II, pp. 9-40. The most outstanding younger branches were the ten acknowledged illegitimate children of the Duke of Clarence, soon to succeed his brother as King William IV.

[3]Wellesley, Speech on Petitions to the Crown (25 Jan., 1821), *PD*, n.s., Vol. 9, col. 108.

[4]A term that originated in the seventeenth century to describe those who claim special enlightenment, especially religious enthusiasts who reject the authority of "old lights"; see Thomas Hubbert, *Pilula ad expurgandam hypocrisin* (London: Lloyd and Cripps, 1650), p. 67.

wisdom, and not much of the sincerity, of such horrors. But the new lights which break in upon the professed enemies of new lights appear to me an object of very well-grounded distrust. I am suspicious of those, who *then* first discover the value of a nation's support, when for some immediate and momentary purpose they happen to *need* it. A lesson so conveniently learned, may no doubt be as conveniently forgotten, when need requires. I shall give credit to these Lords and Gentlemen for their popular principles when I behold them calling forth the people to join with them in any exalted and generous scheme of philanthropy and benevolence. But, as one of the multitude, I give these Noble Personages no thanks that I am summoned to aid them, not in giving freedom to the oppressed, or relief to the afflicted, but in silencing groans with bayonets, and wading up to the knees in the blood of six millions of my countrymen. I complain that, by these new candidates for my favour, no appeal is ever made to any but the mere grovelling and brutish part of my natural Constitution. I am little flattered when I perceive that I am never thought capable of being used for any services but those to which a wild beast would be perfectly adequate—and that my voice is never deemed worthy to be listened to in affairs of State, but when it is hoped, that swelled into rage by savage and malignant passions, it will emit sounds of hatred and ferocity against those over whom, for purposes in which I have no concern, it has been resolved to tyrannize.

But there is one consolatory assurance which may be gathered from the appeal of the Brunswick faction to the British people. The support for which they condescend to stoop so low, they assuredly *need*. It is unquestionably from no common necessity that they fly for help to those for whom, in the days of their pride, they have so little made a secret of their utter aversion and contempt. Perhaps, like other scornful persons before them, they have learned by experience, that very high people may need that assistance which very low people can give. They have little hope of other support, when they will throw themselves upon ours. They feel their weakness, and they feel it with mortification and rage. The feeling is excusable. It is new and strange to them as yet to find any difficulty in keeping their foot on any neck upon which it has once been planted. The loss of power is not familiar to them; it is what they have not yet learned to bear. Every sentence of the famous letter of the Duke of Newcastle betrays a deep and painful sense of humiliation.[5] Ill does he brook to renounce that tone of lofty authority so natural to the Lord of five Boroughs, and descend

[5] Henry Pelham Fiennes Pelham Clinton (1785-1851), 4th Duke of Newcastle, *A Letter to the Right Hon. Lord Kenyon from His Grace the Duke of Newcastle* (London: Hatchard, 1828). He was "lord" of the five boroughs of Aldborough, Boroughbridge, East Retford, Newark, and Nottingham. His letter, dated 18 Sept., 1828, and published also in *The Times*, 23 Sept., expressed deep alarm at the threat of Catholic emancipation to the ancient Constitution; in his view the government's "liberalizing" spirit was extremely dangerous at a time when sedition and treason were stalking abroad.

to the unaccustomed language of complaint and solicitation. His Grace does not easily use himself to the lachrymose tone. It does not sit gracefully upon him. His first efforts in the *comédie larmoyante* have all the inexperienced awkwardness of a beginner.—Amidst the most piteous of his complaints, it is easy to discern how much more to his taste the Aristocratic *sic volo sic jubeo* would be.[6] He probably would not be flattered by being told that he excites the commiseration of others; but he evidently is perfectly sincere in pitying himself.

The Ultra faction[7] are driven to their last resource. It was pleasanter, it was easier to govern the country by the strong arm of power, wielded by an obedient Ministry. For twenty years this scheme of Government had succeeded to their wish; and great was their surprise when they discovered, on a sudden, that it would endure no longer. They laid the blame of this disappointment at first upon those at the helm, who, they thought, having been formerly overpraised for being useful tools, had been puffed up by self-conceit to aspire above their station, and imagine that they might venture to be tools no longer. The new and unexpected difficulty which the Ultras found in governing the country being thus satisfactorily accounted for, they cast their eyes round the circle of the trading politicians of the day, and explored who among the hacks in office, or the hacks who wished to be in office, were the most narrow-minded and illiberal, the most ignorant and inept, and the most destitute of all moral dignity and decent self-respect. Having found that which they sought—having ascertained, as they conceived, which were the individuals who, in a field where such commodities abound, united in the greatest degree all these requisites; being satisfied with the result of their search, they resolved that of these individuals, thus pricked out, their next Ministry should be composed. Accident rather than their own strength gave them the Ministry of their choice; and if jobbing for them, and truckling to them, in any ordinary mode of truckling and jobbing, would have contented them, few Administrations ever did so much, in so short a time, to justify the selection. But no Ministry *dares* do all, which, at the present crisis, the interests of these men require, and their tongues do not scruple to demand. They wanted a Tory Ministry; they have had their wish, and they *cannot find* men who do not shrink from the responsibility of a *bellum internecinum*[8] between the soldiers on one side, and one-third part of the people on the other. Men in conspicuous stations, exposed to the public eye, who know that the *opinion* of mankind at

---

[6]Juvenal (ca. 60-140), *Satires*, VI, 223, in *Juvenal and Persius* (Latin and English), trans. G.G. Ramsay (London: Heinemann, 1950), p. 100.

[7]The extreme anti-Catholic faction, which had exerted strong influence in the previous Tory administrations, found less support in Wellington's ministry.

[8]The phrase goes back to Cicero (106-43 B.C.), Roman orator and statesman, "De domo sua ad pontifices oratio" (xxiii, 61), in *Cicero. The Speeches: Pro archia poeta, Post reditum ad Quirites, De domo sua, De Haruspicum responsis, Pro Planico* (Latin and English), trans. N.H. Watts (London: Heinemann, 1935), p. 206.

least will render them personally answerable for the evils which come upon their country through their means, are not hastily or easily brought to the perpetration of a great crime, to uphold a domination which to them is of no advantage, and satiate passions which they do not share. Since, then, the Ultras can find no other instruments to do their work, they hope at least to make instruments of the people. Their last desperate shift is to terrify their own Minister with that popular voice which they had themselves taught him to despise. What portion of the people fair or foul means will procure to back them in their unhallowed enterprise, a few weeks, or at farthest a few months, will disclose. But it is at least the duty of those who detest it as it deserves not to indulge a sleepy inactivity, nor flatter themselves with the idea that, when wicked men are preparing wicked deeds, it is enough for the good to sit still and silently disapprove. What, in all nations and in all ages, has caused the successes of interested villainy, is the indifference of the well-intentioned. The remark has been often repeated,[9] but it is little attended to; why? apparently because it has not been repeated enough.

I shall, perhaps, continue to address to you a few occasional remarks, as this great drama unfolds itself.

Lamoignon

[9]See, e.g., Edmund Burke, *Thoughts on the Cause of the Present Discontents*, in *Works*, Vol. I, p. 495. Cf. Charles Louis de Secondat, baron de la Brède et de Montesquieu (1689-1755), *Considérations sur les causes de la grandeur des Romains, et de leur décadence* (1734) (Edinburgh: Hamilton, *et al.*, 1751), p. 24; and Jean Jacques Rousseau (1712-78), *Du contrat social, ou Principes du droit politique* (1762), in *Oeuvres complètes*, 2nd ed., 25 vols. (Paris: Dalibon, 1826), Vol. VI, p. 153 (Bk. III, Chap. xv).

··· July 1830 to July 1831···

43. THE FRENCH ELECTIONS

EXAMINER, 18 JULY, 1830, PP. 449-50

In his *Autobiography*, after mentioning his ceasing to contribute to the *Westminster Review* after "Scott's *Life of Napoleon*" appeared in April 1828 (*CW*, Vol. XX, pp. 53-110), Mill says that for "some years after this time" he "wrote very little, and nothing regularly, for publication" (*CW*, Vol. I, p. 136), and his bibliography lists only Nos. 37-42 between "Scott's *Life of Napoleon*" and this leading article on the French Elections of July 1830. In fact he wrote a "treatise" or "tract" on an economic subject, which he submitted to the Library of Useful Knowledge on 23 Jan., 1829 (*EL*, *CW*, Vol. XIII, p. 742), about which nothing else is known. The silence ended when the July Revolution in France, following on the elections, "roused [his] utmost enthusiasm, and gave [him], as it were, a new existence" (*CW*, Vol. I, p. 179). The published result is seen in the flood of articles on France that he wrote in the next four years for the *Examiner*. During this time, Mill says, he "wrote nearly all the articles on French subjects [for the *Examiner*] . . . together with many leading articles on general politics, commercial and financial legislation, and any miscellaneous subjects in which I felt interested, and which were suitable to the paper, including occasional reviews of books" (*ibid.*, pp. 179-81). By October 1832 he was, he told Thomas Carlyle, writing "nothing regularly for the Examiner except the articles on French affairs" (*EL*, *CW*, Vol. XII, p. 125).

In this leading article Mill, in accordance with his belief that the English are ignorant of French affairs (and Continental affairs generally), explains the background of the shift to the left in the recent elections in France and the growing opposition in the country to the regime of Charles X (1757-1836). The previous elections, held in November 1827, had greatly increased the strength of the liberals in the Chamber of Deputies, giving them about two-fifths of the seats, approximately the same number going to the royalist supporters of Charles, and the remainder to the right opposition. This result ended the conservative ministry of comte Jean Baptiste Séraphin Joseph de Villèle (1773-1854), and there followed a period of moderate leadership by the vicomte de Martignac (see No. 45). Displeased by the liberal measures adopted, the King succeeded in 1829 in appointing an ultra-royalist ministry with prince Jules Auguste Armand Marie de Polignac (1780-1847) at its head. Liberal opposition continued to grow, and reached its height in the reply to the King's address at the opening of the session in March 1830, a protest by 221 Deputies, demanding ministers responsible to a majority in the chambers. Charles dissolved the Deputies on 16 May, and announced new elections.

The Charter to which Mill repeatedly refers is the Charte constitutionnelle, *Bulletin des lois du royaume de France*, Bull. 17, No. 133 (4 June, 1814). Granted by Louis XVIII (1755-1824) on his accession, and modified in 1815 after the Hundred Days, it established a new constitution for France that, while guaranteeing political liberties and imposing some limits on the monarch, nevertheless left the direction of the government in his hands. On 20 May, 1830, Charles X had intimated indirectly that he was prepared to use the powers he claimed were granted him by Article 14 of the Charter to govern by ordinance if the Chamber of Deputies failed to support his policies.

When Mill writes, the first stage of the French elections—that of the arrondissement electoral colleges, which elected 258 deputies and were made up of all male residents paying 300 francs a year in direct taxes—had taken place on 23 June; the second stage—that of the departmental colleges, which elected 172 deputies and were made up of the top 25 per cent of the taxpayers, who thus had a double vote—had occurred on 3 July, except in twenty departments (not nineteen as Mill thought).

The death of George IV on 25 June necessitated elections in England at this same time, elections which would replace the government of the Duke of Wellington with that of the 2nd Earl Grey and lead directly into the crisis over the Reform Bill.

This item, which begins the "Political Examiner," headed as title and unsigned, is not in the Somerville College set of the *Examiner*, which begins with 15 Aug., 1830. It is described in Mill's bibliography as "A leading article on the French Elections in the Examiner of 18th July 1830" (MacMinn, p. 10).

THE DEPARTMENTAL, OR GRAND COLLEGES, have now completed their operations throughout all France, except 19 departments. In those departments the elections were postponed by the Government, to afford time for the Court of Cassation to disfranchise a considerable number of electors who had been declared by the inferior Courts entitled to vote.

Exclusive of these nineteen departments, which include Paris, Rouen, and their vicinity, and in which the ministry are sure of a complete defeat, the departmental elections have afforded results as auspicious to the liberal cause as the elections for the *arrondissemens*. The royalists, indeed, still retain a majority, but that majority is greatly diminished. At no election previous to the last had a single liberal candidate been returned by a departmental college. At the last elections in 1827, about one third of the deputies elected by these colleges were liberal. In the present elections the proportion will be much greater. Without reckoning the deputies for the nineteen departments, of which the elections have been adjourned, the opposition had in the late Chamber 34 departmental members; it has now 46.

As the departmental colleges may be said to be composed of the twenty thousand richest men in a population of 30 millions, the great and rapid increase of the strength of the liberal party in these colleges is a still more striking indication of the progress of the public mind, than the liberal majority in the colleges of *arrondissemens*. The most bigotted English Tory cannot affect to see in such a struggle as the present any tincture of Jacobinism, if Jacobinism be, as Burke defined it, "an insurrection of the talents of a country against its property."[1] The insurrection, if such it can be called, is an insurrection of the intelligence and property of the country against an attempt to impose on them a

[1]Edmund Burke, *Mr. Burke's Three Letters Addressed to a Member of the Present Parliament on the Prospects for Peace with the Regicide Directory of France* (1796), *Letter II: On the Genius and Character of the French Revolution*, in *Works*, Vol. IV, p. 424.

ministry who are not only declared enemies to the reform of whatever is bad in the present laws or administration of France, but likewise, as the nation from long experience universally believes, irreclaimably hostile to the existing constitution of their country.

The French nation has been most absurdly reproached, particularly by the *Times* newspaper, for having condemned the Polignac ministry without trial.[2] If Mr. Cobbett were placed at the head of an English ministry, would the *Times* scruple to declare its hostility to his administration, because Mr. Cobbett had never been First Lord of the Treasury before?[3] Men whose whole political life has condemned them, as statesmen and as citizens, are not entitled to be tried over again in the situation of ministers, all measures of national improvement being stopped while the trial proceeds.

The opposition to the Polignac ministry is both of a reforming and of a conservative character. It is a conservative opposition as respects the political constitution of France, established by the Charter, which it defends against the Ministry, and the emigrants and their friends. It is a reforming opposition, as respects the multitude of gross abuses, which the representative system, established by the Charter, has not been able to prevent or extirpate.—The object of the Ministry, on the contrary, is to guard these abuses, to introduce others, and to overthrow either entirely or partially the representative system, which renders the introduction of new abuses extremely difficult, and which now at length seriously menaces the old ones.

The great and leading abuse which exists in France, and from which all the others flow, is the inordinate power of the government,—of the administration, in the common sense,—the crown, and its officers. In England, the ministry are the mere servants of an oligarchy, composed of borough-holders and owners of large masses of property: the abuses of which we complain, exist for the benefit of that oligarchy, not for the private interest or importance of men in office; and any one who should complain of the undue power of the Ministers as such, would be justly ridiculous. But in France, the oligarchy which engrosses all power, and manages and mismanages all public affairs from the greatest to the least, is what has been expressively termed a *bureaucratie*—it is the aggregate body of the functionaries of Government with the Ministry at their head. The power which in Great Britain is shared in Local Corporations, Parish Vestries, Churchwardens, Commissioners of Roads, Sheriffs, Justices of Peace, acting separately and in Quarter Sessions,* and numerous other local officers or bodies,

---

[2]Leading article on France, *The Times*, 17 June, 1830, p. 2.

[3]William Cobbett (1763-1835), radical editor of the *Weekly Political Register*. The British Prime Minister is, by tradition, First Lord of the Treasury.

*We are not here speaking of the judicial powers of these various functionaries, but of their powers of raising and expending public money, of local legislation, of police, and administration in most of its branches.

is in France exclusively exercised by the Government, and by officers appointed and removable at its pleasure. All establishments for education are under the direct superintendance of the Government. Almost all the public works, which in England are executed by voluntary associations of individuals, with all the power and patronage annexed to them, devolve in France upon the Government, partly from the scarcity of capital in France as compared with England, partly from the obstacles which the French laws oppose to all combinations of individuals for public purposes—the extent of which obstacles, and the degree in which the immense natural advantages of France are rendered useless by them, would utterly astonish our readers if we were to lay before them the requisite particulars. The French police has powers over individual security and freedom of action, which are utterly irreconcileable with good government.

The proximate object of the present opposition, so far as it is a reforming opposition, is to limit and curb this all-pervading influence of the Government, by destroying the system of *centralization* (this most expressive word has no synonym in English) from which it takes its rise. There are now many able and influential persons in France, who have studied England and the English Government, not as it is represented in books, but in its actual working and practical effects. They have seen at home the necessity that local affairs should be managed by local bodies; they have seen in England that when a local body is so constituted as to be an oligarchy, it far surpasses in jobbing and mismanagement even the great Oligarchy itself. They consequently desire the same securities for the integrity of the local bodies, which the Charter has provided for that of the general government. The executive officer, the prefect or mayor, they purpose should continue as at present, to be appointed and removable by the King. But their aim is—that the deliberative body, the council of the town, or of the department, should be chosen by the same electoral body which chuses the members of the representative branch of the general government, namely, the 80,000 persons or thereabouts, who pay 300 francs, or 12*l.* per annum of direct taxes.

The avowed purpose for which the Polignac Ministry was formed was, to resist this and all similar improvements. The manifesto which they issued the very day after their election, treated elective municipalities as a relic of Jacobinism. In the same document they announced as the principle of their administration, *point de concessions, point de réaction,*—no further concessions to the public voice, no retractation of the concessions already made.[4] The French nation did not believe them when they said, *point de réaction*: but even on their own showing, they were determined to refuse all concessions. The 80,000 electors and the nation deem concessions indispensable, and the electors would therefore have been guilty of cowardly truckling, if they had not re-elected the

---

[4]"Plus de concessions.—Point de réaction," *Gazette de France*, 10 Aug., 1829, pp. 1-2.

221 deputies who declared to the King that they had not confidence in his ministers.[5]

If even the professed designs of the ministry warranted the general burst of indignation with which their appointment was received, how much more so the designs which the nation, and even their own party, ascribes to them, and which, though not directly avowed, can scarcely be said to be disguised.

The present ministers, to a man, belong to that section of the party calling themselves Royalists, who from the first dissuaded Louis XVIII from granting the Charter, and who have ever been its declared enemies. All the measures of that party, when in power, have been so many encroachments, or attempts to encroach, upon the constitution established by the Charter, and upon the liberties and privileges which it guaranteed. According to the Charter, all the members of the Chamber of Deputies were elected by the 80,000 electors who form the colleges of *arrondissement*.[6] The Royalists added a fourth to the number of the deputies, and that fourth is elected exclusively by the 20,000 richest.[7] By the Charter, one fifth of the Chamber went out by rotation every year.[8] The Royalists passed a Septennial Act.[9] By a law which still subsists, no community of Jesuits can exist on French soil: the Royalist ministry not only connived at the existence of such communities, but threw the education of the greater part of the French youth, and the nomination to the subordinate public offices, almost exclusively into the hands of the Jesuits.[10] This first disgusted with the measures of the court all the most honest and intelligent part of the Royalist party; this it was which threw such men as Montlosier, the ablest literary champion of the royal power, into the ranks of the liberals.[11] A Royalist minister abolished the militia, or national guard, because they refused to turn Manuel out of the Chamber of Deputies, for exercising what in England would be considered a moderate and

[5]For the progress of the address, the vote on its acceptance, and its presentation to Charles X, see *Moniteur*, 15, 16, 17, and 20 Mar., 1830, pp. 296, 300, 303, and 315.

[6]Charte constitutionnelle (1814), Art. 35, p. 203.

[7]Bull. 379, No. 8910 (29 June, 1820). Referred to as the "Law of the Double Vote."

[8]Charte constitutionnelle (1814), Art. 37, p. 203.

[9]Bull. 672, No. 17159 (9 June, 1824). This law abolished the annual election of one-fifth of the Deputies and extended their term of office from five to seven years. The extended term was not to apply until after the next election, i.e., that of 1827.

[10]Louis XV (1710-74) expelled the Jesuits by the Edit du roi, concernant la société des jésuites (1764). Mill, like many of his French contemporaries, was not distinguishing between the Church and the Jesuits, whose renewed presence in France was openly ignored by a Government that had given control over the schools to the bishops (Bull. 664, No. 16774 [8 Apr., 1824]); merged the ministries of ecclesiastical affairs and education under the control of a bishop who was also appointed Grand Master of the University (Bull. 694, Nos. 17617 and 17618 [26 Aug., 1824]); and closed the Ecole Normale.

[11]Comte François Dominique Reynaud de Montlosier (1755-1838), whose pamphlets, especially *Pétition à la chambre des pairs* (Paris: Dupont, 1826), led the judiciary and the Chamber of Peers to declare the illegality of the Jesuits in France.

constitutional freedom of speech.[12] A Royalist Ministry and a Royalist Chamber restored Ferdinand of Spain to absolute power, by the men and money of a people said to be under a constitutional government.[13] A Royalist Ministry and a Royalist Chamber passed the famous law of sacrilege, for punishing the profanation of the sacred elements in the Eucharist,—a law worthy of the days of Calas and La Barre, and which persuaded the civilized world that the reign of despotism was assured for another century, and that France was relapsing into the servitude and superstition of the middle ages.[14]

A Royalist Chamber of Deputies passed the law of primogeniture,[15] which, for the avowed purpose of creating a hereditary aristocracy, offered violence to the strongest and most deeply-rooted sentiment of the most united public mind in Europe. A Royalist Chamber of Deputies passed the law for restraining the press, nick-named by its author, M. de Peyronnet, "une loi d'amour," by which not only all newspapers but all pamphlets and small books were placed under the almost absolute control of the ministry.[16] The hereditary Chamber of Peers rejected both these laws; and a Royalist Ministry attempted to overpower the

[12]Mill seems to confuse two events. The National Guard was abolished by Villèle in April 1827, because there had been anti-government manifestations at a royal review, and one legion, passing in front of the Ministry of Finance, had loudly jeered him (Ordonnance du roi qui licencie la garde nationale de Paris [29 Apr.], *Moniteur*, 1827, p. 617). On 4 Mar., 1823, Jacques Antoine Manuel (1775-1827), a republican Deputy, was ousted by force from the Chamber when, after a speech concerning the execution of Louis XVI, he had refused to comply with a vote for his expulsion. When the sergeant in charge of the National Guard would not obey the order to eject him forcefully, the gendarmes were called in.

[13]In the spring of 1823 French troops had crossed into Spain to aid the forces of the right in the civil war and succeeded in releasing Ferdinand VII who had been virtually held prisoner by the left. By a treaty signed by France and Spain in February 1824, Louis XVIII furnished Ferdinand with an army of occupation 45,000 strong. The French occupation lasted until September 1828.

[14]Bull. 29, No. 665 (20 Apr., 1825). The law was passed after a large number—538 in four years—of thefts of sacred vessels from churches; it was widely regarded by the left as a move towards the re-establishment of the old dominance of the Church. Jean Calas (1698-1762), a Protestant, had been broken on the wheel after being wrongly condemned by eight judges of Toulouse for murdering his son to prevent his conversion to Catholicism. Jean François Le Fèvre, chevalier de La Barre (1747-66), had been executed for mutilating a crucifix.

[15]Projet de loi sur les successions et les substitutions (5 Feb.), *Moniteur*, 1826, p. 168. The proposed law, which would have made equal distribution of property optional (whereas the Civil Code made the gift of the extra portion of the estate to the eldest son optional), was passed by the Chamber of Deputies after a bitter debate, but rejected on 8 Apr. by the Peers.

[16]Projet de loi sur la police de la presse (27 Dec.), *Moniteur*, 1826, p. 1730, presented by comte Pierre Denis de Peyronnet (1778-1854), a politician of ultra-conservative sympathies. In an article in the *Moniteur*, 5 Jan., 1827, p. 2, defending his law for restraining the press, he referred to it as "une loi de justice et d'amour," a nickname henceforth attached to it by the liberals. It was withdrawn by an ordonnance on 17 Apr. (*Moniteur*, 1827, p. 615).

voice of the majority, by creating from among their hacks in the Lower Chamber seventy-six new Peers at one stroke,[17] among all whom there was only one name* not odious or contemptible to all France.

Such is the political history of the party which has raised the Polignac Ministry to power, and by which alone that Ministry is supported. Let us now speak of the individuals. M. de Polignac was one of that portion of the emigrants who, after their return to France, refused to swear to the Charter. M. de la Bourdonnaye proposed that all who had accepted office under Napoleon, after his return from Elba, should be put to death.[18] His successor, M. de Peyronnet, is of ill repute, even in his private character, and the most violent and unbending member of the Villèle Ministry. M. de Montbel is the habitual apologist of that Ministry in the late Chamber. M. de Bourmont is odious to the army, for having gone over to the enemy on the field of battle; and finally, M. de Guernon-Ranville was only known, before his elevation to the Ministry, for having publicly declared that he gloried in being a counter-revolutionist, that is, in being an enemy to all benefits which France has purchased by the sacrifice of an entire generation.[19]

If the intentions of the Ministry are to be judged by the ostentatious declarations of their partizans, they are disposed to carry matters with a higher hand than the most audacious of their predecessors. There is not a royalist journal, including those known to be connected with the Ministry, which does not openly declare that the King will not yield, and that if the Chamber refuses to vote the taxes, they will be levied from the people by a Royal Ordonnance.

[17]Bull. 194, No. 7405 (5 Nov., 1827). It was this creation of peers, forty of whom Villèle had chosen from the loyal majority in the Chamber of Deputies, that had compelled him to call the elections of 1827.

*Marshal Soult. [Nicolas Jean de Dieu Soult, duc de Dalmatie (1769-1851), whose brilliant military career procured him the titles of Marshal in 1804 and Duke in 1807, and secured his popularity in spite of his ready shifts of allegiance as regime succeeded regime.]

[18]Comte François Régis de Labourdonnaie (1767-1839), one of the chief orators of the ultra-royalists, was Minister of the Interior in 1829. In a secret committee, he had proposed the Projet de loi d'amnistie pleine et entière, en faveur de ceux qui, directement ou indirectement, ont pris part à la conspiration du 1er mars, sauf les exceptions jugées indispensables et fixées irrévocablement par ladite loi (10 Nov., 1815), *Archives parlementaires de 1787-1860*, 2nd ser., XV, 212, 222. Napoleon Bonaparte (1769-1821), Emperor of France, returned from exile in Elba to rule during the Hundred Days, 19 Mar. to 22 June, 1815.

[19]Comte Guillaume Isidore de Montbel (1787-1861), conservative deputy since 1827, had become Minister of Public Instruction in August 1829, Minister of the Interior in November 1829, and Minister of Finance in May 1830. He used his considerable eloquence in defence of Villèle, his close personal friend. Comte Louis Auguste de Bourmont (1773-1846), Marshal of France, had already shifted his allegiance from the Bourbons to Napoleon twice, before a final defection to Louis XVIII a few days before Waterloo. Comte Martial Annibal de Guernon-Ranville (1787-1866) became Minister of Public Instruction on 18 Nov., 1829. At his earlier installation as procureur général of Lyons on 26 Oct., 1829, he had described himself as a counter-revolutionary (*Moniteur*, 1829, pp. 1805-06).

According to a mode of interpretation by which any thing may be made to mean any thing, they affirm that one of the articles of the Charter authorizes the King, when he sees urgent necessity, to make laws and levy taxes by his own authority,—that is, that one article of the Charter nullifies all the others. By virtue of this article, according to the ministerial papers, the King is determined, if the Chamber refuses the budget, to reassume absolute power, either definitively, or for the purpose of altering the law of election, and obtaining a Chamber which will be a passive instrument of his will. The liberal papers say that this is mere bravado; that the King will not be so imprudent as to attempt the entire subversion of the established constitution; that if he does attempt to levy taxes, either by proclamation or by the vote of a Chamber not constituted according to law, the people will refuse to pay them; that the courts of justice will support the people in their resistance; that if the King abolishes the courts of justice, establishes others, and endeavours to levy the taxes by force, the army will not support him; and that the struggle which will then take place will be dangerous to no one except the Royalists and the King. The strength and unanimity with which public opinion has declared itself, renders the fulfilment of these predictions, in case the King should endeavour to govern without a Chamber, by no means improbable.

Whether, therefore, the Ministers are to be judged by their avowed intentions, by their personal history, by the great acts of their party, or by its present professions, the renitency of the French nation against their yoke is just and expedient, and their success in putting down the manifestations of public displeasure would be one of the greatest, but fortunately also, one of the most unlikely calamities which could befal France and Europe.

44. PROSPECTS OF FRANCE, I

EXAMINER, 19 SEPT., 1830, PP. 594-5

Between the preceding item (No. 43) and this, the July Revolution had taken place. On 26 July, urged by Peyronnet and with the agreement of Polignac and other ministers, Charles X had issued four ordinances curtailing drastically the liberty of the press, dissolving the newly elected Chamber of Deputies, restricting the number of electors and the number of Deputies, and calling for new elections (Bull. 367, Nos. 15135-8 [25 July, 1830]). He referred to the powers granted by Art. 14 of the Charter of 1814, thus confirming fears that he would use those powers to establish personal government. Three days of riots followed; Charles X revoked the ordinances on 30 July, but it was too late; on 31 July, Louis Philippe, duc d'Orléans, accepted the offer to become Lieutenant-General of the realm; on 2 Aug. Charles X abdicated in favour of his grandson; on 7 Aug. the Chamber of Deputies voted in favour of proposals for a revised Charter, and offered the crown to Louis Philippe on his acceptance of the new version of the Charter (Charte constitutionnelle, Bull. 5, No. 59 [14 Aug., 1830]); and on 9 Aug., in a simple ceremony in the presence of the Deputies and Peers, Louis Philippe, duc d'Orléans, became Louis Philippe, King of the French.

Mill had gone with John Arthur Roebuck (1801-79), a close friend, and others to Paris in the week of 8 Aug., where he "laid the groundwork of the intercourse" he was to keep up "with several of the active chiefs of the extreme popular party" (*Autobiography, CW*, Vol. I, p. 179); he returned to London in the first week of September. For his exuberant letters from Paris extolling the Revolution and the exemplary behaviour of the working class, which he wrote to his father (in large part published in the *Examiner*) giving his impressions of the state of France immediately after the Revolution and the first proceedings of Louis Philippe's government, see *EL, CW*, Vol. XII, pp. 54-63.

This article, headed "Prospects of France. / No. I," is the first of a series of seven under that title in the "Political Examiner" (see Nos. 45, 48, 50, 51, 57, and 61; No. 98 is also related). The articles are described in Mill's bibliography as "A series of essays entitled the Prospects of France and signed S———— in the Examiner of 19th Sept., 26th Sept., 3d Oct., 10th Oct., 17th Oct., 14th Nov., and 28th November, 1830, in all seven numbers" (MacMinn, p. 11).

HOW WILL THE REVOLUTION TERMINATE? This is the question, which every person in England who reads a newspaper has asked, and still continues to ask himself every day. But all do not ask this question in the same spirit, nor with the same hopes and fears.

Those who feel interested in an event which changes the face of the world, chiefly as the security of their own commercial speculations may happen to be affected by it; and those, an equally large class, whose sympathies with their species are of such a character, that in every step which it takes towards the achievement of its destiny, they are more keenly alive to the dangers which beset it, than to the glory and the happiness towards which it is irresistibly advancing; these classes anxiously enquire, whether there will be *tranquillity*?

Those who feel that tranquillity, though of great importance, is not all in all; that a nation may suffer worse evils than excessive political excitement; that if the French people had not valued something else more highly than tranquillity, they would now have been the abject slaves of a priest-ridden despot; and that when tranquillity has once been disturbed, the best way to prevent a second disturbance is to prevent a second disturbance from being *necessary*; with these persons the subject of principal anxiety is this, Will the French establish a good government? And grievous will be their disappointment if, when every thing has been put to hazard, little or nothing shall prove to have been gained.

We will endeavour to contribute such materials as are afforded by a tolerably familiar acquaintance with the history of France for the last forty years,[1] and by

---

[1]Mill had already written three lengthy articles on French history: "French Revolution," *Westminster Review*, V (Apr. 1826), 385-98; "Modern French Historical Works—Age of Chivalry," *ibid.*, VI (July 1826), 62-103; "Scott's *Life of Napoleon*," *ibid.*, IX (Apr. 1828), 251-313. (See *CW*, Vol. XX, pp. 1-14, 15-52, 53-110.)

recent personal observation on the spot, towards the solution of both these questions.

We believe, then, that there will be tranquillity; that there will not be another insurrection; and that there will be no outrages on property, or resistance to the operations of Government in detail, but such as will with the utmost facility be put down, and that, too, by the people themselves, if necessary. But we are also convinced that France is threatened at present even with a greater evil than a second insurrection; and that if the people were to follow the advice of some of our contemporaries, by abstaining from all political agitation, and leaving their destinies to the quiet disposal of their present Ministers and Chambers, they would speedily find that all they had gained by the revolution was, to exchange a feeble despotism for a strong and durable oligarchy.

We believe, however, that the people are becoming aware of this; that they are beginning to understand what are the really important securities for good government; that before long they will make their demands heard in so loud a voice as will compel attention to them; and that they will obtain, gradually perhaps, but certainly, the best form of government which could continue to exist, in the present state of society in France, and with the feelings and ideas at present diffused among the French people.

Concurring as we do most heartily in all the demands of the popular party in France; holding those demands, and the tone in which they are preferred, to be not only unexceptionable but signally and laudably moderate; we of course see no ground for the tone of alarm which a highly influential journal suddenly assumed at the beginning of the present week.[2] The writer in the *Times* cannot possibly be unaware that he is most imperfectly acquainted with the past and present state of France, and the fact is that he hardly ever touches on the subject without betraying gross ignorance of it. He should not therefore be in so great a hurry to decide magisterially, that people of whom he seems to know nothing except that they desire the dissolution of the present Chamber, are a criminal faction. It is a besetting sin of the journal to which we allude, that whether its opinion be founded on knowledge or not, it fancies every man a rogue or a fool who ventures to entertain a different one.

We can assure the writer in the *Times*, without hesitation, that the dissolution of the Chamber is not desired (as he surmises) for the purpose of abolishing the peerage and still further curtailing the functions of the executive. There probably is not a man, certainly there is not a party, in France, whose desire it is that the power of the executive should be further curtailed. On the contrary, it is to the King, Louis-Philippe, that the popular party look, with a confidence not assumed for show, but felt in their hearts, to rid them in proper season of a body which has shewn readiness enough to take power from the Crown, but the greatest

---

[2]See *The Times*, 13 Sept., 1830, p. 2.

reluctance to give to the people any additional securities which it can possibly withhold from them. It is not desired that the Chamber should be immediately dissolved. What is sought is that they should first pass a new election law; that they should then dissolve, and give place to successors chosen under a system of election more favourable to good government than the present.

The whole number of persons having a right to vote at the election of Deputies, does not exceed 88,000. We have seen it asserted that the number of paid places in the gift of the Crown, and to which an elector is admissible, amounts to nearly 50,000. This may be an exaggeration; but when every proper abatement is made, the fact is indisputable that the Government disposes of a sufficient amount of public money to secure, without much difficulty, a majority of the electors; or, what comes to the same thing, the electors, who, in time to come, will have in their own hands the making or unmaking of ministries, have it in their power to distribute the public money, in considerable shares, among themselves and their connexions.

If it be said that, by the retrenchments about to be effected, the means of corruption will be diminished, we answer, that by those very retrenchments, and the accompanying remissions of taxes (the electoral qualification being founded on the amount of taxes paid) the number of voters will be reduced even below what it is at present. The remissions of taxes which have taken place since 1815,[3] have already diminished the number of electors to about four-fifths of what it was when Louis XVIII granted the Charter.

It is obvious, *primâ facie*, that 88,000 electors, in a population of 32 millions, constitute far too narrow a basis for a national representation. But the strenuous and energetic resistance which this body of electors offered to the usurpations of the late Government, appears to have induced many persons, both in this country and in France, to repose almost unlimited confidence in their disinterestedness and public spirit, notwithstanding the contrary presumption founded on their limited number.

To correct this mistake, it is only necessary to repeat an observation, in which the English *Globe*, to its great honour, preceded not only the other English, but even the French journalists. Under the late Government the electors were not yet the governing body. The powers of Government were substantially in the hands of the King; or at least it was yet a question whether the King or the Chambers should be the real sovereign. The King had not yet, like our own King, submitted himself to the necessity of governing in concert with the body who nominate the Chamber, and of dividing with them the produce of the taxes. Nevertheless a king cannot reign alone. Others besides himself must participate in his power,

---

[3]See the budgets for 1819, 1821, 1822 (two), 1823, 1825, and 1826 in *Bulletin*, 7th ser., XI, 41-60; XIII, 41-72; XIV, 417-38; XV, 201-22; XVI, 377-92; and 8th ser., II, 405-22; V, 1-18.

and in the benefits which result from it. But the Bourbons had never had the cunning to ally themselves with the monied class; the only portion of the nation possessing, by the Constitution, any political rights, by the exercise of which they could endanger the power of the sovereign. That stupid race, who, as Bonaparte said of them, had learned nothing and forgotten nothing,[4] were incapable of conceiving one single idea save that of returning to the old regime. Instead of uniting with the new Aristocracy, they had the inconceivable folly to rely for support upon an Aristocracy which had fallen into decay—which had lost all that ever gave it either physical force or moral influence—the titled *noblesse* and the Catholic hierarchy. These classes, reinforced by all whom they could personally influence, formed but an insignificant minority of the 88,000 electors, and the whole weight of the royal power being thrown into the scale, did not suffice to give it the preponderance. The electors would not tolerate a Government in which they had no share, and the King, persisting in his frantic scheme, appealed to the sword, and was defeated.

The case is now altered. The monied class has stepped into the place both of the King and of his allies, the emigrants and clergy. When itself excluded from the Government, this class made common cause with the people. Now, however, it composes the Government: and being a narrow Oligarchy, it has the same interests with any other Oligarchy. The people, when they made the Revolution, certainly did not intend that it should be a mere change of masters; but those whom they have permitted to assume the Government, have already evinced, in a variety of ways, their desire and intention that it should be little more.

Both in France and in England, the late French revolution has been frequently compared to the English revolution in 1688;[5] and there has in fact been up to the present time a striking similitude between the two events. We earnestly hope that they will not resemble each other in their final result.

The English House of Commons, under the Stuarts, was not a much more perfect representation of the people than it is at present. Yet it resisted the Stuarts with the utmost vigour and determination; the most genuine representative assembly could not have evinced more. And why? Because the House of Commons at that time had no separate interest from the people; because it had not yet possessed itself of the powers of government. It fought its own battle against a rival power, the people fought theirs against a tyrannical one. The House and the people marched together in uninterrupted harmony until the common enemy was overthrown. Thus far the conduct of the House of Commons resembled that of the Chamber of Deputies; yet if it had been inferred from their

[4]See the proclamation to the Imperial Guard and the army sent from Juan Bay, 1 Mar., *Moniteur*, 1815, p. 323.

[5]The "Glorious Revolution," in which a coalition of Whigs, Tories, and the Church of England, without violence, replaced James II (1633-1701), the last Stuart King, with his daughter Mary (1662-94) and her husband William of Orange (1650-1702).

intrepid conduct in opposition to tyranny, that they were incapable of abusing the power of Government when placed in their own hands, we have long since been taught by lamentable experience how little foundation there would have been for such an inference.

The revolution of 1688 occurred. The changes which it produced, the new laws which were made to limit the royal power,[6] and the opinions which, for a long time, it was the interest of the new Government to disseminate, have practically had the effect, now acknowledged by every body, of vesting the governing power of this country substantially in the House of Commons. So, in France, it now substantially resides in the Chamber of Deputies: that assembly having, in the first fortnight after the revolution, most expeditiously abolished all those articles of the Charter which imposed any restrictions on their power in favour of the King;[7] while they left to be decided hereafter the great questions which relate to the securities in favour of the people against the misconduct of the Chamber itself.

If the composition of the Chamber be retained nearly as it is, without any material modification in the law of election, the French constitution bids fair to be an exact copy of the English, in all except the fraudulent pretexts and the private immorality by means of which the latter habitually works. It will accomplish its ends without the instrumentality of a Gatton or an East Retford,[8] but the practical results will be much the same, saving the difference in the play of the machinery.

Where 32 millions are governed by the 88 thousand richest, the Government is of necessity a monied oligarchy; and our own Government is substantially of the same character. We have indeed great families who, by the boroughs which they influence, can secure to themselves a greater share of power and of the profits of misrule, than in proportion to their comparative wealth. Of this blessing the French are destitute. But even among ourselves every wealthy man is virtually a sharer in the Government. Every man who can afford to buy land, may obtain more or less influence in a county election; and every man who desires to have a seat in Parliament, can always obtain one by paying the price. The power which every rich man has thus within his reach, is equivalent to power in possession. Though the vices of our Government are as we see them, there is very little actual difference between the situation of a rich man who has a vote, or the means of influencing votes, and of a rich man who has neither one nor the other.

[6]Including the Bill of Rights, 1 William and Mary, Sess. 2, c. 2 (1688); and the Act of Settlement, 12 & 13 William III, c. 2 (1700).

[7]Generally, Arts. 13-23, under the rubric "Formes du gouvernement du roi."

[8]East Retford, like Gatton, was a notoriously "rotten" borough. A Parliamentary enquiry in 1828 had investigated Gatton but it had escaped disfranchisement; East Retford was disfranchised for corruption by the House of Commons but was reprieved by a political fracas and had escaped a second onslaught in 1829.

The French have therefore a genuine example in our Government of the spirit of an aristocracy of wealth, and the fruits which it bears. Let them beware how they suffer such a Government to become consolidated among themselves. It is because we, at our revolution, committed this grand mistake, that we are still, after 150 years, fruitlessly demanding parliamentary reform. The French will not be guilty of a similar error. They will effect their parliamentary reform in two years, perhaps sooner,—not with muskets, but with newspapers and petitions: after which there will be "tranquillity," if that name can be given to the intense activity of a people which, freed from its shackles, will speedily outstrip all the rest of the world in the career of civilization.

The organs of the Engish Oligarchy, the *Post* and the *John Bull*,[9] never fell into so grand a mistake as when they commenced flinging dirt against the new Government of France. For the interest of their employers, they should have upheld that Government by every means in their power. They are committing the same blunder as if they were to declaim in favour of the Jacobites, and against the present Constitution of England and the present settlement of the Crown. The two exiled families, and their respective supporters, are exact models of one another, and the men now in power in France are as exact a copy as could exist in the present day of our own politicians of 1688.

We have unavoidably contented ourselves with generalities in the present article. In the next we shall enter into greater detail.

S———.

45. PROSPECTS OF FRANCE, II

EXAMINER, 26 SEPT., 1830, PP. 609-10

For the context and the entry in Mill's bibliography, see No. 44.

THE CHAMBER OF 1830 was the result of a compromise.[1]

A glance at the history of the last fifteen years will show what was the nature of the compromise, and what were the motives which led to it.

From 1815 to 1830, the Government of the restored Bourbons had proceeded in almost uninterrupted progression from bad to worse: the eighteen months of the Martignac Ministry, a short-lived experiment on the public forbearance, being the only intermission.[2]

---

[9]The *Morning Post* (1772-1937), edited at this time by Nicholas Bryne, while generally supportive of the "Oligarchy," was more a society than a political paper; *John Bull* (1820-92), a Tory weekly of high circulation, edited at this time by Theodore Edward Hook (1788-1841), was so reckless as to be frequently charged with libel.

---

[1]See No. 49, n1, for further comment.
[2]Vicomte Jean Baptiste Sylvère Gay Martignac (1778-1832) was the chief figure in a moderate Ministry which, from January 1828 to August 1829, tried to steer between the Scylla of Charles X and the Charybdis of the Left.

At every step in this downward movement, the Bourbons lost a portion of their adherents. Recent events have made it sufficiently visible how miserable a remnant finally remained. The very soldiers who fought against the people, fought reluctantly, and against their private conviction. Leave out the foreign mercenaries, leave out all whose sole inducement was a mistaken idea of military honour, and Charles X could not perhaps have mustered a hundred men, not priests nor emigrants, who would voluntarily have fired a musket to save his throne.

Thus unanimous were the French, when tyranny was pushed to extremity; when the reign of the Bourbons became incompatible with a government of law, with the security of men's persons against the worst excesses of enraged and terrified power; when, if they had not been overthrown, blood must have flowed in torrents on the scaffold, civil war would have raged in every corner of France, and that wretched family would have been ejected after all, or could have been maintained solely by a despotism worse (if worse be possible) than that of the arch-despot, Napoleon.

So striking a unanimity could not have been generated by a less potent cause. The opposition to the Polignac Ministry was composed of the most heterogeneous materials.

Before the feud between the restored dynasty and the people could come to the issue which we have just witnessed—before the dynasty could have the folly to declare war upon the people with a force insufficient to hold out against them for three days—the dynasty had been, and must have been, deserted, not only by all the friends of good government, but by all the prudent and moderate supporters of bad. The Bourbons had parted with the wisdom of the serpent as well as with the innocence of the dove;[3] and all who had not made a similar renunciation were in the opposite ranks.

The opponents of the Polignac Ministry, though consisting, as we have already observed, of several different shades of opinion and inclination, may be ranged with sufficient accuracy under two great divisions: the old opposition and the new.

At the head of the former was the ancient *côté gauche*: the peers, deputies, and writers, who, in bad times as in good, in a minority of 16 as in a majority of 221,[4] in the sanguinary reaction of 1815 as in the heroic revolution of 1830, were still true to the cause of good government and social improvement: who faithfully and unremittingly watched over the securities, imperfect as they were, which the Charter of Louis XVIII rather promised than afforded; who were ever at their post to resist the jesuitical evasions of the Charter, long before Royal audacity

[3]Cf. Matthew, 10:16.

[4]Mill is probably referring to the very small number of liberal Deputies (sometimes estimated at nineteen), who survived the crushing rightist victory in the election of 1824. For the 221, see No. 43.

ventured on its open violation; whose integrity and self-respect excluded them, as well under a Decazes[5] as a Polignac, from holding office in a Government, the sole object of which was to wield a constitutional monarchy to the ends and in the spirit of a despotism. Such were the leaders of the old opposition. Its followers were all the incorruptible adherents of the good old cause, re-inforced by the thousands of high-spirited and well-educated young men whom every year brought forward into active life, and by numbers who, duped at first, had their eyes opened as the Bourbon Government and the spirit of the age became more and more irreconcileable.

The leaders of the new opposition consisted, first, of the several knots or bands of ejected placemen, who had been successively dismissed from the councils of the restored dynasty, as the game which it was playing came to require more skilful tricksters, or instruments of greater daring and more devoted subserviency. Secondly, of men who, either from personal attachment to the Bourbon family, or from a constitutional or habitual partiality to the strongest side, adhered to the restored Government in all its successful undertakings, and quitted it only when its projects became such as the state of society and opinion rendered impracticable except by force. A third class of the leaders of the new opposition, and one which circumstances have now elevated into unusual consequence, consisted of a school of philosophical and political writers, pure, we believe, for the most part, from any dishonourable ambition, and comprising in their ranks several able *littérateurs* and highly accomplished men, but whose metaphysical doctrines were too closely imitated from Scotland or Germany, and their political opinions from those which are current among genteel people in our own island. Like Madame de Staël,[6] many of whose opinions they inherit, and with whom their most prominent leader, the present Prime Minister of France, is nearly connected,[7] they are ardent sticklers for a representative and constitutional government, but constitutional on the English model. They either supported, or scarcely opposed, the Bourbon Government, when, by the introduction of the double vote, it rendered a national representation, already resting on too narrow a basis, still less popular and more aristocratic than before.[8] But when, by making

[5]Elie Decazes (1780-1860), favourite of Louis XVIII and leading figure in the Government in which he became President of the Council in November 1819.

[6]Anne Louise Germaine Necker, baronne de Staël-Holstein (1766-1817), author and leader of an influential liberal salon.

[7]Achille Charles Léonce Victor, duc de Broglie (1785-1870), statesman and diplomat, and son-in-law of Madame de Staël. He published her *Considérations sur . . . la révolution françoise* (1818). He was officially Minister of Ecclesiastical Affairs and Public Instruction, as Louis Philippe was himself acting as President of the Council. Mill surely also has in mind François Pierre Guillaume Guizot (1787-1874), historian, influential in the liberal opposition through his writings under Charles X, Deputy from 1830, and Minister of the Interior at this time.

[8]See No. 43, n7.

war to restore absolute power in Spain, by an immoral and fraudulent management of the elections, by repeated attempts to stifle the press, by putting down almost all places of general education except those of the Jesuits,[9]—we might say by all the acts of the Villèle Administration, the Bourbons showed themselves openly hostile to every kind of representative government, and to every kind of mental instruction by which men could be fitted for such a government, or led to desire it; then the persons of whom we are speaking, being sincere and strong enemies to the despotism of one, joined the popular cause, to which they have rendered, on not a few important occasions, signal service. This portion of the leaders of the new opposition have, as forming a philosophical party or school, received the name of *doctrinaires*; and, as politicians, bear no remote affinity to the English Whigs, though not stained, like so many of that party, by political duplicity, trick, or *charlatanerie*.

The above picture of the new and old opposition is probably new to most of our countrymen; but this is merely because it is the peculiar character of English nationality, not, like the French, to court the admiration of foreigners, but to treat them and their concerns with something like indifference and neglect. All who have watched the course of French affairs for the last ten years, have witnessed the gradual rise of the new opposition, and know that its constituent elements are such as we have just described.

These, then, are the two great divisions of the seemingly compact and united body which resisted the Polignac ministry, and by that resistance brought on the great events by which the Government of the restored dynasty has been abruptly terminated.

Of these, the old opposition predominates in the nation; but the new opposition predominates in the Chamber of Deputies, and has had the formation of the present ministry. This happened in consequence of the compromise to which, as we observed in the commencement of this article, the present Chamber owes its existence, and which we now proceed to explain.

At the general election in 1827, and at that in 1830, the one and only purpose of the patriotic electors was the overthrow of an administration, whose very existence precluded the slightest hope of a single step in social improvement, and placed in continual danger all the institutions, and all the liberties, to which the French people were most ardently attached. Among those who were united to

[9]For the French intervention in Spain, see No. 43, n13. To win their resounding victory in the elections of 1824, the Villèle ministry had not hesitated to tamper with the voting lists, put pressure on government officeholders, etc. Censorship was imposed in 1819 (Bull. 278, No. 6444 [17 May], Bull. 280, No. 6515 [26 May], and Bull. 284, No. 6648 [9 June]); in 1820 (Bull. 356, No. 8494 [31 Mar.]); in 1821 (Bull. 464, No. 10933 [26 July]); in 1822 (Bull. 510, No. 12253 [17 Mar.], and Bull. 514, No. 12390 [25 Mar.]); and attempted again in 1826 (see No. 43, n16). For the educational measures, see No. 43, n10.

attain this paramount object, all other differences of opinion, however important, were sunk. It was far from certain that by any union of efforts a majority could be obtained: and to risk the defeat of the common end for any object which admitted of postponement, and which was impracticable if the other failed, would have been egregious folly.

In the populous towns, where the number of voters was considerable, and the predominance of the popular party admitted of no doubt, members belonging to the *côté gauche* were returned. But in the poor, remote, and backward provinces of France, where the voters were few in number, composed in great part of functionaries in the pay of Government; and in the great or departmental colleges throughout the country,—it was uncertain whether a majority hostile to the ministry could be obtained. To ensure such a majority, the Liberals almost always endeavoured to select as the popular candidate an individual differing by the slightest possible shade from the obnoxious ministers, provided he would consent to vote against them. By any other selection they would have lost some part of the votes which a candidate of such a character might probably obtain; and have risked the total failure of the paramount object, the exclusion of the ministerial candidate.

In many instances, also, the narrow limits within which the choice of the electors was confined by the conditions of eligibility, did not admit of their making any choice but one which very imperfectly represented their opinion. By the terms of the Charter, half the Deputies of a department must be chosen among the inhabitants of the department, and the whole among persons paying at least 1000 francs (40*l.*) of direct taxes to the state.[10] This, in France, implies no inconsiderable fortune, especially in the poorer departments. And when we mention that there are no less than eight departments in which the totality of the electors, that is, of the inhabitants paying 300 francs or more of direct taxes, falls short of 400, it may be imagined within what narrow bounds the electors were often restricted, in the selection at least of that half of the deputies, whom they were compelled by law to choose from among the inhabitants of the department.

The first which we mentioned of the causes which prevented the popular electors from choosing the men whom the majority of them would have preferred, did not exist in so great a degree in 1830 as in 1827. The popular party were more completely aware of their strength, and could reckon with confidence on a large majority in places where on the former occasion success had been at least doubtful. A considerable proportion of the Deputies who owed their seats to the compromise, would consequently have been ejected from them by men of more decidedly liberal opinions as well as of greater abilities, had not circumstances of which it can only be necessary to remind our readers, rendered it expedient to adopt as a universal rule, the re-election of the 221 who had voted

[10]*Charte constitutionnelle* (1814), Arts. 38 and 42.

for the address condemning the Polignac ministry.[11] Not a few who had lost the confidence of their constituents by their manifest incompetence as legislators, as well as by their inadequacy as representatives of electors sympathising far more than themselves in the feelings and wishes of a vast majority of the French people, are indebted solely to the principle of re-electing the 221, for the advantage which they now possess of assisting in the formation of a new Government: an advantage by no means trifling, as the new Red Book, if the revolutionary era have as yet produced so useful a document,[12] bears ample and unequivocal testimony.

The Chamber of 1830, then, was the result of a compromise; in which, as in all such compromises, the timid and hesitating dictated to the bold and decisive; those least in earnest gave the law to those who were most so. A large proportion, therefore, of the present Deputies, represent the opinion but of a minute and impotent fraction of their constituents. They are far from being the men whom even the present electors would again elect, even under the existing conditions of eligibility; and still further from being such as would be re-elected by the present electors, if those intolerable conditions were abrogated, or so far lowered as to leave any sufficient latitude of choice.

Can it be supposed, for example, that the *centre droit*, a party whose benches in the Chamber are at present only less crowded than those of the ministerial section, the *centre gauche*,—a body composed, in a great measure, of royalists, a little, and only a little more scrupulous or less audacious than the late ministers themselves, and many of whom adhered to the Ministry of Villèle to a later period than the Spanish war—can it be believed that such men would now be pitched upon by electors freed from the usurpation of the double vote[13] (which most of those very men had a hand in fastening upon them), as fit persons to legislate for regenerated France,—for France under a *roi citoyen* in lieu of a *roi cagot*,[14] and demanding good institutions—not a mere mitigation of bad ones?

The present Deputies were elected for the single purpose of overthrowing the Polignac Ministry. For that end they were admirably adapted. They were not chosen to make laws for a regenerated nation; and fitness to make such laws was not at all considered in the nomination of the greater part of them. A large

[11] For details, see No. 43, n5.

[12] The new revolutionary era had not produced a new edition of *Le livre rouge, ou Liste des pensions secrettes sur le trésor public, contenant les noms & qualités des pensionnaires, l'état de leurs services, & des observations sur les motifs qui leur ont mérité leur traitement* ([Paris:] Imprimerie Royale, 1790). The first page of the English Radical exposé of the Civil List, Wade's *The Black Book*, is headed "The Black Book, hitherto Mis-named 'The Red Book.'"

[13] By Bull. 8, No. 67 (12 Sept., 1830).

[14] I.e., a Louis Philippe rather than a bigoted Charles X. Louis Philippe was identified as the Citizen King in a speech to the Peers on 7 Aug., 1830, by Etienne Denis Pasquier, *Moniteur*, 1830, p. 864.

proportion were re-elected for qualities the very reverse of those which the fulfilment of such a duty would require. They were chosen because they could not be accused of being patriots; because they did not sympathise in the feelings of the French people; because their lives had been spent in serving and in worshipping the Bourbons; and because they were known to be capable of abiding by that family in all save the last extremity.

It is not wonderful that men should be in no hurry to resign their seats, who know that this is the last time they will ever fill them. Least of all is this wonderful, when by losing their seats they lose the whole patronage of their department. But it would be wonderful, if any degree of ignorance and presumption in an average English newspaper could surprise us, that the body of the intelligent classes in France should be treated as something approaching to rebels and traitors, because they are eager to get rid of such a Chamber.

S————.

46. MR. HUSKISSON AND THE JACOBIN CLUB
EXAMINER, 26 SEPT., 1830, PP. 611-12

This article comments on rumours (see *Morning Chronicle*, 18 Sept., 1830, p. 2, and 23 Sept., p. 3) about the radical background of William Huskisson, who had died on 15 Sept., after being run over by a train. Headed as title, this leading article in the "Political Examiner" is identified in Mill's bibliography, with No. 47, as "Two short leading articles in the Examiner of 26th Sept. 1830 headed 'Mr. Huskisson and the Jacobin Club' and 'The recent Combination of the [Journeymen] Printers in Paris'" (MacMinn, p. 11).

IN A DISCUSSION which has gone the round of the daily papers respecting the very unimportant fact, whether Mr. Huskisson was or was not a member of the Jacobin club,[1] the *Times* remarks that a speech professing to be delivered by him at that club, was published at Paris in 1790.[2] "In the title of the speech," continues the *Times*, "Mr. Huskisson is described as an Englishman, and a member of the *société* from 1789. The Right Honorable Gentleman had most probably abandoned the society long before it became formidable under the name of the Jacobin club, and hence he is justified in saying that he never attended the sittings of that club but once."[3]

[1]The Jacobin Club, founded in 1789, was originally called La Société des Amis de la Constitution Monarchique. By the end of 1791, it had fallen into the hands of radicals; its meetings were opened to the public, and it became a forum for promoting the Terror. In 1794, after the fall of Robespierre, the Society was disbanded.

[2]*Discours prononcé par M. Huskisson, Anglois et membre de la Société de 1789, à la séance de cette Société, le 29 août 1790, sur les assignats*, in *Mémoires de la Société de 1789*, No. XIV (Paris: LeJay fils, 1790).

[3]*The Times*, 22 Sept., 1830, p. 3.

"A member of the *société* from 1789." This looks very much like a translation of "membre de la société de 1789." If so, the editor of the *Times*, or his informant, is ignorant both of French and of history. Of French, because "a member of the *société* from 1789," if expressed in that language, would stand thus, "membre de la société *depuis* 1789," not *de* 1789. Of history, because he apparently is not aware that there existed a society under the name of "La Société de 1789," more shortly "le club de quatre-vingt-neuf," which was established by seceders from the Jacobin club, and in opposition to it;[4] to defend the original principles of the revolution of 1789, principles which the Jacobin club had by its founders been intended to promote, in opposition to the more democratic views which that club subsequently adopted.

Without pretending to peculiar sources of information, we have always understood that Mr. Huskisson was in fact a member, not of the Jacobin Club, but of the Club of 1789. Our belief is now confirmed, both by his own disavowal of having ever belonged to the former society,[5] and by the apparently ill-translated and ill-understood title-page of his speech, as referred to by the *Times*.

47. THE RECENT COMBINATION
OF JOURNEYMEN PRINTERS AT PARIS
EXAMINER, 26 SEPT., 1830, P. 612

This leader is in response to articles such as those in *The Times*, 8 Sept., p. 4, 10 Sept., p. 2, 11 Sept., p. 2, and 18 Sept., p. 2. The printers of Paris had petitioned the Chamber of Deputies against mechanical printing presses, and when the printers at the Imprimerie Nationale were asked on 1 Sept. to print the order for money to repair the mechanical presses of the Royal Printing House smashed on 29 July, they refused. At a meeting of printers on 3 Sept. a resolution was taken not to work on mechanized presses and consequently some newspapers failed to appear on 3 and 4 Sept. On 4 Sept. Lafayette told the committee of the printers that such combinations of workmen were illegal, and they issued instructions to return to work. Nonetheless fifteen were arrested. On 14 Sept. they appeared before the Tribunal of Correction and were all acquitted. This leading article, following No. 46 in the "Political Examiner," is headed as title. For the entry in Mill's bibliography see No. 46.

THE ALARMS WHICH HAVE BEEN PROPAGATED in England on the subject of this combination were almost entirely groundless.—The workmen, indeed, like many persons of far higher rank and greater acquirements than themselves, fell

---

[4]In August 1789, Mirabeau, Lafayette, J.S. Bailly, and E.J. Sieyès left the Société des Amis de la Constitution and founded the Société de 1789 (also called Les Feuillants). After Mirabeau's death in April 1791 the Society declined.

[5]See Huskisson's letter (7 July, 1830) to "G.P.," *The Times*, 20 Sept., 1830, p. 3.

into the mistake of supposing that machinery, in certain cases at least, was injurious to the general interest, and should be prohibited by law. They accordingly refused to work for those newspaper proprietors who persisted in the employment of steam presses. The *strike* was an offence under the iniquitous combination laws, which still subsist in France, though abolished in England.[1] With this exception, the workmen violated no law. The committee which they appointed, immediately issued a placard, formally disavowing all intention of compassing their end by violence or intimidation. No force was employed against the proprietors of newspapers; and if, for one or at most two days, several newspapers did not appear, it was merely because they had not yet procured workmen, to replace those who had left off work. In three days, at the utmost, affairs resumed their accustomed course, and from that time the newspapers have ceased even to allude to the subject.

We subjoin in confirmation of the above facts, the verdict of the Tribunal of Correctional Police, acquitting the members of the committee:

Considering that,—if it is proved that the committee of the journeymen printers who met at the Barrière du Maine entered into an engagement, by which the journeymen bound themselves not to work in work-shops where there are mechanical presses, and that the meeting therefore assumed the character of an illegal combination, such as is contemplated and prohibited in articles 415 and 416 of the penal code,—it is at the same time proved by the speeches of counsel, and in particular by the explanations given at the trial by the civil and military authorities present at the deliberation, that the committee acted only with a view to preserve order, and in the immediate presence of the authorities;

That, if additions appear to have been made to the resolution subsequently to the moment at which it was carried, this seems to have been the effect of a mistake made by the members of the meeting respecting the extent of their rights;

That the men returned to their work almost immediately, and that the members of the committee, when properly informed on the nature of their rights, recommended to their companions to resume their occupations;

That, if these various circumstances, taken together, do not destroy the fact of the commission of the offence, they at least preclude the supposition of any criminal intention, which intention is the basis of the offences designated by the law;

The Court discharges the accused parties, without costs.[2]

48. PROSPECTS OF FRANCE, III

EXAMINER, 3 OCT., 1830, PP. 626-7

For the background, heading, and bibliographical entry, see No. 44. This article is the first in Mill's Somerville College set in which he has inked in corrections in the margin.

[1]For the French laws, see Code pénal, Bull. 277 *bis*, Nos. 1-7 (12-20 Feb., 1810), Liv. III, Titre II, Chap. ii, Sect. 2.5, Arts. 415-16. For the British laws, see 39 & 40 George III, c. 106 (1800) and 57 George III, c. 19 (1817), which were repealed by 5 George IV, c. 95 (1824).
[2]*Le National*, 15 Sept., 1830, p. 4.

At 145.39-40 "authority in power" is changed to "persons in authority"; in the next number of the *Examiner*, 10 Oct., p. 644, this correction appears in an *Erratum* note.

A CONTEST IS COMMENCING—and if it be a prolonged, it will doubtless be an acrimonious one—between the majority of the Chamber of Deputies and the majority of the French nation.

By the majority of the nation we do not here mean the absolute majority, but the most numerous portion of those who as yet take any part or concern in the struggle. A numerical majority of the entire population are undoubtedly quiescent. The agitation has not yet penetrated so deep. Among the working, (we may call them also the fighting) classes, there is, or was very lately, but one feeling: satisfaction at having achieved the overthrow of a bad government, and confidence, that without their intervention, and by persons more instructed, and having better means of judging than themselves, the constitution will be resettled —in a manner the precise nature of which they do not attempt to predict, but which they feel no doubt will be duly considered, and against which if they should see any reasonable objections, they will be at liberty to propound them. We do not believe that the anticipations or reflections of the great mass of the people of Paris go farther. Any deliberate disregard of their interests, to a degree which would call upon them for further armed resistance, we do not imagine to have once entered into their conceptions. For years past they have been accustomed to hear their sentiments proclaimed, and expression given to their political wants, by the almost unanimous voice of the instructed class. They have not lost their feeling of reliance upon that class: to it the present Ministry, and the adversaries of the present Ministry, alike belong; and in its hands they are willing to leave the decision of the dispute, believing, with a conviction in which we participate, that no government which is, or can be, established in France, will have power to resist the deliberate opinion of the educated part of the public, strongly expressed.

The struggle which is commencing is between the majority of the Chambers and the majority of the educated class; the majority in numbers, in talents, in activity, we believe even in property; and including almost all among the class in easy circumstances, who, in the three memorable days, made any exertions or exposed themselves to any danger in the common cause.

Such being the disputants, it remains to be shewn what is the point at issue. Let no one dream that it is a mere question of who shall be in or out. In our late remarks on the composition of the Chamber of 1830,[1] we sufficiently settled the question of the unfitness of the present men, but unfitness of men is an evil only in proportion to the unfitness of their probable acts. There is a fundamental difference, pregnant with important consequences, between the practical principles of the persons now in power, and those of their opponents.

[1] In No. 45.

The doctrine of the present Chamber and of the Ministry of its choice is, that, the Revolution having been a defensive act, provoked by an attempt to destroy the established Constitution; the existing Charter having been its rallying word, and the maintenance of that Charter its direct object, the people have now obtained this, and ought to be satisfied. Those modifications in the Charter (they add) which the meditations of enlightened men had prepared, and which public opinion had sanctioned, were made by the Chamber, in the first week of its existence, and were assented to by Louis Philippe as the condition of his elevation to the throne. This doctrine respecting the late alterations in the Charter has been several times proclaimed (on one memorable occasion in words of which ours are almost a translation) by Deputies belonging to the majority, and in particular by the two Ministers who take the lead in the Cabinet, and who have the most completely identified themselves with the party predominant in the Chamber.[2]

The first part of their case, as presented by themselves, they have saved their opponents the trouble of refuting, by making an assertion which is inconsistent with it. For if there were alterations in the Charter, respecting the propriety of which the public mind was so maturely made up as to admit of their being carried into effect after a deliberation of two days, without even the forms which are never departed from in the enactment of an ordinary law, it is a proof that, although the Charter was the war cry, and its violation the immediate incentive to resistance, it was not to the Charter, as such, that the people were attached, nor was its maintenance all that they desired. What the people wanted was, securities for good government. If those which the Charter affords, as at present modified, are sufficient, they are in the wrong in wishing for others; but let not this question be got rid of by a side-wind. The whole matter turns upon this. Any argument which does not go to this single point is foreign to the dispute.

But before we state what are the securities for good government which the people would prefer to those afforded by the modified Charter, it is hardly possible to avoid taking some notice of an argument, which, although it would be just as available in behalf of one set of institutions as of another, is yet well adapted to make an impression on certain minds, as it consists of a *phrase*. The current phrase in the mouths of the partisans of the Chamber is, that it is desirable the revolution should stop. This maxim finds favour in the eyes both of those to whom the word revolution is synonymous with insecurity, and of those who, without considering the radical distinction between the two periods, remember that in the days of their fathers the first revolution was succeeded by a second, and the second by a third, until, wearied and without hope, the French people surrendered themselves willing slaves to a military despotism.

[2]See Guizot's and the duc de Broglie's Speeches on the State of France (13 Sept.), *Moniteur*, 1830, pp. 1085-6. As is indicated in the *Moniteur* of 15 Sept., p. 1093, the text of both speeches was the same.

In answer to the profession of a desire to terminate the revolution, the majority of the nation reply, that if by the revolution be meant the fighting in the streets, it is already terminated, and no circumstances but such as are greatly to be deprecated ought, or are likely, to lead to its renewal. Such means, it is to be hoped, will never again be necessary, either for the attainment or for the maintenance of good government: and unless indispensable for that end, nothing that could possibly occur would warrant so hazardous an expedient. But to join heartily in the wish that the revolution may stop, is not quite the same thing as to admit that the political institutions which existed before the revolution are to remain without any material improvement, or that those, whose sole object is that the defects still remaining in the Constitution may be corrected in the mode prescribed by the Constitution itself, are to be deemed sufficiently answered by having it thrown in their teeth that they wish to continue the revolution, when it is time the revolution should terminate.

It is speciously urged that the present moment is a moment of excitement, and that such times are improper for discussing and maturing great constitutional changes. The popular party do not deny this. They allow that a state of violent excitement is one which no rational and well-intentioned person would voluntarily choose for a work requiring slow and calm deliberation. It is for this very reason that they implore the Government not to delay the deliberation until the excitement is such as to be incompatible with slowness and calmness. That it has yet become so, they deny, and deny truly. That it will become so in a few months, if the demands of the reasonable part of the public be not complied with, one must be blind not to see. When justice and the public interest demand the concession of a foot, it is wretched policy to refuse the people an inch lest they should take an ell. Give the entire foot with a good grace: if you withhold what you yourselves think reasonable till it is torn from you by main force, where are you to find moral strength for resisting pretensions of questionable expediency? The people may have confidence in those who obviously intend their good. But they must be idiots if they placed reliance in men who refuse them justice, for fear lest injustice should come of it.

To return, however, to the doctrine that times of political excitement are unfit times for constitutional reforms; we ask, is it possible to cite one single example of constitutional reforms effected in times which are not times of excitement? Reforms in the Government are not what the Government itself is apt spontaneously to originate. When the public are quiet and satisfied, it is not, we may be sure, the persons in possession of power, who will voluntarily come forward to point out faults in the political arrangements which have placed the power in their hands. Popular excitement is the natural indication to persons in authority, that a general wish exists for something which is conceived to be an improvement. It is their duty to defer to that wish by a solemn deliberation, which shall testify that the cause of the people was not prejudged in advance, and shall give hopes that what is now withheld will, if reasonable, be granted, when experience and discussion shall have overcome the scruples of its opponents. It is the duty of the Government to do this, before excitement has grown into passion, wishes into demands, and friendly remonstrance into clamorous hostility.

Those who accuse the popular party of wishing for another revolution, are accused in their turn by that party of not understanding the meaning nor entering into the spirit of the revolution which has already taken place. It is insisted on by the popular newspapers, and re-echoed by thousands in conversation, that the Chamber mistakes the *grande semaine* for a mere change of ministry, and fancies it does enough if it gives to France in 1830, all that France called for in 1829;[3] forgetting that a revolution carries society farther on its course, and makes greater changes in the popular mind, than half a century of untroubled tranquillity. Why were the demands of the people in 1829 so much more moderate than at present? Because what is now past was then to come, and might have been avoided. They asked for as much as they thought could be obtained without a revolution; and with this, rather than draw the sword, they would have been satisfied. What, however, they were content rather to forego, than to purchase at so terrible a price, it does not follow that they are not disposed to claim now when the price has been paid. The bonds of law and government have been broken, and all the perils incurred, to avert which mankind are content to sacrifice their most cherished wishes. France is entitled to require, that one such convulsion, one such dissolution and reconstruction of the machine of society, shall suffice. Proportioned to the fearful dangers of a violent revolution, would be the moral responsibility of those, by whose fault they who have braved those dangers should have braved them in vain. It is of the utmost importance that what is done now should be done once for all. The field is now open; wait but a little while, and it will again be hedged in by the barrier of an established constitution. The questions, on the solution of which by the French people their future good government will depend, *must* be now agitated, must be now decided. Let it be attempted so to decide them that it shall not be necessary again to unsettle them in a year to come. To have turned out one bad government would be a poor equivalent for all the blood which has been shed, if the same operation, in one, or two, or fifty years, should have to be performed again upon another. For the sake even of tranquillity itself, the present is the time so to settle the constitution, that the bad government now happily got rid of shall be the last.

How little there is to inspire terror or mistrust, in the means by which the popular party proposes to accomplish this end, will be seen in the ensuing paper.[4]

S————.

---

[3] See, e.g., *Le National*, 24 Sept., 1830, pp. 1-2.
[4] See No. 50.

49. ANSWER TO BOWRING'S CRITICISM
OF PROSPECTS OF FRANCE, II

EXAMINER, 3 OCT., 1830, P. 627

Immediately following "Prospects of France, III" (No. 48) in the *Examiner* of 3 Oct., p. 627, is a letter from John Bowring (1792-1872), a disciple of Bentham who had been chosen by him to edit the *Westminster Review*; his relations with the two Mills had become difficult in the late 1820s, and they had both withdrawn from the *Westminster*. Bowring's letter, commenting on No. 45, is dated from 5, Millman Street, 27 Sept., 1830, and headed "To the Editor of the Examiner":

The grounds of the unpopularity of the French Chamber of Deputies are obvious. It does not represent the Revolution. The Revolution was the work of the young—of the unopulent. The Chamber has no individual of either of these classes among its members—nor was there one among the electors of the Deputies.

I am greatly surprised that so intelligent a writer as S. should denominate the Chamber of 1830 "the result of a compromise." Nothing can be farther from the fact. The Chamber of 1830 consisted of *the best men* that could be found in the narrow circle of the qualified candidates, wherever popular opinion had any—the slightest—preponderance. The electors did all they could in these circumstances; and in no case, that I know of, did they take a worse where they could have returned a better man. The honor that belongs to them they should be allowed to bear; and it cannot, I think, be denied, that, considering the numerous limitations on the expression of the will of the electors, the Chamber of 1830 was a tolerably fair representation of the elective body.

But the ground of complaint, of just and reasonable complaint, lies far deeper. Not more than one individual in three hundred exercises any proportion of the elective franchise, in France. Deduct two-thirds for women, children, &c., and still not one in a hundred has a voice in the constitutive power of the country. That is, indeed, a grievance, severely and widely felt; and, till some steps are taken for its redress, it is *desirable* that discontent should find expression. I do not mean that a universal, or even a *very extended*, suffrage is demanded by the men of the revolution. The beautiful machinery of the ballot will extract public opinion from a comparatively small portion of society. If the number of electors were quadrupled, I think that would for the present satisfy the French people.

I never have heard from well-informed electors that their "sole object," in the late election, was to upset an "obnoxious ministry:" such narrowness of purpose would have done little credit to their sagacity. Still less that the "liberal electors" sought the candidate who "differed the slightest shade possible from the obnoxious ministers." There were—and I speak from pretty extensive intercourse with the electors of France—no such delicately spun refinements. The electors did the best they could; and I doubt the possibility of your intelligent correspondent's producing a single instance where the liberals—for it is they who are accused of "compromise"—returned a member because he "differed the slightest shade possible from the obnoxious ministers."

That the Chamber is unworthy to represent, and unwilling to develope, the Revolution is, to me, perfectly obvious; that the opinion of a hundred new representatives, many of whom will be chosen from among the young, will greatly improve its character, and liberalize its proceedings, is also clear; that the removal of the corrupt influence of the Polignac administration would tend to the rejection of an immense number of the present Deputies, I hold to be indisputable. The king, whose pride it is to be the king of the people, ought not to delay that appeal to the people which is loudly called for. Among the Doctrinaires, the Whigs, and the Aristocracy of France, there are, for him, many pitfalls and precipices; his strength and his security can only be established by his most intimate alliance with the nation. The reluctance of the Deputies to return to their constituents, grows out of their knowledge that their constituents will now find better servants: and it is truly a grief and a grievance that the "triumphant nation" is not allowed to choose them.

This letter is in turn followed by an editorial comment, "We have communicated the above letter to our correspondent S—, who has furnished us with the following observations in reply:", which introduces Mill's unheaded reply on the same page. Mill's English quotations are from Bowring's letter. This item is not found in Mill's bibliography, but the circumstances mark it as certainly his.

IT RESTS WITH THOSE WHO KNOW THE FACT, to pronounce whether it accords with the statement of your other correspondent or with mine. The expression I made use of is not of my own invention, it is a literal translation from the express words of the French popular newspapers. Which of them has not reiterated, again and again, the expression, "La Chambre de 1830, fut le résultat d'une transaction"; and sometimes, "Le résultat d'une foule de transactions."[1] The assertion that the Chamber was elected for the sole purpose of overthrowing the Polignac Ministry, has been repeated by the same newspapers almost to tiresomeness. Nor does such narrowness of purpose, when fairly considered, reflect any discredit on the electors. The overthrow of the Ministry being the condition on which every thing depended, no sacrifice could have been too great which helped to render it more sure. The people universally felt the importance of re-electing the 221, who, it is notorious, were preferred in cases where even the "narrow circle of the qualified candidates" would have afforded persons in all other respects more acceptable to the majority of the electors.

Your correspondent appears not perfectly to have seized the nature of the "compromise" which was stated to have taken place. He denies that the "Liberals" made any compromise; but who, permit me to ask, are the Liberals? If he accounts all such who were enemies of the late Ministry, undoubtedly they made no compromise with its friends. But the majority of them made—and it is matter of praise, not of blame to them—a compromise with the minority. They elected, not the best man who could be got, but the best who could be sure of uniting all their suffrages; throwing thus the nomination into the hands of that portion of the opposition which differed least from the obnoxious Ministry, wherever there was any chance that the votes of that section of the electors might have it in their power to decide the majority. In the large towns, where the really popular party could afford to dispense with the assistance of semi-liberals, and to which places the enquiries of your correspondent have probably been confined, there was no compromise, because none was necessary. The electors did choose the best men who could be found among the persons legally eligible. But this is no more than I had previously asserted, in the paper to which that of your correspondent is a reply.

It is scarcely necessary to add that I fully concur in your correspondent's estimate of the importance of extending the elective franchise; and I can most

---

[1]This idea was pursued by *La Tribune*: see, e.g., 7 July, 1830, pp. 1-2, and 14 July, pp. 1-2. The closest located wording to Mill's is in *Le Globe*, 13 Aug., p. 1. Similar sentiments are found in "Elections du 12 juillet," *Journal de Paris*, 16 July, p. 1.

confidently add my testimony to his, concerning the very moderate extension which would at present content even the most dissatisfied of the French people.

50. PROSPECTS OF FRANCE, IV
EXAMINER, 10 OCT., 1830, PP. 641-4

The significance of this article for Mill is seen in his recalling in a letter to Tocqueville of 11 Dec., 1835, the argument here and in Nos. 174 and 177 for the representative rather than the delegative responsibility of elected Deputies (*EL, CW*, Vol. XII, p. 288). For the context and entry in Mill's bibliography, see No. 44.

TO COMPLETE THE DESIGN with which this series of papers was undertaken, it remains to explain to our readers the demands of the popular party, with some statement of the grounds on which they are founded.

Perhaps it will rather be expected of us that we should commence by stating what these demands are not, than what they are.

The popular party does not demand a republican government. Every one who is *au courant* of the present state of opinion in France, will affirm that not only there is no party, but possibly not a single individual, who indulges even a wish to disturb the settlement of the crown. Those of our contemporaries in whose daily and weekly columns a republican party figures as the prime mover in all the opposition to the present ministry and chamber, have contrived with singular infelicity to miss the matter.[1] Are they so ignorant, both of France and of common sense, as not to know that the sovereignty of the people does not mean republicanism? Since they are so ill informed of its meaning, we will tell them what it does mean. So far as kingship is concerned, it means simply this—that kings shall be first magistrates, and nothing more: which being the admitted doctrine of the British constitution, and literally realized, as it would be easy to shew, in the practice of the British government, stands sufficiently exculpated, we may be permitted to assume, from the imputation of being a republican principle. It is true that the king, with us, is the chief magistrate of an oligarchy; a form of government which, we must needs admit, the partisans of the "sovereignty of the people" cannot abide. But what offends them is the oligarchy, not the king; the monopoly by a few, exempt from all responsibility, of the substantial powers of the government; not the titles or privileges of the functionary who is its nominal head.

The phrase, sovereignty of the people, is, in our opinion, by no means free from objections; though it expresses, we are aware, just as much, and no more, as the maxim transmitted from generation to generation in Whig toasts, that the

[1]E.g., *Morning Post*, 4 Sept., 1830, p. 2.

people are the source of all legitimate power.[2] We regret as much as it is possible for any one to do, the habit which still prevails in France of founding political philosophy on this and similar abstractions; of which the cause of popular governments stands in no need, and from the misapplications of which that cause sustains great injury. The demonstrable impossibility of practical good government without the control of the people, is all the reason which we require to convince us that the people ought to have the control. When, under the name of divine right, an original title, independent of all considerations of public good, was set up in behalf of monarchs, the friends of liberty naturally reverted to the origin of political society, for the purpose of exposing the imposture. Just opinions on such a subject have this use, that they prevent the mischievous influence of erroneous ones. But the question, in what manner governments may have originated, is henceforth an idle one: the sole business of ourselves is to adapt them to the exigencies of society as at present constituted.

Considered as a practical principle, the sovereignty of the people is moreover susceptible of a mischievous interpretation, though a different one from that which is put upon it by our sapient journalists. It countenances the notion, that the representatives of the people are to the people in the relation of servants to a master, and that their duty is merely to ascertain and execute the popular will: whereas the proper object of comparison is the office of a guardian, who manages the affairs of his ward, subject only to his own discretion, but is bound by a severe responsibility to exercise that discretion for the interest of his ward, and not for that of himself individually. The true idea of a representative government is undoubtedly this, that the deputy is to legislate according to the best of his own judgment, and not according to the instructions of his constituents, or even to the opinion of the whole community. The people are entitled to be secured against the abuse of his trust. This they can not be, unless he is subject to re-election by them, or by a numerous committee of them, at short intervals. But inasmuch as they have chosen him, it is an allowable presumption that they judged him to be a wiser man than themselves, and that therefore it is at least as likely, when there is a difference of opinion, that he should be in the right, as that they should. The elector who declares by his vote that he deems A.B. the fittest man to make laws for his country, and who presumes at the same time to give instructions to A.B., lays claim for himself to a superiority of knowledge and intellect which it is not very likely should be possessed by him so often as once in a hundred times; and to entitle every elector to make the same assumption, the man whom they have chosen their representative must be not the wisest, but the most ignorant and incapable of

[2]"Our Sovereign Lord, the People," a traditional Whig toast of great emotional power. The leading article in *The Times* of 13 Sept., 1830, p. 2, referred to in No. 44, used the phrase "sovereignty of the people" in a way objectionable to Mill, as is evident below.

them all. Now this misapprehension of the true character of popular governments is manifestly promoted, by applying to those governments, or to the principle on which they are founded, the designation "sovereignty of the people."

But the phrase, though it disguises the real foundation of good government, and admits of the practical misapplication which we have just pointed out, admits, so far as we can perceive, of no other; and we do not believe that it is thus misapplied by the French of the present day, though it was by their predecessors, the Jacobins. The truth is, that the phrase itself, though it would probably be placed by most Frenchmen at the head of a treatise on the foundation of government, is little used in the actual strife of parties, except as an equivalent expression to the negation of divine right. Thus, they say that the Revolution of 1830 has firmly established as the basis of the French constitution, the sovereignty of the people; meaning that it has rooted out the principle of legitimacy or divine right, since the king, not owing his throne to a hereditary title, but having been called to it by the people themselves, is precluded for ever from setting up any other claim to the powers which he possesses or may possess, than their expediency. A similar boast was made at our Revolution of 1688, and continued to be repeated until our aristocracy became more afraid of the people than they were of the king.

When the *Times* newspaper expressed its apprehensions, that the party which sought the dissolution of the Chamber of Deputies aimed at a more extensive application of the "sovereignty of the people," by abolishing the Peers, and curtailing the powers of the executive, it displayed great ignorance. The sovereignty of the people—even according to the mistaken application above noticed, which makes the people the judges of every individual measure—does not mean that the people should not have Peers, and a strong executive, but merely that they should not have them unless they like: which, we beg to assure the *Times*, is not exactly the same thing.

We are firmly convinced, that not merely the greater part, but the whole, of the French nation, do wish to have Peers, and an executive strong enough to compel obedience to the laws. Their peerage would not indeed be a hereditary peerage, but one which, as we shall shew, would be more powerful, and more independent even of public opinion, than the present House of Peers, or any hereditary body which could be created in France. As for the throne, we are persuaded that, except the few partisans of the exiled family, there is not a man in France, who, if he could overturn it by a wish, would not leave it where it stands. We speak from considerable opportunities of observation, both among the more active and influential of the young men who now head the popular party, and among the patriots of more established character and more mature years. From the latter, and especially from those who had opportunities of intercourse with the King, we heard nothing but eulogiums on the personal character and public inclinations both of himself and of his heir apparent.[3] The younger men, even those in active hostility to the present ministry, declared that if it had depended solely upon them, they would have raised Louis Philippe to the throne, not before, indeed, but after, the reform of the constitution. Yet these men had no partiality to a monarchy. Almost all Frenchmen resemble republicans in their habits and feelings, but these are republicans in their opinions. They think,—how should they help thinking?—that the progress of events, and of the human mind, is leading irresistibly towards republicanism. They would rejoice, if they thought their country sufficiently advanced to be capable of such a government. But they are convinced that republican institutions would neither be understood nor relished by the mass of the French people. The transition would be too sudden, and would find their minds unprepared. The habits of obedience, formed under a kingly government, could not be all at once transferred to a republican one. They would have no clear conception either of the rights which it conferred, or of the obligations which it imposed. Former reminiscences, instead of guiding, would serve only to alarm them. We are well assured that most of the addresses from the departments,[4] signifying their adherence to the new order of things, testify a kind of horror at the very idea of a republic: and what wonder, when in the minds of the writers it is solely associated with the régime of the proconsuls of the Convention? For these reasons, the speculative republicans, though numerous among the educated class at Paris, and especially among the young men who bore arms in the Revolution, made a complete sacrifice of their republican opinions, and joined heartily in giving effect to the wish of the majority. The conduct of Lafayette was worthy of his previous life. Already, in the former Revolution, he had in like manner renounced his individual inclinations, and though a republican, made sacrifices, greater than which never were made by man, to prevent the establishment of a republic. Nor do we believe that any one of these pure-minded men repents of his acquiescence. We are sure that, even if such a one there be, he would consider the disturbance of the settlement, now when it is definitively made, to be among the highest of crimes.

But the republicans, even such as we have described, form a very small fraction of the party opposed to the ministry. Of the fifteen or sixteen daily newspapers published in Paris, all except four are in the interest of the popular party: the ministerial party has only two; the remaining two belong to the old royalists.[5] The two ministerial papers are the *Journal des Débats*, which

[3]Ferdinand Philippe Louis Charles Henri, duc d'Orléans (1810-42). The "eulogiums" are in the addresses cited in n4 below.

[4]See, e.g., *Constitutionnel*, 12 Aug., pp. 3-4 (Seine-Inférieure), 14 Aug., p. 3 (Rouen), 16 Aug., p. 3 (la ville d'Elbeuf), and 17 Aug., p. 2 (Eure).

[5]The Royalist papers were the *Gazette de France*, founded in 1631, long the paper of record, and the *Quotidienne*, a violent and sensational journal, founded in 1792.

supported even Villèle until M. de Chateaubriand was turned out of place, and the *Messager des Chambres*, which was set up by the Martignac ministry, and was its organ. The same disproportion in numbers between the opposition and the supporters of the ministry, which is seen in the newspapers, is seen every where else; except in the chambers, and perhaps in the timid portion of the monied class. The opposition, however, may be stiled "His Majesty's opposition." It does not include the King in its disapprobation of the ministry. We have heard it affirmed in mixed society, oftener than we can venture to state, that the King is in advance both of the ministers and of the chamber; and we once heard the assertion, that the King, Lafayette, and Dupont de l'Eure,[6] were the only real liberals in France. Why then, it may be asked, does not the King dismiss his ministry? The public feel confidence that he will do so, whenever he shall become convinced that such is their deliberate wish: and it would be scarcely reasonable to require that he should do it sooner.

Having stated what the popular party do not demand, we have to state as briefly as is compatible with the degree of explanation necessary for making the statement intelligible, what their demands really are.—They are comprised under the four following heads:—

1. The conditions of eligibility.
2. Those of the elective franchise.
3. Municipal institutions.
4. The peerage.

In the first place, the popular party demand the entire abrogation of *all* restrictions on eligibility.

The nation, they say, must be wonderfully backward in civilization, or you, its legislators, must be singularly unacquainted with the nation, if you cannot find in all France a body of electors whom you yourselves dare trust with the right of choosing whatever deputies they please. A law to confine the selection of legislators to a narrow class, when not only you cannot be sure that the fittest men will always form part of that class, but when you may be sure that they generally will not, is a clumsy attempt to create an aristocracy in spite of electors who you suppose would not make themselves the instruments of such an attempt if they could help it. There ought to be no conditions of eligibility except the confidence of the electors: if your electors are not fit to be trusted, it is your business to find others who are. Bad electors will find the means of electing bad deputies, under any restrictions which you will dare to impose upon their choice. But good electors will not always be able to choose good deputies, if you compel them to select from a small number of the richest men. Is it so easy a matter to

---

[6]Jacques Charles Dupont de l'Eure (1767-1855) had supported the Revolution of 1789 and been a Deputy of the extreme left from 1817. He was serving as Minister of Justice at this time.

find men qualified for legislation? Are the ablest and most instructed men usually to be met with among the richest? Is it the natural tendency of riches, and of the habits which they engender, to produce vigorous intellects, stored with knowledge and inured to laborious thought? We say nothing of sinister interest; we assume that in the class of qualified candidates the electors will always be able to find the requisite number of individuals, sufficiently accessible to motives of a more generous kind, to prefer the good of the whole above the separate interest of the rich. Yet this is assuming far too much, considering within what narrow limits the choice is confined, by the high pecuniary qualification, coupled with the condition that one half the deputies must be residents in the department where they are chosen.

To pass from these general considerations, to others more specially applicable to the present situation of France:—the adjustment of the qualification of candidates involves the entire question between the gerontocracy and the young men.

The youngest of the present deputies must have been in his twenty-fifth year, at the first return of the Bourbons. There probably is not another example in history of so marked and memorable a disparity between one generation and that immediately succeeding it, as exists between the generation to which the deputies belong, and that which has risen to manhood during the last sixteen years.

The government under which a large majority of the deputies received their early impressions, was not merely a despotism; no other despotism which we have known applied so great a power, or applied it so systematically, to the purpose of degrading the human mind. Not only was the press and every other channel of public discussion inexorably closed, but even in private society, to converse with any freedom on public affairs, was to incur imminent danger of being denounced to the police. All scientific pursuits, but such as had a direct bearing upon the military art, or as contributed to procure the sinews of war, were treated with the most marked discouragement. In particular, all enquiries into the first principles of the moral sciences, as well as all preference of political opinion to personal interest, were, under the name of *idéologie*, the object of avowed contempt and aversion to the low-minded adventurer to whom circumstances had given unlimited power over the French people; and the elimination from the Institute of the department "Sciences Morales et Politiques," was but one specimen among a thousand of the spirit of his government.[7] The very infants were taught to lisp passive obedience, and such was the purpose which dictated the only innovations made by Bonaparte in the catechisms of the priests,[8] in whose hands, with a keen perception of the fitness

[7]See Bull. 243, No. 2257 (23 Jan., 1803).

[8]By Bull. 86, No. 1473 (4 Apr., 1806), Napoleon imposed the uniform use of the *Catéchisme à l'usage de toutes les églises de l'empire français* in place of the various

of such instruments for his end, he replaced the management of education.[9] So acutely, indeed, was he alive to the dangers to which governments such as his are liable from the virtues of mankind, that he is well known to have looked with an evil eye on public functionaries who saved money in his service, because it rendered them less dependant on their places, and less fearful of risking his displeasure. A man who was always in want of money, suited him above all others: of such men he might always be sure.

Putting aside the selfishness, the paltry ambition, the rage of place-hunting, the pliability of conscience, which were the natural out-growth of such a government; it is not very surprising that men who were trained, and passed the best years of their lives, at a time when the human intellect was chained up, should be a puny race. To read their debates is all that is required in order to be satisfied of the prodigious inferiority of their best men to the best men of the generation which preceded them. Where are now the Adrien Duports, the Thourets, the Alexandre Lameths, the Lepelletier Saint-Fargeaus, of the Constitutent Assembly?[10] Need we go farther back, and ask, where are the Gournays and the Turgots?[11] M. de Talleyrand, a venerable name, had his political honesty been on a par with his intellect, is all that survives of that constellation of remarkable men, by which the early period of the first French Revolution was rendered illustrious.[12] Would these men have been taken

---

existing catechisms. The section on duty to one's superiors was an explicit description of the duties of the French citizen to Napoleon.

[9] After the Concordat of 1801, the Church regained much of the predominance in the educational system that it had had before the Revolution, especially in primary education, which was neglected by the Government. The foundation of the Imperial University (by Bull. 91, No. 1547 [20 May, 1806]), which was to regulate the whole teaching body of the Empire, placed education technically under the direct control of the State; but the later legislation, Bull. 185, No. 3179 (17 Mar., 1808), which spelled out the details of the organization, enforced the teaching of Christian precepts in all schools, and gave the approved teaching orders a privileged position within the system. See Arts. 2, 3, 38, and 101.

[10] Adrien Duport (1758-98), member of the Constituent Assembly and of the Triumvirate, legal reformer and advocate of a constitutional monarchy. Jacques Guillaume Thouret (1746-94), four times President of the Constituent Assembly and administrative reformer. Alexandre Théodore Victor, baron de Lameth (1760-1829), revolutionary and then an advocate of a constitutional monarchy. Louis Michel Lepeletier de Saint-Fargeau (1760-93), President of the Assembly in 1790 and member of the Convention.

[11] Vincent de Gournay (1712-59), economist. Turgot, when Controller General of Finance, had introduced liberal economic reforms.

[12] Charles Maurice de Talleyrand-Périgord (1754-1838), statesman and diplomat, member of the Constituent Assembly, Minister of Foreign Affairs 1797-1807, head of the Provisional Government in 1814, Ambassador to the Congress of Vienna, again Minister of Foreign Affairs and President of the Council for a few months in 1815, Ambassador to England 1830-35.

unprepared, and found without a single fixed idea, by events which laid open before them a wider field for legislative improvement than they had expected? Read the discussions in the Constituent Assembly on questions of detailed legislation, and you will learn the difference between the men of the Revolution and those of the Restoration. What other men has the present assembly to be compared even with those of its own members who already figured in the latter period of the first Revolution, with Benjamin Constant and Daunou?[13]

But if the men of forty and upwards, speaking of them as a class, are as poor in intellect and attainments as fifteen years of training under the despotism of Bonaparte could make them, the case is far different with that *jeune France*, of which, as long ago as 1820, Benjamin Constant and other orators of the *côté gauche* boasted as of a generation who would far surpass their fathers.[14] The men who are now between twenty and thirty-five years of age, have received the strongest and most durable of their early impressions under comparatively free institutions. During the period in which they were educated, political discussion has been free, and books have multiplied to an extent and with a rapidity which surprised the French themselves when the particulars were brought before them by Count Daru.[15] The young men have also enjoyed the advantage (it is no trifling one) of living under a government from which they could not, without becoming infamous, accept of place. Being excluded, therefore, from all means of obtaining distinction without the trouble of deserving it, they devoted themselves to serious studies; and (to say nothing of their immense superiority in the higher virtues, above the generation which preceded them), it is among them alone that fit successors will be found in point of intellect, to the best men whom France has produced in the former periods of its history.

By the existing conditions of eligibility, these men are excluded from the

[13]Benjamin Constant de Rebecque (1767-1830), influential writer and liberal politician, became an adherent of the Revolution in 1794 and a member of the Tribunate in 1799; in 1802 he was exiled by Napoleon. A member of the Chamber of Deputies 1819-30, he participated in the deliberations of the leading Deputies during the July Revolution. He had become President of the Legislative Committee of the Council of State in August 1830, although very ill, and was to die in December. Pierre Claude François Daunou (1761-1840), member of the National Convention, chief author of the Constitutions of 1795 and 1799; from 1819 to 1830 he was professor of history and ethics at the Collège de France and in 1830 was reappointed national archivist.

[14]In speeches in the Chamber of Deputies on 5 and 6 June, 1820, Manuel, Laffitte, and Constant had praised the new generation, though they did not use the phrase "jeune France"; the phrase, already in use by 1829 (see the leading article on France, *The Times*, 14 Aug., 1829, p. 2), was given prominence just before Mill wrote this article in a poem by Victor Hugo (1802-85), "A la jeune France," published as a supplement to *Le Globe*, 19 Aug., 1830, pp. 1-2.

[15]Comte Pierre Antoine Daru (1767-1829), successful military administrator during the Revolution and the Empire, in his *Notions statistiques sur la librairie, pour servir à la discussion des lois sur la presse* (Paris: Didot, 1827).

chamber. It is true that the limit in respect of age has been lowered from forty to thirty:[16] but the pecuniary qualification operates as effectually in excluding the young, as in excluding the poor. In a country like France, where fortunes are generally small, and where the law of equal partibility[17] commonly prevents them from descending undiminished to posterity, it is seldom that a man has attained the prescribed degree of wealth before he attains what was originally the necessary age.

In this point of view, therefore, it is even of greater importance than it at first appears, that the qualification for eligibility, if not abrogated, should be greatly reduced. There is another reason of no less moment, which we proceed to mention.

During the last ten years, England has been occupied, with laudable, though not with consistent, good sense, in liberalizing her commercial policy. The conduct of France has been so different from this, that within the same period her commercial legislation, already bad, has been rendered immeasurably worse.[18] In addition to the evils common to all restrictive systems, of rendering commodities scarce and dear by forcing the labour and capital of the community to employ themselves in a less instead of a more beneficial employment, the tariff of 1822[19] is justly chargeable with all the inconvenience and injustice which among ourselves has been imputed to free trade—that of violently altering the channels of industry, and ruining particular classes of producers for the benefit of others. France, thanks to its restrictive laws, has scarcely any external trade; and the vine-growers have been reduced to penury, in order that M. Roy, M. Hyde de Neuville, and a few others having the monopoly of the home market secured to the produce of their vines and of their forests, might accumulate immense fortunes.[20] Now, in a great number of departments, such men as M.

[16]By the Charter of 1830, Art. 31.

[17]The law of equal partibility provided that an estate had to be bequeathed in equal parts to the children, with the option of the gift of an extra share to one of them. It was introduced by the Convention, and took form as part of the Code Napoléon (1803-04) (Bull. 154 *bis*, No. 2653 *bis* [3 Sept., 1807], Livre III, Titre I, Chap. iii, Sect. 3, Art. 745; and Titre II, Chap. iii, Sect. 1, Arts. 913, 915, 919). It was slightly revised by Bull. 90, No. 3028 (17 May, 1826), to give the extra share automatically to the eldest son unless a will provided otherwise.

[18]Pierre Laurent Barthélemy, comte de Saint-Cricq (1772-1854), the director of customs, declared on 25 June, 1822, during the tariff debate, that the Government's policy was "to buy as little as possible from others and to sell them as much as possible" (*Moniteur*, 1822, p. 900).

[19]There were crushing import duties on foreign wheat, iron, woollens, cottons, linens, dyes, hops, livestock, oil, tallow, etc. (Bull. 544, No. 13139 [27 July, 1822]).

[20]Comte Antoine Roy (1764-1847), banker, Minister of Finance, 1819-21 and 1828-29, supporter of Louis Philippe, whose estate was valued at forty million francs. Jean Guillaume Hyde de Neuville (1776-1857), Minister of the Navy, 1828-29, owned extensive vineyards in the Loire Valley.

Roy and M. Hyde de Neuville are the only men who pay a sufficient amount of direct taxes to be eligible to the chamber. In France there are very few large territorial properties which do not consist of vines or of forests. The vine-growers and the consumers together, have never been a match in the Chamber of Deputies, as at present constituted, for the parties interested in a restricted trade. There will never be a free and abundant interchange of commodities between England and France, until the conditions of eligibility are lowered.

The statement and justification of the remaining constitutional changes which the popular party contend for, must be postponed to a succeeding paper.

S————.

51. PROSPECTS OF FRANCE, V
EXAMINER, 17 OCT., 1830, PP. 660-1

For the context and entry in Mill's bibliography, see No. 44.

WE SHALL NOW pass to the demands of the popular party on the three remaining points—the elective franchise, municipal institutions, and the peerage.

We suppose it is scarcely necessary to prove that the destinies of thirty-two millions ought not to be under the absolute control of eighty-eight thousand, or rather of about thirty thousand; for as the poorest and least populous departments are those which return, in proportion to the number of their electors, the greatest number of deputies, a majority of the deputies is returned by a minority of the electors.

We suppose it will be conceded, that it is not very difficult to convert such a representative system as this into a jobbing oligarchy.

Homer required ten voices and ten tongues to enumerate the vessels of the Grecian fleet.[1] We should stand in need of a far greater multiplication of our vocal organs, if we had to enumerate the places which have been filled up, or are to be filled up, by the French ministry. The disposable revenue of France, not mortgaged to the national creditor, is probably the largest in Europe, compared with the average of individual incomes, and maintains, be it said without offence to other governments, the largest and most thriving *bureaucratie* which the world has ever yet seen. Conceive all this turned out of office at one stroke! and the places to be scrambled for: you will have some notion of what the antichamber of a French minister resembles, at eight in the morning, for his levee, a levee in the original sense of the word, is held at that primitive hour. Place, in France, is at

---

[1]*The Iliad* (Greek and English), trans. A.T. Murray, 2 vols. (London: Heinemann, 1924), Vol. II, p. 86 (II, 488-90).

all times in great request, because it is the only kind of unearned distinction which is procurable. In England a man becomes important by wealth, or birth, or fashion, or twenty other adventitious advantages, none of which confer one-tenth of the influence in France, that they do here. But place is a possession of that solid substantial kind, which will ensure consideration to the person who has it, in all states whatever of society; and the fewer his rivals, the greater is his consequence. In England the influence of a placeman is comparatively little, because no mere placeman is so great a man as the Duke of Devonshire, or Mr. Baring, or even Brummell, while his reign lasted;[2] but in France the placeman has no rivals in importance, except those who are so by personal qualities, by integrity, intellect, and acquirements. For consideration of this latter kind, there is no where any great multitude of competitors. The other, a shorter and more commodious road to the same end, is far more trodden by the herd. The French accordingly, although, God knows, not a more worldly-minded people than ourselves, but the reverse, are eminently a place-hunting people. Their own admirable Paul-Louis Courier has made this national characteristic the object of some of his most poignant sarcasms.[3] "Tant qu'il y aura deux hommes vivans," says the clever and *spirituel* Fiévée, "il y en aura un qui sollicitera l'autre pour avoir une place."[4]

On the late occasion, moreover, tax-eating was a pleasure which came recommended to the French electors by all the freshness of novelty. Under the late Government the places were given either to the Faubourg St. Germain, or to those who were affiliated to the Congregation.[5] Now there are some things which men will not do, even to get what they most desire; and one of these things in France is, to go to mass. When these were the terms on which place was offered, he must have been a bold man who would have accepted them; though it must be admitted that M. Dupin, who is not a very bold man, paid the price without even

[2]William George Spencer Cavendish, 6th Duke of Devonshire (1790-1858), very wealthy Whig who became a Privy Councillor in 1827, and was Lord Chamberlain of the Household, 1827-28 and 1830-34. Alexander Baring (1774-1848), head of the family financial house from 1810, conservative M.P., 1806-35. George Bryan ("Beau") Brummell (1778-1840), companion of the Prince Regent and arbiter of fashion until gambling debts forced him into exile in France in 1816.

[3]Paul Louis Courier de Méré (1772-1825), prolific pamphleteer; see, e.g., Lettre II of "Lettres au rédacteur du Censeur," in *Oeuvres complètes*, 4 vols. (Brussels: Librairie parisienne, française et étrangère, 1828), Vol. I, pp. 356-9.

[4]*Correspondance politique et administrative*, 3 vols., 15 pts. (Paris: Le Normant, 1815-19), Vol. I, Pt. 3, p. 22, by Joseph Fiévée (1767-1839), Royalist writer and politician.

[5]The Faubourg St. Germain, the aristocratic quarter of Paris, was a centre for the nobles associated with the Bourbon cause both before and after 1815. The Congregation of the Virgin was an aristocratic lay order of piety, many of whose members had strong royalist sympathies.

being so fortunate as to receive any thing in return.[6] Others, however, though they might be more courageous men in other respects, were not quite so courageous as M. Dupin in defying contempt, and were fain, whatever might be their secret longings, to remain out of place, until the people of Paris were so good as to take up arms in order to turn out another set of placemen and bring these in.

Imagine, now, if you can, the feelings of an elector, who, never having taken a bribe in his life, or known, otherwise than by rumour and conjecture, the pleasure of living upon the earnings of others, beholds for the first time the treasury doors thrown wide open to receive him, and the public purse exhibited to his enraptured gaze, with the strings hanging temptingly loose, and full liberty to thrust in both his hands. Is it likely that this man will send deputies to the Chamber, to vote for retrenchment? In the enthusiasm which succeeds a revolution, perhaps he might. But give him time to acquire the feelings of a placeholder, and make the experiment then. It is not always safe to judge what will be a man's conduct in his own case, by the virtue he shews in the case of other people. Things may be exceedingly improper when done by a bad government, which are very fit to be done by a good one; and what government can be so good, as that which puts ourselves into place?

The virtue of the electors will be put to a hard trial even at the next general election. Having five-and-twenty millions sterling a year, or thereabouts, to dispose of in the lump, the ministers had for once their hands loaded with more gifts than they knew what to do with. After providing handsomely for their brothers and cousins, and the frequenters of their drawing-rooms, and making, it is but fair to add, a considerable number of excellent appointments, they were still able to place a large surplus at the disposal of the deputies. The deputies also had brothers and cousins, and many of them had drawing-rooms, though none, it is probable, had so numerous a *côterie* as Monsieur and Madame Guizot.[7] But after the wants of all expectants down to the fortieth cousin had been amply supplied, a considerable amount of patronage remained on hand, which, unless report has greatly belied the deputies, they have unsparingly employed in making friends in their departments, with a view to their own re-election.

The necessity therefore is evident, of increasing the number of electors, by lowering the electoral qualification. In what degree, is the only question upon which there can be a doubt: and as the solution of this question depends in some degree upon facts which we cannot authenticate, we shall content ourselves with relating what, so far as we could collect, appeared to be the prevalent opinion.

The same kind of persons who, when they hear the sovereignty of the people

---

[6]André Marie Jean Jacques Dupin (1783-1865), well known for his defence of the Gallican Church, had been bitterly attacked in the newspapers for visiting the Jesuits at Saint-Acheul in July 1826 and taking part in a religious celebration.

[7]Elise Dillon (1804-33) had become Guizot's second wife in 1828.

spoken of, make themselves uneasy on the subject of republicanism, are also apt, when there is any mention made of extending the elective franchise, to be disturbed in their minds by the idea of universal suffrage. We shall not here enter into the question, whether it be desirable or not that the suffrage should be universal, which is not quite so simple a question as they imagine; although we should not risk much in undertaking to defend universal suffrage against any arguments likely to be brought against it by persons whom it frightens into fits. With respect to France, however, they may calm their apprehensions. Most thinking persons in France believe indeed that one day the suffrage will be universal; for in France most thinking persons, strange as it may appear, have faith in human improvement. But they reflect that at present no more than a third of the French people can read and write, and they are of opinion that vigorous exertions, continued during a long period, for the improvement and diffusion of education, must precede the extension to the mass of the people of the right of choosing their representatives. If the suffrage were to be universal, they would prefer admitting two stages of election; since it requires less knowledge and discernment to fix on the person who is fittest to elect, than on the one who is fittest to be elected. They affirm, however, that though the people of Paris and a few other large towns may be qualified for such an extension of their political rights, the working classes throughout France are by no means sufficiently advanced even for this step, and they urge the government to take measures for educating the people, with the express view of fitting them for receiving and properly exercising so important a privilege.

With respect to the degree of extension to be given to the suffrage immediately,[8] public opinion does not seem to be completely made up. Much will probably depend on the result of the 130 elections on the point of taking place, to supply the vacancies created by resignations, annullation of elections, refusals to take the constitutional oath, and acceptance of paid offices under the Crown. If the present electors, now called upon for the first time since the revolution to exercise their privilege, exercise it in favour of popular candidates, the public will probably be tolerably well satisfied with the electoral qualification as it is, and will not insist upon any great amount of alteration. If, on the contrary, the electors, either influenced by the alarm which has been industriously spread with respect to the progress of the revolutionary spirit, or by an incipient feeling of a separate interest from the people, should return members who will reinforce the centre, or ministerial party, the doom of the present election law is sealed, and public opinion will require a much greater reduction of the qualification, and multiplication of the number of electors, than would content a large majority at the present moment.

From such information as we possess, we are inclined to expect that the

[8]Under Art. 34 of the Charter of 1830.

popular party will be greatly strengthened by the approaching elections. If so, the hopes of that party will be so great from a dissolution of the Chamber, that we expect to see their efforts directed mainly to that end, and the majority permitted to limit the enlargement of the suffrage almost as much as they please, if on that condition they will compromise the dispute, and consent to a new general election.

It is certain that but a short time ago, a large proportion of the popular party thought that the present electoral qualification, with the suppression of the conditions of eligibility and of the double vote, would form a very tolerable government. We think that they were in the wrong; and we have reason to believe that most of them have since changed their opinion. What misled them was the spirited resistance of the present electors to the Polignac ministry. But this at least shows, how little there is of either faction or fanaticism in their wishes for change. We are firmly persuaded, that the great error which the bulk of the popular party are likely to commit, and the error which they are almost sure to commit, unless their minds become heated by the conflict, is that of resting satisfied with too little concession, with too little security to the people against the abuse of the powers of the government.

The prevailing opinion at present seems to be in favour of extending the suffrage to all who pay 200 francs a year of direct taxes. The qualification is at present 300 francs.[9] M. Mauguin advocated this proposal on the ground that the same incomes which paid 300 francs in 1814, pay only 200 at present, owing not only to the diminution of taxation on the whole, but the substitution, to a considerable extent, of indirect for direct taxes, a policy always favoured by the late government for the purpose of narrowing the electoral class.[10] It does not, however, appear to be known with any approach to accuracy, what number of additional electors would be created by this reduction of the qualification. Of course this point can be ascertained, and means will be taken to ascertain it before any measure is introduced into the Chamber. It is known that the number of *cotes*, or separate accounts with the tax-gatherer, from *one* hundred francs per annum up to 300, amounts to about six or seven times the number of the present electors. As the same individual, however, often pays taxes in several departments, the multiplication of the electors themselves would be in a smaller proportion.

Many persons object, with considerable appearance of reason, to adopting taxation in any shape as the basis of representation. They object to making the

[9]By Art. 40 of the Charter of 1814; not revised in the Charter of 1830.
[10]François Mauguin (1785-1854), lawyer, Deputy from 1827, member of the municipal commission during the July Revolution, was a rival of Odilon Barrot for leadership of the left during the July Monarchy. His speech of 30 Aug. as reported in the *Moniteur* (1830, pp. 999-1000, 1001) does not include a specific reference to the reduction of the qualification to 200 francs, but he was speaking in the debate on an amendment to that effect.

constitution of a country dependent upon its financial system, and consequently upon the fluctuating policy or interested views of an existing government. They see no reason that every time the budget is diminished, the rights of the people should be curtailed. They would adopt some other and more direct means of establishing a property qualification.

But whatever may be the pecuniary conditions which should confer the elective franchise, there is one change which all parties are agreed in demanding, and which we do not believe would be withheld even by the present Chamber. This is the extension of the right of suffrage to the members of the intellectual professions, free from all pecuniary conditions whatever.[11] A qualification by profession, concurrent with a qualification by property, is not new in French law. It already exists in another important case, that of a juryman.[12] A list is annually made out in each department, of the inhabitants of the department qualified to serve on juries. The first part of this list comprises the electors of the department; the second, all judges, advocates, attorneys, surgeons, physicians, professors, and various other classes whose means of livelihood are deemed a sufficient guarantee of their education. The reformers wish that the second part of the list should be included in the first, and perhaps several other professions added to it. You require, say they, in your electors, a certain measure of property, because it is a presumption of a certain measure of education. We cannot suppose you so absurd, as to admit a mere presumption and reject the certainty. You know, that all who practise certain professions must by law have gone through a certain course of education. If the standard of mental cultivation which is sufficient for a judge, an advocate, a physician, or a public teacher, is not sufficient to render a man fit for electing a member of parliament, whom, in the name of common sense, do you expect to find fit for it?

These arguments are so obviously unanswerable, that we do not believe it will even be attempted to attenuate their force. We are convinced that whatever in other respects may be the character of the new election law, one of its provisions will be the admission of all who are qualified to serve on juries, to the elective franchise.

S————.

52. ATTEMPT TO SAVE THE EX-MINISTERS

EXAMINER, 24 OCT., 1830, PP. 673-4

This article comments on the attempts of the Chamber of Deputies to avoid the consequences of having, on 13 Aug., 1830, unanimously approved a resolution (*Moniteur*, 1830, p. 902) accusing of treason the ex-ministers responsible for Charles X's

---

[11]For an example of the demand, see the petition to the Chamber of Deputies from the Société Aide-toi le ciel t'aidera, *Le Globe*, 1 Sept., 1830, p. 4.

[12]Bull. 157, No. 5679 (2 May, 1827).

July ordinances: Polignac, Peyronnet, Guernon-Ranville, and Jean Claude Balthazar Victor de Chantelauze (1787-1859), who had become Minister of Justice in May 1830. On 17 Aug. it had accepted for consideration a motion to abolish the death penalty introduced by comte Alexandre César Victor Charles Destutt de Tracy (1781-1864), defender of liberal causes (*ibid.*, pp. 918-19). On 8 Oct., 1830, it adopted, by a vote of 246 to 21, the Projet d'adresse au roi, proposing a major reduction in the number of capital offences (*ibid.*, pp. 1274-6 and 1278-82), which was enthusiastically received by Louis Philippe on 9 Oct. (*ibid.*, p. 1277). This article, the first in the "Political Examiner," is headed as title. It is described in Mill's bibliography as "A leading article in the Examiner of 24th October 1830, headed 'Attempt to save the ex-ministers'" (MacMinn, p. 12). See also Nos. 68 and 71.

THE FRENCH CHAMBER OF DEPUTIES has voted an address to the King, requesting him to propose a law, for the abolition of capital punishment in all cases of political crime, and in all other cases, except those of a few specified offences, the most dangerous to the safety of society and implying the greatest measure of depravity in the criminal.

Before we give utterance to the doubts and apprehensions which this precipitate, and, we fear, ill-timed resolution, has excited in us, we must request indulgence while we dwell for a few moments on thoughts of a more exhilarating tendency. We cannot restrain our delight and admiration on seeing this noble people afford every day some new and splendid example of its progress in humane feelings and enlightened views. When we recal the pitiable exhibition of our ministry and parliament, on a fragment of this very subject, a few months ago,[1] and contrast it with what we now behold in France, with the leading statesmen of all parties uniting almost as one man to effect this grand legislative improvement, and its principle approved even by the journalists who lament, and the placarders who inveigh against, its retrospective application—it becomes painfully evident how greatly the educated classes in France, on all questions of social improvement to which their attention has been directed, are in advance of the majority of the same classes in England, and how eminently their practising lawyers, whose opinion must have peculiar weight on such a subject, are distinguished in expansion of ideas and elevation of soul from our narrow-minded technicalists.

The comments, which we cannot help making upon the occasion chosen for beginning the mitigation of the French penal law, are made with the most heartfelt wish that the event may prove them misplaced and inapplicable. No

[1]After four debates on 1 Apr., 13 May, 24 May, and 7 June, 1830, the House of Commons voted to abolish the death penalty for forgery, against the wishes of the Home Secretary, Robert Peel, who had argued that, since most forgers were educated people, long incarceration or transportation or both were a harsher penalty than execution. The House of Lords reversed the decision on 13 July. (For the Commons debates, see *PD*, n.s., Vol. 23, cols. 1176-88; Vol. 24, cols. 674-80, 1014-15; Vol. 25, cols. 46-81; for the Lords, *Journals of the House of Lords*, 1830, LXII, 871-2.)

reverence can exceed that which we feel for the constancy of purpose, the unwearied and single-minded philanthropy of such men as Victor de Tracy and Lafayette. They may be better judges of the maturity of the public mind than ourselves, or than the ablest and most enlightened of their own journalists. May they prove so. No one, at least, can mistake the impulses by which *their* course has been determined. As they were in the beginning, so are they now, and will be to the close of their pure and noble career.[2] But it is something new to find the majority of the Chamber marching under their banner. Who compose this majority? The very men who two years ago scouted the same proposition when brought forward by the same individuals. A taste for precipitate reforms is not the failing, of which the rest of the conduct held by these persons since the revolution permits us to accuse them. And wherein consisted the peculiar urgency of the present case? In the circumstance that four men are about to be put upon trial for their lives, by whose guilt more citizens have lost theirs, than usually perish by all other crimes taken together in the course of a century. It is true that these men were ministers. We may be permitted to ask, would as much have been done for four criminals of any other kind? But the fate of a minister concerns all who hope to be ministers. It is well that the zeal which might else, peradventure, have slumbered for some time longer, has been warmed into activity on one subject at least, by motives of a potency so irresistible. Let us hope that this enthusiasm, this generous reliance on the civilization and intelligence of France, will not exhaust itself in one single manifestation. Something of the same spirit will not displease us, when the conditions of eligibility, and the qualification for the elective franchise come to be decided on. Alas! that so great a measure should be presented to a people, so ill prepared, we fear, to receive it, under the auspices of men every one of whose acts is viewed with just suspicion, and on an occasion so well suited to give colour to the worst interpretation.

What becomes of the miserable criminals themselves, whether they die on the scaffold, in gaol, or in dishonoured exile and obscurity, appears to us a matter of consummate indifference. We do not desire their death; though we cannot affect to feel for them any compassion. Our sympathy is with the maimed, the widows and orphans whom they have made. But with the past, punishment has nothing to do. Punishment cannot make that which was, to have never been. The death of the assassin will not bring back to life the victim whom he has slain. Punishment regards the future alone. Safety, not vengeance, is its object, and all thinking men have long been persuaded, that death is far from being the punishment which operates with greatest force upon the minds of delinquents, far even from being the most severe.

The only fit end of punishment is the prevention of crime: but is this truth

---

[2] Cf. the Gloria in the *Book of Common Prayer*.

commonly felt and understood? Are there many, besides persons of cultivated intellects, who have wrought it thoroughly into their convictions, or impressed it deeply upon their feelings? In most minds the idea of punishment has not ceased to be at bottom that of expiation, or the principle of so much pain for so much guilt; the argument most frequently insisted upon even for the alleviation of a penalty, is this, that it is *disproportioned to the crime*. Why is it that murder is almost invariably excepted from the propositions even of philanthropists, for the abolition of capital punishment? Murder is not the crime which it is most difficult to prevent. The feeling which gave birth to the *lex talionis*[3] has not yet died away. The doctrine of blood for blood has sunk deep into the hearts of the vast majority of every people who have been accustomed to see it put in practice. We should not wonder, if there were some persons here who are so foolish as to suppose, that it is thirst for vengeance which makes the Parisian populace cry out, "Death to the ministers."[4] The supposition is too absurd to be worth reasoning upon. If the people desired vengeance, what opportunities of gratification did they not forego during the three days? The very men who had been firing upon them the moment before, were treated as soon as they were disarmed, with the kindness of brothers. Except those of their own number whom they executed for pillaging, it is not known that they put to death a single person, after he had ceased to resist. The officers who gave the orders to fire, remain unmolested to this day. Marmont himself was allowed to retire in quietness, not a voice being raised for his punishment, not a sign given that the idea of his liability to it had entered into any mind.[5] If they cry "death to the ministers," it is because they do not think it vengeance, but justice. Their sons, their brothers, their comrades, have been slain—the ministers, in their eyes, are the murderers. For death, death in their opinion is the proper return. They cannot seize nice distinctions between political murder and common murder. Numbers have suffered death for state crimes while Peyronnet was minister, and they well knew on what multitudes more it would have been inflicted if their enemies had prevailed. It appears to them right, to try the prisoner by his own law. Their feeling, howsoever we may consider it, is a moral one. It is their conscience

[3]The *lex talionis* appeared in Roman Law as early as the Twelve Tables, 451-50 B.C. (see Aulus Gellius [b. ca. 130 A.D.], *The Attic Nights* [Latin and English], trans. John C. Rolfe, 3 vols. [London: Heinemann, 1928], Vol. III, p. 412 [XX, 1, 14]), but is more usually associated with Exodus, 21:24-5.

[4]Hand-written signs demanding "Mort aux ministres" had appeared throughout the populous districts of Paris.

[5]Auguste de Marmont, duc de Raguse (1774-1852), member of a military and revolutionary family, was, in July 1830, the commander-in-chief of the royal guard to whom, on 25 July, Polignac gave the supreme command of the troops in the Paris garrison. Having failed to suppress the July Revolution, he accompanied Charles X into exile and his name was struck off the army list.

which speaks. It is a sentiment of justice, unenlightened, indeed, and misplaced, but in short it is justice, such as they conceive it.

You owe every thing to their sense of justice. It is by their love of justice that your lives and properties are yours at this instant. Never since the beginning of the world was there seen in a people such a heroic, such an unconquerable attachment to justice. The poorest of the populace, with arms in their hands, were absolute masters of Paris and all that it contains; not a man went richer to his home that night. What an instrument, what a safeguard for all that is virtuous have you in such a people! but it is in their moral convictions that you must find your strength. Once forfeit the right of appealing to their justice, and what is there between you and the most enormous evils? Refuse a man favour, and he respects you the more; refuse him what he deems justice, and you excite his indignation. If what the people demand is in itself unjust, withhold it. Real justice is not to be sacrificed to opinion. But it is never unjust to execute upon a real criminal, what was the acknowledged law when he committed the offence. It is only postponing a reform, until it can be effected safely: and this reform, was it for the sake of the criminal that you desired it? No, certainly; but for the sake of the public. And when did a premature and *brusque* attempt to make men better, ever fail of making them worse? It is dangerous in a revolution to trifle with the moral feelings of a people. If you will not give to the people what they think justice, tremble lest they should take it.

We do not express this apprehension lightly. We hope better things from the Parisian people. Indeed, the moment of greatest danger is perhaps past; though there are appearances which, we confess, alarm us. But if, when Polignac was arrested, and brought from Granville to Paris, it had been known that when convicted he would not be put to death, who can answer that an indignant people might not have rendered a trial unnecessary? Spare the lives of political offenders when you can—spare them always, if that be practicable, and we will gladly give you our applause. But before you enact a law interdicting yourselves from inflicting capital punishment, make yourselves sure that no cases will arise, where what you have said you will not do, will be done for you by the avenging hand of the people themselves, preferring, in the fury excited by some outrage against their liberties or lives, what they deem the substance of justice, to the forms.

Do we, then, attempt to set up the rude, undisciplined feelings of untaught minds, as a rule of conduct for men of more enlightened consciences and more exercised understandings? Is the penal legislation of a country to remain for ever a literal copy of the barbarous conceptions of its least civilized inhabitants? Far from it. We only ask, that a purpose, of which we acknowledge the dignity and excellence, should be pursued by the employment of such means as a rational person would adopt in any other case of equal delicacy and difficulty. We cannot conceive any graver or more solemn occasion, than that of a deliberation which is to change the moral sentiments of a whole people. What zeal and perseverance will not be required, to place the objects and principles of punishment in their true light before the people, and to make them familiar with the right grounds of preference, presented in every possible aspect! What an insight into the human heart, to probe to the bottom the seat of the erroneous moral feeling which lies so deeply fixed in it; and what skill in guiding and working upon men for their good, to find the means of loosing the wrong association of ideas, which has wound itself round and round the mind till it has eaten into the substance itself. Nor can the abolition of capital punishment be considered as an insulated question; it involves the revision of your whole penal code. No nation in Europe is provided with unobjectionable secondary punishments. Your most accomplished jurists have enough to do, in fixing, if not their own ideas on the matter, at least those of the public, and you are to recollect, that this last is a condition which, for persons desiring to be the rulers of a free people, is not to be dispensed with. A despot, indeed, has no need of so much trouble. He gives his fiat, and the law is altered; the people, being accustomed to be so treated, acquiesce in the alteration, however disagreeable to them, and in time the new law gives birth to a new state of feeling. But the legislators of France know full well, that the French people are neither children nor slaves, and that they must henceforth be governed with the assent of their reason and of their conscience, or not at all. And was men's reason or their conscience ever yet taken by storm?

By postponing the question of capital punishment, you would have prevented, perhaps, an insurrection; a few months or years later you would have carried your point, and retained, and even strengthened, the hold which it is of so much importance that you should not renounce, upon the moral sentiments of the people. All this you would have gained; but you would not have saved the lives of the ex-ministers. Were their lives, then, of sufficient value, to be saved from the course of law at such a price?

53. THE QUARTERLY REVIEW *VERSUS* FRANCE
EXAMINER, 24 OCT., 1830, PP. 674-5

The stimulus for this leading article came from an unheaded article on the fall of the Bourbons in the *Morning Chronicle*, 14 Oct., 1830, p. 3, which criticized "Political History of France since the Restoration," *Quarterly Review*, XLIII (Oct. 1830), 564-96, by Charles Ross (1799-1860), Conservative M.P. for St. Germains, 1826-32. Both the *Morning Chronicle* and Mill get the title of the article wrong, and mistakenly assume that it was by Basil Hall (1788-1844), a retired naval officer with both scientific and political interests, known for his travel books as well as his articles in the *Quarterly Review*. Among the latter was "Political Condition and Prospects of France" (XLIII [May 1830], 215-42), which probably caused the mistaken attribution and increased the abuse by the *Morning Chronicle* and Mill. Mill's unsigned article, headed as title, immediately follows

No. 52 in the "Political Examiner." The description in Mill's bibliography is of "A leading article in the Examiner of 24 Oct. 1830, headed 'The Quarterly Review and France'" (MacMinn, p. 12), which is identified by MacMinn as this article; however, the title in the *Examiner* of No. 54 is "France and the Quarterly Review," which might imply that the bibliography refers to No. 54 only. For the evidence supporting our conclusion that Mill wrote both, see the Textual Introduction, cvi. The epigraph, which may have been supplied by the editor, Fonblanque, has not been identified.

"We're all a nodding."—Kings.

THE CHRONICLE has some masterly comments on an article in the *Quarterly Review*, entitled "The Political History of France, since the Revolution." This is a subject with regard to which the *Quarterly* is in a false position. Captain Basil Hall served in the quality of evil spirit to Charles X; he marshalled him the way that he should go; he placed the bloody dagger before his eyes,[1] and pointed the road to crime. Charles was hurled from his throne, the sceptre with which he had bruised his people was wrenched from his grasp, but Captain Basil Hall still sits at his desk; the pen with which he outrages reason and disgusts humanity remains in his hand, and he yet asserts his disgraced opinions in the *Quarterly*.

If we rejoiced in the fall of inimical organs, we should certainly observe with complacency the operations of the Charles X of the High Tory Journal; his magnificence is dealing in ordinances so fatal in recoil.

The writer [says the *Chronicle*] honestly avows that it would have afforded him great satisfaction had Charles X succeeded in establishing a despotism. "We certainly wished (he says) that in the struggle, which we had long foreseen, the immediate result might be *the establishment of something like despotic power* in the Throne of France; and we did so because we considered a despotism, in the present condition of the world, as likely to turn out a lesser evil in that mighty country than the other alternative. The past had satisfied us that *if Charles X desired the influence of a dictator, he was incapable of using that influence for any unpatriotic purpose*; that no fretfulness of idle vanity, no fervor of selfish ambition, had tormented his 'chair days;' and that whatever extraordinary power he might obtain, would be held conscientiously, as his only for an extraordinary and temporary purpose—that of endeavouring to lay the foundations of a national aristocracy."[2]

Thus the good intentions of Charles were manifested in his breach of faith and violation of the laws. Innocent love! Amiable forsworn! Benevolent man of violence who attempted to upset the rights of his people all for their good, and was himself upset instead! Good-lack! We trust no kindred soul will steal his

---

[1]Cf. William Shakespeare, *Macbeth*, II, i, 32-43; in *The Riverside Shakespeare*, p. 1319.

[2]*Morning Chronicle*, 14 Oct., 1830, p. 3, quoting Ross, p. 595. Charles X's "chair days" refers to his chairing the Council of Ministers in his apartments at the Tuileries on Wednesdays and Sundays when, from Villèle's departure in 1827 until 1829, there was no titular President of the Council. On Tuesdays and Saturdays the Council met in the offices of, and was chaired by, the ministers in rotation.

purse at Lulworth, with the intention of making an excellent use of the money.[3] When power is reserved from magistrates, it is meant to place it beyond subserviency to their intentions, good or bad; but what exquisite simplicity in not recognising this design, and seizing unlawfully by virtue of good purposes! The *Standard* remarks upon the above text:

We must remark that this King, in reliance upon whose good dispositions the writer wishes for the establishment of a despotic power, is *seventy-five* years old—has passed the allotted period of man's life by five years; but, *non obstante* the probability of his death or dotage, the reviewer would establish a permanent despotism, in reliance upon his good disposition.[4]

The *Chronicle* observes,

The principle which runs through this "Political History of France since the Revolution" is, that the only legitimate object of a Government is to create and preserve a powerful Aristocracy, and the various Ministries since the Restoration are praised or blamed in proportion as they pursued that object. A Church richly endowed, as subsidiary to the maintenance of a rich Aristocracy, is, of course, also an object of the writer's admiration. The more important point—the happiness and prosperity of 30 millions of Frenchmen, and how far such happiness and prosperity are reconcileable with a rich and powerful Aristocracy and a richly-endowed Church—is not deemed deserving of his notice. He admits that the country never was more prosperous than during the period when things were advancing to a crisis which justified the establishment of a despotism:—"Beset as the exiled House was (he says), from the hour of its restoration, with jealousies bitterly conflicting, and perpetually threatening an explosion, it will not be denied that France enjoyed under their rule 15 years of greater prosperity than had ever before fallen to her lot. Such is the fact, 'even their enemies themselves being judges;'[5] never since the foundation of the Monarchy were personal liberty and property so safe. . . . Excluding certain political evils from our view, *that fine country presented, on the whole, a picture of prosperity, which fixed the admiration of Europe.*" But if France, since the foundation of the Monarchy, never exhibited such a picture of prosperity, does not this almost amount to a demonstration, that France was not indebted for that prosperity to the Bourbons, but to the circumstances wherein, during those 15 years, she differed from what she was during the rest of the Monarchy? During the rest of the Monarchy she had a richly-endowed Church and a rich Aristocracy; and during the 15 years she had a comparatively poor Aristocracy and a poor Church; and are we not, therefore, justified in inferring, it was precisely because she had a poor Aristocracy and a poor Church she was so prosperous as to attract the admiration of Europe, notwithstanding she had also foolish Monarchs, who created constant jealousies and heartburnings by their incessant endeavours to bring about the state of things from which the Revolution had liberated her? The Bourbons could not prevent the prosperity which the Institutions, growing out of the Revolution, produced in spite of their endeavours. The country prospered because they were impotent.

"They saw (says the *Quarterly* Reviewer) that the faction (by faction is meant all but the Aristocracy) which had never ceased to labour for the ruin of the Monarchy, were

---

[3]Charles X had arrived at Lulworth Castle on the coast of Dorset on 23 Aug.

[4]*Standard*, 14 Oct., 1830, p. 2.

[5]Deuteronomy, 32:31.

rapidly attaining the utmost height of rebellious audacity—and that the only question was, who should strike the first blow. They saw, that to go on with the Charter of Louis XVIII as it stood, was inevitably to shipwreck the vessel of the State, and they thought to give it a chance by cutting away the masts. The evolution was not successful, and the Monarchy went down." It is questionable how far it may be prudent to accustom people to such phrases as Monarchy going down; for after the first shock which such portentous words are calculated to produce is over, men naturally ask themselves what the words really mean, and they find that the going down of a Monarchy is not such a bad thing. They see, notwithstanding the going down of the Monarchy, thirty millions of people exciting the admiration and respect of Europe by their gallant bearing and their magnanimity—they see them busied in improving their laws and institutions, encouraging education, removing the obstacles in the way of industry—and they see a weak and priest-ridden old man, who could not enjoy in quiet the wealth which this people heaped upon him and his family, but would persist in thwarting those to whose industry he was so deeply indebted, notwithstanding his crime, peaceably conducted out of the country he had outraged, and richly pensioned off. Truly there are worse things in the world, at this rate, than the going down of a Monarchy.[6]

They see, too, that the *going down* of the monarchy has been the rising up of a magistracy; that the *going down* of one king has led to the setting up of a better.

France is prosperous and moral, without a rich church or an aristocracy of boroughmongering capacity; this is the sum of the quarrel with her condition. She wants the main-spring of misrule, but she is deficient in no feature of happiness, wisdom, or virtue, nor is it pretended that she is deficient. She has every production but Lords and Squires, and the magistracy of the brambles. From an article on the decline of science in England, in the same number of the *Quarterly* which contains the pestilent trash quoted, the *Chronicle* extracts this admirable passage:

"Of all the kingdoms of Europe (says the Reviewer) France is undoubtedly the one in which the scientific establishments have been regulated by the most enlightened and liberal principles, and in which science is most successfully cultivated." For scientific and literary establishments, 103,791*l.* is annually voted by the Government. "Nor (says the Reviewer) in her generous care for the respectability and comfort of her scientific men, has France overlooked the most powerful stimulus of genius and industry. All the honours of the State have been thrown open to her philosophers and literary characters. The sage and the hero deliberate in the same Cabinet; they are associated among the Privy Councillors of the King; they sit together in her House of Peers, and in her Chamber of Deputies; they bear the same titles; they are decorated with the same orders; and the arm and the mind of the nation are thus indissolubly united for its glory, or for its defence." Let us turn to Aristocratical, Oligarchical England. "While (says the Reviewer) the mere possession of animal courage (which, of course, a well-fed Aristocracy, in a temperate country like this, can hardly fail to possess), one of the most common qualities of the species, has been loaded with every variety of honour, the possessor of the highest endowments of the mind—he to whom the Almighty has chosen to make known the laws and mysteries of his works—he who has devoted his life, and sacrificed his health and the interests of his family, in the most profound and ennobling pursuits,—is allowed to live in

[6]*Morning Chronicle*, 14 Oct., 1830, p. 3, quoting twice from Ross, p. 594.

poverty and obscurity, and to sink into the grave without one mark of the affection and gratitude of his country. And why does England thus persecute the votaries of her science? Why does she depress them to the level of her hewers of wood and her drawers of water?[7] It is because science flatters no courtier, mingles in no political strife, and brings up no reserve to the Minister, to swell his triumph or break his fall. She is persecuted because she is virtuous; dishonoured because she is weak." "England's liberality to Newton (he elsewhere observes) is the only striking instance which we have been able to record, because it is the only one in which the honour of a title was combined with an adequate pecuniary reward."[8]

We prepare to treat Captain Basil Hall more at length in our next number.

54. FRANCE AND THE QUARTERLY REVIEW

EXAMINER, 31 OCT., 1830, PP. 689-91

This item is a first leader in the "Political Examiner," headed as title. For the context and bibliographical entry, see No. 53. For the attribution of this and No. 53 to Mill, see the Textual Introduction, cvi. In Mill's Somerville College set, the word "insult" has been blotted out from the phrase "to insult the illustrious patriot" at 178.20.

IN OUR LAST PAPER we made an extract from the comments of the *Morning Chronicle*, upon the article on the late French Revolution in the *Quarterly Review*. The reviewer makes a sufficiently pitiful figure in the *Chronicle*'s hands; and there, perhaps, we might have left him, had he not called down upon his own head a still more signal exposure and castigation, by presuming to insult and calumniate the people of England. The reviewer says, that the people of England have not sympathized in the triumph of the French nation over the attempt to abrogate its constitution, and to govern it by open force. He says, that they have regarded the recent changes in France with "stern suspicion," and by so doing, have entitled themselves to as much laudation as he can bestow upon them.[1] Now this assertion, going forth among many other marks of the worst feelings towards the French people, and amidst an immense heap of blunders and misrepresentations respecting French affairs, in a publication known to have a considerable circulation in England, may be productive of very lamentable effects. It is not impossible that the reviewer's confident affirmation that the mass of the English nation are of his opinion, may become known to the leading statesmen and to the journalists of France, and may induce them to believe that

[7]Cf. Deuteronomy, 29:11, and Joshua, 9:21, 23.

[8]*Morning Chronicle*, 14 Oct., 1830, p. 3, quoting "Decline of Science in England and Patent Laws," *Quarterly Review*, XLIII (Oct. 1830), 315-16, 317, 330-1, and 315, by David Brewster (1781-1868), a prominent Scottish scientist and prolific author.

---

[1]Ross, "Political History of France," p. 596.

such is really the fact. If this should take place, the prodigious increase of strength which the expressions of honorable sympathy from the English in the late achievement have given to the disposition to think well of this country, and to keep well with it, might not be permanent, and might be succeeded by a reaction which would be violent in proportion as the previous burst of affection and gratitude (we speak from observation) was cordial, generous, and sincere.

It therefore becomes highly necessary to apprise the French, that the *Quarterly Review* represents the feelings of nobody except the church and the aristocracy: that with the exception of these peculiar and narrow classes, and their hangers-on and retainers, the readers even of the *Quarterly Review* do not read it for the sake of its political opinions: that when the reviewer affirms, that the Revolution has met with no sympathy from the English people, all he really means is this, that it has met with no sympathy from the church and the aristocracy: that the great bulk even of the readers of the review, utterly repudiate and disavow the sentiments of this article, and that it is generally felt that the editor,[2] by inserting it, has committed, with respect to the pecuniary interests of the concern under his management, one of the greatest blunders which he ever made.

It is not our intention, however, to dismiss this creditable effusion with barely the degree of notice rigorously necessary for the purpose for which we adverted to it. We think it may be instructive to exhibit rather minutely what manner of man this is who thus takes upon himself the character of spokesman for the English people. It is true that we have not been gratified by the discovery of one single endowment in the writer qualifying him to have an opinion. But the more scanty his stock of ideas, the apter an illustration is he of the tendency of such as he happens to be master of. These amount to two; Church, and Aristocracy. He can think nothing but church and aristocracy, he can feel nothing but church and aristocracy. These two ideas compose the entire furniture of his skull.

With an intellectual *matériel* of this extent, he turns his attention to France; where he speedily discovers that neither of the idols of his homage exists. This nakedness of the land fills him with dismay. Seeing neither "a powerful church establishment," nor a "wealthy hereditary aristocracy," he sees nothing but a "monarch" and a "mob."[3] Yes, he scruples not to aver, that whatever is not either church or aristocracy, is "mob." He accordingly proclaims his wish that Charles X had succeeded in overpowering the French nation. He regrets that the result of the struggle was not "the re-establishment of something like despotic power in the throne of France:"[4] feeling certain that it would have been used "conscientiously" for one only purpose, that of endeavouring to create a rich landed aristocracy. This, and a powerful church establishment, are the two

---

[2]John Gibson Lockhart (1794-1854), editor of the *Quarterly Review* from 1825 to 1853.
[3]These phrases appear on pp. 594-5 of Ross's article.
[4]*Ibid.*, p. 595. The same passage is quoted in No. 53.

"great absent elements," without which no country is capable of freedom.[5] This maxim in politics is assumed throughout, as one which neither needs, nor is susceptible of, proof; and it is easy to perceive, such is the texture of the writer's mind, that the doctrine really appears to him to be one of those to which the human understanding necessarily and spontaneously assents.

We are thus given to understand that in the opinion of the church and the aristocracy, a church and an aristocracy, each of them the richest and most powerful of its kind, are necessary conditions of what they are pleased to term freedom: and that despotism, naked unmasked despotism, is not only preferable to the want of both or either of these requisites, but is positively the best form of government which can exist in a country not provided with these costly, but indispensable appendages.

It is not, perhaps, very surprising, that the church and the aristocracy should imagine all this. But it does, we confess, somewhat surprise us that in the times we live in, they should expect to find any persons who will receive it on their authority. They may have heard of an opinion which has gone forth rather extensively, that instead of being the *causes* of freedom, a powerful church and aristocracy are the main *obstacles* to it, in the present state of society. They may have heard it whispered that from the days of Themistocles to those of Thomas Jefferson,[6] every nation which has been conspicuous for good government, or eminence in intellect, arts, or arms, (not excepting England itself) has been one in which either a powerful church and aristocracy did not exist, or in which their power was irresistibly controlled by opposing circumstances. They may have been told, that the nations to which at the present moment, the twofold blessing which they brag of, belongs in the most peculiar degree, are those which have passed into a proverb throughout all Europe as the favourite abodes of barbarism and superstition.[7] They may have perceived that in England so far are the merits of the church and the aristocracy as guarantees of freedom from being appreciated, that what the people are seeking is freedom from these very bodies, from their engrossing and irresponsible domination. We can assure them, that they will find few persons besides themselves, who are not very willing just now to listen without either impatience or aversion, to what can be said in behalf of these and similar opinions. Now, if the case be as we state it, we may just submit, whether it might not have been as advisable for such writers as the

[5]*Ibid.*

[6]Themistocles (ca. 527-ca. 460 B.C.), Athenian statesman and general; Thomas Jefferson (1743-1826), 3rd President of the United States of America.

[7]A reference to the Holy Alliance, the name given to the agreement between Alexander I of Russia, Francis I of Austria, and Frederick William III of Prussia, embodied in a treaty signed on 26 Sept., 1815, which envisaged a quasi-mystical union based on Christian principles (attributed to the influence on Alexander I of the Baroness von Brüdener), but which was used to justify reactionary intervention in the internal troubles of other countries. France's secret adherence in 1815 had been made public in 1818.

Quarterly reviewer to make themselves a very little less sure, that their panegyrics upon despotism, in comparison with any other government except that of a church and an aristocracy, would produce exactly the kind of effect which they wish for, upon the public mind.

Thus much with respect to the principles of this performance: what else it consists of is history. We invite attention to its history. The history of the late events comprises, as our readers know, some rather remarkable circumstances. They will, no doubt, feel curious to learn in what manner the reviewer can contrive to turn these to his purposes.

It might have been expected, that a mind of any generosity, though it might be so unfortunate as to see nothing but gloom and desolation in a prospect so full of brightness and joy, would somewhere have exhibited a gleam of human sympathy for a noble people, whose bravery and self-control throw every example of previous heroism into the shade, and exalt, as has been many times exclaimed in our hearing, the dignity of our common nature. The whole population of a vast city, without leaders and without concert, rushing to arms simultaneously with a *divinus furor*,[8] at the first announcement that brute force had usurped the place of law—storming building after building against regular troops—advancing, numbers of them, to certain death, without either ostentation or regret—putting bread into the mouths of their conquered enemies the moment they had thrown down their arms—watching over the safety of every monument of art or taste, with the solicitude of *virtuosi*—executing summary justice upon every one who sullied their cause by appropriating either private or public property—and returning empty-handed and in rags to their humble homes, without once suspecting that they have done any thing extraordinary—this was a spectacle which might have warmed the heart even of a high-churchman. Even the authors of *Blackwood's Magazine*, who, however destitute of principle, are not without occasional touches of generous feeling, could not help paying, at least in their number *immediately* following the events, a just tribute of admiration to the heroic populace of Paris.[9] Some traces of corresponding sensibility in the *Quarterly* reviewer, might have induced a candid opponent to have looked with less severity upon errors which could then have been attributed to no worse cause than a circumscribed and perverted understanding. But no; the same contraction of soul, which can see no freedom but under the protecting hug of a wealthy church and a powerful aristocracy, can feel for no virtue beyond the same narrow pale. It belongs not to a mind constituted like the reviewer's, to

[8]Cicero, *De divinatione*, in *De senectute, De amicitia, De divinatione* (Latin and English), trans. W.A. Falconer (London: Heinemann, 1938), p. 494 (II, 110, 1-4).
[9]"French Revolution," *Blackwood's*, XXVIII (Sept. 1830), 547, by Thomas De Quincey (1785-1859), essayist and autobiographer. By the next issue, De Quincey was referring to "the mobs who now rule at Paris" in "France and England," *ibid*. (Oct. 1830), 703.

believe in the possibility of such virtue. He would not credit his senses, if they testified in its favour. He is in the condition sometimes treated of by the Catholic divines, and termed invincible hardness of heart; a state, in which the sinner is not precluded from a chance of ultimate salvation, being scarcely responsible for disobedience to a summons which his nature does not qualify him to hear.[10]

"Of the transactions of last July," says the reviewer, "we will say nothing, as they are too recent and too much enveloped in mystery, which time alone can unravel, to form the subject of steady contemplation."[11] We are not at all surprised, that he should be anxious to pass over unnoticed the events of July. He is, however, much mistaken, if he imagines that his readers will pass them over. He will find *them* capable not only of admiring the conduct of the Parisians, but also of reflecting upon it. He and his fraternity have used the former revolution as an argument against the people long enough, the present one will be used by the people as an argument against *them*: and the greater has been the success of the well-paid industry which they have employed in heightening and colouring for effect, the excesses of the first revolution, the more eagerly will men enquire and speculate upon the cause which has rendered the present revolution such as it is impossible to calumniate. They will have no help from the reviewer in this investigation. No cause, capable of accounting for such a phenomenon, is to be found in his philosophy.[12] Yet it *has* a cause, though it be one which it was not very likely that such a person as he, should discover:—The people had in the interval shaken off their church and their aristocracy. Such was the blessed effect of this riddance, that all the horrors we are constantly told of, have not been a counterpoise. Those horrors, followed by 25 years of merciless war, which would have been sufficient to brutalize the people of any other country, have been to this people but as a fiery furnace,[13] out of which it has issued in a brighter and purer state of being. And has the catastrophe which was to blot out France from the map of Europe, and extinguish the sun of morality from the universe, come to this? Even so: and to this must the worst revolution come, so it only deliver the nation from the curse of a wealthy church establishment and a powerful aristocracy. A revolution may be bungled, it may be misdirected, the wisest and best of the citizens may perish in its storms, all that is generous, all that is aspiring, all that is enlightened, may seem to be destroyed; yet shall not the hopes even of its most sanguine supporters be ultimately frustrated, if it have

[10]Mill has evidently confused "hardness of heart" with "ignorance." The former is, for Catholic theologians, voluntary and hence sinful. "Invincible ignorance," on the other hand, is not voluntary and not avoidable. On the former, see St. Thomas Aquinas, *Summa theologiae*, I-II, q. 79, aa. 3 and 4; on the latter, *ibid.*, q. 76, a. 2.

[11]Ross, p. 565.

[12]Cf. Shakespeare, *Hamlet*, I, v, 165-6; in *The Riverside Shakespeare*, p. 1151.

[13]See Daniel, 3:11.

achieved this deliverance. The first revolution has rendered the French common people the finest in Europe, and the second revolution has found them so.

We pass to another particular of the reviewer's display.

The events of July are too recent and too mysterious "to form the subject of steady contemplation," or, peradventure, they are too recent and too indisputable to admit of misrepresentation. But he, to whom the events of July appear "enveloped in mystery," is perfectly versed in the most secret acts and inmost designs of every conspicuous person in France for the last fifteen years. Nothing is mysterious to him, except what is plain and intelligible to every one else. The incredulity which cannot swallow, perhaps the best attested facts in history, stands open-mouthed to take in every old woman's tale of treason and conspiracy, which has been got up since 1815 to serve the momentary purpose of a minister, or perhaps only to gratify the readers of the *Quotidienne* by the excitement of a little gentle apprehension. If the reviewer believes half what he says, he believes, we will take upon ourselves to assert, at least twice as much as his informants. If the ex-ministers had but known, when they penned their *Rapport au Roi*, half as much as the reviewer knows, of their own case![14] But there are certain things, which would scarcely occur to any one, who is at a less distance than two hundred miles from what he is talking about.

The liberals, as they used to be called, in the Chamber of Deputies, formed, according to the reviewer, an organized body, unintermittedly occupied in conspiring to dethrone the Bourbons. If the assertion should meet the eye of any one who knows them, we envy his amusement. We think we can figure to ourselves the consternation of the 221, if it had entered into their wildest dreams that any act of theirs could bring on a revolution in France. They have scarcely ceased trembling at it, three months after the event. Their object, it seems, "has been, and is," at once to "delude the nation by the cant of equality," (a word from which they shrink as a pious man avoids the utterance of a blasphemy,) and to "defy it by such an organization of National Guards as invests them virtually with the whole power of the sword."[15] At the same moment appears the *projet de loi* for the "organization" of the National Guard, of which the first article declares, that it consists of all males from 20 to 60 not forming part of the regular army. Need we say a word more?[16]

When men like this reviewer take upon themselves to give their opinion upon a subject, with the facts of which they are wholly unacquainted, and are thrown

---

[14]The Rapport au roi (25 July), prepared for Charles X by the "ex-ministers" (led by Polignac, Peyronnet, Chantelauze, and Guernon-Ranville), was the justification prefixed to the fatal four ordinances (*Moniteur*, 1830, pp. 813-14).

[15]Ross, pp. 593-4.

[16]Enacted finally as Bull. 26, No. 92 (22 Mar., 1831). The reference is actually to Art. 9.

upon such presumptions and conjectures as are suggested *à priori* by the old saws which compose the sum total of their little philosophy, this is the pitiable predicament in which they place themselves.

When we find such a man as this, a man possessing not one of the elements which go towards making up a rational conviction, a man in whose head there is nothing but a besotted terror of the people, and a childish admiration of the privileged classes,—when we find this man setting himself up as a judge not only of actions but of motives, and distributing infamy, as if the execrations of mankind belonged to him to dispose of; we feel ourselves absolved on our side, as he has thought proper to absolve himself, from the conventions which prescribe that whatever may be our secret opinion, our language at least shall express no feeling incompatible with respect for our opponent. This man, who would not venture to call his soul his own, if the church or the aristocracy needed it, dares to stile Lafayette a "wretched traitor."[17] If the man to whom we are replying is sufficiently insensible of the place which he himself holds in the creation, to be unaware of the immeasurable distance which exists in point of virtue between such men as him and such a man as Lafayette, let the contempt of Europe apprise him of it. The gulph is far too wide, for eyes like his to reach across; nor will the dirt flung by hands like his, fall near enough to be even perceptible to the illustrious patriot against whom it is aimed.

It may perhaps be supposed from all this, that the reviewer vows eternal enmity to popular governments, and to the government of France in particular. No such thing. He tells us on the contrary in plain terms, that if they succeed in establishing themselves, he will be in their favour. This we readily believe. We do not question in the least, that he will always be found on the side of power, let it be where it may. The following are his words:

If they go on well—if they do establish a government at once free and firm—if they can in practice enjoy a free press, without its running into licentiousness—and all this, without erecting among themselves a wealthy hereditary aristocracy and a powerful church establishment,—we shall freely admit ourselves to have been grievously mistaken; that we have been accustomed to do the French people gross injustice;—nay, that our whole system of political faith has been wrong, and that the age of miracles is come again.[18]

"A government at once free and firm," is, it appears, the condition, on which the *Quarterly* reviewer will give, to the new order of things in France, his valuable adhesion. In the mean time, does he tell us of any thing, which is to *prevent* the government from being at once free and firm? Nothing whatever; except that it has no wealthy church, or powerful aristocracy; and that neither of the two is very likely to be created, under the government which has now been

[17]Ross, p. 577.
[18]*Ibid.*, pp. 595-6.

established. We concede to him both these points, and consent, as he desires, to await the result of the experiment, well assured of the ultimate suffrages of such men as he, who are always found on the successful side.

But what demon, in what evil hour, suggested to him to name a licentious press, as the peculiar evil from which the possession of a church and an aristocracy can alone render a nation exempt? Audacity of assertion does much, but did he imagine that it could do every thing, when he described the French newspapers as "the most basely libellous press that ever disgraced a civilized age and country"?[19] When a man does not shrink from asserting, because it suits his purpose, that of which the direct contrary is known to be the fact by every one who can even pretend that he has the means of knowledge, there is scarcely any word but one, and that an extremely short one, which expresses without ambiguity the real character of the affirmation. The French periodical press is probably the most decorous in Europe; the most licentious is unquestionably our own. Foreigners are struck with amazement at the malignity and profligacy of the English periodical press. And of what part of it in particular? Of that part which is peculiarly addressed to, and depends entirely upon the support of, the church and the aristocracy. We have observed and we well remember, that every periodical publication in our time, which has systematically attempted to recommend itself to low-minded readers by scandal and detraction, has shewn by its high-church politics among what class it thought it likely that the greatest number of such readers would be found. Attacks on private character or individual peculiarities, are utterly unexampled in a French newspaper; and it never entered into a Frenchman's imagination to conceive the possibility of such publications as the fashionable prints of our time. But the meaning of a "basely libellous press" we suppose to be, one which is not favourable to "a wealthy hereditary aristocracy" nor to "a powerful church establishment."

It has been asserted that the press of the United States of America is licentious. We know not to what degree such is the fact; and the probability is, that the majority of those who parrot the assertion know as little. But the testimony of Jefferson, the head of the democratic party, than whom no one ever underwent in a greater degree the unscrupulous virulence of newspaper opponents, inclines us to believe that the accusation against the press of America is true to a certain extent.[20] Allowing this, it surely is probable that the cause is co-extensive with the effect, and is one of the circumstances common to England with the United States, not one of those which are common to the United States and to France.

---

[19]*Ibid.*, p. 593.

[20]In his Second Inaugural Address (4 Mar., 1805), for example, Thomas Jefferson said, "During this course of administration [his first term] and in order to disturb it, the artillery of the press has been levelled against us, charged with whatsoever its licentiousness could devise or dare" (in *Debates and Proceedings in the Congress of the United States*, Vol. XIV [1804-05], col. 79).

Nor need we search long to discover a perfectly adequate cause. In America as in England, periodical authorship is in the hands of writers who make literature their trade, and pursue it as they would gin-making, in the same sordid spirit, and with the same object, the greatest possible sale of their commodity. In France, on the contrary, it is in the hands of men who labour principally for the respect of their fellow-citizens; who know that their chance of obtaining this, does not depend upon their success in scraping together a greater or a less quantity of money: who belong to the most high-minded and the most highly-cultivated portion of *la jeune France*,[21] and who, if they have any interested motive in their labours, have that of shewing themselves to be fit for those high functions in the State, which are as accessible to them, if properly qualified, as to any other candidate, and which their youth has commonly been spent, as far as in a private station it could, in rendering themselves competent to fill.

But of this on another occasion, and in another manner. It goes too deep into the structure of society, and is connected with too many of the most elevated considerations, to allow of its being mixed up with the exposure which we have thought it useful to perform, of one of the most impotent attempts ever made to palliate a fallen tyranny. That exposure we now consider sufficient. And as the reviewer concludes by congratulating his countrymen that the testimonials of sympathy with France "have been countenanced by hardly one name which any human being will dare to call respectable,"[22] we will give utterance, in return, to our feelings of joy and exultation, that even in a periodical press which so ill represents the better part of the national mind, the writers who have thought they could find their account in exciting odium against the new government of France, form a feeble and insignificant minority. And it is due even to that minority to declare, that so far as we have observed, not one of them has exhibited so grotesque a contrast between the presumption of the design and the miserable poverty of the execution, as the writer of whom we now finally take our leave.

55. FRENCH NEWS [1]
EXAMINER, 7 NOV., 1830, P. 715

This article was prompted by the appointment on 2 Nov. of a new ministry under Jacques Laffitte (1767-1844), the former ministry having fallen as a result of its efforts to save the ex-ministers (see No. 52). It is the first of 107 articles on French politics Mill supplied to the *Examiner* from this date until 31 Aug., 1834, usually on a weekly basis. We have given serial numbers to these; Mill wrote other articles on France (as well as other subjects) for the *Examiner* during this period, to which different titles are appropriate. This article is headed "London, Nov. 6" but, like the others in the series, is untitled and

[21]For the origin of the term, see No. 50, n14.
[22]Ross, p. 596.

unsigned and does not appear in a named section of the *Examiner*. In his bibliography Mill usually groups several of these articles in one entry as here: "The summary of French affairs in the Examiner from 7th November 1830 to 17th April 1831 inclusive: comprising several long articles" (MacMinn, p. 12). These are Nos. 58-9, 62, 64, 66, 68, 71-2, 74, 76, 79, 81, 83, 85, 87, 89, 91, 93, 95-6, and 100. This article continues with paragraphs on German, Dutch, and Belgian affairs that are here omitted because there is no evidence connecting them with Mill other than their presence in the foreign news section. The *Examiner* of 14 Nov., p. 729, indicates an *erratum*: "supposed" should replace "suffered" (here corrected at 181.27).

THE EXPECTED CHANGE in the French ministry has at length taken place. The fraction of the old administration, which was opposed to popular measures, has given way; and after an ineffectual attempt by M. Casimir Périer,[1] to form a ministry of compromise, the vacancies in the Cabinet have been filled by new appointments, said to be made under the auspices of M. Laffitte and M. Dupont de l'Eure.[2]

In this list, which we have given with our foreign intelligence,[3] it will be perceived that M. Odilon-Barrot is not included.[4] It is reported that he was passed over at his own request. Whatever be the cause, we regret it; as he enjoys a far larger share of the public confidence than the young peer who has been preferred to him,[5] and it is of great importance that those who are raised to power by the popular voice, should be men of sufficient weight of character, to retain popularity without the necessity of constantly courting it and sacrificing to it. We fear that this cannot be affirmed of M. de Montalivet. His devotion, however, to the cause of the revolution was proved by his acting a distinguished part in the glorious three days; and it may be hoped, that the high character of M. Laffitte, and especially of M. Dupont de l'Eure, will give weight to any administration in which they are supposed to be the ruling spirits.

M. Mérilhou is an advocate of great reputation and well-known popular principles.[6]

---

[1]Casimir Périer (1777-1832), financier, a reluctant supporter of the change of monarchy, became Minister without Portfolio.

[2]Laffitte had become President of the Council (a position Louis Philippe himself had held in the previous administration) and Minister of Finance (replacing Baron Louis); Dupont de l'Eure remained Minister of Justice.

[3]*Examiner*, 7 Nov., 1830, p. 714.

[4]Camille Hyacinthe Odilon Barrot (1791-1873), a liberal lawyer, had been President of the Société Aide-toi, le ciel t'aidera; active in the July Days, he was appointed Prefect of the Seine. After being elected a deputy he became the leader of the moderate opposition to the Government.

[5]Comte Marthe Camille Bachasson de Montalivet (1801-80), who had become a peer on the death of his brother in 1826, became Minister of the Interior.

[6]Joseph Mérilhou (1788-1856), a liberal lawyer, became Minister of Public Instruction.

M. Maison is the officer who commanded the French expedition to the Morea. His appointment is said by some to be merely a temporary arrangement.[7]

56. IGNORANCE OF FRENCH AFFAIRS BY THE ENGLISH PRESS
EXAMINER, 14 NOV., 1830, PP. 723-4

This article is in response to what Mill considered the ignorant and misleading reporting of French affairs and of English attitudes, particularly by *The Times*. A leading article in the "Political Examiner," headed as title, it is described in Mill's bibliography as "A leading article in the Examiner of 14th Nov. 1830 headed Ignorance of French affairs by the English press" (MacMinn, p. 13). Two *errata* are listed in the *Examiner* of 21 Nov., p. 740: "mere" should read "more" and "set of people to find acts that" should read "sort of people to find out what" (these corrections are made at 183.22 and 183.24-5).

THE CRAZY OUTCRIES OF OUR NEWSPAPERS against the changes in the French ministry, are not calculated to do much honour to England in foreign countries. They will not, however, make so unfavourable an impression upon the French, with regard to our national mind, as might be imagined, since that people, with their usual misapprehension of every thing English, will probably conclude that our daily press is in the pay of the Duke of Wellington. They are by no means aware of the true state of the case, namely, that there is a fund of stupidity and vulgar prejudice in our principal journalists, which needs no extraneous inducements to call it forth; and that our journals, speaking of them generally, are faithful representatives of the ignorance of the country, but do not represent, in any degree, its knowledge or its good sense. One would imagine that, among journalists, a moderately accurate acquaintance with France for the last fifteen years, ought not to be a very rare endowment: if a writer in the newspapers does not know the history of his own times, what, in the name of heaven, does he know? Yet, during the recent struggle in France between the men who made the revolution and the men who were seeking to profit by it, the small number among our journalists who dreaded giving a false and mischievous opinion, dared not to give one at all; while the larger number, who were utterly reckless of the consequences of what they wrote, have made a display of ignorance such as all who knew them would naturally expect. At the head of these was the blundering newspaper which recently asserted that Charles de Lameth, a man who was with

---

[7]Nicolas Joseph Maison (1771-1840), made a general by Napoleon, a peer by Louis XVIII, and a marshal by Charles X, was Minister of Foreign Affairs for only fifteen days from 2 to 17 Nov., 1830, when he became ambassador to Vienna. The expedition to the Morea in 1828 forced Ibrahim Pasha to evacuate the peninsula.

difficulty saved from the September massacres, was a conventionalist:[1] we need scarcely say that we allude to the *Times*, a paper which seldom lets a week pass without affording satisfactory evidence that for it to have any opinion at all on French affairs, is a piece of presumption which nothing can excuse. This paper announces, that the popular party in France, among various other bad qualities, breathes nothing but war against other states, and hatred of England;[2] which assertion it makes with as little diffidence or hesitation as if it really knew any thing about the matter, and enforces the accusation with as much truth and discernment as were displayed in its eulogies on Polignac, in August, 1829,[3] and with a refinement and delicacy of expression which reminds us of its abuse of the same person in August, 1830, when "vagabonds" was the most correct and appropriate term which it could invent to characterize his delinquency and that of his master.[4]

At a time when hundreds of the most influential of our countrymen knew, by personal observation, that there is a kind of *furor* among the French youth for rejecting territorial aggrandizement, and respecting the rights of other nations, and that it is almost enough to be an Englishman in order to be received every where by them with open arms, we shall not dwell upon the peculiar propriety and good sense of the above denunciations. We have no doubt that, so soon as public opinion shall have declared itself in opposition to them, the *Times* will, according to its customary practice, back out of them. In the mean time, it is consoling to recollect, that what is now affirmed of the more popular section of the *libéraux*, is no more than what was laid to the charge of the whole body until a very recent period. It is incredible how long it takes a certain sort of people to find out what they cannot see with their eyes. The *Times*, in its knowledge of history, is just twenty years behind the facts. It is living, not in 1830, but in 1810.

Periodical writers, however, entitled to far greater respect, have adopted, though in an inferior degree, the same tone of alarm; particularly a writer in the *Scotsman*, and one in the *Foreign Quarterly Review*.[5] We do not so much blame these writers, as lament these habits of mind in the English public, of which the

---

[1]Article on French affairs, *The Times*, 10 Nov., 1830, p. 3. Comte Charles Malo François de Lameth (1757-1832), had been President of the Constituent Assembly in 1791. A constitutional royalist, he had fled France in 1792 when the National Convention assumed power. More recently he had been one of the 221 and a supporter of Louis Philippe.

[2]See, e.g., *The Times*, 4 Nov., 1830, p. 2.

[3]See leading articles on p. 2 of *The Times* for 11, 13, and 19 Aug., 1829.

[4]Leading article, *The Times*, 4 Aug., 1830, p. 2.

[5]"French Ministry," *Scotsman*, 10 Nov., 1830, p. 715; "French Revolution of 1830," *Foreign Quarterly Review*, VI (Oct. 1830), 473-91. The latter was by George Cornewall Lewis (1806-63), a fellow student with Mill of John Austin's.

raw speculations of those two publications on the state of France, are a remarkable exemplification. There is no creature in Europe so timid, politically speaking, as your Englishman of the higher or middle ranks, because he is more sensitive than any other specimen of humanity yet known, on the score of insecurity to property. But it appears to us, that his fears are hardly ever in the right place. Formerly, an Englishman used to pride himself on being a friend of liberty, but now his first impulse always is, to take part with power. It never needs any evidence to satisfy him that men are disaffected without cause. If there arise a dispute between a people and an established government, and he (as is usually the case) does not happen to know what it is about, it would be amusing, if an exhibition of imbecility in the most momentous of earthly concerns could excite any but feelings of the deepest seriousness, to see how instantly and undoubtingly it is taken for granted that the people are in the wrong. Of this, the tone of public feeling respecting Belgium is a pregnant example. Most fortunate it is that Charles X was so imprudent as openly to abrogate the constitution of his kingdom, instead of continuing to evade it, and fritter away its provisions in detail. We have been convinced, from the outset, that if that monarch had not taken as much pains as he did to reduce the question to its simplest terms, despotism or not, in such sort that it did not require any knowledge of France to see that he meditated a different kind of bad government from that which we have been accustomed to;—the English, good easy people, would have continued to believe, that none but enemies of England, and zealots for war and conquest, none, moreover but a faction, contemptible in numbers and abilities, doubted the excellence of the Bourbon government, or were dissatisfied with the share of constitutional freedom which that family was willing that France should enjoy.

The purposes of the popular party have been very fully stated at different times in our own pages. The character of those who have held power for the last three months, but who have now been happily ejected from it, we shall take an early opportunity of delineating. Want of space compels us to defer this work for the present.

57. PROSPECTS OF FRANCE, VI
EXAMINER, 14 NOV., 1830, PP. 724-5

For the context and the entry in Mill's bibliography, see No. 44.

WE HAVE TREATED of the demands of the popular party with respect to the conditions of eligibility, and of the elective franchise. We shall next advert to the subject of internal administration.

It is allowed by all philosophers, and felt by all freemen, that securities for the goodness of the Government are not enough; it is also requisite to have as little of it as possible: the Government ought to do nothing for the people, which the people can, with any sort of convenience, do for themselves, either singly or in smaller associations.

The very reverse of this maxim has directed the legislation and administration of France, from the reign of Napoleon to the present time. The principle of the imperial regime, faithfully adhered to by restored legitimacy, was, that the people never should be permitted to do any thing for themselves, which the Government could in any manner contrive to do, or pretend to do, for them.

If a nation could be judged of, from the laws which are made for them by those who hold the right to govern them, not from them, one must needs suppose that the French, being themselves the most stupid of all possible people, were luckily provided with the cleverest of all possible governments. So far as the theory of the French law can be gathered from its practice, the supposition upon which it is founded appears to be, that there is nothing for which the French people *are* fit, nor any thing for which their Government is *not*. The French cannot be trusted to construct a road, or a canal; but the French Government, in addition to its other labours, finds time for making and mending all the roads and canals in France, which consequently are on that scale of shabby magnificence, customary in the doings of governments, being twice as broad, and more than twice as bad, as the canals and roads of any other civilized country. Again, no Frenchman is supposed capable of selecting a school fit to be entrusted with the care of his sons or of his daughters; accordingly the Government ordains that no places of education shall exist, except those subordinate to the department of the French administration called the University, or which are licensed and inspected by its officers; whereby it came to pass, that in a country, in many parts of which even the street-sweepers would think themselves degraded by keeping company with a Jesuit, the Jesuits for several years held in their hands the majority of the establishments for education.[1] Furthermore, the French Government, in order not to be divested of its proper influence in all affairs of importance which are transacted between the Straits of Dover and the Pyrenees, reserves to a sound discretion residing in its own breast, the exercise of a veto on all evening parties, given, or attempted to be given, within the kingdom of France; no one being permitted to receive more than twenty persons at one time into his house without leave of the police.[2] It was under no other than this very law, that the society called *Les amis du peuple* was recently dispersed.[3]

---

[1] For details, see No. 43, n10.

[2] Code pénal, Livre III, Titre I, Chap. iii, Sect. 7, Art. 291.

[3] Les Amis du Peuple, a republican society formed immediately after the July Revolution, was legally dissolved on 25 Sept., 1830, but continued in existence and was behind many of the disturbances during the next eighteen months. It was especially threatening to the government because many of its members were in the National Guard.

But the subject we would chiefly advert to, is one which, next to the constitution of the sovereign body, is the most comprehensive and most important topic of internal policy in all countries whatever, and especially in France; municipal institutions, or the composition of the subordinate legislatures and executives, to whom the authority in matters of purely local regulation is confided.

We are almost certain that there is not any country in Europe except France, in which there exists no vestige of any local authority not emanating from the Crown. We must have recourse to the despotisms of Asia to find a parallel. The municipality, corporation, or *commune*, was the very first free institution which the countries of modern Europe knew. By its means, the citizens emancipated themselves from the condition of serfs of an aristocracy, who seemed sent from Heaven to perpetuate the savage state. To it they owed that security, and that personal independence, which enabled them to accumulate wealth, to train up a high-spirited and numerous armed population, and with that wealth to buy, and with those armed men to demand, a voice in their own government. The associations of chapmen and artificers to manage their local concerns by their own officers, first taught governments to think of the people as a power in the state. To obtain money from these associations did the kings of Europe call together delegates from them, under the name of representatives of the Commons, and conceded to them, one by one, all the privileges, in virtue of which any nation in Europe claims to call itself a free people. In this mode did England, Scotland, Spain, the Netherlands, Sweden, Norway, Denmark, and, we believe, even Poland, acquire such representative constitution as they do now, or did at any former period, enjoy. In France, the crown grew in power faster than the communes, and a despotic instead of a representative government ensued. But if the citizens acquired no share in the management of the state, they retained that of their own local affairs. Town-governments not emanating from the Crown, and, in many provinces, representative assemblies of a more or less popular character, termed States Provincial, with powers very extensive and diversified, subsisted down to the Revolution; when they were abolished by the Constituent Assembly, but replaced by municipal institutions of a still more popular kind.[4] These were swept away by the hand of military usurpation, and a system introduced, founded on the principle of holding all the reins of government in a single hand;[5] a system upheld solely, and for a short time, by the

[4]The Constituent Assembly abolished the provincial assemblies on 26 Oct., 1789 (*Moniteur*, 1789, p. 319); it then divided France into eighty-three departments, subdivided into arrondissements, cantons, and communes, with elected governing bodies at each level (*Moniteur*, 16 Jan., 1790, p. 64).

[5]In February 1800 by Bull. 17, No. 115, Napoleon, as First Consul, introduced a system of direct appointment by himself or his representatives of all administrative officials at all levels. In 1802 electoral colleges were reintroduced but they only elected

préstige of military success, and the impotent attempt to perpetuate which, after the gilding had been rubbed off the chains in which it bound the people, has cost the Bourbons their throne.

In England, the business of local administration is so parcelled out into shares, and cut up into unconnected fragments, that it is hardly either spoken of or thought of, collectively and as a whole. Every parish has its separate government, every corporate town has another, every county has a third; to determine which of the three is the most corrupt, must be left to those who are curious in nice distinctions: local trusts, and commissioners of every variety of denomination, perform a large portion of the public business; for another large and highly important part no provision whatever is made, and when done at all, it is done by the awkward hands of the legislature itself, in the form of an act of Parliament *pro hâc vice*;[6] and finally, a large portion is done, or considered to be done, or considered proper to be done, by the public itself. There is just one possible mode of transacting the public business worse than this, and that is the mode prevailing in France; where every human being, who is empowered to give the most trifling order to the most inconsiderable body of his fellow-citizens, from the *préfet* down to a sort of village watchman called a *garde-champêtre* (the judges excepted), holds that power from the direct appointment of an officer of the crown, holds it during the good pleasure of that officer, and without a vestige of accountability to any other being in human shape; for he cannot even be tried by a court of justice for murder committed in the exercise of his authority, without the previous consent of his official superior, or, in the last resort, of a tribunal called the *conseil d'état*, which deliberates with closed doors, and of which the members are removable at the King's pleasure.

Hence it is, that in France you cannot cross the street without jostling a placeman. Hence it is, that the *bureaucratie* is five times more numerous than the army; for the latter does not exceed 240,000 men, while the officers of government, removable at the pleasure of the crown, amounted in 1818, according to M. Fiévée (and there are few more trust-worthy authorities) to the incredible number of between twelve and thirteen hundred thousand individuals, more than a sixth part of the male adult population of France at that period.[7]

We quote from the *Correspondance Politique et Administrative* of M. Fiévée a passage containing as curious a picture as was probably ever seen, of the real liberties of a country which boasted of a charter, and whose rulers thought the nation extremely unreasonable, because it would not be persuaded that a Chamber of Deputies was liberty. The nation was wiser, and used that one

---

candidates from which the local council, mainly a consultative body, would be appointed (Bull. 206, No. 1876 [4 Aug., 1802], esp. Titre II, Sects. 5, 8, 13).

[6]The state's power to intervene on special occasions was first codified (using this term) by 33 Henry VIII, c. 20 (1541).

[7]Fiévée, *Correspondance politique et administrative*, Vol. III, Pt. 14, p. 34.

liberty, as our ancestors used that of withholding the supplies, for the purpose of obtaining by its means all the other liberties which they had not. Speaking of the prerogatives of the crown, M. Fiévée enumerates that of possessing—

Une justice particulière qu'on appelle *justice administrative* par la nécessité de lui donner un nom, et en vertu de laquelle les douze ou treize cent mille agens soldés de l'administration ne peuvent être traduits devant les tribunaux ordinaires, sans l'autorisation de l'administration; de sorte qu'un percepteur qui, dans l'exercice de ses fonctions, tueroit un comptable, ne pourroit être mis en jugement sans que la royauté y eût consenti. Par le même système, le plus mince agent de la navigation intérieure peut déranger les spéculations du commerce, sans que le commerce puisse s'en plaindre devant une autre justice que la justice administrative; enfin, nos lois ou décrets encore en vigueur disent qu'un fournisseur qui, sur ses billets, a soin d'ajouter son titre de fournisseur après sa signature, ne peut être poursuivi par ses créanciers devant les tribunaux, sans le consentement préalable de la justice administrative; laquelle justice se rend sans publicité par des agens que l'autorité place et déplace à volonté. En un mot, attirer à soi l'examen et le jugement de toute affaire et de toute cause dans lesquelles se prétend intéressé un pouvoir qui se mêle de tout, tel est le matériel de la royauté en France.[8]

Well might M. Fiévée add, "Certes, dans aucun temps et dans aucun pays le pouvoir monarchique n'a eu des attributions aussi étendues."[9] We suppose that there never was any other country on the face of the earth, in which the executive, having made a survey and classification of all matters requiring a judicial decision, set apart from the rest all in which it could itself in any way directly or indirectly be considered a party, and determined, that precisely in those would it also be the judge.*

Let it be granted that the rights and constitution of the legislative body will henceforth secure France (as it certainly ought) against the possibility of a profligate ministry. The people of France conceive, that the general affairs of the nation afford ample employment for any seven persons, even admitting that cabinets henceforth are never to consist of any other than the fittest men. They look back with no pleasant reminiscences to the times when Hamburg could not cut down five trees, the property of the town, without an order from Paris, which took eight months to arrive, nor Holland repair the dykes which alone stood between her and destruction, until permission had been applied for to the *Ministère de l'Intérieur*, and, at the end of six months, obtained.† The people of France are not disposed any longer to keep up, at their expence, a *bureaucratie* twelve hundred thousand strong, spread over the whole country, and who, if not called to account by seven men in seven large buildings at Paris, are not

[8]*Ibid.*, pp. 35-6.
[9]*Ibid.*, p. 36.
*It may possibly increase the weight of M. Fiévée's authority to mention, that when he made these statements he was, and had always been, a strenuous supporter of the ultra-royalist party.
†Fiévée [Vol. I, Pt. 1, p. 25].

accountable at all. Accordingly, the French people, from the Restoration to the present time, have never ceased to demand popular municipalities.

They are willing that the executive power, the right and duty of enforcing obedience to the laws, the chief civil authority in the town or district, should reside, as at present, in officers nominated by the Crown, and removeable by the royal authority. But these functionaries are assisted by deliberative bodies, called *conseils-généraux de département*, or *conseils généraux de commune*. To these bodies, who are at present named by the officer, to whom they act as assessors, belong several functions of very great importance. Among these are the repartition of the taxes, many of which are granted by the Chamber of Deputies in the lump, such and such a gross sum from each department: and, moreover, the supplies required for local purposes are voted by these local bodies exclusively, the legislature interfering no further in the matter than to fix a limit which the aggregate of these supplies shall not exceed; namely, a certain per centage on the general taxes of the department. Now, these councils, it is maintained, ought to be elected by the people; and by a rather extensive suffrage too—a suffrage, perhaps, co-extensive with direct taxation. To this the most moderate of the popular party attach great importance. It would be absurd, they say, to entertain any apprehension of evil from the predominance of the democratic principle in matters of purely local arrangement; while such a constitution of the local bodies would withdraw an immense amount of patronage and corrupt influence from the Ministry, would be a valuable counterpoise to a mere aristocratic constitution of the legislature, would gradually train the people to the management of their own affairs, and help to qualify them for admission, at no distant period, to political privileges more extended than what any party at present would willingly entrust to them.

Not so thinks the Chamber of 1830! A municipal law is in progress, through that chamber, avowedly transcribed, with a few trifling alterations, from the law proposed by Martignac in 1829, with the amendments of the then chamber,—a law, under which the local bodies would be elected by a more restricted suffrage than even the chamber itself—a law, which is tolerable only when compared to a system, in comparison with which any thing would be endurable.[10] Because the French would have accepted this law, bad as it is, rather than fight, the chamber considers it good enough for them after they have fought and conquered. But it will not do; this step has done greater damage to the chamber in public opinion than any other of their proceedings; it was altogether contrary to the expectations

[10]The most significant difference between the Projet de loi sur l'organisation communale (31 Aug.) (*Moniteur*, 1830, p. 1007), introduced by Arnould Humblot-Conté (1776-1845), and Martignac's Projet de loi sur les communes (9 Feb.) (*ibid.*, 1829, pp. 178-81), was the provision that the mayor and his administrative officials be appointed from among the elected councillors. After amendment by the Commission the former was finally enacted as Bull. 25, No. 91 (21 Mar., 1831).

even of those whose distrust of their intentions was the strongest. The ministers themselves, though on every other point the sworn allies of the chamber, have not ventured, on this occasion, openly to approve what they have not felt inclined to dissent from. Not a word has escaped their lips.

One topic more remains to be discussed—the constitution of the Upper Chamber. This, however, must be deferred to the next paper,[11] which will conclude the present series.

S————.

58. FRENCH NEWS [2]
EXAMINER, 14 NOV., 1830, P. 729

This article is headed "London, Nov. 13." For the entry in Mill's bibliography, see No. 55. One correction in the text is explained in n6.

THE FRENCH CHAMBER OF DEPUTIES has postponed the choice of a President, in the place of M. Laffitte, until its number shall be completed by the arrival of the new members.[1] The Government candidate is M. Girod de l'Ain, who has just resigned the office of Prefect of Police.[2] It is believed that the *doctrinaire* party will set up M. Casimir Périer in opposition to M. Girod; but that estimable deputy, who by no means participates in the feelings and purposes of the doctrinaires, and who but two months ago resigned the Presidency on account of ill health, will not, it is believed, allow his name to be employed as an instrument in the hands of a party which has no root in the opinion of the French nation, to oppose the only ministry, in the formation of which, as it now appears, the King and the people could agree.

It is said that the new ministry will introduce an Election Law immediately after the Chamber shall have appointed its President. The provisions of the intended law are expected to be the following: 1st. The entire suppression of all conditions of eligibility—2d. The reduction of the qualification for an elector, from 300 to 200 francs of direct taxation—3d. The admission of the professions now entitled to serve on juries, to the elective franchise, free from any pecuniary condition—4th. If in any department this extension of the franchise shall not

[11]No. 61.

———

[1]On becoming President of the Council, Laffitte had vacated the Presidency of the Chamber of Deputies. Not until the end of November did by-elections bring back to full strength the Chamber, depleted by the resignations after Louis Philippe's accession.

[2]Louis Gaspard Amédée Girod de l'Ain (1781-1847), an Orleanist politician, had been appointed Prefect in August 1830. (For Mill's account of his behaviour, see *EL, CW*, Vol. XII, p. 56.)

produce one elector for every 100 inhabitants, that proportion will be made up from among the persons most highly taxed below 200 francs.[3]

The elections have not been on the whole so popular as some, nor so aristocratic as others, expected. Among the new members are to be found the highly estimable names of Voyer d'Argenson, de Cormenin, Isambert, Barthe,[4] and Odilon Barrot.

The Chamber, since its meeting, has been occupied in disposing of former orders of the day. M. Bavoux's proposition for diminishing the taxes on newspapers, has not been adopted as a whole,[5] but the stamp duty has been lowered from five to four centimes per sheet,[6] and the amount of the security required from newspaper proprietors has been somewhat diminished.[7]

59. FRENCH NEWS [3]
EXAMINER, 21 NOV., 1830, P. 745

This article is headed "London, Nov. 20." For the entry in Mill's bibliography, see No. 55.

THE DEBATE IN THE FRENCH CHAMBER OF DEPUTIES, on the motion for reducing the stamp duties on newspapers, is disgraceful to the Chamber.[1] M. de Villèle's famous *chambre des trois cents*[2] would not have made a more discreditable

[3]The election bill was not in fact presented until 30 Dec., and then in less democratic form; see Nos. 64 and 72.

[4]Marc René de Voyer d'Argenson (1771-1842), was a deputy almost continuously from the Hundred Days to his resignation in 1828. Elected again in 1830, he caused a stir by inserting, in accord with his republican leanings, the phrase "sauf les progrès de la raison publique" when he was sworn in. Vicomte Louis Marie Delahaye de Cormenin (1788-1868), a lawyer, was an opposition deputy and pamphleteer (as "Timon"). François André Isambert (1792-1857), a lawyer, a leading member of the French Society for the Abolition of Slavery, was a liberal deputy. Félix Barthe (1795-1863), a lawyer, had frequently provided legal counsel to liberals prosecuted by the government.

[5]François Nicolas Bavoux (1774-1848), professor of law and a liberal deputy; for his proposition of 17 Sept., see *Moniteur*, 1830, p. 1114.

[6]In the *Examiner* of 21 Nov., 1830, p. 740, a note referring to this item appeared: "In the summary of French news, 'the stamp duty has been lowered from *fifty-four* centimes per sheet,' read 'from *five to four* centimes;' but the statement itself is erroneous, as it was not the stamp duty, but the postage of newspapers which was reduced in that ratio."

[7]Bull. 16, No. 80 (14 Dec., 1830), which resulted from this debate, lowered both the security required from proprietors (Art. 1) and the stamp duty (Art. 3) as well as the postage.

[1]See *Moniteur*, 7, 9, 10, 11 Nov., 1830, pp. 1403-4, 1423-6, 1430-2, 1432-4, 1436-40. See also No. 58, n6.
[2]A reference to the Villèle ministry's safe majority in 1824.

display on this proposition, which was resisted chiefly on the avowed ground of the necessity of curbing the licentiousness of the Press. So rapidly has the new oligarchy succeeded to the worst feelings, and even to the silliest catch-words of its predecessors.

The new ministers, we lament to say, did not support the motion, alleging that they were not prepared to consent to any sacrifice of revenue. This temporizing is very deplorable, as it would be the grossest hypocrisy in the ministers to pretend to suppose that the profuse expenditure of the Bourbon government does not admit of retrenchments far exceeding the trifling revenue afforded by the taxes on discussion.

Several of our newspapers, and their correspondents at Paris, continue to heap abuse upon the popular party.[3] There are no wise and moderate men, according to them, but those who think that 88,000 men should have the power of dividing among them, at discretion, a revenue amounting (independently of the interest of the public debt), to thirty millions sterling; all the rest are firebrands, who seek to throw the world into disorder. The 88,000 electors are the nation. The nation is declared to sympathize with the Chamber, because the 88,000 have generally re-elected the old members: although even the 88,000, when they had no old member to re-elect, have in many instances elected new ones of a very different complexion.

The *Times* takes great pains to represent Mauguin, one of the feeblest declaimers in the Chamber, as the leader of the popular party, and the organ of its sentiments;[4] the real fact being that he is a recent and unexpected proselyte to that party. The *Times* adds, that although an abler man than M. Odilon Barrot, he was never mentioned in the late contest for the ministry. This, in the first place, is incorrect; and secondly, M. Odilon Barrot, if he be not a far abler man than M. Mauguin, ill-deserves the reputation he possesses. The true reason why M. Mauguin was not put forward by the popular party generally, for a place in the ministry, is simply that they did not consider him fit for it.

The chief measures of the Belgian Provisional Government, as specified in their address to the Congress, which we have given in another part of the paper, will form an advantageous contrast to those of the French Chamber.[5]

[3]See, for example, "Private Correspondence. Letter from Our Correspondent at Paris" (13 Nov.), *Morning Post*, 19 Nov., 1830, p. 3; and leading articles, *Standard*, 8 Nov., 1830, p. 3, and 9 Nov., p. 4.

[4]*The Times*, 17 Nov., 1830, p. 2.

[5]See "Foreign Intelligence. Belgium," *Examiner*, 21 Nov., 1830, pp. 741-2. In 1815 the Treaty of Vienna had united the Belgians and Dutch into the Kingdom of the Netherlands. The Belgians resented what they considered the dominance of the Protestant Dutch, and disturbances had broken out on 25 Aug., 1830. On 4 Oct. a provisional government declared independence and on 10 Nov. the National Congress met to draw up a constitution. The chief proposals were that delegates to the National Congress be directly elected, that liberty and equality for all before the law be established, and that

All attempts in favour of the Constitutional cause in the north of Spain appear to be, for the present, at an end.[6]

60. USE AND ABUSE OF THE BALLOT

EXAMINER, 28 NOV., 1830, PP. 754-5

This article is a reminder that while Mill was writing about the progress of the July Revolution, England was experiencing her own crisis over the Reform Bill; the secret ballot was an issue for radicals in both countries. He later became an opponent of the ballot, but continued to use the passage he here quotes from his father's *History of British India* (see *CW*, Vol. XIX, pp. 331-2). This is a leading article in the "Political Examiner," headed as title and described in Mill's bibliography as "A leading article in the Examiner of 28 Nov. 1830, headed, Use and Abuse of the Ballot" (MacMinn, p. 13). Two corrections are indicated by Mill in the Somerville College set, "partial to" is corrected to "protected" (194.34) and "Legislature's" to "Legislator's" (194.36); the first of these is also mentioned as an *erratum* in a note to the *Examiner*, 5 Dec., p. 770.

THE FEELINGS AND PURPOSES of the present Chamber of Deputies in France display themselves more and more plainly every day. We invite attention to one of the most recent of its "*faits et gestes.*"

By the existing laws, no one can follow the business of a printer without a licence from the Government,[1] who hitherto have habitually kept the number so far below the demand, that a licence bears a considerable pecuniary price. A bill was brought in by M. Benjamin Constant, for opening the trade to all who chose to engage in it. The several clauses of this bill were successively voted in the Chamber, by open suffrage: but when the question was finally put, "that the bill do pass," on which, by the regulations of the Assembly, *the votes were taken by ballot*; the same Chamber, which had voted each of the separate clauses, rejected, by a large majority, the entire bill.[2]

One good effect at least will result, it is to be hoped, from this exhibition. We trust that we shall hear no further abuse of the French people for the feelings which they justly entertain towards this despicable body.

---

liberty of the press, of education, of association, and of religion be protected. At the same time a conference of the five great Powers, Great Britain, France, Russia, Austria, and Prussia, met in London.

[6]The final two paragraphs may not be Mill's, but as the first of them, in particular, refers to the text above, they are retained.

---

[1]Bull. 47, No. 395 (21 Oct., 1814), Titre II, Art. 11.

[2]Constant's Proposition tendant à rendre libre les professions de libraire et d'imprimeur was read in the Chamber of Deputies on 11 Sept., and after discussion and reference to a committee, was rejected on 19 Nov. (*Moniteur*, 1830, p. 1072 [introduced], and pp. 1511-12 [rejected]).

When the people first began, after the revolution, to show symptoms of dissatisfaction with the Chamber, most persons in England, taking it for granted, as usual, that if there were any difference of opinion, the people must be in the wrong, were astonished to find the French so capricious, so distrustful, so unreasonably suspicious of their public men. We too are astonished, but from rather a different cause. We marvel at the easy good nature, the unsuspecting credulity with which the severest critics of the Chamber, in August last, allowed themselves to believe that its only fault would be a little slowness, timidity, and irresolution in the accomplishment of reforms. We conversed with several leading men of the popular party shortly after the revolution, and no one of them entertained a suspicion that the motion which the Chamber has now rejected would meet with the slightest resistance.

We must add a few words respecting the ballot. We do hope and trust that the French will now see that the voting in a representative assembly is not one of those cases in which secret suffrage is desirable.

Every person who reflects, for a single instant, on the effect of the ballot, must see that it is simply this: to withdraw the voter from the influence of hopes and fears held out by other persons, and leave him free to act according to those interests and inclinations which are independent of the will of other people. Is it not then obvious, without the necessity of discussion, that the ballot may be good or bad, according to circumstances? It is good where the voter's own interest is to vote right, but when he may be bribed or intimidated by persons whose interest it is that he should vote wrong. It is bad where his own interest is to vote wrong, and where the only means of giving him a sufficient motive to vote right, is *responsibility*, either to the law or to public opinion.

In the election of members of Parliament, under a really popular system of election, the ballot is indispensable. For if the electoral body is sufficiently large, it is the elector's own interest to make a good choice. Responsibility, in that case, is not requisite: the use of responsibility is, to control those who have an interest in doing wrong. If the vote is secret, therefore, it will be honest; but if it be known to his landlord, or to any other person on whom he is dependent, and whose interest it may be that he would make a dishonest choice, dishonest it will probably be.

The very reverse of all this is true, when the votes to be protected are those of members of Parliament themselves. There the danger is not from the interest of those on whom the Legislator may be dependent, but from the Legislator's own interest. Though he be independent of every body else, that is no security for public virtue, when he has the power of making laws in his own favour, and voting the public money into his own pocket. The only check upon a legislator is liability to be turned out for misconduct; and his constituents cannot employ that check unless they know what his conduct is.

The distinction is so obvious, that it might be expected to occur even to the most obtuse: yet in France, as in ancient Rome, the ballot is applied in cases in which it is clearly mischievous; while in England it is not employed in a case in which its employment is indispensable to good government: and we find the *Standard* and the *Times* urging against secret voting at elections,[3] the argument which holds against secret voting in the House, namely, the inestimable value of public opinion as a check, not adverting to the fact that public opinion, though a necessary restraint upon the representatives and trustees of the public, can be no check upon the public itself.

We subjoin a passage from Mr. Mill's *History of British India*, in which the theory of the ballot is clearly and forcibly expounded. We earnestly request the *Standard* to consider this passage with attention, having it deeply at heart that so able a writer should come to a due sense of the value of the only one among the essentials of a real Parliamentary reform, from which he is as yet a dissentient. As for the *Times*, we know the condition, and the only condition, on which we can obtain its concurrence. We shall have its support as soon as we can succeed in persuading it that the majority of buyers are on our side.

There are occasions on which the use of the ballot is advantageous; there are occasions on which it is hurtful. If we look steadily to the end to which all institutions profess to be directed, we shall not find it very difficult to draw the line of demarcation. A voter may be considered as subject to the operation of two sets of interests: the one, interests arising out of the good or evil for which he is dependant upon the will of other men; the other, interests in respect to which he cannot be considered as dependant upon any determinate man or men. There are cases in which the interests for which he is not dependant upon other men, might impel him in the right direction. If not acted upon by other interests, he will in such cases vote in that direction. If however he is acted upon by interests dependant upon other men, which latter interests are more powerful than the former, and act in the opposite direction, he will vote in the opposite direction. What is necessary, therefore, is, to save him from the operation of those interests. This is accomplished by enabling him to vote in secret; for in that case the man, who could otherwise compel his vote, is ignorant in what direction it has been given. In all cases therefore in which the independent interests of the voter, those which in propriety of language may be called his *own* interests, would dictate the good and useful vote; but in which cases, at the same time, he is liable to be acted upon in the way either of good or evil, by men whose interests would dictate a base and mischievous vote, the ballot is a great and invaluable security. In this set of cases is included the important instance of the votes of the people for representatives in the legislative assembly of a nation. It is therefore of the highest importance that they should be protected from that influence. There is however another set of cases in which those interests of the voter, which have their origin primarily in himself, and not in other men, draw in the hurtful direction; and in which he is not liable to be operated upon by any other interests of other men, than those which he possesses in common with the rest of the community. If allowed in this set of cases to vote in secret, he will be sure to vote as the sinister interest impels. If forced to vote in public, he will be subject to all the restraint, which the eye of the community, fixed upon his virtue or knavery, is calculated to produce; and in such cases the ballot is only an encouragement to evil.*

[3]See, e.g., articles of 1830 bearing on the ballot in the *Standard*, 21 Oct., p. 3, and 25 Oct., p. 3; and in *The Times*, 8 Mar., p. 4, 12 July, p. 4, 30 Aug., p. 7, and 23 Oct., p. 2.

*[James] Mill's [*The History of*] *British India* [1818], Book IV, Chap. ix [2nd ed., 6 vols. (London: Baldwin, *et al.*, 1820), Vol. III, pp. 451-2].

61. PROSPECTS OF FRANCE, VII

EXAMINER, 28 NOV., 1830, PP. 756-7

This is the final article in the series beginning with No. 44, *q.v.*

OF THE GREAT CONSTITUTIONAL QUESTIONS, about to become the subject of discussion, and, it is in vain to disguise the fact, of acrimonious dispute, between the men of the restoration and the men of the new revolution, only one remains to be noticed—the inheritableness of the peerage.

We anticipate some difficulty in making perceptible to the English public, of how little comparative importance this matter is; in fact, we foresee that it will be the source of more misapprehension, and more groundless alarms, than questions of ten times as much consequence as really belongs to it. Men in whose eyes a large extension of the right of suffrage would be no more than what Mr. Canning would have called the infusion of a popular spirit into the constitution,[1] will consider the attempt to dispense with a hereditary peerage as a dangerous innovation, establishing the unqualified and formidable ascendancy of the democratic principle. To such a degree are men governed by words rather than things, by forms rather than substance. A house of peers is not necessarily an aristocracy because it is so styled in the traditional phraseology of the British constitution: and the question, whether the French chamber of peers shall be hereditary, does not concern the democratic principle, nor any principle at all except this, that if there be any use in a house of peers, there is use in having one which shall be an object of respect, and not of contempt.

It is well known that for a century or more, the sole idea which the continental nations had of a constitutional government, consisted of the British constitution misunderstood. They took our own word for the theory of our constitution; and were entirely unaware, that the British constitution has no theory. The works of design and intelligence have their laws, but the fortuitous concourse of atoms has no law. Where means have been used to attain an end, an account of the means may be written down, and the record may serve other agents to produce a similar effect: but the seeds of the British constitution fell, sprouted, and grew up, as it pleased God; and the means having pre-existed, ends were found for them by gentlemen in their closets, who seldom proceeded upon any other principle than that of sharing, as fairly as they could, the praises due to all possible forms of government, among the constituent parts of that of England. The doctrine, that the British constitution was a compound of the three simple forms of

---

[1]*Corrected Report of the Speech of the Right Honourable George Canning, in the House of Commons, 25th April, 1822, on Lord John Russell's Motion for a Reform of Parliament* (London: Hatchard, 1822), p. 59.

government, monarchy being represented by the king, aristocracy by the upper house of parliament, and democracy by the lower, a conceit which never could have issued from any head but that of a pedant,[2] passed off among ourselves in a manner characteristically national, that is to say, it served as well as any other form of words to swear by, but never assumed a sufficiently definite signification in our minds, to determine the slightest of our actions. To foreign nations, however, this went forth as the true theory and approved explanation of the British government, and became the received formula for making a constitution. Accordingly (not to lose time in irrelevant examples) the framers of the charter of Louis XVIII having a constitution to make, and desiring to make it properly, called together a number of gentlemen, gazetted them as dukes, barons, and counts, settled pensions on them from the public purse, and said, There is an aristocracy.[3]

This *impromptu* parody on our House of Lords possesses not one of the attributes from which the political importance of its prototype originates. The House of Lords is one of the oldest institutions of England: it is identified with all our historical recollections, and recognized by the traditional doctrines of our government as an essential part of the most stable constitution which ever existed. Its members are likewise the possessors of enormous wealth, in a country in which wealth exercises over the minds of men a command which it possesses among no other people. We are moreover continually told, and most by the greatest admirers of the institution, that all these sources of moral influence are not enough, and that the House of Lords would be in practice reduced to a cypher, if it did not, besides all this, send, by means of corrupt influence, nearly a majority of members to the lower house. If there be a particle of truth in this asseveration, and even though there be none, we have only to suppose that our peerage were but of yesterday, with incomes averaging from five hundred to a thousand a-year, and a reformed House of Commons, and from the political weight which would attach to such a body, we may approximate to a just conception of the present importance which belongs to the mock-aristocratic branch of the French legislature.

If you nickname three hundred gentlemen in various ways,[4] and then declare that they are a branch of the sovereign legislature, equal and co-ordinate with the assembly which represents the people, you must be supposed to intend that they

[2]Actually from that of William Blackstone (1723-80), British legal writer; see his *Commentaries on the Laws of England*, 4 vols. (Oxford: Clarendon Press, 1765-69), Vol. I, pp. 50-2.
[3]When the Charter was proclaimed on 4 June, 1814, it provided for a Chamber of Peers (Arts. 24-34), and subsequently the Chancellor read out a list of names of peers appointed by Louis XVIII to constitute it.
[4]There were approximately 300 French peers in the late 1820s, created by various means with various titles.

should have a will of their own occasionally, and are not to vote always exactly as the other assembly bids. Now, if they refuse to concur with the Commons in any measure which the latter have much at heart, what is to prevent the lower house from voting the upper one a nuisance, and declaring the law to be a law notwithstanding their dissent? The question reduces itself to this: would the people obey? Has the chamber of peers, or can any hereditary chamber, in the situation of France, have a sufficient hold upon the popular mind, for the people to regard a law as less a law because it has not received the concurrence of that chamber? No one, who has any knowledge of France, will answer in the affirmative.

Every thing is new in France, and neither the chamber of peers nor any other institution has any of that stability which belongs to antiquity. It has none of that weight which is derived from the possession of wealth. There is only one remaining source of moral influence, and that is, personal merit and reputation; and of this the chamber is fast losing the little which it ever had. A hereditary body may be as select as an elective one, when first created; and the French chamber did contain some men of mathematical and chemical celebrity, and some of the very few politicians of honourable notoriety whom the revolution and the empire had left:[5] but these are mostly dead, or so old as to be *hors de combat*, and as mathematical and chemical knowledge are not hereditary though the peerage is, their sons are neither wiser nor better than any other men (English eldest sons excepted): the chamber, therefore, would, by this time, have been rather deficient in *notabilités*, had it not been a practice since the restoration to elevate to the peerage every minister to whom it was desired to give an honourable dismissal, and had not the statesmen who were in this predicament been luckily very numerous.[6] The debates, therefore, of the chamber of peers, now that they are open to the public, and reported in the newspapers, display a list of speakers, the perspective of which ten years ago, considering that a revolution has intervened, would have not a little astonished the parties concerned, nearly all of them being of one or more of the many ministries of Louis XVIII. The president of the chamber is Pasquier, the *inévitable*, as he is called, a man celebrated for falling always upon his feet, whatever be the turn in

[5]Among the former were Pierre Simon, marquis de Laplace (1749-1827), the great mathematician, and Claude Louis, comte de Berthollet (1748-1822), the celebrated chemist; among the latter were François Antoine de Boissy d'Anglas (1756-1828), member of the States General, the National Assembly, and a centrist in the Convention, who was made a peer in 1814 after voting for Napoleon's abdication, and Louis Gustave le Doulcet, comte de Pontécoulant (1764-1853), a moderate in the Convention who was outlawed as a Girondin but later became President of the Convention, who was also elevated to the peerage in 1814.

[6]*Figaro* in a parody of the Charter included an Article 24: "Tout ministre chassé par le voeu de la nation est nommé de droit à la pairie" (27 June, 1830, pp. 1-2).

affairs: sometime prefect of police under Buonaparte, and orator to every ministry from the restoration to the commencement of the Villèle government.[7] The principal speakers are Lainé, Decazes, Portalis, Siméon, Roy, Dubouchage, and, we may add, the late Minister of Foreign Affairs, Molé;[8] men highly unpopular when they were formerly in office, and not less so now, saving that the more recent oppressors eclipse the hatred borne to men, some of whom had the redeeming merit (our Shaftesbury had it too)[9] of resisting the worst acts of ministers still worse than themselves.

There are so few people who can see an effect after it has come to pass, that we must not be extremely severe on those who merely cannot foresee it while it is yet to come. Therefore we should not, perhaps, quarrel with the Bourbons for having *rien appris* before the Restoration, if they were found capable of learning any thing thereafter.[10] Now this really was the case: for, in a short time after the formation of the chamber of peers, it occurred to its founders, that it somehow was not so influential a body as the British House of Lords. It struck them that the cause of this must be, that the House of Lords possessed large property, and that the Chamber of Peers was possessed of none. If the seat of the evil was that the peers were without property, this might be cured by giving them property; but it is part of the lot of man that he cannot give what he has not got. The Bourbons, nevertheless, determined to do all they could; and it was enacted that *majorats*, or entails, might be created in the families of peers, and that the peerage should not in future descend to the son of the possessor, unless there had first been created in favour of the son, a *majorat* of a prescribed amount. But to require a

[7]Duc Etienne Denis Pasquier (1767-1862) held high office under Napoleon, Louis XVIII, and Louis Philippe. Napoleon made him a baron; Louis Philippe made him a duke as well as President of the Chamber of Peers.

[8]Joseph Louis Joachim, vicomte Lainé (1767-1835), supporter of Napoleon, then of the Restoration, who, dismayed by the policies of Charles X, supported Louis Philippe in 1830. Joseph Marie, comte Portalis (1778-1858), lawyer, a moderate during the Revolution, held both diplomatic and administrative office under Napoleon and under Louis XVIII, who made him a peer in 1819. Joseph Jérôme, comte Siméon (1749-1842), lawyer, opposed the Revolution and was exiled; he supported Napoleon, and then the Restoration, and was made a peer in 1821. Gabriel Gratet, vicomte Dubouchage (1777-1872), ultra-royalist, succeeded to the peerage in 1823 and became notorious for his right-wing opposition, especially during the reign of Louis Philippe. Louis Mathieu, comte Molé (1781-1855), a moderate royalist, prefect and judge under Napoleon, was made a peer in 1815, and a minister in 1817, but then went into opposition; appointed Minister of Foreign Affairs by Louis Philippe, he had resigned on 2 Nov., 1830.

[9]Anthony Ashley Cooper, 1st Earl of Shaftesbury (1621-83), after a varied career, but usually supporting Cromwell, became a member of the notorious Cabal during the Stuart Restoration. Although constantly involved in intrigue and strife, he was a staunch supporter of the supremacy of Parliament and of religious toleration.

[10]Adapted from Napoleon's characterization of the Bourbons: "ils *n'ont rien oublié ni rien appris*" (see No. 44, n4).

man to transmit to his descendants what he never had, did not seem a very efficacious contrivance for enriching the family. The tarif, therefore, of the peerage, was perforce adapted to the actual fortunes of the peers; and as these did not on the average exceed what would be considered in England a moderate provision for clerks in a public office, the endowment of a baron was fixed at four hundred pounds a-year, and those of the higher grades of nobility in a corresponding proportion.[11] Being now the assured possessors of incomes upon this scale, the peers, it seems to have been supposed, had no longer to fear any want of importance arising from want of wealth. Such was the clumsiness of the original work, and such the clumsy attempt to mend it; but any other remedial application would equally have failed to give life or reality to an institution radically incompatible with the circumstances of France, and of which nothing can ever exist in that country except the forms and the name.

The great error was the original error, of imagining that law-makers are like God, who can create matter as well as arrange it and mould it into form. This extent of power is not conceded to man: he cannot create something out of nothing. It is easy to make the charter of a country assert that an aristocracy exists, but that will not make it exist, if materials are not contained in the country for forming one: the maxim holds equally good of governments and of coats, that they must be cut according to your cloth. There do not exist in France any enormously wealthy families. There exist a large number of persons of moderate wealth. By clubbing these together, you might form a tolerably compact basis for an oligarchical representation, but you are merely ridiculous when you single out a few hundred at random, and affect to call them by the name of peers. The moment when, by adopting the hereditary principle, you give yourself only the ordinary chances of meeting with personal merit, there is not the slightest reason why any three hundred whom you encounter in the street should not have been taken instead of those whom you now have.

It is considered desirable, in France, and in most other countries, that there should exist a second legislative chamber, less democratically constituted than the first, in order that it may be less liable to be acted upon by temporary excitement; strong enough to withstand sudden and hasty impulses of the lower house, but not to resist its deliberate and mature conviction, supported by the public voice. Considered as a general principle of politics, it does not belong to us either to enforce or to combat this maxim: it is sufficient that such are the grounds upon which the institution of a house of peers is commonly defended. Now, in contriving means for this end, it must never be lost sight of, that, in a government which is really, and not nominally representative, the body which

---

[11]Bull. 171, No. 2686 (25 Aug., 1817), required a duke to settle 30,000 francs on his heir, a count 20,000 francs, and a baron 10,000 francs; in 1824 circumstances forced the requirements to be halved (Bull. 688, No. 17462 [10 Feb., 1824]).

the upper house is intended to check is one in which the public will, of necessity, have almost unlimited confidence. It will generally comprise the men of whose talents and of whose integrity the people at large entertain the highest opinion; and the people, moreover, feel the full assurance at each instant, that, if they should see reason to alter their favourable opinion, they will have an opportunity of getting rid of the individual before he has time to betray his trust. Unless, therefore, the upper house shall also possess a moral ascendancy, capable, upon occasion, of counteracting and counterbalancing that of the lower, it will, if new, only be suffered to exist on condition of being absolutely inoperative; although, if old, it might be borne with, as so many other things are borne with, for the toleration of which their age is the only reason.

In order to possess this ascendancy, it must conform to the conditions to which the attainment of moral influence is subject in France. Now, respect is not transmitted from father to son, in France, like an heir-loom. Wealth, by the laws of all countries, is hereditary, and, therefore, where the grand source of respect is wealth, respect also descends in the hereditary line. Where the main source of respect is ancestry, respect is, of course, hereditary. But, in France, wealth is not what confers respect, because it never was what conferred political power; and the respect for ancestry, along with its power in the state, foundered in the storms of the revolution. No nation so utterly despises hereditary distinctions. On the other hand, no people, perhaps, ever set a greater value upon personal ones. Yet, instead of endeavouring to accumulate in the upper chamber the greatest amount of personal distinction possible, the Bourbons, in a spirit of blind imitation, founded it upon a hereditary distinction; and, to complete its insignificance, dubbed its members by the titles of the old *noblesse*, titles so contemned, that perhaps a majority of those who have inherited them, are ashamed to wear them.

If the idea of a peerage necessarily implies hereditary descent, call it a senate: but of this be sure, that it will be efficacious for the purposes for which it is defensible if for any, exactly in proportion as it can be made to consist exclusively of men of established and high reputation. A writer in the *Edinburgh Review* appears to us to misunderstand the matter, when he is afraid that the senators/will generally be the tools of the court, in the hope of being rewarded with the fee-simple of their peerage.[12] It has never been observed that the marshals of France, or our knights of the garter, however able to serve the court, or however willing to do it for hire, have claimed as wages that their *bâton* or their ribbon should descend to their heirs; and this for an obvious reason, that it is easy to bribe them in ways which would excite far less of popular odium. When the chances of birth no longer introduce into the upper chamber, in spite of the

[12]"The Late Revolution in France," *Edinburgh Review*, LII (Oct. 1830), 14-15, by Henry Peter, Lord Brougham (1788-1868), legal reformer, jurist, political leader, and prolific writer.

greatest purity in the new appointments, a majority of the feeble or of the disreputable, it will evidently be far more difficult than now, for the creator of peers to agglomerate other such particles to the same body. But the objection is not only mistaken in principle, it is also singularly inapplicable in point of fact, since it is generally agreed, in France, that the royal prerogative of creating peers,[13] so grossly abused on more than one occasion by the Bourbons, must be subjected to great restrictions, if not entirely done away. More interesting questions having hitherto engrossed the public mind, specific plans have not as yet been suggested for the composition of the senate, but the qualification will probably be that of having served for a given number of years in certain offices, or been re-elected deputy a given number of times; or any other mark which may seem, on consideration, more certainly indicative of the confirmed good opinion of the people.

––––––––––

We have now accomplished our task. The design of these papers was to prepare the English public, or such part of it as might be pleased to listen to us, for the struggle which we knew was approaching between the new oligarchy and the people; to arm them against the misapprehensions, and strengthen them against the false alarms, which were sure to be industriously propagated, and which, in themselves, were not unnatural; to supply facts which we knew that the public were not likely to hear from any other quarter, and without which we are aware that they could not possibly understand the true character of the events which were coming. While we have been thus engaged, the contest has already begun; and all who read the daily newspapers must have seen enough to be convinced that our undertaking was not a useless one. Of the value of our opinions, others must judge, but to the correctness of our facts in every material circumstance, we are certain that any candid person will bear witness who takes the proper means of verifying them. And if, in the mean time, we have only assisted in making it known that France is a subject on which our newspapers, with their vapouring, are profoundly ignorant, and thoroughly to be distrusted, we have not laboured in vain.

S––––––.

[13] See the Charter of 1814, Art. 27.

62. FRENCH NEWS [4]
EXAMINER, 28 NOV., 1830, PP. 761-2

This article is headed "London, Nov. 27." For the entry in Mill's bibliography, see No. 55.

THE CHAMBER OF DEPUTIES having rejected the bill brought in by M. Benjamin Constant to exempt persons desirous of following the business of a printer from the necessity of obtaining a license from the Government,[1] M. Laffitte has declared that the ministers will take up the subject.

M. Laffitte has also introduced a bill for equalizing the pressure of certain taxes which at present press very unequally upon different parts of France.[2] The sentiments and views expressed in the speech with which M. Laffitte prefaced his motion, are generally liberal and enlightened.

With these exceptions, the new Ministry has given no indication of its being animated by a popular spirit; and, unless it is reserving itself for the great struggle which is approaching, on the election law,[3] it will find in a few weeks, that it has thrown away the popularity which is its only strength, to pay its court to an inept and ill-designing majority, who will give it no thanks for what they will consider with truth, as the effect of mere timidity and irresolution.

The retirement of Marshal Gérard from the war department, has modified, and, we regret to say, materially for the worse, the composition of the Ministry.[4] Marshal Soult, the new minister of war, has been, from the beginning of his career, the ready slave of any one who would employ him. He is indeed understood to have been chosen in deference to the general opinion of the army, that there was no other man equally fit for that particular post; but there is not the same excuse for the promotion of Sébastiani, a man almost equally destitute of political integrity, to the Foreign Department:[5] his place as Minister of Marine being supplied by d'Argout, a man fitter for the Guizot or even the Martignac Cabinet, than for a ministry of popular principles.[6]

[1]For details, see No. 60.
[2]For Laffitte's speech of 15 Nov. introducing the bill, see *Moniteur*, 1830, pp. 1475-6; the bill, amended, was enacted as Bull. 29, No. 96 (26 Mar., 1831).
[3]For the initiation of the measure, see No. 58.
[4]Comte Maurice Etienne Gérard (1773-1852), a deputy from 1827, popular minister in the Provisional Government and under Louis Philippe, had to retire because of ill-health, and a slight reshuffling in the administration resulted.
[5]Comte François Horace Bastien Sébastiani (1772-1851), one of Napoleon's generals, was an opposition deputy after 1819. In favour of a dynastic change, he was given the Ministry of Marine in August 1830, and that of Foreign Affairs in November 1830.
[6]Apollinaire Antoine Maurice, comte d'Argout (1782-1858), had served Napoleon and the Bourbons and been made a peer in 1819.

Meanwhile, the Chamber never lets an occasion slip for displaying its anti-popular spirit; and we see no chance that even a moderate and insufficient reform of the law of elections will be conceded to any thing less than intimidation.

Prosecutions multiply against the popular press. M. Guizot, in a recent speech, attempted to draw a distinction between the old-established papers and the new ones, and complimented the former on their comparative moderation;[7] but M. Persil,[8] procureur général in the Cour Royale, an obscure provincial advocate who was selected as successor to M. Bernard of Rennes,[9] when the latter refused to become an instrument in persecuting the press, has now instituted a prosecution against a newspaper of the class which M. Guizot exculpated, the *Journal du Commerce*.[10]

In our next paper we shall make some observations on the ill-advised prosecution of M. de Kergorlay, for his protest against the change of dynasty.[11] For the present, we recommend to the reader's attention, on this subject, the observations of a writer whom we seldom have occasion to commend, O.P.Q., of the *Chronicle*.[12]

The change of Ministry in England[13] has given the greatest satisfaction in France, being considered a pledge of the pacific character of our foreign policy.

63. THE BALLOT
EXAMINER, 5 DEC., 1830, P. 769

Mill here continues his general argument in favour of the secret ballot, replying to a leading article in the *Standard*, 30 Nov., 1830, p. 2, which responded to his assertion in

[7]Speech on the Press (8 Nov.), *Moniteur*, 1830, pp. 1425-6.

[8]Jean Charles Persil (1785-1870), a liberal lawyer, had defended individuals against government prosecution before July 1830, but thereafter became reactionary.

[9]Louis Rose Désiré Bernard (1788-1858), called Bernard de Rennes, a deputy from 1830, had defended the *Journal du Commerce* when it was prosecuted during the Polignac ministry. He had been appointed procureur général, but later chose to transfer to the Court of Appeal.

[10]A generally liberal journal (1794-1848) that changed its name several times.

[11]Mill did not return to this question. Louis Florian Paul, comte de Kergorlay (1769-1856), was an ultra-royalist deputy from 1815 to 1816 and 1820 to 1823, when he became a peer. On 23 Sept., 1830, he wrote a letter to the President of the Chamber of Peers against the new government, printed in the *Quotidienne*, 25 Sept., p. 6. He was tried by the Chamber of Peers and sentenced to six months in prison and a 500-franc fine.

[12]"O.P.Q." was the Rev. Caleb Charles Colton (1780?-1832), a frequent contributor to the *Morning Chronicle* over this signature. See his "France. Important Trial before the Chamber of Peers of Count Kergorlay, Ex-Peer of France, for a Political Libel," *Morning Chronicle*, 26 Nov., 1830, pp. 1-2.

[13]On 16 Nov. the Duke of Wellington had resigned.

No. 60. For further discussion, see No. 65. This item is the first article in the "Political Examiner," headed as title, and described in Mill's bibliography as "The first twelve paragraphs of a leading article on the Ballot, in the Examiner of 5th December 1830" (MacMinn, p. 13). The continuation of the argument, directed against *The Times*, is presumably by Albany Fonblanque (1793-1872), the radical editor of the *Examiner*.

THE STANDARD has met our challenge of last Sunday, by noticing, we must say rather than answering, our argument respecting the Ballot. Its observations are evidently the result of so little consideration, that we advert to them only because, on a subject of such immense and rapidly-increasing importance, discussion can scarcely be carried too far; and also, because a return is due to the courtesy with which we have always been treated by our able contemporary.

Of that courtesy he has afforded us a new instance, in politely allowing to the substance of our observations on the Ballot, the name of an argument,—indeed, he calls it the first argument he ever heard in defence of the Ballot. Without impugning the truth of this assertion, we will make free to suggest, that if he has never before met with any argument for the Ballot, it very probably was because he did not give himself any great trouble to search for one. Indeed, what could be expected, if, as he now informs us, his opinion was predetermined by a consideration which renders all appeal to the merits of the case utterly superfluous. A sufficient objection to the Ballot, in his mind, he says, was its novelty. It has never been tried before, in a like case. And if its never *having* been tried, is a reason why it never *should*, this is a difficulty which is not likely to be soon got over.

On this objection it may be remarked, that if it avail against the Ballot, it would have held equally against steam-coaches.[1] Steam may be an excellent thing in a manufactory, but when was it ever tried in a *like case*?

We need not seriously controvert the proposition, that the plainest dictates of reason are not worthy to be attended to when they recommend any thing which is *new*; nor need we ask, what improvement is there which may not be called an untried one, if that which is tried in private societies within every one's knowledge, and in the political constitution of the only two great or intellectual countries which possess a constitution besides ourselves, is to be set aside without even an examination, on this curious plea.

But these experiments, it seems, are not *like cases*. Does the *Standard* then, really suppose that a political institution was *ever* tried in a *like case*? No two cases in history are alike. This is a logic, by which all reasoning from experience would be rendered impossible. The *Standard* declares itself favourable to a plan of Parliamentary reform which shall restore our old, and therefore, we presume, our *tried* institutions. But does the *Standard* suppose that the state of England when these institutions existed, constitutes a *like case* to the state of England at the present moment? If that be our contemporary's real opinion, we should not

[1]On 15 Sept. the Manchester-Liverpool railway line had opened.

despair of persuading him that any two cases which ever were mentioned together, are like cases.

The *Standard* has very candidly extracted from our columns the passage of Mr. Mill's *History of British India*, from which our argument was drawn;[2] and by the additional publicity which it has given to this passage, it has, we feel assured, done more good to the cause of the Ballot, than it can do harm by such a refutation as it has attempted, though repeated ten times over.

Mr. Mill's proposition, it will be recollected, was this—that the Ballot is bad, where the voter's own interest points in a wrong direction, and where the restraint which public opinion imposes, is indispensable as a check to that interest. But if the voter's own interest accords with the public good, as it must do when the public themselves are the voters, this restraint is not necessary; and the Ballot, consequently, is desirable as often as the voters are liable to be acted upon, either in the way of bribery or intimidation, by the interests of powerful individuals.

On this the *Standard* remarks, that it is not interest, but passion, which, in all save extreme cases, determines the public conduct of the mass. By passion must here be meant, feelings of violent liking or dislike, independent of any calm consideration of the consequences of the vote either to the voter himself or to others.

If it be true that his vote, supposing it to be known to nobody, would be given not from reflection, but from passion, it seems to us, we confess, a singular mode of keeping passion under controul, to make him vote in the face of a multitude, actuated, as is assumed in the supposition, by the very same violent passion.

But this is losing sight of the true question. All the effect which can follow, or is affirmed to follow from the Ballot, is, that the vote will be given to the candidate whom the voter sincerely prefers. A degree of perfection greater than this, it is not possible to attain by any contrivance of polls or ballot-boxes. If it be impossible to constitute any body of electors but such as will sincerely prefer the wrong man, there is an end to all rational attempts at a representative government. But nobody asserts this; and the only question is, what portion of the community, if allowed to chuse the man whom it prefers, is most likely to chuse the right man. Sincere and upright persons may differ on this point; but we should not have imagined that there could have been any difference of opinion respecting the propriety of taking the suffrages in such a manner, that those who you have determined ought to be the chusers, shall *really* be the chusers; and that the power which you have pretended to give to them shall not, through the medium of a system of immorality disgraceful to human nature, be really exercised by a petty oligarchy, on whom nobody would have the face to propose conferring the same power directly and avowedly.

[2]The passage had been quoted by Mill in No. 60.

As for *passion*, as long as men are ill-educated, they will sometimes be too strongly excited to attend to their true interest. But we are apt to think that the passions of men whose interest is right, are less dangerous than the passions of men whose interest is wrong. Amidst all this exaggeration respecting passion, the real fact is, that the passions which extend to entire nations, not collected together in mobs, but insulated in their own homes, are almost invariably, in the present state of civilization, generous and amiable ones. The danger in the present condition of society is not from passion, but from selfish calculation of worldly interest. The universal cry periodically raised, from John o'Groat's House to the Land's End, for the abolition of slavery, is a specimen of popular passion, such as our own day exhibits: humane and disinterested in its ends, and consenting to appear impatient and inconsiderate only because it knows that the assemblies to which it addresses itself possess coolness sufficient to temper the ardour of the hottest enthusiasm.

It is no doubt true that many voters do not, and would not, give their votes upon a judgment of particular public measures, on which they very often are not, and know that they are not, capable of forming a correct opinion. But if they have no private ends of their own to serve, and cannot be made instruments against their conscience for serving the private ends of other people, they will in general vote for the person whom they think most honest, and most capable of judging correctly. And in this they will seldom be mistaken, unless from blind deference to their superiors in rank and education; for, except where they have learned, by bitter experience, that the higher classes have the most miserably petty personal object more at heart than their physical and moral well-being, the fault of the multitude has never been distrust of the rich, but too habitual and implicit a confidence in them.

64. FRENCH NEWS [5]
EXAMINER, 5 DEC., 1830, P. 771

This article is headed "London, Dec. 4." For the entry in Mill's bibliography, see No. 55.

M. LAFFITTE HAS ANNOUNCED to the Chamber of Deputies that he expects to be enabled to present to the Chamber, in the course of the week which will have expired when our paper is published, the financial laws of most immediate urgency, together with a municipal law, and an election law.[1]

---

[1]On 26 Nov. Laffitte proposed to the Deputies (*Moniteur*, 1830, p. 1572) measures to provide a temporary budget that were realized in Bull. 15, No. 79 (12 Dec., 1830), and Bull. 18, No. 83 (5 Jan., 1831). For details on the municipal law, see No. 57, n10. For the previous speculations about electoral reforms, see No. 58; for an outline of the provisions eventually enacted, see No. 72.

Nothing is yet known of the character of the intended municipal law; but the election law, we lament to say, is expected to fall far short of even the very moderate parliamentary reform which we announced a short time ago as being under the contemplation of the French ministry. The electoral qualification, it is now said, will be reduced, not from 300 to 200 francs of direct taxation, but from 300 to 250; and additional electors will be admitted at a lower rate of contribution, in sufficient number to make up, not one elector for every hundred, but one for every two hundred inhabitants. To these will be added, free from any pecuniary conditions, the liberal professions composing the second part of the jury list. The total number of electors will, by this arrangement, be raised, it is supposed, to about 200,000, so that the ratio of the amount of the taxes to the number of the electors will not be three hundred pounds sterling per man, as at present, but about 150*l.* The qualification for eligibility will be lowered from 1000 to 500 francs.

If this be the real scheme of the Ministry, it is a pitiful attempt to compromise with the majority of the Chamber. Why does not M. Laffitte propose a law of election really adequate to produce a good government, instead of the monied oligarchy contemplated by the *hommes du lendemain,*—and leave to the Chamber the entire discredit of making the law a bad one by its amendments? But we expected nothing better when we found that M. de Montalivet was preferred to M. Odilon-Barrot for the most important department of the ministry.[2] There could be no sufficient reason for rejecting M. Odilon-Barrot, excepting that he was thought to be too good for the purposes which it was intended that the ministry should subserve.

We are informed, and the fact is too probable not to be easily credited, that the disgust occasioned by the acts and evident purposes of the men who have got the powers of government into their hands, has resuscitated the republican party. The elevation of Louis Philippe to the throne without first calling together a Congress like that of Belgium,[3] and remodelling the Constitution, has long been regretted; but those who regret that a King and a Court were re-established at all, form, we are assured, a numerous and growing body.

For the present, the national mind seems to be nearly engrossed by exaggerated rumours of warlike intentions on the part of the great continental powers. The French are aware of the power they possess in the sympathies of the people throughout the continent, and the first gun fired should be the signal for the proclamation of federation with the oppressed of the hostile nations.

We shall direct the peculiar attention of our readers to the proposed municipal law, when it makes its appearance.

[2]For details, see No. 55.
[3]For details, see No. 59, n5.

65. CONTROVERSY ON THE BALLOT

EXAMINER, 12 DEC., 1830, PP. 786-7

This article, continuing the discussion in Nos. 60 and 63, responds to the *Standard*, 30 Nov., p. 2, and 8 Dec., p. 2, from the latter of which Mill quotes. The promised reply by the *Standard*, incorporating No. 63, that is referred to by Mill in the opening sentence, actually appeared on 11 Dec., but presumably after this article was completed. This leading article, in the "Political Examiner," is headed as title and described in Mill's bibliography as "An article headed 'Controversy on the Ballot' in the Examiner of 12th December 1830" (MacMinn, p. 13).

THE STANDARD has promised a complete reply to our article of last Sunday, on the Ballot, when it shall have room to re-print the article itself. This mode of carrying on an important controversy reflects credit upon our contemporary's fairness, and is, we confess, very much to our taste. The *Standard* will, we know, readily believe that nothing but the limited space which is at the command of a weekly newspaper, prevents us from affording a similar proof of our regard for truth, by inserting in our columns such of his articles as we think it useful to controvert. They have sufficient claim to such a place on the score of their intrinsic merits. Powers of vigorous thought, however ill disciplined, or however misapplied, scarcely ever run so completely to waste as not to propagate and call forth similar powers in some, at least, of the minds with which they may come in contact.

The *Standard* now affirms, that the Ballot does not ensure secrecy; of this it attempts no proof, except an assertion, that, in the United States, every man's vote is known. There is something, to us, very ridiculous in these appeals from the experience of the human race to the assumed experience of a single country, which not one of the persons so appealing has the assurance to pretend that he knows any thing about. In America, the Ballot may very possibly be an unnecessary protection; for no voter is in a state of dependence, the voters are too numerous to be bribed, and the candidates not in circumstances to bribe. Moreover, the Ballot, in America, may be a mere sham, as at the India House.[1] But when there is a real Ballot, to say that the votes can be known, is a manifest absurdity. The vote can never be known, unless the voter has it in his power to

---

[1]Each year six of the twenty-four Directors of the East India Company retired, and could not be re-elected for one year. But the Chairman drew up a "House List" of recommended candidates, consisting of the names of the six who had retired the previous year; this list was signed by the directors in office and mailed to the members of the Court of Proprietors, who almost invariably balloted for the House List. Consequently thirty Directors were practically assured of life tenure.

shew it. The voter may *tell* it; but his telling it when nobody can ever know whether he tells the truth, will not cause it to be known. Ballot or no ballot, a man's vote may be *surmised* by those who are acquainted with his political opinions; but the *Standard* cannot suppose that any one would be so silly as either to bribe an elector, or lose a respectable tenant on a mere surmise.

After all that has been said, the *Standard* seems even now utterly unable to seize the distinction between the case wherein the ballot is a safeguard to the honest, and that in which it is a cloak to the knave. He cannot even yet see, that the temptation sometimes comes from the interests of people who can influence the voter, and sometimes from the voter's own interests: that in the first case the ballot puts an end to the temptation, while in the second it removes only the restraints. Our contemporary persists in saying, that if the elector needs the ballot to protect him against his landlord, the representative must equally stand in need of it, to remove him from the control of the minister. As if the sovereign body could need protection against the creature of its own will; as if the minister had any means of controlling the legislature, but what the legislature gives him; as if there were any body who does not know that a ministry exists not by commanding the two houses of parliament, but by obeying them. These constitutional fictions belong to a time which is past. Kings and ministers once dictated to the parliament and to the parliament-makers, but have long since sunk down into the humbler office of carving for them.

There is a passage in a late article of the *Standard*, which we cannot let pass without severer reprobation. After accusing the reformers of attaching little comparative importance to bribery, as contrasted with the influence which is exercised by the threat of turning men out of house and home, our contemporary permits himself to say,

At present when it is known that the electors at such places as Stamford can be bought at two or three guineas a-head, it is the duty of the landlord to dispossess all who have proved their corruption by voting against the legitimate influence of a community of political sentiment, and of that interchange of kindnesses which always obtains between a good landlord and his tenants.

We scarcely remember another equally remarkable instance of the doctrines which men will permit themselves to avow respecting their fellow-creatures, when they have unhappily become entangled in a bad cause, and have not manliness or resolution to extricate themselves from it. Here we have it deliberately declared that every tenant who votes in opposition to the will of his landlord, must do so from the motive of bribery, and ought to be treated by other people as if it were legally proved that he had been bribed; and this whatever be the Lord's behest, and whether he be whig, tory, or radical: and such is the undistinguishing sweep of this morality, that the tenants of Lord Radnor or of Sir

Francis Burdett,[2] just as much as those of the Duke of Newcastle,[3] are not only bound to vote as the landlord commands, but are so utterly in the condition of cattle, so incapable of a political opinion, a public sympathy, or even a preference of one man over another, that no possible interpretation can be put upon their disobedience to the lordly mandate, except that they have been bribed in actual money—always providing that the superior whom they have failed to obey, is a good landlord, *judice* the landlord himself.

We make no comment on this doctrine. We leave it to the judgment of its author, who, we have no doubt, in his cooler moments, will recoil from it. But it is a grievous misfortune to be hampered with a Duke of Newcastle, and obliged to prove that his black is white.

66. FRENCH NEWS [6]
EXAMINER, 12 DEC., 1830, P. 795

This article is headed "London, Dec. 11." For the entry in Mill's bibliography, see No. 55. The article concludes with a paragraph of Swiss news, presumably not by Mill.

THE FRENCH MINISTRY has not yet produced the expected municipal and election laws, but M. Dupont de l'Eure has introduced a Bill reducing the number of the Judges in each Court of Assize (as the principal Courts of Justice are called) from five to three.[1] This is a most important improvement, and a step towards getting rid of those multitudinous judicatories which destroy individual responsibility, and neutralize one able judge by associating him with a crowd of feeble or inexperienced colleagues, who either do nothing or worse.

The clergy of all Christian persuasions existing in France, already received

---

[2]William Pleydell Bouverie, 3rd Earl Radnor (1779-1869), a Whig politician of advanced ideas, was M.P. from 1801 until he went to the Lords in 1828. Francis Burdett (1770-1844), a radical and well-known advocate of Parliamentary (and other) reform since 1797, was M.P. for Westminster, 1807-37; he had originally entered Parliament in the Newcastle interest.

[3]Henry Clinton, 4th Duke of Newcastle, had just (3 Dec.) made his famous reply when questioned about his ejection of tenants for voting against his interest, "Is it not lawful for me to do what I please with mine own?" (*PD*, 3rd ser., Vol. I, col. 751). The phrase originates in Matthew, 20:15.

---

[1]The bill passed the Chamber of Deputies by a vote of 186 to 122 on 11 Jan., after four days of discussion, and was enacted as Bull. 21, No. 86 (4 Mar., 1831). Mill is referring to Art. 1.

salaries from the Government: the Chamber of Deputies has just passed a Bill extending the same provision to the ministers of the Jewish worship.[2]

67. THE TRUCK SYSTEM [1]
EXAMINER, 19 DEC., 1830, P. 803

This article comments on the debate in the House of Commons on the Truck System (14 Dec., 1830; *PD*, 3rd ser., Vol. 1, cols. 1133-82) occasioned by the request for leave to introduce "A Bill to Consolidate and Amend the Laws Prohibiting the Payment of Wages in Goods," 1 William IV (16 Dec., 1830), *PP*, 1830-31, II, 559-71. It was brought in by Edward John Littleton (1791-1863), 1st Baron Hatherton, reforming M.P. from 1812 until he entered the Lords in 1835. His bill was enacted as 1 & 2 William IV, c. 37 (1831). For further discussion, see No. 70. This leading article, in the "Political Examiner," headed as title, is described in Mill's bibliography as "An article headed 'Truck System' in the Examiner of 19th December 1830" (MacMinn, p. 13).

ALL MANKIND have long known what an English Parliament is capable of when it means ill. If the debate of Tuesday last is to be regarded as a specimen of what it can accomplish when it means well, we know not what prayer remains for us to put up, unless for a speedy deliverance from it.

It is melancholy to see the immense subject of the condition of the working classes paltered with by miserable trifling. Would not any one suppose, from the speeches in the House of Commons on Tuesday, that what makes the labouring population miserable is, not low wages, but the medium in which wages are paid. Parliament is so wise as to believe, that the labourer will receive a larger remuneration, if prevented from receiving it in the shape in which it is most convenient to the master to give it. Mr. Hume (certainly no enemy to the working people) pointed out the absurdity of this;[1] but nobody, not one man, had sufficient foresight to perceive that Mr. Littleton's bill will infallibly lower wages, instead of raising them.

The object of the bill is to compel the payment of wages in money. Now, money is a portion of the national wealth, which costs much, but produces nothing. It administers to no man's wants. No labourer can subsist upon it, or use it as tools or materials for production. Whatever, therefore, enables the business of the country to be done with less money, increases its productive resources. By being enabled to dispense with the use of money, the employers of labour are enabled to render the whole of their capital available for production—to hire productive labourers to the full amount of their means. But if this bill passes,

---

[2]Bull. 20, No. 85 (10 Feb., 1831).

---

[1]*PD*, 3rd ser., Vol. 1, cols. 1139-52, esp. 1140.

they will be obliged to withdraw a part of their capital from productive employment; to turn off part of their labourers; and what would have been paid to those labourers, if allowed to be paid in the form of goods, they will be obliged to export, for the purpose of merely procuring a circulating medium, wherewith to pay the wages of the remainder of their labourers.

Thus there will be less real means of employment for labourers than before; and the existing poverty of the working people will be aggravated.

Lord Althorp, from whom we expected better things, said, that he would be against interference between employer and workman, if the contract were a free one on the labourer's side; but that it is not so, for the employer can dictate terms to the labourer.[2] But why can the employer dictate terms to the labourer? Only because there is another labourer standing by unemployed, who will accept the terms if his fellow-labourer refuses them. This is what gives the employer undue power; and undue power he will have, so long as there is a greater number of labourers than can find employment. So long as this is the case, the labourer *must* accept any terms which are preferable to the parish allowance; and is it really supposed that the matter will be mended, by declaring that his hard lot shall only be dealt out to him in one particular way? If the laws of Parliament could get the better of the laws of nature, why not fix a minimum of wages; that would, at least, be facing the difficulty boldly. But our legislation resembles a cottage-window in Ireland, with three of the four panes of glass entirely out, and a rag carefully stuffed in to close a trifling breach in the only remaining one.

Then it is asserted that the labourer is dependant by being in his employer's debt; and it is consequently proposed, for the labourer's good, to deprive the employer of any legal means of recovering wages paid in advance. This amounts to neither more nor less than enacting a law, that if a working man is in temporary distress, he shall either go upon the parish or starve. Such is the upshot of all this humanity and philanthropy.

The *Globe* had, on Thursday, an excellent article on this question, which we gladly recommend to universal attention.[3] This is one of a class of subjects which the Editor of that paper has always understood better than any other of our journalists. The speeches of Mr. Hume and of Mr. Hyde Villiers are worth reading.[4]

---

[2]*Ibid.*, col. 1165. John Charles Spencer (1782-1845), Viscount Althorp, M.P. from 1804 until he went to the Lords in 1834 as 3rd Earl Spencer. In November 1830 he had become Chancellor of the Exchequer and leader of the House of Commons in Earl Grey's ministry.

[3]Leading article, *Globe and Traveller*, 16 Dec., 1830, p. 2.

[4]Thomas Hyde Villiers (1801-32), a member of the London Debating Society of which Mill had been the moving spirit, was an M.P. from 1826 until his death (see No. 189). For his speech on the truck system, see *PD*, 3rd ser., Vol. 1, cols. 1159-63.

68. FRENCH NEWS [7]

EXAMINER, 19 DEC., 1830, P. 809

The article is headed "London, Dec. 19." For the entry in Mill's bibliography, see No. 55. The article concludes with a paragraph on Belgian and Swiss news, presumably not by Mill.

THE DEATH OF BENJAMIN CONSTANT is a misfortune to the world.[1] France, since the first revolution, has not produced his equal, taking into account purity of purpose, popular principles, and talents as an orator and politician. His absence leaves a deplorable *hiatus* in the Chamber, which now contains scarcely a man of established reputation and mature years, joined to opinions in harmony with those of the vast majority of Frenchmen between twenty and thirty-five. His health had been for some time declining; but there is no doubt that his death has been hastened by feelings of grievous disappointment at finding France, at the end of four months, from the three days of July last, only at the commencement of, perhaps, a longer and more arduous struggle than that which she appeared to have brought to so glorious and triumphant a consummation. There is reason to fear that the bitterness of these reflections was aggravated by the thought that greater exertions and a more decided tone, on the part of himself and a few others in August last, might have given, perhaps, a materially different character to the settlement of the Constitution.

We are assured that this lamented patriot, almost with his last breath, expressed to the friends who encircled his death-bed, the regret which he felt, while dying, that the revolution of July was *manquée*, and had fallen into the hands of *intrigans*.

His house was surrounded by crowds, similar to those which were congregated round the habitation of Mirabeau in his last moments.

The principal subjects of discussion, in the Chambers, for some time past, have been the organization of the National Guard, and the arrangements for putting the army on the war establishment.[2] As is usually the case, when a nation is what it calls "prepared for war," the French seem to desire nothing so much as an opportunity for convincing their neighbours how well prepared they are. A month ago they were as quiet, as could reasonably be required, on the affairs of Belgium; but now the insurrection in Poland[3] has kindled them into a perfect

[1]Benjamin Constant died on 8 Dec.; crowds of enthusiastic mourners threatened the public peace at his funeral on the 12th (see *Moniteur*, 1830, pp. 1664, 1665, 1689, and 1699).

[2]For identification of the law on the National Guard, see No. 54, n16; Bull. 15, No. 78 (11 Dec., 1830) increased the numbers in the army by 80,000.

[3]The Treaty of Vienna had not ended the partition of Poland among Prussia, Austria, and Russia (Mill's "three Robber-powers"). On 29 Nov., 1830, rioting against Russian domination had broken out in Warsaw.

flame; so great is the difference in the feelings, either of a man or of a nation, according as their red coat is on or off. We have been shocked and disgusted by the language of the leading French papers on the subject of the Polish revolution. The principle of non-intervention, on which they insisted so strongly a few weeks ago, is now scattered to the winds. If a war, unhappily for France and Europe, were shortly to break out, though undertaken by that country, as it probably would be, for no selfish object, we greatly fear that, under its influence, in less than a twelvemonth, the national character would again be perverted, as it was by Napoleon,—the rage for victory and conquest would become again the dominant passion in the breasts of Frenchmen; and the national feeling once turned in that direction, we know the barefaced profligacy, the systematic and unheard-of disregard of every principle of international morality, and of the most sacred rights of independent nations, which made the foreign policy of the directory, and of the empire, a disgrace to civilisation. *That* war began with as much purity of purpose, on the part of the French nation, as the present one will do, if the French government accepts the invitation; which, while we now write, is probably under its consideration, to assist the Poles against the three Robber-powers.

The trial of the Ex-Ministers has commenced.—It is expected that Polignac, and, perhaps, Peyronnet, will be sentenced to death; Chantelauze and Guernon-Ranville to some other punishment.[4] If Peyronnet be put to death, and Chantelauze spared, it will be from other causes than any which will appear on the proceedings; for it is proved, that Peyronnet was averse to the issue of the ordinances, and that Chantelauze was not.

The municipal and election laws are still delayed, but the Ministry has promised speedily to introduce a Bill for the elementary education of the People.[5]

M. Isambert laid a proposition before the Chamber, for reducing the Catholic Church Establishment to the standard of 1802;[6] but this was rejected, without even a public discussion, by virtue of the mischievous regulation which requires that every proposition must be approved by the whole, or a certain portion of the Chamber sitting in *bureaux* or committees, and deliberating in secret, before it can be even read, much less discussed, at the public sittings of the Chamber.[7]

---

[4]See No. 52.

[5]See No. 81.

[6]That is, to the status (to which the Vatican objected) enacted in Bull. 172, No. 1344 (5 Apr., 1802), the result of the Concordat between Napoleon and the Pope of 15 July, 1801.

[7]See Art. 32 of Règlement pour la chambre des députés des départemens (25 June), *Moniteur*, 1814, pp. 711-12. The provision that three of nine bureaus were needed to sanction a measure was provided by Modification au règlement de la chambre (24 Aug.), *ibid.*, 1830, pp. 961-2.

69. THE LABOURING AGRICULTURISTS
EXAMINER, 19 DEC., 1830, PP. 811-12

This article, prompted by the publication of Nassau William Senior's *Three Lectures on the Rate of Wages* (London: Murray, 1830), consists mostly of an extract from that work. Senior (1790-1864), an active member of the Political Economy Club, in 1825 had become the first incumbent of the chair of Political Economy at Oxford (succeeded in 1829 by Whately). The "Poor Laws" in effect at the time of this article went back to 43 Elizabeth I, c. 2 (1601), and included the law of settlement, 13 & 14 Charles II, c. 12 (1662), and the workhouse law, 9 George I, c. 7 (1722). Senior, a member of the Poor Law Commission, wrote its report, which resulted in the famous reform of 1834. This article, headed as title, is described in Mill's bibliography as "An article headed 'The labouring Agriculturists' in the Examiner of the same date [as "The Truck System," No. 67]" (MacMinn, p. 13).

MR. SENIOR, lately Professor of Political Economy at Oxford, has just published three lectures on the Rate of Wages, delivered before that University a few months ago, with the addition of a preface on the Causes and Remedies of the present Disturbances. The preface in particular appears to us calculated to produce the most salutary effects at the present crisis. We extract the following important passage, the doctrines and sentiments of which have our fullest concurrence:

The poor-laws, as administered in the southern districts of England,[1] are an attempt to unite the irreconcilable advantages of freedom and servitude. The labourer is to be a free agent, but without the hazards of free agency; to be free from the coercion, but to enjoy the assured subsistence of the slave. He is expected to be diligent, though he has no fear of want; provident, though his pay rises as his family increases; attached to a master who employs him in pursuance of a vestry resolution; and grateful for the allowance which the magistrates order him as a right.

In the natural state of the relation between the capitalist and the labourer, when the amount of wages to be paid, and of work to be done, are the subjects of a free and open bargain; when the labourer obtains, and knows that he is to obtain, just what his services are worth to his employer, he must feel any fall in the price of his labour to be an evil, but is not likely to complain of it as an injustice. Greater exertion and severer economy are his first resources in distress; and what they cannot supply he receives with gratitude from the benevolent. The connexion between him and his master has the kindliness of a voluntary association, in which each party is conscious of benefit, and each feels that his own welfare depends, to a certain extent, on the welfare of the other. But the instant wages cease to be a bargain—the instant the labourer is paid, not according to his *value*, but his *wants*, he ceases to be a freeman. He acquires the indolence, the improvidence, the rapacity, and the malignity, but not the subordination, of a slave. He is told that he has a

---

[1]Senior is referring to the Speenhamland system originated in 1795 in Berkshire, whereby the wages of poor labourers were indexed to the price of bread and subsidized from the rates.

right to wages, but that he is *bound* to work. Who is to decide how hard he ought to work, or how hard he does work? Who is to decide what amount of wages he has a *right* to? As yet, the decision has been made by the overseers and the magistrates. But they were interested parties. The labourer has thought fit to correct that decision. For the present he thinks that he has a *right* to 2s. 3d. a day in winter, and 2s. 6d. in summer. And our only hope seems to be, that the promise of such wages will bribe him into quiet. But who can doubt that he will measure his rights by his wishes, or that his wishes will extend with the prospect of their gratification? The present tide may not complete the inundation, but it will be a dreadful error if we mistake the ebb for a permanent receding of the waters. A breach has been made in the sea-wall, and with every succeeding irruption they will swell higher and spread more widely. What we are suffering is nothing to what we have to expect. Next year, perhaps, the labourer will think it *unjust* that he should have less than 4s. a day in winter and 5s. in summer;—and woe to the tyrants who deny him his *right*!

It is true, that such a right could not be permanently enforced;—it is true, that if the labourer burns the corn-ricks in which his subsistence for the current year is stored—if he consumes in idleness or in riot the time and the exertions on which next year's harvest depends—if he wastes in extravagant wages, or drives to foreign countries, the capital that is to assist and render productive his labour, *he* will be the greatest sufferer in the common ruin. Those who have property may escape with a portion of it to some country in which *their rights* will be protected; but the labourer must remain to enjoy his own works—to feel that the real rewards for plunder and devastation are want and disease.

But have the consequences of the present system ever been explained to the labourer? Is not his right to good wages re-echoed from all parts of the country? Is he not told— "Dwell in the land, and verily thou shalt be fed?" Does not the Hon. Member, who has affixed this motto to his work,[2] assume that the fund out of which the labourer is to be fed is practically inexhaustible? And can words more strongly imply that his sufferings arise from the *injustice* of his superiors? Have not even magistrates and landlords recommended the destruction, or, what is the same, both in principle and effect, the disuse of the very machines of which the object is to render labour more efficient in the production of the articles consumed by the labourer—in the production of that very fund on the extent of which, compared with the number to be maintained, the amount of wages depends? And is there any real difference between this conduct and the burning of a rick-yard? Threshing-machines are the present objects of hostility, ploughs will be the next; spades will then be found to diminish employment; and when it has been made penal to give advantage to labour by any tool or instrument whatever, the last step must be to prohibit the use of the right-hand.

Have sufficient pains been taken even to expose the absurdity of what appears so obvious to the populace—that the landlords ought to reduce their rents and the clergy their tithes, and then the farmer would give better wages? If the farmer had his land for nothing, still it would not be his interest to give any man more wages for a day's work than his day's work was worth. He could better *afford* it, no doubt, to be paid as a *tax*; but why should the farmer pay that tax more than the physician or the shopkeeper? If the farmer is to employ, at this advanced rate of wages, only whom he chooses, the distress will be increased, since he will employ only that smaller number whose labour is worth their increased pay. If he is to employ a certain proportion of the labourers, however numerous, in his parish, he is, in fact, to pay rent and tithes as before, with this difference only, that

[2]Michael Thomas Sadler (1780-1835), M.P., 1829-32, and social reformer, used this passage from Psalms, 37:3, on the title page of his *Ireland: Its Evils, and Their Remedies* (London: Murray, 1828).

they are to be paid to paupers, instead of to the landlord and the parson; and that the payment is not a fixed but an indefinite sum, and a sum which must every year increase in an accelerated ratio, as the increase of population rushes to fill up this new vacuum, till rent, tithes, profit, and capital, are all eaten up, and pauperism produces what may be called its natural effects—for they are the effects which, if unchecked, it must ultimately produce—famine, pestilence, and civil war.

That this country can preserve its prosperity, or even its social existence, if the state of feeling which I have described becomes universal among the lower classes, I think no one will be bold enough to maintain. That it is extensively prevalent, and that, under the present administration of the poor-laws, it will, at no remote period, become universal in the southern districts, appears to me to be equally clear. But who, in the present state of those districts, will venture to carry into execution a real and effectual alteration of the poor-laws? Remove, by emigration, the pauperism that now oppresses those districts, and such an alteration, though it may remain difficult, will cease to be impracticable.

Again, the corn-laws, by their tendency to raise the price of subsistence, by the ruin which they have inflicted on the internal corn-trade, and the stimulus which they have given to the increase of the agricultural population, have, without doubt, been amongst the causes of the present distress; and if, while the population of England and Wales continues to increase *at the rate of 500 persons a-day*, the introduction of foreign corn is subject, under ordinary prices, to a prohibitive duty, those laws will become every day more mischievous, and less remediable. But the repeal of those laws, however gradual (and only a gradual repeal can be thought of), would, under the present pressure of pauperism, tend to aggravate the agricultural distress. Lighten that pressure, and we may gradually revert to the only safe system—the system of freedom. [Pp. ix-xv.]

Mr. Senior then proceeds to argue, with great force and earnestness, in favour of systematic emigration, as the only feasible mode of removing the immediate pressure of pauperism, and rendering practicable the reform of those abuses in our legislation which have contributed to the growth of the evil. [Pp. xvi-xix.] And we join our voice to his in declaring that it is the most imperative among the duties of the legislation at the present crisis, to inquire and ascertain whether there be any mode of emigration by which our unemployed labourers might be removed from penury to comfort, without, by the same operation, withdrawing so much of our national wealth, as to diminish instead of increasing the wages of those labourers who remain behind. We believe that there is such a mode of emigration; and to this momentous subject, which *must* engage the attention of Parliament speedily and long, we shall return.[3]

70. THE TRUCK SYSTEM [2]
EXAMINER, 26 DEC., 1830, PP. 820-1

In response to a correspondent, "W.M.J.," whose letter is incorporated in the article, Mill here continues the argument of No. 67. The article, headed as title, is in the "Political Examiner," and is described in Mill's bibliography as "An article headed 'Truck System'

[3]The *Examiner* returned to the subject in Feb. (No. 88).

in the Examiner of 26th December 1830" (MacMinn, p. 14). The part of the article following the quotation in full of W.M.J.'s letter is enclosed within square brackets (here deleted), which perhaps imply a different authorship; however, there is no other evidence to support such a conclusion.

WE HAVE RECEIVED a clever letter, signed W.M.J., which, among other observations on our article of last Sunday, relating to the truck system, contends that we were mistaken in considering the payment of wages in goods as a means of economizing the circulating medium. "There is a manufacturer in Sheffield, for instance," says our correspondent, "who pays his wages with drapery goods; but in doing this, how can he be said to dispense with the use of money? If he does not want it to pay wages with, he wants it to pay for the drapery goods with; and there cannot be any difference in the amount, except that which goes to himself for profit."

This is plausible, but unsound. The wholesale transactions of one dealer with another employ very little money. They take place upon credit, either by means of bills of exchange, or mere entries in the books of the several dealers. When these mutual credits come to be liquidated, money is used to pay *balances*, and nothing more. The great demand for money is for the retail transactions; and there can be no doubt that when the employer of labour can contrive to feed and clothe his men by one great purchase, instead of leaving the men to do it by a hundred little purchases, the circulating medium is greatly economized.

Besides, even if it *were* true that the Sheffield manufacturer wanted *money* to pay for the drapery goods, as supposed in our correspondent's hypothesis, he is allowed by law to make this payment in paper. Now, paper performs all the functions of currency, without costing any thing, or absorbing any portion of capital which might else be productively employed. But the manufacturer cannot by law pay his labourers in paper, because bankers may not issue paper of a sufficiently low denomination.[1] Even, therefore, if the truck system did not economize the *currency*, it would still serve to economize the only costly *part* of the currency. It is, as our correspondent partly seems to perceive, a substitute for paper money,—the wisdom of the legislature having thought fit to interdict the more convenient medium.

Our correspondent challenges us to declare our opinions on the subject of currency. We should have done so ere this if we had deemed the occasion favourable, and if we were not, from experience, fully aware that the public attention cannot be advantageously directed to more than two or three great subjects at a time. Now, when we are no longer cursed with a currency, which, being inconvertible into cash, subjected the amount of the circulating medium to the uncontrolled discretion of a close corporation, we deem the question between a paper and a gold circulation to be of immeasurably less importance than is

---

[1]By the provisions of 7 George IV, c. 6 (1826).

attached to it by most writers on either side of the controversy, and probably by our correspondent.

To the Editor of the *Examiner*

Sir,—As a real admirer, I speak sincerely, not in the ordinary cant of newspaper correspondents, of the principles of your journal, I have seen, with pain, your diatribe against the House of Commons for the manner in which it entertained Mr. Littleton's measure against the truck-system;[2] a measure which, as a real friend to the manufacturing labourers, I am actively and zealously engaged in promoting. On their behalf, I request of your impartiality a little space in your columns for this humble effort to counteract what I believe to be the very mischievous tendency of your observations. Allow me to observe, that the conduct of yourself, and other political economists in this matter, is a parody on the foolish maxim —"Fiat Justitia Ruat Coelum;"[3] that you in effect say, abandon not one iota of our stern principles, whatever may be the consequences. In this rigid unbending adherence to a favourite theory, you forget that you are sacrificing the end to the supposed means, and lose sight of the very basis of all your science,—the greatest happiness of the greatest number. What has the House of Commons done? What does it propose to do? Many thousands of labourers complain of the frauds and oppressions they suffer from the truck system, *not sufferings arising from the low rate of wages*, but frauds and oppressions, which the workmen of truck-masters groan under, peculiar to themselves, and which are not shared by the workmen of money-paying masters in the same manufactures in the same districts. To prevent this fraud, we require, that is, we ask for no more than that all contracts between master and workman shall be made, and shall be paid in a medium which does not admit of fraud, and in which the magistrate can understand the rights of, and administer justice between, the parties; instead of in any system of barter, in which it is impossible for the magistrate to know the value that passes between the parties, and consequently impossible for him to do justice to him that is defrauded and oppressed. This is no great restriction on the liberty of contracts. For the truck-master may still keep his store instead of his Tommy-shop, still add the profits of the retailer to those of the manufacturer,—the law merely interfering to provide that the wages of the workman shall be paid in that value which alone the [*sic*] can ascertain, leaves him to have any dealings he pleases afterwards to have with his master. The continuance of the system has produced a violent discontent, hourly increasing: the money-paying masters, unable to compete with the truck-masters, must either follow the same system, adding immensely to this discontent, or, what many of them would do, *stop their works, and turn their men adrift, denouncing the truck system as the cause*. The consequence would be, the instant rising of the men, in riots first directed against truck-masters and their property—and where afterwards, who could calculate? What force could check, what concessions or reasons would soothe or control a mob of a hundred thousand persons, flushed with riot and success, and justly complaining of the apathy of the government and Parliament to their sufferings and complaints? The consequences to the kingdom, who could foresee? What character the mob would assume, or what designs it might be led to entertain? And yet there are political economists who would incur this, rather than yield one iota of their theories, and blame the government for not partaking the same strange temerity.

Is there any thing new or wrong in the principle of legislation which would interfere

[2]For details see No. 67.

[3]"Theodore de la Guard" (Nathaniel Ward), *The Simple Cobbler of Aqqawam in America* (London: Denver and Ibbitson, 1647), p. 13.

with contracts, when the consequences of those contracts may be so prejudicial to others, to the community?

The table of the House of Commons groans with proofs, the experience of centuries shows that the Truck System invariably leads to the grossest frauds; and there is nothing either new or strange in the principle of law that prohibits contracts between parties, even when the parties are perfectly free agents, where those contracts are injurious to public morality.

But the workman is not a free agent. A workman once entered into the employment of a master is not free; his poverty, the lowness of his wages, *the law of settlement*, render it impossible for him to leave his service, to remain one, two, or three weeks idle, to travel to other parishes in search of an employer;[4] and he is obliged, therefore, to submit to the exactions and frauds of an oppressive and fraudulent master. *The workman is not upon equal terms*—And why is he not? Because of the law of settlement, and because of those corn laws, and tithe laws[5] which create a factitious, not a natural superabundance of population, and cause the workman's poverty as effectually as if they were enacted for the express and avowed purpose. We do not wish to controul the laws of nature by acts of parliament; but we do wish, by act of parliament, to relieve the workman from some of the evils of the undue advantages which other acts of parliament have given his employer; and which we are not able to repeal.

You say that the effect of the law would be to lower wages. How is the truck-master's paying in money, instead of in goods, to make the money-paying masters who are still the majority (thank Heaven!) reduce their wages to their men? How is the necessity of purchasing more gold for the extra circulation to diminish the sale of iron, or the quantity of employment which the masters would have to give? If the present masters' capital is unsufficient, of course other capital would flow into the trade to make the supply equal to the demand. If more gold be required for circulation in consequence, (which is very doubtful considering the amount of capital that lies idle) it would, I admit, cost *the country at large* something to get that gold. But is that a price we should hesitate to pay, to get rid of a system which defrauds, oppresses, and degrades the workman, and which has brought the midland counties to the verge of a fearful convulsion? Assuredly not.—At all events, to permit paper, and not to permit truck, would be the proper way to get rid of that burden.

W.M.J.

In the last sentence our correspondent has, in our opinion, approached to the true practical conclusion. "To permit paper," with proper securities for the solvency of the issuers, would effectually abolish the truck system: "not to permit truck," would then be superfluous legislation. Paper-money is the most commodious, and might be made the safest of all modes of economizing a costly medium of exchange. It is found so in Scotland, where the securities against its abuse approach to the utmost limit of completeness and perfection yet reached by any human institution. From the day when the Legislature, instead of fortifying the small-note circulation by the proper securities, thought proper to abolish it,

[4]By Sect. 1 of 13 & 14 Charles II, c. 12 (1662).
[5]The tithe laws, which had been customary by canon law since about the eighth century, were made statutory by 27 Henry VIII, c. 20 (1535); see also 32 Henry VIII, c. 7 (1540), and 2 & 3 Edward VI, c. 13 (1548). In recent years such statutes as 7 & 8 George IV, c. 60 (1827) allowed for composition for tithes.

Parliament has been engaged, as was foreseen and foretold at the time, in an incessant and constantly recurring warfare against all manner of worse modes of effecting that which a properly regulated paper-money accomplishes in a good mode. The truck system is one of those worse modes; and it is worse, simply because, as our correspondent observes, it increases the difficulty of enforcing contracts, and holding parties to the terms of their bargain.

That it is attended with this inconvenience, we have no doubt; but that it can therefore be a cause of impoverishment to the labouring classes in general, we cannot admit. We request the attention of our correspondent to a simple argument. If the truck-master, after paying nominally two shillings a-day to his men, cheats them of sixpence a-day by overcharges in the prices of goods sold at his store, it is evidently the same thing as if he gave to each of them eighteen-pence a-day, and no more. Now, is it not evident, that by giving only eighteen-pence a-day, either directly or indirectly, he is enabled to employ, with a given capital, a greater number of men? And as it is not denied that he now employs men to the full extent of his capital, is it not clear that, if compelled to give two shillings a-day, he must throw a part of his labourers out of employment? The competition of those extra labourers, who would be altogether unemployed if the manufacturer were forced to give really adequate wages, is the true cause which compels the working people to accept wages that are not adequate. To abolish truck would not raise their *real* wages to the standard of their *nominal* ones, but would lower their nominal wages to the level of their real ones; and even lower, unless, by the introduction of paper, the necessity were spared of converting productive capital into idle gold and silver.

We have only room further to assure our correspondent, that he wrongs us in supposing that we are tenacious of a general principle without regarding specific consequences. Every general principle that is worth a rush, foresees and provides for all possible consequences; but a man who is not absurdly confident in his own foresight, looks carefully into details, as we always do, not only to avoid error in the *application* of his principles, but also to guard himself against latent errors in the principles themselves.

71. FRENCH NEWS [8]

EXAMINER, 26 DEC., 1830, PP. 826-7

The implication of the division of the article into two parts (here signalled by a printer's rule) is not clear; the initial two paragraphs of the second part are here included, as being presumably by Mill; the final two paragraphs of that part, dealing with Polish and Belgian news, are excluded. The article is headed "London, December 26." For the entry in Mill's bibliography, see No. 55.

THE FRENCH EX-MINISTERS have been tried, convicted, and sentenced to perpetual imprisonment, and the loss of all honours and distinctions. Polignac is, moreover, pronounced civilly dead. The legal consequence of this part of his sentence is, that his property is not confiscated—that punishment being formally abolished by the charter[1]—but passes to his natural heirs.

Perpetual imprisonment would be a far heavier punishment than death, if it were enforced; but in practice, it is sure to amount, at least in cases of political delinquency, to confinement for two or three years at the farthest.

No disturbances had broken out when the last advices were received, and it was hoped that none would take place. We join most earnestly in this hope; but we have seen, with ineffable disgust, the Parisian populace—the populace of the three days—reproached with bloodthirstiness for demanding that great criminals shall be treated as mean ones have ever been, and as these very persons would have treated the most intelligent and patriotic men in France, if their criminal enterprise had been triumphant.

The greatest possible care was evidently taken by the Peers to avoid putting to the witnesses, during the trial, any question likely to elicit facts unfavourable to the accused.

The ministers have introduced into the Chamber of Peers a bill for the more effectual suppression of the slave-trade.[2] No law could be more indispensable, as the connivance of the Bourbon Government has hitherto been the principal obstacle to the entire rooting out of that abominable traffic.

The ministry have, moreover, introduced a bill into the Chamber of Deputies, granting to the King a civil list of 18 millions a year—about £720,000 sterling. This, which is little more than half the amount of the civil list, which Charles X enjoyed (though he did not think fit to pay his creditors out of it), has given great, and just, dissatisfaction—considering the enormous private fortune of Louis Philippe, and the general wish that no unnecessary pomp should encircle the throne of a citizen king.[3]

From accounts received from Paris, up to Thursday evening, it appears that tranquillity was still maintained, chiefly by the temperance and excellent conduct of the National Guard, aided by the students of the Polytechnique School, and the Schools of Law and Medicine.

Polignac, and his fellow-culprits, are to be confined in the fortress of Ham, in Picardy.

[1]By Art. 57 of the Charter of 1830.
[2]Enacted as Bull. 22, No. 87 (4 Mar., 1831).
[3]Projet de loi qui doit fixer la dotation de la couronne et la liste civile (*Moniteur*, 1830, p. 1733) was presented on 15 Dec.; a commission was appointed on 24 Dec., but the bill was withdrawn because of the outcry.

72. FRENCH NEWS [9]

EXAMINER, 2 JAN., 1831, P. 8

This ninth article on French affairs, headed "London, January 2," is covered by the bibliographical entry in No. 55. Beginning in 1831, Mill's bound set of the *Examiner* in Somerville College contains, on the front fly-leaf of each yearly volume, a list of his own articles, with page numbers. This article is listed as "Article on France." At the same time Mill began the practice of enclosing his own articles in square brackets in his set of the *Examiner*. Of this article, which is divided by rules into three parts, only the first two parts are within brackets, while the third, on Belgian affairs, falls without.

Quand on n'a d'autre politique que de louvoyer selon le temps; quand, sous prétexte de fuir tout extrême, on évite le vrai comme l'extrême du faux; quand on étend l'esprit de conservation à tout, même aux abus, on est fait pour recevoir et non pour dicter des conditions. Assez long-temps les hommes de cette école ont joui d'une influence funeste; assez long-temps les habiles d'entre eux ont corrompu le pouvoir par les suggestions mesquines de leur petite sagesse. Le temps est venu des esprits fermes et des principes décidés.—Revue Française (the Guizot Review) *for January,* 1829. [Vol. VII, p. 268.]

THE ABOVE PASSAGE is a faithful portraiture of the advisers by whom the King of the French is now swayed. By such advisers princes of honest intentions and weak judgment have always been ruined. They will be the ruin of Louis Philippe, who will never more know a tranquil hour while he remains on the throne.

It has been distinctly notified to the King, that he must now choose between the new oligarchy and the people. The alternative has been accepted. He has chosen the oligarchy; and Lafayette, Odilon-Barrot, and Dupont de l'Eure, are consequently no longer in office.

The breach, therefore, between the people and the government is now as wide and as ostensible as it was in the time of Charles X: with this difference, that as the new oligarchy, unlike the old, rests upon a real foundation of wealth and personal importance; as it has not, like the Bourbon Government, the most powerful of the constituted authorities, the Chamber of Deputies, in the ranks of the opposition; as it is not, therefore, obliged to govern in open defiance of all law, or not at all; and as it is not likely to be so ignorant of the universal feelings of the French people as to attempt to force Jesuits and mass-books down their throats; the future struggle, though probably pacific, will be a more arduous one than the preceding, and possibly more prolonged.

The revolution of July has left France almost exactly in the position in which the revolution of 1688 left ourselves. Both revolutions overthrew the doctrine of divine right; put an end to the political influence of the Catholic church; and established the omnipotence of Parliament. Both left the constitution of Parliament a mere oligarchy—but here we trust the parallel will end. The human mind is further advanced in 1830 than in 1688, and the French people have more sense and spirit than to wait a hundred and fifty years before they cry out for Parliamentary Reform in a voice which will carry all before it.

The ignorant and conceited Newspaper which used to stile itself the Leading Journal of Europe, appears to be of opinion that invectives against the Parliamentary Reformers of France are still saleable.[1] It should certainly be the best judge; a successful tradesman is good authority on the tastes of his customers. We derive some consolation, however, from the thought, that ever since his memorable panegyric on the Polignac Ministry, and invectives against the French people for condemning them untried,[2] our contemporary has never allowed a month to pass without attempting some disgusting appeal to the low prejudices, the malignant passions, or the dirty self-interest of the British public; which, within the month ensuing, we have had the satisfaction of seeing him compelled to eat up, bit by bit, to the very crumbs. These things have shaken our faith in the infallibility of our contemporary's judgment in such matters, and have afforded us the satisfactory assurance that the reading public are not altogether in so degraded a state of intellect and feeling, as the daily perusal of his columns, and the reflection how carefully their contents are manufactured for the market, might well have inclined us to suppose.

The introduction of the new Election Law[3] was fixed for Wednesday last; we, therefore, shall soon know whether the Ministry, now deprived of all which constituted its slender popularity, intends to place itself at the head of the oligarchy, or to see-saw between that body and the people. One thing, however, is clear; that the people will no longer be trifled with as they have been. The Chamber, notwithstanding the composition of its deplorable majority, contains within its body many of the popular leaders; and their unaccountable inaction and temporizing has caused us much suspicion and uneasiness. It is now accounted for. Their motive was the same which so greatly lowered the tone of the opposition journals while the Ex-ministers were on their trial. They were resolved, and the resolution does honour to the purity and nobleness of their purposes, to abstain from all which might excite or agitate the minds of the people, until it was certain that France would not be exposed to the dangers and evils of an insurrection for so miserable an object as the blood of four guilty and wretched conspirators. To avert this evil they had the virtue to make the greatest

[1]I.e., *The Times*; see the articles cited below.
[2]Leading article, *The Times*, 17 June, 1830, p. 2, referred to at No. 43, n2.
[3]For Mill's earlier speculation on this law, see Nos. 58 and 64. Introduced on 30 Dec., it was finally enacted as Bull. 37, No. 105 (19 Apr., 1831). It gave the vote to all males twenty-five or over who paid at least 200 francs in direct taxes. (A few others became electors through extraordinary franchises.) To be eligible for election, a man had to be thirty or over, and pay 500 francs in direct taxes. (Again a few more became eligible through peculiar qualifications.) Neither salaries nor expenses were to be paid to deputies. The electors represented about 2.4 percent of the adult male population in 1831; the number of possible candidates was probably less than a tenth the number of electors.

sacrifice which honest public men can make,—that of the favourable moment for advocating their opinions. They would not assume a popular tone, or introduce popular measures, while the fears of their opponents might have ensured a more favourable reception. They postponed the rupture until the enemy were flushed with undeserved success.

The exemplary demeanour of the National Guard during the last week, who with equal firmness and gentleness repressed every tendency to tumult on the part of men whose feelings and purposes were identical with their own; the general tranquillity of the people of Paris, under circumstances of all others the most exciting to a people as susceptible of strong emotions as the French; and the success with which the Law and Medical and Polytechnic Schools ("boys" and "lads," as young men of five-and-twenty are stupidly called by our newspapers),[4] exerted for the preservation of order, the popularity which they owed to their admirable conduct in July last; all this must have shown to every honest man throughout France how little reason there is for apprehending anarchical excesses, and with how little danger political rights might be extended at least to the National Guard, to say nothing of any larger portion of the people of France. To the jobbers and *intrigans*, however, who are at the head of the new oligarchy, these events inspired no other idea than that they were now safe from another Revolution, and might *exploiter* the people of France just as they pleased.

Although the office of Commander of the National Guard was one which no one pretended ought to be permanent, all until now had been apparently agreed in desiring that so long as it could be held by Lafayette it should continue; but as soon as the popularity of Lafayette was not indispensable to keep the people quiet, the Chamber passed a vote abolishing the office, and thereby declaring, in plain terms, that the Government had no further occasion for his services. He forthwith resigned, without waiting until the law which was to remove him should pass through all its stages.[5] Being pressed by the King to resume the office, he refused, except on the two conditions of a more popular Ministry, and a popular Election Law. These conditions having been rejected, Dupont and Odilon-Barrot followed the example of Lafayette, and resigned; together with

[4]The sentence on the ex-Ministers (Polignac, Peyronnet, Guernon-Ranville, and Chantelauze) was pronounced late on 21 Dec. About noon on 22 Dec., when crowds of demonstrators were gathering and cries of "Mort aux ministres" were heard, several hundred students from the law, medical, and polytechnical schools appeared bearing cards reading "Ordre public" and helped the National Guardsmen disperse the crowds. *The Times*, 24 Dec., 1830, p. 3, and the *Spectator*, 1 Jan., 1831, pp. 1-2, applied the term "boys" to the students; *The Times*, 29 Dec., 1830, p. 2, used "lads." Mill, it may be noted, was himself in his twenty-fifth year at this time.

[5]The vote in the Chamber of Deputies on 24 Dec., approving Art. 50 of the law on the National Guard (see No. 54, n16), led to Lafayette's resignation, the reasons for which he explained in a speech on the 27th (*Moniteur*, 1830, pp. 1818, and 1829-30).

Mathieu-Dumas, second in command to Lafayette, and Carbonnel, chief of his staff.[6]

There are now symptoms of a strenuous and united opposition, both in the Chamber and without it. We may hope that now at least the scabbard will be thrown away. Even in the Chamber of 1830, an opposition party headed by Lafayette, and comprising such men as Dupont, de Tracy, de Cormenin, Voyer d'Argenson, de Salverte,[7] Isambert, and Odilon-Barrot, (alas! that we cannot add Benjamin Constant), and backed by almost every man in France under five-and-thirty, is a power which no one dares despise; and, by earnest and well-directed exertions, is sure of ultimate victory.

Since the above observations were written, the Election Law has been presented. It just doubles the number of the electors, making them 180,000 instead of 90,000, and it reduces to 500 francs of direct taxation, the qualification for eligibility.

This is poor enough, but it is more than problematical whether even this will be allowed to pass without further alterations by a Chamber constituted like the present.

73. THE SPIRIT OF THE AGE, I
EXAMINER, 9 JAN., 1831, PP. 20-1

This is the first of a series of articles written, Mill says, "especially to point out in the character of the present age, the anomalies and evils characteristic of the transition from a system of opinions which had worn out, to another only in process of being formed." The articles, he continues, were "lumbering in style, and not lively or striking enough to be at any time acceptable to newspaper readers; but had they been far more attractive, still, at that particular moment, when great political changes were impending, and engrossing all minds, these discussions were ill timed, and missed fire altogether" (*CW*, Vol. I, p. 181). These articles had one positive result: they were read by Thomas Carlyle (1795-1881), Scottish historian and essayist, who praised them as "the first . . . which he had ever seen in a newspaper, hinting that the age was not the best of all possible ages" (*EL*, *CW*, Vol.

[6]Gabriel Mathieu Dumas (1753-1837) had helped Lafayette organize the National Guard in 1789. He fled France as the Revolution accelerated, returning to serve under Napoleon and the Bourbons. Elected a deputy in 1828, he was instrumental in the accession of Louis Philippe, once again organizing the National Guard. Antoine François Carbonel (1779-1861) had risen through the ranks under Napoleon, had been inactive during the Bourbon regime, and had returned to the service under Louis Philippe; he was made a Commander of the Legion of Honour on 31 Oct., 1830, and Brigadier General on 29 Dec.

[7]Anne Joseph Eusèbe Baconnière de Salverte (1771-1839), radical publicist and politician, had been active in public life since 1789.

XII, pp. 85-6), and sought out their author as a "new Mystic." It was the beginning of an anomalous but intense friendship. The title probably echoes William Hazlitt's *The Spirit of the Age; or, Contemporary Portraits* (London: Colburn, 1825), which includes an account of Bentham. Hazlitt (1778-1830), man of letters, had in the *Examiner* itself (1 Dec., 1816, p. 759) referred to Ernst Moritz Arndt's *Der Geist der Zeit* (1805), from which the term probably originates, and had used the English version in the *London Magazine* in April 1820. See also n2 below.

The series of articles has five parts, printed in seven issues (Nos. 77, 82, 92, 97, 103, 107). All appear in the "Political Examiner." The entry in Mill's bibliography reads "A series of Essays headed 'The Spirit of the Age' and signed A.B., in the Examiner of 9th Jany, 23d Jany, 6 Febry, 13th March, 3d April, 15th May, and 29th May 1831" (MacMinn, p. 14). In Mill's Somerville College set, all are indexed and enclosed in square brackets. This first article, listed as "The Spirit of the Age, No. 1," has two corrections: at 233.41, "it *true*, is" is changed to "is *true*, it", and at 234.16, "blew" is changed to "blow".

THE "SPIRIT OF THE AGE" is in some measure a novel expression. I do not believe that it is to be met with in any work exceeding fifty years in antiquity. The idea of comparing one's own age with former ages, or with our notion of those which are yet to come, had occurred to philosophers; but it never before was itself the dominant idea of any age.

It is an idea essentially belonging to an age of change. Before men begin to think much and long on the peculiarities of their own times, they must have begun to think that those times are, or are destined to be, distinguished in a very remarkable manner from the times which preceded them. Mankind are then divided, into those who are still what they were, and those who have changed: into the men of the present age, and the men of the past. To the former, the spirit of the age is a subject of exultation; to the latter, of terror; to both, of eager and anxious interest. The wisdom of ancestors, and the march of intellect, are bandied from mouth to mouth; each phrase originally an expression of respect and homage, each ultimately usurped by the partisans of the opposite catch-word, and in the bitterness of their spirit, turned into the sarcastic jibe of hatred and insult.

The present times possess this character. A change has taken place in the human mind; a change which, being effected by insensible gradations, and without noise, had already proceeded far before it was generally perceived. When the fact disclosed itself, thousands awoke as from a dream. They knew not what processes had been going on in the minds of others, or even in their own, until the change began to invade outward objects; and it became clear that those were indeed new men, who insisted upon being governed in a new way.

But mankind are now conscious of their new position. The conviction is already not far from being universal, that the times are pregnant with change; and that the nineteenth century will be known to posterity as the era of one of the greatest revolutions of which history has preserved the remembrance, in the human mind, and in the whole constitution of human society. Even the religious world teems with new interpretations of the Prophecies, foreboding mighty changes near at hand.[1] It is felt that men are henceforth to be held together by new ties, and separated by new barriers; for the ancient bonds will now no longer unite, nor the ancient boundaries confine. Those men who carry their eyes in the back of their heads and can see no other portion of the destined track of humanity than that which it has already travelled, imagine that because the old ties are severed mankind henceforth are not to be connected by any ties at all; and hence their affliction, and their awful warnings. For proof of this assertion, I may refer to the gloomiest book ever written by a cheerful man—Southey's *Colloquies on the Progress and Prospects of Society*; a very curious and not uninstructive exhibition of one of the points of view from which the spirit of the age may be contemplated.[2] They who prefer the ravings of a party politician to the musings of a recluse, may consult a late article in *Blackwood's Magazine*, under the same title which I have prefixed to this paper.[3] For the reverse of the picture, we have only to look into any popular newspaper or review.

Amidst all this indiscriminate eulogy and abuse, these undistinguishing hopes and fears, it seems to be a very fit subject for philosophical inquiry, what the spirit of the age really is; and how or wherein it differs from the spirit of any other age. The subject is deeply important: for, whatever we may think or affect to think of the present age, we cannot get out of it; we must suffer with its sufferings, and enjoy with its enjoyments; we must share in its lot, and, to be either useful or at ease, we must even partake its character. No man whose good qualities were mainly those of another age, ever had much influence on his own. And since every age contains in itself the germ of all future ages as surely as the acorn contains the future forest, a knowledge of our own age is the fountain of prophecy—the only key to the history of posterity. It is only in the present that we can know the future; it is only through the present that it is in our power to influence that which is to come.

[1]For example, *Babylon and Infidelity Foredoomed of God: A Discourse on the Prophecies of Daniel and the Apocalypse, Which Relate to These Latter Times, and Until the Second Advent* (Glasgow: Collins, 1828), by Edward Irving (1792-1834), the popular preacher, early friend of Thomas Carlyle; *Dialogues on Prophecy*, 3 vols. (London: Nisbet, 1827-29), comp. Henry Drummond (1786-1860), banker and M.P. (1810-13, 1847-60), who endowed the chair of Political Economy at Oxford (see Nos. 69 and 110), and was a founder of the Irvingite church; and *The Abominations of Babylon* (London: Hatchard, 1826), and *Popular Lectures on the Prophecies Relative to the Jewish Nation* (London: Hatchard, 1830), both by Hugh MacNeile (1795-1879), Rector of Albury, at this time an Irvingite.

[2]*Sir Thomas More; or, Colloquies on the Progress and Prospects of Society*, 2 vols. (London: Murray, 1829), by Robert Southey (1774-1843), prolific poet and author, whom Mill met during this period at breakfast parties.

[3]David Robinson (d. 1849), "Letter to Christopher North, Esquire, on the Spirit of the Age," *Blackwood's Edinburgh Magazine*, XXVIII (Dec. 1830), 900-20.

Yet, because our own age is *familiar* to us, we are presumed, if I may judge from appearances, to know it by nature. A statesman, for example, if it be required of him to have studied any thing at all (which, however, is more than I would venture to affirm) is supposed to have studied history—which is at best the spirit of ages long past, and more often the mere inanimate carcass without the spirit: but is it ever asked (or to whom does the question ever occur?) whether he understands his own age? Yet that also is history, and the most important part of history, and the only part which a man may know and understand, with absolute certainty, by using the proper means. He may learn in a morning's walk through London more of the history of England during the nineteenth century, than all the professed English histories in existence will tell him concerning the other eighteen: for, the obvious and universal facts, which every one sees and no one is astonished at, it seldom occurs to any one to place upon record; and posterity, if it learn the rule, learns it, generally, from the notice bestowed by contemporaries on some accidental exception. Yet are politicians and philosophers perpetually exhorted to judge of the present by the past, when the present alone affords a fund of materials for judging, richer than the whole stores of the past, and far more accessible.

But it is unadvisable to dwell longer on this topic, lest we should be deemed studiously to exaggerate that want, which we desire that the reader should think ourselves qualified to supply. It were better, without further preamble, to enter upon the subject, and be tried by our ideas themselves, rather than by the need of them.

The first of the leading peculiarities of the present age is, that it is an age of transition. Mankind have outgrown old institutions and old doctrines, and have not yet acquired new ones. When we say outgrown, we intend to prejudge nothing. A man may not be either better or happier at six-and-twenty, than he was at six years of age: but the same jacket which fitted him then, will not fit him now.

The prominent trait just indicated in the character of the present age, was obvious a few years ago only to the more discerning: at present it forces itself upon the most inobservant. Much might be said, and shall be said on a fitting occasion, of the mode in which the old order of things has become unsuited to the state of society and of the human mind. But when almost every nation on the continent of Europe has achieved, or is in the course of rapidly achieving, a change in its form of government; when our own country, at all former times the most attached in Europe to its old institutions, proclaims almost with one voice that they are vicious both in the outline and in the details, and that they *shall* be renovated, and purified, and made fit for civilized man, we may assume that a part of the effects of the cause just now pointed out, speak sufficiently loudly for themselves. To him who can reflect, even these are but indications which tell of a more vital and radical change. Not only, in the conviction of almost all men, things as they are, are wrong[4]—but, according to that same conviction, it is not by remaining in the old ways that they can be set right. Society demands, and anticipates, not merely a new machine, but a machine constructed in another manner. Mankind will not be led by their old maxims, nor by their old guides; and they will not choose either their opinions or their guides as they have done heretofore. The ancient constitutional texts were formerly spells which would call forth or allay the spirit of the English people at pleasure: what has become of the charm? Who can hope to sway the minds of the public by the old maxims of law, or commerce, or foreign policy, or ecclesiastical policy? Whose feelings are now roused by the mottoes and watch-words of Whig and Tory? And what Whig or Tory could command ten followers in the warfare of politics by the weight of his own personal authority? Nay, what landlord could call forth his tenants, or what manufacturer his men? Do the poor respect the rich, or adopt their sentiments? Do the young respect the old, or adopt their sentiments? Of the feelings of our ancestors it may almost be said that we retain only such as are the natural and necessary growth of a state of human society, however constituted; and I only adopt the energetic expression of a member of the House of Commons, less than two years ago, in saying of the young men, even of that rank in society, that they are ready to advertise for opinions.

Since the facts are so manifest, there is the more chance that a few reflections on their causes, and on their probable consequences, will receive whatever portion of the reader's attention they may happen to deserve.

With respect, then, to the discredit into which old institutions and old doctrines have fallen, I may premise, that this discredit is, in my opinion, perfectly deserved. Having said this, I may perhaps hope, that no perverse interpretation will be put upon the remainder of my observations, in case some of them should not be quite so conformable to the sentiments of the day as my commencement might give reason to expect. The best guide is not he who, when people are in the right path, merely praises it, but he who shows them the pitfalls and the precipices by which it is endangered; and of which, as long as they were in the wrong road, it was not so necessary that they should be warned.

There is one very easy, and very pleasant way of accounting for this general departure from the modes of thinking of our ancestors: so easy, indeed, and so pleasant, especially to the hearer, as to be very convenient to such writers for hire or for applause, as address themselves not to the men of the age that is gone by, but to the men of the age which has commenced. This explanation is that which ascribes the altered state of opinion and feeling to the growth of the human understanding. According to this doctrine, we reject the sophisms and prejudices which misled the uncultivated minds of our ancestors, because we have learnt too

---

[4]"Things as they are" became a catch-phrase for the Radicals, who probably took it from *Things As They Are; or, The Adventures of Caleb Williams*, 3 vols. (London: Crosby, 1794), by William Godwin (1756-1836), philosopher and political writer.

much, and have become too wise, to be imposed upon by such sophisms and such prejudices. It is our knowledge and our sagacity which keep us free from these gross errors. We have now risen to the capacity of perceiving our true interests; and it is no longer in the power of impostors and charlatans to deceive us.

I am unable to adopt this theory. Though a firm believer in the improvement of the age, I do not believe that its improvement has been of this kind. The grand achievement of the present age is the *diffusion* of *superficial* knowledge; and that surely is no trifle, to have been accomplished by a single generation. The persons who are in possession of knowledge adequate to the formation of sound opinions by their own lights, form also a constantly increasing number, but hitherto at all times a small one. It would be carrying the notion of the march of intellect too far, to suppose that an average man of the present day is superior to the greatest men of the beginning of the eighteenth century; yet they *held* many opinions which we are fast renouncing. The intellect of the age, therefore, is not the cause which we are in search of. I do not perceive that, in the mental training which has been received by the immense majority of the reading and thinking part of my countrymen, or in the kind of knowledge and other intellectual aliment which has been supplied to them, there is any thing likely to render them much less accessible to the influence of imposture and charlatanerie than there ever was. The Dr. Eadys still dupe the lower classes, the St. John Longs the higher:[5] and it would not be difficult to produce the political and literary antitypes of both. Neither do I see, in such observations as I am able to make upon my cotemporaries, evidence that they have any principle within them which renders them much less liable now than at any former period to be misled by sophisms and prejudices. All I see is, that the opinions which have been transmitted to them from their ancestors, are not the kind of sophisms and prejudices which are fitted to possess any considerable ascendancy in their altered frame of mind. And I am rather inclined to account for this fact in a manner not reflecting such extraordinarily great honour upon the times we live in, as would result from the theory by which all is ascribed to the superior expansion of our understandings.

The intellectual tendencies of the age, considered both on the favourable and on the unfavourable side, it will be necessary, in the prosecution of the present design, to review and analyse in some detail. For the present it may be enough to remark, that it is seldom safe to ground a positive estimate of a character upon

[5]Eady, a notorious quack doctor and "wall-chalker," formerly bankrupted when a linen-draper at St. Ives, had been subject to a successful action for recovery of £115/11/6 in 1824 (*Examiner*, 29 Feb., 1824, p. 142). John St. John Long (1798-1834) was a popular but untrained medical practitioner, with an office in Harley Street, whose treatments by "friction and corrosion" sometimes had unfortunate effects, leading to trials after the deaths of patients.

mere negatives: and that the faults or the prejudices, which a person, or an age, or a nation *has not*, go but a very little way with a wise man towards forming a high opinion of them. A person may be without a single prejudice, and yet utterly unfit for every purpose in nature. To have erroneous convictions is one evil; but to have no strong or deep-rooted convictions at all, is an enormous one. Before I compliment either a man or a generation upon having got rid of their prejudices, I require to know what they have substituted in lieu of them.

Now, it is self-evident that no fixed opinions have yet generally established themselves in the place of those which we have abandoned; that no new doctrines, philosophical or social, as yet command, or appear likely soon to command, an assent at all comparable in unanimity to that which the ancient doctrines could boast of while they continued in vogue. So long as this intellectual anarchy shall endure, we may be warranted in believing that we are in a fair way to become wiser than our forefathers; but it would be premature to affirm that we are already wiser. We have not yet advanced beyond the unsettled state, in which the mind is, when it has recently found itself out in a grievous error, and has not yet satisfied itself of the truth. The men of the present day rather incline to an opinion than embrace it; few, except the very penetrating, or the very presumptuous, have full confidence in their own convictions. This is not a state of health, but, at the best, of convalescence. It is a necessary stage in the progress of civilization, but it is attended with numerous evils; as one part of a road may be rougher or more dangerous than another, although every step brings the traveller nearer to his desired end.

Not increase of wisdom, but a cause of the reality of which we are better assured, may serve to account for the decay of prejudices; and this is, increase of discussion. Men may not reason, better, concerning the great questions in which human nature is interested, but they reason more. Large subjects are discussed more, and longer, and by more minds. Discussion has penetrated deeper into society; and if no greater numbers than before have attained the higher degrees of intelligence, fewer grovel in that state of abject stupidity, which can only co-exist with utter apathy and sluggishness.

The progress which we have made, is precisely that sort of progress which increase of discussion suffices to produce, whether it be attended with increase of wisdom or no. To discuss, and to question established opinions, are merely two phrases for the same thing. When all opinions are questioned, it is in time found out what are those which will not bear a close examination. Ancient doctrines are then put upon their proofs; and those which were originally errors, or have become so by change of circumstances, are thrown aside. Discussion does this. It is by discussion, also, that true opinions are discovered and diffused. But this is not so certain a consequence of it as the weakening of error. To be rationally assured that a given doctrine is *true*, it is often necessary to examine and weigh an immense variety of facts. One single well-established fact, clearly irreconcilable with a doctrine, is sufficient to prove that it is *false*. Nay, opinions often upset themselves by their own incoherence; and the impossibility of their being well-founded may admit of being brought home to a mind not possessed of so much as one positive truth. All the inconsistencies of an opinion with itself, with obvious facts, or even with other prejudices, discussion evolves and makes manifest: and indeed this mode of refutation, requiring less study and less real knowledge than any other, is better suited to the inclination of most disputants. But the moment, and the mood of mind, in which men break loose from an error, is not, except in natures very happily constituted, the most favourable to those mental processes which are necessary to the investigation of truth. What led them wrong at first, was generally nothing else but the incapacity of seeing more than one thing at a time; and that incapacity is apt to stick to them when they have turned their eyes in an altered direction. They usually resolve that the new light which has broken in upon them shall be the sole light; and they wilfully and passionately blow out the ancient lamp, which, though it did not show them what they now see, served very well to enlighten the objects in its immediate neighbourhood. Whether men adhere to old opinions or adopt new ones, they have in general an invincible propensity to split the truth, and take half, or less than half of it; and a habit of erecting their quills and bristling up like a porcupine against any one who brings them the other half, as if he were attempting to deprive them of the portion which they have.

I am far from denying, that, besides getting rid of error, we are also continually enlarging the stock of positive truth. In physical science and art, this is too manifest to be called in question; and in the moral and social sciences, I believe it to be as undeniably true. The wisest men in every age generally surpass in wisdom the wisest of any preceding age, because the wisest men possess and profit by the constantly increasing accumulation of the ideas of all ages: but the multitude (by which I mean the majority of all ranks) have the ideas of their own age, and no others: and if the multitude of one age are nearer to the truth than the multitude of another, it is only in so far as they are guided and influenced by the authority of the wisest among them.

This is connected with certain points which, as it appears to me, have not been sufficiently adverted to by many of those who hold, in common with me, the doctrine of the indefinite progressiveness of the human mind; but which must be understood, in order correctly to appreciate the character of the present age, as an age of moral and political transition. These, therefore, I shall attempt to enforce and illustrate in the next paper.[6]

A.B.

---

[6]No. 77.

74. FRENCH NEWS [10]
EXAMINER, 9 JAN., 1831, PP. 24-5

For the entry in Mill's bibliography, see No. 55. The article is headed "London, January 9." In the Somerville College index it is listed as "Article on France"; Mill's inked closing square bracket comes before the final paragraph of the article, on Russia and Poland, which is therefore not included.

A VERY MISCHIEVOUS REGULATION of the French Chambers (whose rules are, in many other respects, superior to those of our parliament) requires that all propositions, before they can be publicly discussed, shall be submitted to the Chamber sitting in *bureaux* or committees, and deliberating in secret. Unless three of the nine *bureaux* sanction the proposition, it drops.[1] The *bureaux* have as yet come to no decision on the Parliamentary Reform Bill;[2] and it is said that there have been stormy debates in the secret sittings. No one has the least expectation that the Bill will pass, unless mutilated and made almost worthless.

The popular and the oligarchical party are said to be marshalling and organizing their strength for the approaching contest; and it is added that M. Guizot and his friends, with their usual predilection for half measures, are forming a middle party, and endeavouring to trim the balance. The fault of these men is not in their intentions; and their acquirements and powers of mind no one disputes. Their error is a bigotted and coxcombical devotion to their own ways and their own disciples; and incapacity of conceiving that the government can go on well unless it goes precisely as they have settled beforehand.

75. CONDUCT OF THE UNITED STATES TOWARDS THE INDIAN TRIBES
EXAMINER, 9 JAN., 1831, P. 25

This article was provoked by commentary on the Message of Andrew Jackson (1767-1845), military hero and Democratic President of the United States, 1828-36, in *The Times*, 4 Jan., 1831, pp. 1-2 (the passage concerning the Indians is on p. 2), and by the leading articles on the subject in *The Times*, 5 Jan., p. 2, and the *Standard*, 4 Jan., p. 2. A leading article in "Foreign Intelligence," it is described in Mill's bibliography as "A short article on the conduct of the United States towards the Indian tribes, without heading, in the Examiner of 9th January 1831" (MacMinn, p. 14). In the Somerville College set it is listed as "Article on the conduct of the United States towards the Indians" and enclosed in square brackets; there is one correction: at 236.19, "it" is deleted from the phrase "it is assumed".

[1]For details, see No. 68, n7.
[2]I.e., the Election law. See No. 72, n3.

WE HAVE NO ROOM THIS WEEK for any lengthened observations on the Message of the American President; but we think it an act of bare justice to take the earliest possible notice of some very mischievous remarks which have appeared in the *Times* and in the *Standard* on that portion of it which relates to the removal of the Indians. The facts are as follows:—Several of the States contain within their allotted boundaries the possessions of some of the Indian tribes. These possessions have invariably been held sacred; and the Indians have been protected by law against all attempts to encroach upon them. But in order that the lands now occupied by these tribes may be appropriated and cultivated by civilized men, the Government of the United States has proposed to the Indians to resign their present possessions, and accept others not yet included within the boundaries of any State, and which it is proposed should never hereafter be so included. The Indians will therefore retain these lands for themselves and their posterity. The President informs Congress that several of the Indian tribes have accepted these terms.

Hereupon a loud wailing from the *Times* and *Standard*, on the hardship and injustice sustained by these unfortunate men, in being turned out to make room for the descendants of Europeans. The pity of the reader is invoked for the extermination which is assumed to be their inevitable lot; and the *Times* asks "why should no attempt be made to civilize them?"[1] This wise public instructor scarcely ever touches upon any topic beyond the range of daily conversation without betraying the fact of his knowing nothing whatever about it. The most prodigal expenditure in a Government like ours, professedly for a public object, generally proves nothing but that some of the "proprietors of Parliament,"[2] or their connexions, are to be benefitted thereby. But when a Government like that of America, parsimonious even to excess, devotes money to any purpose, it affords such a proof as it is hardly ever in the power of any other Government to give, of its being deeply in earnest. Now, the Government of the United States has for years expended, for the purpose of civilizing the Indians, sums so large, as to form a very important item in the moderate expenditure of that cheap Government. The conduct of the United States towards the Indian tribes has been throughout, not only just, but noble. The Indians have occasionally been unjustly treated by several of the State Governments, who, like other people, are not the very best of judges in their own cause; but the Federal Government has been the guardian and protector of the rights of the Indians on all occasions, and has

---

[1] 5 Jan., 1831, p. 2.

[2] A remark attributed to Henry Grattan (1746-1820), Irish statesman and orator; see his speech in the Irish Commons on parliamentary reform (15 May, 1797), in *The Speeches of the Right Honourable Henry Grattan*, ed. Henry Grattan (the younger), 4 vols. (London: Longman, *et al.*, 1822), Vol. III, p. 334.

recently been very seriously embroiled with one of the State Governments[3] on their account. We inform the *Times*—of what it should have known without our information, viz.—that one of the chief motives which suggested the removal of the Indians from their present lands was the desire that the State Governments might no longer have sovereign controul over them, and that they might be under the exclusive protection of their "great father," the Government of the United States.

76. FRENCH NEWS [11]
EXAMINER, 16 JAN., 1831, PP. 40-1

For the entry in Mill's bibliography, see No. 55. The article is headed "London, January 16." In the Somerville College set, it is listed as "Article on France"; Mill's square brackets exclude four opening paragraphs on the situation in Poland, and three concluding ones on Dutch and Belgian affairs; and at 238.7, Mill deleted "above" from the printed phrase "Chamber above alone".

THE FRENCH ELECTION LAW has been referred, as usual, to a select committee, the composition of which, if it represents in any degree the intentions of the Chamber, demonstrates that the slender improvements which the bill offers will be pared down to microscopic tenuity. Opinions, still narrower than those of the Guizot party, are represented by no less than four of the nine, and not more than three are supposed to be favourable to the law as it stands.

The municipal law,[1] which originated in the Chamber itself, has been recently returned by the select committee to which it was referred, and stands for discussion at an early period. The local bodies, by the provisions of this bill, are elective by a suffrage tolerably extensive, but all the good which would otherwise result from the law is neutralised by an unfortunate provision—that they are elected for six years, one half being changed triennially.[2] They will thus be far less amenable to public opinion than at present, for being now named and revocable by the government, they may be turned out when public opinion

---

[3]Georgia and the Federal Government differed over agreements with the Lower Creek Indians embodied in the Treaty of Indian Springs (1825) and the Treaty at Washington (1826); the former, which gave the Creeks title to lands beyond the Mississippi in return for Georgia lands, was abrogated by the latter, which allowed them to keep territory within Georgia.

---

[1]For the background of the law, see No. 57, n10. The bill, having been referred to a Commission on 17 Sept., was reported back in amended form on 29 Dec.

[2]By Titre I, Chap. ii, Sect. 1, Art. 17.

declares so strongly against them, as to make their continuance in office a source of unpopularity to the King and Ministry.

The bill for reducing the number of judges in each court of assize from five to three, has passed, after much opposition.[3] Neither side displayed more knowledge of the subject than might have been looked for in our own country under similar circumstances. M. Renouard, the King's Commissioner for introducing the bill, who is not even a member of the Chamber alone showed any sense of the immense importance of the principle of undivided responsibility.[4]

The Ministers are retrenching the public expenditure with good sense and boldness. They have lowered the enormous salaries of the prefects, and have abolished a variety of places, with high-sounding titles and inordinate emoluments, substituting offices with more modest names and more moderate remuneration.

77. THE SPIRIT OF THE AGE, II
EXAMINER, 23 JAN., 1831, PP. 50-2

For the context and entry in Mill's bibliography, see No. 73. In the Somerville College copy, the article is listed as "The Spirit of the Age, No. 2." There is one inked correction, "power in itself, on earth or in hell," being altered to "power on earth or in hell itself" (245.17-18).

I HAVE SAID that the present age is an age of transition: I shall now attempt to point out one of the most important consequences of this fact. In all other conditions of mankind, the uninstructed have faith in the instructed. In an age of transition, the divisions among the instructed nullify their authority, and the uninstructed lose their faith in them. The multitude are without a guide; and society is exposed to all the errors and dangers which are to be expected when persons who have never studied any branch of knowledge comprehensively and as a whole attempt to judge for themselves upon particular parts of it.

That this is the condition we are really in, I may spare myself the trouble of attempting to prove: it has become so habitual, that the only difficulty to be anticipated is in persuading any one that this is not our natural state, and that it is consistent with any good wishes towards the human species, to pray that we may

[3]For its introduction, see No. 66.

[4]Augustin Charles Renouard (1794-1878) became, after the July Revolution, Councillor of State and Secretary General at the Ministry of Justice. For his speech, see *Moniteur*, 9 Jan., 1831, p. 49, wherein he stressed the importance of a judge's feeling directly and solely responsible for a decision.

come safely out of it. The longer any one observes and meditates, the more clearly he will see, that even wise men are apt to mistake the almanack of the year for a treatise on chronology; and as in an age of transition the source of all improvement is the exercise of private judgment, no wonder that mankind should attach themselves to that, as to the ultimate refuge, the last and only resource of humanity. In like manner, if a caravan of travellers had long been journeying in an unknown country under a blind guide, with what earnestness would the wiser among them exhort the remainder to use their own eyes, and with what disfavour would any one be listened to who should insist upon the difficulty of finding their way, and the necessity of procuring a guide after all. He would be told with warmth, that they had hitherto missed their way solely from the fatal weakness of allowing themselves to be guided, and that they never should reach their journey's end until each man dared to think and see for himself. And it would perhaps be added (with a smile of contempt), that if he were sincere in doubting the capacity of his fellow-travellers to see their way, he might prove his sincerity by presenting each person with a pair of spectacles, by means whereof their powers of vision might be strengthened, and all indistinctness removed.

The men of the past, are those who continue to insist upon our still adhering to the blind guide. The men of the present, are those who bid each man look about for himself, with or without the promise of spectacles to assist him.

While these two contending parties are measuring their sophistries against one another, the man who is capable of other ideas than those of his age, has an example in the present state of physical science, and in the manner in which men shape their thoughts and their actions within its sphere, of what is to be hoped for and laboured for in all other departments of human knowledge; and what, beyond all possibility of doubt, will one day be attained.

We never hear of the right of private judgment in physical science; yet it exists; for what is there to prevent any one from denying every proposition in natural philosophy, if he be so minded? The physical sciences however have been brought to so advanced a stage of improvement by a series of great men, and the methods by which they are cultivated so entirely preclude the possibility of material error when due pains are taken to arrive at the truth, that all persons who have studied those subjects have come to a nearly unanimous agreement upon them. Some minor differences doubtless exist; there are points on which the opinion of the scientific world is not finally made up. But these are mostly questions rather of curiosity than of use, and it is seldom attempted to thrust them into undue importance, nor to remove them, by way of appeal from the tribunal of the specially instructed to that of the public at large. The compact mass of authority thus created overawes the minds of the uninformed: and if here and there a wrong-headed individual, like Sir Richard Phillips, impugns Newton's discoveries, and revives the long-forgotten sophisms of the Cartesians, he is not regarded.[1] Yet the fallacies which at one time enthralled the subtlest understandings, might find, we suspect, in the present day, some intellects scarcely strong enough to resist them: but no one dares to stand up against the scientific world, until he too has qualified himself to be named as a man of science: and no one does this without being forced, by irresistible evidence, to adopt the received opinion. The physical sciences, therefore, (speaking of them generally) are continually *growing*, but never *changing*: in every age they receive indeed mighty improvements, but for them the age of transition is past.

It is almost unnecessary to remark in how very different a condition from this, are the sciences which are conversant with the moral nature and social condition of man. In those sciences, this imposing unanimity among all who have studied the subject does not exist; and every dabbler, consequently, thinks his opinion as good as another's. Any man who has eyes and ears shall be judge whether, in point of fact, a person who has never studied politics, for instance, or political economy systematically, regards himself as any-way precluded thereby from promulgating with the most unbounded assurance the crudest opinions, and taxing men who have made those sciences the occupation of a laborious life, with the most contemptible ignorance and imbecility. It is rather the person who *has* studied the subject systematically that is regarded as disqualified. He is a *theorist*: and the word which expresses the highest and noblest effort of human intelligence is turned into a bye-word of derision. People pride themselves upon taking a "plain, matter-of-fact" view of a subject. I once heard of a book entitled "Plain Politics for Plain People." I well remember the remark of an able man on that occasion: "What would be thought of a work with such a title as this, Plain Mathematics for Plain People?" The parallel is most accurate. The nature of the evidence on which these two sciences rest, is different, but both are systems of connected truth: there are very few of the practical questions of either, which can be discussed with profit unless the parties are agreed on a great number of preliminary questions: and accordingly, most of the political discussions which one hears and reads are not unlike what one would expect if the binomial theorem were propounded for argument in a debating society none of whose members had completely made up their minds upon the Rule of Three. Men enter upon a subject with minds in no degree fitted, by previous acquirements, to understand and appreciate the true arguments: yet they lay the blame on the arguments, not on themselves: truth, they think, is under a peremptory obligation of being intelligible to them, whether they take the right means of understanding it or no.

[1]Richard Phillips (1767-1840), bookseller and publisher, strongly attacked Newton and gave support to Descartes in such works as *Essays on the Proximate Causes of the General Phenomena of the Universe* (London: Souter, 1818), and *Protest against the Prevailing Principles of Natural Philosophy* (London: Sherwood, [1830]). For the "sophisms" (concerning vortices) of René Descartes (1596-1650), see his *Principia philosophiae* (1644).

Every mode of judging, except from first appearances, is scouted as false refinement. If there were a party among philosophers who still held to the opinion that the sun moves round the earth, can any one doubt on which side of the question the vulgar would be? What terms could express their contempt for those who maintained the contrary! Men form their opinions according to natural shrewdness, without any of the advantages of study. Here and there a hard-headed man, who sees farther into a mill-stone than his neighbours, and takes it into his head that thinking on a subject is one way of understanding it, excogitates an entire science, and publishes his volume; in utter unconsciousness of the fact, that a tithe of his discoveries were known a century ago, and the remainder (supposing them not too absurd to have occurred to anybody before) have been refuted in any year which you can mention, from that time to the present.

This is the state we are in; and the question is, how we are to get out of it. As I am unable to take the view of this matter which will probably occur to most persons as being the most simple and natural, I shall state in the first instance what this is, and my reasons for dissenting from it.

A large portion of the talking and writing common in the present day, respecting the instruction of the people, and the diffusion of knowledge, appears to me to conceal, under loose and vague generalities,[2] notions at bottom altogether fallacious and visionary.

I go, perhaps, still further than most of those to whose language I so strongly object, in the expectations which I entertain of vast improvements in the social condition of man, from the growth of intelligence among the body of the people; and I yield to no one in the degree of intelligence of which I believe them to be capable. But I do not believe that, along with this intelligence, they will ever have sufficient opportunities of study and experience, to become themselves familiarly conversant with all the inquiries which lead to the truths by which it is good that they should regulate their conduct, and to receive into their own minds the whole of the evidence from which those truths have been collected, and which is necessary for their establishment. If I thought all this indispensable, I should despair of human nature. As long as the day consists but of twenty-four hours, and the age of man extends but to threescore and ten, so long (unless we expect improvements in the arts of production sufficient to restore the golden age) the great majority of mankind will need the far greater part of their time and exertions for procuring their daily bread. Some few remarkable individuals will attain great eminence under every conceivable disadvantage; but for men in general, the principal field for the exercise and display of their intellectual faculties is, and ever will be, no other than their own particular calling or

---

[2] A favourite term of the Philosophic Radicals, used extensively in Jeremy Bentham, *The Book of Fallacies* (1824), in *Works*, Vol. II, pp. 440-8 (Pt. IV, Chap. iii).

occupation. This does not place any limit to their possible intelligence; since the mode of learning, and the mode of practising, that occupation itself, might be made one of the most valuable of all exercises of intelligence: especially when, in all the occupations in which man is a mere machine, his agency is so rapidly becoming superseded by real machinery. But what sets no limit to the *powers* of the mass of mankind, nevertheless limits greatly their possible *acquirements*. Those persons whom the circumstances of society, and their own position in it, permit to dedicate themselves to the investigation and study of physical, moral, and social truths, as their peculiar calling, can alone be expected to make the evidences of such truths a subject of profound meditation, and to make themselves thorough masters of the philosophical grounds of those opinions of which it is desirable that all should be firmly *persuaded*, but which they alone can entirely and philosophically *know*. The remainder of mankind must, and, except in periods of transition like the present, always do, take the far greater part of their opinions on all extensive subjects upon the authority of those who have studied them.

It does not follow that all men are not to inquire and investigate. The only complaint is, that most of them are precluded by the nature of things from ever inquiring and investigating enough. It is right that they should acquaint themselves with the evidence of the truths which are presented to them, to the utmost extent of each man's intellect, leisure, and inclination. Though a man may never be able to understand Laplace, that is no reason he should not read Euclid. But it by no means follows that Euclid is a blunderer, or an arrant knave, because a man who begins at the forty-seventh proposition cannot understand it: and even he who begins at the beginning, and is stopped by the *pons asinorum*, is very much in the wrong if he swears he will navigate his vessel himself, and not trust to the nonsensical calculations of mathematical land-lubbers.[3] Let him learn what he can, and as well as he can—still however bearing in mind, that there are others who probably know much with which he not only is unacquainted, but of the evidence of which, in the existing state of his knowledge, it is impossible that he should be a competent judge.

It is no answer to what has just been observed, to say that the grounds of the most important moral and political truths are simple and obvious, intelligible to persons of the most limited faculties, with moderate study and attention; that all mankind, therefore, may master the evidences, and none need take the doctrines upon trust. The matter of fact upon which this objection proceeds, is happily true. The proofs of the moral and social truths of greatest importance to mankind, are few, brief, and easily intelligible; and happy will be the day on which these

[3]The 47th proposition of Bk. I of the Greek geometer Euclid's *Elements* is the Pythagorean theorem; the *pons asinorum* is the 5th proposition of Bk. I, so called because dunces seldom got over it without stumbling.

shall begin to be circulated among the people, instead of second-rate treatises on the Polarization of Light, and on the Rigidity of Cordage.[4] But, in the first place, it is not every one—and there is no one at a very early period of life—who has had sufficient experience of mankind in general, and has sufficiently reflected upon what passes in his own mind, to be able to appreciate the force of the reasons when laid before him. There is, however, a great number of important truths, especially in Political Economy, to which, from the particular nature of the evidence on which they rest, this difficulty does not apply. The proofs of these truths may be brought down to the level of even the uninformed multitude, with the most complete success. But, when all is done, there still remains something which they must always and inevitably take upon trust: and this is, that the arguments really *are* as conclusive as they appear; that there exist no considerations relevant to the subject which have been kept back from them; that every objection which can suggest itself has been duly examined by competent judges, and found immaterial. It is easy to say that the truth of certain propositions is obvious to *common sense*. It may be so: but how am I assured that the conclusions of common sense are confirmed by accurate knowledge? Judging by common sense is merely another phrase for judging by first appearances; and every one who has mixed among mankind with any capacity for observing them, knows that the men who place implicit faith in their own common sense are, without any exception, the most wrong-headed and impracticable persons with whom he has ever had to deal. The maxim of pursuing truth without being biassed by authority, does not state the question fairly; there is no person who does not prefer truth to authority—for authority is only appealed to as a voucher for truth. The real question, to be determined by each man's own judgment, is, whether most confidence is due in the particular case, to his own understanding, or to the opinion of his authority? It is therefore obvious, that there are some persons in whom disregard of authority is a virtue, and others in whom it is both an absurdity and a vice. The presumptuous man needs authority to restrain him from error: the modest man needs it to strengthen him in the right. What truths, for example, can be more obvious, or can rest upon considerations more simple and familiar, than the first principles of morality? Yet we know that extremely ingenious things may be said in opposition to the plainest of them—things which the most highly-instructed men, though never for a single moment misled by them, have had no small difficulty in satisfactorily answering. Is it to be imagined that if these sophisms had been referred to the verdict of the half-instructed—and we cannot expect the majority of every class to be any thing more—the solution of the fallacy would always have been found and understood? notwithstanding which, the fallacy would not, it is most probable,

---

[4]Such treatises are listed as Nos. 46 and 53 in the *Reports and Prospectus of the Society for the Diffusion of Useful Knowledge* (London: Baldwin, *et al.*, 1830), p. 25.

have made the slightest impression upon them:—and why? Because the judgment of the multitude would have told them, that their own judgment was not a decision in the last resort; because the conviction of their understandings going along with the moral truth, was sanctioned by the authority of the best-informed; and the objection, though insoluble by their own understandings, was not supported but contradicted by the same imposing authority. But if you once persuade an ignorant or a half-instructed person, that he ought to assert his liberty of thought, discard all authority, and—I do not say *use* his own judgment, for that he never can do too much—but *trust* solely to his own judgment, and receive or reject opinions according to his own views of the evidence;—if, in short, you teach to all the lesson of *indifferency*, so earnestly, and with such admirable effect, inculcated by Locke upon *students*,[5] for whom alone that great man wrote, the merest trifle will suffice to unsettle and perplex their minds. There is not a truth in the whole range of human affairs, however obvious and simple, the evidence of which an ingenious and artful sophist may not succeed in rendering doubtful to minds not very highly cultivated, if those minds insist upon judging of all things exclusively by their own lights. The presumptuous man will dogmatize, and rush headlong into opinions, always shallow, and as often wrong as right; the man who sets only the just value upon his own moderate powers, will scarcely ever feel more than a half-conviction. You may prevail on them to repudiate the authority of the best-instructed, but each will full surely be a mere slave to the authority of the person next to him, who has greatest facilities for continually forcing upon his attention considerations favourable to the conclusion he himself wishes to be drawn.

It is, therefore, one of the necessary conditions of humanity, that the majority must either have wrong opinions, or no fixed opinions, or must place the degree of reliance warranted by reason, in the authority of those who have made moral and social philosophy their peculiar study. It is right that every man should attempt to understand his interest and his duty. It is right that he should follow his reason as far as his reason will carry him, and cultivate the faculty as highly as possible. But reason itself will teach most men that they must, in the last resort, fall back upon the authority of still more cultivated minds, as the ultimate sanction of the convictions of their reason itself.

But where is the authority which commands this confidence, or deserves it? Nowhere: and here we see the peculiar character, and at the same time the peculiar inconvenience, of a period of moral and social transition. At all other periods there exists a large body of received doctrine, covering nearly the whole field of the moral relations of man, and which no one thinks of questioning, backed as it is by the authority of all, or nearly all, persons, supposed to possess

[5]John Locke (1632-1704), *Essay Concerning Human Understanding* (1690), in *Works*, New ed., 10 vols. (London: Tegg, *et al.*, 1823), Vol. II, pp. 368-9 (Sect. 18) and p. 372 (Sect. 20).

knowledge enough to qualify them for giving an opinion on the subject. This state of things does not now exist in the civilized world—except, indeed, to a certain limited extent in the United States of America. The progress of inquiry has brought to light the insufficiency of the ancient doctrines; but those who have made the investigation of social truths their occupation, have not yet sanctioned any new body of doctrine with their unanimous, or nearly unanimous, consent. The true opinion is recommended to the public by no greater weight of authority than hundreds of false opinions; and, even at this day, to find any thing like a united body of grave and commanding authority, we must revert to the doctrines from which the progressiveness of the human mind, or, as it is more popularly called, the improvement of the age, has set us free.

In the mean time, as the old doctrines have gone out, and the new ones have not yet come in, every one must judge for himself as he best may. Learn, and think for yourself, is reasonable advice for the day: but let not the business of the day be so done as to prejudice the work of the morrow. "Les supériorités morales," to use the words of Fiévée, "finiront par s'entendre;"[6] the first men of the age will one day join hands and be agreed: and then there is no power on earth or in hell itself, capable of withstanding them.

But ere this can happen there must be a change in the whole framework of society, as at present constituted. Worldly power must pass from the hands of the stationary part of mankind into those of the progressive part. There must be a moral and social revolution, which shall, indeed, take away no men's lives or property, but which shall leave to no man one fraction of unearned distinction or unearned importance.

That man cannot achieve his destiny but through such a transformation, and that it will and *shall* be effected, is the conclusion of every man who can *feel the wants of his own age*, without hankering after past ages. Those who may read these papers, and in particular the next succeeding one,[7] will find there an attempt, how far successful others must judge, to set forth the grounds of this belief.

For mankind to change their institutions while their minds are unsettled, without fixed principles, and unable to trust either themselves or other people, is, indeed, a fearful thing. But a bad way is often the best, to get out of a bad position. Let us place our trust for the future, not in the wisdom of mankind, but in something far surer—the force of circumstances—which makes men see that, when it is near at hand, which they could not foresee when it was at a distance, and which so often and so unexpectedly makes the right course, in a moment of emergency, at once the easiest and the most obvious.

A.B.

[6]Fiévée, *Correspondance politique et administrative*, Vol. III, Pt. 13, p. 136n.
[7]No. 82.

78. FRANCE

EXAMINER, 23 JAN., 1831, P. 55

Here Mill introduces a Paris correspondent, Pierre Martin Maillefer (ca. 1799-?), journalist and member of the Aide-toi Society, whom Mill probably persuaded in August 1830 (see *CW*, Vol. XII, p. 63) to write for the *Examiner* (see Nos. 95, 99, 117). Maillefer's lengthy article (pp. 55-6, dated 11 Jan.) follows the three paragraphs here included. The article, in "Foreign Intelligence," is headed as title. Described in Mill's bibliography as "Paragraphs introductory to a series of letters from France, in the Examiner of 23d Jany 1831" (MacMinn, p. 14), the item is listed on the fly-leaf of the Somerville College set as "Introductory remarks to a French correspondence (by Martin Maillefer)," and Mill's part of the article is enclosed in square brackets.

WE HAVE SUCCEEDED in obtaining the aid of a most valuable correspondent at Paris, whose first letter appears in this day's *Examiner*. England has newspapers enough, which, while hypocritically affecting zeal for Parliamentary Reform at home, make it their daily business to re-echo the most contemptible calumnies propagated by the new Oligarchy against the Parliamentary Reformers of France. The letters of our correspondent will be a faithful picture of the opinions, the feelings, perhaps even the errors, of the younger and more ardent portion of the popular party. Whatever they know, he knows; whatever they feel, he feels; whatever he believes, is believed at least by many of the most active and influential in a party of which he himself is not one of the obscurest members, and of which his position and his sources of information render him an adequate representative.

We are not responsible for all the opinions of our correspondent, nor do we expect that he will never express any sentiments in which we should disagree. But we can answer for the purity and excellence of all the public objects, which he, and his friends, have in view. We cannot, of course, guarantee all the facts which he relates, especially those which are of the nature of anecdotes; but we are certain that he will affirm nothing as true, but what is at least, very generally believed; and it is often of as much, or even of still greater importance and interest, to know what is thought to be true, than what really is so. We are convinced, in short, that as nothing will be disguised in these letters, both the faults and the virtues of the French character, and of the popular party in particular, will be exhibited in them, with the utmost fidelity and *naïveté*; and that here, and no where else, will the English reader be enabled to judge the more *exaltés* of the young patriots of France from their own lips. The very first letter, and the picture which it exhibits of public opinion in France, exemplify at once the virtues and the failings most natural to the French people, those connected with great susceptibility and mobility of character. In the most sanguinary excesses of the first revolution, as a word would rouse the popular fury, so a word would calm it: and now, with manners and habits infinitely softened and improved, the French retain the same excitability of spirit: the most lively gratitude and affection towards public men who wish, or seem to wish their good; suspicion and distrust, easily conceived, and easily renounced; political tergiversation punished for a time by bitter resentment, but very slender and inadequate services accepted as a full atonement.

The correspondence will not be continued every week, but as often as events may require and space permit, or as the reception which it meets with from the public, may seem to justify.

79. FRENCH NEWS [12]

EXAMINER, 23 JAN., 1831, P. 57

This article is headed "London, January 23." For the entry in Mill's bibliography, see No. 55. In the Somerville College copy, the article is listed as "Article on France"; and Mill's square brackets enclose the part of the article here included (two further paragraphs comment on Polish and Hanoverian affairs).

DURING THE LAST WEEK, the French Chamber of Deputies has been principally occupied with a bill relating to the Sinking Fund; in one clause of which, the Ministers have sustained what appears to us a merited defeat.[1] They proposed, that the nation should pledge itself never to cancel any portion of stock until the whole was redeemed; but to continue paying the interest upon the stock which is bought up, to augment the fund for the redemption of the remainder. As M. Gautier observed, this would be to throw the whole burthen of paying off the debt upon the present generation, although in all probability the next will have greater resources, and fewer demands upon its finances for extraordinary expense.[2] The clause was thrown out, members of both oppositions speaking and voting against it.

General Lamarque made another of his vehement exhortations to war.[3] He appears to resemble the other Bonapartist officers in their military mania, though not in their baser attributes, the low selfishness and imbecile vanity, which

[1]Mill is referring specifically to the debate and vote (17 Jan.) on Art. 7 of Projet de loi relatif à l'amortissement; see *Moniteur*, 1831, p. 119.

[2]Jean Elie Gautier's speech of 11 Jan. on the sinking fund is reported *ibid.*, pp. 76-8. Gautier (1781-1858), deputy 1824-31, first sat as a royalist, but spoke against the law of censorship in 1827 and subsequently was one of the 221.

[3]On 15 Jan., *ibid.*, pp. 109-10. Maximilien Lamarque (1770-1832) had joined the army in 1791 and fought with brilliance until he went into exile in 1815. Returning in 1818, he was elected in 1828 to the Chamber of Deputies, and made a name for himself as one of the orators of the opposition. He was quickly disillusioned with Louis Philippe's policy of peace at all costs, against which he spoke, favouring going to the aid of Poland.

distinguish almost the whole of Napoleon's *parvenu* nobility. M. Mauguin followed with a speech of considerable ability, full of just observations on the character of foreign governments, particularly of the English, the Aristocratical character of which he perfectly understands; but too much in the same warlike tone.[4] That able and highly-principled paper, the *Courrier Français*, has answered both speeches in an article, which, we trust, will be read in every corner of France.[5]

Addresses from the People and from the National Guard of different parts of France to Lafayette, lamenting his retirement,[6] and to the King, demanding popular institutions,[7] are now to be found in every number of the French newspapers, and they seem to be as numerous from what were thought the backward parts of France, as from any others.

80. THE QUARTERLY REVIEW ON THE POLITICAL ECONOMISTS
EXAMINER, 30 JAN., 1831, P. 68

Mill in this article replies to "The Political Economists," *Quarterly Review*, XLIV (Jan. 1831), 1-52, by George Poulett Scrope (1797-1876), liberal M.P. for Stroud, 1833-68, geologist and writer on economics. The item, headed as title, appears in the "Literary Examiner." It is described in Mill's bibliography as "An article headed 'The Quarterly Review on the Political Economists' in the Examiner of 30th January 1831" (MacMinn, p. 15). It is listed as title and marked as Mill's in the Somerville College set.

THE NUMBER JUST PUBLISHED of the *Quarterly Review*, contains an article headed "The Political Economists," which exhibits some proofs of thought and talent, and more of arrogance and self-sufficiency. In criticizing, sometimes with and sometimes without ground, various doctrines of various Political Economists, from some part or other of whose writings, however, he has derived every valuable idea, relevant to the subject, which his article contains, he is careful to assure the reader on every topic which he successively takes in hand, that not a word of sense has been spoken upon it by any of his predecessors: after which he proceeds to lay down the true theory of the subject, with an unhesitating and undisguised confidence in his own infallibility, which is not altogether becoming in one who contends that those who have hitherto written on this extensive and complicated science, many of whom he will not pretend to have been any way his inferiors in mental endowments, have fallen into so many errors.

[4]*Ibid.*, p. 111.
[5]"De la paix et de la guerre," *Courrier Français*, 17 Jan., pp. 1-2.
[6]See, e.g., *Le National*, 17 Jan., p. 4, 18 Jan., p. 3, 19 Jan., p. 3, and 21 Jan., p. 3.
[7]See, e.g., *ibid.*, 17 Jan., p. 4, for the address from the Meurthe, mentioned in Nos. 81 and 85.

Though we have said thus much in dispraise of the spirit in which this article is conceived, our object in noticing it is to draw attention to one portion of it, which is on the whole praiseworthy: we mean the concluding pages,[1] in which the writer strongly insists upon the insufficiency and sterility of all inquiries which relate to the means by which a community may obtain the greatest accumulation of commodities possessing exchangeable value, unless followed up by the inquiry how far the particular nature of those commodities, and the manner in which they are distributed among the different members of the community, are conducive to human happiness in the largest sense and upon the most extended scale. He adds (and on this important truth he dwells at some length, and in a spirit honourable to his feelings,) that the wealth of a country is upon a footing most favourable to human happiness, just in proportion to the number of persons whom it enables to obtain, by their bodily and mental exertions, a comfortable subsistence; while on the contrary, a further increase of the wealth of particular individuals beyond this point, makes a very questionable addition to the general happiness; and is even, if the same wealth would otherwise have been employed in raising other persons from a state of poverty, a positive evil.

These are precisely our opinions, and it is in the spirit of them that we would wish all legislation to be directed, so far as is consistent with that secure enjoyment, by every man, of the fruits of his industry, or that of his ancestors, which is an essential condition of all human prosperity. But we know not whence the reviewer has derived the idea, that the political economists of the present day are adverse to these views; nor do we see much good sense in his complaint that the science, as it at present exists, is founded upon a wrong principle, because it professes to inquire only how a nation may be made rich, not how it may be made happy. It is not usual to find fault with mathematics, for being conversant only with lines, and angles, and planes, and solids, and numbers; nor is it ever surmised that mathematical science is founded upon a wrong basis, because mankind cannot be made happy by means of that science exclusively. The truth is, that there are, among those who have studied political economy, the same two kinds of men, into which the students of any other subject whatever may be divided: there are the men who know nothing except political economy, and the men whose ideas and whose feelings habitually comprehend the whole range of moral and political truth. This latter class of political economists the reviewer will find to be unanimously, or almost unanimously, of his opinion; and it is no fault of political economy if the other sort of persons, who have studied that and nothing else, judge of all practical questions exclusively by the considerations which their own subject presents to them, simply because they are incapable of appreciating any others; no more than the art of dancing is responsible for the

[1]Pp. 43ff.

individual absurdity of the dancing-master in Molière—"La philosophie est quelque chose; mais la danse, monsieur, la danse!"*

We have said thus much, because we are really sick of the crazy outcries against the political economists, which seem to be rather increasing than diminishing, at the very time when the public is almost unanimously adopting most of the opinions which principally excited the original uproar against them. It is unworthy of a man like this reviewer, who has really studied the subject sufficiently to have perceived, or at any rate to have profited by, the immense merits of the writers whom he attacks, thus to mingle his voice in the vulgar howl of ignorance against knowledge.

81. FRENCH NEWS [13]

EXAMINER, 30 JAN., 1831, P. 72

This article is headed "London, January 30." For the entry in Mill's bibliography, see No. 55. The article is listed in the Somerville College copy as "Article on France"; Mill's brackets indicate that only the first six paragraphs of this article are by him (it continues for six more paragraphs on Russia, Poland, and Hanover).

THE KING OF THE FRENCH, if a letter in the *Courrier des Pays-bas* is authentic, has had the inconceivable silliness of announcing to the Belgian Congress, that if they elect for their king the son of Eugène Beauharnais, he will not be recognized by the French Government.[1] The sole apparent motive of this act of imbecility, is fear lest some of the few remaining Bonapartists should think of setting up that individual as King of France, in consequence of his father's connexion with the object of their admiration and regret. This perfectly squares with the accounts we have heard of the panic terror into which Louis Philippe was thrown, by a letter which appeared in France from Joseph Bonaparte, asserting, with an obstinacy

---

*[Jean Baptiste Poquelin Molière (1622-73), *Le bourgeois gentilhomme* (Paris: Le Monnier, 1671), I, ii; p. 13.] Mr. Herschel, in his excellent Discourse, just published, on the Study of Natural Philosophy, most justly and wisely observes, that it is impossible to know any one even of the physical sciences well, without knowing all of them. The same observation is still more emphatically true of the moral sciences; but it is no reproach to the completeness of each individual science within its own limits. [John Frederick William Herschel (1792-1871), *A Preliminary Discourse on the Study of Natural Philosophy* (London: Longman, *et al.*, 1830), p. 132. Mill reviewed the work two months later; see No. 94.]

---

[1]For the background, see No. 59, n5. The letter to the Belgian government was from Count Sébastiani, then Minister of Foreign Affairs (*Courrier* [formerly *Courrier des Pays Bas*], 25 Jan., 1831, p. 1). Eugène Rose de Beauharnais (1781-1824), known as prince Eugène, was the only son of Napoleon's wife Josephine by her first marriage. His eldest son, Auguste Charles Eugène Napoléon, duc de Leuchtenberg (1810-35), was a candidate for the Belgian throne.

worthy of a more legitimate line, the claims of his nephew, the Duke of Reichstadt, to the throne.[2] Such is Louis Philippe's terror of the Bonapartists, that he dares refuse them nothing which they ask for; he has numbers of them about his house and person like tame mastiffs, not knowing, in his foolish fear, that the Bonapartist partakes far more of the nature of the spaniel, and is ever ready to lick the hand which feeds him.

We mentioned last week that addresses were pouring in from the departments, complaining of the conduct of government, and calling for more popular institutions. One of the best of these was from the admirable department of the Meurthe;[3] to this several public functionaries, among others the *Préfet*, and the *Procureur du Roi*, were parties.[4] For this the *Préfet* has been dismissed, and the *Procureur du Roi* reprimanded.

The Ministry have been defeated on their bill for altering the mode of levying a portion of the direct taxes. The subject was well and fully discussed on both sides, and it appears to us, on consideration, that the opponents of the measure were in the right.[5]

A Political Economy Society has been formed at Paris, consisting of thirty-six deputies of all parties, to meet once every week for the purpose of discussing among themselves such questions likely to come before them in their legislative capacity, as require a peculiar acquaintance with political economy.

The Ministry have at length introduced the promised bill for the elementary instruction of the people. It establishes a school in every commune, nearly upon the footing of the excellent parish schools in Scotland; and we doubt not that it will equal in its results that memorable example of great effects produced by small means.[6]

Another bill has been introduced by the Ministers, to remove the censorship of the theatres, and provide for the trial and punishment of such offences as may be committed by means of theatrical performances. Like our libel law, this bill is somewhat vague and indefinite, but it is to be hoped that French juries will temper it by a large and liberal interpretation.[7]

---

[2]Joseph Napoléon Bonaparte (1768-1844), eldest surviving brother of Napoleon, lived in exile after 1815. His letter from New York (18 Sept., 1830), addressed to the Chamber of Deputies, but never received by it, is in Anon., *Biographical Sketch of Joseph Napoleon Bonaparte* (London: Ridgway, 1833), pp. 111-16.

[3]The protest to the King (2 Jan., 1831), appeared in *Le National*, 17 Jan., p. 4.

[4]The Préfet was Stanislaus Michel François Vallet de Merville (1767-1833), who had been appointed in August 1830; the procureur du roi was Jean Baptiste Jorant.

[5]The debate centred on the bill's tendency to centralization and to invasion of privacy. On 21 Jan., 1831, the bill was sent back to the commission for further preparation. The Ministry was defeated only on Art. 1 (see No. 62).

[6]Projet de loi sur l'instruction primaire (20 Jan.), *Moniteur*, 1831, p. 136.

[7]Projet de loi relatif à la répression de délits commis par la voie des représentations théâtrales (19 Jan.), *ibid.*, 1831, pp. 131-2; the bill was dropped at the end of the session. (British libel law was based on common, not statute, law.)

82. THE SPIRIT OF THE AGE, III [Part 1]

EXAMINER, 6 FEB., 1831, PP. 82-4

For the context and entry in Mill's bibliography, see No. 73. In the Somerville College set the article is listed as "The Spirit of the Age, No. 3," and is marked with enclosing square brackets.

THE AFFAIRS OF MANKIND, or of any of those smaller political societies which we call nations, are always either in one or the other of two states, one of them in its nature durable, the other essentially transitory. The former of these we may term the *natural* state, the latter the *transitional*.

Society may be said to be in its *natural* state, when worldly power, and moral influence, are habitually and undisputedly exercised by the fittest persons whom the existing state of society affords. Or, to be more explicit; when on the one hand, the temporal, or, as the French would say, the *material* interests of the community, are managed by those of its members who possess the greatest capacity for such management; and on the other hand, those whose opinions the people follow, whose feelings they imbibe, and who practically and by common consent, perform, no matter under what original title, the office of thinking for the people, are persons better qualified than any others whom the civilization of the age and country affords, to think and judge rightly and usefully.

In these circumstances the people, although they may at times be unhappy and consequently discontented, habitually acquiesce in the laws and institutions which they live under, and seek for relief through those institutions and not in defiance of them. Individual ambition struggles to ascend by no other paths than those which the law recognizes and allows. The ruling powers have no immediate interest in counteracting the progress of civilization; society is either stationary, or moves onward solely in those directions in which its progress brings it into no collision with the established order of things.

Society may be said to be in its *transitional* state, when it contains other persons fitter for worldly power and moral influence than those who have hitherto enjoyed them: when worldly power, and the greatest existing capacity for worldly affairs, are no longer united but severed; and when the authority which sets the opinions and forms the feelings of those who are not accustomed to think for themselves, does not exist at all, or, existing, resides anywhere but in the most cultivated intellects, and the most exalted characters, of the age.

When this is the posture of affairs, society has either entered or is on the point of entering into a state in which there are no established doctrines; in which the world of opinions is a mere chaos, and in which, as to worldly affairs, whosoever is dissatisfied with any thing or for any reason, flies at once to an alteration in the conditions of worldly power, as a means for obtaining something which would remove what he deems the cause of his dissatisfaction. And this continues until a moral and social revolution (or it may be, a series of such) has replaced worldly power and moral influence in the hands of the most competent: when society is once more in its natural state, and resumes its onward progress, at the point where it was stopped before by the social system which it has shivered.

It is the object of the present paper, and of that by which it will be immediately followed,[1] to demonstrate, that the changes in the visible structure of society which are manifestly approaching, and which so many anticipate with dread, and so many with hope of a nature far different from that which I feel, are the means by which we are to be carried through our present transitional state, and the human mind is to resume its quiet and regular onward course; a course as undisturbed by convulsions or anarchy, either in the political or in the moral world, as in the best times heretofore, but far more favoured than any former period in respect to the means of rapid advancement, and less impeded by the effect of counteracting forces.

To begin with the conditions of worldly power.

There are two states of society, differing in other respects, but agreeing in this, that worldly power is habitually exercised by the fittest men. One is, when the holders of power are purposely selected for their fitness. The other is, when the circumstances of society are such, that the possession of power of itself calls forth the qualifications for its exercise, in a greater degree than they can be acquired by any other persons in that state of society.

The former state was exemplified in the best constituted republics of antiquity, and is now realized in the United States of America: the latter prevailed throughout most of the nations of Europe in the middle ages.

In the best of the ancient republics all offices, political or military, which were supposed to require peculiar abilities, were conferred upon those who, in the opinion of the best judges, the educated gentlemen of the country (for such the free citizens of Athens, and, in its best times, of Rome, essentially were) possessed the greatest personal qualifications for administering the affairs of the state, and would administer them according to the best ideas of their age. With how much wisdom the choice was usually made, is evidenced in the case of Athens, by the extraordinary series of great men by whom the affairs of that little commonwealth were successively managed, and who made it the source of light and civilization to the world, and the most inspiring and elevating example which history has yet produced, of how much human nature is capable. In the case of Rome, the same fact is as certainly demonstrated, by the steady unintermitted progress of that community from the smallest beginnings to the highest prosperity and power.

---

[1]Mill presumably is referring to the fourth instalment (No. 97), not merely to the continuation of the third instalment (No. 92).

In the United States, where those who are called to power, are so by the general voice of the whole people, experience equally testifies to the admirable good sense with which the highest offices have been bestowed. At every election of a President, without exception, the people's choice has fallen on the person whom, as all impartial observers must admit, every circumstance that the people knew, pointed out as the fittest; nor is it possible to name one person preeminently qualified for the office, who has not, if he was a candidate, obtained it. In the only two cases in which subsequent experience did not confirm the people's judgment, they corrected the error on the very first lawful opportunity.[2]

But supposing that, in communities constituted like the United States, the holders of power were not really, as in fact they are, the most qualified persons; they are at least those whom the people imagine to be so. The people, consequently, are satisfied with their institutions, and with their rulers; and feel no disposition to lay the blame of their private ills upon the existing order of society, nor to seek the improvement of their circumstances by any means which are repugnant to that order.

In addition to these instances, where the management of the affairs of the community is in the fittest hands because those hands are deliberately selected and put in charge of it, there is another class of cases, in which power is not assigned to him who is already the fittest, but has a strong tendency to render that person the fittest to whom it is assigned. The extreme case of this state of society is that of a Highland clan: and all other small societies of barbarous people are in the main similar. The chief of a clan is despotic, so far as custom and opinion and habit can render him so. He is not selected for any qualities of his, for his office is in all cases hereditary. But he is bred to it, and practised in it from his youth upwards; while every other member of the community is bred to, and practised in, something else, and has no opportunity of training himself to that. The position, moreover, of the society itself, does not admit of the chief's being utterly destitute of the necessary qualifications for leading the clan in battle, and guiding them in council. It is the condition of his existence and theirs, that he should be capable of maintaining himself in circumstances of considerable difficulty. As men generally contrive to acquire the faculties which they cannot possibly do without, the head of a clan is scarcely ever absolutely unfit for governing: the clansmen are fit for executing, and sometimes for advising, but seldom for commanding. The leader, therefore, is still the fittest, or at the least as fit as any one else: and the essential character of a natural state of society is realised, for the people have confidence in those who manage their affairs.

Between these two states of society, that in which capacity raises men to power, and that in which power calls forth their capacity, there is this important

[2]Both John Adams (1735-1826), 2nd President of the United States (1797-1801), and his son, John Quincy Adams (1767-1848), 6th President (1825-29), served a single term.

difference, that the former state does not contain in itself the seeds of its own dissolution. A society which is directed by its most capable members, wheresoever they are to be found, may doubtless come to an end, as is shown by many instances, but at least its dissolution is never the direct consequence of its own organization, since every new intellectual power which grows up, takes its natural place in the existing social order, and is not obliged to break it in pieces in order to make itself way. But when the possession of power is guaranteed to particular persons independently of their capacity, those persons may be the fittest to-day and the most incapable to-morrow: and these social arrangements are exposed to certain destruction, from every cause which raises up in the society itself, fitter persons for power than those who possess it. For although mankind, in all ages except those of transition, are ever ready to obey and love those whom they recognize as better able to govern them, than they are to govern themselves, it is not in human nature to yield a willing obedience to men whom you think no wiser than yourself, especially when you are told by those whom you do think wiser, that they would govern you in a different manner. Unless therefore this state of society be so constituted as to prevent altogether the progress of civilization, that progress always ultimately overthrows it—the tendency of civilization being on the one hand, to render some of those who are excluded from power, fitter and fitter for it, and on the other hand (in a way hereafter to be explained) to render the monopolizers of power, actually less fit for it than they were originally.

Now, the proposition which I am about to prove is, that the above is a correct account of the process which has been going on for a considerable length of time in modern Europe:—that the qualification for power has been, and is, anything rather than fitness for it, either real or presumed: that nevertheless the holders of power, for a long time, possessed, from the necessary circumstances of society, greater fitness for it than was possessed by any other persons at that time; which fitness they have for some time been losing, while others through the advancement of civilization have been gaining it, until power, and fitness for power, have altogether ceased to correspond: and that this is one great cause, so far as political circumstances are concerned, of the general dissatisfaction with the present order of society, and the unsettled state of political opinion.

From the earliest periods of the nations of modern Europe, all worldly power has belonged to one particular class, the wealthy class. For many centuries the only wealth was land, and the only wealthy were the territorial aristocracy. At a later period, landed wealth ceased to be so greatly engrossed by a few noble families, and manufacturing and commercial wealth grew by little and little into large masses. Worldly power, under which expression I include all direct influence over the worldly affairs of the community, became proportionably diffused. It then belonged to two classes, but to them exclusively, the landed gentry, and the monied class; and in their hands it still remains.

For many ages these were felt by all to be the proper depositories of power, because they possessed, on the average, such qualifications for it as no other members of the community, in the then state of civilization, could rationally hope to acquire. It cannot, for example, be imagined that the villeins or serfs, or even the smaller freeholders, in those ages in which nothing was to be learnt from books, but all from practice and experience, could be so fit for commanding the nation in battle, or deliberating on its affairs in council, as those who had been taught to look to these as their appointed functions and occupations, who had been trained to fitness for them in every way which was suggested by the conceptions of those times, and who from constant practice, possessed at least the same kind of superiority in their business, which an experienced workman possesses over one who has never handled a tool.

It is not pretended that the barons were in themselves very fit for power, or that they did not use it very ill; they did so, as history testifies, to a frightful extent: not that I agree in one-half of all that is said in their disparagement by many who, if cotemporary with them, would most probably have admired them, having no standard of approbation but the ideas of their own age. But those may be in themselves very unfit, than whom, nevertheless, an uncivilized age affords none fitter: and power, which is not accountable to those interested in its being properly employed, is likely to be abused, even though it be held by the most capable persons, not in a rude age only, but in the most highly civilized one. This is one of those principles which being true in all states and in all situations in which man has been found, or in which we can rationally expect to find him, must be allowed the paramount importance which is due to it, whatever be the state of society that we are considering. This may not always have been duly adverted to by the historical school of politicians (by whom, be it understood, I mean the really profound and philosophic inquirers into history in France and Germany, not the Plausibles, who in our own land of shallowness and charlatanerie, babble about induction without having ever considered what it is, relying on that rhetoric which is defined by Plato as the art of appearing profoundly versed in a subject to those who know nothing at all about it).[3] I say, those who have endeavoured to erect an inductive philosophy of history, may be charged with having taken insufficient account of the qualities in which mankind in all ages and nations are alike, their attention being unduly engrossed by the differences; but there is an error on the other side, to which those are peculiarly liable, who build their philosophy of politics upon what they term the universal principles of human nature. Such persons often form their judgments, in particular cases, as if, because there are universal principles of human nature, they imagined that all are such which they find to be true universally of the people of their own age and country. They should consider that if there are some

---

[3]Plato (427-347 B.C.), *Gorgias*, in *Lysis, Symposium, Gorgias* (Greek and English), trans. W.R.M. Lamb (London: Heinemann, 1953), pp. 290-2 (456^b-457^b).

tendencies of human nature, and some of the circumstances by which man is surrounded, which are the same in all ages and countries, these never form the whole of the tendencies, or of the circumstances, which exist in any particular age or country: each possesses, along with those invariable tendencies, others which are changeable, and peculiarly its own; and in no age, as civilization advances, are the prevailing tendencies exactly the same as in the preceding age, nor do those tendencies act under precisely the same combination of external circumstances.

We must not therefore (as some may be apt to do,) blame the people of the middle ages for not having sought securities against the irresponsible power of their rulers; persuading ourselves that in those or in any times, popular institutions might exist, if the many had sense to perceive their utility, and spirit to demand them. To find fault with our ancestors for not having annual parliaments, universal suffrage, and vote by ballot, would be like quarrelling with the Greeks and Romans for not using steam navigation, when we know it is so safe and expeditious; which would be, in short, simply finding fault with the third century before Christ for not being the eighteenth century after. It was necessary that many other things should be thought and done, before, according to the laws of human affairs, it was possible that steam navigation should be thought of. Human nature must proceed step by step, in politics as well as in physics. The people of the middle ages knew very well, whether they were oppressed or not; and the opinion of the many, added to the fear of vengeance from some injured individual, acted in a certain, though doubtless by no means a sufficient, extent, as a restraint upon oppression. For any more effectual restraint than this, society was not yet ripe. To have thrown off their masters, and taken others, would have been to buy a still worse government at the price of a convulsion: to contrive, establish, and work the machine of a responsible government, was an impossibility in the then state of the human mind. Though the idea had been conceived, it could not have been realized. Several antecedent stages in civilization had previously to be passed through. An insurrection of the peasants against their feudal lords, could, in the nature of things, have only been, what it actually was, a Jacquerie:[4] for any more rational effort there was needed a power of self-restraint for the purpose of union, and a confidence in each other, which they are not to be blamed for not having, since it could only be the slow result of a habit of acting in concert for other purposes, which, in an extensive country, can only co-exist with a high state of civilization. So soon as any portion of the people did acquire this habit of acting together, they did seek better political securities, and obtained them: witness the rise of the free cities, and

---

[4]The insurrection in 1358 of the French peasants in the Ile de France and Beauvais, involving the burning of châteaux and great atrocities, gave its appellation, derived from the common peasant's name, Jacques, to subsequent violent rural disorders.

corporations, all over Europe. The people therefore of the middle ages had as good a government as the circumstances of the middle ages admitted; their affairs were less badly managed, in that bad age, by their masters, than they could have managed them for themselves. The army of Godefroi de Bouillon in the first crusade, was not quite so efficient an instrument of warfare as that of the Duke of Wellington, in 1815: but it was considerably more so than that of Peter the Hermit, which preceded it.[5]

From these remarks it will be seen how greatly I differ, at once from those, who seeing the institutions of our ancestors to be bad for us, imagine that they were bad for those for whom they were made, and from those who ridiculously invoke the wisdom of our ancestors as authority for institutions which in substance are now totally different, howsoever they may be the same in form. The institutions of our ancestors served passably well for our ancestors, and that from no wisdom of theirs; but from a cause to which, I am afraid, nearly all the good institutions which have ever existed, owed their origin, namely the force of circumstances: but the possessors of power in the present day are not the natural successors of the possessors of power in that day. They may show a valid title to inherit the property, perhaps, of the ancient Barons; but political power descends, as will be found in the long run, by a different law.

(The conclusion of this Paper in our next.)[6]

83. FRENCH NEWS [14]

EXAMINER, 6 FEB., 1831, P. 88

This article is headed "London, February 6." For the entry in Mill's bibliography, see No. 55. In the Somerville College set the article is listed as "Article on France" and square brackets enclose the part here printed; the excluded parts are the first three paragraphs, on Belgium and Poland, and the concluding paragraph, on the French Chamber of Peers passing the bill that was enacted as Bull. 20, No. 85 (10 Feb., 1831), allowing ministers of the Jewish religion to be paid from public funds (see No. 66).

THE UNSETTLED STATE OF BELGIUM, and the approaching struggle in Poland, appear to occupy and agitate the French people far more than that which is of

[5]Godefroi de Bouillon (ca. 1060-1100), son of Eustace II, comte de Boulogne and a descendant of Charlemagne, who, as commander of the First Crusade, captured Jerusalem in 1099, and was idolized in later sagas for his feats. Peter the Hermit (ca. 1050-ca. 1115), a French monk who stirred up the poor for the first wave of that crusade, and led one of the five sections to massacre in 1096; with a few surviving followers, he joined the second wave, led by Godefroi, in 1097.

[6]See No. 92, which, however, appeared not on 13 Feb. in the next issue of the *Examiner*, but in that of 13 Mar.

greater importance to human kind than the very existence of Belgium and Poland taken together—their own struggle for good institutions.[1]

The French are not, as is sometimes asserted, fond of war, but they have not the deep-rooted abhorrence of it, which so large a proportion of ourselves have; it is one of our few points of national superiority. The French are kept out of unjust war, not by a proper sense of its evils, but by a sentiment of national morality, which forbids infringement upon the rights of other nations. But it is obvious, that they would be ready, at the present instant, to seize hold of any just or plausible ground of quarrel, however trivial, for taking part with the Poles, whom they consider as engaged in the same cause with themselves; and as in reality, defending their own frontiers. When once the sword shall be drawn, and the five hundred thousand French soldiers, now under arms, shall, with a successful general at their head, be overrunning Europe, it is quite impossible to foresee for how long a period the progress of civilization, and that of good institutions all over the world may be stopped, or even for how large a space it may be thrown back.

84. THE MUNICIPAL INSTITUTIONS OF FRANCE
EXAMINER, 13 FEB., 1831, PP. 98-9

This article was occasioned by the discussion of the municipal reform law, already frequently alluded to by Mill (see, e.g., Nos. 57 and 76). It is headed as title and printed in the "Political Examiner." Described in Mill's bibliography as "An article headed 'The Municipal Institutions of France' in the Examiner of 13 Febry. 1830 [*sic*]" (MacMinn, p. 15), it is listed as title and marked with square brackets in the Somerville College set.

DEBATES OF GREAT INTEREST AND IMPORTANCE are now taking place in the Chamber of Deputies, on the proposed municipal law. Our daily journalists, being altogether unaware of the importance of this as of almost every other topic beyond the range of every-day conversation, allow the public to remain utterly unacquainted, both with the debates themselves, and with the facts necessary to understand them. We shall briefly state the nature of the existing municipal institutions of France, and of the alterations proposed to be made in them by the present Bill.

France is divided into departments, and each department into arrondissements. Each arrondissement is likewise divided into cantons; but of this last subdivision it is unnecessary to say any thing further in this place. Below the canton, there remains only the division into communes or townships, consisting of a town or village, with the lands appertaining to it.

[1]For the background on Belgium, see No. 59, n5; on Poland, No. 68, n3.

At the head of each department is a prefect, at the head of each arrondissement a sub-prefect, and at the head of each commune a mayor. The prefect and the sub-prefect are the delegates of the executive, the subordinate agents or instruments of the general government; and are therefore, very properly, named by the Crown. The mayor has also to perform various duties, judicial and administrative, which are delegated to him by the general government, but he is considered as the representative, not so much of the Crown as of the commune; appointed, not so much to take care that the commune performs its duties, as to see that it obtains its rights; and is therefore supposed to be, and generally is, one of the principal inhabitants of the place. Nevertheless, under the odious system of centralization introduced by Napoleon, and carried still farther by the restored Bourbons, the principle of which was to annihilate every atom or vestige of power not emanating from the central government, the mayors as well as the prefects and sub-prefects are named by the executive.[1] In all communes exceeding, we believe, 3,000 inhabitants, they are appointed directly by the Crown; where the population is below that number, by the prefect of the department.

In addition to the prefect, the sub-prefect, and the mayor, there are also bodies, consisting of from twenty to thirty of the principal inhabitants or thereabouts, and termed, *conseils généraux de département*, *conseils d'arrondissement*, and *conseils communaux* or *municipaux*. These bodies are not boards, sitting constantly, but a kind of local parliaments, holding a session of about a fortnight once every year, and meeting for special purposes at any other time, if called together by the prefect, the sub-prefect, or the mayor, respectively. The duties of these councils are to determine what rates shall be levied for the local purposes of the department, the arrondissement, and the commune, and to what objects they shall be devoted; to audit the accounts of the preceding year; and to assess on each inhabitant of the department his proper share of the direct taxes of the department; for the chambers only determine upon certain general data what sum shall be paid by each department on account of each tax (*impôt foncier*, *impôt mobilier*, and *portes et fenêtres*). The departmental council afterwards shares out this demand among the several arrondissements, the council of each arrondissement among the several communes, and the council of each commune among the inhabitants.

Such are the functions of the various local councils. Their nomination emanates exclusively from the executive. They are named in every case by the Crown, or its delegate and representative, the prefect. Such were the liberties of France under the restoration! and yet there are slaves, both in this country and in France, who aver that the charter of 1814 was faulty by not giving sufficient power to the Crown!

[1]See No. 57, n5.

The present bill, which originated with the Chamber of Deputies, not with the ministry, relates to the mayors, and the communal councils, exclusively, and has for its object, not to make any change in their functions, but to alter the mode of their nomination. There is a crying demand for a law for the former of these purposes, as the functions of the councils comprehend but a small proportion of that large part of the business of government, which can be most conveniently and unexceptionably performed by local representative bodies. But any extension of their powers would be pure evil, while they continue, as at present, to be named by the government: for if any part of the people's business is to be transacted by persons, in the selection of whom they have no voice, it is better that it should be done at Paris, by the ministers and the Chamber, who are at least under the influence of the opinion of a larger public, and who are supposed to be controlled and restrained by the nation whom they profess to represent.

By the present bill, the municipal councils are to be elected by the most highly-taxed inhabitants of the commune, in a number amounting on the average to about one-thirtieth part of the population.[2] The mayors are to be named as heretofore, by the King or the prefect, but they must be selected from among the municipal councillors.[3] The mayor is to retain his functions for three years, the members of the council for six, one half going out every three years, but being immediately re-eligible.[4]

The debates on the bill afford a tolerable foretaste of those on the approaching electoral law,[5] and it might be added, of those in our own House of Commons on the bill for Parliamentary Reform.[6] The popular party contend that the suffrage for the local councils ought to be extended to all who are rated for direct taxes, and are able to read and write. They say, that the proposed law will throw the powers of the local councils in the smaller communes entirely into the hands of landed proprietors, who, though a numerous class in France, will yet, if invested with a monopoly of power, exercise it for their separate interests; and will, in particular, make it their grand object to throw the local expenses off the land, and levy them by *octroi*, or taxes on raw produce imported into the town or village, which obviously fall, with enormously disproportionate weight, upon the poorer classes, and those who have nothing to support them but their labour. This would be a monstrous evil. It is admitted that in a new country, rent, not being the result of labour, is the most proper fund from which the necessities of the state can be

---

[2]Titre I, Chap. ii, Sect. 1, Art. 11.
[3]Titre I, Chap. i, Art. 3.
[4]Titre I, Chap. i, Art. 4, and Chap. ii, Sect. 1, Art. 17.
[5]See No. 72, n3, for the details of this law.
[6]Mill is referring to the impending debate on "A Bill to Amend the Representation of the People in England and Wales," 1 William IV (14 Mar., 1831), *PP*, 1830-31, II, 197-218, which was defeated in Committee on 21 Apr. For subsequent Bills leading to 2 & 3 William IV, c. 45 (7 June, 1832), the First Reform Act, see Nos. 107, n2, and 174.

supplied: in France this has already been done to a large extent, and to undo it would be a mere confiscation of the earnings of the productive and industrious, to put into the pockets of a class which in France, we admit, is also for the most part productive and industrious, that which it has in no respect earned.

In answer to this are brought forward all the stale common-places, which are heard whenever a demand is made for irresponsible power; that men of considerable property are alone fit for managing any of the affairs of the public, they alone having a stake in the country, and being the exclusive possessors of intelligence. These insolent assumptions, which we fear mankind will be condemned to hear for a considerable time longer, were refuted by the speakers on the popular side, with an ability and soundness which we wish we could expect to see equalled in our own Honourable House next month. We rejoice at the proofs afforded by these debates of the growing strength of the popular party in the nation. Three highly esteemed deputies, MM. Marchal, Thouvenel, and Gaëtan de la Rochefoucault, who had never belonged to the *extrême gauche*, have made able and energetic speeches, in which they ally themselves expressly and in the strongest manner with the popular cause.[7] The speech of M. Daunou, and that of M. Isambert, were excellent.[8]

As usual, the party which calls itself moderate, had all the intemperance to itself. It is astonishing to us how the popular leaders find patience to bear up, without any attempts at retaliation, against the reproaches heaped upon them every day by an insolent and corrupt oligarchy, whose shameless greed of places and dignities has equalled or surpassed anything previously known even in the worst times of the Restoration.

85. FRENCH NEWS [15]

EXAMINER, 13 FEB., 1831, P. 106

The article is headed "London, February 13." For the entry in Mill's bibliography, see No. 55. The item is listed as "Article on France" in the Somerville College set, with the paragraphs here included surrounded by square brackets; the article begins with a paragraph, here excluded, on Belgian affairs.

[7]Pierre François Marchal (1785-1864), a deputy from 1827, joined the 221 and supported Louis Philippe; his speech on the municipal government bill (29 Jan.) is in *Moniteur*, 1831, pp. 206-7. Pierre Sébastien Barthélemy Thouvenel (1782-1831), a doctor, also a deputy from 1827, one of the 221 and a supporter of Louis Philippe; his speech of 31 Jan. is *ibid.*, pp. 227-8. Marquis Frédéric Gaëtan de La Rochefoucauld-Liancourt (1779-1863), a moderate constitutionalist, who also was a deputy from 1827, one of the 221 and a supporter of Louis Philippe, favoured the abolition of slavery but not the new Electoral Law. His speech of 1 Feb. is *ibid.*, p. 223.

[8]For the speeches of Daunou (31 Jan.) and Isambert (1 Feb.), see *ibid.*, pp. 215-16 and 228-9.

THE GOVERNMENT OF LOUIS PHILIPPE appear to be trying a course of experiment how much the patience of the French people will bear. We mentioned in our last paper the dismissal of M. Merville, the prefect of Meurthe, for signing an address, in which wishes were expressed for more popular institutions.[1] This was followed by the resignation of the sub-prefect, the mayor, his deputy, and many officers of the national guard.[2] Another prefect has since been dismissed for his democratic inclinations, M. Pons de l'Hérault, prefect of the Jura.[3] Such was this magistrate's popularity, that a few days previously, on a mere rumour that he had been, or was about to be recalled, the people of the neighbouring country thronged into the town, the streets were crowded with people; deputations waited upon the prefect from all quarters to ascertain the fact; and a petition to the King, not to remove M. Pons, was actually sent to Paris, and must have crossed his dismissal on the road.[4]

The King has taken off the mask: and in his answer to an address from Gaillac, a town of some consequence in the south of France, has dropped at length his hypocritical adulation of the people and the revolution, and, for the first time, adopted the cant of the stationary or stagnation party.[5] He has thus (whether from cowardice and weakness, or from original evil intention, we know not, nor need we care,) made his determination to stand, or, as we devoutly trust will be the case, to fall, with the new oligarchy. Posterity at least will know, if contemporaries do not, on whose head the responsibilty should rest of all the evils which may result from another struggle, followed by another convulsion.

86. THE BUDGET

EXAMINER, 20 FEB., 1831, PP. 113-14

Here Mill turns his attention to the British House of Commons, where, on 11 Feb., John Charles Spencer, Lord Althorp, introduced the budget (*PD*, 3rd ser., Vol. 2, cols. 403-18). The intentions behind the proposals, stated Spencer, were to reduce the burden on the poor, which could best be done by improving manufactures and thus increasing employment; to increase revenue by lowering duties and thereby increasing consumption; and to improve the distribution of taxes by spreading over the whole community those which fell on only one part. He proposed to abolish 210 offices, many in Ireland; to

[1]For earlier discussion, see Nos. 79 and 81.

[2]The sub-prefect has been identified only as the chevalier de Landrian; the mayor was Nicolas André Esprit Tardieu (1790-1843); and his deputy, Louis Victor Chenut.

[3]André Pons de l'Hérault (1772-1853), a supporter of the Revolution and then of Napoleon, during a career of mixed fortunes had always favoured reform. He had been appointed Prefect of the Jura after the July Revolution.

[4]The town into which the people thronged was Lons-le-Saunier; the petition (undated, but ca. 1 Feb.) is in the Archives Départementales du Jura, cote M 12.

[5]*Moniteur*, 1831, p. 205.

reduce duties on beer, leather, cider, and sugar; to reduce taxes on newspapers, coal, tallow candles, printed calicoes, glass, and tobacco; and to increase the tax on wine, timber, raw cotton, and passengers by steam. He also proposed to impose a one-half percent duty on the sale of funded property, but the outcry over this last proposal caused its immediate withdrawal. The debate continued on 14 Feb. in both Lords and Commons (see *ibid.*, cols. 492-539).

The item, the first in the "Political Examiner," is headed as title. It is described in Mill's bibliography as "An article headed 'The Budget' in the Examiner of 20th February 1831" (MacMinn, p. 15), and is listed as title and marked with square brackets in the Somerville College set.

THE BUDGET HAS GIVEN A SHOCK to the influence of the Ministry, from which, it seems to be the general persuasion that they will hardly recover. All that class of politicians, so numerous in times of difficulty, who, in the civil dissensions of the seventeenth century, were termed "waiters upon Providence,"[1] are beginning to desert the falling house. They are "losing their confidence in the Ministry," which from them always means, their confidence in its continuing in place. Those whose respect for a Cabinet is proportioned to their opinion of its durability, have lowered the quota of their respect to three months at most.

It cannot be denied withal, that the present Budget evinces large views of public good, an enlightened perception of the pernicious working of our fiscal system, a discriminating selection of the worst parts of it to be first got rid of, which it would be injustice to compare for a moment with any of the feeble aspirations of preceding financiers: but, unhappily, these generous and enlarged projects of improvement are deformed with blunders of so portentous a magnitude, as have caused all that is admirable in the general scheme to be passed over with little attention and no gratitude: and unhappily the Ministers, who like the remainder of the Parliamentary herd, if they are capable of receiving, are incapable of originating truth and good sense, are indebted to others for all their enlightened views; while their blunders, alas! are all their own.

The taxes which are taken off are such as all who were acquainted with their operation, had long since pointed out as some of the very worst which disgrace our fiscal code. These which are to be laid on, the Ministers, as ministers are wont, reserved *in petto*, to be first announced in Parliament, when it was too late to retract with any dignity; and of course, they underwent no other consideration or scrutiny than such as could be given them by the feeble, infantine, ministerial, parliamentary minds of their official originators.

Although the tax of one-half per cent. on the transfer of stock has been abandoned, which was the least foolish course a ministry could adopt, which had been so foolish as to propose it; the question which it involves is too deeply

---

[1]For the term, see Hume, *History of England*, Vol. VII, p. 227.

important, and too certain to recur again in some other shape, to be let pass without a few words of remark.

A tax on stock is partial taxation; it is taxation imposed upon that class whose property is, from its very nature, more precarious, less protected by the feelings which ordinarily attach to property, and more tempting to financial cupidity, than any other; and it is taxation in breach of a direct Parliamentary pledge, as clear as words could make it, which formed as essential a part of the national contract with the fundholder, as the rate of interest.[2]

To the assertion, that the proposed tax is partial taxation, in other words, confiscation, aggravated by a direct breach of faith, Ministers had no answer to make, but that they intended to impose a similar tax on the transfer of land, and that their measure was no more a breach of national faith than was the income tax.[3]

Neither of these pleas in justification, will bear a moment's thought. The land and the funds together, form a very small portion of the national wealth; and a tax which falls upon them both, and upon nothing else, is partial taxation no less than if it fell only upon one or other of them. A large portion of the funds, moreover, change hands as many times in a year as land does in a century, and would therefore, under the show and pretext of exact equality, be taxed unequally in the ratio of one hundred to one. The allusion to the income tax is actually silly. The income tax was a *general* measure. The national creditor never stipulated for exemption from bearing his due share, proportional to his property, of the public burthens. He stipulated that he should not be made to pay it in *such a way* as should enable a profligate ministry and parliament, under the fraudulent pretence of calling upon him for his share, to call on him for more than his share, and place the nation in the disgraceful predicament of a debtor saying to his creditor, God forbid I should refuse you the interest of my debt, but I am free to call part of it a *tax*, and under that name I mean to keep it in my own pocket.

If the fundholder is not taxed in the same proportion to his property as other people, it is in the power of Parliament to make the matter certain, by laying on a uniform tax in proportion to property. But if inequalities in the pressure of taxation are to be made up for, as this scheme proposes, by partial taxes on those who are supposed to be undertaxed, there is so much unavoidable uncertainty,

---

[2]The words appear in the Acts authorizing the raising of money by a bond issue on the credit of the Consolidated Fund; see, e.g., 28 George III, c. 26 (1788): "and moreover, that no Money to be lent upon the Security of this Act shall be rated or assessed to any Tax or Assessment whatsoever."

[3]A reply by Spencer (11 Feb., 1831), *PD*, 3rd ser., Vol. 2, cols. 446-7. The wartime taxes referred to both as income and property taxes were established by 38 George III, c. 60 (1798), and 39 George III, c. 13 (1799), and repealed in effect by 56 George III, c. 65 (1816).

and so much room for sophistry and quibble, in discussing whether the fundholder pays his share or less than his share, that he is the ready victim of any minister, who with plunder in his heart and jesuitry on his lips, should come down to Parliament with a proposition for throwing two-thirds of the public burthens upon the shoulders of a single class; and that, too, the only class whose property the nation has, by a special obligation, engaged itself to protect.

So far is this from being a hypothetical danger, urged merely for effect, and unlikely to be realized, that the very tax proposed realizes it as far as it goes. For can there be a more impudent assumption than that the fundholder does not pay his due share of the taxes? The rich, truly enough (and sufficiently to our discredit) are more lightly taxed than persons of small, or middling fortunes; but the poor fundholder pays the same taxes as any other poor man, and the rich fundholder pays the same as any other rich man. The fundholder pays all the assessed taxes. He pays all the taxes on consumption. He pays the legacy duty in common with the public in general; this the landholders, in their two Houses of Parliament, have taken good care that their land should *not* pay. There remain only the taxes which fall peculiarly on the land. Now, without saying any thing of their amount, which has been so grossly exaggerated; or of the counterbalancing advantage of low wages, which, to the greatest national detriment, is occasioned by those very taxes; is there a man in the country who does not know that there has been enacted a Corn Law for the declared purpose of *compensating*, and *more* than compensating, the landholders for all these taxes, at the cost of three times the amount, taken from the pockets of all the other classes of the community, the fundholder included? But the lion's share of the plunder of the people does not content our rent-eating oligarchy; they would have the whole, and, doubtless, will make a desperate effort to seize and engross it, by means of the approaching Sham Reform. This at least is certain—that if, when the facts which prove the contrary are so flagrant and notorious, the impudent pretence is made, that the landlords bear more than their share of the taxes, and the fundholders less, it is a sufficient proof how abundantly needful the stipulation was, which formed part of the contract with the fundholder, that he should not be called upon to pay any tax, unless in common with all the rest of the community; for if a pretext can be found for imposing a partial tax upon him now, when, in the name of Heaven, can such a pretext possibly be wanting?

The other taxes which are to be laid on, are all more or less objectionable. The tax on raw cotton is less mischievous certainly than that on calicoes; but it is justly chargeable, though not quite in an equal degree, with nearly all the vices which a tax can have, together with the accidental one of being a *new* tax, and therefore disturbing previous expectations and arrangements. It falls heavier on the poor than on the rich; it impedes the increase of intercourse with foreign countries; it renders larger capitals necessary, for carrying on all the branches of manufacture in which cotton is used; it compels the keeping up of two establishments, one to levy the tax, and another to pay back as much (according to some) as two-thirds of it; and it occasions all the frauds inseparable from a system of drawbacks. And while we are on the subject of drawbacks, we may just remark, how much eagerness is always shown to prevent a tax from falling upon our exports, that is to say, upon foreigners, while our own people are suffered to be taxed *à merci et à miséricorde*, without a tithe of the complaints. This keen anxiety for the interests of our merchants, and indifference to that of the consumers, is quite in keeping with all the rest of the working of our aristocratical government.

The tax on steam-boat passengers is as indefensible an impost, viewed on general principles, as can easily be conceived; and it will, besides, most injuriously affect existing interests. Our fear is, that it is not sufficiently high to prevent the influx of Irish, which degrades and pauperizes our labourers; for if it were, nothing could exceed the delight and gratitude with which we should hail even so bad a means of effecting so virtuous an end.

The modification of the duties on timber is highly objectionable as an increased burthen upon a necessary of life and a material of all manufactures; while it has *not*, at least if the newspapers have rightly reported it, the redeeming merit of removing the inequality of taxation between Baltic and Canada timber.[4] If it accomplished this, it would of itself save the country a sum of one million annually, which is now as completely lost and sacrificed as if it were thrown into the sea, or into the fire. But the measure, we fear, is so distant an approach to this equalization, that its effect in removing the evil of a forced and unprofitable employment of capital, will scarcely be perceived.

But if these were the best of all taxes, instead of ranking among the worst, could the ministers hope to gain the least credit with the public for merely shifting the burthen which oppresses us from one shoulder to the other, when we are all firmly convinced that such retrenchments are possible, as would have enabled taxes of this amount to be dispensed with altogether? What retrenchment, however, is to be expected from a ministry, which expatiates on its own economy in cutting off an Irish Postmaster-General, or a Lieutenant-General of the Ordnance, while it levies nine thousand additional soldiers to fight Swing;[5] not having the common sense which would have taught any plough-boy, that Swing will range the country for ever, if he continues at large until regular troops can catch him; nor foreseeing, what has since been boasted of by the Attorney-General,[6] that the common officers of justice would quietly go to

---

[4]See, e.g., leading articles in the *Morning Chronicle*, 12 Feb., p. 4, and *The Times*, 12 Feb., p. 3.

[5]The name used to personify the rick-burning and other current disturbances in the agricultural areas mostly of the south.

[6]Thomas Denman.

the spot, and take the offenders and try them and hang them without the smallest impediment.

A Ministry, whose fears can thus far overmaster their reason, may possibly be sincere in making the monstrous assertion, that the public service does not admit of any diminution of taxation.[7] But where was Mr. Hume when this was said? Had such a doctrine been advanced by a Goulburn or a Herries, what bounds could have been set to his indignation?

The Ministry should have taken off the duty on cottons, on sea-borne coals, on candles, on glass, and reduced those on newspapers and advertisements,[8] without laying on any new tax at all, until they had time to see, first, what expenditure they could retrench, and next, how much revenue they would actually lose. The loss of revenue is never equal to the amount of the nominal sacrifice, because a portion of what the consumers save is sure to be expended in some other taxable article. These taxes in particular, as they take from the consumer very much more than they bring into the public treasury, would, when remitted, have set at liberty a much larger income than the nominal amount of the tax, and would consequently have increased in more than the usual degree, the produce of the other taxes. The abolition of the duty on glass, by leading to a large export of that article, would have caused increased imports, and an increase of the customs revenue. Neither must it be forgotten, that trade and manufactures are now extremely prosperous, and that an increase of revenue is naturally to be looked for from that cause alone. The equalization of the duties on wines, one of the best of Lord Althorp's propositions, might have been persevered in; and as the abolition of the duty on glass would, we are informed, have been nearly a compensation to the wine merchant, for the small increased duty on Spanish, Portuguese, and German wines, a large increase of consumption and of revenue might have been expected, and a great extension of commercial intercourse with France, leading to manifold advantages, and not without a beneficial effect on the revenue.

If all these sources of increased revenue, together with such retrenchments as the proprietors of Parliament could be induced to permit, proved insufficient to supply the deficit occasioned by the repeal of so many taxes, it would have been a trifling evil to make up the deficiency for a single year by the issue of, certainly, far less than a million of exchequer bills. In the meantime, public attention would have been drawn to the possible necessity of a new tax; the merits and defects of all those which could occur to any one, would have been fully canvassed, and the least objectionable, or the least unacceptable, might have been chosen; unless a Parliamentary Reform, occurring in the meantime, should bring about (as, if not a mere imposture, it undoubtedly would) such

[7]Spencer, speech of 11 Feb., cols. 404-6.
[8]For the concluding two, part of the "taxes on knowledge," see No. 177, n2.

retrenchment as would have rendered not these alone, but many others of our taxes altogether unnecessary.

It is not too late, even now, for the Ministers to adopt this course; but we fear there is little chance of it.

In giving up the proposed tax on the transfer of land and stock, the Ministry have abandoned the intended reduction of the duties on tobacco, and the abolition of those on glass. The first we do not lament; as we have no hope that a reduction, which would still have left a duty of 600 per cent. would have had the effect expected from it, and which alone could justify it,—the prevention of smuggling. The change of determination with respect to the duty on glass, we deeply regret.

87. FRENCH NEWS [16]
EXAMINER, 20 FEB., 1831, PP. 121-2

This item is headed "London, February 20." For the entry in Mill's bibliography, see No. 55. The item is listed as "Article on France" and enclosed in square brackets in the Somerville College set.

THERE HAS BEEN A SLIGHT DISTURBANCE AT PARIS, in consequence of an attempt of some old royalists to celebrate mass for the soul of the Duc de Berri on the anniversary of his assassination; on the occasion of which celebration royal honours were paid, or believed to be paid to the bust of the Duke of Bordeaux.[1] This so incensed the people, that they broke into the church, where they destroyed most of the *matériel* of the celebration, sparing, however, the painted windows and the pictures, and afterwards proceeded to the house of the Archbishop of Paris, which they completely gutted, throwing the furniture into the Seine.[2] Tranquillity seems afterwards to have been completely restored. Several of the royalist leaders have been arrested. Some say, that their absurd demonstrations were connected with ulterior designs. They are sufficiently stupid to have meditated such, but they are also sufficiently stupid to have acted as they have done for mere bravado, without any serious designs.

[1]Charles Ferdinand de Bourbon, duc de Berry (1778-1820), second son of Charles X, was assassinated on 13 Feb., 1820. His wife, Marie Caroline Ferdinande Louise de Bourbon (1798-1870), to everyone's surprise and to the delight of the legitimists, proved to be pregnant and subsequently produced Henri Charles Ferdinand Marie Dieudonné, comte de Chambord, duc de Bordeaux (1820-83), in whose favour Charles X abdicated during the July Revolution.

[2]Hyacinthe Louis de Quélen (1778-1839), Archbishop of Paris since 1821. For accounts of the disturbances, see "Service du duc de Berry," *Constitutionnel*, 15 Feb., p. 2, and "Bulletin de la journée," *ibid.*, 16 Feb., p. 2.

The discussion on the municipal law still continues.

The Budget for the year has been presented.[3] It exhibits some retrenchments on the ordinary expenses, and a considerable amount of extraordinary ones, rendered necessary by placing the army on the war establishment.[4] These are to be provided for by the sale of a small part of the enormous extent of forests belonging to the state.[5]

We learn from M. Laffitte's statement, a most satisfactory fact, that, notwithstanding the late and present commercial embarrassments, and the temporary privations which they must have caused to the middle and working classes, the produce of the taxes on consumption exhibits a decided increase; and this although, or perhaps because, the duties on wine, which compose a large part of the whole amount, have been considerably reduced.[6]

The ministry have lately afforded a poor earnest of their disposition towards a relaxation of the restrictive system, by which France partially renounces the use of the natural productiveness of her land and capital. They have re-established the Board of Trade, under the presidence of M. de Saint-Cricq, the Vansittart of France.[7]

88. THE EMIGRATION BILL

EXAMINER, 27 FEB., 1831, PP. 130-1

Mill is commenting on "A Bill to Facilitate Voluntary Emigration to His Majesty's Possessions Abroad," 1 William IV (22 Feb., 1831), *PP*, 1830-31, I, 463-75, introduced on 22 Feb., 1831, by Henry George Grey (1802-94), Viscount Howick, later 3rd Earl Grey, an M.P. from 1826 until he succeeded to the peerage in 1845, who was Under-Secretary for the Colonies 1830-33. For his speech on the Bill, see *PD*, 3rd ser., Vol. 2, cols. 875-906. The Bill was well received by the Commons, but was lost when Parliament was dissolved in April 1831. The item, headed as title, appears in the "Political Examiner." Described in Mill's bibliography as "An article headed 'The Emigration Bill' in the Examiner of 27th February 1831" (MacMinn, p. 15), the item is listed as title and enclosed in square brackets in the Somerville College set.

THE GOVERNMENT HAS INTRODUCED a bill for facilitating voluntary Emigration, by creating a board of commissioners, authorised to contract with individuals or with parishes, on the security of their poor-rates, for conveying pauper labourers, with their own consent, to Canada or Australia.

---

[3]Introduced on 11 Feb. by Laffitte, the budget was finally enacted as Bull. 46, No. 115 (16 Oct., 1831).

[4]For the Act, see No. 68, n2.

[5]On 11 Feb., the ministry had introduced a Bill to that effect that became Bull. 28, No. 95 (25 Mar., 1831).

[6]*Moniteur*, 1831, pp. 295-8.

[7]Nicholas Vansittart, 1st Baron Bexley (1766-1851), Chancellor of the Exchequer from 1812 to 1822, had a reputation for complicated financial borrowings.

In so far as this measure evinces a just conception of the great cause of low wages, excessive competition for employment; and in so far as the board which it will call into existence, may be considered as a commission for inquiring into the means of rendering the vast productive resources of our colonies available for the employment and comfortable subsistence of the unemployed poor of our own country; to that extent Lord Howick's bill is an indication of laudable dispositions and an earnest of improvement. Our praise can go no farther.

We have no faith in the efficacy of any plan of emigration, which, for every labourer whom it removes, implies the permanent alienation of a portion of the national capital. Lord Howick states that the expense of the emigration of a labouring man, his wife, and two children, is sixty-six pounds, and that their maintenance as paupers costs twenty-five pounds annually; on which text he proceeds to dissert upon the benefits of his plan, saying that an annuity of twenty-five pounds may be redeemed, by the advance of a sum falling short of three years' purchase.[1] But this is not a fair statement of the question. It assumes that the whole expenditure of the country on account of poor-rates is pure uncompensated outgoing, without any return. Now this, we admit, is to a great degree the case at present, but it is so merely from mal-administration; and mainly from the established mode of managing the poor piecemeal, by each parish within itself. Undoubtedly every pauper should be *chargeable* solely to his own parish, but there is no reason in the world why he should be *set to work* within that parish exclusively, where perhaps there is no employment for him of a more productive character than drawing gravel. If we had duly-constituted municipal councils, or, in default of such institutions, an officer named by the Crown in each county, and bound to find employment for all the paupers of the county, on public works, in agriculture, in manufactures, in any manner in short in which their labour could be turned to greatest account; or what would be still better, if the poor of the county were farmed by open competition to private contractors, proper securities being taken that no pauper should be mulcted of his due allowance or otherwise oppressed; no one, we believe, who has considered the subject, will doubt, that the paupers of England might be made to reproduce annually the whole amount of their maintenance, in the same manner as other labourers reproduce theirs with considerable profit. In this way the annuity of twenty-five pounds a-year would be redeemed by the advance of that sum once only; and therefore the present measure, which requires an advance of sixty-six pounds for the same purpose, is unthrifty and unadvisable.

Objections of detail present themselves in great numbers against the proposed mode of facilitating emigration: but the consideration which we have just stated applies to the principle, and appears to us to be decisive.

Yet we are friends to emigration; and are persuaded that from it, in conjunction with other measures, material relief might be afforded to the

[1] Grey, speech of 22 Feb., col. 878.

labouring classes from the pressure of their own excessive competition for employment. But, to be entitled to this praise, the scheme must be such as to pay the expenses of a second body of emigrants from the produce of the labour of the first.

Every one admits that the labour of a man in England produces very little; that the labour of a man in Australia or Canada produces very much; and that every labouring man, who could be removed from England to either of these colonies, would, by his change of abode, occasion an increase of the produce of the world, which would suffice in two or three years to repay, with interest, the expense of his passage. Here then, by general admission, is on the one hand a value lost, namely what the pauper would have produced at home, together with the expenses of his passage; on the other hand, a value created in the colony, exceeding the value lost; and it is actually given up as an insoluble problem, to make a portion of the gain available to cover the loss! It is an insult to the human understanding to pretend that there are no means of making emigration pay for itself. If the emigration of a moderate number of labourers in the prime of life were defrayed by an advance from the treasury, and a portion of what was added to the produce of the colony by their labour, were exacted in the form of a tax, and appropriated to form a fund for further emigration, a perennial stream of emigrants might be kept up without further expense to the mother country, until Canada, South Africa, and Australia were fully peopled. Whether this drain could be rendered sufficiently large to prevent overflow—whether emigration on this principle could ever be sufficient to relieve over-population at home—can scarcely be known before trial; but the grounds of hope are amply sufficient to render a trial not only advisable, but imperative.

The best mode which we have seen proposed, of enabling emigration to pay its own expenses, is that to which Mr. Robert Gouger, and Mr. Tennant, the member for St. Alban's, have so perseveringly called the public attention—that of fixing a price upon waste land, the highest which could be levied without so crowding the inhabitants as to lower wages below their highest rate.[2] There is no difficulty or disadvantage in this measure. The government of the United States

[2]Robert Gouger (1802-46), proponent of Edward Gibbon Wakefield's system of emigration, edited Wakefield's anonymously published pamphlet, *A Letter from Sydney, the Principal Town of Australasia. Together with an Outline of a System of Colonization* (London: Cross, *et al.*, 1829), where the specific recommendation is given on pp. 169-80, and in the Appendix, pp. iii-xxiv. Gouger was secretary in 1830 of the National Colonization Society, the moving force behind the establishment of the colony of South Australia. Charles Tennant (1796-1873), M.P. 1830-31, was author of several pamphlets on emigration that cover the issues Mill mentions; see, e.g., *A Letter from Mr. Charles Tennant to Sir George Murray, on Systematic Colonization* (London: Ridgway, 1830), and *Letters Forming Part of a Correspondence with Nassau William Senior, Esq. Concerning Systematic Colonization, and the Bill Now before Parliament for Promoting Emigration* (London: Ridgway, 1831).

raises a considerable annual revenue from the sale of unappropriated land; to the great benefit of the inhabitants, which benefit would be still greater if the tax were higher, as it is almost certain that the population of the back settlements is even now far more widely dispersed than is consistent with the most productive employment of their labour. The same principle has been adopted in part by the present ministry, in the colonies of New South Wales and Van Diemen's Land. All that is wanting is, that the minimum price of waste land should be higher; that the system should be established by act of parliament, not by a mere regulation, revocable at the pleasure of any colonial minister; and finally, that the produce of the sales of land should be wholly devoted to emigration, and to the emigration of *young couples*, in order that the greatest effect may be produced on the future growth of population, by the removal of the smallest number of individuals.

89. FRENCH NEWS [17]
EXAMINER, 27 FEB., 1831, P. 136

This article is headed "London, February 27." For the entry in Mill's bibliography, see No. 55. The item is listed as "Article on France" and enclosed in square brackets in the Somerville College set.

THE LATE TUMULTS IN PARIS have been viewed by all parties in France in a far more serious light than the accounts at first received in this country made them appear to merit. Moderate, time-serving newspapers, and moderate, time-serving deputies, have now publicly declared their conviction on the following points:—That it is now obvious that the National Guard, and the middle classes, at least, of Paris, are not satisfied with the present state of the government, either in respect to men or measures;—That, until they obtain a government with which they are satisfied, the feeling of security will not revive;—That until there is security, the labouring population will be without work, will be dissatisfied, a prey to agitators, and ready for continual tumults: which tumults, so long as they do not endanger human life or private property, the National Guard will give themselves as little trouble as possible to suppress. All this has been obvious to every man of common sense for the last six months; and the popular journals have been dinning it into the ears of the King and the Chamber since August last. But they would not listen to Reason, when she came with a gentle whisper; and now they must be fain both to hear and feel her, returning with a loud shout and a thundering blow.

One point is now admitted by the unanimous voice of all parties—the necessity of dissolving the Chamber. This measure, so odious to the majority a few days since, is now pressed on by them with indecent precipitation, to escape from the approaching debate on the electoral law, and have the opportunity of presenting themselves once again to the same narrow body of constituents, which elected them before, and by which they believe that they will be re-elected. The *côté gauche* are now the opponents of an immediate dissolution. They were always so. From the beginning they demanded that the Chamber should (to use their own phrase) make its last will and testament before it expires; should determine, by an election-law, to whom the estate which it leaves behind, its constitutional authority, shall descend.[1]

The commission, or select committee, on the electoral law, has presented its report.[2] This proposes to lower the electoral qualification from 300 to 240 francs of direct taxes: and that of eligibility from 1000 to 500. Trifling as is this diminution of the qualification of an elector, it seems that it will increase the number of the voters to 210,000; and though nothing short of a million of electors ought to be accepted by the sincere Reformers, either in this country or in France, even as a compromise, the chances of some improvement in the composition of the Chamber even from so inadequate a Parliamentary Reform, if adopted previous to the dissolution, are sufficient to be worth a hard struggle.

The usual quantity of absurd misapprehension has displayed itself in England on the subject of the troubles in Paris. The hatred of the populace to the *fleurs-de-lis* is partly understood; but their antipathy to the crosses, and to the priesthood, is, not unnaturally, somewhat less intelligible to Englishmen who have never stirred from their fire-side, nor imbibed any ideas but those which it suited the purpose of some person or other to carry thither. All persons who have conversed with the working population of Paris must have been forcibly struck with the intensity of their hatred to the Jesuits, and to *les mauvais prêtres* (as they phrase it) generally; a hatred which has partly for its cause, and partly for its effect, a notion that those against whom it is directed are capable of the worst of crimes; and we have ourselves repeatedly heard persons of the lowest class, subsequently to the revolution in July, expressing their fears that if Louis Philippe persisted in going about without an escort, some Jesuit would be found to assassinate him. But the very persons in whom these feelings appeared to be strongest, always qualified the expression of them, by the unsolicited and unsuggested acknowledgment, that there must be both religion and priests. Even at the summary funeral of the victims of July, who were laid under ground by the collected people in the very place where they fell, a priest was sent for to perform the usual ceremonies. The people of Paris, from the highest to the lowest, have ceased to hate Christianity, and are tired of listening to ridicule of it: but they detest mortally a political religion; and, although their minds are more open than they have been for above a generation, to religious feelings and ideas generally, they are averse from the Catholic religion, and ready, in a moment of

---

[1]See the leading article in *Le Globe*, 17 Aug., 1830, pp. 1-2.
[2]On 22 Feb. (*Moniteur*, 1831, pp. 373-8).

excitement, to make the most violent demonstrations of hatred to the Catholic priests. As for the crosses which have been pulled down from the tops of the steeples, it may not be amiss to state that they were put up only a very few years ago by the Bourbons, at the expense of the people, and to their vehement dissatisfaction.

The King seems, of all men in France, to be the least capable of rightly interpreting the passing events. He has chosen a moment like this for dismissing from their offices, Odilon-Barrot, the Prefect of the Seine, and Baude, the Prefect of Police.[3] The *Times* says that Odilon-Barrot is dismissed for being too liberal, and Baude for not being liberal enough; and regards the whole proceeding as a specimen of mere trimming;[4] but if this were the case, why was the precise moment selected for removing Baude, at which he had just delivered a speech reconciling him with the popular party?[5] That speech is the true cause of his dismissal. He is removed from the same motive as Odilon-Barrot. He is removed because the King wishes to show that he can be *firm*; as Charles X was firm when he issued the ordinances.[6] The rule with Kings is to drive the people to extremity, and then to face their fury by way of showing firmness, and avoiding the humiliation of a retreat. Weak men never take it into their heads to be firm, until the time is come, when it is absolutely necessary to be pliant. Their firmness consists in braving real dangers, for fear of imaginary ones. The feeble King of the French is terrified at giving votes to the million richest among thirty-two millions, but rather than yield an inch to the other thirty-one millions in arms, *impavidum ferient ruinae*. Alas! a fool can be as *tenax propositi* as Horace's hero.[7]

One of those evil counsellors whom nature seems to have formed as the appointed means to bring the mighty to their ruin, as apt guides to hurry princes and potentates blindfold to the edge of the precipice, and leave them to destruction, exhorts the Aristocracy of England, in an intercalary *Quarterly Review*, to act as the old King of France did, and as the new King of France intends to do—to be *firm*.[8] Those who would never yield to aught but fear, are tauntingly exhorted not to yield to that. Obstinate cleaving to the taxes, unflinching adherence to the interest of their pockets, constitutes Roman virtue in

[3]Jean Jacques Baude (1792-1862) had been a liberal pamphleteer and journalist and was one of the signers of the publishers' protest against the Ordinances. He was Prefect of Police from December 1830.

[4]*The Times*, 25 Feb., 1831, p. 2.

[5]*Moniteur*, 19 Feb., 1831, pp. 337-9.

[6]For the details, see the headnote to No. 44.

[7]Horace (65-8 B.C.), *Carmina*, III, iii, 8 and 1, in *Odes and Epodes* (Latin and English), trans. C.E. Bennett (London: Heinemann, 1914), p. 178.

[8]See Robert Southey, "Moral and Political State of the British Empire," *Quarterly Review*, XLIV (Jan. 1831), 261-317, particularly the conclusion.

the eyes of some people. But if the Aristocracy of England are sufficiently unaware of their present situation to hearken to such counsellors, they little know what is in store for them. If the English and the new French government are destined severally to give another lesson to the world on the incapacity of oligarchies, howsoever constituted, to learn wisdom from experience, the trial must be submitted to: but at least those who shall provoke it shall do so knowingly, and must hold themselves prepared to suffer the natural consequences of their own folly.

90. THE PARLIAMENTARY REFORM BILL
EXAMINER, 6 MAR., 1831, P. 147

One of Mill's few direct contemporary comments on the British reform agitation of 1830-32, this article appeared in the "Political Examiner" under the heading "[From a Correspondent]." It is described in his bibliography as "Paragraphs on the Parliamentary Reform Bill headed 'from a Correspondent' in the Examiner of 6th March 1831" (MacMinn, p. 15); in the Somerville College set it is listed as "Article on the Reform Bill" and enclosed in square brackets, with one inked correction, "had had" to "had led to" (277.23).

IN ESTIMATING the nature of the change which Lord John Russell's Bill,[1] if adopted, will produce in the practical working of the Constitution, it is necessary to look somewhat closely at the specific character of the abuses by which our government has hitherto been deformed.

These are of two kinds: 1st, private jobs, for the benefit of individuals possessing Parliamentary influence.—2dly, bad laws, and great naval and military establishments, for the benefit of the higher classes generally.

We expect that the proposed Reform will almost entirely extinguish private jobs. The supporters whom the Minister secures by the direct expenditure of the public money are seldom those who are returned by numerous constituencies. It is worth while, for a minister to purchase a vote in parliament by giving a place to the son or younger brother of a borough patron; it is seldom worth while for the sake of two votes, to give valuable consideration to each man of the majority of the influential landholders of a county. Westmoreland is an exception; but Westmoreland is, in reality, a close borough.[2] County members are seldom the

---

[1] John Russell (1792-1878), later 1st Earl Russell, parliamentarian from 1813, was Paymaster of the Forces in 1830 when he helped draft the Reform Bill (see No. 84, n6), which he introduced in the Commons.

[2] In 1832 Westmorland, which had 4392 registered electors, belonged mostly to the Earl of Lonsdale.

paid and regular supporters of an administration; they seldom receive any thing out of the taxes, and are therefore generally friends to retrenchment; but they are, more than any other class of the members of Parliament, the stedfast and unbending supporters of bad laws. For bad laws do not exist for the benefit of borough proprietors, but of the landed, or the landed and monied classes at large. The same may be said of large military and naval establishments, the chief cause of the magnitude of the public burthens.

The proposed Reform will take the nomination of a majority in Parliament from two hundred aristocratical families, and will give it to the Aristocracy generally; for, without the protection of the Ballot, it is absurd to suppose that the nominal electors, except in a few places like Westminster, will be less subject to undue influence than at the present moment.[3] Instead of our own old oligarchy, we shall have a French oligarchy: the undue power, instead of being unequally divided,—a large mass being held by one very great man, and small portions by a number of small men, will now be more equally divided among the higher classes at large; but subject to no greater responsibility than at present; with the same sinister interests, and under a more specious appearance.

Heretofore a Minister, hard pressed by public opinion, could carry with him a large portion of the borough members, who, to save their place, would at times separate themselves from their *order*. Hereafter an immense majority of the House will be the mere men of their order, or would be so, were they not controlled by the irresistible spirit of the age.

If the proposed Reform had been introduced in quiet times, and had led to no ulterior changes, we question whether the alteration which it would have made in the composition of the Houses would have been in any respect an improvement. But with an excited public, and a public fully possessed with the importance of the Ballot, the members whom this measure will send to Parliament *must* represent, in a considerable degree, the real feelings of their nominal constituents, or the cry for the Ballot will become absolutely irresistible. If we gain this Bill, therefore, we shall gain all; and every nerve ought to be strained by every Reformer throughout the nation, for the success of the ministerial measure.

If there were no other reason for giving it the most strenuous support, the consternation which it has spread among the whole tribe of the people's enemies would be a sufficient one.

[3]Westminster, which had the largest number of voters of any urban constituency, was one of thirty-seven "scot and lot" boroughs; i.e., all male householders paying municipal tax were enfranchised.

91. FRENCH NEWS [18]

EXAMINER, 6 MAR., 1831, P. 155

For the entry in Mill's bibliography, see No. 55. The unheaded item is listed as "Article on France" and these two paragraphs are enclosed in square brackets in the Somerville College set.

THE FRENCH CHAMBER OF DEPUTIES has lowered the qualification of an elector from 300 to 200 francs of direct taxes;[1] which will give a constituency of about 200,000, or rather more than double the present number. The Chamber, however, has refused to give votes to advocates, physicians, attorneys, notaries, or judges, unless qualified by paying the same amount of taxes as other people.

The Centres, who were eager for a dissolution when they thought that it could take place under the pre-existing election law, have now resumed their previous attitude of hostility to it. No one can guess whether the declared intention of the Government to dissolve the Chamber will even now be persevered in; so timid and rash (no uncommon conjunction) is the King, and so truckling his Ministry. The destinies of France are in the hands of men more than nine-tenths of whom are not fit to have any part in the government of a parish.

92. THE SPIRIT OF THE AGE, III [Part 2]

EXAMINER, 13 MAR., 1831, PP. 162-3

This article, headed "The Spirit of the Age, / No. 3, *concluded*," is introduced by the following notice: "[*It was by mistake that we announced, several weeks since, that this series would conclude with the present paper. It will extend to several numbers more, though the pressure of more urgent matter will not enable us to continue it from week to week.*]" The notice presumably refers to the remark at the end of No. 82, "The conclusion of this Paper in our next." For the entry in Mill's bibliography, see No. 73. In the Somerville College set, it is listed as heading and enclosed in square brackets.

IT IS NOT NECESSARY for me to point out that until a comparatively recent period, none but the wealthy, and even, I might say, the hereditarily wealthy, had it in their power to acquire the intelligence, the knowledge, and the habits, which are necessary to qualify a man, in any tolerable degree, for managing the affairs of his country. It is not necessary for me to show that this is no longer the case, nor what are the circumstances which have changed it: the improvement in the arts of life, giving ease and comfort to great numbers not possessed of the degree of wealth which confers political power: the increase of reading: the diffusion of

---

[1]By Titre I, Art. 1 of Bull. 37, No. 105 (19 Apr., 1831) (see No. 72, n3).

elementary education: the increase of the town-population, which brings masses of men together, and accustoms them to examine and discuss important subjects with one another; and various other causes, which are known to every body. All this, however, is nothing more than the acquisition by other people in an inferior degree, of a few of the advantages which have always been within the reach of the higher classes, in a much greater degree: and if the higher classes had profited as they might have done by these advantages, and had kept their station in the vanguard of the march of improvement, they would not only at this moment have been sure to retain in their hands all the powers of government, subject perhaps to severer conditions of responsibility, but might possibly even have continued for a considerable time longer to retain them on the same footing as at present. For ample experience has proved that mankind (who, however prone they may be, in periods of transition, to even groundless suspicion and distrust, are as strongly addicted at all other times to the opposite extreme of blind and boundless confidence), will bear even great excesses of abused power, from those whom they recognize as fitter to hold the reins of government than themselves.

But the higher classes, instead of advancing, have retrograded in all the higher qualities of mind. In the humanizing effects of civilization they have indeed partaken, and, to some extent, in the diffusion of superficial knowledge, and are so far superior to their predecessors: but those predecessors were braced and nerved by the invigorating atmosphere of a barbarous age, and had all the virtues of a strong will and an energetic active mind, which their descendants are destitute of. For these qualities were not the fruits of an enlightened education skilfully pointed to that end, but of the peculiar position of the holders of power; and that position is no longer the same.

All is not absolutely unfounded in the notion we imbibe at school, from the modern writers on the decline of the ancient commonwealths, that luxury deadens and enervates the mind. It is true that these writers (whose opinion, truly, was the result of no process of thought in their own imitative souls, but a faint impression left by a ray of the stoic philosophy of Greece and Rome themselves, refracted or bent out of its direction by the muddy medium through which it had passed) were wrong in laying it down as a principle that pleasure enervates; as if pleasure, only to be earned by labour and won by heroic deeds, ever did or ever could enervate the mind of any one. What really enervates, is the secure and unquestioned possession, without any exertion, of all those things, to gain which, mankind in general are wont to exert themselves. This secure and lazy possession, the higher classes have now for some generations enjoyed; their predecessors in the same station and privileges did not enjoy it.

Who, for example, that looks over the catalogue of the Kings who have reigned in Europe for the last two centuries, would not conclude, from that and the nature of the case combined, that the station of a hereditary king was the very most unfavourable to be found in this sublunary world, for the acquisition of any talents for governing? Is not the incapacity of the monarch allowed for, as an inevitable inconvenience, even by the most strenuous supporters of monarchy; represented at best as an evil susceptible of palliation, and preventing other evils far more fatal? From the beginning of the eighteenth century it has passed into a philosophic truism, that kings are generally unfit to govern, and likely even to delegate their power not to statesmen, but to favourites, unless forced to choose those Ministers whom the public voice recommends to them. Yet this maxim is far from being borne out by history. A decided majority of all the kings of England previous to the Revolution, will be found to have been men who, in every endowment belonging to their age, might be compared to the best men in it. The same may be said of the Emperors of Germany, and even of the Kings of France, of Spain, the Dukes of Burgundy, and so on. Would you know why? Think of Edward II and Richard II.[1] In that turbulent age, no rank or station rendered the situation of a man without considerable personal endowments, a secure one. If the king possessed eminent talents, he might be nearly absolute: if he was a slave to ease and dissipation, not only his importance was absolutely null, but his throne and his life itself were constantly in danger. The Barons stood no less in need of mental energy and ability. Power, though not earned by capacity, might be greatly increased by it, and could not be retained or enjoyed without it. The possessor of power was not in the situation of one who is rewarded without exertion, but of one who feels a great prize within his grasp, and is stimulated to every effort necessary to make it securely his own.

But the virtues which insecurity calls forth, ceased with insecurity itself. In a civilized age, though it may be difficult to *get*, it is very easy to *keep*: if a man does not earn what he gets before he gets it, he has little motive to earn it thereafter. The greater the power a man has upon these terms, the less he is likely to deserve it. Accordingly, as Mr. Hallam has remarked, Great Britain has had since William III no monarch of more than ordinary personal endowments;[2] nor will she ever more, unless the chapter of accidents should open at a page inscribed with very singular characters. We may add, that the House of Peers has produced, since the same epoch, hardly any remarkable men; though some such have, from time to time, been aggregated to the order. As soon as these facts became manifest, it was easy to see a termination to hereditary monarchy and hereditary aristocracy: for we never shall again return to the age of violence and insecurity, when men were forced, whatever might be their taste for incapacity, to become men of talents in spite of themselves: and mankind will not always

---

[1]Edward II (1284-1327), King of England 1307-27, and Richard II (1367-1400), King of England 1377-99, both weak monarchs who lost the crown.

[2]Henry Hallam (1777-1859), *The Constitutional History of England from the Accession of Henry VII to the Death of George II*, 2 vols. (London: Murray, 1827), Vol. II, pp. 496-7.

consent to allow a fat elderly gentleman[3] to fill the first place, without insisting upon his doing something to deserve it. I do not undertake to say in what particular year hereditary distinctions will be abolished, nor do I say that I would vote for their abolition, if it were proposed now, in the existing state of society and opinion: but to the philosopher, who contemplates the past and future fortunes of mankind as one series, and who counts a generation or two for no more in marking the changes of the moral, than an age or two in those of the physical world, the ultimate fate of such distinctions is already decided.

There was an intermediate stage in the history of our own island, in which it was yet a question whether the Crown should share in the government of the country as the master of the aristocracy, or only as the first and most powerful of its members. Though the progress of civilization had given to the gentry of England, personal security independently of honourable exertion, it had not yet given them undisputed power. They were nothing, except through the Parliament, and the Parliament as yet, was nothing, except through their energy and talents. The great names by which the seventeenth century of English history has been immortalized, belonged almost without an exception to the same class which now possesses the governing power. What a contrast! Think, good heavens! that Sir John Elliot, and John Hampden, and Sir John Colepepper, and Sir Thomas Wentworth, were *country gentlemen*—and think who are the parliamentary leaders of that class in our own day: a Knatchbull, a Bankes, a Gooch, a Lethbridge![4] Think even of the most respectable names among the English landholders of our time, such as Lord Wharncliffe, or Mr. Coke.[5] The

[3]The reference is probably to George IV (1762-1830), who, after serving from 1811 to 1820 as Regent during periods when his father, George III, was mad, ruled 1820-30; his fatness was a subject of frequent satirical comment.

[4]The contrast is between, on the one hand, the great parliamentary figures in the early seventeenth century: John Eliot (1592-1632), M.P. 1614 and again 1624; John Hampden (1594-1643), who became an M.P. in 1621 and eventually a Colonel in Cromwell's army; John Colepeper (d. 1660), who began as a supporter of the popular party but later served both Charles I and Charles II; and Thomas Wentworth (1593-1641), Earl of Strafford, who, having defended the subjects' rights against the king, became a defender of the royal authority, and was impeached and executed; and on the other hand, the weak country representatives in the nineteenth century: Edward Knatchbull (1781-1849), Tory M.P. 1819-30, an opponent of corn-law reform and Catholic emancipation; George Bankes (1788-1856), Tory M.P. 1816-23, 1826-32, appointed to the Board of Control in 1829, and Junior Lord of the Treasury and a commissioner for India (1830); Thomas Sherlock Gooch; and Thomas Buckler-Lethbridge (1778-1849), 2nd Baronet Lethbridge, M.P. 1806-12, 1820-30, and Colonel of the 2nd Somerset Militia.

[5]James Archibald Stuart-Wortley-Mackenzie (1776-1845), Lord Wharncliffe, was a Tory M.P. 1801-26, when his support for Catholic emancipation cost him his seat; then, as a peer, he moved from opposing parliamentary reform to persuading his fellow peers to accept it. Thomas William Coke (1752-1842), Earl of Leicester, known for his agricultural improvements, was a Whig M.P. almost continuously from 1776 until 1833; he favoured reform but also supported the corn laws and agricultural interests generally.

remainder of the great politicians of that age, the Bacons, the Cecils, the Walsinghams, the Seldens, the Iretons, the Pyms, the Cokes, were mostly lawyers.[6] But what lawyers, and how strikingly distinguished, as well by their origin as by the range of their faculties and acquirements, from our successful Barristers, our Sugdens and Copleys![7] They were almost to a man, the younger or even the elder sons of the first families among the English gentry: who studied the law as being what it then in some degree was, a liberal profession, a pursuit fit for a gentleman, and not for a mere drudge; exercising at least the higher faculties, by the comprehension of principles, (though frequently absurd ones), not the mere memory, by the heaping together of unconnected details: and who studied it chiefly that it might serve them in fulfilling the exalted mission, to which they were called by an ambition justly to be called noble, since it required of them great sacrifices, and could be gratified only by the accomplishment of what was then nearest to their country's weal.

Applied to these men, the expression, natural leaders of the people, has some meaning: and then and then only it was that our institutions worked well, for they made this country the nurse of more that is exalted in sentiment, and expansive and profound in thought, than has been produced by all other countries in the modern world taken together, until a recent period. The whole of their effect is now the direct contrary—to degrade our morals, and to narrow and blunt our understandings: nor shall we ever be what we might be, nor even what we once were, until our institutions are adapted to the present state of civilization, and made compatible with the future progress of the human mind. But this will, I trust, more clearly appear, when, in the next paper, the historical survey which I have here taken of the conditions of worldly power, shall also have been taken of the conditions of moral influence.

A.B.

---

[6]Nicholas Bacon (1509-79), eloquent and learned lawyer, holder of many public offices, including that of Lord Keeper of the Great Seal (1558), and his son Francis Bacon (1561-1626), the great philosopher and statesman, nephew of William Cecil (1520-98), Lord Burghley, one of the most powerful statesmen of the sixteenth century; Francis Walsingham (ca. 1530-90), diplomat and Secretary of State; John Selden (1584-1654), learned author and parliamentarian; Henry Ireton (1611-51), general in Cromwell's army and his deputy in Ireland; John Pym (1584-1643), M.P. and parliamentary spokesman on constitutional and religious questions; and Edward Coke (1552-1634), great legal authority and parliamentarian.

[7]Edward Burtenshaw Sugden (1781-1875), Baron St. Leonards, legal writer and M.P., had become Solicitor-General in 1829; and John Singleton Copley (1772-1863), Baron Lyndhurst, at one time a holder of Jacobin views, had become a Tory, Solicitor-General in 1819, Attorney-General in 1824, and Lord Chancellor in 1827.

93. FRENCH NEWS [19]
EXAMINER, 13 MAR., 1831, P. 171

This article is headed "London, March 13." For the entry in Mill's bibliography, see No. 55. In the Somerville College set the item is listed as "Article on France" and the first five paragraphs are enclosed in square brackets (the final three paragraphs concern German and Polish affairs and their effect in Paris).

THE FRENCH CHAMBER OF DEPUTIES has adopted the article of the proposed election-law, which lowers the qualification of a deputy from 1000 to 500 francs of direct taxes.[1]

With this improvement in the conditions of eligibility, and the reduction which has already been voted in the elective franchise, there is room to hope for some improvement in the composition of the Chamber, when the new law shall come into operation. It is, therefore, of the greatest importance that the existing Chamber should be promptly dissolved. But doubts are thrown out as to the King's disposition to adhere to the intentions which his Ministers have expressed on this subject. It is surmised that the present Ministry will be turned out, and another appointed from the ranks of the centre; and that a prorogation, instead of a dissolution, will take place. It is certain that M. Mérilhou has been obliged to resign, because he refused to dismiss M. Comte, *Procureur du Roi*, one of the wisest and most virtuous men in France.[2]

There would be something ludicrous, were it not a subject for the deepest melancholy, in the panic terrors and woful plight of the individual whom the Revolution of July has hoisted up to an eminence which he is utterly incapable of creditably filling. He is now suffering under the embarrassments which his own folly, and that alone, has brought upon him; he is feeling the consequences of first raising the hopes of an excitable and confiding people, and then utterly disappointing them.

We know nothing better fitted to convince the French of the ignorance and baseness of the English newspaper writers, than the tone they have assumed with respect to the present party differences in France. Men who are shouting in favour of a plan of Parliamentary Reform, far outrunning anything which the most ardent of the French Reformers have even ventured to suggest, for immediate adoption,—a plan which adds 500,000 at one blow,[3] to a constituent

[1]Art. 59 in Titre V (see No. 72, n3).

[2]François Charles Louis Comte (1782-1837), radical publicist, lawyer, and politician, was son-in-law of J.B. Say, the economist and friend of the Mills, with whom J.S. Mill had stayed in 1820 and 1821, and whom he had again met in August 1830. Procureur du roi près le tribunal de la Seine from September 1830, Comte was dismissed on 12 Mar., 1831.

[3]I.e., Russell's Reform Bill (identified at No. 84, n6).

body already very numerous, when the question in France is, whether, in a much larger population, a few more or a few less than 200,000 in all, shall be admitted to the elective franchise—these very writers treat as the wildest of democrats men who do not go a quarter of *their* length in democracy, on the mere word of those who are the avowed enemies of all Reform whatever!

The probabilities of war seem, in the general apprehension, to have increased: in ours they are diminishing. The French may be assured, that the English people will approve of their *enforcing* the principle of non-intervention against the despotic powers, but will disapprove of their *violating* that principle, in order to crusade in support of the subjects of other states against their governments, however just the resistance of such subjects may be, or however certain their destruction, if not aided from abroad. The French have their character for moderation and pacific inclinations still to acquire; and should they go to war on grounds in any respect doubtful, those grounds are sure to be interpreted to their disadvantage.[4]

94. HERSCHEL'S PRELIMINARY DISCOURSE

EXAMINER, 20 MAR., 1831, PP. 179-80

John Frederick William Herschel, 1st Baronet (1792-1871), astronomer, son of the astronomer Sir William Herschel and President of the Astronomical Society 1827-32, was a brilliant theorist as well as observer and discoverer of stars. This review appears in the "Literary Examiner," headed: *"Lardner's Cabinet Cyclopaedia, Vol. XIV. A Preliminary Discourse on the Study of Natural Philosophy. By John Frederick William Herschel, Esq. A.M., late Fellow of St. John's College, Cambridge, &c. &c. &c."* The work had been published in London by Longman, *et al.*, in late 1830. Described in Mill's bibliography as "Review of Herschel's Discourse on the Study of Natural Philosophy, in the Examiner of 20th March 1831" (MacMinn, p. 15), the item is similarly listed ("Review of Herschel's Discourse on the Study of Natural Philosophy"), and enclosed in square brackets, in the Somerville College set.

THIS WORK has afforded us great pleasure, and greater hope. It evinces a reach of thought, for which the physical researches of the present day are quite inapt to supply adequate occupation. A greater destiny is reserved for Mr. Herschel. It is his to aspire, and not in vain, to the character of the philosopher—to whom the mere man of science is but a pioneer.

If the utility of the *very* modern physical inquiries were to be estimated solely by the intrinsic value of their *results*, by the direct use which has been made, or from their nature ever can be made, of the truths which those inquiries have elicited, we know not that the labours of a *savant* would be deserving of much higher commendation than those of a bricklayer; and we much doubt whether, if

[4]For background, see No. 59, n5, No. 68, n3, Nos. 81 and 83.

there had not been made a single scientific discovery in the last hundred years, mankind, taken in the mass, would have at this moment enjoyed one jot less of happiness than they actually do. Mere physical comforts and enjoyments, not the most valuable part of happiness, are the best which such knowledge *could* bestow, while it is too apparent in how niggardly a measure it has dealt out even those, to an immense numerical majority in the most civilized nations; and even the fortunate individuals on whom it has most lavished its gifts, have most frequently found in them not enjoyment, but only *means* of enjoyment, from which they have never known how to extract real happiness—nor ever will, until their minds are as highly cultivated as their bodies are: until moral and social science have attained the same perfection as physical science: until the theory and practice of education are lifted out of their present depressed and degraded posture: until human beings have learned how to cultivate and nurture their own susceptibilities of happiness, and have made such arrangements of outward circumstances, as shall provide that the means which each adopts of seeking his own well-being, shall no longer damage that of the remainder of his species.

To this blessed consummation, physical science is capable of contributing invaluable assistance; not, however, by the truths which it discloses, but by the process by which it attains to them. It is an example, and the only example, of a vast body of connected truth, gradually elicited by patient and earnest investigation, and finally recognized and submitted to by a convinced and subdued world. If the broad and fundamental differences which exist among the minds which have sought with greatest diligence for truths of a higher order, may be traced, as they clearly may, to differences in their *methods*, or modes of philosophising; if the uncertainty which hangs over the very elements of moral and social philosophy, proves that the means of arriving at the truth in those sciences are not yet properly understood—that the minds of the majority of inquirers are not yet so formed as to be capable of the successful pursuit of those truths which are essential to the proper use and application of all other knowledge; whither can mankind so advantageously turn, in order to learn the proper means, and to form their minds to the proper habits, as to that branch of knowledge in which, by universal acknowledgment, the greatest number of truths have been ascertained, and the greatest possible degree of certainty has been arrived at?

But physical science has not yet been converted to this its noblest use. Men of science are usually as little conscious of the methods by which they have made their greatest discoveries, as the clown is of the structure of his eye, or the process by which he has learnt to see. With the exception of the analysis of the syllogism, which was performed long ago by the ancients, scarcely any thing has yet been contributed towards an accurate dissection of the mode in which the human understanding arrives at the discovery and the verification of truth. Bacon afforded merely a few hints, which it has scarcely even yet been attempted to improve and follow up: for such scattered suggestions as can be gleaned from books of later date, mankind are indebted to metaphysical writers, not to physical; to Locke and Brown,[1] rather than to Newton or Davy.[2] Men of science have even, in our own country at least, rather more than their share of the vulgar prejudice against such researches. An inquiry into the nature of the instrument with which they all work, the human mind, and into the mode of bringing that instrument to the greatest perfection, and using it to the greatest advantage, has usually been treated by them as something frivolous and idle: as if the rules of philosophising did not stand fully as much in need of a philosophical foundation, as any of the particular truths which have been, or may be, attained by the observance of them.

From this prejudice, which essentially belongs to minds of the most limited range (though, perhaps, of microscopic vision within that range) Mr. Herschel is wholly exempt; and his work contains (we speak advisedly) a clearer and less incomplete view of the nature of philosophical truth, of the evidence on which it rests, and the means of discovering and testing it, than is to be found in any work which has yet been produced. To point out in what particulars it appears to us to fall short of what is still to be looked for and hoped for, would be inappropriate to the nature of a notice like the present: but there is nothing which may not be hoped for from the author of such a work, if he perseveres in the course of thinking into which he has here entered; and his vast and profound knowledge in every department of physics has enabled him, in this volume, to supply any one who may take up the inquiry where he has left it, with a rich fund of the most apt examples, capable alike of illustrating, and of suggesting, the most profound and important views on the operation of the intellect in philosophising.

The first chapter, being the most vague, is, as usually happens in such cases, the least valuable. There are some points in the higher metaphysics on which we should differ from the author: but these are precisely such as have least to do with the general course of his speculations. The *spirit* of the work is admirable. We never met with a book so calculated to inspire a high conception of the superiority of science over empiricism under the name of *common sense*—of the advantage of *systematic* investigation, and high general cultivation of the intellect. And we quote with delight the following noble passage; showing that one who, by the consent of all our scientific men, is placed first, or among the first, in the knowledge of all which physical science can teach, yet feels that there are truths far more important to human happiness than all these which it is

[1]Thomas Brown (1778-1820), disciple of Dugald Stewart and a leading exponent of the Scottish school, was Professor of Moral Philosophy at Edinburgh from 1810.

[2]Sir Humphry Davy (1778-1829) became Professor of Chemistry at the Royal Institute in 1802; in 1812 he was knighted, largely for his work in isolating certain elements (potassium, sodium, chlorine) by the agency of the galvanic battery; he is best known for the development of the safety-lamp in 1815.

the highest boast of physical science that it may assist in training the mind to be capable of investigating and applying. The first part of the treatise, which is devoted to setting forth the "General Nature and Advantages of the Study of the Physical Sciences," is wound up as follows:

Finally, the improvement effected in the condition of mankind, by advances in physical science as applied to the useful purposes of life, is very far from being limited to their direct consequences in the more abundant supply of our physical wants, and the increase of our comforts. Great as these benefits are, they are yet but steps to others of a still higher kind. The successful results of our experiments and reasonings in natural philosophy, and the incalculable advantages which experience, systematically consulted and dispassionately reasoned on, has conferred in matters purely physical, tend of necessity to impress something of the well weighed and progressive character of science on the more complicated conduct of our social and moral relations. It is thus that legislation and politics become gradually regarded as experimental sciences; and history, not as formerly, the mere record of tyrannies and slaughters, which, by immortalizing the execrable actions of one age, perpetuates the ambition of committing them in every succeeding one, but as the archive of experiments, successful and unsuccessful, gradually accumulating towards the solution of the grand problem—how the advantages of government are to be secured with the least possible inconvenience to the governed. The celebrated apophthegm, that nations never profit by experience, becomes yearly more and more untrue. Political economy, at least, is found to have sound principles, founded in the moral and physical nature of man, which, however lost sight of in particular measures—however even temporarily controverted and borne down by clamour, have yet a stronger and stronger testimony borne to them in each succeeding generation, by which they must sooner or later prevail. The idea once conceived and verified, that great and noble ends are to be achieved, by which the condition of the whole human species shall be permanently bettered, by bringing into exercise a sufficient quantity of sober thought, and by a proper adaptation of means, is of itself sufficient to set us earnestly on reflecting what ends *are* truly great and noble, either in themselves, or as conducive to others of a still loftier character; because we are not now, as heretofore, hopeless of attaining them. It is not now equally harmless and insignificant whether we are right or wrong, since we are no longer supinely and helplessly carried down the stream of events, but feel ourselves capable of buffetting at least with its waves, and perhaps of riding triumphantly over them; for why should we despair that the reason which has enabled us to subdue all nature to our purposes, should (if permitted and assisted by the providence of God,) achieve a far more difficult conquest; and ultimately find some means of enabling the collective wisdom of mankind to bear down those obstacles which individual short-sightedness, selfishness, and passion, oppose to all improvements, and by which the highest hopes are continually blighted, and the fairest prospects marred. (Pp. 72-4.)

95. FRENCH NEWS [20]

EXAMINER, 20 MAR., 1831, P. 186

This item is headed "London, March 20." For the entry in Mill's bibliography, see No. 55. The piece is identified as "Article on France" and these two paragraphs are enclosed in square brackets in the Somerville College set.

A CHANGE HAS TAKEN PLACE in the French ministry. Laffitte has resigned; Mérilhou was out of office already; the others, who composed the dregs of the late Cabinet, remain in office, though with some shuffling and changing of places, under the new Premier, M. Casimir-Périer, who takes the department of the interior. Louis, the most narrow-minded and inept of Bonaparte's clerks, resumes the post of minister of finance, which he held in the administration of Guizot, and in two of the numerous ministries of Louis XVIII.[1] His nephew, Admiral De Rigny, who commanded the French fleet at Navarino, becomes minister of marine.[2]

From the letter of our Paris correspondent,[3] it will be seen what the popular party think of this ministry; they conceive, and do not hesitate, through their various organs, to declare, that it is the Polignac ministry of the new government, and will bring that government to the same abrupt termination as that which preceded it. We trust not; for as it is the second blow which makes the quarrel, so it is the second convulsion which annihilates future stability. But if there be such a convulsion, we are as fully convinced that the incredible folly and weakness of Louis Philippe, and the grasping selfishness of his worthy majority, are the sole cause of it, as we are that the wisdom of our public will lay the whole blame upon those who are contending for a Parliamentary Reform about half as extensive as that which an English King,[4] and a cabinet of English Noblemen, have thought it safe and necessary to propose to an English Parliament, amidst the acclamations of the people from the Orkneys to the Land's End.

96. FRENCH NEWS [21]
EXAMINER, 27 MAR., 1831, PP. 202-3

This item is headed "London, March 27." For the entry in Mill's bibliography, see No. 55. Exceptionally, Mill here comments also on Italian news, as he indicates in the listing in the Somerville College set, "Article on France and Italy"; Mill gives the page number as 201, rather than 202-3, but the paragraphs here included are enclosed in Mill's square brackets.

IT APPEARS THAT THE CHANGE OF MINISTRY in France has made no alteration in the intention of dissolving the Chamber.

[1] Baron Joseph Dominique Louis (1755-1837) had served the financial interests of Louis XVI, Napoleon, and Louis XVIII. Minister of Finance under the Provisional Government, he had continued to hold the appointment until November 1830.
[2] Henri Gauthier, comte de Rigny (1782-1835). The battle of Navarino, 20 Oct., 1827, was the decisive event in establishing the independence of Greece.
[3] "M." (Pierre Martin Maillefer), "Foreign Intelligence," *Examiner*, 20 Mar., 1831, pp. 184-5.
[4] That is, William IV (1765-1837), the third son of George III, who in 1830 had become King on the death of his brother, George IV.

The most recent news from Italy[1] seems to imply that the Austrian Government has no purpose of interfering with the new order of things any where in Italy, except the duchies of Parma and Modena—grounding their pretended right of interference upon the circumstance, that these duchies are held, the one by an Austrian princess, the other by an Austrian prince,[2] and revert, on failure of direct heirs, to the reigning line. If this be the limit of the interference—though the violation of justice, and the rights of every independent people to change their government, is the same on the smaller scale as on the larger one, the emancipation of Italy will be no way retarded by this act of usurpation. All that is important is, that there should be a state in Italy, governing itself, and sheltering the exiled patriots of the other states. Round that nucleus the whole of Italy will in time cluster itself. That three or four towns more or less should be included this year or the next, in the independent Italian state, is of little account, when every one sees that all Italy will join it on the first opportunity, and that, in the mean time, Italian patriotism and Italian intellect will find in Italy itself a place, not only of refuge, but of healthy nourishment and growth.

97. THE SPIRIT OF THE AGE, IV
EXAMINER, 3 APR., 1831, PP. 210-11

For the context and entry in Mill's bibliography, see No. 73. The article is listed as "The Spirit of the Age, No. 4" and enclosed in square brackets in the Somerville College set.

IT HAS BEEN STATED, in the preceding paper,[1] that the conditions which confer worldly power are still, amidst all changes of circumstances, the same as in the middle ages—namely, the possession of wealth, or the being employed and trusted by the wealthy. In the middle ages, this form of government might have been approved, even by a philosopher, if a philosopher had been possible in those ages: not, surely, for its intrinsic excellence; not because mankind enjoyed, or could have enjoyed, the blessings of good government under it: but there are states of society in which we must not seek for a good government, but for the least bad one. It is part .of the inevitable lot of mankind, that when they themselves are in a backward state of civilization, they are unsusceptible of being well governed.

---

[1]In February, there had been popular insurrections in Bologna, Modena, and Parma; when they spread to the Papal States, Pope Gregory XVI called for help, and on 21 Mar. Austrian troops entered Modena, suppressing the uprising.
[2]Maria Louisa (1791-1847), Duchess of Parma, and Francis IV (1779-1846), Duke of Modena.

---

[1]I.e., in Nos. 82 and 92, especially the former.

But, now, mankind are capable of being better governed than the wealthy classes have ever heretofore governed them: while those classes, instead of having improved, have actually retrograded in capacity for government. The abuses of their power have not diminished, though now showing themselves no otherwise than in forms compatible with the mildness of modern manners, and being of that kind which provokes contempt, mingled with resentment, rather than terror and hatred, as of yore.

Such of the above propositions as required illustration appearing to have sufficiently received it in the foregoing paper, I proceed to take a similar survey of the changes which mankind have undergone in respect to the conditions on which moral influence, or power over the minds of mankind, is dependent.

There are three distinguishable sources of moral influence:—eminent wisdom and virtue, real or supposed; the power of addressing mankind in the name of religion; and, finally, worldly power.

It is not necessary to illustrate the manner in which superiority of wisdom and virtue, or in which religion, pre-engages men's minds with the opinions and feelings in favour of which those authorities declare themselves. It is equally superfluous to insist upon the influence exercised over the minds of men by worldly power. The tendency of the human mind to the worship of power, is well understood. It is matter of common complaint, that even the Supreme Being is adored by an immense majority as the Almighty, not as the All-good; as he who can destroy, not as he who has blessed. It is a familiar fact, that the vulgar, in all parts of the world, have in general little or no rule of conduct or of opinion, but to do as their betters do, and to think as their betters think: and this very word *betters*, is a speaking proof of the fact which we allege—meaning, as it does, not their *wisers*, or their *honesters*, but their *richers*, and those placed in authority over them.

All persons, from the most ignorant to the most instructed, from the most stupid to the most intelligent, have their minds more or less under the dominion of one or other, or all, of the influences which have just been mentioned. All bow down, with a submission more or less implicit, to the authority of superior minds, or of the interpreters of the divine will, or of their superiors in rank and station.

When an opinion is sanctioned by all these authorities, or by any one of them, the others not opposing, it becomes the received opinion. At all periods of history in which there has existed a general agreement among these three authorities, there have existed *received doctrines*: a phrase the sense of which is now almost forgotten. The most marked character of such periods is a firm confidence in inherited opinions. Men cleave with a strong and fervent faith to the doctrine which they have imbibed from their infancy: though in conduct they be tempted to swerve from it, the belief remains in their hearts, fixed and immoveable, and has an irresistible hold upon the consciences of all good men.

When, on the contrary, the three authorities are divided among themselves, or against each other, a violent conflict rages among opposing doctrines, until one or other prevails, or until mankind settle down into a state of general uncertainty and scepticism. At present, we are in a mixed state; some fight fiercely under their several banners, and these chiefly the least instructed; while the others (those few excepted who have strength to stand by themselves) are blown about by every breath, having no steady opinion—or at least no deep-rooted conviction that their opinion is true.

Society, therefore, has its natural state, and its transitional state, with respect to moral influence as well as to worldly power. Let us bestow a few words upon the natural state, and upon the nature of those varieties of the social order in which it has hitherto been realized.

It is in states of society in which the holders of power are chosen by the people (or by the most highly civilized portion of the people) for their supposed fitness, that we should most expect to find the three authorities acting together, and giving their sanction to the same doctrines. As men are raised to worldly power for their supposed wisdom and virtue, two of the three sources of moral influence are united in the same individuals. And although the rulers of such societies, being the creatures of the people's choice, have not, *quâ* rulers, that ascendancy over the minds of the people, which power obtained and held independently of their will, commonly possesses; nevertheless, the station to which they are elevated gives them greater opportunities of rendering their wisdom and their virtue visible, while it also fixes the outward stamp of general recognition upon that merit, which would otherwise operate upon each mind only in proportion to its confidence in its own power of discriminating the most worthy.

Accordingly, in the best-constituted commonwealths of the ancient world, this unity of moral influence did to a very great degree exist. And in the great popular government of our own times, it exists with respect to the general doctrines of the constitution, and many maxims of national policy, and the list of received doctrines is increasing as rapidly as the differences of opinion among the persons possessing moral influence will allow.

I say, only the *best-constituted* commonwealths of antiquity—and chiefly Athens, Sparta, and Rome—because, in the others, the form of the government, and the circumstances of society itself, being in a perpetual flux, the elements of moral influence never remained long enough in the same hands, to allow time for constitutional doctrines, or received maxims of policy, to grow up. But, in the three commonwealths which I have named, such constitutional doctrines, and such received maxims of policy, did exist, and the community was intensely attached to them.

The great authority for political doctrines in all these governments was the wisdom of ancestors: their old laws, their old maxims, the opinions of their ancient statesmen. This may sound strange to those who have imbibed the silly persuasion, that fickleness and love of innovation are the characteristics of popular governments. It is, however, matter of authentic history. It is not seen in reading Mitford, who always believed his prejudices above his eyes[2]—but it is seen in reading Demosthenes, who shows in every page that he regards the authority of ancestors, not merely as an argument, but as one of the strongest of arguments; and steps out of his way to eulogise the wisdom of the ancient laws and lawgivers, with a frequency which proves it to have been the most popular of topics, and one on which his unequalled tact and sagacity taught him mainly to rely. All the other Athenian orators, down to the speeches in Thucydides; Cicero, and all that we know of the Roman orators; Plato, and almost all the monuments which remain to us of the ideas of Athens, Sparta, and Rome, teem with evidence of the same fact.[3] In all this there is nothing but what the known constitution of human nature would have enabled us to surmise: it is precisely what marks these commonwealths to have been in a natural state of society. When a government, whether it be a popular one or not, works well for the people among whom it exists, and satisfies their highest conceptions of a good social order, there is naturally a strong, and generally a very just, reverence for the memory of its founders. This would not have been thought strange three-quarters of a century ago. Robertson, the historian, speaks with the utmost simplicity, of "that attachment to ancient forms, and aversion to innovation, which are the unfailing characteristics of popular assemblies."[4] Europe had not then entered into the state of transition of which the first overt manifestation was the breaking out of the French revolution. Since that epoch, those near-sighted people who can see nothing beyond their own age, have mistaken that desire of novelty, and disregard of the authority of ancestors, which characterise an age of transition, for the properties of a popular government: just as if the same symptoms did not constantly attend every change, no matter of what nature, in

[2]*History of Greece* (1784-1810), 10 vols. (London: Cadell and Davies, 1818-20), by William Mitford (1744-1827), anti-Jacobin monarchist, M.P. intermittently 1785-1818.

[3]For praise of the wisdom of ancestors in these authors, see, e.g., Demosthenes (384-322 B.C.), *De falsa legatione*, in *De corona and De falsa legatione* (Greek and English), trans. C.A. and J.H. Vince (London: Heinemann, 1926), pp. 420-6 (268-76); Thucydides (ca. 460-399 B.C.), *Thucydides* (Greek and English), trans. Charles Forster Smith, 4 vols. (London: Heinemann, 1919-23), Vol. I, p. 144 (I, lxxxv, 1), and p. 252 (I, cxliv, 4); Cicero, *Pro T. Annio Milone*, in *Cicero: The Speeches. Pro T. Annio Milone, In L. Capurnium Pisonem, Pro M. Aemilio Scauro, Pro M. Fonteio, Pro. C. Rabinio Postumo, Pro M. Marcello, Pro. Q. Ligario, Pro rege Deiotaro* (Latin and English), trans. N.H. Watts (London: Heinemann, 1953), p. 98 (XXX, 83); and Plato, *Laws* (Greek and English), trans. R.G. Bury, 2 vols. (London: Heinemann, 1926), Vol. I, p. 294 (716^{b}ff.).

[4]*The History of the Reign of the Emperor Charles V* (1769), in *Works*, 6 vols. (London: Longmans, *et al.*, 1851), Vol. III, p. 379, by William Robertson (1721-93), Scottish historian whose works Mill read avidly as a child.

the spirit of the age; as if we might not be quite sure that there was as much scoffing at the wisdom of ancestors in the Court of Augustus,[5] as in the National Convention of France.

The authority of ancestors, so deeply reverenced at Athens and Rome, was the authority of the wisest and best men for many successive generations. If, instead of upholding and applauding the ancient maxims, the ablest and most experienced contemporaries had affirmed them to be the rude conceptions of barbarians, the many would have lost their faith in them, and would have been as we are now. Nor had authority more than its just weight: it did not supersede reason, but guided it: for every relic which remains to us, of what was addressed to the Athenian Demos, for example, by their orators and politicians, is full of strong sense, cogent argument, and the most manly and forcible appeals to the reason of the people. The speeches of the great orators, and those in Thucydides, are monuments of long-sighted policy, and keen and sagacious observation of life and human nature, which will be prized as long as the world shall endure, or as wisdom shall be understood and appreciated in it.

It is well known that respect and deference for old age formed a conspicuous feature both in the public and private morality of the ancient commonwealths: and there is no surer mark of a natural state of society in respect to moral influence. So deeply, however, have the notions and feelings of an age of transition taken root among us, that if there are some who wonder that this reverence should no longer exist, there are probably many more who wonder that it should ever have existed, and view it as a sort of superstition, or as one of the numerous oddities of those peculiar people, the ancients: if, indeed, they believe it at all; for it may be almost a misapplication of terms to say that a man believes a fact, although he may never dream of doubting it; as religious writers know well, when they treat of what they call practical infidelity. We can hardly be said to believe that, which we do not conceive with any distinctness or vivacity. What we read of Greece and Rome is so remote from what we have ever seen; we are helped by so few familiar analogies to penetrate our minds with its spirit, and make ourselves, as it were, at home in it, that some strength of imagination is requisite to conceive it with the intensity and life which is essential to any thing deserving the name of belief. We do not believe ancient history, we only fancy we believe it—our belief deserves no higher name than simple acquiescence—it scarcely amounts to more than that conventional assent, which we give to the mythology of the same nations.

Unquestionably, if the mental state of the old men of the present day were their natural state, there would be little reason for paying much deference to their modes of thinking. But narrowness of mind, and obstinate prejudice, are not the necessary, or the natural concomitants of old age. Old men have generally both

[5]Gaius Julius Caesar Octavianus Augustus (63 B.C.-14 A.D.).

their opinions and their feelings more deeply rooted than the young; but is it an evil to have strong convictions, and steady unfluctuating feelings? It is on the contrary, essential to all dignity or solidity of character, and to all fitness for guiding or governing mankind. It constitutes prejudice, only when society is at one of those turns or vicissitudes in its history, at which it becomes necessary that it should change its opinions and its feelings. There is but little wisdom in any one head, whatever quantity there may be in the society collectively, when the young are wiser than the old. We should not forget that, in the natural state of things, the old would, as a matter of course, be further advanced than the young, simply because they have been longer on the road. If this be not the case at present, it is because we have come to a bend in the road, and they not knowing it, continued to advance in the same line, got to the wrong side of the hedge, and allowed even the hindmost to pass them by. If the old know less than the young, it is because it is hard to unlearn; but society, fortunately, has not so frequent need to unlearn, as to learn.

All old men might have, and some old men really have, knowledge which it is altogether impossible that a young man, however great his capacity, should possess a very large measure of, namely, that which is derived from personal experience. There are some states of civilization in which this is every thing—rude states, it is true. In these, accordingly, the authority of age is almost unlimited. Nowhere is it so great as among the North American Indians: for there, the knowledge and judgment of every man must be nearly in proportion to the length of his individual experience, as the cunning of a fox may be not inaccurately measured by his years. Among the Greeks and Romans, though, in comparison, highly civilized nations, wisdom, notwithstanding, was less the fruit of speculative study, than of intercourse with the world, practice in business, and the long habit of deliberating on public affairs. It was there a recognised maxim, that old men were fittest to devise, and young men to execute.

In an age of literature, there is no longer, of necessity, the same wide interval between the knowledge of the old, and that which is attainable by the young. The experience of all former ages, recorded in books, is open to the young man as to the old; and this, doubtless, comprises much more than the individual experience of any one man; but it does not comprise all. There are things which books cannot teach. A young man *cannot*, unless his history has been a most extraordinary one, possess either that knowledge of life, which is necessary in the most difficult and important practical business, or that knowledge of the more recondite parts of human nature, which is equally necessary for the foundation of sound ethical and even political principles, but which is almost the exclusive privilege of him who, like Ulysses, has been πολύτλας:[6] which he, whose mind

---

[6]"Much-enduring" is the epithet frequently applied by Homer to Ulysses; see, e.g., *Odyssey* (Greek and English), trans. Augustus Taber Murray, 2 vols. (London: Heinemann, 1919), Vol. I, p. 182 (E, 171).

has not passed through numerous states, both moral and intellectual, cannot find out by himself—though he may undoubtedly take upon trust from other minds, such faint, uncertain, and shadowy conceptions, as we have of a plant or an animal about which we have merely read. It is true that our old men, educated as they were, have little enough of all these advantages; but young men *cannot* have them. If they are not in the old men, they are nowhere.

That the habits of old men are fixed, their principles riveted, and that they swerve not easily from them, instead of a defect, should naturally be the highest recommendation. It would be so, if the habits which they acquired in their youth, were still suitable to the state of the human mind in their old age. When it is otherwise, indeed, the greater flexibility of the young, their greater accessibility to new ideas and new feelings, all which would otherwise be termed unsteadiness, renders them the sole hope of society. But this is nothing to be proud of, or to rejoice at; it is one of the great causes which combine to render this state of transition a most dangerous passage to society. The indispensable requisites for wise thinking and wise conduct in great affairs, are severed from each other: they are apart, and are not all found in the same men; nay, they are found in two sets of men, who are, for the most part, warring with each other. The young must prevail, though it were only by outliving their antagonists; but the most important of the qualifications for making a good use of success, are still to be acquired by them during the struggle. In turbulent times, knowledge of life and business are rapidly obtained; but a comprehensive knowledge of human nature is scarcely to be acquired, but by calm reflexion and observation, in times of political tranquillity; for when minds are excited, and one man is ranged against another, there are few who do not contract an invincible repugnance, not only to the errors of their opponents, but to the truths to which those errors are allied. Through this state, however, we must struggle; and happy will be the day when it will once more be true, that with length of years cometh wisdom,[7] and when the necessary privations and annoyances of declining life shall again, as heretofore, be compensated by the honour and the gratitude due to increased powers of usefulness, fittingly employed.

A.B.

98. THE PROSPECTS OF FRANCE

EXAMINER, 10 APR., 1831, PP. 225-6

Though similar in title to the series "Prospects of France" (beginning with No. 44), this article is distinct from it. Mill was concerned now to defend the Revolution of 1830 from accusations that it had not lived up to the expectations of its supporters (a problem that was to recur in Britain after the Reform Act of 1832). The article, the first in the "Political

[7]Cf. Job, 12:12.

Examiner," is headed as title. Unlike the earlier series of articles, which were all signed "S—.", this is unsigned. Described in Mill's bibliography as "An article headed 'The Prospects of France,' in the Examiner of 10th April 1831" (MacMinn, p. 15), the item is listed as "Prospects of France" and enclosed in square brackets in the Somerville College set; though not within the square brackets, the epigraph is here included.

> War is a game which, were their subjects wise,
> Kings would not play at; nations would do well
> To extort their truncheons from the puny hands
> Of heroes, whose infirm and baby minds
> Are gratified with mischief; and who spoil,
> Because men suffer it, their toy—the world.[1]

THE SITUATION OF FRANCE at present is extremely critical, and it is of the utmost importance that it should be rightly understood.

It is not to be denied that, up to this moment, the Revolution of 1830 has brought forth none but bitter fruits;—the ruin of hundreds of opulent families; thousands of industrious workmen thrown out of employment; perpetual apprehension of internal tumults or foreign war; the most grievous disappointments; the most violent political dissensions; and, finally, a Government not more democratic in its constitution—not more popular in its spirit—and, by the necessity of its false position, not less oppressive and anti-national in its acts, than that of Charles X. Seeing this, the enemies of free institutions throughout Europe insultingly exclaim, "What has France gained by her Revolution?" and men look grave, and dilate on the fresh example now afforded of the miseries inevitably attendant even on the most legitimate and best-conducted popular insurrections.

To all this, the answer is, that the circumstances of France and the character of the French nation are grievously mistaken, if it is imagined that the people of France made their Revolution under the conception that it was a thing to *gain* by. There is no country, probably, in the world, where the evils of a popular convulsion are more highly estimated, or more nervously dreaded, than in France. *Can* it be otherwise, after the events of the last forty years? It is well known that evils with which we are only acquainted through description, and by means of general terms, scarcely ever affect our imagination with the same proportionate force with which they influence our reason. There are, probably, very few persons in Great Britain who are not convinced that a convulsion in our own country, with its enormous masses of indigent intelligence, and its utter absence of individual sympathies binding together the high and the low, would be a far more terrible catastrophe than a Revolution in France. There are few of us, moreover, who are not convinced in our understandings, that such an event is upon the cards; and yet, so little is the thought, or its attendant emotions, familiar

[1]William Cowper (1731-1800), *The Task: A Poem in Six Books* (London: Johnson, 1785), pp. 190-1 (V, 187-92).

to us—so little are we used to contemplate a Revolution at home as in the category of possible phenomena—that our reason only, not our imagination, believes in the possibility; and we eat, drink, and sleep, with our accustomed regularity, and perform all the round of daily occupations with our wonted tranquillity, knowing and saying all the while, that we are on the brink of an abyss. But such is by no means the case in France. There, even in the midst of that exemplary populace, the "people of property" lock up their strong boxes at every knocking at the door, and hear the roar of anarchy and devastation in every breeze. "The burnt child dreads the fire," is an every-day truth; but there is an Italian proverb still more accurately suited to their case—"The scalded dog fears cold water."

L'ordre public in France is a talismanic expression,[2] which has power not only to raise, but to charm down the most potent spirits. And it is as much in the interest of one as the other of the two rival idols, Order and Liberty, that the *hommes du mouvement*[3] protest against the "lame and impotent conclusion"[4] which the Stationaries are desirous of putting to the Revolution of July.

The Stationaries had nothing to do with the Revolution of July. Not one name of note in their ranks was allowed by its owner to be compromised until the struggle was over. The same terror which now rouses them, then paralysed them. They disliked the late Government—they disliked the Ordinances[5]—but they dreaded the people, and the leaders of the people, far more. The Revolution was the work exclusively of the *hommes du mouvement*; of those with whom the Government which has emanated from the Revolution is at open war. And why of them, and them alone? Not because they were what is absurdly called *Revolutionists*; as if there were, or ever had been, since the first institution of Governments, any human being who was a Revolutionist. No; but because they alone united a wish for good government, with courage to brave the necessary dangers of the struggle for it; because all the professed Liberals, them alone excepted, were either too lukewarm in their patriotism to be inclined to make any sacrifice for obtaining or preserving free institutions, or else had the misfortune to labour under a panic terror of democracy, which made them tremble at the idea of calling forth the mass of the population to contend against the common enemy. The same lukewarmness, or the same timidity, renders the same men the upholders and instigators of the present Government in its deplorable system of

---

[2]See, e.g., Louis Philippe, Proclamation du roi (15 Aug.), *Moniteur*, 1830, p. 907.

[3]There had developed in France two groups, commonly referred to as "les hommes du mouvement" and "les hommes de la résistance"; the former wished for more democratizing reforms including, for many, the establishment of a republic, and the latter were for consolidating the present situation. Both, in Mill's view, were acting in the name of law and order.

[4]William Shakespeare, *Othello*, II, i, 161; in *The Riverside Shakespeare*, p. 1213.

[5]See No. 44.

statu quo. Under their guidance, the Government has made an enemy of every man in France, who either stirred, or would have dared to stir, a finger or a foot to place that Government where it is.

But what better is to be looked for, when it is assumed as the fundamental principle of politics, that government exists, not to protect men's persons and property, and to forward their advancement in civilization, but to uphold a hereditary monarchy; and that to this end all progressive and gradual extension of popular rights is to be avoided, lest in the end it should prove to be a step towards republicanism? Louis Philippe cannot forget that those who desire that the present narrow oligarchy of electors should be widened, are headed by men who believe that a constitutional monarchy, though desirable for France at present, and for a long time to come, is at the best no more than a means of transition, to educate the people for a republic. It is in vain that these very leaders—when they were strong and he was weak—when they might have assumed the government, instead of resigning it to him—magnanimously sacrificed their private and speculative opinions, and consented to accept such a monarchical constitution as should be compatible with the progressive improvement which had been the aim of their whole lives. Louis Philippe, like other kings, made his option in favour of those who were attached to monarchy as an end, not a means, or who were ready to attach themselves to any established government; and, by a natural consequence, his throne is now surrounded almost exclusively by the hired supporters of every government which would pay them—the timid supporters of every government as long as it will stand—and some whose virtue, having never before been assailed by any powerful seductions, wore a goodly appearance, but who have surrendered the citadel at the first summons—have eaten up their words—have broken with their friends and with their principles, and proclaimed themselves in the face of Europe guilty of tergiversation so shameless, as might surprise and grieve their bitterest enemy.

The aversion of the new oligarchy to improvement, is not confined to constitutional changes. If we are truly informed, they do not seek to disguise, either in public or in private, the coldness with which they look upon all aspirations for benefitting mankind on a large scale, or for the further advancement of civilization; but especially for improving the condition of the most numerous and poorest class—a class which, according to them, is as well off as nature and the constitution of society permit it to be, and has no business to be dissatisfied while *their* property is secure, and they have the disposal of the taxes. Every one, moreover, who reads their parliamentary debates, must perceive that personality and intemperance in discussion are nearly confined to the *moderates*, who have been most justly, as well as cleverly, called *des hommes furieux de modération*.[6] Their opponents have far too much good sense

---

[6]Lafayette, Speech on the Events of 14 Feb. (20 Feb.), *Moniteur*, 1831, p. 358.

and magnanimity to retaliate; and whoever wishes for examples of that kind of oratory, in which both what is said, and the manner of saying it, indicates the greatest and the truest moderation, should read the speeches of MM. Mauguin and Odilon Barrot, in the recent debate on the Patriotic Associations.[7]

It is unfortunate in a thousand ways for all Europe, that the question of peace and war should have come at this moment to complicate the difficulties of the present position of France, to place the popular party, in the estimation of many who would otherwise have sympathized with them, manifestly in the wrong, and to expose all that has been gained, and all that might hereafter have been gained, to new and countless hazards.[8] The defeat of France would stop the march of civilization for another half century: successful she could not be, in less than three or four campaigns; in that time, the ignominy of invasion, and the inevitable horrors of war and devastation, would again rouse the national antipathies which a peace of unusual length has so greatly mitigated; while, instead of soldier-citizens, five hundred thousand military ruffians, demoralized and brutalized like those of Napoleon, might once more overspread Europe, and after enslaving foreign countries under the forms of liberty, might return prepared to be the tools of any new usurper in inflicting still worse slavery upon their own.

We must be just, however, to what is called (incorrectly) the war party in France. They do *not* advocate a crusade for liberty, or a war of propagandism. They know well that the improvement of a nation is not advanced, but retarded, by popular institutions imposed upon it by foreign force. It is not in the power of any one to affirm, with probability, that a nation would be benefitted by a constitutional government, until it puts forth its strength and seizes one; for, whatever be the forms of a government—unless it be vigorously upheld by a preponderance of the physical and intellectual strength of the nation itself, sufficient to overmatch all domestic attempts at its overthrow, it must, as the condition of its existence, be carried on, substantially, in the spirit and with the machinery of a despotism. The so-called war party have not the folly to think of quixotizing through all Europe, giving liberty to nations by the sword. But they say that when a nation *has* put itself in motion—when it *has* shown itself eager for liberal institutions, and ripe for them, by subverting all domestic opposition,

---

[7]For Mauguin's speech of 29 Mar., see *ibid.*, pp. 659-60; for Odilon Barrot's of 30 Mar., see *ibid.*, pp. 669-70. In those uncertain times, many had joined extra-governmental associations for the protection of France from disorder and foreign intervention. On 19 Mar., the Government had ordered office holders to resign from l'Association Nationale, one of the most important, and was attempting to dissolve them all on the grounds that they were no longer necessary and were usurping the Government's responsibilities.

[8]The popular party in France were belligerently demanding that France send troops to protect both Belgium against the Dutch and the East European powers, and the Italian states against the Austrians.

vanquishing the strength of an established Government, and giving itself, by its own strength, without foreign aid, a constitution more favourable to the progress of civilization,—that then no one ought to be permitted to rush down upon it with the overpowering strength of another nation not equally advanced, not equally prepared for an improvement in its government, and overwhelm a united people by superiority of brute force. They say that non-intervention by one nation in the affairs of another should be laid down by France as an inflexible rule, which she should herself observe, and of which she should enforce the observance on all other Governments. And this, they assert, is the true interest of France herself; and it is in this view mainly, we may say solely, that they contend for it.

The existence, they say, in France, of a government founded on popular will, and established on the ruins of legitimacy and divine right, must necessarily give an impulse to the democratic spirit throughout Europe, by which, if not restrained, the thrones of all absolute monarchs will be every year more and more undermined, and, in no long period, certainly overthrown. The reason and the instinct of those monarchs will therefore join in indicating to them as the sole chance of saving their existence as despots, to extinguish the spirit of liberalism in France. The consequent struggle, the French are aware, will be an arduous and a perilous one: but those, at least, who are called the war-party, believe it to be as inevitable as was the still more terrific struggle in 1792. In this contest they would have for their natural allies the people of every country in Europe which aspires to free institutions. But what, they ask, will be our situation, if we allow all to whom we might appeal in the hour of need to be crushed, one after another, not by their own governments, but by the armies of foreign despots; who will then have no enemy but us, and who, after keeping us for an indefinite period in perpetual agitation, and a state of habitual preparation for war, implying most of the evils of actual war, without its advantages, will seize the first favourable moment for pouring their troops across our frontiers, and reducing us to the necessity of fighting for our very existence at our own doors, and on our own soil? It is therefore that Lafayette, and the numerous body whose opinions he represents, contend for the enforcement, by arms, if necessary, of the principle of non-intervention.[9]

And if France had been a united nation, headed by a government which could trust the people, which the people trusted, and which was able and dared to call forth the national enthusiasm, this would have been the true policy of France, and its almost infallible result would have been not war but peace. When France declared that the entry of foreign troops into Belgium would be considered a declaration of war, all Europe applauded, and the Cabinets reluctantly acquiesced. Yet France was then almost without an army, and many of her

[9]See, e.g., Lafayette's Speech on External Affairs (28 Jan.), *Moniteur*, 1831, pp. 193-4.

frontier fortresses were in a state almost incapable of defence. But the imposing unanimity which reigned in the July revolution, struck terror into the Powers, and they feared to stir. It is Louis Philippe, and his Chambers, that have marred this glorious position. It is they who, by placing themselves in a state of hostility against the spirit of the nation, have destroyed the *préstiges* of its power, and impressed the despotic governments with the gratifying assurance that it has too much upon its hands at home to be formidable abroad. This being the melancholy fact, the attempt to enforce non-intervention against Austria in the case of the Papal states would probably lead to war; and the co-operation of such a spiritless people as that of Romagna, in case of future hostilities, is so little worth, that it would be unwise in France to accelerate such a calamity in order to save them. Her policy now is to throw her shield over Belgium and Switzerland;[10] leave events in other countries to take their course; and, if war is coming, wait till it comes.

99. PARAGRAPH ON FRANCE
EXAMINER, 10 APR., 1831, P. 232

This unheaded editorial comment refers to a letter signed "M" from the *Examiner*'s Paris Correspondent, Pierre Martin Maillefer, in which Maillefer points to the growth of a republican spirit in France, anticipates a republic with Lafayette at its head, and ends with a bitter denunciation of the corruption and duplicity of Louis Philippe's government and a personal attack on the king and Casimir Périer. The letter (pp. 231-2) is headed "Foreign Intelligence. (From the Correspondent of the *Examiner*)" and dated 2 Apr. The item is not included in Mill's bibliography, but is listed as "Paragraph on France" in the Somerville College index. Though the page number is there given as 233, this paragraph on p. 232 is enclosed in square brackets in the bound set.

THE STATE OF FEELING amongst the young men of France, and the most estimable of the old patriots, is pourtrayed in the letter of our Parisian correspondent. There are no new events of importance of which he does not treat.

100. FRENCH NEWS [22]
EXAMINER, 17 APR., 1831, P. 249

This item is headed "London, April 17." For the entry in Mill's bibliography, see No. 55. The item is listed as "Article on France" and enclosed in square brackets in the Somerville College set.

[10]In the spreading enthusiasm of 1830, several Swiss cantons had elected reformist governments, and liberals and radicals alike were campaigning for a federal state, which they thought would be more progressive than the existing federation of states.

THE FIFTEEN YEARS OF THE RESTORATION never furnished anything approaching to the deplorable exhibition which the French Government is making in the face of Europe, on the trial of the pretended Republican Conspirators of December.[1] The prosecution cannot establish the most trifling point. The witnesses who were most relied on, are brought forward, and have nothing to say; complaining in many cases, that the eagerness of the Judge before whom they made their preliminary depositions, had converted the merest trifles into facts of the gravest import. It is evident that the government has kept innocent men in prison for several months, and now puts them on trial for their lives, on no evidence whatever; proceeding upon idle reports, and the suggestions of its own morbid and unmanly apprehensions. One of the witnesses summed up his opinion of the whole affair, in words which are borne out by every fact which has transpired: "There are two sorts of men who have exaggerated these tumults: terrified men, who take alarm at every thing, such men as may now be seen exhibited at the *Théâtre des Variétés*; and some others, who were willing to stake the lives of their fellow-citizens against a ribbon, or a place. But they will reap nothing from it but infamy."[2]

The Chamber of Deputies have refused to adopt the amendment, by which the Peers had cut off a large proportion of the new electors;[3] but it has adopted, on the proposition of M. Casimir Périer, an additional article,[4] which provides that the electoral lists shall be made out from the tax-books of 1830, instead of 1831; which will prevent the new taxes, now about to be imposed, from operating to augment still further the number of electors. This distrust and jealousy of the people, shown at the very moment when the hand of the tax-gatherer is to be thrust deeper into their pockets, has created the most lively dissatisfaction among all but the admirers of the "*juste milieu*," or *statu-quo* system.

[1]For the riots in December, see No. 72, n4. Godefroi Eléonore Louis Cavaignac (1801-45) and Auguste Joseph Guinard (1799-1874), republicans, commanders in the artillery of the National Guard, were accused with seventeen others of giving weapons to the people during the disturbances demanding the death of the ex-Ministers. The prosecutors were MM. Miller (b. ca. 1789), appointed avocat-général in 1830, and Hardouin (b. ca. 1789), a conseiller at the Cour Royale de Paris since 1821. The trial had begun on 6 Apr., 1831.

[2]Godefroy Levasseur (an artillery captain), testimony at the trial on 10 Apr., 1831, *Le National*, 11 Apr., p. 3.

[3]The amendment (adopted by the Peers on 30 Mar. and rejected by the Deputies on 9 Apr.) had excluded the *centimes additionnels* (the annually adjusted tax always levied in addition to the basic tax) from the calculation of a voter's qualification, thus lowering the potential electorate by about 70,000 names. (The Peers acquiesced on 16 Apr.)

[4]Titre VII, Art. 79 (Bull. 37, No. 105 [19 Apr., 1831]).

101. CAVAIGNAC'S DEFENCE

EXAMINER, 24 APR., 1831, P. 266

For the background, see No. 100, n1. This paragraph introduces a translation that is given in App. A. It is the first item in the "Foreign Intelligence" of the *Examiner*, subheaded "France." Not listed in Mill's bibliography or in the Somerville College set, the translation is acknowledged as his by Mill in a letter to Thomas Carlyle of 25 Nov., 1833 (*EL, CW*, Vol. XII, p. 194); there can be little doubt that the introductory paragraph is also his.

THE PRETENDED REPUBLICAN CONSPIRATORS have been acquitted, and carried in triumph through the streets of Paris. Our daily papers being unable to find room at the present juncture for French news of any interest or importance, but only for loose talk and idle speculation, we think it a duty to present our readers with a translation of part of M. Cavaignac's defence; that they may see what manner of men those are whom the satellites of power load with abuse, whom the government has not feared nor been ashamed to put on trial upon a capital charge, and who, it has been supposed by good-natured, timid friends of freedom, both in this country and in France, must needs be firebrands and sowers of sedition, seeing that the citizen king and his government cannot rest in their beds on account of them.

102. FRENCH NEWS [23]

EXAMINER, 24 APR., 1831, P. 267

This item, headed "London, April 24", is not covered by the inclusive entry in Mill's bibliography cited at No. 55, which ends at 17 Apr. However, it is listed as "Article on France" and enclosed in square brackets in the Somerville College set.

THE CHAMBER OF DEPUTIES is prorogued, and will shortly be dissolved. Thus, in the two greatest nations in the world, general elections will simultaneously take place, and the new legislative bodies will be simultaneously called upon to determine the future constitution of their country.[1]

The speech of Louis Philippe[2] expresses his determination to maintain the charter, and speaks of the good disposition of foreign powers towards France: it is empty and formal, and precisely such a speech as might have been concocted by our last administration.

[1]Prorogued 20 Apr., it was dissolved on 31 May; the election took place at the beginning of July. In England, Grey had been defeated on 21 Apr., and William IV had dissolved Parliament at his request. The election took place immediately.

[2]Adresse du roi (20 Apr.), *Moniteur*, 1831, p. 855.

103. THE SPIRIT OF THE AGE, V [Part 1]

EXAMINER, 15 MAY, 1831, P. 307

For the context and entry in Mill's bibliography, see No. 73. The article, listed as "The Spirit of the Age, No. 5" and enclosed in square brackets in the Somerville College set, is also there corrected in eleven places: "which, it" is altered to "which it" (305.20), "pale, because" to "pale because" (305.26), "Now, when" to "When" (305.39), "that, situate . . . of the rivals . . . him, even . . . chair," to "that (situate . . . of rivals . . . him even . . . chair,)" (306.6-9), "mankind, the" to "mankind, and the" (306.11), "of menacing" to "for menacing" (306.12), "low." to "low;—" (306.14), "them; and" to "them and" (306.20), "but when" to "but where" (306.22), "indisputably" to "undisputably" (306.25), and "irretrievable—except" to "irretrievable except" (307.5). These are all accepted here.

IN COMMENCING THIS SERIES OF PAPERS, I intended, and attempted, that the divisions of my discourse should correspond with those of my subject, and that each number should comprehend within its own limits all which was necessary to the expansion and illustration of one single idea. The nature of the publication, which, as being read by more persons capable of understanding the drift of such speculations (and by fewer, in proportion, who are unfit for them) than any other single work, I considered myself fortunate in being enabled to adopt as a vehicle for my ideas, compels me to limit the length of each article more than is compatible with my original plan. I can no longer always hope that every paper should be complete within itself; and the present number, had it appeared in its proper place, would have formed the continuation of the last.

In endeavouring to give an intelligible notion of what I have termed the *natural* state of society, in respect of moral influence—namely, that state in which the opinions and feelings of the people are, with their voluntary acquiescence, formed *for* them, by the most cultivated minds which the intelligence and morality of the times call into existence; and in drawing attention to the striking differences between this *natural* state and our present *transitional* condition, in which there are no persons to whom the mass of the uninstructed habitually defer, and in whom they trust for finding the right, and for pointing it out; I have hitherto illustrated the former state only by the example of those commonwealths, in which the most qualified men are studiously picked out because of their qualifications, and invested with that worldly power, which, if it were in any other hands, would divide or eclipse their moral influence: but which, placed in theirs, and acting partly as a *certificate* of authority, and partly as a *cause*, tends naturally to render their power over the minds of their fellow-citizens paramount and irresistible.

But it is not solely in such societies that there is found a united body of moral authority, sufficient to extort acquiescence from the uninquiring, or uninformed majority. It is found, likewise, in all societies where religion possesses a sufficient ascendancy, to subdue the minds of the possessors of worldly power, and where the spirit of the prevailing religion is such as excludes the possibility of material conflict of opinion among its teachers.

These conditions exist among two great stationary communities—the Hindoos and the Turks; and are doubtless the chief cause which keeps those communities stationary. The same union of circumstances has been hitherto found only in one *progressive* society—but that, the greatest which had ever existed: Christendom in the middle ages.

For many centuries, undivided moral influence over the nations of Europe, the unquestioned privilege of forming the opinions and feelings of the Christian world, was enjoyed, and most efficiently exercised by the Catholic clergy. Their word inspired in the rest of mankind the most fervent faith. It not only absolutely excluded doubt, but caused the doubter to be regarded with sentiments of profound abhorrence, which moralists had never succeeded in inspiring for the most revolting of crimes. It is certainly possible to feel perfectly sure of an opinion, without believing that whosoever doubts it will be damned, and should be burnt: and this last is by no means one of those peculiarities of a natural state of society which I am at all anxious to see restored. But the deep earnest feeling of firm and unwavering conviction, which it pre-supposes, we may, without being unreasonable, lament that it was impossible, and could not *but* be impossible, in the intellectual anarchy of a general revolution in opinion, to transfer unimpaired to the truth.

The priesthood did not claim a right to dictate to mankind, either in belief or practice, beyond the province of religion and morals, but the political interests of mankind came not the less within their pale because they seldom assumed the authority to regulate those concerns by specific precepts. They gave the sanction of their irresistible authority to one comprehensive rule, that which enjoined unlimited obedience to the temporal sovereign: an obligation from which they absolved the conscience of the believer, only when the sovereign disputed their authority within their peculiar province: and in that case they were invariably triumphant, like all those to whom it is given to call forth the moral sentiments of mankind in all their energy, against the inducements of mere physical hopes and fears.

The Catholic clergy, at the time when they possessed this undisputed authority in matters of conscience and belief, were, in point of fact, the fittest persons who *could* have possessed it—the then state of society, in respect of moral influence, answers to the description of a *natural* state.

When we consider for how long a period the Catholic clergy were the only members of the European community who could even read; that they were the sole depositaries of all the treasures of thought, and reservoirs of intellectual delight, handed down to us from the ancients; that the sanctity of their persons permitted to them alone, among nations of semi-barbarians, the tranquil pursuit of peaceful occupations and studies; that, howsoever defective the morality which they taught, they had at least a mission for curbing the unruly passions of mankind, and teaching them to set a value upon a distant end, paramount to immediate temptations, and to prize gratifications consisting of mental feelings above bodily sensation; that (situate in the position of rivals to the temporal sovereign, drafted chiefly from the inferior classes of society, from men who otherwise would have been serfs, and the most lowly among them all having the road open before him even to the papal chair,) they had the strongest motives to avail themselves of the means afforded by Christianity, for inculcating the natural equality of mankind, and the superiority of love and sacrifice above mere courage and bodily prowess, for menacing the great with the only terrors to which they were accessible, and speaking to their consciences in the name of the only superior whom they acknowledged, in behalf of the low;—Reflecting on these things, I cannot persuade myself to doubt that the ascendancy of the Catholic clergy was to be desired, for that day, even by the philosopher; and that it has been a potent cause, if even it was not an indispensable condition, of the present civilization of Europe. Nor is this an apology for the vices of the Catholic religion: those vices were great and flagrant, and there was no natural connection between them and the more civilizing and humanizing features in which all that there was of good in it resided. We may regret that the influence of the priesthood was not superseded by a better influence: but where in those days did any such influence exist?

I conclude, therefore, that, during a part of the middle ages, not only worldly power, as already shown, but moral influence also, was undisputedly exercised by the most competent persons; and that the conditions of a natural state of society were then fully realized.

But the age of transition arrived. A time came when that which had overmatched and borne down the strongest obstacles to improvement, became itself incompatible with improvement. Mankind outgrew their religion, and that, too, at a period when they had not yet outgrown their government, because the texture of the latter was more yielding, and could be stretched. We all know how lamentably effectual an instrument the influence of the Catholic priesthood then became, for restraining that expansion of the human intellect, which could not any longer consist with their ascendancy, or with the belief of the doctrines which they taught.

The more advanced communities of Europe succeeded, after a terrific struggle, in effecting their total or partial emancipation: in some, the Reformation achieved a victory—in others, a toleration; while, by a fate unhappily too common, the flame which had been kindled where the pile awaited the spark, spread into countries where the materials were not yet sufficiently prepared; and instead of burning down the hateful edifice, it consumed all that existed capable of nourishing itself, and was extinguished. The germs of civilization to come were scorched up and destroyed; the hierarchy reigned stronger than ever, amidst the intellectual solitude which it had made: and the countries which were thus denuded of the means of further advancement, fell back into barbarism irretrievable except by foreign conquest. Such is the inevitable end, when, unhappily, changes to which the spirit of the age is favourable, can be successfully resisted. Civilization becomes the terror of the ruling powers, and that they may retain their seat, it must be their deliberate endeavour to barbarize mankind. There has been, since that day, one such attempt, and only one, which has had a momentary success: it was that of a man in whom all the evil influences of his age were concentered with an intensity and energy truly terrific, less tempered by any of its good influences than could appear possible in the times in which he lived—I need scarcely say that I refer to Napoleon. May his abortive effort to uncivilize human nature, to uncultivate the mind of man, and turn it into a desolate waste, be the last!

It remains to trace the history of moral influence in the nations of Europe, subsequently to the Reformation.

104. MLLE LEONTINE FAY [1]

EXAMINER, 15 MAY, 1831, P. 310

This, Mill's first artistic notice, perhaps not by chance on a French actress, was followed in the next *Examiner* by a fuller account (see No. 106) of the talents of Jeanne Louise Baron (called Léontine) Fay (1810-76), who had begun with children's roles. Her London repertoire included some sixteen plays in thirteen appearances, with Mlle Fay playing in two or even three of the playlets each evening, including three performances each of *Yelva, ou L'orpheline russe*; *Louise, ou La réparation*; *Valérie, ou La jeune aveugle*; *Le Quaker et la danseuse*, and *Une faute*. She was engaged in London by Pierre François Laporte (1799-1841), actor and theatrical entrepreneur, who managed the King's Theatre in the Haymarket, 1828-31 and 1833-41, bringing there such Italian operas as *La sonnambula*, *I puritani*, and *Norma*. The article, headed "French Theatre, Haymarket," appears in the "Theatrical Examiner." It is described in Mill's bibliography as "A paragraph on Mlle Léontine Fay, in the Examiner of 15th May 1831" (MacMinn, p. 16), and listed ("Paragraph on Madlle Léontine Fay") and enclosed in square brackets in the Somerville College set.

M. LAPORTE, whose French company is usually as miserable a *travestie* of the French stage as his company at the Opera-house frequently is of an Italian Lyric theatre, has made atonement for all past faults by engaging (alas! only for ten nights) Mademoiselle Léontine Fay; an actress, to see whom, would be of itself a sufficient motive, were there no other, for journeying to Paris. In all these scenes from domestic life, whether of tragic or of comic interest, which are the reigning character, and the peculiar charm of the French stage, this lady is pre-eminent.

We shall speak of her at greater length in our next paper; meanwhile, we can only entreat our readers, who are capable of understanding a theatrical performance in the French language, to see her, and admire for themselves.

105. THE CROIX DE JUILLET
EXAMINER, 15 MAY, 1831, p. 313

This article responds to a leading article on French affairs in *The Times*, 11 May, 1831, p. 2, which criticizes the French reaction to the Croix de Juillet, a decoration instituted by Bull. 17, No. 81 (13 Dec., 1830). The article, headed "London, May 15," is described in Mill's bibliography as "An article on the Croix de Juillet in the Examiner of the same date [as No. 104], standing as the summary of French news" (MacMinn, p. 16); it is listed as "Article on France" and enclosed in square brackets in the Somerville College set, where one correction (here adopted) is made: at 308.29, "incapable of, comprehending" is altered to "incapable of comprehending".

A LAW, passed in the late session of the French Chamber of Deputies, had decreed a peculiar decoration to those who had fought for the freedom of their country in the three days of July. A commission was appointed, which, by a careful and protracted investigation, ascertained who were the parties entitled to this national testimonial; and it was supposed that nothing further was necessary to authorise them to wear it: but no; the medal bears the words, "*donné par le roi*," and no one is to receive it without taking an oath of fidelity to Louis Philippe. Against this the majority of the parties entitled to the decoration have protested: have refused to accept it, subject to these conditions; and asserted their right, and their intention, to wear it free from any conditions whatever, by virtue of the law, and of the decision of the commission of national rewards.

For this *The Times* soundly rates them, in the stile in which a nurse scolds a self-willed child; and threatens them with the ridicule of Europe for their frivolity. *The Times* might have spared itself the pains of demonstrating, by another conclusive proof, that it is not only utterly ignorant of, but utterly incapable of comprehending, the national character of the French. The last of our public writers who still holds fast to the idle phrases of "our lively neighbours," "our volatile neighbours,"[1] has great need of putting himself to school before he gives lectures to a people who, as all mankind know, except himself, have undergone some rather remarkable metamorphoses since the days of their grandfathers. Is it necessary to repeat, once more, that the French of the present

[1] The phrases Mill alludes to in this paragraph have not been found in any recent editorial on French affairs in *The Times*; however, "our lively neighbours" appears in Richard Chenevix, "Comparative Skill and Industry of France and England," *Edinburgh Review*, XXXII (Oct. 1819), 363. (Cf. Chenevix, "English and French Literature," *ibid.*, XXXV [Mar. 1821], 164.)

day are a far more serious people than the English; that their national character is grave, earnest, and enthusiastic; that frivolity has fled from them with its parent aristocracy, and that the gibes of forty years ago might now, with far greater justice, be retorted by "our volatile neighbours" against ourselves?

If the writer in *The Times* knew any thing of *la jeune France*,[2] he would know that, by all the more ardent and generous portion of it, a ribbon, a title, a favour, a distinction of any kind proceeding from a king, or a court, is held in supreme contempt. He would know that the medal of July is the only decoration sanctioned by the French law, which nine-tenths of the combatants of the three days of July would accept: and that, because it does not proceed from a King: because it is not a mark that they have dangled in an ante-chamber, and mingled in the crowd of place-hunters, and candidates for court favour: it is the reward of a specific service, attached to that service by inflexible law, and not by a man's flexible will. Deprive it of this character, and you place it on a level with the Cross of St. Louis, or that of the Legion of Honour,[3] which have been made the prize of sycophancy and favouritism by successive governments, until it is considered a degradation to accept them. When the Schools, and the National Guard, with one accord, declined the crosses which the King had offered to confer upon a certain number of the most deserving, the reason which they *gave* was, that no one of them was more deserving than the rest: the reason which every one knew to be the real one, was contempt for the prostituted distinction. Yet to this the King, unauthorised by the law, thought fit to assimilate the testimonial of a grateful nation to the heroes of July.

Not less offence was given by the oath of fidelity to the King, exacted from men, two-thirds of whom are, from conviction, and without disguise, republicans. A government may have a right to annex conditions to its favours, but not to its justice: it may treat those who will not swear to uphold it, as disqualified for serving it, but not as excluded from the reward of services previously performed. They may disapprove of the existing constitution, but their hands aided to build it up: the deeds which France has thought worthy of a national testimonial were not the less done by them, and a service to their country is entitled to its appointed reward, even though it were achieved by men who have no attachment to their King. It is contended, and justly, that an oath of allegiance may be exacted from a public functionary, but from a private citizen never. These men might have been public functionaries if they would, there are many of them to whom places were offered; but they preferred to retain the freedom of their individual opinion, and upon that no government, they assert,

---

[2]For the origin of the phrase, see No. 50, n14.
[3]The Order of St. Louis, founded by Louis XIV in 1693 to recognize military merit, had been abolished during the Revolution, partially rehabilitated during the Restoration, and finally done away with in 1830; the Legion of Honour, instituted by Napoleon in 1802, rewarded military and civic service.

has a right to encroach, by requiring a profession of faith from the labourer before adjudging him worthy of his hire.[4]

106. MLLE LEONTINE FAY [2]
EXAMINER, 22 MAY, 1831, PP. 325-6

For background, see No. 104. This article, headed "French Theatre," appears in the "Theatrical Examiner." It is described in Mill's bibliography as "An article on Mlle Léontine Fay in the Examiner of 22d May 1831" (MacMinn, p. 16), and is listed ("Article on Madlle Léontine Fay") and enclosed in square brackets in the Somerville College set.

IT IS DIFFICULT to characterise or to criticise the performances of Mademoiselle Léontine Fay, because it is difficult to try by any standard that which might itself serve as a standard for trying every thing we could liken to it. It is impossible to describe what is her style, or in what character she excels; because she is not one of those persons who have a style, or who excel in any particular parts. If she were, she could not be, as she is, a woman of genius. An actor may distinguish himself in a certain line of characters, from a natural similitude in the turn of his own thoughts and feelings, to those which he is required to represent; or from possessing some incidental endowments, for the display of which such parts afford a peculiar scope. Or he may attain the semblance of greater variety and more abundant resources, by the mere ape-like quality of imitation: by the faculty of making his own voice, and his own face and limbs, reproduce the sounds, the motions, and the attitudes, which he has happened to hear and see. But what is hearing or seeing, without understanding? If he imitate the mere signs, without well knowing and intimately feeling what they are signs of, it matters not how accurately he may observe, nor how ample may have been his opportunities of observing; no care and pains will prevent a thousand inconsistencies from creeping in, or a thousand of the finer traits from escaping his notice. Let the most careful penman attempt to copy a long passage, in a language of which he does not understand one word, and we doubt whether, even if he were a Chinese, he could help making a hundred mistakes in spelling before the end.

A great actor must possess imagination, in the higher and more extensive meaning of the word: that is, he must be able to conceive correctly, and paint vividly within himself, states of external circumstances, and of the human mind, into which it has not happened to himself to be thrown. This is one of the rarest

[4]Cf. Luke, 10:7.

of all endowments; which is the reason why there are so few great dramatists and great actors. But he who is thus endowed, if he can act one character, can act all characters; at least, all which are in nature. And this is what is meant by the universality of genius. Let him who wishes it to be practically illustrated, go to see Mademoiselle Léontine Fay.

There is no mystery in this. If the actor were really such a person as the author conceived, and were really placed in the situation which the play supposes, he would actually have the thoughts and feelings which the author has pourtrayed: or else, the dramatist has not done his duty,—his conception is not in nature. But it rarely happens that the actor resembles the person he represents; and he never is in the precise situation. Yet, if he possesses sufficient sensibility and imagination to conceive vividly the character and the situation, this vivid conception will of itself suggest to him the very thoughts and feelings which he himself would have if he were such a character, and were placed in such a situation. He will think them and feel them, not indeed in so lively a manner as if the case really were his own, but vividly enough to represent them in the true colours of nature. This is the secret of great histrionic as well as of great dramatic genius; and we suspect that the other fine arts might equally be included in the assertion.

By this test, the sensibility and imagination of Mademoiselle Léontine Fay must be of the highest order. From the deepest tragedy to the gayest comedy, she identifies herself with every part, until you would swear that it, and it alone, was her own nature: that is, if the part *be* in nature. We apprehend, indeed, that in what are commonly called tragedies, or in the hotchpotch of buffoonery and caricature which men call a farce, she would be sadly at fault; for she has nothing conventional; and if she cannot find in herself something which answers to the words of the author, and from which those words might emanate, she would probably be more embarrassed in attempting to utter them than the feeblest and most insipid personage who ever tuned her voice to the sing-song of the theatre. Wherever feeling and taste are hindrances instead of helps, we are persuaded that Mademoiselle Léontine would fail. But this is seldom the case in the little dramas of the modern or recent French stage, in which alone she ever performs. These are of various degrees of merit, but they are always pictures of the real feelings of real human beings; they paint from the life, and not from faded paintings of manners and habits which never existed, or which have passed by. The genius of Mademoiselle Léontine ranges through several hundreds of such pieces, some of them exquisite, all natural and true; some calling forth a part of her wonderful powers; a few, very few, affording adequate scope to the whole.

For ourselves, had we written a drama of real life, whether of serious or comic interest, we should not desiderate any higher proof of its being true to nature throughout, than that it was such a piece as Mademoiselle Léontine could play.

107. THE SPIRIT OF THE AGE, V [Part 2]
EXAMINER, 29 MAY, 1831, PP. 339-41

This article is the last in the series beginning with No. 73 (*q.v.*), though the concluding paragraph makes it clear that Mill had further articles in mind; as late as October 1831, he was telling Sterling of his plans "(when the Reform Bill shall have past) to resume [his] series of papers headed the Spirit of the Age" (*EL, CW,* Vol. XII, p. 80). The article is headed: "The Spirit of the Age. / No. V. (*concluded.*)" and in the Somerville College set is similarly listed ("The Spirit of the Age, No. 5 concluded") and enclosed in square brackets.

IN THE COUNTRIES which remained Catholic, but where the Catholic hierarchy did not retain sufficient moral ascendancy to succeed in stopping the progress of civilization, the church was compelled, by the decline of its separate influence, to link itself more and more closely with the temporal sovereignty. And thus did it retard its own downfal, until the spirit of the age became too strong for the two united, and both fell together to the ground.

I have said that the three sources of moral influence are, supposed wisdom and virtue, the sacerdotal office, and the possession of worldly power. But in Protestant countries, the authority of the ministers of religion, considered as an independent source of moral influence, must be blotted out from the catalogue. None of the churches which were the successors of the Catholic church in the nations in which the Reformation prevailed, succeeded, as churches, to any portion of the moral influence of their predecessor. The reason is, that no Protestant church ever claimed a special mission from the Deity to itself; or ever numbered among the obligations of religion, that of receiving its doctrines from teachers accredited by that particular church. The Catholics received the priest from God, and their religion from the priest. But in the Protestant sects, you resorted to the teacher, because you had already decided, or because it had been decided for you, that you would adopt his religion. In the popular religions you chose your own creed, and having so done, you naturally had recourse to its ministers;—in the state religions, your creed was chosen for you by your worldly superiors, and you were instigated by conscience, or, it may be, urged by motives of a more worldly nature, to resort for religious instruction to the minister of their appointment.

Every head of a family, even of the lowest rank, in Scotland, is a theologian; he discusses points of doctrine with his neighbours, and expounds the scripture to his family. He defers, indeed, though with no slavish deference, to the opinion of his minister; but in what capacity? only as a man whom his understanding owns as being at least more versed in the particular subject—as being probably a wiser, and possibly, a better man than himself. This is not the influence of an interpreter of religion, as such; it is that of a purer heart, and a more cultivated intelligence. It is not the ascendancy of a priest: it is the combined authority of a professor of religion, and an esteemed private friend.

What I have said of the Scottish church, may be said of all Protestant churches, except state churches (which the Scottish church, notwithstanding its national endowment, is not). It may be said of all dissenters from our own establishment; except, indeed, those who inherit their religion, and adhere to it (not an uncommon case) as they would to any other family connexion. To the followers of the Church of England, a similar observation is wholly inapplicable: those excepted, who would abide by that communion for its doctrine, were it a dissenting sect. The people in general have not, nor ever had, any reason or motive for adhering to the established religion, except that it was the religion of their political superiors: and in the same ratio as their attachment to those superiors has declined, so has their adherence to the established church. From the time when the Church of England became firmly seated in its temporalities; from the period when its title to the fee-simple of our consciences acquired the sanctity of prescription, and when it was enabled to dispense with any support but what it derived from the stable foundations of the social fabric of which it formed a part; it sunk from its independent rank, into an integral part, or a kind of appendage, of the aristocracy. It merged into the higher classes: and what moral influence it possessed, was merely a portion of the general moral influence of temporal superiors.

From the termination, therefore, of that period of intellectual excitement and hardy speculation which succeeded the crisis of the Reformation, and which was prolonged in our own country to the end of the seventeenth century;—that moral influence, that power over the minds of mankind, which had been for so many ages the unquestioned heritage of the Catholic clergy, passed into the hands of the wealthy classes, and became united with worldly power. The ascendancy of the aristocracy was not so dictatorial and enthralling as that of the Catholic priesthood; because it was backed in a far inferior degree by the terrors of religion: and because unity of doctrine was not maintained, by the same powerful means, among the dominant class itself. Nevertheless, the higher classes set the fashion, as in dress, so in opinion. The opinions generally received among them, were the prevalent ones throughout the rest of the nation. A bookish man here and there might have his individual theories, but they made no converts. All who had no opinions of their own, assumed those of their superiors. Few men wrote and published doctrines which the higher classes did not approve; or if published, their books were successfully cried down, or at best, were little read or attended to. Such questions, and such only, as divided the aristocracy, were (modestly) debated by the people: whose various denominations or divisions were each headed by an aristocratic *côterie*. Even the Dissenters made amends for their preference of a vulgar religion, by evincing a full measure of pliability and acquiescence in all that concerned politics and social life; though the banner they in general followed, was that of a section of the aristocracy less wedded than the other section to the monopoly of the sect which possessed advowsons and archbishoprics.

The wealthy classes, then, from the revolution downwards, possessed all that existed both of moral authority and worldly power. Under their influence grew up the received doctrines of the British constitution; the opinions, respecting the proper limits of the powers of government, and the proper mode of constituting and administering it, which were long characteristic of Englishmen. Along with these arose a vast variety of current opinions respecting morality, education, and the structure of society. And feelings in unison with those opinions, spread far, and took a deep root in the English mind.

At no time, during this period, could the predominant class be said, with truth, to comprise among its members all the persons qualified to govern men's minds, or to direct their temporal interests, whom the state of society afforded. As a whole, however, that class contained, for a long time, a larger share of civilization and mental culture, than all other classes taken together. The difficulties, to men of merit and energy, of lifting themselves into that class, were not insuperable; and the leading and active spirits among the governing body, had capacity to comprehend intellectual superiority, and to value it. The conditions, therefore, of a natural state of society were for some time, upon the whole, tolerably well fulfilled.

But they have now ceased to be fulfilled. The government of the wealthy classes was, after all, the government of an irresponsible few; it therefore swarmed with abuses. Though the people, by the growth of their intelligence, became more and more sensible of whatever was vicious in their government, they might possibly have borne with it, had they themselves remained as they were formerly, unfit, and conscious of their unfitness, for the business of government. But the comparative freedom of the practical administration of our Constitution—the extensive latitude of action which it allowed to the energies of individuals—enabled the people to train themselves in every habit necessary for self-government; for the rational management of their own affairs. I believe it would be impossible to mention any portion whatever of the business of government (except some parts of the defence of the country against external enemies), of which the exact counterpart is not, in some instance or other, performed by a committee chosen by the people themselves: performed with less means, and under incomparably greater difficulties, but performed unexceptionably, and to the general satisfaction of the persons interested. It is notorious that much of the most important part of what in most other countries composes the business of government, is here performed wholly by voluntary associations: and other portions are done by the government in so clumsy and slovenly a manner, that it is found necessary to have recourse to voluntary associations as a subsidiary resource.

When the people were thus trained to self-government, and had learned by experience that they were fit for it, they could not continue to suppose that none but persons of rank and fortune were entitled to have a voice in the government, or were competent to criticise its proceedings. The superior capacity of the higher ranks for the exercise of worldly power is now a broken spell.

It *was* in the power of those classes, possessed as they were of leisure and boundless opportunities of mental culture, to have kept themselves on the level of the most advanced intellects of the age; not to have been overtopped by the growth around them of a mass of intelligence, superior, on the average, to their own. They might also have preserved the confidence of the people in the integrity of their purposes, by abating each abuse, in proportion as the public conscience rose against it. They might thus have retained, in right of their virtue and intellect, that moral ascendancy which an intelligent people never long continues to yield to mere power. But they have flung away their advantages.

I have already adverted to the decline of the higher classes in active talent, as they became enervated by lazy enjoyment. In the same ratio in which they have advanced in humanity and refinement, they have fallen off in energy of intellect and strength of will. Many of them were formerly versed in business: and into the hands of such, the remainder committed the management of the nation's affairs. Now, the men of hereditary wealth are mostly inexperienced in business, and unfit for it. Many of them formerly knew life and the world: but their knowledge of life is now little more than the knowledge of two or three hundred families, with whom they are accustomed to associate; and it may be safely asserted, that not even a fellow of a college is more ignorant of the world, or more grossly mistakes the signs of the times, than an English nobleman. Their very opinions,—which, before they had passed into aphorisms, were the result of choice, and something like an act of the intelligence,—are now merely hereditary. Their minds were once active—they are now passive: they once generated impressions—they now merely take them. What are now their political maxims? Traditional texts, relating, directly or indirectly, to the privileges of their order, and to the exclusive fitness of men of their own sort for governing. What is their public virtue? Attachment to these texts, and to the prosperity and grandeur of England, on condition that she shall never swerve from them; idolatry of certain abstractions, called church, constitution, agriculture, trade, and others: by dint of which they have gradually contrived, in a manner, to exclude from their minds the very idea of their living and breathing fellow-citizens, as the subjects of moral obligation in their capacity of rulers. They love their country as Bonaparte loved his army—for whose glory he felt the most ardent zeal, at a time when all the men who composed it, one with another, were killed off every two or three years. They do not love England as one loves human beings, but as a man loves his house or his acres.

Being such persons as has now been described, and being at last completely found out by the more intelligent, they no longer retain sufficient moral influence to give, as heretofore, vogue and currency to their opinions. But they retain—and the possessors of worldly power must always retain—enough of that influence, to prevent any opinions, which they do not acknowledge, from passing into received doctrines. They must, therefore, be divested of the monopoly of worldly power, ere the most virtuous and best-instructed of the nation will acquire that ascendancy over the opinions and feelings of the rest, by which alone England can emerge from this crisis of transition, and enter once again into a natural state of society.

A few months before the first of these papers was written, it would have seemed a paradox to assert that the present aera is one of moral and social transition. The same proposition now seems almost the tritest of truisms. The revolution which had already taken place in the human mind, is rapidly shaping external things to its own form and proportions.

That we are in a state of transition, is a point which needs no further illustration. That the passage we are in the midst of, will conduct us to a healthier state, has perhaps been rendered probable in the preceding papers, to some few who might otherwise have questioned it.

But it greatly imports us to obtain a far deeper insight into the futurity which awaits us, and into the means by which the blessings of that futurity may be best improved, and its dangers avoided.

How shall we attain this insight? By a careful survey of the properties which are characteristic of the English national mind, in the present age—for on these the future fate of our country must depend.

But "fit audience," even "though few,"[1] cannot be found for such discussions, at a moment when the interests of the day and of the hour naturally and properly engross every mind. The sequel of these papers must therefore be postponed until the interval of repose, after the present bustle and tumult. I shall resume my subject as early as possible after the passing of the Reform Bill.[2]

---

[1] John Milton (1608-74), *Paradise Lost* (1667), Bk. VII, l. 31; in *The Poetical Works* (London: Tonson, 1695), p. 180.

[2] The elections returned a substantial majority for Grey and the Reform Bill. After Parliament resumed on 14 June, the second version was brought in, "A Bill to Amend the Representation of the People in England and Wales," 2 William IV (25 June, 1831), *PP*, 1831, III, 9-46.

108. DEATH OF THE ABBE GREGOIRE
EXAMINER, 5 JUNE, 1831, P. 360

In this, Mill's first obituary notice, he memorializes Henri, abbé Grégoire (1750-1831), a leading radical and former politician. The Archbishop of Paris, Quélen, having refused him the last rites unless he agreed to renounce his oath to the civil constitution, they were performed without the renunciation by abbé Marie Nicolas Sylvestre Guillon (1760-1847), a priest, writer, and practitioner of medicine during the Revolution. At first no church was permitted to receive his body, but eventually he was buried, to the accompaniment of fiery speeches, in the cemetery of Montparnasse. These unheaded paragraphs are described in Mill's bibliography as "An obituary notice of the abbé Grégoire in the Examiner of 5th June 1831, included in the summary of French news" (MacMinn, p. 16); in the Somerville College set they are similarly listed (without the "An") and enclosed in square brackets.

THE CELEBRATED ABBÉ GRÉGOIRE has recently died, after an illness of some length, and in extreme old age. The Archbishop of Paris refused to authorize the sacraments to be administered to him, or the funeral service to be performed, considering him as a schismatic, who had not made his peace with the Church. Clergymen, however, were found to perform these offices, in spite of the Archbishop. His schism consisted in having conformed to the ecclesiastical establishment of the Constituent Assembly, and having accepted the office of a Constitutional Bishop. M. Grégoire never renounced the Roman Catholic faith, but adhered to it openly throughout the reign of Terror, either from conviction, or because he scorned submission to an odious tyranny. Few characters have been the subject of greater calumny; none ever were more highly respected by all to whom they were really known. In 1819, the estimation in which his country held him was evinced in his being returned to the Chamber of Deputies, without any solicitation on his part, by the department of the Isère. This provoked a furious debate on the meeting of the Chamber; and his election was finally pronounced void, on a point of form.

M. Grégoire was a Member of the Convention when Louis XVI was tried.[1] Being absent on deputation, he forwarded his vote in writing; it was for a verdict of guilty, but against capital punishment: and he persuaded three colleagues, who were joined with him in the same mission, to do the like.[2] He was, and remained to the last, a firm Republican; and was one of the first persons in France (along with Brissot,[3] and others) who made any public exertions for the mitigation and final extinction of Negro slavery.

[1]Louis XVI (1754-93) was tried and executed in January 1793.
[2]Grégoire's colleagues were Marie Jean Hérault de Séchelles (1760-94), Grégoire Marie Jagot (1751-1838), and Edouard Thomas Simon (1740-1818).
[3]Jean Pierre Brissot (called de Warville) (1754-93), lawyer and radical reformer, was one of the founders in 1788 of the Société des Amis des Noirs.

109. ATTACK ON LITERATURE
EXAMINER, 12 JUNE, 1831, PP. 369-71

This lengthy defence of state pensions for literary worthies was prompted by a leading article, "Literature and Patronage," in the *Brighton Guardian*, 8 June, 1831, p. 2, from which the quotations, unless otherwise noted, are taken. The *Brighton Guardian* responded, and Mill replied (see No. 111). The article is the first in the "Political Examiner," and is headed as title. It is described in Mill's bibliography as "A leading article headed 'Attack on Literature' in answer to the Brighton Guardian; in the Examiner of 12th June 1831" (MacMinn, p. 16); it is listed as title and enclosed in square brackets in the Somerville College set.

IN THE YEAR 1824, a Society was instituted, under the name of the Royal Society of Literature. With what definite views it was established, or what purposes of utility the association, as such, has ever promoted, we know not; and the members themselves, possibly, know as little. There were annexed, however, to the Institution, ten pensions, of a hundred guineas each, from the Privy Purse; to be held by as many persons, distinguished in the world of letters. And the individuals who were first selected to hold these moderate stipends were the following (we quote from the *Englishman's Magazine*):[1]

Samuel Taylor Coleridge; the Rev. Edward Davies; Dr. Jamieson, the indefatigable compiler of the Scottish Dictionary; the Rev. T.R. Malthus; Matthias, the author of the *Pursuits of Literature*; James Millingen, Esq.; Sir William Ouseley; William Roscoe; the Rev. Henry J. Todd; and Sharon Turner.*

[1]"Extraordinary Case of the Royal Associates of the Royal Society of Literature," *Englishman's Magazine*, I (June 1831), 264. The beneficiaries were Samuel Taylor Coleridge (1772-1834), poet and philosopher; Reverend Edward Davies (1756-1831), master of a grammar school at Chipping Sodbury, better known for his *Celtic Researches on the Origin, Traditions, and Language of the Ancient Britons* (1804); Dr. John Jamieson (1759-1838), antiquary and philologist, friend of Walter Scott, who had compiled a two-volume *Etymological Dictionary of the Scottish Language* (1808); Thomas Robert Malthus (see No. 17); Thomas James Matthias (1754?-1835), probably best known for his *Pursuits of Literature* (1794-96), a satire on many authors, but whose scholarly Italian translations were his best works; James Millingen (1774-1845), archaeologist, who had compiled works in English, French, and Italian, on coins, medals, Etruscan vases, etc.; William Ouseley (1767-1842), orientalist, author of *Persian Miscellanies* (1795) and *Oriental Collections* (1797-1800); William Roscoe (1743-1831), historian, author of several works, including a *Life of Lorenzo de' Medici* (1795) and an edition of Pope's *Works* (10 vols., 1824); Reverend Henry John Todd (1763-1845), editor of Milton, Spenser, and Johnson's *Dictionary*, author of numerous original works including a life of Cranmer (1831); Sharon Turner (1768-1847), historian, whose best known work was his *History of the Anglo-Saxons from Their First Appearance to the Norman Conquest* (1799-1805).

*The *first* account of the affair appeared in *The Law Magazine*. ["Events of the Quarter," *The Law Magazine; or, Quarterly Review of Jurisprudence*, V (Jan. and Apr. 1831), 523.]

Perhaps no act of the late King, which is known to the public, was altogether so creditable to him as the grant of these pensions. While the debates on the Civil List are fresh in the recollection of our readers,[2] we need scarcely remind them, that, of what is called the Privy Purse, a large part is granted by Parliament avowedly for purposes of liberality and munificence. These pensions were among the best examples which England had long seen, of well-directed munificence. They were too inconsiderable to excite the cupidity of tax-eating idlers. Several of the persons on whom they were bestowed, were in circumstances which rendered the accession to their incomes of real importance. The individuals were not selected on any narrow or exclusive principle; but had distinguished themselves in different modes, and in different walks of literature and philosophy. All, however, were men of reputation in their several departments; all, as writers, had proposed to themselves higher objects than merely to amuse; and none of them could possibly have acquired affluence, or even respectable subsistence, by such works as those to which they had dedicated themselves. A. or B. may think some of the number undeserving of what was bestowed upon them, and may imagine that he himself could have pointed out individuals better entitled to be so provided for. This was inevitable. We ourselves, as well as other people, could have suggested emendations in the list; but the giver was not bound to please us, or to please A. or B., but to satisfy the body of educated and cultivated Englishmen: and taking, as is proper, for the standard, the prevalent opinions and feelings, at the time when the grant was made, of the bulk of those whose approbation had the best title to be considered, it would be difficult to point out ten persons, the selection of whom, as the objects of the Royal liberality, would have been in every respect so unobjectionable.

These pensions, however, his present Majesty has, it appears, seen fit to discontinue. It, undoubtedly, rests with the King himself to decide in what manner that portion of his revenues which is set apart for acts of generosity, can be most worthily employed; and it is proper that, in the choice of objects, he should follow his own opinion, and not ours. On this subject it would be disrespectful to express more than regret, and our firm conviction that the one thousand guineas per annum which the Privy Purse will save by the stoppage of this annual bounty, will be expended, we know not how indeed, but most assuredly in a less useful manner, and for the benefit of less meritorious persons. We might be permitted to add, (what has been insisted upon with great force by some of our contemporaries) that when the odious Pension List, the wages of political, if not even of personal prostitution—the purchase-money of despotic power—the fragments of a nation's spoil which the feasters have flung from their richly-furnished table to allay the hunger of some of the baser and more

---

[2]In the House of Commons on 28 Mar., 12 and 14 Apr., 1831 (*PD*, 3rd ser., Vol. 3, cols. 1102-12, 1253-5, 1371-85).

subordinate of their tools;—when this monument of iniquity has just been screened from revision, on the ground that, although there had been no promise, persons naturally expect to keep what they have once got;[3]—the moment is ill chosen for resuming the scanty pittance which men, whose lives had been devoted to usefulness, had every rational ground to calculate upon retaining for their few remaining years. But it is in this spirit that an English government usually economizes. Whatever is enormous and unearned, it leaves undisturbed to the possessors. Its retrenchments bear uniformly and exclusively upon the ill-paid and the deserving.

But, as Rousseau well observes, one bad maxim is worse than a thousand bad actions,—because it leads to ten thousand.[4] A report that Lord Grey, at the instigation of Lord Brougham, had tendered to Mr. Coleridge a grant of two hundred pounds from the Treasury (which, however, Mr. Coleridge declined),[5] has furnished the *Brighton Guardian* with the occasion of an article, equal in length to half a page of *The Times*; the Vandalism of which, inconceivable, if *any* Vandalism could be inconceivable, provokes us to take up the pen. The matter with which the article is filled, is indeed, or should be, very little formidable, did the writer merely state the opinion of one rather perverse individual. But, unfortunately, this perverse person is but one man who is bold enough to utter what the whole tribe of the dunces are intimately persuaded of in their hearts, but do not dare to avow. They will soon, however, pluck up courage to proclaim and act upon it, if they find themselves countenanced by one or two persons (as this writer has proved himself to be) not untinctured with letters. It is, therefore, of some importance to analyse a performance, more abounding in the ideas and feelings characteristic of uncultivated minds, than is often the case with the productions of an understanding even superficially cultivated.

The object of the writer is to establish, that men of letters ought, in no case, to be provided for at the national expense. And though this is, in our opinion, a mischievous error, it is shared by too many superior men in the present day, to be matter of serious reproach to any one. It is a maxim in perfect harmony with the *laissez faire* spirit of the prevailing philosophy—with the idea by which, either consciously or unconsciously, nine-tenths of the men who can read and write, are at present possessed—viz. that every person, however uneducated or ill-educated, is the best judge of what is most for his own advantage, better even than the man whom he would delegate to make laws for him. The scope of the received doctrines is, to make mankind retrograde, for a certain space, towards the state of nature; by limiting the ends and functions of the social union, as strictly as possible, to those of a mere police. The idea that political society is a

---

[3]See "Pension List," *The Times*, 2 June, 1831, p. 2.

[4]Adapted from Jean Jacques Rousseau, *Julie, ou La nouvelle Héloïse* (1760), in *Oeuvres complètes*, Vol. VIII, p. 168 (Pt. 1, Letter 30).

[5]See *The Times*, 3 June, 1831, p. 2.

combination among mankind for the purpose of helping one another in every way in which help can be advantageous, is yet a stranger to the immense majority of understandings.

But if the conclusion at which this writer arrives, is common to him with many wiser men than himself, this is not precisely the case with the premises by which he supports it; for he goes the full length of averring that literary men are of no use; that the improvement of mankind is not, in the slightest degree, owing to them or their writings; and that we should be as far, or farther, advanced in wisdom and virtue than we now are, if the whole tribe had long since become extinct.

He begins by accounting for the high estimation in which literary men are held. It arises, he says, from the fact, that "literary men are the penholders of society, and they praise themselves and praise their pursuits." In part also it is "a sort of traditionary sentiment." After the breaking up of the Roman empire, all the knowledge of past times existed in a dead language; and was accessible only to literary men, who, consequently, met with "respect, and even veneration." "There was, at the period of what is called the revival of learning in Europe, a considerable mine of valuable knowledge opened by literary men." This, however, is no longer the case; because, peradventure, we now know everything; or, at least, one of us knows no more than another. Literature "is praised and honoured for what it once did,—not for what it now does." He then holds forth as follows:

Do literary men, or does literature now improve and instruct mankind? To a certain extent, we admit that it does both. But amusement is afforded to thousands of people by Punch in the street, by a clown at the theatre, and by the shows at Vauxhall; and we have never heard any person venture to assert, that a fellow playing on Pan-pipes, making faces, performing extraordinary leaps, or rattling his chin till it sounded like a pair of symbols [cymbals],[6] was a proper object for the national bounty, and ought to be pensioned in his old age, if he dissipated the halfpence or shillings he collected from the crowds. A man who writes a novel, or a play, or a poem, in respect of amusement, and in respect of being entitled to public rewards, is on the same footing as a mountebank or a puppet-showman. It is very possible that this amusement may be combined with some sentiments that may make the heart better; and it is equally possible, which we believe is in fact more generally the case, that the amusement is only made the vehicle of perverted sentiments, of conveying impurity into the mind, and of promoting the cause of vice, rather than of virtue. The use of literature, then, comes to consist in the truth and accurate knowledge which it contains. Unfortunately, however, those who have taught mankind truth have been prosecuted, not pensioned. De Foe, Horne Tooke, Thomas Paine,[7] and a

[6]Mill's square-bracketed correction.

[7]Daniel Defoe (ca. 1659-1731), journalist and novelist, employed by the government as a writer, was fined and imprisoned in 1702; John Horne Tooke (1736-1812), philologist and politician, a supporter of John Wilkes, was several times tried for his opinions; and the publication of the writings of Thomas Paine (1737-1809), English-born political philosopher and revolutionary propagandist in the United States and France, led to prosecutions for libel (see Nos. 4 and 9).

number of other writers, who have been the means of making useful, moral, and scientific truths known to the world, have been punished by the government, not rewarded. Governments always have been, and ever will be,—precisely because they are the offspring of conquest or of fraud, not of reason,—ready to prohibit literary men from searching after truth; so that if we should admit that literature, in the abstract, might be harmless, existing literature must have been mischievous. That system of corruption, which we are all now eager to pull down, has in fact long been supported by the majority of literary men. By all who have been pensioned,—by all who have sought any other patronage than that of the public, this miserable system has been favourably regarded, and they have endeavoured, and do endeavour, to uphold it.

Now, if this man's insight into human nature, and into the future destination of mankind, does not enable him to form the conception of any other government than one which is "the offspring of conquest or of fraud, not of reason"—if his mind is fully made up that the human race shall for ever, in spite of themselves, have their necks under the feet of men disposed to restrain and persecute those who search after truth—it is natural that he should look with small favour on any literary labours which such governments are likely to esteem deserving of reward. For our part, we do not hold it to be a law of nature that governments shall endeavour to stop the progress of the human mind. We do not believe that, even in the present vicious constitution of political society, the majority of civilized governments have any such purpose, or are actuated by any such spirit. And we look forward to a time, and no very distant one, in which all the more vulgar and subordinate purposes of government will merge in one grand purpose of advancing the progress of civilization. Proceeding upon premises so different from those of our contemporary, no wonder that we should quarrel with his conclusion.

We must, however, [says he,] go a step further in speaking of literature, and say that it has little or no influence over the progress of society. It is the consequence, not the cause, of civilization. Literary men and philosophers may flatter themselves that they possess a great power over the hearts and minds of their fellow-men, and over the progress of society; but experience teaches a different lesson. Man is taught by events, not by books, which too often obscure the most plain facts.

For "it is now upwards of three hundred years since Sir Thomas More made those beautiful observations on punishing theft by death;"[8] and theft still continues to be thus punished. "It is now also a hundred and thirty-nine years since Sir Dudley North published his Discourses on Trade;"[9] and he wrote in vain, till there arose "a want of markets for our produce:" and "it is upwards of two hundred years since Lord Bacon taught that man was but the minister and

[8]In *A Fruteful and Pleasaunt Worke of the Beste State of a Publyque Weale, and of the New Yle Called Utopia* (London: Vele, 1551), pp. [41-2] (Bk. I), by Thomas More (1478-1535).
[9]*Discourses upon Trade* (London: Basset, 1691), pp. 10-24, by Dudley North (1641-91), merchant and financier, M.P., one of the earliest advocates of free trade.

interpreter of nature;"[10] notwithstanding which, literary men are constantly recommending alterations in the structure of society; which, according to this writer, is a gross absurdity, since "human society, in its complicated relations, is as much a part of creation as minerals or flowers;" a proposition which is about as good an argument against improvements in the social science, as it would be against improvements in mining or horticulture.

So, because a man of genius may have an idea too far in advance of his age to gain many converts in it, men of genius have no more influence upon the destinies of society than dunces have. Because Sir Thomas More did not convince mankind of the barbarism of capital punishment, the labours of Beccaria, of Voltaire, of Bentham, of Romilly, in the same cause, have been useless and of none effect.[11] Because Sir Dudley North perceived the advantages of free trade, while the politicians of the world, both practical and theoretical, did not read him, or were too stupid, or too much engrossed by other subjects, to understand him, *therefore* the truth which he detected would by this time have been incorporated in our laws, if Adam Smith, and Say, and Ricardo,[12] and all men resembling them, had never existed. And this, because "man is taught by events, not books;" and events, it seems, never have any need of an interpreter; their language is as intelligible to any blockhead, who is not deaf, as to the greatest genius. If Newton had never lived, his next-door neighbour, no doubt, might have seen an apple fall, and in due time would have evolved the *Principia*,[13] for man is taught by events.

This "ignorance of what mankind owe to books" (if we may borrow an expression from Mr. Coleridge)[14] is most pitiable. We contend, in opposition to

[10] Francis Bacon, *Novum Organum* (1620), in *Works*, new ed., trans. Basil Montague, 16 vols. (London: Pickering, 1825-36), Vol. XIV, p. 31. (This edition gives the wording cited.)

[11] Cesare Bonesana, marchese di Beccaria (1738-94), Italian jurist and economist who influenced Bentham, best known for *Dei delitti e delle pene* (Leghorn: n.p., 1764). François Marie Arouet Voltaire (1694-1778), leading French philosopher, whose relevant writings include "Des lois," Chap. xlii of *Précis du siècle de Louis XV* (1752), "De la peine de mort," Sect. x of *Commentaire sur le livre Des délits et des peines par un avocat de province* (1766), "Des proportions," Chap. x of *L'homme aux quarante écus* (1767), and "Du meurtre," Art. III of "Prix de la justice et de l'humanité" (1777), in *Oeuvres complètes*, 66 vols. (Paris: Renouard, 1817-25), Vol. XIX, p. 379, Vol. XXVI, pp. 229-31, Vol. XL, pp. 60-7, and Vol. XXVI, p. 271, respectively. Bentham, *Rationale of Punishment* (1830), in *Works*, Vol. I, pp. 441-50, 525-32. Samuel Romilly (1757-1818), legal reformer, M.P., Solicitor-General 1806-07, associate of Bentham, *Observations on the Criminal Law of England, as It Relates to Capital Punishments* (London: Cadell and Davies, 1810).

[12] Adam Smith (1723-90), Scots political economist and moral philosopher, who was, like Jean Baptiste Say and David Ricardo, an advocate of free trade.

[13] I.e., Newton's *Philosophiae naturalis principia mathematica* (London: Royal Society, 1687).

[14] Coleridge, *The Friend*, 3 vols. (London: Rest Fenner, 1818), Vol. II, p. 306.

our contemporary, that mankind, instead of not being indebted to men of highly-cultivated intellects for any of the steps of their progress, are indebted to them for every step. Events might have spoken, or even cried aloud, but they would have spoken a foreign language: mankind could not have profited, and do not profit, even by the lessons of their personal experience, until a man of genius arises to construe those lessons for them. Before the press existed, the leading minds of a nation could bring themselves into contact with the national mind only by means of speech. The forum, the theatre, the pulpit, the school, were then the sources of illumination and mental culture. Since the discovery of printing, books are the medium by which the ideas, the mental habits, and the feelings, of the most exalted and enlarged minds are propagated among the inert, unobserving, unmeditative mass. And we challenge our adversary to a historical trial of the fact. From the Reformation to the present Parliamentary Reform Bill, he will not find one great moral or social improvement, the origin of which cannot be distinctly traced to the labours of men of letters. No one man of genius, it is probable, was ever indispensable; because, what he did, it is likely might have been done by some other: but by another man of genius. Had it not been for a few great minds, mankind would never have emerged from the savage state. Let the series of great minds be once broken off, and it is not clear that we shall not relapse into barbarism.

But mark the pseudo-metaphysical theory, which serves as a pedestal to this fine philosophical system. "Instead of society being modelled on, or formed by, the opinions of literary men or philosophers, all their opinions, as far as they are correct, are modelled on what they behold in the world. Every thought they possess, if correct, is a mere copy of external nature; and yet it is assumed, that by some little legerdemain arrangement of their reflections, they influence the course of the intellectual world:" and, we presume, whatever is "in the world," and in "external nature," is as visible to one man's optics as to another's. This style of philosophizing will carry us far. Every picture which Raphael ever painted, "if correct, is a mere copy of external nature;" of that nature, too, which we can see with our bodily eyes, not solely with those of our minds: *argal*, every man who has eyes, could have painted the *Transfiguration*.[15] Lavoisier's discovery of the composition of water,[16] was "modelled on what he beheld in the world;" the hydrogen and the oxygen were always before us, in every rivulet, and in every cistern, "and yet it is assumed, that by some little arrangement" of retorts and gas apparatus, he "influenced the course" of the science of chemistry, and of the arts to which it is applied.

[15]The *Transfiguration*, begun in 1519 and left unfinished, was the last painting of Raphael Sanzio (1483-1520).
[16]Antoine Laurent Lavoisier (1743-94), French chemist, whose work on hydrogen led to his discovery in 1783 of the composition of water.

Finally, our contemporary adds:

It is clear, we think, whether looked at theoretically or as a matter of fact, that literature and literary men are of no more use to society, no more instrumental in promoting its improvement, than is any other class or any other art; and therefore, we conclude, no more to be pensioned and provided for out of the people's purse than is the weaver, for his skill in cloth-making. The best reward for both is the common market of the world; and what will not sell there is worth no man's labour.

From this we may learn, that the sale of a book is always in exact proportion to its utility; and mankind are as well able to discern, and as eager to seek, that which will enlarge and elevate their minds, as that which will please and beautify their bodies. The person whose mind is capable of conceiving an opinion of this sort, must be a precious observer of his age and of human nature.

If we were now to state our own opinion with respect to a public provision for literary men, we should suggest to this writer a distinction which, it would seem, is not "heard of in his philosophy."[17] We should remind him, that there are literary men, and literary works, whose object is solely to give immediate pleasure, and other literary men and literary works that aim at producing a permanent impression upon the mind. The first we should, with him, regard as being on the same footing in respect to public rewards, with "a mountebank or a puppet-showman:" not because amusement in itself is not a worthy object of pursuit, but because it is one for which mankind are always willing to pay the full value. Accordingly, the amusement of the poor, who cannot afford to pay for it, *is* a fit object of public provision; and doubtless, as civilization advances, will be considered so.

In addition, however, to these writers, whose aim is only to please mankind, there is another sort, who endeavour to educate them: to batter down obstinate prejudices; to throw light on the dark places; to discover and promulgate ideas, which must be meditated for years before they will be appreciated; to form mankind to closer habits of thought; to shame them out of whatever is mean and selfish in their behaviour; to elevate their tastes; to inspire them with nobler and more beneficent desires; to teach them that there are virtues which they have never conceived, and pleasures beyond what they have ever enjoyed. These, by the leave of our contemporary, are the labours, for which "the best reward" is not always "the common market of the world." This is a literature which deserves a public provision, and which, unfortunately, is too apt to require one; because such are not the services which mankind are apt at first to requite with either their money or their thanks.

But no enemy to a cause ever did more for its injury, than is done to this cause by its friends, when they talk of giving "encouragement to literature."[18] The

[17]Cf. Shakespeare, *Hamlet*, I, v, 166; in *The Riverside Shakespeare*, p. 1151.

[18]Leading article on literary pensions, *Morning Chronicle*, 3 June, 1831, p. 2; cf. the article in the *Englishman's Magazine* cited in n1 above.

phrase grates upon our ears. Literature needs no encouragement. The man who engages in literature from the motive of money, is false to his mission. It is the curse of literature, that it is a trade. He who would inspire others with high desires, must himself be inspired with them. He would teach mankind to love truth and virtue for themselves, and shall *he* need any other stimulus than the love of truth and virtue, in order to inculcate them? What is due to literary men is not encouragement, but subsistence. They ask not to be rewarded,—they ask to be kept alive, while they continue to enlighten and civilize the world. They ask this, in order that they may not, like so many of the first men of our own country, be compelled to renounce or suspend the labours for which none others are fit, and devote their lives to some merely gainful occupation, in order that they may have bread to eat: or still worse, that they may not be compelled by penury and dire dependance, which eat up so many minds fit for better things, to prostitute their noble calling by base compliances—to pander to selfishness and malignity, instead of wrestling with them; to give utterance to the opinion which they hold not, to counterfeit the emotion which they feel not, to find justification for the evil-doer, instead of bringing him to shame—to become confounded with the meanest of mankind, by sycophancy and base hypocrisy—or if they sink not to this depth of infamy, at least to waste their highest powers, by mixing among the herd of those who write merely to amuse.

It is most true, as our contemporary affirms, that the majority of our literary men have long been of the low description, which we have just attempted to characterize. But why is this? For several reasons, one of the chief of which is, that such men, in this country, have *not* any public provision. In Germany and France, where, through the universities and various other institutions, a man of letters or science easily obtains, by the sacrifice of a small part of his time, a respectable subsistence—there, even under arbitrary governments, the lettered class are really the highest and most cultivated minds of their several nations. With us, they are dependant, for subsistence, upon the sale of their works, and must consequently adapt themselves to the taste of those who will buy. The buying class, until lately, have been the aristocracy: which explains why, as our adversary says, our corrupt institutions have "long been supported by the majority of literary men." When, subsequently to this, the mass of the people became buyers, books were written which were addressed chiefly to them. As the people had not the sinister interests of the aristocracy, the writings which were addressed to them did not assume the same particular form of noxiousness and wickedness, as those which were written for the ruling classes: but they assumed other forms. And so it will be, if, by the Reform Bill and its consequences, all the corruptions of our government are done away. The people, as well as the aristocracy, like better to have their opinions confirmed, than corrected. The people as well as the aristocracy prefer those who chime in with their feelings, to those who endeavour to improve them. After the Reform Bill as before, it will be easier and more gainful to take men as they now are, with their vices and weaknesses, and to give them the food which pleases their vitiated palates, than to form their tastes and their constitutions to healthier nourishment. And such will be the character of all literature, which is got up for "the common market of the world;" until mankind shall have attained a degree of civilization, to which Parliamentary Reform may remove some of the obstacles, but which of itself it gives not, nor ever can give.

But to prevent these evils, it is not necessary that any thing should be added to the fiscal burdens by which we are already weighed down. It is not requisite that the people should be taxed to give pensions to men of literature and science. The endowments of our universities, now squandered upon idle monks, are an ample fund already existing; a large portion of which (the Fellowships) already is expended under that pretext, and is of right appropriate to that purpose and to no other. And a time, we trust, is coming, when to that, and no other purpose, it will be applied.

110. WHATELY'S INTRODUCTORY LECTURES
ON POLITICAL ECONOMY

EXAMINER, 12 JUNE, 1831, P. 373

This is Mill's first notice of an author he often referred to, Richard Whately (1787-1863), cleric and prolific writer on religion, philosophy, and political economy, who was Drummond Professor of Political Economy at Oxford from 1829 until he became Archbishop of Dublin from 1831 until his death. The review, which appears in the "Literary Examiner," is headed "*Introductory Lectures on Political Economy: being part of a Course delivered in Easter Term, 1831. By Richard Whately, D.D., Principal of St. Alban's Hall, Professor of Political Economy in the University of Oxford.* [London: Fellowes, 1831.] 7*s.*" It is described in Mill's bibliography as "A review of Whately's Introductory Lectures on Political Economy; in the Examiner of the same date [as No. 109]" (MacMinn, p. 16), and is similarly listed (without the "A") and enclosed in square brackets in the Somerville College set.

BY THE STATUTE relative to the Professorship of Political Economy endowed by Mr. Henry Drummond, it is prescribed, that the Professor shall hold his office only for five years; and that he shall annually publish at least one of his lectures.[1] By virtue of the first provision, the late able and excellent Professor, Mr. Senior, has resigned the chair, and has been replaced by Dr. Whately; who now, in

---

[1]Henry Drummond founded in 1825 a chair of Political Economy at Oxford; the third of his stipulations sets the five-year limit (though re-election was possible after two years out of office), and the fourth requires the publication of at least one of a minimum of nine lectures delivered each year (broadsheet, dated 25 Apr., 1825, from the Delegates' Room, Bodleian Library G.A. Oxon c. 41 [52]).

compliance with the second injunction of the founder, lays before the general public not one lecture merely, with which scanty measure he might have contented himself, but the first eight discourses, comprising the introductory division of his course.

If the English Church, and its Universities, possessed many such members as Dr. Whately; or if the few whom it does possess, exercised the influence which such men might be expected to exercise, over the general spirit of the body; the prospects of the Church in this era of general reformation would be very different from what they are. And of this no one seems better aware than Dr. Whately himself. An author who writes in earnest, if he writes much, cannot help betraying, to an intelligent reader, the predominant feeling of his own mind. Now, in Dr. Whately, the predominant feeling evidently is a consciousness and regret, that nearly all the most important branches of useful knowledge are possessed, in the present age, by various other persons indeed, but not by that profession which is set apart and paid for the purpose, or under the pretext, of civilizing and cultivating the human mind. And he is deeply anxious that these persons, whose duty and vocation it is to teach, should be prevailed upon to learn; in order that they may be at least upon a level with those who are under no peculiar or professional obligation of possessing knowledge. To impress upon them, both the propriety and the prudence of thus bestirring themselves, is the purpose which, more than any other, his labours, as an author, always seem to have in view. And a highly laudable purpose it is: though it might have been somewhat less prominent, without any loss to the general reader, who has neither a rectory nor a fellowship to preserve, and who desires knowledge for its own sake, and not on the score that it has become indispensable to the safety of tithes.

In all other respects, this production is excellent. We know of no existing work to which we can refer our readers for so clear, cogent, and analytical a refutation of the fallacies, and exposure of the perverse feelings, which disincline many weak, and some intelligent persons, from the study of a branch of knowledge pre-eminently important to all the best interests of mankind. We do not assert that the author has exhausted the subject; nor can it ever be exhausted. We even think that he has left unsaid several matters of importance, in order to have room for others which his lay readers, at least, could have better dispensed with. For example: he contends at great length against what he terms the false and dangerous impression, that Political Economy is unfavourable to religion. But where, we ask, was such an impression ever entertained, except at Oxford? and who would have suspected that it was entertained even there, if the Professor had not betrayed the secret? But, since he assures us that such is the fact, we are compelled to give credit to him; and to believe, that, in that ancient seat of learning, the race of theologians still survives, who condemned the discoveries of Galileo,[2] inoculation, and the emetic, and who are firmly persuaded that God

[2]Galileo Galilei (1564-1642), Italian mathematician, astronomer, and physicist, condemned by the Catholic Church for his observations confirming the Copernican theory.

never intended mankind to know any thing more than what *they* know, on any subject whatsoever, moral or physical.

We have no where seen the good qualities of Dr. Whately's manner of writing displayed to greater advantage than in this work. Among these we may mention, as the most valuable, first, that he is pre-eminently clear; and, secondly, that we may almost always learn from his writings much more than what we sought for in them. The first excellency he possesses, because he is perfectly master of all the steps in his own deductions. The second he owes to habits of *general* observation and reflection, by which (whatever be the subject on which he writes) he is supplied with materials, applicable indeed to his immediate purpose, but also covering a much larger extent of ground than that on which he happens to be building. It is by this test, more than by any other, that we distinguish the mind of general culture from that which is merely cultivated at one or two points. Every one must have known men and writers, who, if they confine themselves to what they are fit for, accomplish it excellently well, but without either using in the construction, or dropping by the way, one single idea which could possibly be of use for any purpose *in rerum naturâ* save that one. Dr. Whately is a man of a different description; and, consequently, all his works, even those with the most unpromising titles, are valuable.

111. REPLY OF THE BRIGHTON GUARDIAN TO THE EXAMINER

EXAMINER, 19 JUNE, 1831, P. 387

Here Mill responds to "Literature and Patronage," *Brighton Guardian*, 15 June, 1831, p. 2, which replied to No. 109. The article, headed as title, appears in the "Political Examiner." Described in Mill's bibliography as "An article headed 'Reply of the Brighton Guardian to the Examiner'; in the Examiner of 19th June 1831" (MacMinn, p. 17), the article is listed as title and enclosed in square brackets in the Somerville College set.

THE BRIGHTON GUARDIAN has honoured our article of last Sunday by a reply. His opinion is not changed; and as the manner in which he has again presented it has produced no change in ours, we have no wish that the discussion should proceed farther. The question will full surely reproduce itself often enough; connected, as it is, with principles which lie still deeper, and for which we may hereafter be called upon to do battle, not solely with our present antagonist, but with some of the strongest tendencies of the age. But as our contemporary, whose tone in conducting the controversy is temperate and decorous, thinks that he has reason to complain of ours, we are unwilling to quit the subject without attempting to remove this impression.

We admit that we wronged our contemporary in representing him to have asserted, that literary men are of no use. He merely affirmed (what, however, is substantially the same) that they do not, in any material degree, influence the opinions or sentiments of mankind; and this he now repeats, calling in, as his voucher, a writer in the *Edinburgh Review*, who says of men of genius, that they are "only the first to catch and reflect the light, which, without their assistance, must, in a short time have become visible to those who were far beneath them."[1] We well remember the passage: but we do not think that our contemporary derives much additional strength from such backers. The stronger should not lean for support upon the weaker. The doctrine, in the mind of the Edinburgh Reviewer, was but one of those crude and thoughtless paradoxes, which unsettled and juvenile minds think it clever to fling out at random: but in the mind of our contemporary, we are bound to allow that to all appearance it forms part of a connected course of thought. An opinion thus adopted belongs to a far higher quality of mind, but to one of which the aberrations are pregnant with far greater evil. Almost the only dangerous error is systematic error.

We must have looked at our contemporary's productions with as perverse an eye, as we think he has at his subject, if we had, as he accuses us, classed him "with the tribe of dunces." He will find, on reperusing our remarks, that we expressly *distinguished* him from that class. But we could not help testifying our sense of the immense advantage which he enjoyed, in having the whole tribe of dunces on his side: for we well know how numerous, potent, and united a body these are. And we know, that, in an age of transition, in which mankind have just found out that their guides have lost their way, the spell of intellectual superiority is broken, or greatly impaired, and the dunces are prone to believe that they are fully competent to their own guidance, and that instruction and intellect are no such mighty matters, after all. We are not blind to the danger, or to the ridiculousness, of the self-worship to which literary men are liable in common with all other possessors of power; but we deem the self-idolatry of ignorance rather more ridiculous and dangerous still; and the regret we felt at finding it countenanced by one who, in no sense, belongs to the ignoble fraternity, alone provoked us to the warmth of language of which our contemporary complains.

Be it remembered, that, lofty as are the claims which we have set up in behalf of genius, we have never asserted that men are entitled to consideration merely because they labour with the pen, rather than with the hod. The honour due to any man depends not upon his occupation, but upon the spirit in which he pursues it, and the qualities of mind which he evinces in carrying it on. Nor have we said one word in exaltation or vindication of the common herd of *littérateurs*, respecting whom our opinion, in the main, coincides with that of our contemporary. The whole mind of a reading nation is reflected in its literature; and we claim admiration solely for the nobler parts of both. But the highest literature is the food of the highest minds, without which they wither and die.

---

[1] Thomas Babington Macaulay (1800-59), "Dryden," *Edinburgh Review*, XLVII (Jan. 1828), 3.

The *Globe* of Thursday last contains an excellent article on the subject of this controversy, to which we have great pleasure in calling the attention of our readers.[2]

112. FLOWER'S MUSICAL ILLUSTRATIONS
OF THE WAVERLEY NOVELS

EXAMINER, 3 JULY, 1831, PP. 420-1

Eliza Flower (1803-46), composer, was the closest friend of Harriet Taylor (1807-58), whom Mill had met in the summer of 1830. Eliza and her sister, Sarah (1805-48), were protégées of W.J. Fox (1786-1864), the Unitarian preacher and journalist, who had contributed to the first number of the *Westminster Review* and was one of Mill's closest associates in the early 1830s; he had been instrumental in introducing Mill and Harriet. Flower set to music psalms and religious poems (probably the best known was one for which her sister composed the verses, "Nearer, My God, to Thee"), as well as secular works. The first of the Waverley novels by Walter Scott (1771-1832) appeared in 1814. See also Nos. 155, 197, 201, and 229. The article, in a section called "Musical Review," is headed: "*Musical Illustrations of the Waverley Novels, dedicated (by permission) to Sir Walter Scott, Bart. By Eliza Flower.* [London: Novello, [1831].]" Described in Mill's bibliography as "A review of Miss Flower's Musical Illustrations of the Waverley Novels, in the Examiner of 3d July 1831" (MacMinn, p. 17), the article is similarly listed (without the "A") and enclosed in square brackets in the Somerville College set.

WE OMITTED TO NOTICE THIS PUBLICATION among the musical novelties of the last month. Our apology is, that the music is of too high a character to be judged of hastily. Much of it, indeed, cannot fail to please, even at the first hearing: but, at the first hearing, it would most surely be underrated.

It displays taste and sensibility of the highest order, and no common genius—if the creation of that which is at once original and beautiful be the privilege of genius. Nothing can be conceived more unlike the everyday music which the composers for the common market copy from one another. So little are this lady's compositions the result of imitation or memory, that they do not even resemble the works of the great masters. They have a character of their own; distinctly and strikingly individual; compounded, it should seem, of the peculiarities of the poetry, and those of the composer's mind: founded on a strong conception of the meaning and spirit of the poetry; but adding so much to it, that the inspiration she gives is almost equal to that which she receives. One who can feel poetry so vividly, if she be as well accustomed to clothe her conceptions in the language of words as in that of melody, would surely give

---

[2]*Globe and Traveller*, 16 June, 1831, pp. 2-3.

birth to poetry of her own, not inferior to that with which she has inseparably associated these most characteristic airs.

As the title implies, all the songs are selected from the Waverley Novels, and are most aptly chosen. Their character is extremely various; and the music rises and falls with the poetry. In proportion as more invention and resource is required, more is shown: the composer easily supplies all that the simpler and more ordinary subjects require; but she puts forth her strength in grappling with the more difficult ones. Yet the airs which are least poetical in themselves—or, rather, of which the poetry is of the least elevated kind—will probably be the more generally pleasing, for precisely the reason which makes Goldsmith[1] a more popular poet than Milton, or a landscape of Claude a more general favourite than the *St. Sebastian* of Guido.[2] Among this portion of the songs, we would particularly recommend to attention the serenade from the *Pirate*, "Love wakes and weeps;"[3] and a sweet air called "The Song of Annot Lyle."[4] Nothing can be simpler, and at the same time less common-place, than this little melody. There is one very unusual interval in it, which gives a peculiar tinge to the whole, and which is scarcely ever found in modern music: though it is to be met with in one or two of the best Scottish airs.

The pieces which we ourselves most admire are the following three:—No. 5, "Meg Merrilies' Chaunt," a wail over a dying person. No. 8, "The Death of Madge Wildfire;" every one must remember that most affecting passage, perhaps, in the most pathetic tale of the whole Waverley series.[5] The music consists of four different movements, of which the first two are beautiful melodies, of a somewhat subdued character; followed by two others most characteristically wild—the last of which declines into the loveliest passage, perhaps, in the whole volume. (P. 43.)

There is one other song of the same elevated character, No. 2, "The Lady in St. Swithin's Chair." This is an example of what we sometimes, though rarely, meet with—first-rate ballad music; that is to say, an air sufficiently simple not to seem too lofty for the plainer and merely narrative parts of a ballad, and which

---

[1]Oliver Goldsmith (1728-74), poet and playwright.

[2]Claude Gelée (called Lorrain) (1600-82), landscape painter much admired by the Romantics; Guido Reni (1575-1642) painted several canvases of St. Sebastian.

[3]No. 13, "Serenade 'Love Wakes and Weeps,'" p. 58, based on a ballad in Walter Scott, *The Pirate*, 3 vols. (Edinburgh: Constable, 1822), Vol. II, Chap. x, pp. 237-8.

[4]No. 11, "Annot Lyle's Ballad," p. 54, based on a ballad in Scott, *A Legend of Montrose*, in *Tales of My Landlord*, 3rd ser., 4 vols. (Edinburgh: Constable, 1819), Vol. IV, Chap. xiii, pp. 277-8.

[5]No. 5, "Meg Merrilies' Chaunt," p. 21, based on a ballad in Scott, *Guy Mannering*, 3 vols. (Edinburgh: Constable, 1815), Vol. II, Chap. vi, p. 87; and No. 8, "Death of Madge Wildfire," p. 34, based on a ballad in Scott, *The Heart of Mid-Lothian*, in *Tales of My Landlord*, 2nd ser., 4 vols. (Edinburgh: Constable, 1818), Vol. IV, Chap. iii, pp. 67-71.

yet, when the words rise into energy and dignity, rises with them, and sustains them with a majesty equal to their own. But the highest flight of imagination is at the close of this ballad, in the music of the stanzas describing the appearance of the night-hag.

> She shudders and stops, as the charm she speaks!
> Is it the moody owl that shrieks?
> Or is that sound, betwixt laughter and scream,
> The voice of the demon that haunts the stream?
>
> The moan of the wind sunk silent and low;
> The roaring torrent has ceased to flow;
> The calm was more dreadful than raging storm,
> When the cold grey mist brought the ghastly form![6]

We envy the real lover of music the pleasure which he will receive from the accompaniment of the former of these stanzas, and from the melody of the latter, which changes to another strain of great sweetness in itself, and admirably embodying the character of the words.

Among the livelier pieces, our greatest favourite is No. 4, the "Song of Norman the Forester," in the *Bride of Lammermoor*.[7] These, perhaps, resemble one another too much, at least in their rhythm: but each in itself is pretty, and suited to the words.

No. 1 is a quartette;[8] and several others terminate in quartettes or trios. These we have not yet had an opportunity of hearing properly executed: the melody, however, (as in so many of Mozart's concerted pieces)[9] shews itself in the accompaniment. No. 1, even as a mere instrumental piece, will please all lovers of chaste and expressive music.

One of the songs, No. 6,[10] is avowedly a mere adaptation of a beautiful French air. The melody is as characteristic of the words as if it had been written for them; and it is extremely well arranged.

---

[6]No. 2, "Rose Bradwardine's Song; or, St. Swithin's Chair," p. 6, based on a ballad in Scott, *Waverley*, 3 vols. (Edinburgh: Constable, 1814), Vol. I, Chap. xiii, pp. 188-90.

[7]No. 4, "Norman the Forester's Song," p. 18, based on a ballad in Scott, *The Bride of Lammermoor*, in *Tales of My Landlord*, 3rd ser., Vol. I, Chap. iii, p. 81.

[8]No. 1, "Hail to Thee, " p. 2, based on a ballad in Scott, *Waverley*, Vol. II, Chap. i, p. 14.

[9]Wolfgang Amadeus Mozart (1756-91), one of Mill's (and everyone's) most admired composers.

[10]No. 6, "Louis Kerneguy's Song," p. 25, based on a ballad in Scott, *Woodstock*, 3 vols. (Edinburgh: Constable, 1826), Vol. III, Chap. ii, pp. 38-9.